Focusing on the disciplines of economics, sociology, political science, and history, this book examines how American social science came to model itself on natural science and liberal politics.

Professor Ross argues that American social science receives its distinctive stamp from the ideology of American exceptionalism, the idea that America occupies an exceptional place in history, based on her republican government and wide economic opportunity. Under the influence of this national self-conception, Americans believed that their history was set on a millennial course, exempted from historical change and from the mass poverty and class conflict of Europe. Before the Civil War, this vision of American exceptionalism drew social scientists into the national effort to stay the hand of time. Not until after the Civil War did industrialization force Americans to confront the idea and reality of historical change. The social science disciplines had their origin in that crisis and their development is a story of efforts to evade and tame historical transformation in the interest of exceptionalist ideals.

Professor Ross shows how each of the social science disciplines, while developing their inherited intellectual traditions, responded to changes in historical consciousness, political needs, professional structures, and the conceptions of science available to them. Hoping first in the Gilded Age to sustain fixed laws of nature and history, social scientists in the Progressive Era linked American history to Western liberal history and its modernizing forces to capitalism, democracy, and science. But they hastened to subject that history to scientific control and tried to carve out a realm of nature that would perpetuate exceptionalist ideals. By the 1920s, driven to harder versions of technological control, the social sciences had transmuted the dismaying uncertainties of history into controllable natural process.

This is the first book to look broadly at American social science in its historical context and to demonstrate the central importance of the national ideology of American exceptionalism to the development of the social sciences and to American social thought generally.

# The Origins of American
# Social Science

# IDEAS IN CONTEXT

*Edited by Richard Rorty, J. B. Schneewind, Quentin Skinner,
and Wolf Lepenies*

The books in this series will discuss the emergence of intellectual traditions and of related new disciplines. The procedures, aims, and vocabularies that were generated will be set in the context of the alternatives available within the contemporary frameworks of ideas and institutions. Through detailed studies of the evolution of such traditions, and their modification by different audiences, it is hoped that a new picture will form of the development of ideas in their concrete contexts. By this means, artificial distinctions among the history of philosophy, of the various sciences, of society and politics, and of literature may be seen to dissolve.

For titles published in the series, see page following the Index.

This series is published with the support of the Exxon Education Foundation.

# The Origins of
# American Social Science

Dorothy Ross

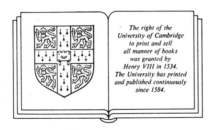

The right of the
University of Cambridge
to print and sell
all manner of books
was granted by
Henry VIII in 1534.
The University has printed
and published continuously
since 1584.

CAMBRIDGE UNIVERSITY PRESS

Cambridge

New York   Port Chester   Melbourne   Sydney

Published by the Press Syndicate of the University of Cambridge
The Pitt Building, Trumpington Street, Cambridge CB2 1RP
40 West 20th Street, New York, NY 10011, USA
10 Stamford Road, Oakleigh, Melbourne 3166, Australia

First published 1991

Printed in the United States of America

*Library of Congress Cataloging-in-Publication Data*
Ross, Dorothy.
The origins of American social science/Dorothy Ross.
p.   cm.
Includes bibliographical references and index.
ISBN 0-521-35092-1
1. Social sciences – United States – History.   2. Economics – United
States – History.   3. Sociology – United States – History.
4. Political science – United States – History.   I. Title.
H53.U5R67      1990
300′.973 – dc20                                          90-37441
                                                            CIP

*British Library Cataloguing in Publication Data*
Ross, Dorothy
The origins of American social science.
1. United States. Social sciences, history
I. Title
300.973

ISBN 0-521-35092-1 hardback

*To John and Ellen*
*who grew up with this book*

Travellers in Switzerland who stepped across the Rhine where it flowed from its glacier could follow its course among medieval towns and feudal ruins, until it became a highway for modern industry, and at last arrived at a permanent equilibrium in the ocean. American history followed the same course. With pre-historic glaciers and medieval feudalism the story had little to do; but from the moment it came within sight of the ocean it acquired interest almost painful. . . . Science alone could sound the depths of the ocean, measure its currents, foretell its storms, or fix its relations to the system of Nature. In a democratic ocean science could see something ultimate. Man could go no further. The atom might move, but the general equilibrium could not change.

Henry Adams
*History of the United States of America*, vol. 9

# Contents

# Acknowledgments

Because scholarship is a collaborative effort, I am keenly aware how much this book owes to the work of predecessors and colleagues. I have cited their contributions in my text and footnotes, but I have undoubtedly omitted some intellectual debts incurred over the long course of writing this book. Let me express my general gratitude to the community of scholars and friends whose work, and often personal support, have contributed to this book.

I owe particular thanks to my former colleagues at the University of Virginia, where this book was written, for intellectual stimulation and encouragement. Theodore M. Porter gave the text a searching and skeptical reading and Stephen Innes performed the same service on the early chapters. Richard Rorty, Michael Holt, Mark Thomas, Olivier Zunz, and Joseph Kett read all or part of the manuscript and made very useful suggestions. To the enlightening discussion of the Faculty Seminar on hermeneutics chaired by Ralph Cohen, and to the timely reminders of Erik Midelfort, I owe whatever reflexivity this text has achieved.

I thank equally my other professional associates who commented on the manuscript. Louis Galambos, my new colleague at Johns Hopkins, gave the text a searching and sympathetic reading; Peter Novick, David Hollinger, and Amy Stanley commented extensively on the early chapters; Barbara Laslett read the text with an eye to sociology and gender studies; Howard Seftel did the same for economics; and Donald Dewey read the section on Knight. The book has benefited substantially from the criticisms and suggestions of all my readers, even when I have chosen not to take their advice. Finally, I want to express my gratitude to my editor at Cambridge, Frank Smith, for not only improving the text, but for knowing just what to say to allay an author's anxieties.

A number of people and institutions have helped in other ways to make this book possible. A large part of the early research was supported by the National Science Foundation, Grant No. SES-7923830, and I am pleased to be able to reward the patience of Ronald Overmann, director of the section on the history and philosophy of science. Some of the later writing and research was supported by the Sesquicentennial Fund of the University of Virginia. To the Library of Congress and the staff of its Stack and Reader Division, I owe special thanks for the opportunity to research and write this book amid the library's splendid resources. The staffs of the libraries I have used to do manuscript research have also been exceedingly helpful. I will single out here only the staff at the University of Chicago Special Collections, Robert Rosenthal, curator, whose riches in the history of American social science required several visits.

Once I started to write, bound to the ancient typewriter, the secretaries at the University of Virginia, Lottie McCauley, Kathleen Miller, and Ella Wood, transcribed the succeeding drafts onto a word processor; I am grateful to them for dedication and good humor beyond the call of duty. My research assistant during the last few years, Charles Evans, ably performed a multitude of tasks.

Finally, I want to thank my husband, Stanford G. Ross, for a reading of the text at once skeptical and sympathetic, and most especially, for the satisfactions of our life together, that make this book, and everything else, possible.

Johns Hopkins University

# Abbreviations used in the footnotes

*AAAPSS*  Annals of the American Academy of Political and Social Science

*AER*  American Economic Review

*AHAAR*  American Historical Association Annual Report

*AHR*  American Historical Review

*AJS*  American Journal of Sociology

*APSR*  American Political Science Review

*ASR*  American Sociological Review

*DAB*  Dictionary of American Biography

*EW  John Dewey: The Early Works*, 5 vols. (Carbondale: Southern Illinois University Press, 1967–75)

*JAH*  Journal of American History

*JHBS*  Journal of the History of the Behavioral Sciences

*JHS*  Journal of the History of Sociology

*JHUSHPS*  Johns Hopkins University Studies in History and Political Science

*JPE*  Journal of Political Economy

*LW  John Dewey: The Later Works, 1925–1953* (Carbondale: Southern Illinois University Press, 1981–    )

*MW  John Dewey: The Middle Works, 1899–1924*, 15 vols. (Carbondale: Southern Illinois University Press, 1976–83)

*PAEA*  Publications of the American Economic Association

*PAPSA*   Proceedings of the American Political Science Association
*PPASS*   Papers and Proceedings of the American Sociological Society
*PSQ*   Political Science Quarterly
*QJE*   Quarterly Journal of Economics

# Introduction

American social science bears the distinctive mark of its national origin. Like pragmatism or Protestant fundamentalism or abstract expressionism, social science is a characteristic product of modern American culture. Its liberal values, practical bent, shallow historical vision, and technocratic confidence are recognizable features of twentieth-century America. To foreign and domestic critics, these characteristics make American social science ahistorical and scientistic, lacking in appreciation of historical difference and complexity. To its supporters, the drive for scientific method, freedom from the vagaries of history, and practical utility in American society have been praiseworthy goals marred by too-frequent lapses, but they have been equally singled out as its characteristic features. What is so marked about American social science is the degree to which it is modeled on the natural rather than the historical sciences and imbedded in the classical ideology of liberal individualism.

The distinctive character of American social science has necessarily had a profound effect on social practice and social thought in the United States. A historical world is a humanly created one. It is composed of people, institutions, practices, and languages that are created by the circumstances of human experience and sustained by structures of power. History can be used to achieve a critical understanding of historical experience and allows us to change the social structures that shape it. In contrast, the models of the social world that have dominated American social science in the twentieth century invite us to look through history to a presumably natural process beneath. Here the social world is composed of individual behaviors responding to natural stimuli, and the capitalist market and modern urban society are understood, in effect, as part of nature. We are led toward quantitative and technocratic manipulation of nature and an idealized liberal vision of American society. As twentieth-century American culture becomes increasingly disoriented in time and its social ethic becomes increasingly eroded, it behooves us to look closely at this ahistorical strategy.[1]

My focus will be on three core disciplines of American social science – economics, sociology, and political science. I begin in Part I with the origin of the social sciences in eighteenth-century Europe and early nineteenth-century America. These two chapters introduce the historical and conceptual scaffolding from which my argument is constructed and necessarily condense a great deal of material in a small space. The main body of the book, proceeding at a less demanding pace, is about the formative decades of the social-science disciplines in America, roughly 1870 to 1929. Although they began that period much influenced by German historical models, American social scientists determined by the end of it to orient their disciplines toward natural science. A still higher point of scientific aspiration was reached in the 1950s, when quantitative modeling, systems analysis, functionalism, and behavioral science gained wide currency, but the decision to seek out a natural scientific path and the underlying view of the social-historical world as a realm of natural process had already been forged by the 1920s.

I believe that American social science owes its distinctive character to its involvement with the national ideology of American exceptionalism, the idea that America occupies an exceptional place in history, based on her republican government and economic opportunity. Both this national self-conception and the social sciences themselves emerged from the late eighteenth- and early nineteenth-century effort to understand the character and fate of modern society. The successful establishment of republican institutions and the liberal opportunity guaranteed by a continent of virgin land, Americans believed, had set American history on a millennial course and exempted it from qualitative change in the future. America would forestall the mass poverty and class conflict that modernity appeared to be creating in Britain. Before the Civil War this vision of American exceptionalism drew the social sciences into the national effort to stay the hand of time.

---

1 Among a large literature of criticism of American social science, I have been most influenced by Kenneth Bock, *The Acceptance of Histories; Toward a Perspective for Social Science* (Berkeley: University of California Press, 1956); Richard J. Bernstein, *The Restructuring of Social and Political Theory* (New York: Harcourt Brace Jovanovich, 1976) and *Beyond Objectivism and Relativism: Science, Hermeneutics and Praxis* (Philadelphia: University of Pennsylvania Press, 1983); Warren J. Samuels, "Ideology in Economics," in *Modern Economic Thought*, ed. Sidney Weintraub (Philadelphia: University of Pennsylvania Press, 1977), 467–84; William E. Connolly, *The Terms of Political Discourse*, 2nd ed. (Princeton, N.J.: Princeton University Press, 1983). See also Peter T. Manicas, *A History of Philosophy of the Social Sciences* (Oxford: Blackwell Publishers, 1987).

Social scientists found fixed laws of history and nature that would perpetuate established national institutions.

The experience of civil war and rapid industrialization and the decline of religious assurance precipitated a national crisis and forced Americans to an understanding of history in the modern sense: history as a process of continuous, qualitative change, moved and ordered by forces that lay within itself. Under the impact of industrialization and the rise of class conflict, Americans confronted the possibility that the country would follow the same historic course that Europe did and that permanent classes, even socialism, might develop here. As a result, many social scientists revised the idea of American exceptionalism. They argued that the realization of American liberal and republican ideals depended on the same forces that were creating liberal modernity in Europe, on the development of capitalism, democratic politics, and science. America's unique condition did not block the full effects of modernity on this continent, but rather supported it.

Given the long investment in the exceptionalist ideal, however, it is not surprising that the effort to carry America into Western liberal history was not complete or unequivocal. Some social scientists had some success in the effort to orient their studies toward history. There would be less interest in drawing the scientific trajectory of mainstream social science if there had not been from the beginning an alternative impulse, occasionally working beneath the surface or in open conflict with mainstream patterns. But the main body of social scientists tried to carve out within or beneath history a realm of nature that would ward off the lingering fears of decline and insure the realization of a harmonious liberal society sometime in the future. In this liberal model history acted within a narrow range and to the extent it opened America to change it triggered the fear of change, as well, so that many social scientists hastened to subject history to scientific control.

By the second decade of the twentieth century, the rapid development of industrial society, the deepening response to change, and then the experience of World War I led to a new sense of discontinuity with the past and to accelerating historical transformation. Under those conditions, American social scientists sought harder kinds of technological control. They invented pluralist, behaviorist, and statistical models of a liberal world in perpetual flux, yet perpetually recreating its American form. As the past receded, the dismaying uncertainties of history were transmuted into controllable processes of nature.

To explain the scientific and liberal stance of American social science by examining Americans' understanding of history and response to historical change may seem a roundabout procedure. There are rough and ready answers closer at hand. American social scientists have been apt to see the

scientific aspiration of American social science as merely an outgrowth of
the original scientistic impulse of the social sciences. But a glance across time
and national boundaries shows us that science could take different forms
in dealing with sociohistorical events. In the eighteenth century and a good
part of the nineteenth, science was loosely understood as systematic natural
knowledge, and its models of scientific method ranged from the inductive-
deductive method of Newton to the critical philology of Herder and the
Göttingen Gelehrten. Various species of historico-evolutionary empiricism
were added to the list with Comte, Spencer, and Darwin. All these models
were available to American social scientists, and from the early nineteenth
century they found points of attraction across the entire range. More critical demands were made upon scientific method toward the end of the
nineteenth century, but these new scientific standards did not foreordain the
result. The ancient rule that method be appropriate to its subject matter
continued to leave wide room for interpretation, especially when the subject
matter of the social sciences was – and had been from the outset – history
itself. The particular kind of scientific stance American social scientists chose
cannot be explained without resort to their particular kind of historical
consciousness.

Another frequent explanation for the distinctive characteristics of American social science is that they simply mirror the unique characteristics of
American society. American social science is uniformly liberal because
American society and political culture are uniformly liberal. American social
science is practical and technocratic because its citizens are practical democrats and value technology. As against the latter we will see that American
social science was not developed by practical Yankees, but by an increasingly academic class, rooted in moral philosophy, and committed to the values
of an elite segment of American society. If they were concerned with
practical power, it was because they generally felt themselves somewhat
distant from it.

The liberal interpretation of American society and politics likewise misses
the complexities of American experience. American liberal thinkers, most
notably Louis Hartz, have urged that American political culture was wholly
liberal from its inception and defined liberalism as acquisitive individualism.
American exceptionalism rested on its liberal character, for the absence of
feudalism led to the absence of socialism and locked American politics into
liberal consensus.[2] I argue in this book, however, that the consensual
framework of American politics that developed in the late eighteenth and

---

2 Louis Hartz, *The Liberal Tradition in America* (New York: Harcourt, Brace & World,
   1955).

early nineteenth century formed out of the intersection of Protestant, republican, and liberal ideas around the idea of America. Inscribed in that national ideology were not only liberal market values, but Protestant and republican ambivalence toward capitalist development and historical change. It created not a stable liberal consensus, but a continuing quarrel with history. The exceptionalist framework stimulated, as well as contained, conflict and its power of containment was repeatedly tested and defended. If socialism did not develop in America as a major political force, industrialization still raised the problem of class conflict and the threat of socialism. Under the pressures of American exceptionalism, the problem and the threat loomed large and shaped the social scientists' liberal response. They redefined the American exceptionalist ideal in wholly liberal terms and read back those terms to the origin of the Republic. The Hartzian view of American experience is itself a product of that liberal revision of American exceptionalism.

Moreover, the uniqueness of American experience among the Western countries has been exaggerated, for each national history has been shaped by the interaction of common and unique factors. The social sciences that developed in the European countries have also had ties to liberalism and have sought to become scientific. But these common factors have been shaped by the historical cultures in which they emerged, so that in each country, the social-science disciplines took on somewhat different political tasks and located themselves somewhat differently between what we in America call the humanities and the natural sciences. German culture was most deeply shaped by historical understanding, and so too the social scientific models of *Wissenschaft* within it, from the liberal Roscher and Weber to the radical Marx and Mannheim. In France, history has shared influence with rational philosophy and positive science, but has continued to shape *les sciences humaines* since the days of Tocqueville and Comte. England, like America, has been less influenced by historical thinking than the continental countries, but also less swayed than the United States by the model of the natural sciences. Independent disciplines of sociology and political science did not arise to join with economics as a distinctly scientific genre of knowledge; instead economics, philosophy, politics, and history largely retained their nineteenth-century alliances as university studies.

These relationships between the Western countries cannot, however, be placed along a single continuum. We will find, for example, that there were similarities between American and continental social science that were lacking in England, similarities that reflected the late nineteenth-century sense of national crisis and concern with historical change that the United States shared with Germany and France. We will also find that the lingering

American desire to escape history that separated its historical consciousness from Europe in the early nineteenth century brought it closer to Europe's modernist historical consciousness in the early twentieth century. To map out the similarities and differences between American and European social science, however, would require another book. Once we see how America's distinctive national ideology and social scientific task emerged from European social science, I will return only occasionally to the comparative context, in order to highlight American developments.

I should make clear, therefore, lest there be any room for doubt, that my examination of the ideology of American exceptionalism is a critique of this idea of American uniqueness, not an endorsement. While claiming to describe the American world as it was, exceptionalism instead distorted that world, providing a simplistic and idealized vision of the United States and exaggerating American uniqueness. The idea of American difference and the ideology of American exceptionalism has nonetheless played an extremely important role in American life and deeply shaped the structure of social and political thought. This ideology has, I believe, made American experience *more* different from that of other countries than would have been the case had Americans developed a more differentiated view of themselves. In this limited sense, I plead guilty to a species of American exceptionalism. But my intention in singling out this ideology for historical critique is to render it less effective in the future.

The approach I have taken to this study is designed to capture a central line of development in American social science, not the whole story of the social sciences in America. It is an attempt to uncover a fundamental and deeply imbedded dynamic in American social science, a dynamic that links it at its core to American history and that becomes visible only when the underlying values and premises of social scientists are surveyed over a long stretch of that history.

My approach is, therefore, that of intellectual history, that kind of intellectual history which seeks to reconstruct the discourse within which social scientists worked.[3] I understand discourse as conversation, developed over time, centering around certain problems, setting the terms of discussion for those who enter into it, and at the same time responding to the different

---

3 My understanding of discourse draws upon J. G. A. Pocock, "The Concept of a Language and the *métier d'historien*: Some Considerations on Practice," in *The Languages of Political Theory in Early Modern Europe*, ed. Anthony Pagden (Cambridge University Press, 1987), 19–38; James Tully, ed., *Meaning and Context: Quentin Skinner and His Critics* (Princeton, N.J.: Princeton University Press, 1988), pts. 1, 2, 4; David Hollinger, "Historians and the Discourse of Intellectuals," in *New Directions in American Intellectual History*, ed. John Higham and Paul Conkin (Baltimore: Johns Hopkins University Press, 1979), 42–63.

intentions of participants. Discourses are numerous and overlapping, though I will confine the term here to the disciplinary traditions of discussion that grew up around the problems of modern society, polity, and economy, and to the national discussion of America's exceptional place in history.

Such an approach to intellectual history necessarily reaches out in two directions. A discourse is composed of a language, a special idiom or rhetoric, and of acts of utterance by those who participate in it. Hence we can distinguish between the language of a discourse and the way it is actually spoken. A language provides a distinctive logic and rhetorical armory, hence a particular set of possibilities and limitations. But it may be used to express different ideas, it may be used for tactical purposes, and it may produce effects on its participants and audience other than the ones intended. Discourse understood in this way also reaches out to the contexts in which language is formed and propagates. Language emerges from life and orients people to living; it is not separable from the history that surrounds it. The problems that provoked the conversation of American social scientists and the intentions they pursued in that conversation arose from the disciplinary and historical contexts within which they lived. The focus on discourse will therefore lead me to situate their language in the economic, political, and social institutions that formed their historical world. On occasion we will find that a spoken language becomes the ideology of a political class, discipline, or profession.

I have presented social scientific discourse by focusing on the leading figures who, at each historical juncture, carry the discourse forward. They are the people who have grappled closely with the problems their discourse set for them and emerged with characteristic or revealing resolutions of those problems. Often, though not always, they have been the most influential figures in their own or later generations. At each juncture I have tried to present as many voices as are necessary – and only as many as are necessary – to show the major lines of advance, some significant variations, and occasionally, the exceptional person who proves the rule. As the story moves into the twentieth century and the social sciences enlarge, the cast of characters inevitably becomes more selective and incomplete. My selection has been informed by reading a great deal, but by no means all, of what American social scientists wrote during these years, and aided by a rich body of secondary studies. By and large, I have chosen to critique the standard canon of American social science by analyzing the standard canon, rather than enlarging it, although I have noted carefully where the boundaries have been set.

In defining economics, sociology, and political science as the core social sciences, I have not systematically included history, psychology, and anthropology, disciplines which have often had a partial allegiance to the social sciences. I have paid considerable attention to the historical discipline because it so thoroughly overlapped the study of politics in the nineteenth century, and because it was centrally concerned in the retreat from history of the other social sciences. I have paid less attention to psychology and anthropology because their origins in the biological sciences and natural history gave them a different set of concerns; during the formative decades of the social sciences in America, they were only partially and indirectly involved in the common discourse about American exceptionalism. I have, however, brought them into my discussion when they become central to the social scientists' discussions. The development of pragmatism by John Dewey and the influence of functional and then behaviorist psychology are treated here as central features of the social scientific discourse. Anthropology played a less prominent role, as a model of critical method, as a support for evolutionary and racial theories, and then through Boasian cultural anthropology, as a solvent of evolutionism.

I should note also that I have, partly for the sake of convenience, used the terms "social science" and "social scientists" as collective terms throughout the book for the different traditions and kinds of thinkers with which I am dealing. We can recognize the unitary, though differentiated, phenomenon these terms represent, even though the collective designation did not come into common use until the early twentieth century in the United States. The otherwise specific historical contexts delineated in the book should prevent any anachronistic implications from arising.[4]

Like all the books I consider in these chapters, this book, too, is shaped by the intentions of its author and the discourse to which those purposes are tied. The reconstruction of the past is always a dialogue with the past, whether acknowledged as such or not, and I believe the writing of history has something to gain from pursuing the dialogue more self-consciously. On one level, my purpose in writing this book is relatively simple. As a scholar of American intellectual history, I would like to integrate the study of the social sciences more fully into the study of American culture, so that students of history will find the subject more accessible and so that we can

---

4 The terms "social science" and "social sciences" emerged in the late eighteenth century as one designation for the new political and moral sciences. At times during the nineteenth century, it was more closely associated with a specific kind of social science – the theory of Charles Fourier or Comte, the remedial work of the British and American social science associations – than with the disciplinary traditions established in the universities. See Peter R. Senn, "The Earliest Use of the Term 'Social Science,' " *Journal of the History of Ideas*, 19 (1958): 568–70; Georg G. Iggers, "Further Remarks about Early Uses of the Term 'Social Science'," ibid., 20 (1959): 433–6; Fred R. Shapiro, "A Note on the Origin of the Term 'Social Science,' " *JHBS*, 20 (January 1984): 20–2.

consider more carefully just what happened in America when social thought was partially transformed into social science.

My larger purpose, for which I hold out less hope of success, is that by demonstrating the extent to which social scientific choices were rooted in history, I can suggest that those choices are open to reexamination. Social scientists may have had "good reasons" for choosing their scientistic path, but they were reasons consistently hemmed in by their historical intentions. Given hindsight, we may find that there are better reasons for choosing differently. My own view is that the separation between history and the social sciences at the turn of the century, and the contemporaneous retreat among historians from their colleagues' synthetic concerns, were disadvantageous for both history and the social sciences.

These judgments and concerns place this study in sympathy with two movements in American historiography over the past twenty years or so, which partly overlap: one, the effort to use systematic methods and social scientific theory more extensively in historiography; the second, the rise of a vigorous new, left historiography, which has used Marxist theories against the liberal tradition of the American historical profession. These are diverse movements, and I do not feel allegiance to all aspects of them. A fair number of social and social scientific historians are attracted to the natural science model of the social sciences and uncritically try to import it into historiography; some left historians seem to me to sacrifice too much of the complexity and ambiguity of history to theory. But in general , my sympathy with these new directions has led me to regret that so much of twentieth-century social science is historically vacuous and to see how scientism and liberal ideology have interacted to enforce political and ahistorical constraints on social thinking. Part of the professional bargain made in the early twentieth century, after a considerable amount of acrimonious debate, was to let each specialized field of sociohistorical knowledge go its own way. That too was a historical choice.

The largest single intellectual stimulus for this book has come from the work of J. G. A. Pocock. Though it emerged from a different disciplinary and political context than those upon which I was drawing, *The Machiavellian Moment* converged in important ways with those contexts and spoke powerfully to the desire to broaden American intellectual history beyond the confines of conventional liberal interpretation. More important, I recognized in *The Machiavellian Moment* the origin of my social scientists. Pocock's work gave me the central problem of American social science – the fate of the American Republic in time. It also showed me the historical form that problem took, a discourse that shaped the way Americans experienced history, even as it was reshaped by that experience. In the end, these ideas of history and American history sustained me during the long period of composition, for they forced me to grapple, at a deeper level than I had anticipated, with my understanding of the American Republic and the problem of historical relativism. Such grappling is the only answer there is to the historian's endless regress of contextuality. The hermeneutic circle, for all the limitations it places upon knowledge, gives us access to the happenings of history and the experience of life.

# PART I

European social science in
antebellum America

# 1

◁══════════════════════════════════════▷

# The discovery of modernity

The social sciences began in America by importing and adapting models of political economy, political science, and sociology developed in Europe in the eighteenth and early nineteenth centuries. These were new ways of understanding the historical world, born out of a new kind of historical consciousness and shaped by the emerging contours of capitalist society.

The social sciences originated in the eighteenth century in an effort to understand the character and future of modern society. Montesquieu's *Spirit of the Laws* (1748), Adam Smith's *Wealth of Nations* (1776), Condorcet's *Outline of an Historical View of the Progress of the Human Mind* (1795), and J. G. Herder's *Ideas towards a Philosophy of History* (1784–91) were exemplary texts of the new sciences. Premised on a decisive difference between modern society and its feudal and ancient forerunners, they envisioned social sciences that would guide modern society into the future. The effort to create social sciences was bound up with the discovery that history was a realm of human construction, propelled ever forward in time by the cumulative effects of human action, and taking new qualitative forms.[1]

---

1 The claim that the social sciences originated in a historical question, namely the character and future of modern society, has been generally made for sociology and its classic nineteenth-century texts: Philip Abrams, "The Sense of the Past and the Origins of Sociology," *Past and Present*, no. 55 (May 1972): 18–19; Theda Skocpol, "Sociology's Historical Imagination," in *Vision and Method in Historical Sociology*, ed. Theda Skocpol (Cambridge University Press, 1984), 1–2, 20. That the claim holds good for economics and political science and their exemplary eighteenth-century texts, as well, can be seen in Duncan Forbes, "'Scientific' Whiggism: Adam Smith and John Millar," *The Cambridge Journal*, 7 (August 1954): 643–70; Keith Michael Baker, *Condorcet* (Chicago: University of Chicago Press, 1975), chaps. 4–6; Isaiah Berlin, *Vico and Herder* (New York: Viking, 1976). Although Montesquieu lacked a sense of the cumulative movement of history in time, he was a central figure in the recognition of history as a human construction. See, in addition to Berlin, Friedrich Meinecke, *Historism*, trans. J. E. Anderson (London: Routledge & Kegan

3

This understanding of history was a late and complex achievement of the modern West. At the end of the Middle Ages, history was not intelligible in terms of human actions. The ultimate causes and meaning of historical events on earth were understood by Christian minds to lie in the supernatural world, in the sequence of eternal Christian time within which earthly history was enacted. The long dominance of that view and the heritage of ancient idealism had sharply limited the understanding of historical change. Within the medieval framework, the timeless realm of nature was subject to rationality and law, but the succession of particular events that constituted history could only be understood as pure chance; as repetitive and hence timeless custom; as devolution or decay from the ideal, rational forms which essentially defined human existence; or as the occasional scene of divine action.[2]

The modern understanding of history was one aspect of the broader movement toward secularization. The Christian view that eternal time was punctuated by an ascending sequence of sacred events was projected into secular time, imparting a degree of meaning and progressive organization to history. At the same time, the changing earthly world was slowly loosed from the eternal world of God and His immutable truth, and secular modes of understanding the particular configurations of human history gained authority. Change could then be understood as a succession of qualitatively different phenomena, not merely as random variations, or the surface appearance of essentially unchanging things, or the recurring cycle of an endless wheel. The past became both qualitatively different from and causally linked to the present. It was not until the early nineteenth century that this understanding of history as a continuous procession of qualitative changes came fully into view and that many European thinkers began to interpret the whole of reality, including what had earlier been conceived as absolute and unchanging, in contextual historical terms. I will call this new view of history "historicist" and this new interpretive tendency, "historicism."[3]

Paul, 1972), chap. 3. These texts have been chosen in part for their importance to the social sciences in America and in part to illustrate the diversity of the tradition. I believe my argument would hold as well for such other exemplars as Adam Ferguson, Hume, Turgot, Vico, and Kant.

2 J. G. A. Pocock, *The Machiavellian Moment* (Princeton, N.J.: Princeton University Press, 1975), pt. 1.

3 This definition follows Hayden V. White, "On History and Historicisms," Introduction to *From History to Sociology. The Transition in German Historical Thinking*, by Carlo Antoni (Detroit: Wayne State University Press, 1959), xv–xxviii. Conceptions of historicism more closely attuned to German romanticism and German experience are developed by Meinecke, *Historism*, and Georg G. Iggers, *The German Conception of History* (Middletown, Conn.: Wesleyan University Press, 1968). A more limited philosophical definition of

The social sciences and historicism emerged together from a number of early modern cultural traditions. Despite the ancient separation between the rational understanding of nature and the particularistic understanding of historical events, both these approaches to the human world converged in the eighteenth-century discovery of modern society and in the work of Montesquieu, Smith, Condorcet, and Herder. Humanists and legal scholars began first to decipher the ways in which literature, art, and law varied between nations and across time and to explain those differences by natural and historical circumstances. Debate between the champions of ancient and modern culture and national conflicts over political power mobilized these traditions and made the difference of the past increasingly visible. The pioneer works of Montesquieu and Herder were among the fruits of this scholarship. Insisting on the qualitative differences between nations, they explored the roots of those differences in physical conditions, cultural influences, and historical experience. Herder, unlike Montesquieu, placed those differences fully in the dimension of time, so that each nation, rooted in a long-standing culture, had to work out its destiny in the new forms available to every age.[4]

The revival of civic humanism in Renaissance Italy and early modern Europe generated another source of historical understanding. Living still in the timeless world of rational forms and eternal salvation, Italian patriots revived the civic humanist ideal, that human beings fully realized themselves in political activity. The republic was the ideal polity, founded on and sustained by the balanced participation of the one, the few, and the many. This was a brave attempt to realize universal values in historical time and hence a decisive step toward investing historical time with meaning. As the creation of time, however, the republic would suffer the inevitably destructive effects of time. The virtuous republic was only a moment in a recurrent cycle of corruption and decay.

In their efforts to protect the republic from decay, republican thinkers over the next centuries came to an increasingly sophisticated understanding of historical causation. By the mid-eighteenth century, Whig and republican thinkers in Britain and France had begun to sense a paradoxical historical

historicism, which specifically excludes the historian's "historical sense," is discussed in Maurice H. Mandelbaum, *History, Man, and Reason: A Study in Nineteenth Century Thought* (Baltimore: Johns Hopkins University Press, 1971), pt. 2. A still more limited, and tendentious, definition of historicism was popularized by Karl Popper in *The Poverty of Historicism* (London: Routledge & Kegan Paul, 1957).

4 Donald R. Kelley, *Foundations of Modern Historical Scholarship* (New York: Columbia University Press, 1970); J. G. A. Pocock, *The Ancient Constitution and the Feudal Law* (Cambridge University Press, 1957); Berlin, *Vico and Herder*, 42–52, 147–51, 167–9; Meinecke, *Historism*, chaps. 3, 9.

outcome: The simple agrarian historical conditions that secured the health of the republic belonged to the primitive past and the modern civilization, commerce, and refinement which Europe was calling progress produced republican decay. In response to this impasse, the social and historical thinkers of the Scottish Enlightenment, most notably Adam Smith, abandoned the republic for commercial improvement and turned the republican cycle into a multistage theory of historical progress. The message of Smith's new science of wealth was that modern Western society could for a long time to come escape the stasis or decline that had befallen all other societies by freeing the transformative energies of commerce and industry.[5]

The development of natural science through direct observation and manipulation of natural phenomena also contributed to the new perception of modern historical progress. In the influential program of Francis Bacon, the new men of science would improve and reconstruct life on earth along a progressively enlightened course. By the eighteenth century, the sweeping discoveries of Newton seemed to renew Bacon's promise. Enlightenment social thinkers found the progress of the practical arts and of science the most convincing evidence that modern society, heir to the cumulative gains of reason, would not succumb to barbarism or decay as its predecessors had. Upon this insight, Condorcet constructed a theory of progress as the advance of reason and proposed that social science light the way to the future.[6]

Science contributed in still another way to the modern conception of history by linking rational intelligibility to the particular configurations of history. In order to apply the new "experimental" method to the human world, David Hume urged observation of the "uniformity among the actions of men, in all nations and ages." By marking how in certain constant circumstances, the unchanging propensities of human nature gave rise to constant consequences, and under given variations, varied in given ways, empirical laws could be discovered comparable to the laws scientists discovered in nature. This procedure was congenial with a tendency already at work in the older natural law tradition, which moved from the ideal laws of conduct revealed by "right reason" toward exploration of the relative action of reason in the imperfect conditions of human existence. Montesquieu,

---

5 Pocock, *Machiavellian Moment*, pts. 2, 3; Forbes, " 'Scientific' Whiggism"; J. G. A. Pocock, "Cambridge Paradigms and Scotch Philosophers: A Study of the Relations between the Civic Humanist and the Civil Jurisprudential Interpretation of Eighteenth-Century Social Thought," in *Wealth and Virtue: The Shaping of Political Economy in the Scottish Enlightenment*, ed. Istvan Hont and Michael Ignatieff (Cambridge University Press, 1984), 235–52.
6 J. B. Bury, *The Idea of Progress* (New York: Macmillan, 1932), chaps. 2, 5–7, 11; Baker, *Condorcet*, chap. 6.

Hume, and Smith were following that path when they explored the diverse rationality of human action under different circumstances. As Enlightenment thinkers became increasingly concerned with the problem of progress, they focused on that second and changing "nature" formed by manners, customs, and institutions. Although Smith assumed certain universal psychological propensities, like the propensity to barter, and posited universal laws of exchange, like the relationship of price to supply and demand, he was concerned with the progressive course of human development. He came to see that "all the arts, the sciences, law and government, wisdom and even virtue itself" were rooted in the economic organization of society, and hence changed as civilization progressed through the stages of hunting, herding, agriculture, and commerce.[7]

The social sciences were imbued at their inception with a new understanding of history and with high expectations of modernity. They approved the historical supports of modern society – commercial development, science, and in most cases, the representative state. Drawing on the Enlightenment understanding of civilization developed in Scotland and France, they defined modernity as diversification, in which the rude and simple structures of primitive and feudal life gave way to complexity, multiplying comforts, and multiplying values. Generated by the division of labor, as Adam Smith showed, and abetted by the advance and specialization of the sciences, diversification created a world in which individuals could choose multiple goals and realize varied potentialities. The social sciences were to be agents of improvement. Developed in the utilitarian milieu of the Enlightenment and in the moral discourses of the Scottish and German universities, their programs were in the broadest sense practical and moral. In their focus on the diverse realm of economic activity, practical arts, and refined enjoyments – a world of private values as opposed to the classical realm of political action – they discovered society and began to consider it the essential and most inclusive ground of human activity.[8]

From the outset the social sciences were also committed to using tools

---

7 Meinecke, *Historism*, 101–4; Duncan Forbes, *Hume's Philosophical Politics* (Cambridge University Press, 1975), chap. 4; Andrew S. Skinner, "Science and the Role of the Imagination," in *A System of Social Science. Papers Relating to Adam Smith* ([Clarendon Press] Oxford University Press, 1979), 14–15; Forbes, "'Scientific' Whiggism," 655–7. Smith's quotation is from his lectures on jurisprudence, cited in Ronald L. Meek, *Social Science and the Ignoble Savage* (Cambridge University Press, 1976), 126.

8 Montesquieu belonged to an early and moderate phase of the Enlightenment. Herder was a partial exception, both accepting and rebelling against Enlightenment values. He believed in free self-determination as against a coercive state, the progress of humanity, and progress of the arts and sciences, but the diversity he valued was grounded in romantic holism rather than economic functionalism. See Berlin, *Vico and Herder*, 145–216.

provided both by natural science and by historical and cultural investigation. Their task of understanding the future tendency of history as well as their eighteenth-century sources yoked them to both universal laws of nature and particularistic understanding of historical culture and institutions. Condorcet sought to develop a statistical social science, based on mathematical laws of probability, that would provide the means for rational decision-making in politics. Smith followed Newton in searching for simple laws underlying widely varying phenomena, but he also imbedded those laws in a historical account of the economic, political, and social conditions that gave rise to commercial society and sustained it. Herder proposed an empirical, historical science that would use psychology and the study of language and culture to facilitate progress, primarily through education. His writings effected an uneasy synthesis between universal laws of nature, the differing circumstances of race, geography, and culture, and the moral purposes individuals and peoples enacted in history.[9]

The discovery of modernity remains to this day the fundamental context in which to understand the social sciences, for the future of modern society remains their central question; diversification remains central to their understanding of modern society; moral and utilitarian goals continue to shape their programs; and diverse conceptions of scientific method still bridge general law and particularistic investigation. As history changes, however, new contexts emerge: the programs of the eighteenth-century originators of social science were transformed in important respects by the dynamic history that they had been among the first to recognize. By the early nineteenth century, the French Revolution and its contentious aftermath, the accelerated development of capitalism, and the growth of romanticism deepened the modern understanding of history and quickened the urgency with which social scientists examined the fate of modern society.

Although the eighteenth-century pioneers of social science had recognized the historical existence of modern society, most of them had not viewed all of human existence from a historicist perspective. For Montesquieu history still remained, like nature and divinity, essentially immutable, its distinctions and changes occurring as variations within a static framework. The Enlightenment idea of progress, with its confidence in human powers and unidirectional sense of time, marked a major step in the

9 Baker, *Condorcet*, pt. 1; Skinner, "Science and the Role of the Imagination"; Forbes, "'Scientific' Whiggism"; H. B. Nisbet, *Herder and the Philosophy and History of Science* (Cambridge: The Modern Humanities Research Association, 1970), chaps. 1, 2; F. M. Barnard, *Herder's Social and Political Thought* (Oxford: Oxford University Press [Clarendon Press], 1965), chaps. 6, 7.

direction of historicism, but progress still often remained the product of extrahistorical causes. For Condorcet, the law at work in history was the human ability to reason by combining sensations and ideas, and thereby to reason "according to the sentiment of virtue and the immutable law of right." The progress of civilization was the result of the "necessary development of human faculties," not of history. Smith's account of the rise of commercial society recognized both the "natural" progression of civilization through economic stages and the force of historical contingencies and unintended consequences, as when the alliance of monarchs and burghers against feudal lords increased the strength of cities and the commercial class. Smith's account could be read as a "natural" or "philosophical" history, in which the events of history were only the particular "accidents" through which a natural course of progression worked itself out. Or his account could be read as fundamentally historicist, so that the progressive order and the contingent actions that could subvert or encourage it existed equally within the open framework of history.[10]

The French Revolution, particularly the failures of that revolution, had a major effect in moving European thinkers toward historicism. As the Revolution fell into tyranny and reaction, the millennial and apocalyptic hopes it had aroused were projected into the secular future. Humanity was cast fully into history and salvation fully into historical time. Immanuel Kant, at the end of his life, as well as G. W. F. Hegel, expressed the new recognition that history alone was the arena in which humanity must work out its destiny.[11]

Romanticism also provided a fuller appreciation of the particular configurations of the historical world. Emerging in reaction to the Enlightenment attempt to subject all reality to universal and mechanistic general laws, the Romantics grounded value and sought intelligibility in the individuality and diversity of historical existence. The German *Aufklärar* anticipated the romantic reaction and the French Revolution stimulated romanticism and historicism all over Europe. As the Revolution carried its conflicts and

10 Mandelbaum, *History, Man, and Reason*, chap. 3; Baker, *Condorcet*, 346. For a naturalistic reading of Smith, see Dugald Stewart, "Account of the Life and Writings of Adam Smith," in Smith, *Essays on Philosophical Subjects*, ed. W. P. D. Wightman and J. C. Bryce (Oxford: Oxford University Press [Clarendon Press], 1980), 292–6, and Andrew S. Skinner, "Natural History in the Age of Adam Smith," *Political Studies*, 15 (February 1967): 32–48. For an interesting reading of Hume and Smith as historicists, see Don Herzog, *Without Foundations* (Ithaca, N.Y.: Cornell University Press, 1985).

11 M. H. Abrams, *Natural Supernaturalism: Tradition and Revolution in Romantic Literature* (New York: Norton, 1971); White, "On History and Historicisms," xv–xix; Immanuel Kant, *On History*, ed. Lewis White Beck (Indianapolis, Ind.: Bobbs-Merrill, 1963).

French rule across the continent, its universal claims were countered with a new awareness of the individuality of different cultures and histories.[12] Historicism accentuated the diversity and contingency of the human past and future. In this new context, sharper tensions emerged between the complex particularity of history and the natural models of lawful regularity that had joined together in the social scientific program.

Historicism imposed on Western Europe – and on the social sciences – an immense historical and synthetic task, but before we examine it, we must understand that the task was made more difficult by the ideological contention that at once overtook it. In the aftermath of the French Revolution and the wake of industrial development, commercial classes challenged the traditional landowning class for political power and worker riots and radical protest challenged both. Fears of political and social revolution galvanized the social scientists' inquiry into the fate of modern society and reshaped their ideological bearings.

The term "liberal" was first adopted in the early nineteenth century by English and continental radicals who sought to destroy the remains of feudal and mercantilist power in the state and to place justice, representation, and economic activity on individualistic bases. The social sciences that had emerged in the eighteenth century belonged to the broad stream of social and political thought that was antecedent and tributary to liberalism. The eighteenth-century originators of social science were members of the social world of the reform-minded aristocracy and educated middle class, functionaries, professors, doctors, lawyers, and clerics who wanted to throw off the traditional restraints placed on reason and initiative. Their visions of society, polity, and economy acknowledged a central place for the rights, powers, or potentialities of the individual person.[13]

The liberalism that emerged in the early nineteenth century absorbed the Enlightenment's view of modern civilization as a realm of progressive diversification and its faith in commercial development, science, and representative government. Deriving social value and authority from the individual, liberals constructed an individualistic and libertarian political

---

12  Meinecke, *Historism*; Iggers, *German Conception of History*; Lionel Gossman, *Medievalism and the Ideologies of the Enlightenment: The World and Work of LaCurne de Sainte-Palaye* (Baltimore: Johns Hopkins University Press, 1968); Thomas Preston Peardon, *The Transition in English Historical Writing, 1760–1830* (New York: AMS Press, 1966).

13  N. T. Phillipson, "Culture and Society in the 18th Century Province: The Case of Edinburgh and the Scottish Enlightenment," in *The University in Society*, 2 vols., ed. Lawrence Stone (Princeton, N.J.: Princeton University Press, 1974), 2:407–48. Dorothy Ross, "Liberalism," *Encyclopedia of American Political History*, 1984 ed., 2:750–63, lists the sources from which my account of liberalism is drawn.

language. Liberalism was, and still is, subject to differing interpretations and is put to different uses, depending upon what implications are drawn from the view that the individual is "self-possessed." John Locke for example, a primary source of liberal theory, used a universalistic language capable of democratic as well as libertarian interpretation, when he argued that individuals stand in a state of nature, as before God, free and equal and that "every man's soul belongs unto himself." But Locke also emphasized the propertied bases of liberty. Reflecting the commercial capitalism of his day, he used property as a metaphor for all natural rights, whether of body, soul, or mind, or of material possessions made one's own by labor. Moreover, he anchored in natural right the inequality of property that resulted from the use of money. The protection of property became the central reason men agreed to form a government.[14]

The divergence between the humanistic and commercial bases of liberalism has been compounded by the divergence between the negative and positive implications of freedom. Liberalism emerged from a judicial mode of thought in which liberty was understood as a specific grant or right bestowed by law, ultimately by the law of God or nature. This was a negative liberty, which left the person free from coercive authority to pursue specific activities and relationships. Still, liberty depended positively on an accountable government of laws to protect the individual's natural rights. Adam Smith retained a strong sense of the proper, if limited, legislative functions of government and sought liberal supports for citizenship. In the nineteenth-century English liberal tradition, however, government could be consigned to little else beyond securing individual rights from the interference of others. Not only was the individual self-possessed, but a society composed of autonomous individuals pursuing their own interests was self-sustaining. In the very different German Kantian tradition, individual self-realization and the harmony of society were understood to require the positive actions of the state.[15] Liberalism everywhere presented an unsteady balance of conflicting tendencies. Its humanistic implications could be limited by its economic bias. Its individualistic premises could deny conceptions of public good and erode the virtues necessary to sustain society and polity. The liberalism about to emerge in early nineteenth-century England,

14 John Dunn, *The Political Thought of John Locke* (Cambridge University Press, 1969); Richard Ashcraft, *Revolutionary Politics and Locke's "Two Treatises of Government"* (Princeton, N.J.: Princeton University Press, 1986); C. B. Macpherson, *The Political Theory of Possessive Individualism* (Oxford: Oxford University Press [Clarendon Press], 1962).
15 Pocock, "Cambridge Paradigms and Scotch Philosophers"; Donald Winch, *Adam Smith's Politics* (Cambridge University Press, 1978); James J. Sheehan, *German Liberalism in the Nineteenth Century* (Chicago: University of Chicago Press, 1978).

traditionally called "classical" liberalism, and critically, "possessive individualism," had a negative and economic bias.

In the political upheavals and social conflicts of the early nineteenth century, the program of liberal progress that had emerged from the eighteenth century – and the social sciences along with it – came under increasing challenge. Capitalist development was already producing consequences Adam Smith had not foreseen; the postrevolutionary order was everywhere contested. Liberals found themselves vulnerable to the conservative charge that liberalism created not a harmonious order but political chaos, social disorganization, and the exploitation of labor; only an organically integrated society, conservatives claimed, founded on the mutual duties of classes and the consensual ties of religion could be stable and just.

Auguste Comte accepted a good part of this organicist critique in formulating his social theory and grafted it onto the stem of liberal social science. Comte retained the division of labor as a characteristic feature of modern society and he also retained Condorcet's faith in the progress of reason, turning it into a three-stage historical law. Like the conservatives, however, Comte believed that modernity was creating social and moral fragmentation. History could not be rolled back and the traditional organic order reinstated, but liberal progress was itself producing the force that would create social order. The present age would see the triumph of scientific thinking, culminating in the science of sociology, and scientific rationality would command agreement. Comte's liberal readers branched off at this point in his argument, urging the conscious use of science by a technocratic state to order the modern differentiated society. Comte himself went on to a conservative conclusion: a hierarchical, authoritarian society integrated by the scientific construction of organic institutions.[16]

In Germany the liberal social science program generally took a more statist and conservative stance, influenced both by nationalism and the organicist critique of liberalism. The longing among the middle class for political unification and the German experience, in which modern forms had been introduced by central monarchs in opposition to feudal centers of power, led German liberals to think that both liberty and social order were the creation of the state and its rule of law. As demands for mass suffrage increased and class conflict widened, liberals grew increasingly fearful. The multiplying interests of society had to be brought under the unifying authority of the constitutional state. At the same time, Kantian and Hegelian

---

16 Lucien Levy-Bruhl, *The Philosophy of Auguste Comte* (London: Swan, Sonnenschein, 1903); Harriet Martineau, ed., *The Positive Philosophy of Auguste Comte* (New York: C. Blanchard, 1855).

idealism tended to exempt the real state from critical attack. Hence German writers who formulated social science programs in the early nineteenth century hesitantly drew conservative German political traditions toward liberalism, and were themselves drawn toward acceptance of authoritarian national rule. By mid-century, such mediating liberals had laid the foundation for an empirical science of politics; practical, administrative sciences for the instruction of state officials, and a juristic science of the *Rechtsstaat*, the ideal state as embodied in public law.

Liberal economists, too, followed that mediating path. Inspired by the strong historiographical tradition developing in the universities, Wilhelm Roscher claimed that English political economy had become disengaged from historical reality. Economics had to be studied as part of national life, like all else in history, an organic whole. Roscher founded the tradition of historical economics in Germany that accepted an active state role in the liberal economy as a necessity of national history.[17]

Although Germany spawned an array of relatively conservative and organicist social sciences, it also spawned the most radical variant. Karl Marx, allying himself with the working class, turned Hegelian idealism, the liberal progress of British political economy, and the organicist critique of the conservatives into a radical science of history. If the capitalist market was producing a deformed and contentious integration, only the full development of capitalism would produce the economic abundance and the revolutionary force necessary to create communism. Ultimately, communism, not the market, would allow the harmonious integration of society and release the full individuality of its members.[18]

Contested on the right and left, liberal social science stiffened its defenses. Indeed, contention entered the liberal camp itself, as capitalist progress appeared to be producing not Smith's widespread improvement, but industrial crises and rootless poverty for the vast majority of England's working class. In 1798 the Reverend Thomas Malthus demonstrated that human population tends to increase much faster than food supply, so that the laboring population, which always multiplied more rapidly when subsistence improved, tended always to be reduced to the level of necessary subsistence. Aimed at the perfectionist hopes of the postrevolutionary

17 Leonard Krieger, *The German Idea of Freedom* (Boston: Beacon, 1957); Sheehan, *German Liberalism*; Otto Butz, *Modern German Political Theory* (New York: Doubleday, 1955); Charles Gide and Charles Rist, *A History of Economic Doctrines*, 2d ed. (Lexington, Mass.: Heath, 1948), bk. 4, chap. 1.
18 Gerald A. Cohen, *Karl Marx's Theory of History: A Defense* (Princeton, N.J.: Princeton University Press, 1978). J. D. Y. Peel, *Herbert Spencer* (New York: Basic, 1971), chap. 3, suggests one origin of Marx's harmonial ideal in radical liberalism.

utopian radicals, Malthus' pessimistic forecast was understood to strike down even the moderate hopes of the liberal economists.[19]

David Ricardo soon compounded liberal fears by adding to Malthus' law of population his own law of the diminishing returns on land. As less productive land was brought into cultivation, Ricardo said, land rents rose, raising the price of food, forcing capitalists to raise wages and take lower profits. Ricardo's conclusion was widely understood as a historical prediction of diverging class interest and the emergence of a stationary state when arable land was exhausted. It was, however, a cautionary tale, a hypothetical model of market forces holding technological improvement constant, designed in part to show the invidious basis of aristocratic support of the Corn Laws.

A banker, stockbroker, and member of Parliament, engaged throughout in the practical debates in which the liberals fought for control over economic policy, Ricardo went to the most contested point in political economy when he took the differential rate of profit as his problem. Sharpening Smith's method of hypothetical analysis into a formidable analytical and polemical tool, Ricardo focused political economy on Smith's theoretical model, lifted from the history of civilization and the bodies of historical data in which Smith had imbedded it. When Ricardo and his followers removed their economic theory from this historical framework, they not only reduced the science to its abstract elements but reduced history to the progressive course of liberal society deducible from them.

The liberal economists who followed Ricardo took over his method but sought to overturn what appeared to be his dire predictions. Focusing on the mechanization of British industry going on around them, and countering the working-class spokesmen who were putting Ricardo's analysis to radical use, the liberal economists showed that capital accumulation and technological progress were the driving forces of capitalist progress and would in the long run sustain Smith's hopes for market society. Their apologetic intentions also led them to expand the moral underpinnings Smith had given the market. The virtues bred by capitalist labor now permeated the system. Capital accumulation was defined as the product of abstinence, and neo-Malthusians promised slow improvement for the working class if it practiced sexual, as well as economic, abstinence. John Stuart Mill summed up this classic formulation of liberal economics in his *Principles of Political Economy* (1848), and softened its Victorian shadows by predicting the spread of

19 Maxine Berg, *The Machinery Question and the Making of Political Economy* (Cambridge University Press, 1980), pt. 1; Gide and Rist, *History of Economic Doctrines*, bk. 1, chap. 3.

cooperative industries and turning the stationary state into an era of modest comfort and continuing moral improvement.[20]

Shortly after Comte and Mill, Herbert Spencer put the last piece of liberal social science in place by developing a liberal version of sociology from the sociological materials implicit in Smith's political economy. Spencer's chief inspiration came from the radical republican politics of his youth and its ideal of cooperative individualism. His model of social organization came not from the organic institutions of traditional society Comte valued, but from the voluntary associations of the early industrial towns. On that fast-receding ground, he tried to construct for the liberal vision of history its largest vindication. He conferred upon the idea of progress through differentiation, which he learned from Smith, the status of a cosmic law of evolution: All things evolved from undifferentiated homogenous things into differentiated heterogenous things. Drawing out the vision of harmony implicit in Smith's liberal ideal, he pictured the functionally integrated, contractual, industrial society as a cooperative as well as competitive world, one which would produce altruism in its members and a peaceable world order. Spencer both softened the message and widened the authority of liberal political economy to counter its opponents left and right.[21]

At the same time that ideological conflict was generating competing versions of social science, social scientists were also responding to the problems posed by historicism. As the construction of human action, history was subject to the frailty and contingency upon which human events

20 Gide and Rist, *History of Economic Doctrines*, bk. 3, chap. 2; Berg, *Machinery Question*; J. S. Mill, *The Principles of Political Economy* (Toronto: University of Toronto Press, 1965 [1848]); Samuel Hollander, *The Economics of David Ricardo* (Toronto: University of Toronto Press, 1979) supports the hypothetical view of Ricardo's analysis and his continued belief in Smith's larger historical vision. Although Hollander disputes the specific origin of Ricardo's distributional analysis in the corn-law debate, he does not disprove its origin in the larger context of social conflict, which made distribution a central issue, nor the importance of the Corn Laws in focusing and developing Ricardo's analysis.
21 Herbert Spencer, *The Principles of Sociology*, 3d ed., 3 vols. (Westport, Conn.: Greenwood Press, 1975 [1897–1906]), vol. 1, pars. 215–17, 260. On the Smithian and radical sources of Spencer's theory see Peel, *Herbert Spencer*, 136–40, 217–23. Peel argues that it was only later in the nineteenth century, as liberalism itself changed and Spencer did not, that his views took on a conservative valence. American sociologists have most often traced the conservative character of sociology to the conservative tradition of Comtian sociology and conservative function of organicism. One consequence of that attribution is to maintain the libertarian purity of the American liberal tradition. See Robert A. Nisbet, *The Sociological Tradition* (New York: Basic, 1966) and Leon Bramson, *The Political Context of Sociology* (Princeton, N.J.: Princeton University Press, 1961). On the multiple political valences of mechanical and organic metaphors in social science, see Theodore M. Porter, "Natural Science and Social Theory," in *Companion to the History of Modern Science*, ed. R. C. Olby (London: Routledge & Kegan Paul, 1989).

turned. As a process of continuous, qualitative change, it also presented the constant challenge of novelty. What stable bases for understanding and praxis could be found in the historical world? Indeed, how could any values be secured? Adapting their eighteenth-century program to the task, early nineteenth-century social scientists found answers in progress, law, or an idealist conception of reason. With these tools they subdued the unsettling implications of historicism and also limited their perception of historical change.

The idea of progress could lessen the uncertainty of human agency and historical flux by anchoring a better future in longstanding historical causes or current historical transformations. In a still Christian culture, progress could compensate for the intolerable imperfections of the world. Neither the virtues of the past nor its failures need be regretted if both were helping to create an ever-higher level of civilization. But the idea of progress also weakened historical understanding. Particularly in those liberal social sciences in which the rationalist values of the Enlightenment dominated, the historicist appreciation of past cultures was less fully developed than in the conservative or radical social sciences. Opposed as they were to the liberal capitalist present, Comte and Marx envisioned history as a three-stage process in which the future would incorporate the organic community of earlier cultures in a new and higher form.

Beset on either side by these claimants to the past and impatient for change, nineteenth-century liberals turned increasingly to the future. Such successors of Adam Smith as Dugald Stewart and James Mill associated history with Tory defense of the past. Like Jeremy Bentham they believed a modern society had nothing to learn from the past and should go instead directly to the universal principles of human nature. It was in this political context that Ricardian political economy, with its analytic system of principles abstracted from history, took hold. For those engaged in understanding the historical course of progress, the whole past could be telescoped into a single stage which progress was leaving behind. Sir Henry Maine strengthened this two-stage liberal imagination when he characterized premodern societies as organized by status and modern societies by contract.[22]

If progress was one mechanism for counteracting the disturbing implications of historicism, another was scientific law. Eighteenth-century social

---

22 J. W. Burrow, *Evolution and Society* (Cambridge University Press, 1966); George W. Stocking, Jr., *Victorian Anthropology* (New York: Free Press, 1987); Stefan Collini, Donald Winch, and J. W. Burrow, *That Noble Science of Politics* (Cambridge University Press, 1983). There was a tendency even in Smith for the premodern stages to coalesce into a single, traditional stage antithetic to liberal, progressive modernity. See Berg, *Machinery Question*, 136–44.

scientists propounded the laws of nature as "rules through which divine governance flowed," thus fusing the scientific view of law as observed regularities in nature with the older religious concept of natural law as the agency by which God governed the natural world. By the early and mid-nineteenth century, the divine presence was generally discounted, but the characteristics of divine law – its necessity, uniformity, and action as a governing agency – most often continued to adhere to the laws scientists discovered in nature. Even many scientists and thinkers who accepted Hume's critique that scientific laws were merely observed phenomenal regularities, continued to think of scientific laws as necessitarian rules inhering in the structure of nature.[23]

This reification of scientific law was a product of both insecurity and confidence, reflecting both the need to rely on nature as divinity receded and a growing assurance in the scope and power of scientific investigation. At the same time, ideological conflict placed a premium on scientific authority. Social scientists and philosophers began to assert the special claims of natural science to knowledge and to extend its scope from nature to history. Although Comte coined the term positivism for his entire system, it became associated more closely with his general claims for scientific knowledge, particularly as they were defined by John Stuart Mill.

Drawing on the Enlightenment conclusion that only phenomena could be known, positivism asserted that scientific knowledge was the only certain knowledge, and therefore that it was the preferred form of knowledge. In the eighteenth century, and often in the nineteenth, the term science was applied to any systematic study in much the same way that Germans used the term *Wissenschaft* for all their scholarly disciplines. Positivism, however, applied a more selective standard of knowledge derived from natural science. For Mill, the Newtonian model of science, as it existed in the oldest and most developed physical science, astronomy, was paradigmatic. Newton's method required that scientists go directly to nature to observe phenomena, seek underlying causes and reach generalizations through induction, and finally arrange those generalizations in logically systematic form, so that verifiable conclusions could be deduced from them. The achievement of synthetic, deductive form was for Mill the decisive mark of science.[24]

Mill was, however, uncertain as to how far the social sciences could attain this form. Political economy, he believed, had already done so. By abstracting from the complexity of human motives and history a few basic motives

---

23 Mandelbaum, *History, Man, and Reason*, 87–8.
24 Ibid., 10–13, 167–8, 197–8; Leszek Kolakowski, *The Alienation of Reason* (New York: Doubleday, 1968); John Stuart Mill, *A System of Logic*, bk. 6: "On the Logic of the Moral Sciences," (Indianapolis, Ind.: Bobbs-Merrill, 1965 [1843]).

and a few basic facts of land and population, it had been able to derive a deductive model of the economy. From its principles one could deduce consequences that had the predictability and necessity of scientific law. Mill emphasized that to predict consequences in any particular situation, and to predict the course of historical development, it was necessary to take into account not only these scientific principles but also the complex array of human and historical factors that political economy had deliberately excluded from its model. To draw conclusions in concrete circumstances was not a science but an "art," one that had also to take account of human values. Mill himself, however, failed to heed that caution and like so many of his colleagues, projected an account of the future from the premises of political economy alone.[25]

In sociology, positivism supported an empirical science of social progress. Comte formulated a pluralistic view of science and argued that sociology, the most advanced because the newest of the sciences, need not take synthetic deductive form. Through historical study sociology discovered empirical laws of social progress, such as the law that the human mind progressed from animistic to metaphysical to scientific thinking. So long as such empirical laws conformed to what might be rationally deduced from the principles of human nature, Mill said, they could serve as the basis of a scientific sociology. Spencer's law that history evolved from undifferentiated homogeneity to differentiated heterogeneity could claim a similar positivist warrant from empirical historical evidence and conformance to natural laws of evolution at work throughout biological and physical nature.

Positivist sociology tended to turn all of history into a closed system. Although critics have focused on the distant influence of Aristotle or the authority of organic metaphors in the romantic and Darwinian nineteenth century, the underlying premise for the practice of treating "society" or "history" as a unitary organism was the belief in deterministic natural laws. Just as the "economy" had tended to become a closed system of variables from whose action all change in the system could be deduced, so too did society. Once the chief dynamic factors had been specified, rooted in nature, and the trajectory of their action set, history developed by an inner logic along a precharted course, substantially immune to the contingencies of historical change.[26]

25  Mill, "On the Logic of Moral Sciences"; idem, *Principles of Political Economy*, bk. 4.
26  While the organic and mechanical metaphors bore varied meanings, their closed, systematic character and consequent historical reductionism were identical. See Anthony D. Smith, *The Concept of Social Change* (London: Routledge & Kegan Paul, 1973); Peel, *Herbert Spencer*, 166–73. The source of the critique of social science as Aristotelian, organismic, and hence reductionist is Frederick J. Teggart, below, chapter 10, and Kenneth E. Bock, *The Acceptance of Histories* (Berkeley: University of California Press, 1956).

According to Mill, politics was the field least likely to become a science. Just as Mill continued to call the social sciences after their eighteenth-century title of moral sciences, so he continued to think of the polity as the most inclusive category and most subject to variable human motives, hence least likely to yield to reduction. Mill thought that an intermediate science of political ethology, which linked universal principles of human nature to national character, might open the way, but his suggestion was never followed. Instead a variety of studies took the name of political science, all of them based to some degree on empirical generalization from history. Henry Buckle was one of the few to claim positivist status for his empirical laws of history; for most, political science was understood in the looser sense of science as systematic knowledge.[27]

The historicism that underlay the early nineteenth-century social sciences thus existed in considerable tension with positivistic scientific methods. Positivism, moreover, was not the only force working counter to historicism. In those social sciences under the influence of philosophical idealism, an assurance of historical necessity could also be provided by the cunning of reason. Hegel's philosophy of history showed the development of reason at work in the complex dialectical processes of historical change and moving toward realization in an ideal national state. Although on one level Hegel stimulated historical studies through his acute demonstrations of historical development, the belief that there was a plan of historical development reducible to rationalist logic also limited the complexity of history and locked the German historical sciences of the state into a fixed teleology. Hence everywhere in Europe, historicism stimulated social theorists to contain its vast dynamic within the categories of progress, law, or reason.[28]

The chief exception, yet one which in its own way followed similar motives and analogous strategies, were the historians. Those engaged in preserving the records of the past and in writing history wanted to develop a coherent account of history from the particulars themselves. Instead of looking for general laws, they sought to locate and explain the actions of significant "historical individuals" – persons, institutions, nations – formed by the unique configurations of history. Their claim to provide a true account of the past was, like that of the scientific positivists, compounded of both insecurity and confidence: a need to rely on history now that it comprised the ultimate ground of existence and a growing confidence in the

---

27 Mill, "On the Logic of the Moral Sciences"; Collini, Winch, and Burrow, *That Noble Science.*
28 White, "History and Historicisms," xix–xxiii. See also G. A. Wells, *Herder and After* (The Hague: Mouton, 1959), chap. 4, pts. 2, 4.

arsenal of critical methods, centering on philology, by which they could evaluate evidence so as to recover the different contexts of the past.

German university scholars were the first to set out and practice this historicist program. Inspired by an Identity-philosophy, in which metaphysical or divine reality was located inside history and expressed in every individual configuration of history, Leopold von Ranke made the depiction of history "as it really was" the highest task. By immersion in primary sources, constant critical sifting of evidence, and a process of romantic or mystical insight, historians would be able to disclose the progressive course of development hidden in the empirical substance of history. From Ranke, Barthold Niebuhr, and other practitioners, the influence of this program spread to the less professionalized historiographical communities of France and England.[29]

By the mid-nineteenth century, therefore, more positivistic variants of social science and a more historicist historiography began to assume distinct and sometimes conflicting identities. In Germany, Ranke charged that Hegel's rationalistic system violated the empirical standards of historiography, while in England Buckle's attempt to discover deterministic laws of history was criticized by practicing historians. At the same time positivist sociologists like Comte and Spencer caricatured historiography as the mere chronicling of kings and wars, mired in a hopeless superficial facticity. Positivist laws were thought to exist somewhere below the empirical substance of history. Comte's sociology included a richer historical base than Spencer's, and Marx's unlike either Spencer or Comte, worked from close contextual study of historical sources. But Comte and Spencer both urged sociologists to look beneath the events chronicled by historiography and did not feel obliged to test their theories against the full complexity of the historical record. Genuine induction and analysis from the massive empirical data of history was thought a wasteful and hopeless task.[30] Yet substantial areas of congruence and contiguity remained – the tensions between historicist and ahistorical tendencies were often muted; historicist social thinkers like Alexis de Tocqueville and Marx continued to embrace both; and the work of political science and history intertwined around the study of national political institutions.

29 Lewis D. Wurgaft, "Review Essay: The German Conception of History," *History and Theory*, 8, no. 2 (1969): 404–18; Leonard Krieger, *Ranke* (Chicago: University of Chicago Press, 1977); Herbert Butterfield, *Man on His Past* (Cambridge University Press, 1955), chaps. 2, 4.

30 Iggers, *German Conception of History*, 43; T. W. Heyck, *The Transformation of Intellectual Life in Victorian England* (New York: St. Martin's, 1982), 133–7; Mandelbaum, *History, Man, and Reason*, 88–9, 130–2.

The early nineteenth century was a critical period in the formation of the social sciences in Europe. Under the pressure of social conflict, the liberal social sciences of the Enlightenment split into conflicting ideological programs and liberal social scientists defensively reasserted their vision of modern social harmony. In contrast to historiography, major spheres of social science became more abstract and systematic, seeking positivistic scientific laws to stabilize the uncertain course of history and gain the authority of nature for their contested social programs.

The different cultural and historical circumstances of each country weighted these factors differently, producing different kinds of historical consciousness and different social science traditions, rooted in the peculiarities of each national history. Germany's romantic Enlightenment and fragmented political condition cast its historical imagination into the past and future and made German social thinkers and historians the pioneers of historicism. Oriented to the state, the German academic class tied historicism to national purpose. In England, however, a strong sense of the continuity of political institutions made historicism less pronounced. Allied to the growing power of the middle class and its liberal programs, classical political economy became the prototypical and most fully developed English social science. It is not surprising, therefore, that as we move to the United States, we will find the different social sciences developed in Scotland, England, France, and Germany taking another distinctive course.

# 2

# The American exceptionalist vision

Americans participated in the discovery of modern society that occupied European social thinkers in the late eighteenth and early nineteenth centuries, but put that discussion and its social scientific discourse to a partially distinctive use. Many of the cultural components that developed in Europe into historicism were also present – Protestant Christianity, the secular Enlightenment, republican political discourse, and romanticism. Yet historicism did not develop contemporaneously in America and indeed made little headway until late in the nineteenth century. Engaged in founding and defining their national existence, Americans developed from these cultural resources a different historical consciousness, and with it a variant social scientific tradition.[1]

## The national ideology of American exceptionalism

If America did not follow Europe into historicism, one major factor was that Americans regarded their own revolution, unlike the French, as a success. Americans understood the success of the Revolution and the establishment of republican government in the Constitution as events in Christian and republican time. Protestant Americans already had available a Christian paradigm to which the establishment of the new nation could be assimilated. Reformation prophecy allowed them to believe that the millennium was a progressive historical period on which the Reformed world was about to enter, and the Puritan errand to New England moved the scene of that hope to the New World. When national independence was won, fervent Protes-

---

1 For a more complete discussion of this conception of American historical consciousness see Dorothy Ross, "Historical Consciousness in Nineteenth Century America," *AHR*, 89 (October 1984): 909–28.

tants identified the American Republic with the advent of the millennial period that would usher in the final salvation of mankind and the end of history. American progress would be the unfolding of the millennial seed rather than a process of historical change.[2]

In republican historical perspective, the successful establishment of republican government was a more ambiguous event. In eighteenth-century Britain, as modern civilization appeared to erode the basis for citizenship, republican thinkers had divided. While the "Court" party compromised their republican values in favor of progress, suggesting that history could be managed, "Country" republicans held fast to the ideal of the virtuous republic and sought to stay or turn back the hand of time through calls for a return to first principles. The characteristic stance of the Country republican was to exert virtue against history, and republican virtue still carried, besides the force of independent citizenship, the Machiavellian sense of *virtù*, the ability to impose one's form and will upon historical events through manly action. Americans were influenced by both schools, and often adapted the strategies of the Court to the goal of the Country, to protect republican values against the corrosion of time.

After the adoption of the Constitution, this goal appeared within reach. The founders self-consciously constructed a new kind of enlarged, balanced, and democratic republic that appeared to have solved the ills that had always destroyed republics in the past. The cyclical view of history of classical republicanism began to give way to the possibility of perpetual life. Following the lead of the Scottish social thinkers, Americans assumed a position somewhere between the agrarian and commercial stages of development and concluded that republican institutions and their huge reservoir of land insured an agrarian basis and republican progress virtually in perpetuity. America would progress, but unlike the nations of the past, it would not grow old. American republicans turned Smith's historicist account of stages of progress into a vision of how America could escape historical change.[3]

The millennial investment of the American Republic turned the past into

---

2  Ernest Lee Tuveson, *Redeemer Nation* (Chicago: University of Chicago Press, 1968); Sacvan Bercovitch, *The Puritan Origins of the American Self* (New Haven, Conn.: Yale University Press, 1975); Nathan O. Hatch, *The Sacred Cause of Liberty* (New Haven, Conn.: Yale University Press, 1977). Theodore Dwight Bozeman, *To Live Ancient Lives: The Primitivist Dimension in Puritanism* (Chapel Hill: University of North Carolina Press, 1988), casts some doubt upon the millennialist orientation of the first generation of participants in the Puritan mission, but not of the generations that followed.

3  J. G. A. Pocock, *The Machiavellian Moment* (Princeton, N.J.: Princeton University Press, 1975), chaps. 13, 14; Gordon S. Wood, *The Creation of the American Republic* (Chapel Hill: University of North Carolina Press, 1969), 6–8, chaps. 13, 15; Drew R. McCoy, *The Elusive Republic: Political Economy in Jeffersonian America* (Chapel Hill: University of North

prologue and the future into fulfillment of America's republican destiny. Reinforced by nationalism and Protestant religiosity, transmuted as secularization proceeded into a "civil religion," the linkage proved remarkably resilient through the nineteenth century. Indeed, the tie between republic and divine providence, once established, set up tensions that reinforced the fusion. The fear that republics must decline was not entirely vanquished by the idea of progress. For many, the secular conditions that maintained the republic postponed rather than eliminated the possibility of decline. The fall of the Roman Republic in class conflict and tyranny continued to haunt the American political imagination.[4] Moreover, once accepted, divine help itself generated human uncertainty. God, after all, can never be fully grasped in human terms, and sinful rejection of God was a common human experience.

The republican rhetoric of corruption formed an alliance with the jeremiad, the ritualized confession that God's people had fallen away, and the cycle of anxiety and assurance they jointly set in motion could be self-perpetuating. It was during the War of 1812 and again in the 1820s and 1830s, when anxiety was highest about the ability of a new generation to sustain the virtuous republic of the founders, that a new burst of evangelical piety and nationalism sealed the millennial identity.[5] If the failures of the French Revolution forced Europeans to ground their values in the forward movement of history and opened them to the dangers of historical time, the success of the American Revolution allowed Americans to seek moral assurance in divine protection and subjected them to the anxieties of millennial time.

Under the aegis of this special dispensation, American writers often linked their national history to the account of Anglo-Saxon liberty developed in England. American self-government was attached to a continuous inheri-

---

Carolina Press, 1980). The dominant conception of the future Rush Welter found in antebellum popular discourse did not project qualitative change. "The future would be an occasion only for the elaboration and extension of institutions the Americans had already introduced." *The Mind of America, 1820–1860* (New York: Columbia University Press, 1975), 8, pt. 1. For a view of American historical consciousness that intersects with the one presented here, but emphasizes fluctuating and personal "attitudes toward the past" (p. 123), see David Lowenthal, *The Past Is a Foreign Country* (Cambridge University Press, 1985), chap. 3.

4 Dorothy Ross, "The Liberal Tradition Revisited and the Republican Tradition Addressed," in *New Directions in American Intellectual History*, ed. John Higham and Paul Conkin (Baltimore: Johns Hopkins University Press, 1979), 121–5.

5 Hatch, *Sacred Cause of Liberty*, chaps. 2, 3; Steven Watts, *The Republic Reborn: War and the Making of Liberal America, 1790–1820* (Baltimore: Johns Hopkins University Press, 1987), particularly pp. 283–9; Fred Somkin, *Unquiet Eagle: Memory and Desire in the Idea of American Freedom, 1815–1860* (Ithaca, N.Y.: Cornell University Press, 1967); James H. Moorhead, *American Apocalypse: Yankee Protestants and the Civil War, 1860–69* (New Haven, Conn.: Yale University Press, 1978), 10–11, 49.

tance that went back to the Teutonic tribes that vanquished Rome. Its institutions were carried by the Saxons to England, preserved in Magna Carta and the Glorious Revolution, and planted in the colonies, where it reached its most perfect form in the American Revolution and Constitution. The American Republic was the latest link in the chain of Teutonic liberty, and the exemplar of liberty to the world. Originally this view of liberty was understood as a chain of immemorial custom, and it still encouraged a flattened conception of historical change by reading current institutional forms back into earlier periods. The millennial destiny required the same static logic and ancient lineage. The American Republic could hardly be understood as the product of merely local, temporary conditions, but had to be assimilated to a long-standing continuity of universal import.[6]

A complementary strategy, looking forward rather than back, was to stress the millennial "newness" of America. In this connection the vast continent of virgin land that offered America an escape from republican decay assumed increasing, and mythic, importance. Since the time of discovery, Europeans had projected utopian fantasies onto the New World; John Locke could, as a matter of course, envision it as his state of nature. In the Romantic nineteenth century, the West was endowed with the energies of dynamic nature and became increasingly identified with America's millennial future. By moving ever westward and subduing nature, Americans could become an empire for liberty and regenerate their virtue. They could relegate history to the past while they acted out their destiny in the realm of nature. Drawing on the perpetually self-renewing dynamism of nature, they could develop in space rather than in time.[7]

6 H. Trevor Colbourn, *The Lamp of Experience* (Chapel Hill: University of North Carolina Press, 1965); David Levin, *History as Romantic Art* (Stanford, Calif.: Stanford University Press, 1959), chap. 4; Herbert Butterfield, *The Englishman and His History* (New York: Archon Books, 1970 [1944]); J. G. A. Pocock, *The Ancient Constitution and the Feudal Law* (Cambridge University Press, 1957). Reginald Horsman, *Race and Manifest Destiny* (Cambridge, Mass.: Harvard University Press, 1981) distinguishes between a softer version of this Anglo-Saxon racialism, which took root in New England and its cultural hinterland, and a more virulent and expansionist racism that began to develop in the 1830s and 1840s.

7 Henry Nash Smith, *Virgin Land* (Cambridge, Mass.: Harvard University Press, 1950); R. W. B. Lewis, *The American Adam* (Chicago: University of Chicago Press, 1955); Leo Marx, *The Machine in the Garden* (Oxford University Press, 1964); David W. Noble, *Historians against History: The Frontier Thesis and the National Covenant in American Historical Writing since 1830* (Minneapolis: University of Minnesota Press, 1965); Major L. Wilson, *Space, Time, and Freedom; The Quest for Nationality and the Irrepressible Conflict, 1815–1861* (Westport, Conn.: Greenwood, 1974). Andrew Martin Kirby suggests that the ideological move into space has created a geographically undifferentiated continent, analogous to the undifferentiated history of American time: "The Great Desert of the American Mind: Concepts of Space and Time and Their Historiographic Implications," in *The Estate of Social Knowledge*, ed. Jo Anne Brown and David Van Keuren (Baltimore: Johns Hopkins University Press, forthcoming).

This vision of the unique place America occupied in history was the core of a set of ideas I will call American exceptionalism. Standing at the westernmost culmination of European history, the United States would not follow Europe into a historical future. American progress would be a quantitative multiplication and elaboration of its founding institutions, not a process of qualitative change. Still prehistoricist, tied to God's eternal plan outside of history, American exceptionalism prevented Americans from developing a fully historicist account of their own history through much of the nineteenth century and limited the extent to which they could absorb European historicism. Historicist tendencies in American culture were not absent, as we shall see, but they had to contend against this larger prehistoricist framework. As "nature's nation,"[8] and as God's, America could more easily be seen as the domain of eighteenth-century natural law: The course of American history followed the prescriptive norms of nature.

American exceptionalism implied a particular kind of political economy as well as a particular kind of historical stance. America, unlike Europe, would forestall the mass poverty and class conflict that modernity appeared to be creating in Britain. American republican politics were rooted in the civic humanist ideal of political participation and in the Country opposition to Walpole's "modern" government, and hence inherited their mistrust of the political consequences of commercial development. The financial speculation that replaced devotion to the public good by fevered search for private gain; the standing army that replaced a citizens' militia with a specialized force tied to the Crown; the political factions bought through bribery: All these violated the citizen's independence and virtue, founded on landed property and arms, essential to republican liberty. The ideal of the Country party was Sparta, not Athens. Country republicanism thus offered a rich vocabulary with which to castigate paper credit, privatization of interests, specialization of occupations, and the rise of manufacturing, a vocabulary quickly put to use in America when Hamilton proposed that the new country become a mercantilist trading and manufacturing nation like Britain. Doubts about the consequences of industrialization in Britain, particularly those raised by Thomas Malthus, soon compounded these republican fears of capitalist progress.[9]

8  Perry Miller, *Nature's Nation* (Cambridge, Mass.: Harvard University Press, 1967).
9  The literature on republicanism versus liberalism is mammoth, based on Pocock's *Machiavellian Moment* and the counters by Joyce Appleby, summed up in her *Capitalism and a New Social Order* (New York: New York University Press, 1984). There are now powerful critiques of the excesses of both. On Appleby see John Ashworth, "The Jeffersonians: Classical Republicans or Liberal Capitalists?" *Journal of American Studies*, 18 (Summer 1984): 425–35; Donald Winch, "Economic Liberalism as Ideology: The Appleby Version," *Economic History Review*, 38 (Spring 1985): 287–97. The best critique of Pocock is also an

Many Americans, however, were also drawn to the wealth and individuality generated by commercial development and as the new republic entered a period of rapid geographic and economic expansion, liberal values gained increasing ground. Moreover, republicans shared with liberals some of the basic premises of political economy, for they too valued productive labor as the source of national wealth and propertied independence as a spur to labor. If shored up by Protestant virtue and community, individual self-interest could create wholesome wealth. Smith had already shown how labor and enterprise could join private to public good. Enterprising republicans could extend the virtues of property from yeoman agrarians to all productive laborers and strengthen the distinction between the natural course of trade and those excessive manifestations of greed and speculation loosed by government power and capitalist credit.

What sealed this reconciliation of republican and liberal ideals were the exceptional conditions of the American continent. Jefferson, Madison, and many in their generation overcame their fears on the grounds that America was, and in the foreseeable future would remain, different. Malthus' calculations might hold true for an old country like Britain, but in America vast stores of fertile land guaranteed that production of food outstripped population growth. Moreover, the country could expect for the foreseeable future to remain predominantly agrarian. Ignoring the growing population of slaves, defining their own freedom against black bondage, they imagined America to be peopled by landowning or aspiring farmers generating crops for market and artisanal workmen in possession of their own tools. Under these conditions, the individual property holder would remain the backbone of both republican government and liberal economy.

By the 1840s and 1850s merchant elites were organizing the construction of railroads and mechanized industries, which were drawing in heavy waves of Irish and German immigration, but even the most outspoken advocates of manufacturing envisioned a "middle landscape" of integrated agriculture and industry. So long as western lands remained available for settlement and kept wages high, economic independence would be widely available and wage labor need be only a temporary condition in the life-cycle of the industrious workman. Blurring the distinction between the new wageworker and the independent producer through the concepts of social mobility, capital accumulation, and property ownership, Americans could

important effort to suggest the points of convergence between liberal and republican values and politics, despite the areas of divergence in their languages: Jeffrey C. Isaac, "Republicanism vs. Liberalism? A Reconsideration," *History of Political Thought*, 9 (Summer 1988): 349–77. See also James T. Kloppenberg, "The Virtues of Liberalism: Christianity, Republicanism, and Ethics in Early American Political Discourse," *JAH*, 74 (June 1987): 9–33.

continue to believe that widespread independence would provide the basis for republican government. Republican government in turn would allow the liberal market to distribute its benefits widely. This symbiotic relationship between the liberal market economy and republican political institutions would hold the class conflict of European history at bay.[10]

American exceptionalism was thus a connected body of interwoven ideas – indeed other dimensions, like America's mission to the world, could be plotted – and one whose scope has been difficult to specify. Fundamentally, American exceptionalism was a nationalist ideology, an idea of America in a country whose national self-conception had to be intellectually formed from the experience of gaining national independence. Explicitly argued at times of national and political crisis during the late eighteenth and early nineteenth century, it quickly entered into popular literary, religious, and political discourse, and was so widely diffused that its premises often went unstated and its conclusions were often merely celebrated.[11]

Besides supplying a nationalist rhetoric, American exceptionalism also permeated political discourse in antebellum America, providing the frame-

10 My view of the symbiotic relationship that developed in antebellum America between republicanism and liberalism derives from McCoy, *Elusive Republic*; Cathy Matson and Peter Onuf, "Toward a Republican Empire: Interest and Ideology in Revolutionary America," *American Quarterly*, 37 (Fall 1985): 496–531; Eric Foner, *Tom Paine and Revolutionary America* (New York: Oxford University Press, 1976); Thomas Bender, *Toward an Urban Vision* (Lexington: University of Kentucky Press, 1975); John Ashworth, *"Agrarians" and "Aristocrats": Party Political Ideology in the United States, 1837–1846* (London: Royal Historical Society, 1983); William B. Scott, *In Pursuit of Happiness: American Conceptions of Property from the 17th to the 20th Century* (Bloomington: Indiana University Press, 1977); and Isaac, "Republicanism vs. Liberalism?" Watts, *The Republic Reborn*, argues for the wholesale transformation of republican into liberal political culture during the War of 1812. The evidence in the book, however, suggests the interlocking of Protestant, republican, and liberal ideas, with American exceptionalism serving as guarantor of the whole. The dialectic Watts describes certainly does not end at the conclusion of the War of 1812. For similar evidence, and a useful corrective to Watts, see J. David Lehman, "Political Economy and the Response to the Panic of 1819 in Philadelphia," unpublished paper, 1989.

11 The construction of this national self-conception has not been fully charted. Key elements are provided by Bercovitch, *The Puritan Origins of the American Self*; idem, *The American Jeremiad* (Madison: University of Wisconsin Press, 1978); Hatch, *Sacred Cause of Liberty*; Somkin, *Unquiet Eagle*; Richard W. Van Alstyne, *Genesis of American Nationalism* (Waltham, Mass.: Ginn, 1970). Anne Norton, *Alternative Americas: A Reading of Antebellum Political Culture* (Chicago: University of Chicago Press, 1986), argues that from the late eighteenth century forward, the South created a different conception of American nationalism, which rejected New England's millennial identification of the American Republic; rather, Southern nationalism was rooted in agrarian and maternal metaphors and emphasized the separation of church and state. Although suggestive, the book ignores considerable Southern evidence to the contrary. There were many variants, Whig and Democratic as well as denominational and regional, existing under the construct of the idea of America.

work within which the two major parties operated. The major parties formed in the 1790s and again in the 1820s and 1830s over disagreements about how best to realize the exceptionalist promise, each defining the terms of that promise and the threats to its fulfillment in different ways. The Democrats, forming around Andrew Jackson, believed the American exceptionalist ideal was threatened by encroaching aristocracy. The chief defense of liberty Jackson offered was the democratization of suffrage and office-holding, strong executive action on behalf of the popular will, and a low-tariff, small government economic policy that opposed any "special privilege." The Whigs feared Jackson's demagogic executive tyranny as the peculiar corruption to which the demos was liable. Like the founders and such British liberals as John Stuart Mill, they stressed the need for the natural aristocracy of education and talents to play a special role in government. Their national leadership favored a high tariff and government promotion of economic development on the grounds that it would enlarge economic opportunities for everyone.[12]

To say that the exceptionalist framework expressed a political consensus is to ignore the majority of adults, black and female, who were altogether excluded from the formal political process, as well as those radical or conservative segments of antebellum society that rejected part or all of the exceptionalist vision. But exceptionalism did constitute the predominant language of politics. It became a presumptive consensus, if not a consensus in fact, deriving its normative force both from its dominant position in political discourse and from its roots in national ideology.

Even then, the consensual basis of American political culture can be misleading. As a national ideology, American exceptionalism was an intellectual construct, the work of cultural and political elites, and hence it had to be propagated, learned, and accepted by the diverse strata of American society. Neither its dissemination nor its affirmation could be taken for granted.[13] Moreover, as the dominant framework of politics, it did not so much define agreement as stimulate conflict. Beneath the sharp ideological conflicts of Jacksonians and Whigs, even beneath the more ordinary political

12 The literature on the antebellum party system is vast. Marvin Meyers, *The Jacksonian Persuasion* (New York: Random House, 1960), remains a good introduction as does Daniel Walker Howe, *The Political Culture of the American Whigs* (Chicago: University of Chicago Press, 1979). Recent studies that link political ideology and social and political experience are Ashworth, *"Agrarians" and "Aristocrats,"* and Michael F. Holt, *The Political Crisis of the 1850's* (New York: Wiley, 1978).
13 Jean Baker, "From Belief into Culture: Republicanism in the Antebellum North," *American Quarterly*, 37 (Fall 1985): 532–50; Daniel Walker Howe, "Classical Education and Political Culture in Nineteenth Century America," *Intellectual History Group Newsletter*, 5 (Spring 1983): 9–14.

disagreements over "more" or "less," there were centrifugal tendencies at work. For the Protestant, republican, and liberal ideals joined in American exceptionalism formed an unsteady alliance. Organic conceptions of community, virtue, and the public good often survived alongside faith in the improving power of individual self-interest, just as fears of decline lingered beneath the vista of progress. The promise of liberty, harmony, and relative equality had constantly to meet the test of actual conditions. The major political parties most often mobilized and contained these sources of dissent, but the millennial anxieties and ambivalence toward capitalist progress and historical change that were imbedded in American exceptionalism sometimes escaped the consensual framework. Dissent always carried the possibility of becoming "un-American." Hence political consensus in America was not a given fact but something that was constantly threatened and had constantly to be maintained. It was not the opposite of conflict but its constant ground.

### Antebellum contexts of social science

Given the roots of American exceptionalism in the debate over modernity and its dialectic of consensus and conflict, America was fertile soil for the new social sciences. Interest in developing the social sciences appeared both among those anxious to define and maintain the American exceptionalist vision and those anxious to modify or refute it.

The chief source of opposition to the national ideology and its political implementation was itself the great "exception" in American history – the slaveholding South. Mobilized by the Tariff of 1828, which threatened the South's economic interest and forecast its declining political power in the national government, and frightened by the Nat Turner rebellion of 1830 and growing abolitionist agitation, Southern politicians and intellectuals mounted a defense of their slave society, which culminated in the 1850s in distinctive conservative versions of political theory, political economy, and sociology.[14]

The most famous was John C. Calhoun's *Disquisition on Government*

---

14 Drew Faust, *A Sacred Circle* (Baltimore: Johns Hopkins University Press, 1977), discusses the Southern intellectuals who mounted a proslavery argument qua intellectuals, including William Gilmore Simms, James H. Hammond, Edmund Ruffin, Nathaniel Beverley Tucker, and George Frederick Holmes. A survey of a wider group of Southern writers, which includes a number of those working within the social science traditions, finds them obsessed with the problem of historical decline and the Roman example: James C. Britton, "The Decline and Fall of Nations in Antebellum Southern Thought: A Study of Southern Historical Consciousness, 1846–1861" (Ph.D. dissertation, University of North Carolina at Chapel Hill, 1988); on Rome, see 290.

(1851). Like all the Southern writers, Calhoun recognized the growing conflict between workers and capitalists generated by Northern economic development, a conflict which Calhoun's republicanism had prepared him to expect in "an advanced stage of wealth and civilization," and he offered the South as a balance wheel in what could only be a self-destructive conflict. But his central concern was the sectional imbalance between North and South. Arguing at first that the Constitution allowed states to nullify federal legislation, he came in the end to advocate a more drastic revision of the Constitution: government by "concurrent majority," the agreement of all major sectional and class interests in any legislation, perhaps through the mechanism of a dual presidency. Calhoun's reasoning and language remained fully within republican political science; he offered a compromise with the Northern liberal economy in the Country spirit: containment of the disruptive effects of capitalist dynamism within a strengthened structure of political checks and balances.[15]

Southern economists also continued to operate within their parent tradition and also sought to modify the American exceptionalist framework, rather than abrogate it altogether. Thomas R. Dew, professor at William and Mary College and perhaps the ablest of the proslavery economists, followed David Ricardo in predicting an increasing resort to inferior soils, higher food prices, higher wages, and lower profits. This causal chain justified the concentration of an older country like England on manufacturing and of a newer country like America on agriculture; it proscribed the tariff as an artificial restraint on the natural course of trade and an artificial transfer of wealth from the agrarian West and South to the manufacturing Northeast; and it forecast the eventual decline of America once it became an advanced manufacturing nation. Indeed the somber Ricardian analysis seemed to strike deep chords in the Country fear of ultimate decline once the agrarian basis of republican government was gone, chords that Southern critics of the free-labor economy were eager to amplify. Dew argued that slavery was justified as a civilizing form of control of inferior peoples, a superior labor system in agriculture, and a guarantor of republican liberty for all whites, rich and poor. When Northern capitalism created millions of impoverished workers who would attack property rights, as the poor had done in Greece and Rome, the conservative slaveholding South would be the only defense left for the Republic: "firm and resolute as the Spartan band at

15 John C. Calhoun, *A Disquisition on Government* (Columbia, S.C.: A. S. Johnston, 1851); Richard Hofstadter, *The American Political Tradition* (New York: Knopf, 1948), chap. 4; Pauline Maier, "The Road Not Taken: Nullification, John C. Calhoun, and the Revolutionary Tradition in South Carolina," *South Carolina Historical Magazine*, 82 (January 1981): 1–19; Ross, "Historical Consciousness," 919–20.

Thermopylae." Like Calhoun, Dew made slavery a bulwark of American exceptionalism.[16]

Only the Southern pioneers in sociology of the 1850s questioned the basic premises of American exceptionalism, a token of the heterodox possibilities in sociology's organic vision. Regarding political economy as the science of Northern free-labor society, they looked to the early socialists or to Auguste Comte for the model of a science of society that would project a wholly different historical course.[17] George Fitzhugh's *Sociology for the South, or the Failure of Free Society* (1854) began at the central point: The rise of capitalism had produced "something new under the sun" and its philosopher Adam Smith, looking only at those few who were benefiting from this novel development, announced that henceforth society would operate on the novel principle of every man for himself and march forward to the millennium. Against this liberal historicism, Fitzhugh reverted to the old Tory vision of a timeless world of prescriptive custom. Free-labor principles were only an aberration – "a little experiment . . . tried for a little while in a little corner of Europe." In fact, "there is no new thing under the sun." Slavery had always existed in human society, instituted by God and founded in the social nature of man and family government. "When society has worked long enough, under the hand of God and nature, man observing its operations, may discover its laws and constitution." Fitzhugh granted, however, that while there had been no real, no moral, progress in history, there had been progress in the mechanic arts. His final anomaly was to retain the new world of railroads, banks, and cities, enclosed in autarkic provincial units, led by a landed aristocracy and organized around a graded system of dependent labor. America was not an exception, and did not need to be, because world history itself embodied a timeless order that could contain capitalism.[18]

16 The best recent study of antebellum as well as Southern political economy is Allen Kaufman, *Capitalism, Slavery, and Republican Values: Antebellum Political Economists, 1819–1848* (Austin: University of Texas Press, 1982); on Dew, see chaps. 5–6. See also the indispensable source on the history of American economics, Joseph Dorfman, *The Economic Mind in American Civilization*, 5 vols. (New York: Viking, 1946–59), vol. 2, chaps. 31–2; the quotation is on p. 907.

17 L. L. Bernard, "Henry Hughes, First American Sociologist," *Social Forces*, 15 (December 1936): 154–74; Harvey Wish, "George Frederick Holmes and the Genesis of American Sociology," *AJS*, 46 (March 1941): 698–707; Theodore D. Bozeman, "Joseph LeConte: Organic Science and a 'Sociology for the South,'" *Journal of Southern History*, 39 (November 1973): 565–82. A Northern utopian anarchist who was led to sociology by his search for social harmony also made connection with Southern writers: Harvey Wish, "Stephen Pearl Andrews: American Pioneer Sociologist," *Social Forces*, 19 (May 1941): 477–82.

18 George Fitzhugh, *Sociology for the South* (Richmond, Va.: A. Morris, 1854), 8, 70–1, 151–2, 176; Eugene D. Genovese, *The World the Slaveholders Made* (New York: Pantheon, 1969), pt. 2.

Southern social science, for all its ingenuity, went down to defeat with the Confederacy. The timeless slave order asserted by Fitzhugh, or the Comtean historical development toward an organic slave society projected by George Frederick Holmes, could not carry much weight after the Civil War. The idealized image of slave society survived in the disguised form of nostalgic fiction, and William Dean Howells ironically noted the resemblance of Southern sociology to the Gilded Age critique of capitalism, but the pro-slavery argument could not bear direct emulation. The few originators who survived the Civil War led chastened and marginal intellectual lives.[19]

The second great source of antebellum opposition to American excep-tionalism – the radical working class – also mounted a social scientific attack on capitalism, in this case, through the labor leaders, journalists, and re-formers involved in workingmen's politics. Arguing that a "vast disparity of condition" had developed in America, a disparity that became more acute during the depressions of the 1830s, they believed that America was not in fact an exception, but was already reproducing the class system of Europe. The most radical of that group was the machinist Thomas Skidmore, who in 1829 declared that every man and woman had an equal right to property in the state of nature and hence an equal right to property in society. Because the original government had failed to secure that right, government must now redistribute all property equally and ban inheritance; it must provide everyone with an education and an equal portion at the age of eighteen. With common property and factories owned communally, Skidmore's agrarian remedy effected a total reorganization of society.[20]

Most of the working-class writers, however, believed that the liberal economy could be made to realize the exceptionalist ideal with less drastic changes. The Loco-Foco wing of New York Democratic politics aimed their Country fears at the chartered banks. William Leggett, their chief theorist, regarded American government and the liberal market as "the simple order of nature" in politics and economy, corrupted only by monopoly privilege. With Jackson and his men in the White House, he expected the natural order to be restored.[21] A more egalitarian and antimarket conception of republican commonwealth persisted alongside the dominant liberal-republican syn-

---

19 William Dean Howells, *A Hazard of New Fortunes* (1890), in the character of Colonel Woodburn; Lester D. Stephens, *Joseph LeConte, Gentle Prophet of Evolution* (Baton Rouge: Louisiana State University Press, 1982); Jonathan M. Wiener, "Coming to Terms with Capitalism: The Postwar Thought of George Fitzhugh," *Virginia Magazine of History and Biography*, 87 (October 1979): 438–47.
20 Sean Wilentz, *Chants Democratic: New York City and the Rise of the American Working Class, 1788–1850* (New York: Oxford University Press, 1984); Joseph L. Blau, *Social Theories of Jacksonian Democracy* (New York: Macmillan, 1947), chap. 25; Dorfman, *Economic Mind*, vol. 2, chaps. 23–4, particularly pp. 641–5.
21 Dorfman, *Economic Mind*, 2:653–4; Meyers, *Jacksonian Persuasion*, chap. 9; the quotation is on p. 193.

thesis, however. Articulated by radical workers and self-sufficient farmers, sometimes joined to the language of "equal rights," it was drawn into the Civil War defense of free-labor society, only to revive in the Gilded Age as a radical critique of industrial capitalism.[22]

The most complex of the Loco-Foco spokesmen, Orestes Brownson, did not have much lasting influence, but is revealing of the efforts to formulate social scientific dissents to American exceptionalism. Influenced by both Calhoun and Henri de Saint-Simon, a precursor of Comte, Brownson enacted in his own conflicted mind the Democratic party's union of Southern slave-holders and radical Northern workingmen around a common antagonism to Northern capitalists and African Americans. Believing that capitalism was indeed impoverishing the free worker and that majority-rule politics merely manipulated workers in the capitalists' interest – believing that he lived in Saint-Simon's time of historical disintegration, which required a new form of order – Brownson was driven in 1840 to accept Skidmore's plan for the equal redistribution of property. But unlike Skidmore he saw that such a scheme would produce violent class war, and soon shrank from the furor it created. He abandoned his former hope in the restoration of an egalitarian natural order and, converting to Catholicism, sought the hierarchical stability it could impose on the destructive effects of capitalism. Brownson ended as a Northern counterpart to Fitzhugh, an exemplar of polar opposition to the exceptionalists' centrist fusion of nature and history.[23]

At the same time that dissenters explored the critical resources of the social sciences, political, cultural, and economic elites drew the social sciences into the service of American exceptionalism. The doubts that European theorists like Malthus and Ricardo raised about America needed to be countered and the exceptionalist vision validated against domestic critics on the left and right. Moreover, partisan political conflict raised class-related issues about governance and economic policy that were tied to different readings of the exceptionalist heritage. Within that centrist framework, the national ideology and its social scientific validation could legitimate existing power arrangements by asserting that the American exceptionalist ideal was current reality. It could also generate expansive democratic ideals that mobilized as well as contained dissent, and in this function, too, social science played its part.

---

22  Wilentz, *Chants Democratic*, 182–9; Chester M. Destler, *American Radicalism, 1865–1901* (Chicago: Quadrangle Books, 1966 [1946]); William E. Forbath, "The Ambiguities of Free Labor: Labor and the Law in the Gilded Age," *Wisconsin Law Review*, 1985: 767.
23  Dorfman, *Economic Mind*, 2:661–7; Blau, *Social Theories of Jacksonian Democracy*, chap. 22; Arthur M. Schlesinger, Jr., *Orestes A. Brownson* (Boston: Little, Brown, 1939).

The centrist social science discourse was profoundly shaped by the political and cultural milieux in which it developed. The men of affairs who wrote on social science were often drawn into the subject in the interest of public policy and often divided by affiliation to one of the two major parties. In broadest terms, the Whigs were the party of the "respectable classes," drawing together those who were benefiting and those who thought they stood to benefit from commercial-industrial development. They also attracted evangelical groups who urged the same ethic of self-disciplined autonomy that served the liberal economy. The Democrats, as befitted a coalition resisting the Whig design for development, claimed the right to individual and local diversity. The Democrats developed the rhetoric of nature; the Whigs stressed the importance of historical institutions and the value of education against the potentially radical claims of natural rights.[24]

Beyond the party system, the cultural context that most influenced American social science was the antebellum college, a milieu heavily religious and increasingly elitist in tone. Although regional and religious differences existed, the collegiate model developed in New England spread throughout the North, West, and South. The colleges were generally founded or annexed by denominational clerical bodies and their aim was to preserve Christian learning and morality in a society undergoing rapid secular change. Although the clergy suffered a loss of status in the antebellum decades, and their ranks and the colleges were open to the aspiring sons of poor farmers, clerics remained professionals, whose classical education allied them with gentlemen. Some of the older colleges such as Harvard, Yale, and Columbia were long tied to a local or regional upper class, and as the sons of wealthy Northeastern merchants began to attend the smaller colleges in the 1850s, the colleges became more closely identified with the wealthy classes.[25]

The social role the colleges conceived themselves as playing, therefore, was conservator of the social authority as well as the Christian belief of the respectable elite. As capitalist development led to economic discontent and

24 See above n. 12. On the parties as matrices of culture, see particularly Howe, *Political Culture of the American Whigs*, and Jean H. Baker, *Affairs of Party; The Political Culture of Northern Democrats in the Mid-Nineteenth Century* (Ithaca, N.Y.: Cornell University Press, 1983).
25 Richard Hofstadter and C. DeWitt Hardy, *The Development and Scope of Higher Education in the United States* (New York: Columbia University Press, 1952); Frederick Rudolph, *Mark Hopkins and the Log* (New Haven, Conn.: Yale University Press, 1956), 76–7; Donald H. Meyer, *The Instructed Conscience* (Philadelphia: University of Pennsylvania Press, 1972); Peter Dobkin Hall, *The Organization of American Culture, 1700–1900* (New York: New York University Press, 1982), chaps. 3–5; Ronald Story, *The Forging of an Aristocracy* (Middletown, Conn.: Wesleyan University Press, 1980).

protest, as white male suffrage widened, and as Democrats and Whigs became mass parties run by professional politicians, cultural and economic elites found themselves increasingly excluded from participation in the political arena. Turning in part to private cultural institutions to recover their influence, they exerted the power conferred by their education and status against the dangers of leveling democracy, and believed the survival of the Republic virtually depended on their success. As lay trustees, they were often the force that pushed the colleges to introduce courses in political economy, history, and politics into the still largely classical curriculum.[26]

Both the religious and elitist tone of the colleges gave them close ties to Whig political culture. As the party of the respectable classes, the Whigs must have been preponderantly the party of the colleges' trustees, faculty, and students. The two cultures certainly shared the concern for popular virtue and moral improvement, and the Whig attempt to circumscribe natural rights and promote moral restraint was fully embraced in the colleges.

The intellectual framework in which social science was taught in the colleges was moral philosophy, that mediate realm between theology and natural philosophy within which the eighteenth-century Scottish sciences of man and society had developed. Understood as a science of the principles and obligation of duty, moral philosophy studied human affairs as the realm within which individuals sought moral improvement. Politics, civil polity, and political economy were included as adjuncts to or chapters within the course in moral philosophy, which was taught in the senior year as the capstone of higher education, usually by the clerical president of the college.[27]

Moral philosophy was for the Presbyterian Scots a half-way house between Christian assurance and critical secular inquiry, as was the commonsense realism that American colleges also imported. Commonsense theorists accepted Locke's empiricist critique of knowledge, but argued that

26  Story, *Forging of an Aristocracy*, chap. 7; Hall, *Organization of American Culture*, chaps. 5, 8–10. There is useful information on the introduction of economics and social science courses throughout the nineteenth century in *Breaking the Academic Mould: Economists and American Higher Learning in the Nineteenth Century*, ed. William J. Barber (Middletown, Conn.: Wesleyan University Press, 1988).

27  Meyer, *The Instructed Conscience*; Wilson Smith, *Professors and Public Ethics* (Ithaca, N.Y.: Cornell University Press, 1972); Daniel Walker Howe, *The Unitarian Conscience* (Cambridge, Mass.: Harvard University Press, 1970). On the relation between moral philosophy and American social science see Gladys Bryson, "The Emergence of the Social Sciences from Moral Philosophy," *International Journal of Ethics*, 42 (April 1932): 304–8; idem, "The Comparable Interests of the Old Moral Philosophy and the Modern Social Sciences," *Social Forces*, 11 (October 1932): 19–27; idem, "Sociology Considered as Moral Philosophy," *Sociological Review*, 24 (January 1932): 26–36.

it did not have to lead to the idealism of George Berkeley or the skepticism of David Hume. Rational reflection upon the truths of experience, including elementary moral intuitions – the common sense of mankind – validated both the common physical world and the fundamental truths of morality and divinity embodied in Christianity. In the American colleges common-sense realism encouraged the belief in Baconian empiricism as the proper method of all the sciences; indeed Newton's method was assimilated to this trust that empirical observation would yield, through rational reflection upon its evidence, the highest truths of science. It also supported belief in the harmony between science and religion, keeping the advance of science within the Christian purview.[28] The flourishing state of these doctrines, like the religious domination of the colleges and the lingering millennial identification of America, bespeaks the deep Protestant religiosity of nineteenth-century American culture and its slow movement toward a secular concept of nature and history.

## Lieber's collegiate political science

We turn finally to the principal social science traditions formed in the political and collegiate milieux of antebellum America and their fundamental attachment to the discourse of American exceptionalism. Political science was probably the first to appear in America, though ironically it remained less developed as a systematic study than political economy. The founding of the Republic had been a striking exercise of republican political science, described as such by Madison and Hamilton in *The Federalist Papers*, and members of that generation, like John Adams and John Taylor of Caroline, continued the original discussion into the early nineteenth century.[29] Once republican institutions were established, however, political thinking was largely drawn off into political practice. The principles of American government were elaborated in the form of judicial decisions, congressional debate, party speeches, and journalism. The colleges could have offered the opportunity for more sustained reflection, but they also shied away from partisan controversy. The most profound political conflicts of the period were produced by sectionalism, and even in the South, the systematic

28 Bruce Kuklick, *The Rise of American Philosophy* (New Haven, Conn.: Yale University Press, 1977), chaps. 1–2; James Turner, *Without God, Without Creed* (Baltimore: Johns Hopkins University Press, 1985), chaps. 2–3; Theodore Dwight Bozeman, *Protestants in an Age of Science* (Chapel Hill: University of North Carolina Press, 1977), chap. 1; George H. Daniels, *American Science in the Age of Jackson* (New York: Columbia University Press, 1968).
29 On the use of "political science" by the founders, see Alexander Hamilton and James Madison, *The Federalist Papers*, nos. 9, 18, 31, 37, 44, 66.

challenges to established republican principle it stimulated, like Calhoun's *Disquisition*, emerged in the political arena.

Political science also remained a scattered and diffuse body of knowledge, variously attached to political economy, history, philosophy, and statecraft. In the American colleges political instruction was linked to elementary description of American political institutions, included in study of Latin and Greek or surveys of Western history, or combined with moral philosophy.[30] Given the timidity of the colleges, the practical energy of American politics, and the diffuseness of the subject, it is perhaps not surprising that the most influential formulation of political science before the Civil War should be the work of a German immigrant. Exploiting the resonances between German understanding of the state and American Whig culture, Francis Lieber forged a lasting link between the two in American political science.

Lieber became an ardent republican in Napoleonic Prussia, only to be branded a dangerous radical when autocratic government returned. Hounded from one German university to another by the secret police, he acquired a fragmentary education in the new Kantian philosophy. Under Barthold Niebuhr, pioneer historicist and disciple of Machiavelli's republicanism, he developed a respect for historical method. Lieber fled to Boston in 1827, where he sought some avenue of support among the old Federalist and new Whig Boston elites. He found his German brand of middle-class constitutional liberalism quite consonant with the ideas of his new friends. His belief in natural rights grounded in natural law was placed within a conservative respect for state authority and social institutions. He had little sympathy for the increasing attacks from the left on the narrowness of English suffrage or on the class basis of property rights in America. His most influential disciple, President Theodore Dwight Woolsey of Yale, remarked that "in his political judgments he was more of an Englishman or of a republican than anything else. We wonder ... how there could have been any froth of liberty in his youth which brought suspicion upon him."[31]

The moral emphasis of Lieber's German tradition also took root easily in American soil and in this, as in all his work, he had a keen eye for

30  Stefan Collini, Donald Winch, and John Burrow, *That Noble Science of Politics* (Cambridge University Press, 1983); Anna Haddow, *Political Science in American Colleges and Universities, 1636–1900* (New York: D. Appleton, 1939).

31  Frank Friedel, *Francis Lieber, Nineteenth Century Liberal* (Baton Rouge: Louisiana State University Press, 1947); Bernard Edward Brown, *American Conservatives: The Political Thought of Francis Lieber and John W. Burgess* (New York: Columbia University Press, 1951); Theodore Dwight Woolsey, "Introduction" to *On Civil Liberty and Self-Government*, by Francis Lieber, 3d ed., ed. Theodore Dwight Woolsey (Philadelphia: Lippincott, 1877), 8–9. On Niebuhr's republicanism see Carlo Antoni, *From History to Sociology* (Detroit: Wayne State University Press, 1959), 124–5.

convergences that would allow him to take hold. Still, the colleges were suspicious of a liberal Episcopalian who never lost his German accent, and he was forced for years to work from a chair in history and political economy at South Carolina College. Here in 1838–9 his first major treatise used the Kantian distinction between universal law and political practice to carve out a subject called "political ethics," which would focus on the conscientious action required of citizens, thus turning his German idealism to the account of republican virtue.[32]

Lieber began by laying out the philosophic basis of politics in a Kantian formulation of Whig doctrine. Natural rights did not inhere in the lone individual, in a mythical state of nature; people were social beings who derived primordial, natural rights from their (social) humanity. What they had right to was the progressive fulfillment of their individual and social natures as members of society. In Kant's teleological terms, man's "destiny is civilization ... the cultivation, development and expansion of all our powers and endowments." The means to this end were provided by the spur of necessity, the liberal economy, and most importantly, the juristic state. Like Kant, Lieber saw the national state as the highest form of social life to which man was destined, and government as a natural extension of the family and a positive good. When in 1857 he escaped South Carolina to an appointment at Columbia College in New York, he gave vent to the antislavery feelings he had submerged and became during the Civil War a leading Republican and staunch advocate of nationalist programs. After the war his synthesis of the Kantian and Whig view of government and of German and American nationalism were fundamental to the new political science.[33]

Although Lieber expounded a positive view of government, it was still a limited government that he urged. First he distinguished society, the ongoing matrix of humanity and primordial rights, from the state, defined as the nation or people as a whole in their political capacity and the seat of constituent sovereignty. "Men cannot exist without the state; men never have existed without the state," Lieber said. But at the same time Lieber gave to individual conscience and social decision the right to hold the state and its

---

32 Francis Lieber, *Manual of Political Ethics*, 2 vols., ed. Theodore Dwight Woolsey (Philadelphia: Lippincott, 1875 [1838–9]).
33 Ibid. 1:127, 180–1; idem, *On Civil Liberty*, chaps. 3–4. The roots of American political science in German idealism, from Lieber to World War I, were well laid out by Thomas I. Cook and Arnaud B. Leavelle, "German Idealism and American Theories of the Democratic Community," *Journal of Politics*, 5 (August 1943): 213–36. Most often, however, this line of development has been considered an anomalous growth on a liberal natural rights tradition: Sylvia D. Fries, "*Staatstheorie* and the New American Science of Politics," *Journal of the History of Ideas*, 34 (July–September 1973): 391–404.

creature, government, to their lawful authority and to rebel if necessary. To fulfill their proper role as means, state and government had to protect primordial human rights and civil liberties. Like Burke, Lieber combined a social view of political rights with a liberal conception of constitutional government. The English and American traditions of voluntary action, local self-government, and protected civil liberties and property rights were the true principles of government, the only ones which balanced the claims of the jointly individual and social nature of man. The centralized French system of majoritarian democracy was the historical model to be avoided at all costs.[34]

In *Civil Liberty and Self-Government* (1853), Lieber's most popular text, he "endeavored to reconcile the historic development of the state with its philosophic ground." Believing it was necessary to test philosophic principle against historical fact, he increasingly saw his task in political science as a historical one.[35] He summed up this view in his inaugural lecture as professor of history and political science at Columbia.

Political science treats of man in his most important earthly phase; the state is the institution which has to protect or to check all his endeavors, and in turn, reflects them. It is natural, therefore, that a thorough course of this branch should become, in a great measure, a delineation of the history of civilization, with all the undulations of humanity, from that loose condition of men in which Barth found many of our fellow beings in Central Africa, to our own accumulated civilization.

Lieber had a sophisticated understanding of historical methods, including a sensitivity to language and the desire to put history to analytical use. The proper method for the study of history he called "social analysis ... the separation of the permanent and essential from the accidental and superficial, so that it becomes one of the keys by which we learn to understand better the present." Thus he approved the new tendency in historiography to minute and exact study as well as the new efforts to discern the laws of human society, and focused the highest study of history on institutions and the larger movements of history. His historico-politics defined a broad field on which scholars interested in history and politics could converge.[36]

---

34 Lieber, *Political Ethics*, 1:214–17; 2:162–76; idem, *On Civil Liberty*, 38–40 and chaps. 22–35.
35 Francis Lieber, "History and Political Science Necessary Studies in Free Countries," in *The Miscellaneous Writings of Francis Lieber*, 2 vols., ed. Daniel Coit Gilman (Philadelphia: Lippincott, 1880), 1:339–40; and Brown, *American Conservatives*, 30–1.
36 Lieber, "History and Political Science," 344, 367; idem, "On History and Political Economy, as Necessary Branches of Superior Education in Free States," *The Miscellaneous Writings*, 1:179–203, particularly 192, 203; James Farr, "Hermeneutic Political Science: The Forgotten Lesson of Francis Lieber," *History of Sociology*, 6–7 (1986–7): 65–74.

In *Civil Liberty and Self-Government*, Lieber discovered from his examination of Western history that political progress culminated in the conservative Whig principles of American constitutional government. American civil liberties were embodied in the Anglo-American common-law tradition and in its self-governing institutions. Again, the French revolutionary resort to abstract doctrine was the bad example. The popular governments of England and America, with their interconnected system of institutions and their "articulated liberty," were the highest forms achieved by history. "To last long – to last with liberty and wealth – is the great problem to be solved by a modern state," and only the "institutional self-government" developed by the Teutonic peoples could do it. Writing a few years before Sir Henry Maine denominated the "Aryan" political tradition and its historical path, Lieber regretted the absence of any single term to characterize this accrued political heritage and settled on the term "Anglican" principles of liberty – "the leading subject of Western history and the characteristic stamp and feature of our race, our age, our own country and its calling." He thus joined his political theory to Teutonic history and a defense of American exceptionalism.[37]

It is worth noting that Lieber's sanguine view of the American Republic was not shared by his friend, Alexis de Tocqueville. Lieber was one of Tocqueville's principal informants on his tour of America in 1831 and became his lifelong correspondent. Despite Lieber's personal misgivings about the provincial world in which he had been forced to cast his lot, probably because of that necessity, he never explored the corrosive implications of his friend's analysis. Tocqueville saw America as an exemplar of the principle of democracy that also awaited Europe, an exemplar to be admired and feared. He admired those social bases of American democracy that preserved the stability of republican government and the average comfort and good sense of the people. But he predicted American democracy would not produce distinction in any of the fields of human achievement, and he feared the absence of those class structures that supported, at the same time that they constrained, individual identity. The dynamics of democratic individualism could undermine true individuality, turning the body of independent citizens into an undifferentiated mass of self-centered and unimaginative conformists. Here, Tocqueville brought to completion the republican "sociology of liberty" he inherited from Montesquieu, showing the paradoxical outcome for republican liberty of the individual's dependence on society, as Rousseau had earlier shown it for the individual psyche. Tocqueville's warnings were noticed and sometimes answered by

37 Lieber, *On Civil Liberty*, 22, 204–14, 300, 319, 361–2.

the Whig elite, but were more widely read by the skeptical postwar genera-tion. Lieber was deemed a more suitable mentor for collegiate youth.[38]

## Native traditions of political economy

The intent of centrist political economy, like that of Lieber's political science, was to reaffirm America's Protestant and republican version of liberal progress against domestic dangers and foreign doubts. From Hamil-ton's "Report on Manufactures," discussion of policy differences over tariffs, banking, and currency was grounded in the more fundamental discourse about American exceptionalism. The first systematic treatises and the two competing schools of antebellum political economy emerged from the period of economic distress that was set off by the Napoleonic Wars. New England merchants and bankers and their clerical allies responded to the depression and popular unrest by promoting the teaching of political economy in the New England colleges. With their economic interests tied to free trade with Britain, and their pessimistic Calvinist and Federalist heri-tage, the New England elites were anxious to exploit the conservative uses of classical economics. They agreed with their British sources that "political economy . . . will be found to have pre-eminence over the other sciences, in acting as a sedative, and not as a stimulant to all sorts of turbulence and disorder." Most of the Northern free-trade theorists were clerical or lay participants in this defensive collegiate enterprise. Although instruction was intermittent and most often folded into moral philosophy, their texts moved with New England cultural influence through most of the North and West.[39]

The most popular antebellum text was written by Francis Wayland, the clerical president of Brown University. Openly apologetic in tone, Wayland praised the usefulness of merchants and bankers, opposed government efforts to regulate them or popular infringement of their property rights, and stressed the natural harmony of interest between them and the whole community. In keeping with his conservative Calvinism, Wayland's Amer-ican exceptionalist premises were restrained: Millennial nationalism could raise popular expectations and thereby discontent. Still, he appeared to

---

38 Melvin Richter, "The Uses of Theory: Tocqueville's Adaptation of Montesquieu," in *Essays in Theory and History*, ed. Melvin Richter (Cambridge, Mass.: Harvard University Press, 1970), 74–102; Haddow, *Political Science in American Colleges*, 248–9.
39 Michael J. L. O'Connor, *Origins of Academic Economics in the United States*, Introduction by Michael Hudson (New York: Garland Publishing, 1974), chap. 3; the quotation is on p. 92; Dorfman, *Economic Mind*, vol. 2, chaps. 25–7.

exempt America from the operation of Malthusian principle and doubted it prescribed "the condition of man which his Creator intended." Population depended on capital formation and in America capital was increasing faster than population, so that real distress was "very rare." The laborer was paid enough for family subsistence, unless he was immoral and lazy. Wayland had been influenced by the French economist J. B. Say, whose text had preceded his own as the Northern college favorite and who stressed the productive role of capital and the harmony of interest between economic sectors and classes.[40]

Wayland also took over Say's use of "consumption" as a major category of organization, coordinate with production, exchange, and distribution. Like Say, he included under consumption the spending of both individuals and states, assimilating both to the same system of natural principles, and emphasized the moral dimension of consumer choices and government expenditures and taxes. Recast in the exceptionalist idiom, this emphasis on moral consumption became a characteristic feature of American political economy.[41]

Amasa Walker was a free-trade theorist who put the elements of Wayland's text into more hopeful form. Walker, who was a businessman, taught political economy for many years before setting down his ideas in 1866. Malthus' predictions, he argued, were belied in America by the increasing productivity of land and by the natural causes that limit population far short of starvation. One could already see that process at work in the declining birthrate of the native American working-class population. If governments did not hamper the economy – bestowed no special privileges, avoided onerous taxation and making war – and if individuals saved wisely and spent for productive and moral purposes – what Walker called "right consumption" – peace and plenty would be achieved. After quoting a poem with rich millennial overtones, he concluded

It may not be wise to expect the quick attainment of such a result, or worth while to prepare our robes for such an ascension of humanity; but just as far as the consumption of wealth can be affected by human laws, or customs and agreements, in so far may this end be approached in every day of time.

40 Francis Wayland, *The Elements of Political Economy* (New York: Leavitt, Lord, 1837), 327–9, 340; O'Connor, *Origins of Academic Economics*, 120–35, 172–90; Paul Conkin, *Prophets of Prosperity* (Bloomington: Indiana University Press, 1980), 28–30; Charles Gide and Charles Rist, *A History of Economic Doctrines*, 2d ed. (Lexington, Mass.: Heath, 1948), 118–33.
41 Wayland, *Elements*, bk. 4. Cf. Jean-Baptiste Say, *A Treatise on Political Economy*, trans. C. R. Prinsep (Philadelphia: John Grigg, 1827), bk. 3.

Walker's was an expansive version of the American exceptionalist faith.[42]

The early nineteenth-century economic distress that mobilized Northern free-trade economists also produced a protariff response. Daniel Raymond, a Baltimore lawyer, argued that republican government must take positive action, chiefly through a protective tariff, to prevent the excessive inequality which could result from capitalist development. With such protection, the natural laws of the market would operate and America would lead the world to Christian redemption. Raymond's text was the first major work to set out the "American system" of political economy. Against classical British economics, with its free-trade cosmopolitanism and its meager Malthusian and Ricardian hopes for ordinary people, these economists mounted a nationalist revolt that would sustain the millennial hopes of American exceptionalism.[43]

The American school had its chief support in the mid-Atlantic states, particularly Pennsylvania, where small-scale manufacturing flourished. Matthew Carey, an Irish republican who settled in Philadelphia and founded one of the country's leading publishing firms, was one of the early architects of this transformation of Hamiltonian mercantilism into republican nationalism.[44] For a time in the 1820s, Friedrich List, a liberal emigré fleeing German repression, was his protégé. List was already an advocate of a common protective tariff for the fragmented German states and warmed to the nationalist program he found in Philadelphia. Projecting a text in English and seeking a university appointment, he was less fortunate than Lieber in finding a new home. When he returned to Germany, he published *Das Nationale System der Politischen Oekonomie* (1841), a founding text of German nationalist economics.[45] His example joins that of Lieber in showing early lines of congruence in the liberal nationalism of Germany and America.

The American school of political economy became central to the Whig party program and Henry C. Carey, Matthew's son and successor, became its leading theorist. Henry Carey began writing during a period of Whig-Democratic compromise over the tariff and in his first major treatise in 1837–40 he supported free trade. But his real purpose was to defend an

42 James P. Munroe, *A Life of Francis Amasa Walker* (New York: Henry Holt, 1923), chap. 1; Amasa Walker, *The Science of Wealth* (Boston: Little, Brown, 1866), particularly 464–6.

43 Kaufman, *Capitalism, Slavery, and Republican Values*, chaps. 3–4; Ernest Teilhac, *Pioneers of American Economic Thought* (New York: Macmillan, 1936); Conkin, *Prophets of Prosperity.*

44 Arnold W. Green, *Henry Charles Carey: Nineteenth Century Sociologist* (Philadelphia: University of Pennsylvania Press, 1951), chap. 1; A. D. H. Kaplan, "Henry Charles Carey: A Study in American Economic Thought," *JHUSHPS*, ser. 49, no. 4 (1931): 11–12.

45 Gide and Rist, *History of Economic Doctrines*, bk. 2. chap. 4.

expansive version of American exceptionalism. Ricardo had reached his conclusions by holding improvements in technology and productivity constant, but Carey believed that the working of the economic system could be understood only if its progressive character was taken into account. Returning to Smith's initial formulation of how wealth multiplies, he concluded it afforded a glowing prospect. Labor creates capital and capital increases the quality of labor, producing constantly greater quantities of goods. In this dynamic situation, while the value of the product is measured by labor, the value of capital, which is stored labor, is measured by the cost of reproducing it. Thus capital always commands relatively less of the product, labor necessarily more, and in the overall increase in quantity of goods, both interests are harmonized.[46]

Like Smith, Carey placed the production of wealth at the center of liberal progress. As capital increases,

men are enabled to benefit by the co-operation of their neighbours, and habits of kindness and good feeling take the place of the savage and predatory habits of the early period. Poverty and misery gradually disappear, and are replaced by ease and comfort. Labour becomes gradually less severe, and the quantity required to secure the means of subsistence is diminished, by which he is enabled to devote more time to the cultivation of his mind. His moral improvement keeps pace with that which takes place in his physical condition, and thus the virtues of civilization replace the vices of savage life.

Although these natural laws worked to carry humanity forward to civilization, there had been constant historical obstructions to their operation. A great deal of his four-volume treatise was taken up with historical and statistical analyses designed to show that the recurrence of poverty and brakes on capital formation were due not to Malthusian or Ricardian laws but to the limiting conditions imposed by human moral and political failures. Dynastic wars, excessive taxation, and personal vice were for Carey, as for so many American republicans, the villains of history. Only the United States, secondarily England, and France lagging behind as a poor third, offered that "security of person, and perfect freedom of action" that allowed the full play of economic progress. Indeed the refutation of Malthus constituted only the penultimate chapter of the treatise. The final chapter was reserved for a critique of Tocqueville, and his groundless fears for the American future. Tocqueville had not seen the true dynamic of American progress. Democracy was not the causal agent, but the result of the more basic conditions of American political economy. Yet more than any other

46 Henry Charles Carey, *Principles of Political Economy*, 3 vols. (Philadelphia: Carey, Lea & Blanchard, 1837–40), vol. 1.

factor, it was republican government that allowed the laws of nature to work unobstructed in America.[47]

Carey's sanguine view of American progress took a further turn in the 1840s. A man of considerable wealth, he expanded his father's publishing business and invested his capital in the burgeoning coal mines and enterprises of Pennsylvania. Noticing his own losses and the country's economic decline after the lowered tariffs of the 1830s and their rise after the higher tariff of 1842, he found a similar pattern in history. In *The Past, the Present and the Future* (1847), Carey argued that the British policy of free trade had deflected the progressive course of civilization. By diverting funds and labor into trade – expensive, long-distance commerce – rather than allowing cities and their contiguous countryside to exchange goods, Britain had forced whole countries into overspecialized colonial poverty and depressed the level of capital formation and prosperity. The undisturbed process of division of labor, he now realized, operated according to a beautiful law of association. Association was based on "the division of land and the union of men," the tendency to both increased individual independence and united cooperation in corporate enterprise and regional exchange, which formed the true balance of civilization. Britain's commercial policy had disrupted the operation of that law and had now to be deposed. "Westward, the star of empire wends its way...It is the great work reserved for the people of these United States."[48]

For the next twenty years Carey acted as one of the leading spokesmen for Pennsylvania protariff interests, writing journalism and political argument, and then in 1858–60 he published a major statement of his system as *The Principles of Social Science*. His concern for the interaction between political, social, and economic factors in the chain of improvement was carrying him into sociology. As Herbert Spencer found confirmation for his Smithian view of progressive differentiation in the embryology of K. E. von Baer, Carey found his law of association confirmed in the natural history of Goethe and Arnold Guyot. In all organisms, great individuality in the parts denoted a high level of organization. Not only economic processes but all of "societary organization" conformed to his law of association. Indeed so did all of nature. Undergirded by the laws of motion and heat, elaborate material metaphors now replaced much of the historical analysis of the earlier books.[49]

47 Ibid. Quotations are in 1:341 and 2:462.
48 Kaplan, "Henry Charles Carey," 46–8; Henry Charles Carey, *The Past, the Present and the Future* (Philadelphia: Henry Carey Baird, 1847), 138, 446.
49 Henry Charles Carey, *Principles of Social Science*, 3 vols. (Philadelphia: Lippincott, 1858–60), especially vol. 2, chap. 2.

Carey must have been drawn to this positivist formulation not only by the authority it provided for his partisan policies, but by his strong religious predilections. That the laws of political economy were such as a just God would decree had always been a major theme of his work: "The great Architect of the universe was no blunderer," as Malthus and Ricardo would make Him. As he reached out from political economy to society he grasped the assurance offered by a universal structure of law. Like Spencer, but independently of him, Carey developed a sociology from Smithian economics, turning the historical account of increasing differentiation into a law of social evolution. At least in England and the free states of North America, sociology originated in a liberal attempt to maximize the harmonious possibilities of the capitalist order. After the Civil War, a considerable number of American economists would follow that same path into sociology.[50]

Before the Civil War Carey had a wide following in Whig journalistic and political circles and the highest reputation abroad of any American economist. But in America free-trade advocates controlled national policy and the free-trade theorists who ruled the Northern schools dismissed him as a partisan tariff advocate. The American school dominated the University of Pennsylvania and established beachheads elsewhere – Frances Bowen at Harvard was a Carey disciple – but never captured the large academic market. After the war Carey injured what was left of his reputation by supporting greenback currency when so many of the respectable elite favored resumption of specie payment. His monetary policy was consistent, however, with the stance he and the American school of economists had always taken. Seeing the interests of the manufacturer and the workingman as perfectly allied, Carey, like his workmen, favored the looser credit, accelerating growth, and rising wages that an expanding currency could provide. His whole theory had turned on his view of the worker not as a poor wage earner, but as the laboring man improving his condition, hardly distinguishable from the farmer, small businessman, or manufacturer in his ability to amass capital.

There was considerable irony in Carey's expansive optimism. He was one of a group of aggressive entrepreneurs who developed Pennsylvania coalfields against the warning of geologists that the coal beds would not permit economical mining. The result was frequent failure and low profits for the owners, turning Carey into a champion of high tariffs. The result was

---

50 Ibid., 232; Green, *Henry Charles Carey*, 79, 145–55. Carey had, however, read Comte and it appears from *Past, Present, and Future*, 212–27, that he also derived his law of association in dialogue with Tocqueville's analysis of French "Solidarité." In the final statement of his theory, *The Unity of Law* (Philadelphia: Henry Carey Baird, 1872), Carey annexed the principle of the persistence of force cited in Youman's popular science.

also low wages, unemployment, and dangerous working conditions for the workers. Carey seems to have been one of the better employers, but like his colleagues, he opposed unions and strikes, and looked to natural law to remedy most of his workers' ills. He uttered his theories, of course, while living an elegant life among the Philadelphia elite, honored by his peers at a lavish, testimonial dinner under the banners "Protection to American Labor" and "Harmony of Interests."

Despite the unequal costs of optimism, the opportunities created by rapid exploitation of the continent and the fervent belief that God "was no blunderer," surely in America, joined many workmen as well as capitalists to Carey's expansive view. After the Civil War, as we are about to see, the common hope began to fade that the average worker would be a mobile propertied citizen or even, as Wayland implied, a stable worker in decent poverty. In that harsher world, Carey's easy assurance of harmonious progress seemed inadequate and his influence quickly dissipated.[51]

## Conclusions

Before the outbreak of the Civil War, Americans had imported, elaborated, and transformed the social scientific traditions that had originated in eighteenth- and early nineteenth-century Europe. From the outset Americans shared Europeans' concern for the future of modern society, but believed that their republican institutions and natural advantages would allow them far more than Europe to realize the liberal promise of modernity. Republican political science and liberal political economy were centrally connected to this national ideology of American exceptionalism and were developed by those within the dominant political dialogue who defended it, as well as by those class and sectional spokesmen who dissented from it.

Despite the existence of radical and conservative versions of social science, the traditions that established the strongest institutional base before the Civil War, and the foundation upon which postwar disciplines developed, came

51 Anthony F. C. Wallace, *St. Clair, A Nineteenth Century Coal Town's Experience with a Disaster-Prone Industry* (New York: Knopf, 1987), 65–70, 184, 194–200, 400; Green, *Henry Charles Carey*, 22–5, 89, 172–92; Francis A. Walker, "Recent Progress of Political Economy in the United States" (1888), in Walker, *Discussions in Economics and Statistics*, 2 vols., ed. Davis R. Dewey (New York: Augustus M. Kelley, 1971 [1899]), 1:321–39. Carey's antebellum liberalism is difficult for twentieth-century historians to place. In Dorfman, *Economic Mind*, vol. 2, chap. 29, his theories appear to be the capitalist apologetics of a wealthy opportunist; in Hudson's Introduction to O'Connor, *Origins of Academic Economics*, Carey and his American school colleagues are presented as materialistic idealists whose closest post–Civil War affinity is with the reformist historical economists.

from cultural, political, and business elites who occupied the center and right of the liberal-republican consensus. These were for the most part men of Whig, rather than Jacksonian, political and cultural sympathies, whose work was strongly shaped by the defensive, moralistic stance of the denominational colleges in which they often taught. They found strong affinities with the moderate liberalism and nationalism of early nineteenth-century German political and economic thinkers as well as with British political economy.

In political economy Americans preferred Smith's optimism to the somber theories of Malthus and Ricardo that had emerged from early industrial poverty and conflict. The liberal-republican formulation of American exceptionalism was closer to the moral world of the Scottish Enlightenment than to the classical liberalism of contemporary Britain. Among the conservative Southern elite, with its feudal pretensions and fears of republican decline, Ricardo's dire predictions could appear tenable, but in the North political economists argued that the continent of virgin land and the free course of capitalist development would circumvent English fears. If the conservative text of Wayland offered workmen only a modest subsistence, the American school of Henry Carey and more optimistic free-trade economists like Amasa Walker – as increasingly the politicians of both major parties – stressed the opportunity open to all workmen to amass capital and implied that property and independence would be widely distributed. As industrial development quickened in the 1840s and 1850s, Northern economists clung to the preindustrial vision of widely distributed productive resources, both legitimating capitalist development and perpetuating the expansive ideals of American exceptionalism. At that moment, an optimistic liberal turned the American ideal – much as Spencer had turned the English – into a cosmic sociology.

Francis Lieber allied political science with the limited Whig version of political rights as against the egalitarian thrust of Jacksonian democracy. His praise of Anglican political principle made the checks on majoritarian democracy in the American Constitution the very definition of liberty. He assumed, too, that government would be led by "public men," who would act like, if they were not born as, gentlemen. Still, he offered political rights and political education to all citizens, depicting the choice of political action as an individual decision rather than a class role, in this respect, at least, affirming the mass political participation that had emerged in antebellum America.[52] It was left to his Gilded Age successors, claiming a

52 Lieber, *Manual of Political Ethics*, vol. 1, bk. 1, chap. 5; vol. 2, bk. 5, chap. 4 and bk. 6, chap. 1.

new realism, to turn Whig elitism into a class and vocational ideology, just as postbellum economists would gradually harden the class lines left deliberately indistinct in antebellum theory.

Americans found most congenial those strains of European social science that allowed them to preserve their institutions unchanged, and even radical and conservative dissenters most often turned to a timeless nature or eternal history. Lieber's German model of political science combined Kantian idealism with genuine historicism, though he focused on the continuity of the Teutonic history of liberty and depicted American republican institutions as a fixed point of political wisdom. By means of these permanent principles of American governance, he created a bridge between political science and institutional history as well as a means of protecting the Republic from decline.

Political economists sought to maintain or restore the American continent to the reign of natural law. Although Southern apologists had to accommodate this vision to slavery, Northern free-trade economists who followed Smith or Say had less difficulty making the republic into the self-denying guardian of capitalist progress and the economy into a school for republican citizenship. The nationalist protariff economists, for whom republican government had a positive as well as a negative role to play in the economy, could have grounded state action fully in history, as the German historical economists were beginning to do in the 1840s. Instead they conceived of their tariff remedy as a temporary expedient that would restore the force of benign natural law. Both protariff and free-trade economists attributed the progressive character of civilization to the working of natural laws; when history did appear, it was likely to be as a realm of error, superstition, and corruption. Like the Enlightenment liberals whose values they shared, they believed the past was an impediment to progress.

Throughout, American social scientists understood the laws of nature as Europeans had in the eighteenth century, as the rules through which God governed the world. They were prescriptive rules that set the norm for "right consumption" and that reflected the Calvinist severity or the liberal mercy of the particular deity invoked. The outspoken positivism of Mill or Comte was virtually nonexistent before the Civil War. In the Gilded Age, to which we now turn, secular naturalism and historicism would begin to undermine this early modern conception of natural law and to threaten the principles of American exceptionalism.

# PART II

The crisis of American
exceptionalism, 1865–1896

# 3

## Establishment of the social science disciplines

Before the Civil War the social sciences, like most of the loosely constructed fields of humane learning in America, had led a fragmented existence. Economics and combinations of history and politics had established presences in the antebellum colleges, though subordinate to clerical influence and the moral philosophy curriculum, while men of affairs took up these subjects as part of the larger policy debates of the era. After the war, growing wealth, university expansion, and increasing specialization of labor and knowledge opened the way to the establishment of independent social science disciplines. What galvanized social science practitioners into self-consciousness and gave the new disciplines their American shape was a crisis in the national ideology of American exceptionalism, which gathered force through the Gilded Age. On one level the crisis was connected to the problem of intellectual authority, as science increasingly discredited the apologetic stance and naive resort to divine providence of the established voices in American culture. On another level, the crisis grew out of the social and political challenges of the Gilded Age, as Civil War and Reconstruction and then rapid industrialization appeared to test whether America could sustain the principles that defined her place in history.

### The Gilded Age crisis

Among the Whiggish class of clerics and men of affairs whose centrist versions of social science had predominated in education and politics, there were some who responded quickly and forcefully to the wide-ranging cultural and social upheavals of the Gilded Age. The more cosmopolitan among them, what I will call a gentry class – largely northeastern in residence, well-educated, liberal or heterodox in religion – were alert to the challenge natural science presented to religious orthodoxy.[1] Whether born into this class or entering it through education, the gentry also thought of themselves as elite guardians of the American Republic and were thus sensitive to threats to the exceptionalist ideal created by political and economic change. In the two decades after the Civil War, they set out to establish their authority and social vision by creating modern universities that would promulgate scientific truth and social science disciplines that would place the old principles of American exceptionalism on unassailable scientific ground.

The problem of intellectual authority developed during the 1860s and 1870s, as the harmony between science and religion declared by virtually all segments of Protestant Christianity proved increasingly difficult to maintain. By mid-century, the synthesis of physics and chemistry in the principle of the conservation of matter, new theories of thermodynamics, and advances in physiology and biology that were bringing fundamental facts of organic and human life under scientific explanation, all suggested that natural science had the power to provide a total worldview. At the same time, through technology, science was literally remaking the world. While antebellum Americans had imagined a "machine in the garden," Gilded Age Americans saw the rails of commerce and industry impose a new order upon the garden altogether. American society was reaching the point of integration, Thomas Haskell suggested, when people became aware that human events were caused not by personal intentions and actions close at hand, but by impersonal, distant, and less apparent causes, and hence turned for authority and practical power to the impersonal explanations of natural science.[2]

Against the widening reach of science, American religious spokesmen had

1  The importance of this class in the establishment of social science disciplines was noted by John Higham, *History* (Englewood Cliffs, N.J.: Prentice-Hall, 1965), chap. 1; and Robert L. Church, "Economists as Experts: The Rise of an Academic Profession in the United States, 1870–1920," in *The University in Society*, ed. Lawrence Stone, 2 vols. (Princeton, N.J.: Princeton University Press, 1974), 2:571–609; and developed by Thomas L. Haskell, *The Emergence of Professional Social Science* (Urbana: University of Illinois Press, 1977), chap. 4. The secular, cosmopolitan mentality of the people active in this movement is identified by David D. Hall, "The Victorian Connection," in *Victorian America*, ed. Daniel Walker Howe (Philadelphia: University of Pennsylvania Press, 1976), 81–94, and its base in the northeastern upper class is analyzed by Peter Dobkin Hall, *The Organization of American Culture, 1700–1900* (New York: New York University Press, 1982), pt. 3. The terms "gentry," and even more "cosmopolitan gentry," carry awkward connotations from English history, but nonetheless describe a localistic upper class, not aristocratic, open to attainments and sometimes educated to cosmopolitan sympathies.

2  Hall, "Victorian Connection"; Frank M. Turner, *Between Science and Religion* (New Haven, Conn.: Yale University Press, 1974), chap. 2; Haskell, *Emergence of Professional Social Science*, chap. 2.

to take an increasingly defensive posture, warning their charges away from the irreligious implications of some developments in natural science, German biblical criticism, and the theories of Auguste Comte and Herbert Spencer. Like forbidden fruit, heterodox naturalistic influences stole in nonetheless, particularly from Germany and England. German universities attracted some nine thousand Americans during the century after 1815, the great bulk of them between 1870 and 1900. Unlike English universities, German universities applied no religious test, and their Protestant culture, although liberal, escaped the American censure of Catholic and libertine France. Most important, the German universities were the most advanced in the world. American students there learned to value the discovery of natural knowledge and to dismiss dogmatic speculation. Equally important for Americans was that respected group of English liberals, led by John Stuart Mill, whose defense of science and positivism reached Americans in books, journals, and personal exchange.[3]

To the educated American gentry, science began to appear not only as the most authoritative modern knowledge, but as a courageous source of free inquiry, as against an authoritarian, outmoded religion, and their anticlericalism increased as the American churches grew more defensive. Although Christians had long exerted influence over "respectable" opinion, after the Civil War some orthodox Protestants began to take their religious precepts more aggressively into politics. They aimed their program against the Roman Catholic Church, as well as irreligion, but their defense of orthodoxy seemed to the cosmopolitan gentry to place them equally on the side of reaction with the Roman Church, which was also tightening its defenses against modern culture during these years.

Many Gilded Age social scientists participated in this conflict. Francis Amasa Walker, raised as an abolitionist by his economist father, was first antagonized by the conservative clerics' defense of slavery and in the 1870s mobilized to fight Protestant prayer in public schools. Lester Frank Ward had a similar abolitionist reaction. He also learned anti-Catholicism from his evangelical parents and as he moved toward naturalism, he gradually found his anticlerical objections to apply to the orthodox evangelicals who were trying to force their views into public law. Introduced to the works of Thomas Paine and Voltaire ("I have never read a more instructive book"),

3 Charles C. Cashdollar, "Auguste Comte and the American Reformed Theologians," *Journal of the History of Ideas*, 39 (January 1978): 61–80; Jerry Wayne Brown, *The Rise of Biblical Criticism in America, 1800–1870* (Middletown, Conn.: Wesleyan University Press, 1969); Jurgen Herbst, *The German Historical School in American Scholarship* (Port Washington, N.Y.: Kennikat Press, 1972), chap. 1; Charles E. McClelland, *State, Society and University in Germany, 1700–1914* (Cambridge University Press, 1980); Hall, "Victorian Connection."

he formed a National Liberal Reform League in 1869 to fight religious dogmatism. In Massachusetts in the early 1870s, Carroll Wright dubbed the orthodox Congregationalists who opposed his efforts to liberalize religion and improve public education, the "Catholic" element.[4]

A conflict between scientific naturalism and religion was thus independently underway when the American debate over Charles Darwin's *Origin of Species* added fuel to the fire. As Darwin's challenge to Christianity came more fully into view in the 1870s, so too did the antagonism between the new positivism of the liberal gentry and the defensiveness of orthodoxy.[5] The gentry grew increasingly militant over control of the colleges. Andrew Dickson White had resisted his pious father's importunities from childhood and appreciated religious liberality as a graduate student and diplomatic assistant in Europe. When in 1866 he became the founding president of Cornell University, he insisted on its secular character, urged a nonsectarian model for all of higher education, and wrote extensively on the warfare between science and theology. William Graham Sumner, an Episcopal minister who had studied in Germany and England, came to Yale in 1872 to teach the social sciences. When the clerical president of Yale forbade him to assign Spencer's *The Study of Sociology* to undergraduate students, Sumner publicly attacked the clerically dominated moral philosophy curriculum that held the social sciences subordinate. The history of learning, he declared, showed one subject after another freeing itself from "metaphysical speculation" and becoming independent sciences.[6]

4 George M. Marsden, *Fundamentalism and American Culture* (New York: Oxford University Press, 1980), chap. 2; James P. Munroe, *A Life of Francis Amasa Walker* (New York: Holt, 1923), 276–8; Clifford H. Scott, *Lester Frank Ward* (Boston: Twayne, 1976), 136–9; Lester F. Ward, *Young Ward's Diary*, ed. Bernhard J. Stern (New York: Putman, 1935), 234, 239, 313–35; James Leiby, *Carroll D. Wright and Labor Reform* (Cambridge, Mass.: Harvard University Press, 1960), 24.

5 When John W. Draper abridged his Comtian *History of the Intellectual Development of Europe* (1863), he added a scathing chapter on Catholic reaction and the latest Darwinian martyrs. Published as the *History of the Conflict between Religion and Science* (1874), it became the best seller in Youman's popular science series. Donald Fleming, *John William Draper and the Religion of Science* (Philadelphia: University of Pennsylvania Press, 1950), 125–34.

6 Glenn C. Altschuler, *Andrew D. White – Educator, Historian, Diplomat* (Ithaca, N.Y.: Cornell University Press, 1979), chaps. 1–4; Andrew D. White, *The Warfare of Science* (New York: D. Appleton, 1876); idem, *New Chapters in the Warfare of Science* (New York: D. Appleton, 1888); idem, *A History of the Warfare of Science with Theology in Christendom* (New York: D. Appleton, 1896); idem, "The Relation of National and State Governments to Advanced Education," *Journal of Social Science*, 7 (September 1874): 299–322; William Graham Sumner, "Sociology," *Princeton Review*, 57 (November 1881): 303; Donald Bellomy, "The Molding of an Iconoclast: William Graham Sumner, 1840–1885" (Ph.D. dissertation, Harvard University, 1980), chap. 14; Frank M. Turner, "The Victorian Conflict between Science and Religion: A Professional Dimension," *Isis*, 69 (September 1978); 356–76.

The gentry intellectuals who attacked religious control did not want to destroy the harmony between religion and science but to recast it. Positivist science was to set the terms of the agreement rather than orthodox religion. Few of them actually became agnostics; most adjusted the basis of their Christian faith to avoid cognitive conflict with natural science. For all of them, however, the influence of positivism forced for the first time in America a divorce between natural knowledge and revealed Christianity and a determination to develop natural knowledge on its own terms.

At the same time that the Gilded Age gentry was beginning to reexamine basic truths in the naturalistic light of science, the events of history were forcing them to look closely at the accepted truths of American exceptionalism. The Civil War generated a powerful sense of nationalism and a new dedication to the Republic. Many Northerners with Whig commercial inclinations, as well as many former Jacksonians committed to the uncorrupted reign of natural economic law moved into the Republican party and emerged from the war with a new sense of the importance of national unity and strength. The northeastern gentry particularly, who had been forced to the margins of antebellum politics, became prominent participants in the fighting and organization of the war, and sought ways afterward to extend their leadership. And while the war opened the promise of new national strength, it also chastened these young nationalists with its brutal lessons in power, organization, and tragic necessity.[7]

What the war taught was soon compounded many times over by the disruptive effects of industrialization. The massive economic and social dislocations set underway by industrial development and the corruptions of American politics it stimulated were profoundly disillusioning. As journalists, academics, and professionals who sought an active role in politics after the war, the gentry ran immediately into the brokerage of political power by professional politicians, the increasing influence of urban political machines with their immigrant labor voters, and the corrupt intrusion of capitalist money into the political process.

Perhaps the hardest fact they had to face was the existence of a permanent working class, increasingly tied by machine processes to wage labor and to the vicissitudes of the business cycle. In the chaotic postwar years and in the long depression from 1873 to 1877, the new working class made its existence known in palpable ways: in greatly increased numbers of impoverished workers seeking jobs and relief, in the formation of local and national unions, dissident political parties, strikes, and violence. The radical republi-

---

7 Hall, *Organizaton of American Culture*, chap. 11; George M. Fredrickson, *The Inner Civil War* (New York: Harper & Row, 1965).

can, equal-rights tradition revived in labor organizations, launched an attack on the "wage system" of industrial capitalism, and proposed to realize the ideal of independence through cooperative industry. Lassallean and Marxist socialism, as well as anarchism made their first appearance in a few working-men's groups and German immigrant communities. Coming on the heels of the Commune of Paris in 1870–1, and culminating in the nationwide railroad strikes of 1877, class conflict in America broke through the exceptionalist armor of the gentry class. The hope that America could progress without changing, that she could escape the corruption and class conflict in which republics had declined and toward which capitalism moved, seemed threatened.

The consequence of scientific naturalism and historical upheaval was a deep sense that America had changed. For the first time Americans were forced into an awareness of historicism as a premise of their own world. The historicist theories of Hegel, Comte, and Spencer now began to be taken seriously as analytical structures that underlay the course of American as well as European history. Historicist methods that promised to capture the complex particularity of human affairs gained new authority. The larger numbers of students who took graduate studies in German universities augmented historical influences.[8] In historico-politics John W. Burgess began to grapple with the implications of "historical and revolutionary forces," and the economist Francis Walker, to find a way to take account of the differentiated empirical reality of industrial society. The crisis of American exceptionalism was at bottom a crisis over the reality and the concept of change, and if we follow out the pervasive ramifications of that crisis we can reconstruct the course of American social science.

The experience of change produced, to begin with, a new impulse toward realism in wide areas of American culture, and particularly in social thought. According to Roger B. Salomon, realism was a product of the sense that past and present had become "discontinuous," that the inherited cultural traditions no longer applied to current reality, so that reality must be sought in what was "existing, comprehensible, visible, palpable; the scrupulous imitation of nature." With the old religious framework in tatters and a new world at their doors, Sumner declared in his inaugural lecture that "the traditions and usages of past ages are broken, or at least discredited. New conditions require new institutions and we turn away from tradition and prescription to reexamine the data from which we learn what principles of the social order

8 The classic study of the influence of German education on the rise and decline of a historical school of social science in the United States treated historicism as an exotic German import that "was bound to fail" (p. x), but did not explore the American context of historicism: Herbst, *The German Historical School in American Scholarship*.

are *true*, that is are conformed to human nature and to the conditions of human society."

Francis Walker, too, wanted to turn to facts. Wounded in the Civil War and following his father's footsteps into political economy, he was glad that "the world has lost its taste for a priori politics." The postwar world required "stern and practical inquiry into the workings of government" and "the facts of society." Indeed, "We must regard liberty no longer as a female, but as a fact," hence not as a romantic ideal to be wooed, but as something concrete, to be seized in particular pieces. Walker confessed to retaining his father's faith "in a good time coming, and in glorious days of liberty, equality and fraternity that shall surely be," but the old idealism could no longer serve as a guide to the hard reality. "Realism was the aesthetic of disinheritance; it solved the problem of the torn thread of time by offering scissors for cutting it into even tinier shreds. In a world of change a kind of stasis could be achieved by, so to speak, atomizing time."[9]

Realism helped to set American social science on a deliberately "masculine" course. Disdaining romantic fantasy, realism abandoned the subjective authorial voice for the objective things in themselves. In the gendered language of Victorian culture, hard facts and hard science were masculine, and sentiment, idealism, and the imaginative constructions of literature were feminine. Since the time of Comte and John Stuart Mill social scientists have felt the attraction of both realms, but the realist desire to eliminate subjectivity, as well as the desire for scientific authority, have repeatedly cast the social scientific enterprise in masculine terms.[10]

Realism reinforced the empirical thrust of the commitment to natural knowledge. Baconian empiricism had been the reigning methodology of American science, resting on a philosophy of commonsense realism, and although new philosophical currents would shape the restructuring of Gilded Age social science, they would not alter its underlying empirical thrust. In this context, Gilded Age social scientists made increasing use of statistics. Before the Civil War, American statistical work developed on the English model, as descriptive statistics of social groups and as a rudimentary

---

9 The analysis of realism is from Roger B. Salomon, "Realism as Disinheritance: Twain, Howells and James," *American Quarterly*, 16 (Winter 1964): 531–44; quotations are on 532–2. Robert C. Bannister, Jr., called attention to the importance of Salomon's "disinheritance" for Sumner and his generation in "William Graham Sumner's Social Darwinism: A Reconsideration," *History of Political Economy*, 5 (Spring 1973): 89–109. Sumner's quotation is in Bellomy, "The Molding of an Iconoclast," 251; Walker's, in Francis A. Walker, "Mr. Grote's Theory of Democracy," *Bibliotheca Sacra*, 25 (October 1868): 687–90.
10 Although he subsumes the category of gender in the rivalry between literature and science, Wolf Lepenies suggests its importance to the development of the social sciences in *Between Literature and Science: The Rise of Sociology* (Cambridge University Press, 1988).

science of natural laws, in which numerical regularities in social phenomena were thought to yield natural laws at work in society. At mid-century in England, and more powerfully in Germany under the aegis of historicism, statistics came to be viewed as a scientific method for analyzing the diversity of social phenomena. For the Germans statistics was a method of mass observation useful for dealing with the inherent diversity and indeterminacy of human phenomena, producing the generalizations of historical science rather than laws of nature.[11] In the Gilded Age the German view of historical statistics began to have some influence, but American social scientists were more likely to join their interest in social diversity to positivist conceptions of natural law, as they joined American history to American nature.

Through empirical method social scientists hoped to discover fundamental laws at work alike in nature and history. Sumner expected his study of "data" to yield "principles of the social order that are *true*." Indeed, their dawning awareness of historical change, their sense of living in a natural and historical world that must generate its own principles of order, made them, like the earlier European positivists, more dependent than before on the force of scientific law. Sumner admitted that social science had not yet produced much, but "there is a scientific substratum . . . principles and laws which are inevitable and perfect in their operation – which underlies all these social sciences . . . It is a matter of faith with me."[12]

For American social scientists these new attitudes toward nature and history had a special meaning. Faced with mounting evidence of historical change and no longer able to call on providential power, they had to confront the possibility that changes could alter the exceptionalist course of American history. They began what would prove to be a long effort to accommodate to that possibility. They admitted the erosion of some of those peculiar characteristics that made America different from Europe and united American history more systematically to the universal course of natural law and Western historical development. But on a more fundamental level, they remained wedded to the exceptionalist vision and its prehistoricist conceptions of time. They redrew the lines of American uniqueness and turned natural law and historical principle into unchanging bases for the

---

11 Theodore M. Porter, *The Rise of Statistical Thinking, 1820–1900* (Princeton, N.J.: Princeton University Press, 1986); Victor L. Hilts, "*Aliis exterendum*, or, The Origins of the Statistical Society of London," *Isis*, 69 (September 1978): 21–43; Theodore M. Porter, "Lawless Society: Social Science and the Reinterpretation of Statistics in Germany, 1850–1880," in *The Probabilistic Revolution*, ed. Lorenz Kruger, Lorraine Daston, and Michael Heidelberger (Cambridge, Mass.: MIT Press, 1987), 351–75; Robert C. Davis, "Social Research in America before the Civil War," *JHBS*, 8 (January 1972): 69–85.
12 Bellomy, "The Molding of an Iconoclast," 253.

established course of American history. So far as possible, change was contained and history rendered harmless. Indeed, the sense of crisis that pervaded the Gilded Age was itself the product of the exceptionalist historical consciousness not yet accommodated to the necessity of change. Fears of the decline of the Republic and apocalyptic images of impending doom and reborn millennial hope still shaped the historical imagination of these social scientists and bespoke the strength of the republican-millennial vision in the face of change.[13]

The social and intellectual crisis in American exceptionalism was also a class crisis. The uncertainty in intellectual authority and the runaway corruption and conflict hit directly at the status and function of the gentry class, a dilemma they met by reasserting their sociopolitical and cultural authority. Indeed, the mentality of this Gilded Age gentry is often called "mugwump," for its efforts to replace corrupt politicians with the disinterested leadership of the "best men," namely themselves. Faced with the specter of class conflict, they both feared for their established position and welcomed their opportunity for leadership. As Andrew Dickson White proclaimed, "The time is surely coming ... when disheartened populations will hear brilliant preaching subversive of the whole system of social order ... the only safeguard is in a thorough provision for the checking of popular unreason, and for the spreading of right reason."

The new gentry self-consciousness reflected the sharper class lines that began to form in the 1870s, producing not only a more clearly delimited working class but also a much larger stratum of great wealth at the top of society. The educated gentry had always been a part of or allied to the commercial class through birth, patronage, and education, and although angered by the arrogance and lawlessness sometimes displayed by the new capitalists, interest and outlook drew them together. Increasingly through the Gilded Age, the northeastern gentry and the new capitalists intermingled and began to form a national upper class. With this wealth and power at its upper reaches, the educated elite could seek new influence. Already aware of themselves as a kind of republican natural aristocracy and as Whiggish moral

---

13 On the Gilded Age sense of crisis, see Dorothy Ross, "The Liberal Tradition Revisited and the Republican Tradition Addressed," in *New Directions in American Intellectual History*, ed. John Higham and Paul Conkin (Baltimore: Johns Hopkins University Press, 1979), 121–5. A study of American political science discusses the origins of the discipline in a Gilded Age crisis caused by historical change and the effort to realize the values of an earlier American republic, though it does not focus on the intervening factor of historical consciousness: Raymond J. Seidelman with Edward Harpham, *Disenchanted Realists: Political Science and the American Crisis, 1884–1984* (Albany: State University of New York Press, 1985).

stewards, they emerged in the Gilded Age as both the conscience of the capitalist class and the voice of "right reason" to the nation at large.

They also began to think of themselves as professionals, whose authority and expertise had in part an older kind of social source, in status and higher education, and in part a new source in their specialized, expert social function. The basis of their new authority was to be modern scientific knowledge. As clerical leadership became increasingly discredited, the cosmopolitan gentry were uniquely placed to offer themselves as a modern alternative. In contrast to the politicians, labor leaders, and businessmen who raised divisive claims, the gentry could call on the authority of modern science to command agreement. Science allowed them to speak with the voice of universal rationality, while bestowing special authority on its elite class of practitioners.[14]

With their mugwump ideal, the gentry hoped that the expanding work of government after the Civil War would be done by men knowledgeable in scientific principles and at first sought careers in government. Francis Walker learned his economics chiefly from his father, dabbled in law and political journalism, and then rose quickly in Washington from deputy to the Commissioner of Revenue to Superintendent of the Census in 1870. Carroll Wright as chief of the Bureau of Labor Statistics in Massachusetts in the 1870s and in Washington in the 1880s turned his position into a base for serious study of the labor problem and a platform for social science expertise. Around John Wesley Powell, chief of the U.S. Geological Survey, were a group of natural and social scientists, including Lester Frank Ward, who believed scientific expertise in government could be a major force for the commonweal. But in the end, federal and state governments were slow to develop central administrative apparatus and proved less quickly amenable to gentry scientific authority than did the colleges.[15]

Taking their cue from the gentry group of natural scientists who had been pushing American scientific institutions toward greater professional rigor, mugwump intellectuals began to urge academic reform. Trained in history

---

14 Above, note 1; Andrew D. White, *Education in Political Science* (Baltimore, Md.: John Murphy, 1879), 34–35. On gentry, class-based professionalism, see Dorothy Ross, "Professionalism and the Transformation of American Social Thought," *Journal of Economic History*, 38 (June 1978): 494–9. There is an interesting discussion of the class-based, community-oriented scientific institutions that drew together New York City scientists in the 1870s and 1880s before academic specialization broke them apart, in Douglas Sloan, "Science in New York City, 1867–1907," *Isis*, 71 (March 1980): 35–76.

15 Munroe, *Life of Francis Amasa Walker*, chaps. 1–3; Leiby, *Carroll D. Wright*, chaps. 3–4; Michael Lacey, "The Mysteries of Earth-Making Dissolve: A Study of Washington's Intellectual Community and the Origins of American Environmentalism" (Ph.D. dissertation, George Washington University, 1979), chaps. 1, 5.

and politics, Andrew White took over Cornell University in 1866; the chemist Charles William Eliot became President of Harvard in 1869; the geographer Daniel Coit Gilman opened the Johns Hopkins University in 1876, while advocates of social science disciplines like William Graham Sumner at Yale and John William Burgess at Columbia gained key academic appointments. Allying themselves with a new group of worldly and wealthy alumni, they constructed on the old college system a secularized apex of modern university instruction that began to set the standard for higher education.[16]

At the same time, the gentry moved on other fronts to bring social science to bear on the mounting crisis. The American Social Science Association (ASSA), modeled on the British National Association for Promotion of Social Science, was founded in 1865 jointly by the scientific and university reformers and by gentry reformers at work in charity organizations, government, and politics. During the 1870s and early 1880s it served as a catalyst for the work of both reformers and academic social scientists, who were broadly united by class and social outlook. In the 1880s the coalition of gentry activists and academics began to divide, however, as functional standards of competence became increasingly important and as ideological controversy pushed the academics into retreat from overt advocacy. The ASSA became the "mother of associations," as it presided over, and was dismembered by, the founding of specialized, functionally oriented professional organizations like the National Council of Charities and Corrections and the American Economic Association. The new universities, with their offer of stable careers, increasing control over access to specialized knowledge, and modicum of professional autonomy would displace the practical vocations as the locus of authority in the new social science disciplines.[17]

The gentry intellectuals of the 1870s presided over a watershed in the development of the social science disciplines in America. The Civil War and

---

16 Haskell, *Emergence of Professional Social Science*, chap. 4; Bellomy, "The Molding of an Iconoclast," chap. 6. An older generation of clerical academics, like Theodore Dwight Woolsey and Noah Porter at Yale and John Bascom at Williams College and the University of Wisconsin, had already begun to absorb German ideals of advanced scholarship and to make the colleges hospitable to them. Their religious ties, however, placed distinct limits on the degree of innovation they could tolerate and left it to the more secular gentry to break the antebellum mold. See Louise L. Stevenson, *Scholarly Means to Evangelical Ends* (Baltimore: Johns Hopkins University Press, 1986). The standard work on university reform is Laurence R. Veysey, *The Emergence of the American University* (Chicago: University of Chicago Press, 1965).

17 Haskell, *Emergence of Professional Social Science*; Mary O. Furner, *Advocacy and Objectivity* (Lexington: University of Kentucky Press, 1975), chaps. 1–2; Lawrence Goldmann, "Experts, Investigators, and the State in 1860: British Social Scientists through American Eyes," paper presented at the Wilson Center, Washington, D.C., September 1986.

rapid industrialization – very much like the French Revolution and industrialization earlier in France and England – introduced a new turn toward
positivism, historicism, and class consciousness. As in Victorian Europe,
realism emerged as a way of coping with the new industrial world. But the
gentry still stood at the beginning of the Gilded Age crisis in American
exceptionalism and hardly began to appreciate the demands that these new
orientations toward value and knowledge would place upon them. Their
understanding of these imperatives and their response to them would remain
shaped by the exceptionalist heritage. At the outset their overriding concern
was to show that the social sciences could reconfirm the traditional principles of American governance and economy and replace religion as a sure
guide to the exceptionalist future.

## Historico-politics and republican principle

The model of historico-politics established by Francis Lieber provided the
foundation for most Gilded Age political science, but there was one brief
effort in the 1870s to establish a somewhat different historical-political
science that bears examination. Although Lieber looked for principles
validated by cumulative historical experience, a few Americans, influenced
by positivist scientific ideals, hoped for the discovery of laws of historical
development like those formulated by Comte and Spencer. Although Henry
Adams fits uneasily in that, or in any single category, his brief foray into
academic history in the 1870s belongs in that positivist camp. At Harvard
Eliot and his modernizing allies hired Adams, then a young cosmopolitan
turned political journalist and reformer, who claimed no special knowledge
of his designated field of medieval history. Adams soon discovered that
the medieval bases of American institutions could be given a scientific
foundation.[18]

In the mid-nineteenth century, detailed research provided the Teutonic
chain of descent with new scientific warrant. By 1871 Sir Henry Maine in his
study of *Village Communities in the East and West* could link the English
village community, born of the Saxon hundred and the German mark, with
village communities in India, themselves vestiges of ancient Indian forms.
Adopting the term "Aryan" from the philological analysis of Indo-
European languages descended from the Sanskrit, Walter Bagehot and
Maine a few years later claimed this lineage for the Aryan race. The Teutonic

18 Robert L. Church, "The Development of the Social Sciences as Academic Disciplines at
   Harvard University, 1869–1900" (Ph.D. dissertation, Harvard University, 1965), 1:90–9.

chain, and America along with it, became part of a potent synthetic view of Western history.[19]

To Henry Adams, one of the great attractions of "what is called Aryan or Indo-European law," was that it could become a "tolerably complete science and one of no little value to mankind." If systems like Comte's were premature, Adams believed they exemplified a healthy scientific impulse toward the discovery of laws of social development. Moreover, the Aryan science of liberty confirmed American institutions. In his own research he tried to show that for a brief time under Alfred, the Saxon hundred served as the basis for a confederate state based on republican principles, an anticipation, as it were, of the natural course of development of British and American institutions.[20]

Adams' thought, however, was too complex to be long contained within Cambridge academic routine or the Aryan theory of political liberty. In 1876 he returned to Washington and tried to gauge what Americans themselves had done with those principles through a history of the early years of the Republic. He was more shaken than many of his contemporaries by the force of history and its ironic course and sought persistently, if metaphorically, for controlling scientific laws. His resort to scientism reflected the lingering power of the American fusion of history and nature. In a rich metaphorical passage, whose images we will see throughout this book, Adams explained his belief that American democracy required a science of history.

Travellers in Switzerland who stepped across the Rhine where it flowed from its glacier could follow its course among medieval towns and feudal ruins, until it became a highway for modern industry, and at last arrived at a permanent equilibrium in the ocean. American history followed the same course. With pre-historic glaciers and medieval feudalism the story had little to do; but from the moment it came within sight of the ocean it acquired interest almost painful.... Science alone could sound the depths of the ocean, measure its currents, foretell its storms, or fix its relations to the system of Nature. In a democratic ocean science could see something ultimate. Man could go no further. The atom might move, but the general equilibrium could not change.

Here in the language of science and the image of a "democratic ocean" was the potent vision of millennial America, which his family had harbored for

19  George P. Gooch, *History and Historians in the Nineteenth Century* (Boston: Beacon, 1959 [1913]), 320, 369–70.
20  William H. Jordy, *Henry Adams, Scientific Historian* (New Haven, Conn.: Yale University Press, 1952), 113–20; Henry Adams, "The Anglo-Saxon Courts of Law," in *Essays in Anglo-Saxon Law*, ed. Henry Adams (Boston: Little, Brown, 1876).

generations: America as an unchanging realm of nature, that had left behind the structured, changing European past; America as the final repository of law and the end of history; America as dynamic atomistic movement contained within a larger stasis.[21]

Adams was never able himself to discover what the scientific laws of historical development might be. But several in his intellectual milieu did formulate during the 1870s positivist laws of historical progress that incorporated the Teutonic theory. Adams sent his Cambridge friend Oliver Wendell Holmes into investigation of the Saxon origins of the English common law, resulting in his famous lectures of 1881. An admirer of Spencer, Maine, and current anthropology, Holmes found progression in the common law that echoed these evolutionary theories. He has been remembered by later generations for his belief that the life of the law is in experience, not in deductive logic, but experience in this positivist Cambridge context yielded evolutionary laws. John Fiske, a contemporary of Holmes at Harvard Law School in the 1860s and almost appointed to the Harvard history department in the 1870s, had absorbed the same positivist and Teutonist literature. Fiske managed to link Spencer's cosmic law directly to Aryan history: The federated republic perfectly reflected the impulses to both coherence and differentiation, association and individuation, central power and individual liberty visible in the development of all natural forms.[22]

The overt positivism advocated by Henry Adams and realized by Fiske and Holmes did not sink academic roots in the 1870s and 1880s. Religious opposition gave way slowly so that independent temperaments like Adams and Holmes sought careers outside academia, while the earnest young Fiske was denied entrance. By the 1890s, however, clerical control was in retreat and A. Lawrence Lowell, an inheritor of Cambridge positivism, would revive the tradition and pass it on to the political scientists.

The conception of historico-politics that dominated the 1870s and 1880s was the tradition of Francis Lieber, who linked the Teutonic chain to the methodological premises of historiography rather than to those of natural science. Lieber's search for the principles of political progress imbedded in the history of civilization and his emphasis on a strong national state gave his

21 On Adams the historian, see J. C. Levenson, *The Mind and Art of Henry Adams* (Stanford, Calif.: Stanford University Press, 1957); and Jordy, *Henry Adams, Scientific Historian*. The quotation is from Henry Adams, *History of the United States of America*, 9 vols. (New York: Scribner, 1890), 9:225.

22 On Cambridge positivism, see Mark DeWolfe Howe, *Justice Oliver Wendell Holmes*, 2 vols. (Cambridge, Mass.: Harvard University Press, 1957), vol. 1, chap. 5; vol. 2, chap. 5. On Holmes's Spencerian framework, see also Grant Gilmore, *The Ages of American Law* (New Haven, Conn.: Yale University Press, 1977), 41–67.

political science new relevance in the wake of Civil War nationalism and the onset of exceptionalist crisis. When Lieber died in 1867, he had already had a major impact upon "the most thoughtful students of politics" according to Daniel Coit Gilman, a postwar promoter of his work. Lieber's most influential disciple was probably Theodore Dwight Woolsey, the clerical president of Yale, who taught his ideas in courses in history, politics, and international law. After he retired in 1872, he issued new editions of Lieber's works and published his own reinterpretation.[23]

Andrew White had been a student of Woolsey, and after his European historical studies he returned to Yale for a master's degree in 1856 just as Woolsey was enthusiastically adopting Lieber's text. White's interest in politics had been aroused by the native tradition of civic humanism and heightened by the accelerating conflict over slavery. Francis Wayland inspired him to accept the chair in history at the University of Michigan in 1857, by declaring that "the country was shortly to arrive at a 'switching-off place' toward good or evil; that the West was to hold the balance of power, and to determine whether the country would prove a blessing or a curse in human history."[24]

White was also inspired by Thomas Arnold, Regius professor of history at Oxford. Arnold's critical historiographical method and sophisticated understanding of institutions, as well as his Teutonism, his belief that nations develop according to historical laws, and his presentist aim to bring historical understanding to bear on contemporary political problems all formed common ground with Lieber's conception of political science and provided a platform on which American historians could link their study to his. White claimed his primary purpose in teaching history was to promote "better training in thought regarding our great national problems." After an interlude in active politics, he took over Cornell University in 1867 and promptly announced, on paper at least, a "School of Political Science" that embraced history, politics, law, and economics, as well as lectures on "social science"

23 Daniel Coit Gilman, "Introductory Note" to *On Civil Liberty and Self-Government*, by Francis Lieber, 4th ed., ed. Theodore Dwight Woolsey (Philadelphia: Lippincott, 1901); Theodore Dwight Woolsey, "Introduction" to *On Civil Liberty and Self-Government*, by Francis Lieber, 3d ed., ed. Theodore Dwight Woolsey (Philadelphia: Lippincott, 1877); idem, *Political Science*, 2 vols. (New York: Scribner, Armstrong, 1877); Stevenson, *Scholarly Means to Evangelical Ends*, chap. 7. On the post–Civil War rise of nationalist political theories, see Chapter 2, n. 33, and Mark E. Neely, Jr., "Romanticism, Nationalism, and the New Economics: Elisha Mulford and the Organic Theory of the State," *American Quarterly*, 29 (Fall 1977): 404–21.
24 Andrew Dickson White, *The Autobiography of Andrew Dickson White*, 2 vols. (New York: Century, 1905), 1:256–62; 2:384; White to Daniel Coit Gilman, February 2 and March 5, 1883, Gilman Papers, Johns Hopkins University; Andrew Dickson White, "How I Was Educated," *Forum*, 2 (February 1887): 572–3.

as the scientific treatment of what were called the dependent, delinquent, and defective classes. Political science, in other words, was the generic term for all the social and historical sciences. Charles Kendall Adams, White's student, carried on this conception and presided over the establishment of a school of political science at Michigan in 1881.[25]

By that date, John W. Burgess had given "the political sciences" an added prominence. Burgess too was drawn toward politics by his Civil War experience. Then, as a student of Julius Seelye at Amherst College, he read Lieber and upon graduation enrolled in Columbia Law School to study with him. Forced to withdraw because of illness, he decided instead to read law in a private office and then studied history and *Staatswissenschaft* in Germany. In 1877 he went to Columbia, where a group of trustees and faculty around Samuel Ruggles, a wealthy New York cosmopolitan interested in modernizing the college, recognized Burgess as a fitting successor to Lieber. By 1880 he and the liberal trustees had launched a school of political science. Cast along the inclusive lines White had conceived, Burgess' larger permanent staff and ambitious graduate program immediately set a new standard for the field.[26]

Herbert Baxter Adams was moving in a similar direction. Adams too had read Lieber under Seelye at Amherst and studied both political science and history in Germany. His major professor was Johannes Bluntschli at Heidelberg, himself an admirer of Lieber, who joined the idealist and historical branches of *Staatswissenschaft* into a single theory of the state. Applying for a position at Johns Hopkins University, Adams said he wanted "to pursue historical researches and to contribute something to Political Science." With Gilman he began a graduate seminar and then publication series in "history and political science." Spurred on by Burgess' success at Columbia, he hoped for more money to construct "a great school of History and Politics," one that would "command for her graduates the Washington situation," so that "when experts are needed . . . they will be taken from this university," but Gilman did not have the money to provide.[27]

25 Thomas Arnold, *Introductory Lectures on Modern History* (New York: D. Appleton, 1845); Duncan Forbes, *The Liberal Anglican Idea of History* (Cambridge University Press, 1952); Anna Haddow, *Political Science in American Colleges and Universities, 1636–1900* (New York: D. Appleton-Century, 1939), 189–92, 205–8.
26 John W. Burgess, *Reminiscences of an American Scholar* (New York: Columbia University Press, 1934); Albion Small, "Fifty Years of Sociology in the United States (1865–1915)," *AJS*, 21 (May 1916): 728n.; R. Gordon Hoxie et al., *A History of the Faculty of Political Science, Columbia University* (New York: Columbia University Press, 1955); D. G. Brinton Thompson, *Ruggles of New York* (New York: Columbia University Press, 1946).
27 John Martin Vincent, "Herbert Baxter Adams," in *American Masters of Social Science*, ed. Howard Odum (New York: Holt, 1927), 99–130; Richard T. Ely, "A Sketch of the Life and Services of Herbert Baxter Adams," in *Herbert Baxter Adams: Tributes of Friends*, ed. John

Adams held on, however, to his vision of the joint field. When his coveted professorship was offered in 1890, he was chagrined to learn that it was to be in "American and Institutional History." The term "American history," he told Gilman, conveyed neither the cosmopolitan scope of his teachings, nor his aim.

What I really represent in this University is the practical union of History and Politics. That combination is the main strength of my department. The spirit of my work and of our University Studies in Historical and Political Science has been commended in this country and in Germany because it illustrates precisely that intimate blending of historical and political science which Bluntschli and Lieber, Arnold and Freeman regarded as inseparable. The term "Institutional History" or "Historical Politics" fairly expresses the spirit of the motto printed upon our University Studies and Seminary wall.

The motto was taken from Freeman, Regius professor at Oxford, disciple of Arnold, and a fulsome Teutonist: "History is past politics, and politics are present history."[28]

Given the widening crisis in American exceptionalism after the Civil War, it is clear why Lieber's version of historico-politics would be so attractive among the reforming university gentry. Its task was to verify, strengthen, and preach those Teutonic principles of civil liberty that now seemed threatened by change. The historical activists could offer to reformulate traditional American principles on the firmer ground of science, preserving the past while guiding America into the future. Burgess feared that "unless a sounder political wisdom and a better political practice be attained, the republican system may become but a form, and republican institutions but a deception."

When the American gentry went abroad, they confirmed their native fears and the broad lines of their solution. The moderate German liberals like

Martin Vincent et al., *JHUSHPS*, extra vol. 23 (1902); H. B. Adams to Gilman, May 21, 1876, quoted on 32 in W. Stull Holt, "Historical Scholarship in the United States, 1876–1901: As Revealed in the Correspondence of Herbert Baxter Adams," *JHUSHPS*, ser. 56, no. 4 (1938); H. B. Adams to Gilman, March 4, 1887, Herbert Baxter Adams Papers, Johns Hopkins University; H. B. Adams to Gilman, December 13, 1890, Gilman Papers.

28 H. B. Adams to Gilman, December 19, 1890, Adams Papers. Note that this letter was omitted from the Holt collection. Historians have generally ignored the connection between history and political science, though it is discussed in David Van Tassel, "From Learned Society to Professional Organization: The American Historical Association, 1884–1900," *AHR*, 89 (October 1984): 941–54. I have argued for the joint origins of history and political science in "On the Misunderstanding of Ranke and the Origin of the Historical Profession in America," in *Leopold von Ranke and the Shaping of the Historical Discipline*, ed. Georg G. Iggers and James M. Powell (Syracuse, N.Y.: Syracuse University Press, 1990). On Freeman see Stefan Collini, Donald Winch, and J. W. Burrow, *That Noble Science of Politics* (Cambridge University Press, 1983).

Bluntschli from whom they learned were even more consumed by the threat of class conflict and mass democratic politics and were also developing a historical political science that would withstand those threats. In France, too, Burgess was inspired by the example of the new Ecole Libre des Sciences Politiques and its mission of defending the Third Republic. The establishment of historico-politics in America was part of the wider effort of Western educated classes to defend a precarious liberalism by reinvigorating their cultural tradition.[29]

For the political scientists, the mugwump program to develop a leadership class and an expert civil service was part of their professional as well as their class intention. With a dash of wishful thinking, Charles Kendall Adams asserted that "popular opinion is always shaped and guided by the educated classes ... there is much greater need of good leading than of good following." Burgess at first taught part-time in the law school and hoped to use it as a base for professional education in government, but he quickly despaired of its narrow focus. When New York State passed a civil-service reform law, and when he toured the elite training program at the French Ecole, he proposed to the Columbia trustees a graduate school of civil service. Less sanguine than he about the rapid transformation of American politics, the trustees approved instead a school of political science, noting that instruction in its principles was still needed, regardless of the availability of careers in the civil service.[30]

As it turned out, Columbia's graduates found places in the burgeoning university system far more frequently than in the lagging government service. At Johns Hopkins, too, although Henry Baxter Adams hoped to furnish experts to Washington, his graduates went rather into university teaching or into new professional positions in journalism and social services. Like Burgess, however, he kept alive the ideal of a professional government service as part of the broader campaign for a trained leadership class. Dominating Adams' seminar room was a large map of the United States, on which he marked the location of his successful graduates. Woodrow Wilson remembered him as a great "Captain of Industry."[31]

29 John W. Burgess, "The Study of the Political Sciences in Columbia College," *International Review*, 12 (April 1882): 346; James J. Sheehan, *German Liberalism in the Nineteenth Century* (Chicago: University of Chicago Press, 1978), 19–21, 87–9, 106, 114, 150, 156; Thomas R. Osborne, *A "Grande Ecole" for the "Grands Corps"* (Boulder, Colo.: Social Science Monographs, 1983).

30 Charles Kendall Adams, "The Relations of Political Science to National Prosperity," Address delivered at the opening of the School of Political Science of the University of Michigan, October 3, 1881, pp. 4, 18; Hoxie, *History of the Faculty of Political Science*, 11–15.

31 Vincent, "Herbert Baxter Adams," 118–19; Ely, "A Sketch of H. B. Adams," 46.

The historico-political scientists set out to strengthen their science by using the critical historical method developed most fully in Germany. Grounded in philology and the historiographical program of Ranke, this conception of historical method as a science providing real access to the past had made its way to America through the influence of study abroad and American adaptations. The influence of Thomas Arnold and of Ranke, English and German institutional history, the new Teutonist studies, and growing acquaintance with biblical criticism all contributed to the view that critical historical method would discover the facts of history. The gentry political scientists were not, as has long been thought, nominalistic historical positivists, believers that historians could discover "facts alone, with no generalizations and with a renunciation of all philosophy." Rather they believed that the facts, when contemplated, would yield those underlying principles that guided political progress. With philosophical grounding in commonsense realism or idealism, they believed – as Ranke's identity philosophy allowed him to believe – that the historian could discern in the facts the underlying principles of progress.[32]

The gentry political scientists had several versions of this scientific program to save republican principle. Burgess was an Hegelian idealist who believed that the state was "the product of the progressive revelation of human reason through history." The task of political science was first to arrange "the facts of history in the forms and conclusions of science," and then to discern in those facts "political ideals not yet realized." These ideals in turn "become principles of political science, then articles of political creeds, and at last, laws and institutions." The process of "philosophical speculation" was thus "the most important element in political science, because it lights the way of progress." In practice, that meant that Burgess organized the curriculum around political and legal institutions, and political and economic theory, all studied historically, while his research program focused on the comparative examination of modern political institutions.[33]

Burgess' Hegelianism gave him a strong sense of historical change in dealing with some topics, as we shall see in a moment, but it also allowed him to see republican civil liberty as the ultimate constitutional form of the state. The ideals cum principles of political science cum historical realities he

---

32 Above, Chapter 1, n. 29; Carl Diehl, *Americans and German Scholarship, 1770–1870* (New Haven, Conn.: Yale University Press, 1978). The quotation is from W. Stull Holt, "The Idea of Scientific History in America," *Journal of the History of Ideas*, 1 (June 1940): 356–7; for a more extended critique of that view, see Ross, "On the Misunderstanding of Ranke."

33 Burgess, *Reminiscences*, 52–4; idem, *Political Science and Comparative Constitutional Law*, 2 vols. (Boston: Ginn, 1890), 1:67; idem, "Political Science and History," *AHR*, 2 (April 1897): 407–8; Haddow, *Political Science*, 178–82.

most praised were the traditional ones of limited self-government. With citation to Freeman and the Teutonist literature, he declared the modern nation state "the creation of Teutonic political genius" and argued that among those states, American political institutions most fully solved the problem of liberty. Once the perfect form of reason had been attained, change could not affect principle.[34]

Burgess' static conception of republican principle probably gained strength from his legal training. Like Woolsey and many others in the new field, Burgess had studied law, and American legal scholars before Holmes regarded constitutional principles, like the law of nature, as fixed. Legal principle had always to be adjusted to "the advancing spirit of each age." But doing so, according to Theodore Dwight, dean of Columbia's law school, was no different from applying the "settled and determined principles" of mathematics to the differing, complex circumstances of mechanics. To Dwight, historical study was necessary and useful, but it disclosed unchanging principle.[35]

For Herbert Adams, a commonsense realist, the way to validate the traditional principles of civil liberty was to trace their long lineage through historical research. Faced with evidence of change all around him, Adams and his students embarked on community studies around New England that would show the unbroken continuity of American and English institutions. Continuity for Adams assured the conservative course he and his gentry peers wanted to steer. "In the improvement of the existing social order, what the world needs is historical enlightenment and political and social progress along existing institutional lines. We must preserve the continuity of our past life in the State . . ." His desire that "the political history of the world should be read as a single whole" also reflected the tendency of newly secular intellectuals to look to the historical world for philosophical coherence.[36]

More than political stability and philosophic unity, continuity maintained the vision of unchanging principle that linked America to divine purpose. Although Adams was thoroughly exposed to historicism in his German studies and recognized history as the ground on which American principles must be vindicated, his work remained shaped by the prehistoricist mentality of American exceptionalism. Unlike the interpenetration of continuity

34 Burgess, *Political Science*, 1:38–9, 53, 57, 68, 174–83, 264.
35 Theodore W. Dwight, *Inaugural Addresses of Theodore W. Dwight and George P. Marsh in Columbia College* (New York: Columbia University Trustees, 1859), 31, 38–40; Gilmore, *Ages of American Law*, 34–60.
36 Ross, "On the Misunderstanding of Ranke"; Herbert Baxter Adams, "Is History Past Politics?" *JHUSHPS*, ser. 13, nos. 3–4 (1895): 74, 80–1.

and change in nineteenth-century English Whig histories and idealist German historiography, Adams' continuity was unchanging. The one defense he made of his search for Teutonic germs of American institutions was that the New England towns could not have sprung up merely from Puritan virtue or the rocky New England soil, as though by "spontaneous generation." There had to be seeds, he said, "old English and Germanic ideas, brought over by Pilgrims and Puritans, and as ready to take root in the free soil of America as would Egyptian grain which had been drying in a mummy-case for thousands of years." This improbable simile expresses as well as anything could Adams' determination to protect American principle from the corrosive effects of time; it had always been and must always remain the same.[37]

Charles Kendall Adams showed the same inclination to seek out timeless principle in history, though his was the more threatening cyclical principle of republican rise and decline. "The history of civilization is one continuous story of development," he said. "Before this fact all artificial distinctions between different periods of history and different kinds of history fade away." Continuity meant that "we are not under that exceptional protection which von Holst has sneeringly said was long supposed to be vouchsafed by the kindness of a partial Providence to Americans as well as to women and children." If von Holst's gibe was meant to jar Americans into abandoning millennial time and entering the world of historical change, however, it rather led Charles Kendall Adams back to the cyclical republican fate. "We are under the same rigorous laws that have shaped the destinies of nations on the other side of the Atlantic . . . our tendencies are essentially the same that have shown themselves in other republics." In his historical research program, as in much of Andrew White's, the history of Europe was rehearsed to show the dire consequences awaiting dereliction from republican principle.[38]

For Herbert Adams and Burgess, the major figures in historico-political science, republican principle had also to be strengthened to serve conservative political purposes in the Gilded Age. Like Lieber and their Whig

---

37 Herbert Baxter Adams, "The German Origin of New England Towns," *JHUSHPS*, ser. 1, no. 2 (1882): 8; Dorothy Ross, "Historical Consciousness in Nineteenth Century America," *AHR*, 89 (October 1984): 909–28. After examining Adams' historical work, John Higham concluded that "he cared only about continuity and took no interest whatever in change." John Higham, "Herbert Baxter Adams and the Study of Local History," *AHR*, 89 (December 1984): 1229.

38 Charles Kendall Adams, *A Manual of Historical Literature* (New York: Harper, 1882), 17–18; idem, *Democracy and Monarchy in France* (New York: Holt, 1874); Andrew Dickson White, *The Greater States of Continental Europe: A Syllabus* (Ithaca, N.Y.: Cornell University Press, 1874), particularly pp. 5–9.

forebears, they wanted to protect established institutions from the demos by subordinating individual rights to history and the community. In looking for survivals, Herbert Adams stressed not the New England town meeting with its link to Jacksonian popular sovereignty, but rather the communal limits on individual liberty. He found traces in New England of "the old system of cooperative husbandry and common fields which are the most peculiar features of a German village community." From this economic cooperation he concluded that "Plymouth was not settled upon the principle of squatter sovereignty – every man for himself – but upon communal principles of the strictest character ... The life principle enduring in these apparently dead forms of land tenure is the sovereignty of the community over its individual or associate members."

If we can see in the condemnation of "every man for himself" resistance to working-class demands, there are also indications that Adams saw capitalist lawlessness too as individual selfishness. "There is and always has been, a moral element in the business world, in the relations of capital and labor, master and servant.... Doctrines of selfishness and individualism are now supplemented by conceptions of generosity and public spirit." Adams much preferred Henry Drummond's view of evolution as "a struggle for the life of others" to Spencer's equation of the biological and economic struggle for existence. But Adams' reform efforts were largely limited to mugwump charity reforms and programs in popular education which shied away from direct class appeals.[39]

Burgess turned the Whig program in a more conservative direction. Like Lieber, he grounded rights and limited government in the state, "the people in ultimate sovereign organization"; the true republic was a democratic state with an aristocratic government, an aristocracy of merit like the American judiciary. Civil War nationalism, however, turned this Whig vision toward a powerful and conservative national government. For Adams Civil War and Reconstruction had dampened national enthusiasm: He called the Teutonic principle of local self-government a "wholesome conservative power in these days of growing centralization." Burgess became a champion of national power and far more than Lieber or Adams subordinated the

39 H. B. Adams, "The German Origin of New England Towns," 14–15, 33, 37; Herbert Baxter Adams, "Arnold Toynbee," *The Charities Review*, 1 (November 1891): 13–14; Ely, "A Sketch of H. B. Adams," 36–8; Records of the Historical and Political Science Association and of the Seminary of History and Politics, October 19, 1894, Johns Hopkins University. For an account of Gilded Age social science that emphasizes its organicist premises and values, see Guenther Brandt, "The Origins of American Sociology: A Study in the Ideology of Social Science, 1865–1895" (Ph.D. dissertation, Princeton University, 1974).

individual to the state.[40] He inveighed against "the pernicious doctrine of natural rights, according to which each individual or the population of any section is practically authorized to determine in what his or its rights consist." Only "the Nation's *will*" could transform the ethical feeling of the individual into rights. "Until this happens, however, the assertion of rights is but an ignorant boast or a disloyal threat." The voice here is not merely that of a conservative Whig, but of one who had lived painfully through the Civil War. The son of a Tennessee slaveholder and unionist Whig who could not offer his son safety from the crosscurrents of war, Burgess went through a harrowing period of fear and deprivation. When he made his way north, he transferred his allegiance to the triumphant nation. He knew through personal experience that the assertion of individual or sectional conscience was a futile gesture when it countered the aroused national will.[41]

Burgess' Civil War nationalism taught him the power of history as well, for the nation and its Constitution were produced by "historical and revolutionary forces," not legal ones. The American Constitution was the work of a revolutionary convention expressing the national will of the people, not the creation of the legal action of the states in ratification. Precisely to prevent such revolutionary eruptions of history in the future, he counseled, the amending power in the Constitution should be made simpler. He was delighted that historical developments were reducing the states to mere administrative units of the national government. If America had already solved the problem of liberty, he wrote, its future destiny was to find the proper balance between centralization and decentralization in government. In regard to the federal executive, "adjustment to modern conditions is still in progress."[42] Burgess saw American nationalism as still in the process of formation; in this realm alone history was the bearer not of the same ancient principles but of qualitative change toward a still unrealized ideal. His bifurcated vision points clearly to the lingering power of American exceptionalism amidst the beginning of a new appreciation of historicism.

Unfortunately for Burgess, history was about to change precisely that sphere of civil liberty which he believed to be fixed. The rise of radical sentiment and Progressive reform led him to harden his defense of private property rights as central to the American tradition of liberty. His reform

40 Burgess, *Political Science*, 1:66, 72; 2:365–6; Herbert Baxter Adams, "Cooperation in University Work," *JHUSHPS*, ser. 1, no. 2 (1882): 89.
41 John W. Burgess, "The American Commonwealth: Changes in Its Relations to the Nation," *PSQ*, 1 (March 1886): 17; idem, *Reminiscences*, chaps. 1–3.
42 Burgess, *Political Science*, 1:90, 98–108, 150–4; 2:38–40, 319; idem, "The American Commonwealth."

interest was limited to municipal and civil-service reforms that would purify politics and to complaints of "our prodigality with the suffrage." He later felt particularly betrayed by the income tax, for it was authorized by the process of constitutional amendment, the process by which the sovereign nation exercised its will and spoke the voice of history. Burgess' strategy of grounding property rights in the historical state ironically worked both ways. If the individual was now dependent on the constitutional decree of the state for rights, the state was also dependent on the combined action of individuals in history. "Back of the Constitution," he complained, "were, or at least ought to be, the sound principles of political science, which deals with things according to their nature, and not as a jugglery of artificial names." Aided by his Hegelian idealism, Burgess had so fully identified the rational and the real that logically he had no recourse from the verdict of history.[43]

In their attempts to fix in history the proper blend of authority and private rights, as in their social and scientific programs, the historico-political scientists of the 1870s and early 1880s are easily seen as a transitional generation. They were moved by social, historical, and philosophical conceptions that partook of both the early nineteenth-century republic and the changing industrial world of the coming century. But as we shall see, the generations that followed them were equally transitional, not merely because historical time always presents the task of synthesizing old and new, but because every generation of American social scientists would accept the apologetic task bequeathed them by American exceptionalism and only partially resolve the conflicting claims it entailed.

During the two decades after the Civil War, historico-politics provided nonetheless a relatively stable context for the establishment of political science as a field of systematic knowledge. The joint field overlapped a spectrum of scholars interested in more exclusively historical study to those more oriented toward contemporary politics. Even in the joint programs, either history or politics predominated. While most of the university students of politics practiced some version of historico-politics, many historians, descended from the older tradition of history as belles lettres or sceptical of political activism, projected different conceptions of their field. Herbert Adams and Andrew White founded the American Historical Association in 1884 as a vehicle for the study of both history and politics, and scholars and activists whose interest was in contemporary politics gave

43 John W. Burgess, "The Ideal of the American Commonwealth," *PSQ*, 10 (September 1895): 404–25; idem, *The Reconciliation of Government with Liberty* (New York: Scribner, 1915), 368.

papers at the meetings, but from the beginning there were some tensions. For a time, however, specialists in both fields generally coexisted peaceably. Their common belief in Teutonic principles of self-government as well as their common commitment to historical method allowed them to see – in Wittgenstein's well-used phrase – a family resemblance in their work.[44]

## Exceptionalism revised in political economy: Francis Walker

The free-trade tradition of political economy that had come to dominate the colleges before the Civil War continued its influence well into the Gilded Age. Down to 1900 the leading college textbooks remained those of Francis Wayland, Amasa Walker, and Walker's disciple, Arthur Latham Perry, a clerical teacher of political economy at Williams College and free-trade activist. Among men of affairs, the widest reputations were held by men of this old school: Perry; Edward Atkinson, a Boston businessman and economic writer; and David Ames Wells, a government official and publicist on revenue, trade, and railroads. These men reworked the exceptionalist free-trade tradition in part as a practical response to the rise of machine industry. Atkinson, a pioneer in textile manufacture, and Wells, an inventor and acute observer, early concluded that mechanized production required greatly increased markets and therefore the elimination of trade barriers. They argued for long-term benefit against manufacturing interests who had succeeded during the Civil War in erecting a protective tariff.[45]

Free laws of the market stood sentinel not only against manufacturers seeking special privileges, but increasingly against greenbackers, labor reformers, and after 1879, when Henry George's *Progress and Poverty* burst on the scene, proponents of a single tax to expropriate the unearned increment on land. For economists still grounded in the antebellum fusion of divine and natural law, another source of defense against the visible poverty and class conflict of the Gilded Age was the call on divine intention. Atkinson declared that if one believed in God, one must believe "that this is the best world that could have been made . . . that the struggle for existence, hard and severe as it seems to us, must be the necessary school by which man could have been elevated above the beasts of the field." From beginning to

---

44 Ross, "On the Misunderstanding of Ranke."
45 Joseph Dorfman, *The Economic Mind in American Civilization*, 5 vols. (New York: Viking, 1946–59), vol. 3, chaps. 1, 3; Daniel Horowitz, "Genteel Observors: New England Economic Writers and Industrialization," *New England Quarterly*, 48 (March 1975): 65–83; Broadus Mitchell, "David Ames Wells," *DAB*, 19: 637–8; Harold F. Williamson, *Edward Atkinson: The Biography of an American Liberal, 1827–1905* (Boston: Old Corner Book Store, 1934), chaps. 1–2.

end of Perry's popular text, God made frequent appearance. "If the footsteps of providential intelligence be found anywhere upon this earth, if proofs of God's goodness be anywhere discernible, they are discernible, and are found in the fundamental laws of society." The more appearances belied their faith, the stronger their faith had to be.[46]

Indeed Perry's text codified the expansive version of antebellum exceptionalism as it was becoming visibly obsolete. He admired the optimistic forecasts and class harmonies portrayed by Walker and Carey, shorn of their tie to the tariff, and framed his text on Bastiat's definition of economic exchange as exchange of services. On Ricardo's law of diminishing returns he was willing to follow classical theory rather than Carey, for he had an internationalist vision that took into account increases in the quality of land being brought under cultivation across the globe. On Malthus, however, the exceptionalist basis of his optimism held fast. Malthus' so-called law was simply unproven, a travesty on divine will, and a denial of workers' upward mobility. In the 1870s and 1880s Perry became even more explicit in the face of worsening protest: "In the United States the greatest freedom prevails; there is nothing to hinder any laborer from becoming a capitalist."[47]

Although this older tradition remained, the cosmopolitan gentry began to establish economics as a discipline independent of moral philosophy and the old tariff wars. One of Eliot's first decisions at Harvard in 1869 was to take the teaching of political economy away from the old Careyite moral philosopher Francis Bowen and appoint a free-standing professorship of political economy, the first in the country. The chair went in 1871 to Charles F. Dunbar, editor of the *Boston Daily Advertiser* and an alumnus of the Harvard Law School. Supported by local businessmen for his free-trade views, Dunbar quickly adopted the new scientific role and refrained from public advocacy. At Yale in 1872 Sumner replaced Woolsey as professor of political and social science and Francis A. Walker was appointed professor of political economy and history in Yale's Sheffield Scientific School. Although Sumner dealt partly with political economy in his teaching and writing, Walker's main work was in economics, in Sheffield and in graduate courses in the college. In 1876 he added part-time lectures at the new Johns Hopkins University, while keeping a hand in government work.[48]

46 Williamson, *Edward Atkinson*, 243, quoting from Atkinson's *The Industrial Progress of the Nation* (1890); Arthur Latham Perry, *Elements of Political Economy* (New York: Scribner, 1866), 26, 76, 126.
47 Dorfman, *Economic Mind*, 3:56–63; Perry, *Elements*, 74–166; 1873 ed., 158–66; 1883 ed., 239–40, 247.
48 John B. Parrish, "Rise of Economics as an Academic Discipline: The Formative Years to 1900," *Southern Economic Journal*, 34 (July 1967): 1–16; Church, "Economists as Experts," 577; idem, "The Development of the Social Sciences," chap. 1.

Like the professors of historico-politics, the gentry political economists wanted to strengthen the established course of American history by giving it a sounder scientific basis. Dunbar's first article in 1876 was an assault on the entire previous body of work in American political economy. Dismissing Carey's theory as a failure, and other American efforts as theoretically derivative, narrowly tied to specific problems, or bogged down in partisan politics, he asserted "the United States have, thus far, done nothing toward developing the theory of political economy."[49]

Although Walker and Sumner would not be so sweeping, they shared the standards by which Dunbar found the American tradition wanting. Their standards of modern science required at the outset that they make political economy a "positive" science as Mill defined it, one which should have no ties to the theological and ethical premises of moral philosophy. The deity so much called upon in previous American texts disappeared from theirs. Although Dunbar did not have to fight the battle against moral philosophy at Harvard, we have already seen that Sumner undertook it at Yale, and Walker had besides to get free of the influence of his pious father. In his *Political Economy* (1884), he urged the economist to have nothing to do with ethics and keep his sentiments altogether out of sight. Yet when he came at the end, as his father had, to the subject of consumption, he could not help calling for "a great moral philosopher," quickly adding that it must be a philosopher "strictly confining himself to the study of the economic effects of these causes, peremptorily denying himself all regard to purely ethical, political, or theological considerations." Once again, the covert ties of economic theory to Victorian ethics remained unremarked.[50]

Gentry science, in economics as in historico-politics, also placed new emphasis on empiricism. There was already a long tradition of empirical inquiry in political economy. Policy issues like currency, banking, and the tariff had produced from the beginning a literature of factual investigation as well as theoretical argument, informed by statistics, some undertaken by state agencies. Amasa Walker began the practice, which Perry expanded, of including in his college text sections of historical and policy analysis on banking and currency, trade and tariffs, and taxation. In their pamphlets and books, Wells and Atkinson were noted for their attempt to use the facts of current economic life, particularly statistics. Atkinson reflected the American tradition of commonsense realism when he opened his book, *Facts and*

49 Charles F. Dunbar, "Economic Science in America, 1776–1876" (1876), in *Economic Essays* (New York: Macmillan, 1904), 16.
50 Francis A. Walker, *Political Economy* (New York: Holt, 1884), 15–16, 305.

*Figures, The Basis of Economic Science* (1904), with the motto, "Figures never lie unless liars make figures."[51]

The concern for facts of the Gilded Age economists was in many ways an extension of that tradition. Walker had learned from his father, been assistant to Wells, and taught himself on the job at the Census Bureau. But the gentry economists were also influenced by new empirical currents from historiography and approached the task with a new methodological awareness. Dunbar had already in 1876 a strong sense of empirical and historical investigation as one method of classical economics. Following Mill he regarded empirical research as a means of testing, rather than originating, generalizations and as a means of applying economic laws to the different special conditions of real life. These tasks, he thought, were becoming increasingly important. The center of economic discussion was now in Germany, he said, and he lamented the absence in America of expertise not only in "abstract science," but also "in philology," and "the more recondite historical investigations." In his own work in theory and banking he concentrated so much effort on historical research that his younger colleague Frank W. Taussig sensed a "streak of antiquarianism" in him. Sumner, too, who was trained in philology at Göttingen, believed that economics had made good progress as a deductive science, but henceforth must adopt the surer if slower method of induction. His major works in political economy were histories of currency and the tariff in America. For Dunbar and Sumner, as for many of the orthodox economists who succeeded them, empirical search for the facts promised only to deepen the fundamental principles of classical political economy and cement the union of nature and history.[52]

For Walker, the empirical tendency in economics had the critical thrust of the historicist opponents of classical economics, but before we examine it, we need to recognize that for all the gentry economists, the universal laws of the market, however extended or modified, carried the force of positivist law. Indeed, for the American economists, the positivists' emphasis on unbending law had particular force, for they saw that the whole previous effort of American political economy had been to escape the rigors of Malthusian and Ricardian analysis. The recognition that America was changing in the Gilded Age was the central problem of all the gentry social scientists, and for the political economists, change meant that America could

---

51 Dorfman, *Economic Mind*, 3:49–50 and chap. 1; Edward Atkinson, *Facts and Figures, the Basis of Economic Science* (Boston: Houghton Mifflin, 1904).
52 Dunbar, "Economic Science in America," 2, 22–3; Frank W. Taussig, "Introduction" to *Economic Essays* by Charles F. Dunbar, xi; Bellomy, "The Molding of an Iconoclast," 284–5.

no longer opt out of the direction of history the classical economists predicted.

That perception was central to Dunbar in his opening salvo of 1876. The United States held the position, "unique among the great powers, of a people developing a rich and virgin territory." From that fact the conclusion was often drawn that if the operation of economic laws "be not actually suspended in the United States, they can at any rate be disregarded with comparative safety." Such a misconception may have gotten by when we were a youthful country, but "as our condition approaches more and more to that of old countries," that will no longer be the case. "In such a country as we may reasonably believe this will be fifty years hence, and with the dangerous forces now growing within our democracy fairly developed.... it will then no longer be possible for statesmen or scholars to ignore or neglect those economic laws which determine the consequences of our actions." Walker too went out of his way to accept, as his father had not, the universal sway of Malthusian and Ricardian laws, carefully showing that they did not necessarily determine the actual trend of population or rent unless other factors were taken into account. In the changed industrial world of the Gilded Age, exceptional conditions of American history could no longer provide wholesale exemption from the stern laws of classical political economy.

When T. E. Cliffe Leslie, an eminent English political economist, sur-veyed the subject in America in 1880, he bemusedly noted the distinguishing characteristics of the tradition as rejection of Malthus, the heavy admixture of a "theological element," approval of the tariff among even reputable economists, and the faulty provincial doctrines of Henry George. Like the message of von Holst that Charles Kendall Adams carried to the historians, to give up the special protection providence gave to women and children, Cliffe Leslie's critique challenged the economists to face the real conditions of nature and history in America.[53]

Walker, the most eminent and creative of the gentry economists, most fully took up Cliffe Leslie's challenge. Economic science had to rest on the fundamental laws of classical political economy, he believed; Americans could not simply abrogate them. Yet these laws had to be made permeable to the real conditions of modern industrial life. More than that, they had to be made sympathetic to the real needs of workers, for Walker's understanding of historicism was decisively shaped by his political purpose. Empiricism

53 Dunbar, "Economic Science in America," 25, 29; Francis A. Walker, *The Wages Question* (New York: Holt, 1876), 107–8; 224–7, 367–71; T. E. Cliffe Leslie, "Political Economy in the United States," *Fortnightly Review*, n.s. 28 (October 1880): 488–509.

offered a method of loosening the harsher restraints of classical law and opening the way for mild action on behalf of the working class. As the heir of his father's expansive version of American exceptionalism, he emerged from the Civil War with strong democratic sentiments, and was sympathetic to working-class protest in the 1870s.

Walker picked up quickly on the strain of moderate criticism already at work among English economists seeking to accommodate their discipline to industrial protest. Following J. E. Cairnes, he pointed out that laissez-faire was not a scientific law but rather a practical maxim of policy. As such, it could not automatically be applied in all situations, for economics, as Mill had said, was a hypothetical science and its conclusions were only true in the absence of disturbing causes. Economists therefore had to "ascertain the character of those subordinate causes, whether mental or physical, political or social, which influence human conduct in the pursuit of wealth." Such factors were like the astronomer's discovery of a new planet, "the attraction of which, operating on all the heavenly bodies within the sphere of its influence will cause them more or less to deviate from the path which had been previously calculated for them."[54]

By the 1870s Cairnes's modest statement was swamped by a wider attack on classical theory in the name of historicism. Moved partly by the influence of English historicism through Comte and Maine, and partly by the increasing prominence of the German historical school and its attack on British theory, English economists like Cliffe Leslie and John Kells Ingram argued that the deductive method of classical economics necessarily simplified and distorted reality. Walker echoed this critique in 1879. What classical economists left out was precisely what history made plain – the effects of economic and social structure, of national differences, and of actual conditions.[55]

Walker turned his combination of universal law and conditional facts to the redemption of the American exceptionalist ideal under the changed industrial conditions of the Gilded Age. In *The Wages Question* (1876), he reformulated how the basic shares of wealth were determined so as to legitimize the fundamental action of the market and allow hope to the hard-pressed laborers. On the determination of rent and interest, he followed the accepted theories of Ricardo and Smith: Rent was determined by the differential productivity of land, interest by the supply of and demand for capital. But profit, he argued, was a payment for the entrepreneurial

54 Francis A. Walker, "Cairnes' 'Political Economy,'" in *Discussions in Economics and Statistics*, 2 vols., ed. Davis R. Dewey (New York: Augustus Kelley, 1971 [1899]), 1:279–85.
55 A. W. Coats, "The Historist Reaction in English Political Economy, 1870–1890," *Economica*, n.s. 21 (May 1954): 143–53; Francis A. Walker, "The Present Standing of Political Economy," in *Discussions*, 1:301–18.

function and determined analogously to rent by the differential in the productive efficiency of entrepreneurs. Walker thus made profits a legitimate return for skill, rather than the expropriation of a surplus created by labor as the socialists claimed.

Finally, Walker reassessed wages. One of the chief defenses of economic conservatives against the protests of labor had become the wages-fund theory, that workers were paid out of the fixed fund of circulating capital available at any point in time. Efforts to raise wages, therefore, were futile, merely forcing more of the wage fund to some workers and depriving others. Walker argued that workers were paid not from a fixed fund of capital on hand, but progressively over the course of production and at a rate anticipating ultimate returns, hence a rate reflecting anticipated increases in production. The worker became the residual legatee of the constant growth in productivity exceptionalists had always expected of the American economy. The whole point of his argument, he concluded, was to show that

the remuneration of hired labor finds its measure not in a past whose accumulations have been plundered by class legislation and wasted by dynastic wars, but in the present and the future, always larger, freer, and more fortunate.... Surely it is not a small matter that the laborer should find the measure of his wages in the present and the future, rather than in the past!

With these echoes of Carey and his father, Walker reaffirmed the expansive version of American political economy, with its twin message of resignation to the laws of the capitalist market, in expectation of its generous rewards under the liberal-republican order.

Yet the familiar ideal now rested on the classical structure. If workers gained from increasing production, they had still to counter Malthusian pressures through control of the birthrate and moral improvement. And in the actual conditions of modern industrial life, even in America, they could not always win out. Using the empiricist critique of classical economics, Walker pointed out that the system worked fairly when there was perfect competition, but this was often not the case. Economists like Bastiat and Perry had masked the differences between commodities and services in the market, but labor could not always move freely to maximize its situation. Once a class of laborers had been degraded by bare subsistence wages, it lacked the energy and power to seek its best gain in the market. The large textile mill was "one vast machine which rolls on in its appointed work, tearing, crushing, or grinding its human, just as relentlessly as it does its other, material.... Personality disappears ... apathy soon succeeds to ambition and hopefulness." Employers often did not recognize their own best interest and took advantage of such workers. They had sunk beneath the sphere in which the beneficent laws of competition could operate.[56]

Dire as was Walker's description, the direct remedies he proposed suggested that the disease was not fatal: the influence of public opinion on employers and provision by the state of primary education, sanitary legislation, factory acts – particularly for women and children – and savings banks. Strikes, as a form of insurrection, might be needed in rare and extreme cases, but they were best left to spontaneous action. Trade unions were not generally necessary in America, where the great body of workers remained sound and alert to their interests. If economic law did not always work perfectly in America, the disturbing causes remained subordinate ones. The exceptionalist idea was threatened by infirmity, but saved.[57]

Walker was the first economist to work out distinctly the concept of perfect competition, a concept that became central to the marginal economists' definition of market equilibrium. Although the marginalists would envision the market as a moving equilibrium, Walker's model remained the static Newtonian universe of Cairnes. Competition was "the order of the economic universe, as truly as gravity is the order of the physical universe, and . . . not less harmonious and beneficent in its operation." The older conception of natural law as necessary force and moral norm thus anchored his vision, even as he recognized that historical causes could hamper the operation of law and that historical remedies would be necessary to counter them.[58]

Walker did begin to open America somewhat to history. Not only the promise of natural law worked in America, but also the particular factors which blocked its operation. Fortunately for Walker, the liberal-republican institutions that had thus far kept the working class sound – general education, free access to trade and land ownership, and full civil and political rights – were also, he believed, still at work to prevent degradation. Still, new steps must be taken; to some degree, the realization of the exceptionalist ideal depended on historical struggle. And to some degree, the ideal itself had begun to change. Even in Wayland's niggardly version of American exceptionalism, the honest workman in America was assured a decent family subsistence. He could not be forced by natural causes into degradation. Walker's laborer was still amassing capital but he was carrying on a harder struggle; he could be defeated and his destined escape from the working class was nowhere explicitly stated. The antebellum ideal of wide access to in-

---

56 Walker, *The Wages Question*, pt. 2, and 359, 411; Bernard Newton, *The Economics of Francis Amasa Walker* (New York: Augustus Kelley, 1968), 87.
57 Walker, *The Wages Question*, chaps. 15–19, and 398, 406.
58 Newton, *The Economics of F. A. Walker*, 24, 26, 77, 103; Walker, *Political Economy*, 228.

dependent ownership moved perceptibly toward the reduced and distant hope of the classical neo-Malthusians.

## The beginnings of sociology: Sumner and Ward

While Walker moved tentatively to give the expansive version of American exceptionalism a more realistic basis, William Graham Sumner, his colleague at Yale, moved aggressively to justify a more constricted version. From his appointment in 1872, Sumner addressed a public audience, ranging broadly over the political, economic, and social sciences, chiefly to combat tariff and currency heresies and the perennial threats of popular democracy. He soon clashed publicly with Walker and their conflicts contributed to Walker's decision to leave Yale in 1881 for the presidency of the Massachusetts Institute of Technology. Sumner went on to forge his conservative economic and political ideas into a science of sociology.[59]

No compelling tradition of sociology had been established in America before the Civil War, but in the postwar decades, Sumner at Yale and Ward in Washington both tried to develop sociological theories on the model of Comte and Spencer. Sociology was to be a science of the laws of history, hence the laws that governed the progress of civilization. Both of them believed America was in crisis, her traditional heritage threatened with extinction, and turned to the widest field available on which to ground their hopes.

Sumner's ideal came partly from his English artisan father, a member of the Methodist, temperance culture in which respectability meant taking care of oneself and one's own. He early accepted classical economic doctrine in the simplistic form presented by Harriet Martineau and never doubted its logic. On one level, Sumner's sociology was an extrapolation of the historical vision imbedded in classical economics, as Carey's had earlier been an extension of his more optimistic political economy. But Sumner's sociology, like his broad chair at Yale, also reflected his attachment to historico-politics. He had learned Whig principles of government from Lieber and Woolsey at Yale and when he later at Oxford read Hooker's *Ecclesiastical Polity*, "It suited exactly those notions of constitutional order, adjustment of rights, constitutional authority, and historical continuity, in which I had been brought up.... It reawakened ... all my love for political science." In the early seventies, faced with popular calls for government action, he recast that tradition in a more conservative mold. Like Burgess, he grounded rights

---

59 Bellomy, "The Molding of an Iconoclast," 317–24. As the footnotes throughout this chapter attest, I am greatly indebted to Bellomy's learned and insightful thesis.

entirely in the historical state where they were circumscribed by established judgments and institutions. Property rights and a strictly limited government were fixed in the American Republic and sociology was to vindicate political as well as economic conservatism.[60]

Sumner's studies in historico-politics and in German philology had interested him in history and at Oxford he became intrigued by Buckle's attempt to discover the laws of history through empirical study. It was Spencer's methodological prologue, *The Study of Sociology* (1872), which convinced him that a science of history was possible. Sociology could discover the laws underlying the surface events of history, but its method must be historical and statistical induction. He thought Spencer himself too speculative and insufficiently inductive. Yet Sumner's method always remained at odds with his conclusions. Though praising German historical economics for its method, he had to condemn its relativistic conclusions. Perhaps statist economics was appropriate to German conditions, he once ventured, then immediately added that statist economics could never anywhere be justified. Herbert Adams, too, when he encountered Arnold Toynbee's historical economics, demurred from its relativistic implications. The facts of history had to yield universal principles or laws.[61]

Sumner's general conception of sociology lacked specific form until the Gilded Age crisis forced him to try to salvage his heritage. As Donald Bellomy has shown, what brought Sumner's ideas together was his heated reaction to the violent railroad strikes of 1877. Before the strikes he believed that America was still "far from having reached any such state" as the classical economists predicted for an "old" country. After the strikes, he saw that "the peculiar circumstances have been steadily, if not rapidly, passing away, and that they must surely pass away with time, until we come into the same position, and have the same problems to deal with, as other old and fully developed nations." That traumatic realization was the catalyst that joined his conservative economics and politics into a new sociology.[62]

Sumner made the Malthusian-Ricardian dynamic – what he called the man-land ratio – the primary law of social-historical evolution. It was "the iron spur which has driven the race on." The result of that struggle to amass capital and enlarge the sphere of comfort was the survival of the fittest, those

---

60 [William Graham Sumner], "Sketch of William Graham Sumner," *Popular Science Monthly*, 35 (June 1889): 261–4; Bellomy, "The Molding of an Iconoclast," chaps. 2, 7.

61 [Sumner], "Sketch of William Graham Sumner," 263–6; Bellomy, "The Molding of an Iconoclast," 252–3, 284–8, 305–9; H. B. Adams, "Arnold Toynbee," 14–15.

62 Bellomy, "The Molding of an Iconoclast," chap. 10, and pp. 263, 396. The first quotation is from Sumner's *North American Review* article, "Politics in America, 1776–1876" (1876); the second from an unpublished essay, "The Strikes" (1878).

whose energy, intelligence, and virtue won them a reward from nature. Attached to this economic dynamic were "differences in the industrial, political and civil organization which are produced all along at different stages of the ratio of population to land." In a condition of underpopulation, the great majority were yeoman farmers, differences in wealth were moderate and social mobility easy; consequently, a spirit of equality and political democracy were generated. But in a condition of overpopulation, competition for reward was fierce, divisions of wealth and social class pronounced, and a more aristocratic political temper engendered. Here surely was the history of the United States and the threat that America was becoming an "old" country.

Still, for the time being, he believed, advances in transportation had brought new land into cultivation and relieved "the pressure in the oldest countries and at the densest centers," producing a general tendency toward equality and a long period of relative ease in the perpetual struggle for existence. Yet this prospect immediately called forth the time-honored language of republican jeremiad: all could be lost in "extravagant governments, abuses of public credit, wasteful taxation, legislative monopolies and special privileges, juggling with currency, restrictions on trade, wasteful armaments on land and sea." Or all could be lost in the most hideous possibility of all, the rise of communism and nihilism, fed on the false sense of equality common in America. "The old classical civilization fell under an eruption of barbarians from without. It is possible that our new civilization may perish by an explosion from within."[63]

Not since Dew and the Southern Ricardians had such an ambiguous vision of American progress been formulated. For Sumner too, republican and classical economic fears combined to turn the American promise into a temporary and fragile reprieve on the road to a painful European future. Sumner did not project an end to the process, stationary or otherwise – the Ricardian future simply forecast ever greater rewards of civilization and ever more "terrible" punishment as the struggle grew fiercer. It is not surprising that he eventually became one of the few members of his generation to doubt the idea of progress.

In addressing a popular audience in 1883, however, under the title *What Social Classes Owe to Each Other*, there was a telling inconsistency. On one level he did not blink at the harshness and asymmetry of the struggle to "get capital." Indeed, he revelled in it. Those who fell to the bottom deserved to be there. "If employers withdraw capital from employment in an attempt to

63 William Graham Sumner, "Sociology," *Princeton Review*, 57 (November 1881): 309–10, 315, 317, 319–21.

lower wages, they lose profits. If employees withdraw from competition in order to raise wages, they starve to death." Yet he ignored the European future awaiting America and returned to American exceptionalism. The mobility of the American workman and his "independent and strong position in the labor market" meant that here class warfare, with its trade unions and strikes, was not necessary. As a class, American employers "have no advantage over their workmen. They could not oppress them if they wanted to do so. The advantage, taking good and bad times together, is with the workmen." The average workman in America could get some capital and qualify as a respectable capitalist. Sumner disingenuously left his reader basking in the old vision of America as the land in which the promise of liberal economic progress was fulfilled. When forced to recognize that one day its unique hope would be ground down by the wheels of time, he preferred to turn his face away.[64]

Sumner dwelt instead on applying the tenets of classical liberalism to political, as well as economic, principle. In the Middle Ages, he said, following Maine,

society was dependent, throughout all its details, on status, and the tie, or bond, was sentimental. In our modern state, and in the United States, more than anywhere else, the social structure is based on contract.... Contract, however, is rational ... realistic, cold and matter-of-fact.... [It] gives the utmost room and chance for individual development, and for all the self-reliance and dignity of a free man.

Hence a free man could not "take tips." He could ask of government only a minimal protection of his historically based rights. To ask for more was to destroy his standing as an "independent citizen" and to throw the republic open to plutocracy. Sumner's tract was a tour de force in the integration of republican, Whig, and liberal history around a new conception of libertarian individualism.[65]

The other major attempt of the 1880s to forge a science of sociology was made by Lester Frank Ward, and it was based on a different law of historical progress. As a young convert to positivism, Ward adopted the scientific view of progress developed by the French philosophes and Comte and propagated by such English liberals as Mill, T. H. Huxley, and John Tyndall. The chief dynamic force in history was the advance of knowledge; scientific rationality, as the most advanced form of knowledge, was the key to future

---

64  William Graham Sumner, *What Social Classes Owe to Each Other* (Caldwell, Idaho: Caxton Printers, 1978 [1883]), 77, 84, 86, 110.
65  Ibid., 23–4.

progress. Since Jefferson and his generation, the advance of knowledge had been a central feature of progress, but before the Civil War it did not form the underlying structure of history. To the extent that the idea of progress bore specific marks, it bore the character of the Scottish Enlightenment, which placed economic forces at the base of progress and showed how politics, society, and culture were intertwined with it; or, following American Protestantism and German idealism, progress was seen as essentially a moral phenomenon, dependent on the advance of specifically religious and moral forces. The proponents of natural knowledge in Ward's generation like White and Sumner were perhaps the first Americans to develop the view of scientific progress in their battle against religious control. What is important about Ward is that he constructed his entire sociology on its frame.[66]

The centrality of this issue to Ward arose from its resonance with the ethos of self-improvement. No less than Sumner's, Ward's sociology was an artisanal strategy of self-help writ large, in one case the effort to "get capital," in the other, to "get education." Ward's background was even poorer than that of Sumner. Like his heroes Lincoln and Horace Greeley, he was a product of the improving Whig culture in its most egalitarian form.[67] "Perhaps the most vivid impression that my early experience left on my mind was that of the difference between an uneducated and an educated person." He embarked on a program of self-education which began with the classics of five languages and basic mathematics, and went on to a dozen other fields. As a young government clerk after the Civil War, he became a positivist and fought the resurgence of orthodox Christianity. "We are near to one of those great culminating epochs," he said in 1869, when the rationalistic element in history will have to defend itself from the superstitious or be subjugated by it. The apocalyptic struggle between Christ and anti-Christ that shaped his early evangelical training now shaped his rationalist history. He began a treatise to be titled "The Great Panacea,"

---

66 Dorothy Ross, "American Social Science and the Idea of Progress," in *The Authority of Experts*, ed. Thomas L. Haskell (Bloomington: Indiana University Press, 1984), 157–61. Ward's early adoption of this view of progress is best seen in his journal, *The Iconoclast*, published in Washington, D.C., 1870–1.

67 In my "Socialism and American Liberalism: Academic Social Thought in the 1880's," *Perspectives in American History*, 11 (1977–8): 28, I mistakenly traced Ward's paternity to the Democratic Loco-Foco tradition, rather than to the egalitarian wing of the Whig tradition, an error unfortunately relied upon by Raymond Seidelman with Edward J. Harpham, *Disenchanted Realists, Political Science and the American Crisis, 1884–1984* (Albany: State University of New York Press, 1985), 28.

which would attempt to prove that happiness was created by progress, progress by knowledge, and knowledge by education.[68]

In 1875 Ward came under the influence of John Wesley Powell and his circle of government scientists and turned to studies in natural science. In a few years he joined Powell's Geological Survey as a paleobotanist. It was apparently in Powell's milieu that he began to read Comte seriously and to see that the crisis of knowledge was also a crisis in the governance of society. Class conflict intruded itself upon his cosmic consciousness both through public events and contact with his brother, Cyrenus Osborne Ward, a labor radical who through the 1870s advocated industrial cooperation and then communism as the fruition of the historic tendency toward democracy and republicanism. Ward concluded that his own scheme of progressive evolution was the only antidote to revolution.[69]

Ward set about rewriting his treatise and the result was *Dynamic Sociology*, an account of the evolution of matter, organic forms, mind, man, and society. Intelligence was a product of biological evolution and gave human beings the ability to alter nature to their own purposes. Following distinctions drawn by Kant and Comte, he believed human action was purposive, and hence allowed humanity to direct the course of its own progress. His view of social progress was a liberal version of Comte's: Science could provide the direction and order the fragmenting liberal society needed. Ward accepted the liberal market economy as a progressive force in civilization and with it a neo-Malthusian view of slow progress that would ultimately allow the working class to develop cooperative industry. But Malthus' insight was true on a higher level, for the capacity to acquire knowledge increased arithmetically, while the need for it increased geometrically. "This swarming planet will soon see the conditions of human advancement exhausted, and the night of reaction and degeneracy ushered in, never to be again succeeded by the daylight of progress, unless something swifter and more certain than natural selection can be brought to bear upon the development of the psychic faculty." The second volume of *Dynamic Sociology* was entirely devoted to intellectual progress, a reprise of "The Great Panacea." Progress would culminate in "sociocracy," the study of

68  L. F. Ward, *Young Ward's Diary*, 57–8; idem, *Glimpses of the Cosmos*, 6 vols. (New York: Putnam, 1913–18), 3:147–8, 150–5; idem, "The Situation," *The Iconoclast*, March 1870. See also Gillis J. Harp, "Lester Ward: Comtean Whig," *Historical Reflections*, 15, no. 3 (1988): 523–42.
69  Scott, *Lester Frank Ward*, 84–6; Lacey, "The Mysteries of Earth-Making Dissolve," chap. 2; L. F. Ward, *Glimpses of the Cosmos*, 3:150–5; Cyrenus Osborne Ward, *The New Idea* (New York: Cosmopolitan Publishing Co., 1870); idem, *A Labor Catechism of Political Economy* (New York: Trow Printing Co., 1878).

social laws and the art of applying them so as to produce order and progress. Sociocracy was to replace politics as the mechanism of social governance.[70]

Sumner and Ward thus proposed very different conceptions of law for a science of sociology. Sumner's natural laws of the economy and society retained the normative force of older concepts of natural law. The purpose of sociology was to derive "the rules of right social living from the facts and laws which prevail by nature in the constitution and functions of society." Although Sumner denied such laws contained any inherent "oughtness," the free will they allowed was the free will always assumed in the Christian tradition of natural law, the freedom to sinfully or mistakenly disobey. Certified by history as well as nature, "the institutions whose growth constitutes the advance of civilization have their guarantee in the very fact that they grew and became established. They suited man's purpose better than what went before." Hence, one could flout these laws, but only at the cost of going "backward."[71]

Ward, on the other hand, following Comte rather than Spencer, believed that human purposes were as much a part of nature as the blind process of natural selection. History, society, and culture were governed by laws, and therefore were subject to human direction. Ward retained the faith that scientific laws expressed a necessary relation between cause and effect and inhered in the real nature of things, despite the contrary arguments of Comte and Mill. But on the issue of human intervention, Ward became Sumner's chief antagonist during the 1880s. His brief for the application of intelligent reform to the problems of modern society was the first major statement in American social science of the new liberalism, a revision of classical liberalism that expanded its conception of individual liberty, social conscience, and public powers. The Progressive reformer Frederic C. Howe probably did not exaggerate when he wrote Ward in 1912 that "the whole social philosophy of the present day is a formative expression of what you have said to be true." *Dynamic Sociology* accepted the capitalist economy and evolutionary rather than revolutionary change. The general liberal trend of history was satisfactory and the sociocracy in which it culminated was a substitute for socialism. History in Ward's view was partially constrained by social laws and established institutions; it was open only to limited, liberal change.[72]

Sociocracy was also the first formulation in American social science of the

70 Lester Frank Ward, *Dynamic Sociology*, 2 vols. (New York: Johnson Reprint, 1968 [1883]), particularly 1:16, 60, 704ff.; 2:205–10.
71 Sumner, "Sociology," 303–4, 312, 322–3; idem, *What Social Classes Owe to Each Other*, 134–5.
72 L. F. Ward, *Dynamic Sociology*, 1:89, 159–60; idem, "Professor Sumner's Social Classes," (1884) in *Glimpses of the Cosmos*, 3:301–5; Scott, *Lester Frank Ward*, 91–5, 98, 129, 168.

concept that history was subject to scientific control. Having opened up history to change, Ward not only limited its scope, but immediately subjected it to the domination of positivistic science. Although Ward's conception of history escaped the determinism of many positivists, it retained the positivists' faith that society was fundamentally like physical nature and hence open to mechanical manipulation. He was calling not simply for intelligent action in dealing with human problems but for social engineering, the rational deployment of inanimate forces from above. Ward claimed that

the operations of a state constitute a department of natural phenomena, which, like other natural phenomena, take place according to uniform laws. The pure science, then, consists in the discovery of these laws. The intermediate, or inventive, stage embraces the devising of methods for controlling the phenomena so as to cause them to follow advantageous channels, just as water, wind, and electricity are controlled. The third stage is simply the carrying-out of the methods thus devised.

Ward's conception that politics could become the manipulation of social laws "just as water, wind, and electricity are controlled" reflected no special study on his part of political theory or history, but rather the antipolitical bias of the desire for scientific control.[73]

As an autodidact, Ward seems to have missed entirely the methodological strain of German and English historicism influencing his formally educated contemporaries; unlike Sumner, he found no difficulty in applying Spencer's method. Although he borrowed Comte's progressive historical framework, he never absorbed Comte's historicist appreciation of the past or his central focus on the discovery of historical laws. With his naturalistic background, Ward believed that sociology had to be grounded in the biological foundations of human nature. Because desire was the basis of action, and because individuals sought to maximize happiness in the satisfaction of desire, it was "the true force in the sentient world." The primary motive forces of human nature – the preservative, reproductive, aesthetic, moral, and intellectual appetites – were thus the "social forces" which it was the province of

---

73 Lester Frank Ward, "The Claims of Political Science" (1884), in *Glimpses of the Cosmos*, 3:334; see also L. F. Ward, *Dynamic Sociology*, 2:156, 249–52, 395. Bernard Crick, *The American Science of Politics* (Berkeley: University of California Press, 1960), began the tradition of reading back from the antipolitical scientism of later American political science to Lester Frank Ward, naming him a, if not *the*, founder of the discipline. Ward had a diffuse influence on his generation, but no very specific influence on the students of historico-politics who established political science in America. Crick's analysis is a clever and still devastating critique of scientism in American political science, but it suffers from overkill. Crick assumes a mindless liberal consensus in America that scientism merely reflects. For reference to a similar view of American social science, see the citation below to Geoffrey Hawthorn, Chapter 7, n. 43.

sociology to study. Social institutions seemed aggregative units through which these forces worked. Order was a problem of rational coordination; progress, a problem of learning.

For Ward, like the Enlightenment liberals and the exceptionalist devotees of nature in America, history was a chronicle of error, and progress meant approach to the rational regime of nature. "Nearly all suffering is occasioned by the violation of natural laws through ignorance or error respecting those laws," Ward said. There were no irreconcilable conflicts of interest or value that could not be harmonized by scientific rationality. The Enlightenment utopianism that moved his brother to communism was just below the surface of Ward's sociocracy.[74]

If we are to understand this Gilded Age appropriation of the radical Enlightenment and its mechanistic conception of scientific control, we must recognize its uses to America's prehistoricist mentality under siege.[75] Ward's apocalyptic metaphors, lifelong interest in religion, and faith in the ability of science to see into the real nature of things betrayed his underlying attachment to divine power. Ward sought in scientific law an assurance of order in a natural universe suddenly removed from God. If human beings had to order their own affairs, the process was open to chance and failure. Only by subjecting history to scientific control could progress be assured.

The idea that human reason can guide and direct human life, David Hollinger has suggested, has been a powerful cultural ideal at least since it was articulated for the Anglo-American world by John Stuart Mill. Formed in response to the modern recognition of human agency and the limits of human knowledge, this "cognitivist" ideal has emphasized the power of scientific knowledge and its applicability to human affairs. Although Hollinger defines the cognitivist ideal broadly as faith in reason and a *wissenschaftliche* science, American social scientists often defined it in positivist terms

74 L. F. Ward, *Dynamic Sociology*, 1:464–8, 174–6; 2:244.
75 There have been two major attempts to interpret the Enlightenment rationalism of the new liberal social scientists in America. Cushing Strout, "The Twentieth-Century Enlightenment," *APSR*, 49 (June 1955): 321–39, dealt with the Progressive descendants of Ward and concluded on p. 326 that "the historical sense has been blunted in them by a utopian, technocratic rationalism." Strout's implicit causal analysis is that they were seduced by modern science and the machine. My argument here is that causation runs the other way, that technocratic scientism was attractive to them because of their prehistoricist, exceptionalist mentality. David W. Noble, in *The Paradox of Progressive Thought* (Minneapolis: University of Minnesota Press, 1958), 106–13, 134–7, 246–8, dealt with Ward as a founder of the Progressive generation, who falls under the general indictment of clinging to eighteenth-century modes of utopian thought and avoiding a real understanding of history, until World War I destroyed the idea of "absolute progress." Noble's study deserves more attention than it has received, although the problem Noble raised requires a more differentiated analysis, centered on the underlying dynamics of historicism and the political implications of historical change rather than the idea of progress.

and narrowed it to social engineering. Ward expressed in an eighteenth-century language of mechanical contrivance an ideal that in time took on a harder technocratic edge.[76]

As substantive models for sociology, both Ward and Sumner had mixed success. Sumner admitted in 1881 that once having laid down the basic principles of classical economics and constitutional liberty, he did not know how to proceed. In 1889 he confessed he had "spent an immense amount of work" on sociology, all of it "lost because misdirected." His mixed methodology and ambivalence about progress surely contributed to his difficulties, although later, as we shall see, he constructed a more adequate framework for his tragic vision. After 1883 Ward continually absorbed new perspectives but he no longer set the agenda for sociology. His utilitarian psychology gave him little insight into the distinctively social aspects of psychology and society, which would ultimately become the focus of the field.[77] In 1906 after academic sociology was firmly launched, he was finally offered a chair at Brown University, where he taught sociology under the rubric, "A Survey of All Knowledge."

## Conclusions

The crisis in American exceptionalism widened throughout the Gilded Age, but its first result in the 1870s and early 1880s was the establishment of historico-politics and political economy as disciplines independent of the older moral philosophy tradition, and tentative efforts to establish sociology on the same basis. The cosmopolitan gentry were the architects of this development; in quest of social authority, they moved into government positions, mugwump reform activity, university reform, and the academic social science disciplines. They began to explore a number of strategies, some more successful than others, by which their more positivist conception of natural knowledge and their new awareness of historical change might be given effect, and their inherited exceptionalist vision of America nonetheless saved.

In political economy as in historico-politics the gentry resolutely banished overt reliance on divine guidance, hitherto the fundamental support of an eternal natural and historical order in America. They were thrown into

---

76 David A. Hollinger, "The Knower and the Artificer," *American Quarterly*, 39 (Spring 1987): 42–5.
77 Sumner, "Sociology," 322; [Sumner] "Sketch of William Graham Sumner," 266; L. F. Ward, *Glimpses of the Cosmos*, 5:1. For an excellent discussion of Ward's theory, early and late, see Robert C. Bannister, *Sociology and Scientism* (Chapel Hill: University of North Carolina Press, 1987), chap. 1.

greater reliance than before on the order discernible within nature and history. Aware that America could not claim exemption from the operation of universal laws and principles, they had to find in the dynamics of history and nature the basis for preserving America's special liberal-republican order. If the exemption previously claimed for America was the result of historical circumstances and institutions that were now changing, then new ways had to be found to reassert continuity.

The students of historico-politics had ready to hand the Teutonic principles of civil liberty as a guarantee of American republican institutions. Although embarked on a historical research program with deep roots in German and English historicism, Herbert Adams and John Burgess resorted to unchanging "germs" and normative ideal principles to perpetuate a view of American constitutional government as fixed and unchanging. The Whig principles of property rights, limited majoritarianism, and elite governance were not only necessary to the current crisis, but must be fortified to withstand the new demands for widened democracy and "equal rights," although Adams placed lighter restrictions than Burgess on popular democracy. Adams' continuity and unity of history, like Burgess' progressive development of reason, provided history with the normative power needed for the task.

In his version of political economy qua sociology, Sumner followed much the same strategy, grafting together the normative principles of classical political economy and the unchanging principles of Teutonic civil liberty. For all of them, history enacted a change from primitive to civilized, from despotic to constitutional governments, but American history enacted and perpetuated the highest forms of this progressive experience. If Burgess had a real sense of ongoing change in national historical structures, and Sumner had a presentiment that American conditions could not in the end withstand the changing course of history, these limited incursions of historicism made their determination to hold onto American exceptionalism all the more striking.

Only Francis Walker in economics and Lester Ward in his pioneer version of sociology, in the interest of a limited liberal activism, opened up some space in their view of America for genuine historical change. Walker saw that industrialism, even in America, forced some workers to fall outside the beneficent action of the natural laws of the market. In the real circumstances of history, competition was imperfect and human agency was free to take remedial action. Ward too showed that history was not completely subservient to the natural laws of biological evolution; scientific knowledge allowed modern men and women to direct historical progress to their own purposes. Yet for Walker, history remained a realm of subordinate causes, an auxiliary realm of progress but not its principal source. Moreover, the universal laws of the market continued to work best in America, where special conditions and republican institutions remained to counteract the ill effects of industrialization and to make trade unions and class conflict most often unnecessary. Like Sumner, Walker began to see the worker in America as a wage laborer, pressed by the same natural forces that weighed on his European counterpart, but chose to stress the opportunity for improvement in terms that echoed the anachronistic antebellum ideal.

Ward left American history more open to change than any of his contemporaries and therefore hastened to show that it could be brought under the control of positivist science. History was a process of change because it was, like nature, a realm of law, and like human nature, a realm of rational adaptation to law. To the extent that history generated change it must be controlled by scientific rationality, its wayward conflict reduced to the predictable consequences of social manipulation. Although Ward generally presented his theory as a means to save cosmic progress rather than as a means to save America's peculiar place in history, his vision seems nonetheless an outcome of the exceptionalist faith in natural law and need for absolute assurance in the face of historical uncertainty.

Although their strategies varied with their disciplinary traditions, the new directions taken by the gentry social scientists constituted recognizable and remarkably similar variations on the antebellum themes of American exceptionalism. To the extent that a consensus was forming among the gentry social scientists, it formed as it had in the antebellum colleges, around the center and right of the political spectrum. If America could no longer escape industrialization as it was known in Europe, Walker and Ward as well as Sumner and Burgess believed America could still escape the prolonged class conflict of Europe and the necessity for radical change. But we can also see the outlines emerging of a new liberal and a new conservative response to the possibility of change in America. Nurtured in millennial piety and the abolitionist crusade, Ward and Walker's egalitarian sentiments sharply distinguished them from Burgess and Sumner. If Walker clung to the exceptionalist ideal, it was the expansive version of that ideal he tried to maintain. Ward was the most thorough egalitarian of his cohort, on race and gender as well as class, a stance not unconnected to his location outside academia. Although he placed great faith in an expert elite, he also wanted widened popular access to knowledge and a legislature thoroughly learned in social science.[78]

During the 1870s and early 1880s, these differences among the cosmopoli-

78 L. F. Ward, *Dynamic Sociology*, 1:23, 37; 2:398–9.

tan gentry were muted. In historico-politics, where the militantly conservative Burgess and the cautious Adams held sway, there was little sign of ideological controversy, even in the late eighties and nineties. In economics, however, and soon after in sociology as it established an academic presence, the controversy begun by Walker, Ward, and Sumner escalated far beyond the bounds the cosmopolitan gentry had set. In these disciplines, the gentry expectation that the crisis in American exceptionalism could be contained by the authority of science was quickly challenged by a new scientific voice claiming that change in America was leading toward socialism.

# 4

The threat of socialism in
economics and sociology

The static principles of American exceptionalism were no sooner refurbished
and restated than they came under attack. During the 1880s and 1890s the
widening crisis of American exceptionalism destroyed the consensus within
which the first wave of Gilded Age social scientists had worked. Open
conflict developed across the sociopolitical landscape, as groups of capitalists, workers, farmers, and the middle class fought for economic advantage
and the power to shape the future. Social scientists soon joined the struggle,
forcing a reconsideration of exceptionalist American principle and with it
the character of their disciplines and the proper role of the social scientist.

## The socialist threat

During the 1880s and early 1890s a series of worker, farmer, and middle-
class protests waxed, waned, and re-formed, flowing separately and together,
all seeking to wrest some measure of power from industrial and financial
capital. To many observers in the middle and upper classes, this eruption
from below took on the formidable shape of socialism. The failure of
socialism to secure a permanent and substantial presence in America has
made it easy to forget that its fate was still an open question in this period.
Nor was socialism exclusively identified with the theories of Karl Marx but
still gave equal if not greater prominence to the cooperative ideals of
Christian and bourgeois socialists. While socialist groups formed variously
around gradualist, communitarian, statist, and revolutionary goals, advanced
liberals increasingly embraced collectivist means and ends. With the bound-

aries of both liberalism and socialism shifting, it was not clear where the increasing call for social action would end.[1]

Among workingmen, socialist unions attracted some native-born as well as foreign workers, but the native tradition of worker protest itself moved in the same direction. Seeking modern collective means to embody their traditional goals of economic independence and meaningful republican citizenship, working-class leaders charged the older language of American exceptionalism with a new, critical edge. Extending the radical abolitionists' critique of industrialism as a form of slavery, they envisioned a commonwealth of workers' cooperatives that would destroy the wage system and the capitalist class at one stroke. The rapid rise in the mid-1880s of the Knights of Labor, who articulated this ideal, seemed a portent of radical change. According to Francis Walker, the Knights' success was regarded as a likely and immense fact by friend and foe alike.[2] The fruits of capitalist inequality – class conflict, labor organization, and industrial violence – became the dominant "social question" of the time, and the possibility of its socialistic solution appeared for the first time in America as a realistic possibility.

Although the Knights' strength collapsed quickly in 1887, there was little respite in the onslaught of protest. Trade-union organization and strikes continued, and in the late eighties, farmer protests, drawing on the equal-rights tradition, began to organize in the South and prairie states around producer cooperatives and electoral politics. Middle-class dissenters meanwhile assumed a presence in the respectable press probably larger than their numbers. As spokesmen for social harmony, they developed the cooperative and egalitarian ideals implicit in their Christian and political traditions and proposed schemes ranging from voluntary cooperatives and labor arbitration to Henry George's single tax, Christian socialism, and the nationalist version of socialism advocated by Edward Bellamy. In 1892 the Populist party drew together farmer, labor, and middle-class radicals around a program of government control of transportation and finance and a call for such use of "the power of government – in other words, of the people" as seemed fit, "to the end that oppression, injustice and poverty shall eventual-

---

1 On the rise of socialism and the fluid relations between socialism and liberalism in the 1880s, see Dorothy Ross, "Socialism and American Liberalism: Academic Social Thought in the 1880s," *Perspectives in American History*, 11 (1977–8): 5–79.
2 Francis A. Walker, "The Knights of Labor," in *Discussions in Economics and Statistics*, 2 vols., ed. Davis R. Dewey (New York: Augustus M. Kelley, 1971 [1899]), 2:321–37. See also Richard T. Ely, "American Labor Organizations," *The Congregationalist*, January 6, 13, 20, 1887.

ly cease in the land."[3] When in 1896 the Populists endorsed the Democrat William Jennings Bryan for President it was not clear whether their sting had been pulled or whether radicalism had permeated the Democratic party and thereby mainstream American politics.

Against this threat from below, capitalists mounted an increasingly organized and sophisticated campaign. Wherever skilled trades could not bring some degree of monopoly power to bear, capitalists attacked labor organization, hired private mercenaries, called in the power of the states and national government to break strikes, and began systematically to mobilize political party support. The capitalists had allies among those in the middle and working classes whose worldview, interests, and respectable status tied them to capitalism. In the new industrial world, they argued, if widespread ownership was impossible, the freedom to labor was still available, and it was, as classical economists had always claimed, the individual ownership of labor power that constituted the basis of liberty in a liberal society. America's unique political economy and exceptionalist historical promise rested only on the widespread individual opportunity to compete for wealth, and so long as that opportunity remained open no special attention need be paid to egalitarian or harmonious results. If the protesters retained the old liberal-republican exceptionalist ideal and in order to save it, tried to alter capitalism through collectivism, the capitalists and their allies redefined that ideal as possessive individualism and retained the capitalist market intact. Both sides claimed to be the true heirs of the original American promise.

Both sides also felt threatened, but it was the capitalists who commanded the larger resources. With power over jobs, the press, churches, universities, and whole towns, cities, and states, they used carrots and sticks to disarm their opponents and win broader support. Not the least of their strengths was the ability to cast their program as a defense of American tradition. Both collectivists and possessive individualists transformed the antebellum exceptionalist vision, but only the radicals openly advocated historical change and accepted class struggle as legitimate in America. The conservatives could claim to retain capitalism, republican institutions, and individual opportunity, proscribing transformative change as "un-American."

The interplay of protest and conservative reaction reached its first peak in the depression and strikes of 1873 to 1877. The second peak occurred with the depression of 1885, the rapid growth of the Knights of Labor, and the national eight-hour day demonstrations and Haymarket riot of May 1886.

3 "Platform of the Populist Party, July 4, 1892," in *Documents of American History*, 7th ed., 2 vols., ed. Henry Steele Commager (East Norwalk, Conn.: Appleton-Century-Crofts, 1963 [1934]), 1:593–5.

These events set off a hysterical reaction in respectable public opinion and led to antilabor and antiradical campaigns, which ran into 1888. The finale was enacted during the mid-1890s: The depression of 1893–7, a series of major strikes, notably Homestead in 1892 and Pullman in 1894, the march across the nation of Coxey's army of unemployed in 1894, the rise of the Populists, and the presidential campaign of 1896, all brought conflict, anxiety, and reaction to fever pitch.[4]

The polarizing ideological conflict soon appeared within academic social science and followed closely the peaks of public protest and reaction. The field of economics, and behind it, sociology, formed the front line of battle on the social question, attracting the more liberal and radically inclined of the younger social scientists. For the most part, however, radicalism did not enter economics and sociology through recruitment into its ranks of new social types. Born roughly between 1850 and 1870, the younger social scientists were generally sons of the well-to-do, native-born, Protestant middle class or recruits to that class from the poorer ranks of respectable Protestantism. They were Whig or Republican in culture if not formal affiliation, and many of them sons or grandsons of ministers. Hence they came from the same broad stratum that had dominated centrist social science since the early nineteenth century.

The academic acceptance of meritocratic scientific standards worked very slowly to open the social sciences to different segments of American society, for informal mechanisms of control continued to exclude them. A few newcomers did manage to break in – Thorstein Veblen, for example, son of Norwegian farmer immigrants, and Edwin R. A. Seligman, of German-Jewish parentage. But few such people entered academic ranks during the Gilded Age. Prejudice against Jews and Catholics pervaded the genteel environment of the universities almost as thoroughly as racial discrimination against African Americans. Seligman's roots in the wealthy, assimilated German-Jewish community of New York City allowed him to become an

---

4 This analysis of Gilded Age class conflict draws on, but does not altogether follow, Robert Wiebe, *The Search for Order, 1877–1920* (New York: Hill & Wang, 1967); David Montgomery, *Beyond Equality: Labor and the Radical Republicans, 1862–1872* (New York: Knopf, 1967); Alan Dawley, *Class and Community: The Industrial Revolution in Lynn* (Cambridge, Mass.: Harvard University Press, 1976); Melvin Dubofsky, *Industrialism and the American Worker, 1865–1920* (Arlington Heights, Ill.: AHM, 1975); Leon Fink, *Workingmen's Democracy: The Knights of Labor and American Politics* (Urbana: University of Illinois Press, 1983); J. H. M. Laslett, *Labor and the Left: A Study of Socialist and Radical Influences in the American Labor Movement, 1881–1924* (New York: Basic, 1970); Howard Quint, *The Forging of American Socialism: Origins of the Modern Movement* (Indianapolis, Ind.: Bobbs-Merrill, 1964 [1953]); Chester M. Destler, *American Radicalism, 1865–1901* (Chicago: Quadrangle Books, 1966 [1946]); Lawrence Goodwyn, *Democratic Promise: The Populist Moment in America* (New York: Oxford University Press, 1976).

early exception. Women, already deeply involved in charitable and reform activities, were a natural constituency for the social sciences, but one that could threaten the masculine image of the social scientists' effort to achieve realism, science, and professional standing. During the 1870s and 1880s women were rarely admitted to graduate study, either in America or Europe, although we will see that situation dramatically change in the 1890s.[5]

The group of young economists who led the drive for a new political economy – John Bates Clark, Henry Carter Adams, Richard T. Ely, Edmund J. James, Simon Patten, and E. R. A. Seligman – were, except for Seligman, part of a distinctive segment of the native respectable Protestant culture. They were sons of evangelical families of New England heritage that valued moral conscience in social and political as well as personal life.[6] Throughout the nineteenth century, evangelical and pietistic Protestant traditions had produced activists who cultivated tender consciences, sought

5 Marcia Synnott, *The Half-Opened Door: Discrimination and Admissions at Harvard, Yale and Princeton, 1900–1970* (Westport, Conn.: Greenwood, 1979); Harold S. Wechsler, *The Qualified Student: Selective College Admission in America* (New York: Wiley, 1977); Kenneth Manning, *Black Apollo of Science: The Life of Ernest Everett Just* (New York: Oxford University Press, 1983); Rosalind Rosenberg, *Beyond Separate Spheres: Intellectual Roots of Modern Feminism* (New Haven, Conn.: Yale University Press, 1982); Margaret Rossiter, *Women Scientists in America: Struggles and Strategies to 1940* (Baltimore: Johns Hopkins University Press, 1982).
6 For a more detailed discussion of the social and cultural background of the historical economists, see Ross, "Socialism and American Liberalism," 15–22, 69–70, and Mary Furner, *Advocacy and Objectivity: A Crisis in the Professionalization of American Social Science, 1865–1905* (Lexington: University Press of Kentucky, 1975), 49–57. Specifically on Adams and Ely, see: Ephraim Adams, *The Iowa Band* (Boston: The Pilgrim Press, 1901 [1868]); A. W. Coats, "Henry Carter Adams: A Case Study in the Emergence of the Social Sciences in the United States, 1850–1900," *Journal of American Studies*, 2 (October 1968): 179–85; Richard T. Ely, *Ground under Our Feet* (New York: Macmillan, 1938), chap. 1; Benjamin G. Rader, *The Academic Mind and Reform: The Influence of Richard T. Ely in American Life* (Lexington: University of Kentucky Press, 1966), 1–7. Clark's father, the only businessman among them, retained the Congregational piety of his missionary minister father. Clark's maternal grandfather was also a minister. On Clark, see John R. Everett, *Religion in Economics: A Study of John Bates Clark, Richard T. Ely, and Simon N. Patten* (Morningside Heights, N.Y.: King's Crown Press, 1946), 26–8; *John Bates Clark: A Memorial* (New York: privately printed, 1938), 5–10; Rev. James Seegrave to Rev. A. H. Clark, June 23, 1910, John Bates Clark Papers, Columbia University Library. On James see E. J. James, "Reverend Colin Dew James," *Journal of the Illinois State Historical Society*, 9 (January 1917): 450–69; Steven A. Sass, *The Pragmatic Imagination: A History of the Wharton School, 1881–1981* (Philadelphia: University of Pennsylvania Press, 1982), chap. 3. On Patten, see Daniel M. Fox, *The Discovery of Abundance: Simon N. Patten and the Transformation of Social Theory* (Ithaca, N.Y.: Cornell University Press, 1967), and Sass, *The Pragmatic Imagination*, chaps. 3, 4. On Seligman, see Joseph Dorfman, "Edwin Robert Anderson Seligman," *DAB*, Suppl. 2, 606–9.

the salvation of the whole community, and emphasized the millennial underpinnings of the American Republic. These activists demanded of themselves and their countrymen moral purity and social renewal. They supplied the abolitionist zeal of the antebellum North, a zeal that disrupted the colleges in the 1830s and 1840s and then moved into the Republican party and the Civil War crusade to save the Union. During the Gilded Age crisis, the heirs of that cultural tradition, sometimes its literal descendents, were again roused to assert the organic and egalitarian values imbedded in dissenting Protestant Christianity.[7]

Unlike the cosmopolitan gentry, the advance guard of naturalism in Victorian America, these evangelical Christians felt no real conflict between science and religion. They accepted the growing authority of naturalism and recognized its divergence from orthodox belief. Neither Adams nor Ely could attain the conversion experiences their parents wanted of them and Adams abandoned clerical studies when he could not adhere to doctrine. But they identified Christianity with the spirit rather than the letter of the law. Christian idealism allowed insight into moral and spiritual truths as science allowed discovery of natural truth, and the two must be brought into an ethical, not a literal, harmony. Francis Walker and Lester Ward, who had earlier inherited the same pietistic, evangelical tradition, exhibited its moral values, but under the influence of positivism could not perform that idealist mediation. During the 1880s, while talking to popular audiences, the younger economists unselfconsciously retained reference to providence or the Creator, while in their professional work they increasingly kept to naturalistic boundaries.

The importance of the oppositional Christian conscience to these young economists – in the case of the outsider Seligman, the moral orientation of reformed Judaism – is demonstrated by its absence among the younger economists who chose to follow in the path of the conservative gentry founders. J. Laurence Laughlin, Frank W. Taussig, Arthur T. Hadley, and Henry W. Farnum were all sons of successful business or professional men who felt well served by the economy. There was no moral enthusiasm in their background. Farnum, for example, who was educated abroad as a

---

7 Ross, "Socialism and American Liberalism," 17–22; Furner, *Advocacy and Objectivity*, 45, 49–50; Jean B. Quandt, "Religion and Social Thought: The Secularization of Postmillennialism," *American Quarterly*, 25 (October 1973): 390–409; and James M. McPherson, *The Abolitionist Legacy: From Reconstruction to the NAACP* (Princeton, N.J.: Princeton University Press, 1975). George M. Fredrickson, "Intellectuals and the Labor Question in Late Nineteenth Century America," unpublished paper, emphasizes the importance of Civil War nationalism in the creation of this school of "social Christians."

young gentleman, "felt keenly the obligations which this fact placed upon him," but his paternalistic philanthropic instincts, like his father's, flowed in respectable channels.[8]

The evangelical economists were also much influenced by German historical economics. Historical economics was originally a creation of the moderate, organic tradition of German liberalism. In the late 1860s and 1870s, when the German version of the "social question" came to the fore, the historical school took on radical overtones. The inability of English laissez-faire economics to deal with the massive poverty of the laboring class was a major catalyst for their program. All of them regarded socialism as the characteristic product of modern industrial society and the central problem of contemporary economic statecraft. They contemplated moderate statist reform and were motivated by concern for the organic unity of society and the imperial state. But they were sympathetic to the claims of socialism and believed state action was necessary to assert the commonweal against capitalist selfishness. Economics was an ethical, as well as a historical, science. Some voluntarily assumed the name first thrust upon them in scorn, of *Kathedersozialisten* or "socialists of the chair."[9]

The young radical economists all took their graduate degrees in Germany and absorbed the historical economists' sympathy with socialism. Their native heritage of Whig organicism, Republican nationalism, and college moral philosophy easily meshed with the German tradition. We have seen that in the hands of Burgess and Sumner, this Whig-Republican tradition could be used to fortify a strong, conservative national state that would be the guardian and sole arbiter of individual property rights. But in the more egalitarian sectors of Whig-Republican political culture, the assertion of community over individual rights could be brought to bear against capitalist individualism and the organic ideal could lead out to the new liberalism and beyond, to socialism. The *Kathedersozialisten* focused and strengthened the more radical inclinations of the young economists.

Conversely, the young classical economists, like their mentors, continued to think of historical economics as only a subordinate method, supportive of

8 Furner, *Advocacy and Objectivity*, 54–7; Ray B. Westerfield, "Henry W. Farnum," *DAB*, Suppl. 1, 293–5.
9 John Rae, "The Socialists of the Chair," *Contemporary Review*, 38 (February 1881): 19–25; Charles Gide and Charles Rist, *A History of Economic Doctrines*, 2nd ed. (Boston: Heath, 1948), 383–449; Fritz K. Ringer, *The Decline of the German Mandarins: The German Academic Community, 1890–1933* (Cambridge, Mass.: Harvard University Press, 1969), 128–51; Kenneth D. Barkin, *The Controversy over German Industrialization, 1890–1902* (Chicago: University of Chicago Press, 1970), 1–12, 138–47; Abraham Ascher, "Professors as Propagandists: The Politics of the *Kathedersozialisten*," *Journal of Central European Affairs*, 23 (October 1963): 282–302.

the classical paradigm. Laughlin, Taussig, and Hadley took their advanced degrees from Charles F. Dunbar and William Graham Sumner at Harvard and Yale, and when Taussig and Hadley went abroad, they ignored or refuted the heterodox message of historical economics. Farnum, after graduating from Yale, took his doctorate at Strasbourg and devoted his whole career to historical economic studies, but like Sumner, he used history to elaborate the classical structure.[10]

The more radical young economists thus early condemned the inequality being generated by industrial capitalism in America as in Europe and identified themselves with the working class. Clark may have first become aware of industrial poverty as a boy in Providence or during his study in Germany. As early as 1877 he was bitter about American industrial conditions and drew on anthropological metaphors to liken the treatment of workers to cannibalism and slavery. Adams too was deeply moved by the poverty he saw in Baltimore in the middle seventies and turned his sense of religious calling into a mission to abolish want. Ely claimed that on his return from Germany in 1880, while tramping the streets of New York looking vainly for a job, "I took upon myself a vow to write in behalf of the laboring classes."[11] In taking this stance, they were introducing a new element into mainstream political discussion in America.

Since the early nineteenth century, the exceptionalist consensus had been based on the premise that in America liberal-republican institutions produced individual liberty, relative equality, and social harmony. In the American vision, whether Whig or Jacksonian, failures in the realization of this ideal could be understood as failures to keep capitalist and republican institutions on their true course. But the magnitude of those failures in the Gilded Age lent themselves less easily to that treatment, particularly by those of tender conscience. For the evangelical economists, as for working-class and middle-class dissenters, the socialist critique of capitalism showed that capitalist individualism destroyed egalitarian and fraternal values. The socialists shattered the harmony envisioned in antebellum exceptionalism, pitting liberty against equality, individual self-interest against the common good.

When Darwinian naturalism gained currency and the competitive individualism of classical economics and Spencerian sociology was seen in the

---

10 Furner, *Advocacy and Objectivity*, 55; Westerfield, "Henry W. Farnum."
11 John Bates Clark, "How to Deal with Communism," *New Englander*, 37 (July 1878): 540; Henry Carter Adams to his mother, June 12, 1876; February 11, October 22, December 23, 1877; January 27, 1878, Henry Carter Adams Papers, University of Michigan; Ely to Labadie, August 14, 1885, in "The Ely-Labadie Letters," ed. Sidney Fine, *Michigan History* 36 (March 1952): 17.

garish light of "Nature red in tooth and claw," the logic of the socialist indictment rang true. "There exists a necessary antagonism between the actions of men when directed by personal motives, and their action when made to conform to the social interest," Henry Carter Adams argued. Still, "There must be, for organisms of an advanced development, a higher law than the law of personal struggle for existence."[12] The young economists sought a higher social ethic to contain the inequality and selfishness generated by capitalist individualism. If they found it in the communal organicism and democratic collectivism of their native traditions, they also found inspiration in the socialists' egalitarian and fraternal ideals and saw in cooperative socialism the realization of their original liberal-republican hope.

As a new social ethic broke through the boundaries of the exceptionalist political consensus and the gentry social science program, so too did a deepening awareness of historical change. Born into the era of Civil War and rapid industrialization, the younger generation could see the new American reality more clearly than their predecessors. The growing authority of naturalism opened them more decisively to the historicist message of European historiography and social theory, while their Christian idealism allowed them, as it had the Germans, to submerge divine reality within history and its changing forms. More of them too studied in Germany. But the new element prominent in the rhetoric of the 1880s and 1890s was evolution. In the work of Sumner, Walker, and John W. Burgess, if Darwinian influence appeared at all, it supplemented the idea of historical change that had grown out of ample pre-Darwinian sources. For the younger men, the triumph of Darwinian evolution was now broadly visible and it became more central to their world view.[13] Biological evolution so compellingly transformed the understanding of all natural phenomena into changing forms that even the American identity could not escape.

## Historicist challenge and exceptionalist response from Ely to Clark

When the young historical economists on the left addressed political economy, they began as had their predecessors with the problem of American exceptionalism. Industrialization, they believed, had permanently changed American society. "The days of diffusion are limited," Clark said, "and

---

12 Henry Carter Adams, "Relation of the State to Industrial Action" (1887), in *Two Essays by Henry Carter Adams*, ed. Joseph Dorfman (New York: Augustus M. Kelley, 1969), 72–3.
13 Cf., e.g., [William Graham Sumner], "Sketch of William Graham Sumner," *Popular Science Monthly*, 35 (June 1889): 266, with Ely, "American Labor Organizations."

those of concentration are at hand." Industrialism opened America to the same future that had earlier engulfed Britain and was now transforming the continent of Europe. In the millennial republican logic, that portent called up images of the closing period of the millennium – apocalyptic upheavals and the ushering in of the Kingdom of God – images that ran through the literature of crisis and utopian transformation of the Gilded Age. The young evangelical economists, assimilating their new historicism to their inherited American vision, followed the path of European thinkers earlier in the nineteenth century and cast their millennial hopes into history. The transformative power of the Kingdom of God would give the American promise new historical form.[14]

"Present institutions contain in themselves the germs of a progress that shall ultimately break the limitations of the existing system," said Clark. There is "an undercurrent flowing calmly and resistlessly in the direction of a truer socialism ... directed by the Providence which presides over all history." The evangelical expectation was even more explicit in Ely's writings and in the private words of the more scholarly and cautious Adams. "Keep off the track! The train of progress is coming! Prepare the way!" cried Ely, watching the rapid rise of the Knights of Labor. "It rests with us so to direct inevitable changes that we may be brought nearer that kingdom of righteousness for which all good Christians long and pray."[15]

Clark, Adams, and Ely specifically linked the new future to socialism. Their ideal was the cooperative commonwealth, with its familial definition of egalitarian and fraternal values. As Clark declared in 1879:

The beauty of the socialistic ideal is enough to captivate the intellect that fairly grasps it. It bursts on the view like an Italian landscape from the summit of an Alpine pass, and lures one down the dangerous declivity. Individualism appears to say, "Here is the world; take, every one, what you can get of it. Not too violently, not altogether unjustly, but, with this limitation, selfishly ... For the strong there is much, and for his children more; for the weak there is little, and for his children, less." True socialism appears to say, "Here is the world; take it as a family domain under a common father's direction. Enjoy it as children, each according to his needs; labor as brethren, each according to his strength. Let justice supplant might in the distribution.... The beautiful bond which scientists call altruism, but which the

14 John Bates Clark, "The Nature and Progress of True Socialism," *New Englander*, 38 (July 1879): 571; Kenneth M. Roemer, *The Obsolete Necessity: America in Utopian Writings, 1888–1900* (Kent, Ohio: Kent State University Press, 1976), 3, 16–22, 54–5, 87–96; Dorothy Ross, "The Liberal Tradition Revisited and the Republican Tradition Addressed," in *New Directions in American Intellectual History*, ed. John Higham and Paul Conkin (Baltimore: Johns Hopkins University Press, 1979), 121–5.
15 Clark, "Nature and Progress of True Socialism," 579, 570, 572. Ely, "American Labor Organizations."

Bible terms by a better name, will bind the human family together as no other tie can bind them.

Clark's socialist ideal would embody "the old struggle for personal independence, translated to a higher plane of organic life."[16]

Adams too was aware of transforming and enlarging the old exceptionalist ideal into new historical form. In his published writings he used the vocabulary of German historical economics and modern historical analysis, but the language of his home and school had been republican. His father had been a leader of the "Iowa Band" of antislavery Congregational ministers sent out by the American Home Mission Society to save the free West, and when young Adams wrote him from Germany to explain why he now called himself a socialist, he instinctively slipped into the language of republican history. The American and French revolutions, he began, had abolished tyrants, caste, and privilege, and bestowed suffrage on all. But they did not establish economic equality. "Under existing institutions, those who labor have no property and with difficulty gain the bare means of existence, while those who do not labor live in opulence and own the soil." That inequality must be removed, he warned. "Either you must establish a more equitable division of property and produce, or the fatal end of democracy will be despotism and decadence."

The history of Greek Democracy and Roman Republicanism shows that these once prosperous nations went to ruin on the rock of unequal distribution of products in the contract between the rich and the poor.... We are in the midst of a great social problem – to stand still is impossible, and there is but one path, and to that path there are but two directions, one to go on, the other to go back. To go on is to extend our theoretical equality to actual equality.

The millennial-republican jeremiad carried Adams forward into a socialistic future. Equal citizenship would be expanded into "economic republicanism."[17]

The cooperative commonwealth was an attempt to transform the liberal-republican antebellum ideal to meet new conditions. An economy cooperatively owned and managed under the supportive aegis of the state was an ideal that harkened back to the individualism of a producers' democracy and at the same time pointed forward to the collectivism of democratic socialism. Adams, Ely, and particularly Clark continued to value the individual independence and moral strength that competitive exertion in the capitalist

16 Clark, "Nature and Progress of True Socialism," 580, 567. See also Richard T. Ely, *French and German Socialism in Modern Times* (Freeport, N.Y.: Books for Libraries Press, 1972 [1883]), 186–8; H. C. Adams to his Mother, April 7, 1884, Adams Papers.
17 H. C. Adams to his Father [late summer, 1879], Adams Papers.

economy could create. Wherever genuine competition could be made to work, they hoped to retain it. By the same token, state action would be used only where necessary: to raise the plane of competition, regulate monopoly, or enforce the rights of labor as workingmen increasingly gained control of industry. Ely was the most enthusiastic statist, in one text subscribing to Elisha Mulford's conception of the state as a divine institution, with blanket sovereignty over the national economy and "the welfare of the people." In the end, they believed, capitalism would be transformed; sustained by collectivist democracy, workers would gain control of productive resources. During the late 1870s and early 1880s the young historical economists, like many social thinkers in western Europe and America, were poised on the still shifting ground between liberalism and socialism. The direction in which they would develop their ideas would depend not only on their own mixed predilections, but on the response they would find in the American academic world.[18]

They first had to gain an academic foothold, well aware of the opprobrium that awaited those sympathetic to socialism in capitalist America.[19] Their future as political economists rested on their ability to be accepted into a professional fraternity hitherto dominated by moderate and conservative versions of American exceptionalism and classical economics. They had keen professional ambitions, whetted by the high status and public importance of their German professors.[20] Following the lead of their German models who had formed the *Verein für Sozialpolitik* in 1872 to advance their reformist economic program, the young historical economists took the professional offensive in America.

Richard T. Ely, who taught political economy in Herbert Baxter Adams' department of history and politics at Johns Hopkins, emerged as the most radical spokesman. Still comfortable with the role of evangelical preacher, he made contact with Christian reformers and started writing widely for the popular and religious press. In the assertive professional atmosphere of

18  Ross, "Socialism and American Liberalism," 35–7, 52–3; Richard T. Ely, *An Introduction to Political Economy* (New York: Chautauqua Press, 1889), 30.
19  When Adams, still in Germany and hoping to be appointed at Johns Hopkins, wrote his first article on socialism, he confided, "There are one or two things slightly socialistic in it and the thought came, dare I put them in? Will it not endanger my position at Baltimore? That was but for a moment. Endanger it or not I will write what I believe." Adams to his Mother, January 18, 1879, Adams Papers.
20  Furner, *Advocacy and Objectivity*, chap. 2, identifies the conservative young economists as "careerist" in distinction to the ethical orientation of the reformist economists, but I doubt that the two schools differed regarding careerism. See Ross, "Socialism and American Liberalism," 16; and Dorothy Ross, "The Development of the Social Sciences" in *The Organization of Knowledge in Modern America, 1860–1920*, ed. Alexandra Oleson and John Voss (Baltimore: Johns Hopkins University Press, 1979), 118–21.

Johns Hopkins, he also turned his entrepreneurial and didactic impulses into professional channels. He fired the opening salvo in an article in 1884, which turned historicism onto economic theory itself. In "The Past and the Present in Political Economy," he relegated classical political economy to the late eighteenth and early nineteenth century and claimed the future for the historical school.[21] The older generation of economists, led by Sumner and Simon Newcomb, mathematician, astronomer, and part-time economist who also lectured at Johns Hopkins, mounted a counterattack that was taken up by the conservative press.

In the midst of this controversy Ely proposed organizing a professional association "to combat the influence of the Sumner crowd."[22] Recognizing that laissez-faire was the least common denominator to gather together the critics of classical economy, Ely united Francis A. Walker, who had begun the revisionist effort the previous decade; the professionally trained economists of his own generation sympathetic to historical economics; Christian social reformers like Washington Gladden; and students of historico-politics favorable to the German school like Andrew White and Charles Kendall Adams. In September 1885 they formed the American Economic Association (AEA) and issued a nonbinding statement of principles, which approved state economic action, called on economists to turn from the older "speculative" economic methods to historical ones, and named the "conflict of labor and capital" the central problem of modern economics.[23] The group succeeded in its purpose of capturing the professional initiative for the new economists. Sumner was deliberately not invited to join the AEA and the older traditional economists like Dunbar shunned the association. The younger classical economists at Harvard and Yale – Laughlin, Taussig, Hadley, and Farnum – stayed out as well. When *Science* asked the economists to debate the issues that divided them, the historical economists had the largest voice.[24]

From the beginning of the public controversy in 1884, Ely's assertive stance raised the fundamental questions that historical economics posed for

21 Richard T. Ely, "The Past and Present of Political Economy," *JHUSHPS*, 2d ser., no. 3 (March 1884): 5–64.
22 The controversy set off by Ely's article and the formation of the American Economic Association that grew out of it are discussed in detail in Furner, *Advocacy and Objectivity*, chap. 3. The quotation is from Ely to Seligman, June 9, 1885, E. R. A. Seligman Papers, Columbia University Library.
23 Richard T. Ely, "Report of the Organization of the American Economic Association," *AER*, 1 (March 1886): 5–46.
24 Reprinted in Henry Carter Adams et al., *Science Economic Discussion* (New York: The Science Co., 1886).

the discipline: Did historicism force a change in the principles of American exceptionalism? Did it require a change in the methods and substance of classical economics? What relation did economic knowledge have with ethics and what social role did that relation require the economists to play? On all these issues, the historical economists discovered differences among themselves as well as between themselves and the classical economists. Moreover, they had to explore these issues in the increasingly heated environment of the mid-1880s.

From his first statement, Ely argued that the changing character of history – "industrial progress and new economic formations" – rendered classical economics obsolete. Only a historical economist could deal adequately with historical reality. Using the German school as a model, he claimed that historical economics should become predominantly inductive, building up fewer generalizations from the close study of facts. German economists had not yet discovered any laws as powerful as those of David Ricardo or Thomas Malthus, but in time they would. One such historical law had in fact been formulated by Adolph Wagner already: Given the increasing interdependence of modern civilization, there followed the law of the increasing function of government in the economy. Ely did not clearly identify himself with the methodological position of Wagner, who believed the classical structure still provided a useful tool of analysis, or with that of Gustav Schmoller, who urged only historical study of economic institutions, so that the fate of the classical structure of laws was not clear. But his aggressive statement gave the impression that classical economics' bias toward laissez-faire must be wholly discarded and its laws substantially revised in the light of changing historical circumstances.[25]

Ely's colleagues were anxious to assert that historical economics meant to build upon, rather than discard, the work of the past. Yet they too made clear their belief that historicism required a fundamental reorientation of economic science. Newcomb and Hadley persisted in defending classical economics as a system of universal natural laws, which developed like the laws of physical science, by deduction from verified premises and the testing of hypotheses against empirical fact. But Henry Carter Adams replied that economics could not operate like a physical science, because it dealt with an evolving social reality, and James urged that as "scientific progress in neighboring fields" had shown, the appropriate model for economics was "the jural and politico-philosophical sciences." Classical economics carried the scientific imprimatur of John Stuart Mill, but the historical school could

25 Ely, "The Past and Present of Political Economy."

call on historical German models of social science, and indirectly, the most powerful scientific stream of the Gilded Age, that of evolutionary biology.[26]

The economists quickly realized, however, that airing their disagreements in public jeopardized the professional status they sought for their discipline and they hastened to find grounds on which both deductive theorists and inductive historians could recognize the validity of each other's work. The clearest statement of the basis for compromise was presented to the AEA in 1887 by W. J. Ashley, a historical economist at Oxford, who was shortly to move to Toronto and then Harvard.

The question at issue between the deductive and historical economists is not that of the truth or falsehood of the main Ricardian doctrines. . . . From the side of the abstract economists it is now freely granted that these doctrines are only hypothetically true, that they are true only so far as certain conditions are granted. From the other side . . . it is confessed that so far as they are realized [i.e., certain conditions] the doctrines based upon them are true.[27]

This formulation left a place in historical economics for classical theory and in classical economics for the empirical investigation of economic conditions. So far as it went, this formulation could be accepted by everyone from Dunbar on the right to Adams on the left.

The mutual permission from both camps to let the other proceed solved the issue on the professional level, but it did not solve the substantive issue. For the question remained, Ashley pointed out, which was the most promising way to proceed. The abstract economists believed that their doctrines expressed "tendencies far greater than any other," and therefore it was wise for economists to expand their theories by deduction so far as possible and only secondarily study those conditions that would allow their application to real life situations. But historical economists believed that

the actual state of affairs in every particular industry, trade, country, and how it came to be so [and the direction in which it was developing], is best discovered by historical and statistical inquiry – an inquiry in which the old doctrines will furnish a useful standard of comparison, and in some cases suggest influences that have been at work, but in which they will after all play a quite subordinate part.[28]

The question at bottom was whether deductive theory or historical inquiry described the most potent forces of modern economic life, and those most relevant to understanding the industrial world growing up around them. On

26 *Science Economic Discussion*, especially 24–5, 92–7, 101–3.
27 W. J. Ashley, "The Early History of the English Woolen Industry," *PAEA*, 2 (September 1887): 9; *Science Economic Discussion*, 105.
28 Ashley, "Early History of the English Woolen Industry," 9–10.

that question, disagreement continued to surface. When the economists discussed at the AEA how to teach economics, for example, the relative weight, priority, and consequence of teaching deductive versus historical economics immediately entered the discussion.[29]

In the debates of the eighties and nineties, however, it was not simply a theoretical or methodological issue that was at stake. A great deal of the energy that animated the methodological difference and kept it alive came from the sociopolitical vision with which each side was allied. The most frequent and repeated debates at AEA meetings were sociopolitical conflicts between the two camps – over government regulation and ownership of industry and the rights of labor. Ely stated that the one certain law of historical economics was the increasing function of government in the economy and he left the degree of that function open. More impulsive and less analytical than Clark or Adams, Ely was both more positive and more ambivalent on the subject of socialism, so that every doubt he expressed was balanced by praise, and every assertion that his goal was a conservative alternative to socialism was matched by a call for such incorporations of socialism as would transform society. His assurance that among the historical economists "there is not a single one who could be called an adherent of socialism, pure and simple," was hardly calculated to quiet fears. As Farnum cleverly noted in a politically charged review, "If a man should march in a socialistic procession, bearing a red flag with the inscription 'I am no socialist,' he could hardly pick a quarrel with the newspapers for reporting him as a socialist."[30]

Hence the more moderate members of the school were anxious to dissociate themselves, as Seligman said, from "any imagined Katheder-Socialistic tendencies." Seligman too regarded the social question as the central issue of modern economics and in the mid-1880s hoped that cooperation on a wide scale might be its solution, but he sought a middle ground well short of socialism.[31] In the *Science* debate Adams, who con-

---

29 Simon N. Patten, "The Educational Value of Political Economy," *PAEA*, 5 (November 1890): 7–36, and "Discussion," *PAEA*, 6 (January–March 1891): 102–15; W. J. Ashley, "The Historical School, a Retrospect," *PAEA*, 10 (March 1895): 117–18; "The Teaching of Economics in the Secondary Schools: A General Discussion," ibid., 119–38; "Discussion – The Relation of the Teaching of Economic History to the Teaching of Political Economy" and "Discussion – Methods of Teaching Economics," *PAEA: Economic Studies*, 3 (February 1898): 88–101, 105–11.

30 Ely in *Science Economic Discussion*, 70; Henry W. Farnum, "Review of Richard T. Ely, *The Labor Movement in America*," *PSQ*, 1 (December 1886): 686–7. For examples of political debate, see *PAEA*, 3 (July 1888): 44–51; 6 (January–March 1891): 102–15; 8 (January 1893): 62–76; 82–7.

31 On Seligman, see Ely, "Report of the Organization of the AEA," 28 and Chapter 6, below.

tinued to cherish cooperative socialistic goals, carefully formulated his program as an extension of the Anglo-Saxon conception of liberty.

The sociopolitical conflict also shaped the discussion of the proper scope of economic science and the proper role of the economist. In Mill's classic formulation, the "science" of economics was separate from the "art" of applying its principles to specific public problems, an art that must include political and ethical considerations. Although the classical economists adhered to Mill in theory, the normative and necessitarian character they often assigned to economic law made it impossible to separate the science of economics from its policy implications. Nor did the classical economists often try to do so. In the *Science* debate, however, fear of socialism pushed the young defenders of classical economics into an untenable position of self-denial. Hadley argued that economists could tell legislatures what cannot be done, because that was within the realm of science. It was only positive state action that was excluded under the category of art. Taussig even suggested that the sphere of state economic action be given over entirely to sociology or political science.

The historical economists had no difficulty arguing that this separation was artificial. As Adams said, political economy was both an analytical and a "constructive science" whose purpose was "to discover a scientific and rational basis for the formation and government of industrial society." Economics was only one of several social sciences concerned with social progress, but of course, echoed Richmond Mayo-Smith, a moderate sympathetic to the historical school, economics must direct state action and "say what will be the consequences of such action, and whether it will be for good or evil."[32]

To accept the prescriptive policy role of the economist, however, opened up another problem. Ely insisted that to advise and prescribe norms for the most satisfactory economic organism was inherently an ethical task. Economic standards of judgment should not be merely materialistic but Platonic: Economists should prescribe "rules and regulations for such a production, distribution, and consumption of wealth as to render the citizens good and happy." Moreover, economics was concerned not with economic arrangements as they existed at present, presumably unchangeable, but with what ought to be in the future, a matter open to historical choice. Ely claimed both these ethical tasks exclusively for historical economists, for it was only they who recognized the injustice of the present industrial system and wished to abandon the narrow classical laws of wealth for a full

---

32 *Science Economic Discussion*, Hadley, 92–7; Taussig, 34–8; Adams, 99–103; Mayo-Smith, 119–22.

consideration of the economic conditions of humane social progress. The Platonic task, for Ely, was accessible to the reason of Christian idealism, and hence a task suitable for science to undertake, in alliance with Christian reformers.[33]

The older school could hardly accept that formulation. In America as in England, classical economics had always implicitly claimed a moral universe. The idea that only historical economics held to high ideals of morality and justice was not easily borne. But the morality of the classicists had been written as scientific fact into their description of economic law. Their legitimacy as economists had rested on their profession of science, not their ideals. Particularly in the United States, where the economists had been trying to free themselves from the domination of the clerical colleges and moral philosophy, the direct identification with ethics summoned up a moralistic and impractical clerical connection they wished to avoid. And in the polarizing ideological context of the Gilded Age, it could destroy altogether their claim to disinterested science.

The economists' debate over the theoretical, political, and professional implications of the new historicist program was part of the wider conflict in the society at large over the future of American society, and its resolution followed the course of the wider social outcome. Despite the historical economists' sympathy with socialist ideals and the working class, they shared the exceptionalist heritage and the respectable middle-class identification with, and vulnerability to, capitalist power. They too retreated from socialism. The tide began to turn in May 1886, when the Haymarket riot sent shock waves through the upper and middle classes. John Bates Clark had been the most divided and was the first to turn. When the Haymarket reaction hit, and he was publicly berated by Hadley for spreading "socialistic fallacies," Clark began an intense effort to rethink his position and by 1887, to change it.[34]

The political upheavals of 1886 at first led Adams and Ely to even stronger statements of labor support. Adams had stated his program in the *Science* debate as an extension of liberal doctrine. Private property which affects the lives of others and exerts a public influence must be subject to public regulation. Moreover, through the judicial recognition of collective bargaining, workers must be given proprietary rights in their jobs. We must part company with "constructive socialism," he concluded, because "our entire juridical structure is against it, and it is easier to bring our industries into harmony with the spirit of our law than to re-organize our society from top

33 *Science Economic Discussion*, 44–56; Ely, "Past and Present of Political Economy," 58, 48.
34 Ross, "Socialism and American Liberalism," 35–79.

to bottom, industries included." By using the historicist strategy of Wagner, subjecting the capitalist economy to the norms of his national historical culture, and by choosing a judicial strategy of regulation, Adams was able to both retain and transform America's liberal tradition. "There can be no permanent solution of the labor problem," he declared, "so long as the wages system is maintained."[35]

In the midst of the southwestern railroad strike of 1886, Adams made so impassioned a statement of these ideas that he roused the ire of Cornell benefactor, Russell Sage. Eased out of his Cornell appointment, he turned his hopes to Michigan, where President James Burrell Angell was already questioning him on his "leanings." In his next public statement of his program, Adams retreated on the "proprietary rights" of labor. "To admit that the state should control labor relations is to admit the essential point in socialism"; in contrast, his own program was based on individualism. Adams received a permanent appointment at Michigan.[36]

Ely too continued to preach in favor of labor in the midst of the crisis, and despite the criticism his speeches brought, Daniel Coit Gilman promoted him to associate professor at Johns Hopkins in 1887, probably because of his strong support in the religious community. But his ordeal had just begun. Sensitive to the criticisms of originally sympathetic colleagues like Clark and Adams, Ely started a practice of submitting drafts of his work to them and others for review, and Clark obliged with detailed criticisms of his unclear and indeterminate "language," pointing out "passages which seem to me to have a somewhat elastic meaning and to suggest possibilities of radical views." As Clark confided to Adams, he wanted Ely to draw "clear lines where the socialistic leaning stops. On most points he is really sound, and it is a pity to sink himself under the odium of semi-socialism." For a time Ely appeared to eschew the subject of socialism and take greater care.[37]

35 *Science Economic Discussion*, 80–91; "A Symposium on Several Phases of the Labor Question," *The Age of Steel*, 59 (January 2, 1886): 20.
36 Furner, *Advocacy and Objectivity*, 135–7; Henry Carter Adams, "The Labor Problem," *Scientific American Supplement*, 22 (August 21, 1886): 8861–3; Angell to Adams, March 19, 1886; March 12, 1887; Adams to his Mother, May 3, October 14, October 28, 1886; March 8, March 13, 1887, H. C. Adams Papers; Adams to Angell, March 15, 1887, James B. Angell Papers, University of Michigan; H. C. Adams, "Relation of the State to Industrial Action," 133.
37 Ely, "American Labor Organization"; Richard T. Ely, "Conditions of Industrial Peace," *The Congregationalist*, 39 (August 1887), 638–44; Richard T. Ely, "Land, Labor and Taxation," *Independent*, 39 (December 1, 8, 15, 22, and 29, 1887) and 40 (January 5, 1888). "You could advocate all that you usually do and not be attacked much. I think the trouble with these articles is the lack of distinguishing between the natural enlargement of state functions, and the doctrinarian policy of pushing such enlargement toward a goal." Clark to Ely, March 17, 1891, Richard T. Ely Papers, State Historical Society of Wisconsin. For further evidence of professional pressure, see also Clark to Ely, November 14, 1887;

But his concern was nothing if not dogged. In 1891 he thought he saw the climate of reaction temporarily recede and started again to urge social progress through a combination of "socialism and individualism."[38] Soon he had moved to the University of Wisconsin and was writing in the midst of a new wave of radical discontent and respectable anxiety. In 1894 a trustee of the university publicly accused him of siding with labor, favoring socialism, counseling union organizers, and threatening to boycott a printer doing university business for not adopting a union shop. The charges led to a public trial of Ely by the university regents, and while he was exonerated and the board issued a ringing defense of academic freedom, Ely achieved these results by denying that the charges were true and declaring that had he held such views and engaged in such activities, he would have no right to teach in the university. Ely, like Adams, gave up the effort to transform the national ideology to include some measure of socialism.[39]

As Mary Furner has shown, the professionalizing process itself had acted to discourage radicalism and dampen fundamental conflict. Professionalism required at least the appearance of objectivity, an elusive attribute that generally meant absence of bias and hence neutrality as between biased contending parties. In the heated political context of the Gilded Age, where deviations from conventional exceptionalist norms were painfully visible, the historical economists' overt ethical stance, sympathy with labor, and tendencies toward socialism made their objectivity suspect and endangered the professional project. Professional pressures soon led the AEA to drop its statement of principles and bring in the classical economists, although Sumner remained permanently outside. Even before the public attack on Ely, as we have seen, his professional peers pressed him toward moderation and they ultimately abandoned him. When he began again on his old course in 1891 and in 1892 scheduled the AEA meeting in conjunction with the popular, religiously oriented meeting of Chautauqua, he was forced to resign his post as secretary of the association. In case after case of university pressure brought against social scientists in the 1880s and 1890s, the con-

January 24, February 7, 1888; April 23, May 28, 1891; H. C. Adams to Ely, November 20, 1887, Ely Papers; Clark to H. C. Adams, January 24, 1888, Clark Papers; Ely, *Introduction to Political Economy*, 6.

38 Records of the Historical and Political Science Association and of the Seminary of History and Politics, May 1, 1891, Johns Hopkins University; Richard T. Ely, "Socialism: Its Nature, Its Strength and Its Weakness," *Independent*, 43 (February 5–July 2, 1891); idem, *Introduction to Political Economy*, 236–39; idem, *Outlines of Economics* (New York: Hunt and Eaton, 1893), 308; idem, *Socialism, an Examination of Its Nature, Its Strength and Its Weakness, with Suggestions for Social Reform* (New York: Thomas Y. Crowell, 1894).

39 Rader, *The Academic Mind and Reform*, chap. 6, and 167–79, 200–13; Furner, *Advocacy and Objectivity*, chap. 7; Ross, "Socialism and American Liberalism," 64–79.

servative and moderate professional leaders carefully parceled out their support, making clear the limited range of academic freedom and the limited range of political dissent they were willing to defend. A degree of professional autonomy was achieved by narrowing its range.[40]

It was thus of central importance, and an ironic consequence of the historical school's challenge, that it stimulated the most gifted theorist of their generation, John Bates Clark, to abandon his early inclination toward historical economics and to join forces with marginalist theoretical currents from Europe that were revitalizing the deductive school. The desire to legitimate the capitalist market in the face of radical challenge was the major element in Clark's thinking.[41] Indeed from the beginning Clark had responded to the socialist challenge by trying to reconceptualize the market economy so as to "find a place in the system for the better motives of human nature" and to "apply at all points the organic conception of society." The market was itself a great social organism operating by a "beautiful law" that appropriated to each what was adapted to his use, distributing "useful commodities, molecules of social nutriment, unerringly" through the social system.

It was through this effort at organicist idealization that Clark developed independently the central idea of marginalist economics. Value is based in utility, he said, and the "quantitative measure of utility" is expressed in market price. Putting absolute utility to one side, he identified "effective utility" as the "power to modify our subjective condition, under actual circumstances." Here he began to recognize that value was determined at the margin of diminishing returns. Developed in classical economics by Ricardo as a theory of rent on land, the marginalist concept could be applied to all economic factors. Once value was based on utility, it was possible to see that all values were set by the same mechanism, for the diminishing utility of any increment would always cause its price to be set by the last, the marginal, increment an agent felt it worthwhile to buy. The myriad subjective estimates of utility were coordinated by society through the mechanism of price. "Market value is a measure of utility made by society considered as

---

40 Furner, *Advocacy and Objectivity*, chaps. 4–5; Ross, "Socialism and American Liberalism," 45–64.
41 Clark's political motivation is recognized both by those who accept a strong connection between the marginalist paradigm and liberal capitalist ideology – see Ronald L. Meek, "Marginalism and Marxism," in "Papers on the Marginal Revolution in Economics," *History of Political Economy*, 4 (Fall 1972): 503 – and by those who reject such a connection – see Joseph Schumpeter, *History of Economic Analysis* (Oxford University Press, 1954), 870.

one great isolated being ... great and complex, indeed, but united and intelligent."[42]

While seeking to legitimate the competitive market, however, Clark also recognized that historical change had at one point subverted it. In the crucial competition between employers and workmen over the distribution of profit, large consolidated business corporations had come to face divided workmen, and in that situation of "predatory competition," employers enriched themselves at the expense of labor. It was that historical subversion of the market that led Clark to posit a historical evolution of society toward a cooperative commonwealth.[43]

In late 1886 and 1887, however, Clark retreated from the idea of a socialist American future. He began to think that the economic conditions of the past hundred years and the Ricardian vision along with them were only temporary. The rapid industrialization America experienced in the Gilded Age, like the early years of industrialization in England, were an aberrant period, already passing. History showed that a historical economics was not necessary. Ricardo, Clark said,

saw before him an interval of contest that must of necessity, sooner or later, come to an end; while we see approaching a period of union which gives a promise of indefinite continuance.... History will aid us by furnishing a point of departure, and by indicating the direction of social development, but not by giving facts from which any possible induction can give the principles which we seek.... The materials for study lie in the present and the immediate future.[44]

History was moving beyond its hundred-year period of class conflict to one of consolidation, where union organization and arbitration would equalize the power of labor and capital. In that consolidated economy, competition was still at work, and therefore could be expected to govern lawfully the price and distribution of products.

With the competitive market now restored, Clark first applied marginal analysis to the idea of profit. Beyond "the wages of directive labor" there was a "pure" profit, he said, the "bonus" which was causing so much social strife. But "pure profit is a vanishing sum." When particular factors like the settlement of a fertile continent, or invention, or the trade cycle created unnaturally high profits, other managers and capitalists were attracted to the

---

42 John Bates Clark, *The Philosophy of Wealth* (Boston: Ginn, 1886), iv, chaps. 4–5. The quotations are from pp. iv, 84, 87, 74, 78, 82, 85. Clark first stated his concept of "effective utility" in "The Philosophy of Value," *New Englander*, 40 (July 1881): 457–69.
43 Clark, *Philosophy of Wealth*, chap. 9.
44 John Bates Clark, "The Limits of Competition," *PSQ*, 2 (March 1887): 47.

field, and competition in time reduced this pure profit to nil. "The view of social evolution which these conclusions afford is that of progress toward equity between men, promoted by combinations, but guaranteed by the deeper and more general influence of competition itself. Injustice is diminishing, and that by natural law." During the 1890s Clark bent his efforts toward producing a fully articulated marginalist theory of distribution that would show wages as well as profits determined by the market estimate of its marginal contribution to the product. In his treatise on distribution in 1899 he demonstrated that the market dispensed liberal justice: It gave "to every agent of production the amount of wealth which that agent creates."[45]

Clark and his marginalist allies were engaged in an effort to justify the capitalist economy in less contested terms than those provided by classical theory. In classical economics, value had been defined by labor, the economy driven by capital accumulation, self-interest transmuted to public good by an "invisible hand," and distribution governed by class relations. With all these ideas under radical attack and often turned to radical purposes, Clark and the marginalist economists found a different way of conceiving the market economy. Basing value in utility, they viewed the market as a mechanism for the satisfaction of human wants and driven by consumer desires. Through the adjustment of prices, the resources of society were allocated to produce the maximum utility to consumers, with the maximum possible efficiency. The same price system that allocated to different goods their appropriate value in consumption also distributed to the different productive "factors" or classes the appropriate value of their services and assets.[46]

Given his assumption of maximum utility, allocational efficiency, and just distribution, Clark could face squarely the inegalitarian consequences of the liberal economy. Industrialization was producing a large working class of reduced skill, he said, and making it harder for workers to cross the barriers of education and wealth into independent ownership. At the same time, higher standards of education and wealth were uniting the professional and capitalist class. In the same issue of the *Political Science Quarterly* in which Clark began to publish his new ideas, Theodore W. Dwight, professor of law at Columbia and grandson of Timothy Dwight, reminded his young colleagues of "Harrington and His Influence upon American Political In-

---

45 John Bates Clark and Franklin H. Giddings, *The Modern Distributive Process* (Boston: Ginn, 1888), iv, 35, 45–50; John Bates Clark, *The Distribution of Wealth* (New York: Macmillan, 1899), v.

46 A. K. Dasgupta, *Epochs of Economic Theory* (Oxford: Blackwell Publisher, 1985), chap. 6. For continued discussion of the ideological meanings of marginalist economics, see below, Chapter 6.

stitutions and Political Thought." Apparently drawing on Dwight's emphasis on the idea of natural aristocracy, Clark concluded that "The outline of the coming industrial state has the shape neither of despotism nor of democracy; it is the outline of a true republic." Clark was willing to accept as Harrington had not been, that in future, increasing concentration of capital would create "vast and evergrowing inequality." But the market republic was saved by the cornucopia of goods it would produce. Workers' pay might double or quadruple "within a century or two" and allow them increasing access to goods and personal property. Where some benefits flowed to all, a sense of justice and even of fraternity would prevail.[47]

If Clark's new marginalist economics allowed him to rehabilitate the moral legitimacy of the capitalist market, it also allowed him to reconstitute the timeless domain of American exceptionalism. He had achieved his marginalist vision of the economy, he said, by putting "actual changes out of sight, intentionally and heroically." He showed America leaving history behind and entered upon a state of perpetual progress under natural law that gave "promise of indefinite continuance." In a nice coincidence, Dwight at the same moment called attention to "the prime feature of Harrington's scheme." It was that "the republic, like the glorious luminaries ... may go onward with steady and melodious motion forever."[48]

As Clark expanded his marginalist analysis, he came to realize that he was developing a "static" theory of the capitalist market as it worked under an ideal, hypothetical condition of perfect competition. "Natural standards of values, and natural or normal rates of wages, interest, and profits are, in reality, static rates. They are identical with those which would be realized if a society were perfectly organized, but were free from the disturbances that progress causes." Clark urged that in time, economics would require a dynamic theory to accompany his static one. The two had been intermingled in classical economics and could now be separated. His static theory, however, was normative. Historical changes were mere "disturbances." In another nice coincidence, Clark chose the metaphor of the ocean to explicate his meaning. "However stormy may be the ocean, there is an ideal level surface projecting itself through the waves, and the actual surface of the turbulent water fluctuates about it." In this figure, progress could only be

47 Clark and Giddings, *Modern Distributive Process*, 4–10, 41; John Bates Clark, *Social Justice without Socialism* (Boston: Houghton Mifflin, 1914), 51, 45–6; idem, "The Society of the Future," *Independent*, 53 (July 18, 1901): 1651; idem, "The Scholar's Political Opportunity," *PSQ*, 12 (December 1897): 598; Theodore W. Dwight, "Harrington and His Influence upon American Political Institutions and Political Thought," *PSQ*, 2 (March 1887): 1–44.
48 John Bates Clark, *Essentials of Economic Theory* (New York: Macmillan, 1907), vii; Dwight, "Harrington and His Influence," 39–41.

likened incongruously to surface fluctuations or to "mountains of new water" raising the whole level of the sea.[49]

The ocean has no history and no structural features. The classical economists, though they abstracted their doctrine from the full complexity of history, retained as their chief categories the physical factors of production – land, labor, and capital – and the historical classes that owned them. Ricardo's law of diminishing returns was understood to reflect a historical process of cultivation across the earth and the march of liberal progress embodied a dramatic conflict of classes that would someday end in a stationary state.

In the marginalists' neoclassical world, these distinctive historical features dissolved. All values were determined by individuals calculating marginal utilities in the interconnected markets of capitalist society. The vision of competing individuals, freely exercising their wills and maximizing their goals through market choice, tending continually through surface fluctuations to reach an equilibrium of "natural" values, was an ideal liberal world. It was also the American exceptionalist world writ large, with Henry Adams' democratic ocean recreated in liberal terms and the dynamic energies perpetually renewed in nature replaced by the dynamism of insatiable individual wants. The radical historicist challenge had produced a conservative ahistorical response, restating in the form of marginalist theory the American exceptionalist desire to escape qualitative historical change and redefining the exceptionalist ideal as possessive individualism, stripped of the egalitarian implications it had borne in its original antebellum form.

### The sociologists' quarrel: Small versus Giddings

The sociologists acted out a similar conflict amidst the reverberating effects of the economists' quarrel. Sociology, the last developed of the social sciences, gained only a toehold in the universities in the 1880s. The positivist bias of William Graham Sumner's and Lester Frank Ward's evolutionary theories hampered their inclusion in institutions still freeing themselves from clerical control. Sumner himself was silenced for some years by a nervous breakdown and Ward was still an academic outsider. There was, however, a growing reformist "social science" of experts in charities and corrections and of social gospel ministers addressing the "social question." Through the

---

49 John Bates Clark, "The Future of Economic Theory," *QJE*, 13 (October 1898): 9; idem, *Distribution of Wealth*, vi, 76, 409, 418–19.

1880s leading figures from the ASSA lectured in the universities on the dependent, delinquent, and defective classes, and reform-minded clerics began to teach courses in "social ethics."[50] When in the 1890s, university expansion and growing secular influence opened new possibilities for sociology, its practitioners had to define their subject from disparate sources and negotiate all the while treacherous political shoals.

When the University of Chicago opened its doors in 1892, President William Rainey Harper, surely the most entrepreneurial biblical scholar America ever produced, gave the first chair in sociology in the country to Albion Woodbury Small. Two years later Columbia University, at the urging of Seth Low, created a similar chair for Franklin H. Giddings. Small was a Baptist minister who came to sociology from historico-politics and brought to it the ethical and reformist aims of the social gospel ministry.[51] Giddings, originally a journalist, came to sociology from economics and had collaborated with John Bates Clark in his turn to a marginalist legitimation of American capitalism.[52] Not surprisingly, they presented sociologists at the outset with very different models of their discipline and replayed the economists' quarrel.

After his clerical studies, Small studied historical economics and *Staatswissenschaft* in Germany. When he returned to Colby College as professor of history in 1882, he taught students to "recognize the more obvious and general laws which historical evolution illustrates" while at the same time learning to gather evidence themselves and deduce from it "definite and legitimate conclusions." Such training would produce broadminded men of affairs who could "estimate rightly the forces that modify society." But in a few years he began to feel that history yielded only "solemn conclusions which are not convincing" or a "litter of facts." These feelings were re-

50 Luther Lee Bernard and Jesse Bernard, *The Origins of American Sociology* (New York: Thomas Y. Crowell, 1943), pt. 9; Anthony Oberschall, "The Institutionalization of American Sociology," in *The Establishment of Empirical Sociology*, ed. Anthony Oberschall (New York: Harper & Row, 1972), 187–251.

51 The best work on Small is Vernon K. Dibble, *The Legacy of Albion Small* (Chicago: University of Chicago Press, 1975), although it treats Small's ideas as unchanging throughout his life and hence misses the tensions that immobilized him. The standard sources of biographical information are Small's own "Fifty Years of Sociology in the United States (1865–1915)," *AJS*, 21 (May 1916): 721–864; and Edward Cary Hayes, "Albion Woodbury Small," in *American Masters of Social Science*, ed. Henry W. Odum (New York: Holt, 1927), 149–87. See also Richard J. Storr, *Harper's University: The Beginnings, A History of the University of Chicago* (Chicago: University of Chicago Press, 1966).

52 John L. Gillen, "Franklin Henry Giddings," in *American Masters of Social Science*, 191–228; R. Gordon Hoxie et al., *A History of the Faculty of Political Science, Columbia University* (New York: Columbia University Press, 1955), 284–303.

inforced when in 1889 he went to Johns Hopkins to study under Herbert Baxter Adams and Richard Ely.[53]

The "solemn conclusions" from history Small found unconvincing were apparently the unchanging and conservative principles of American exceptionalism. Like the other German-trained, evangelical scholars of his generation, Small had a new appreciation of historicism and a new social ethic. In his Johns Hopkins dissertation he argued against the view that American nationality was created by the Declaration of Independence; it was instead a product of the historical development of the whole people over the following decades. Indeed, the Declaration no more established nationality than it "made absolute and universal equality the will of the people in 1776." In his syllabus of European history, he noted that "No specially favored country has been able to establish the ideal order in miniature."[54]

The difficulty for Small was what would take the place of traditional exceptionalist principles. With his interest in the "progressive recognition of social needs," he could have, like his younger contemporaries Frederick Jackson Turner and Charles Beard, tried to create a social and economic history relevant to praxis. Instead Small began reading philosophies of history from Augustine to Buckle, as well as the "systematic sociology" of Comte, Spencer, Ward, and the German organic theorist, A. E. F. Schäffle. Sociology, he concluded, was "the natural successor, heir and assign of the worthy but ineffective 'Philosophy of History,'" providing a "conspectus of the correlation of the forces that have given human society its present character."[55]

As cleric, Small also thought sociology the heir and assign of his evangelical expectations. He closed his first sociology course at Colby with a sermon in which he presented sociology as the means to the goal of Christianity – the Kingdom of God on earth, the "condition of human society in which the principles of divine righteousness pervade and control social or economic activity." As with Ely, Clark, and Adams, his millennial hopes were cast into history.[56]

53 Dibble, *Albion Small*, 28–30, 232. Small, "Fifty Years of Sociology," 767, 729–34; idem, "Course of Study in Sociology" [n.d.], Herbert Baxter Adams Papers, Johns Hopkins University.
54 Albion W. Small, "The Beginnings of American Nationality: The Constitutional Relations between the Continental Congress and the Colonies and States," *JHUSHPS*, 8th ser., nos. 1–2 (January–February 1890): 1–77; idem, "Von Holst on American Politics," *The Civil Service Reformer*, 4 (December 1888): 141; idem, *Syllabus: Introduction to the History of European Civilization* (Colby, Maine: Colby University, 1889), 87.
55 Small, "Course of Study in Sociology," H. B. Adams Papers; Dibble, *Albion Small*, 30–2; idem, "The Relations of Sociology to Economics," *JPE*, 3 (March 1895): 173.
56 Albion W. Small, "Sermon," *The Dawn*, 2 (November 1890): 302. In Albion W. Small and George E. Vincent, *An Introduction to the Study of Society* (New York: American Book

Small conceived the task of sociology in three parts. The first part, Descriptive Sociology, used an inductive "historical and analytical" method to separate out "the accidental and permanent" features of society. History "deals preferably with the order and sequence of events, and with the exhibition of cause and effect"; sociology "treats the same facts rather as exhibiting normal or abnormal conditions, permanent or temporary forms of social structures and functions." Moreover, unlike economics, sociology must organize "all the positive knowledge of man and of society" to gain a holistic perspective. Like Ward, he wanted sociology to deal with all the principal wants of human nature or the "social forces": health, wealth, sociability, knowledge, beauty, and rightness.[57]

As the reference to "normal" and "permanent" social forms suggests, Small's historical-sociological world still lay partly imbedded in the eternal Christian one. The task of Statical Sociology was to formulate the "equilibrium of a perfect society." Society contained an "immanent ideal" that could be found through "inspection and induction, not . . . speculation." Sociological method "takes account of the demonstrated facts and forces of society. . . . From this material it derives systematized knowledge of the neglected economies of life, and thereupon a symmetrical ideal of the social life in which immanent social potencies shall be realized." The ideal was created by history in its ongoing progress toward the Kingdom of God and could be discerned through the sociological study of history. Still, if history held within it the potential of an ideal order, human will must create it. The third task of sociology, Dynamic Sociology, was to investigate the ways and means "for changing the actual into the ideal." Small's sociology, like Ely's historical economics, was an ethical science. He praised books on the historical development of modern capitalism which were "not afraid of being written down as unscientific for reflecting upon a future or ideal social order," for drawing conclusions about "the directions in which or the means by which we should seek for change."[58]

When Small outlined this conception of sociology he had no substantive theory of history to present. But he already knew the direction social change

---

Co., 1894), bk. 2, there is an account of "The Natural History of a Society," written by Vincent, that traces the simultaneous progress and decline from a village community to industrial city. See Dibble, *Albion Small*, 21. Small himself tended to keep to the forward progress of historical development and avoided the traditional language of decline.

57 Albion W. Small, "The Era of Sociology," *AJS*, 1 (July 1895): 1–15; Small and Vincent, *Introduction*, 62–5, 172–82.

58 Small and Vincent, *Introduction*, 66–70; Small, "The Relation of Sociology to Economics," 182; idem, "Review of John A. Hobson, *The Evolution of Modern Capitalism*; Ernst von Halle, *Trusts, or Industrial Combinations in the United States*; and Henry Dyer, "The Evolution of Industry," *AJS*, 1 (September 1895): 223, 227–8.

should take. "Sociology looks to the equalization of social relations." The ideal within modern society was one of mutuality and of personal realization for all its members, and this ideal made sociology "the ally of any class which is temporarily at a disadvantage against any other class." Indeed, sociology was called into existence by socialism, which has "mercilessly exposed social evils, but ... has not been equally positive in proposal of remedies.... Socialism is nevertheless a challenge which society cannot ignore.... Considering the role that Socialism has played in nineteenth century thought, Sociology appears to have come into existence less from choice than from necessity. In the Hegelian idiom, conventionality is the thesis, Socialism is the antithesis, Sociology is the synthesis." Small looked to sociology to formulate some way less "visionary" and radical than socialism to reach his Christian socialist goals. It would produce a comprehensive philosophy of history and a surer path to progress than the materialism and inequality enacted by industrial capitalism and mirrored by classical economics.[59]

As Small well knew in 1894, the inclusion of socialism in any synthesis whatsoever was a dangerous path for an American academic. He vacillated throughout his text as to how serious the pathology of American society was, whether structural institutions should be indicted or the blame placed primarily upon individuals and faulty socialization.[60] If his own judgment was uncertain, he was also under heavy crossfire at Chicago. The chairman of the economics department at Chicago was the conservative J. Laurence Laughlin, who made no secret of his contempt for sociology. Small was also dean of the faculty of arts as well as chairman of the sociology department and well aware of Harper's desire not to alienate the wealthy Chicagoans on whom the university depended. Small himself valued the contacts his university position gave him with leading Chicago businessmen and was one of the founders of the Chicago Civic Federation, an effort to mobilize the leadership of the city for civic goals.

At the same time, Small was in close contact with Christian reformers. He was proud of his own cautious forays in reform, most notably as a member of the Federation's commission to mediate the Pullman strike in 1894 and seek passage of an arbitration law in Illinois. As a proponent of scientific reform, however, he was anxious to preempt the clerical amateurs and to separate sociology from the stigma attached to the radicals in the religious

59 Small and Vincent, *Introduction*, 78–9, 40–1.
60 Ibid. 267–72, 298–301.

movement. He urged Ely to break with the radical social gospelers and probably decided to found his *American Journal of Sociology* in 1895 to head off their plans for a journal of Christian sociology.[61]

Under these cross-pressures, Small staked out a precarious centrist path for the sociologist to follow. Although he declared unequivocally the ethical aim of sociology, he criticized throughout the premature efforts of reformers to construct social remedies without adequate social knowledge. The synthetic science of society was still far off, and "zealous prophets of righteousness" were doing more harm than good. "If institutions are defective they are the reflection of defective social knowledge, and . . . much information must be gathered about many things before safe substitutes for prevailing social conclusions can be derived." Small's historical holism, with its radical demand for a more comprehensive knowledge than economics provided, also had a quietist use, one that echoed Spencer's warning against the remote and unintended consequences of social reform. For Small's ethical sociologist, investigation, not prescription or activism, was the proper social role.[62]

Franklin Giddings at Columbia produced a positivist philosophy of history that identified the actual and the ideal. Giddings was the rebellious child of an evangelical preacher, who rejected his strict puritanical upbringing and was early won over to positivism. As a disciple of classical economics and Spencerian sociology, he believed that society progressed slowly, and only under the moral discipline of individual exertion. By the middle 1880s Giddings was increasingly preoccupied with the social question. Although the range of voluntaristic actions he could offer the working class was not very different from Sumner's, Giddings wanted to play a positive role. He became active in support of workers' cooperatives which functioned on strictly voluntaristic principles and was even more enthusiastic about profit sharing, which was "cooperation initiated and controlled by capitalist employers." After Haymarket he founded a monthly, *Work and Wages*, which offered workers condescending advice on the proper uses and abuses

---

61 Small to Harper, July 13, 1894, President's Papers, University of Chicago; Small, "Fifty Years of Sociology," 768–9; idem, "The Era of Sociology," 15; idem, "The Civic Federation of Chicago: A Study in Social Dynamics," *AJS*, 1 (July 1895): 79–103; Small to Ward, April 10, 1895, and May 25, 1895, in "The Letters of Albion W. Small to Lester F. Ward," ed. Bernhard J. Stern, *Social Forces*, 12 (December 1933): 170–2.
62 Small and Vincent, *Introduction*, 19; Herbert Spencer, *The Study of Sociology* (New York: D. Appleton, 1874), 21–2. Only the radical uses of Small's holism are discussed by Ernest Becker in *The Lost Science of Man* (New York: Braziller, 1971).

of labor organization and warnings that the unemployed were "defective" working people.[63]

Coming into contact with John Bates Clark in 1886, the two found instant sympathy. Giddings published Clark's new ideas in *Work and Wages* and added to Clark's marginalist restatement of profits and wages his own confirmation of competition as a universal evolutionary process. He had never doubted the moral legitimacy of the capitalist market and Clark's elegant new proofs could only strengthen his conviction. Giddings moved toward sociology in the hope that he could "put the Science of Political Economy into a philosophical form and broaden its method, do something toward the practical solution of the labor question, and throw out some ideas that I am cherishing on the subject of government and public policy."[64]

Giddings conceived of sociology in Spencerian terms. If Small entered sociology trailing his normative Christian idealism, Giddings trailed Spencer's evolutionary monism, with its assumed identity between physical and social "force" and its normative natural law. With this view of evolution, there was no need for a special ethical function in science. As he declared against Ely in 1888,

if the economist, pursuing the study of the actual, faithfully describes the economic natures and practices of the most advanced men, he does, in so doing, forecast the economic idea. . . . whatever of moral obligation it may be the function of economic science to disclose, will stand out and speak for itself. There will be no need of dogmatism or exhortation.

The evolutionary positivist had only to describe progressive action to render moral judgment. Government action could be useful only if it supported capitalist progress along the line of "cumulative liberty."[65]

The laws Giddings found at work throughout evolution were the inter-

---

63 Gillin, "Franklin Henry Giddings," 196–9; Frank A. Ross, "Franklin Henry Giddings," *DAB*, Suppl. 1–2, 339; Franklin H. Giddings, *Railroads and Telegraphs: Who Shall Control Them?* (Springfield, Mass.: The Manufacturer and Industrial Gazette, 1881); idem, "Co-operation," in *The Labor Movement: The Problem of To-Day*, ed. George E. McNeill (Boston: A. M. Bridgman, 1887), 508–31, particularly 524. In *Work and Wages*, see idem, "Work and Wages," 1 (November 1886): 8; idem, "Who and What Are the Unemployed?" 1 (December 1886): 6; idem, "Two Views of the Labor Movement," 1 (May 1887): 5–6; idem, "Education the Solution," 1 (September 1887): 6.
64 Ross, "Socialism and American Liberalism," 45–6; Clark and Giddings, *Modern Distributive Process*; Giddings to Lester F. Ward, June 23, 1887, in "Giddings, Ward, and Small: An Interchange of Letters," ed. Bernhard J. Stern, *Social Forces*, 10 (March 1932): 307.
65 Franklin H. Giddings, "The Province of Sociology," *AAAPSS*, 1 (July 1890): 66–77, particularly 73; idem, "Sociology and Political Economy," *PAEA*, 3, no. 1 (March 1888): 39; idem, *Outline of Lectures on Sociology* (Philadelphia: Wm. J. Dornan, 1891), 17–18.

twined laws of natural, social, and sexual selection. Together they conformed individuals within groups to the predominant social pattern, and determined which groups and societies survived. Conscious human purpose might widen the variation of social forms available, but it was selection that controlled the outcome. The economic struggle for existence was accompanied by sociological processes of association, aggregation, and differentiation, by which racial differences and the division of labor issued in ethnic and class divisions. Races varied in ability and hence capacity for progress, so that England and its colonies moved to the forefront. In the "sifting" process that selection enforced, different classes were formed in society, and "differences of ability correspond closely to differences of social function, and roughly to differences of economic condition." But Giddings also stressed the altruistic consequences for human nature produced by modern social interdependence. He looked forward to the emergence of an "ethical society," peopled by diligent, respectable workmen, and philanthropic elites.[66]

As Giddings neared the end of his optimistic Spencerian epic, however, he lamented that progress itself, by its constant change and stimulation of activity and ambition, created suffering and degeneration. Indeed, he sharpened the picture to familiar lines. Industrial society can over-develop the "mercenary spirit" and threaten to separate absolutely the wealthy from the poor, throwing government "wholly into the hands of those who control the material means of existence.... That a plutocratic spirit is a real cause of social disintegration, is beyond reasonable doubt. It played its unworthy part in the fall of the Roman Empire and in the ruin of the medieval republics. It seriously menaces the future of our own free institutions." But industrial society was not, fortunately, wholly of this plutocratic type.

In the simple democracies of colonial America, and of the early western migration beyond the Alleghenies, there was a virile moral life that kept all other interests in a reasonable subordination.... Not the factory and the mart, but the church, the common school, and the freemen's meeting, were the real centres of social activity. ... It was the rare fortune of the American people that in its formative days the quick moral life of such communities left a deep impress on the larger life of the nation. The impress has not been effaced, but the clear lines of its beauty have been broken and confused.

Evolutionary naturalism came to a poignant halt in the Gilded Age crisis of American exceptionalism. As for Sumner, liberal optimism warred with exceptionalist fear that progress would efface "the clear lines" of the

66 Giddings, *Outline of Lectures on Sociology*; idem, *The Principles of Sociology* (New York: Macmillan, 1896), 299–360, particularly 328–9, 341.

beautiful American past. Under the tutelage of Clark rather than Ricardo, Giddings hoped that the altruism being generated by evolutionary law would restore the old "virile moral life" and the republic go on forever, but he could not quite shake his fear of decline.[67]

Within this Spencerian evolutionary framework, Giddings looked for what made individuals into social creatures. He was not satisfied that biological need or economic interest alone could account for social conduct, but looked for the secret of society in association. In 1896 in his *Principles of Sociology*, he announced that the psychological fact of association on which all of sociology rested was reducible to "consciousness of kind," the most elementary form of social consciousness, which attracted like to like. He developed this idea from Adam Smith's discussion in *The Theory of Moral Sentiments* of "sympathy" or "fellow feeling," the act of imagination by which we place ourselves in the situation of another, and thereby "become in some measure the same person with him, and thence form some idea of his sensations, and even feel something which, though weaker in degree, is not altogether unlike them." Giddings transformed this feeling of sympathy into a conscious perception of likeness. He discerned in it the clue not only to what draws individuals into social association, but also to what draws groups apart, creating the invidious pattern of association humanity has constructed, with its "race hatreds and class prejudices." In going back to Smith's "sympathy," Giddings had found the classical conception of liberal society, and drawn from it a double-edged sword fit for the modern industrial world. His evolutionary theory put these invidious conflicts on the road to ultimate extinction, but in the interim, it fixed them in natural law.[68]

Although Small thought sociology was the fundamental social science because it was comprehensive, Giddings thought sociology was fundamental because it was the science of the elementary psychological principle of consciousness of kind and its social transformations. Small recognized the need of a "historical and analytical method" to uncover the social forces at work in history, but Giddings sought to construct an evolutionary science without history. "Sociology stands at the opposite end of the scale of social science from history." Yet his analyses concerned evolutionary changes over time that were clearly drawn from history. After struggling with this problem, referring at one time to Dilthey and another time to the categories of Mill and Comte, he tried to have it both ways. Sociology, like political

---

67 Giddings, *Principles*, 347, 355–6.
68 Ibid.; idem, "Preface to the Third Edition," (New York: Macmillan, 1926), ix–xvii; Adam Smith, *The Theory of Moral Sentiments* (London: G. Bell, 1892 [1759]), 3–10.

economy, abstracted out of social experience a primary principle and traced it through all its manifestations; but in addition, sociology showed how this principle combined with others to create the concrete phenomena of the real world.[69]

While Giddings and Small were formulating their views in the early 1890s, scholars who were interested in sociology found themselves divided and uncertain. When Ira Howerth, a student at Chicago, sent queries to all those academics loosely connected with the new subject in 1894, he found a "chaotic condition of social thought." What sociology was and what relation it held to either its neighboring or constituent fields was widely disputed. When the forty respondents were presented with Small's division of sociology into descriptive, static, and dynamic, nine agreed and fourteen opposed it, and not all the nine proponents appeared to define the divisions the way Small did, nor all the opponents to take Giddings' position. Perhaps the most significant finding of Howerth's survey, however, was that despite the substantive disagreement, three-quarters of those polled thought sociology was or was becoming a science, defined as a "systematized body of knowledge," and the great majority thought it should occupy a separate university department. Professional ambitions obviously outran intellectual development.[70]

The discussion of the survey at the AEA and a programmatic paper by Small quickly pitted Small's conception of sociology against Giddings'. In part, the conflict concerned the scope and method of sociology. Only a comprehensive historical sociology, Small claimed, was "adequate to the task of direction of social cooperation." But sociology could not be a science of the whole, Giddings countered. In his *Principles* he ridiculed Small's "inventory" method as "a tiresome endeavor to enumerate all the motives that actuate man ... as if all motives were of coordinate importance to sociology. The result is not the reasoned knowledge that is science."

Small countered with a long, acerbic review of the book. Giddings retained the broad scope of sociology as a synthetic study of the evolution of society, Small complained, but at the same time narrowed it to a study of

69 Franklin H. Giddings, "Sociology as a University Study," *PSQ*, 6 (December 1891): 649, 653–5; idem, "The Province of Sociology," 68; idem, "The Relation of Sociology to Other Scientific Studies," *Journal of Social Science*, 32 (1894): 144–50; idem, *Principles*, 39–40.
70 Ira W. Howerth, "Present Condition of Sociology in the United States," *AAAPSS*, 5 (September 1894): 260–9. A survey of textbook use in sociology up to 1901 found forty-two courses using Small and Vincent and thirty-two using Giddings. Since the survey was cumulative, and Small and Vincent had a two years' edge on Giddings, the split may have been about even at the turn of the century. J. Graham Morgan, "Courses and Texts in Sociology," *JHS*, 5 (Spring 1983): 55.

only those phenomena arising out of the associational impulse. Human evolution could hardly be explained on the basis of this single motive. Giddings' methodology was likewise confused. The only proper method to study society and evolution was the inductive method, a method not of "inventory," but of reasoned classification on which generalizations might be based. In the spirit of American Baconian empiricism, Small denied that there was any difference between the marginalists' method and his own inductive one – they were merely making "a larger generalization of facts than has previously been accomplished." Giddings' method, however, was wholly speculative, his "consciousness of kind," a "pre-Platonic metaphysical fabrication."[71]

As in economics, the debate over historicism and sociological method was fueled by underlying political disagreement. After the AEA debate, Giddings instigated, if he did not write himself, an editorial in the *Popular Science Monthly*, which ridiculed the Christian socialist variety of sociology as a fad for cranks, labeled Small's chair at Chicago one of "social science," and claimed the first chair of genuine sociology for Giddings,

who holds that social ethics can never teach us what social relations ought to be until sociology has analyzed and classified them as they are; discovered how, through an evolutionary process, they came to be as they are; and explained in terms of natural causation why they are what they are, and not in all respects what we might wish them to be.

Moreover, he asserted, the AEA discussion had concluded in Giddings' favor that sociology was "a science of what is and has been, sharply distinguished from social ethics."[72]

Small made clear what he thought of the ethical implications of Giddings' consciousness of kind. "Sufficiently integrated and differentiated, it gives us the battle-field and the torture-chamber and the slave-pen and the sweat-shop!"[73] But Small, caught in the crossfire of the mid-1890s, had tried to avoid conflict by retreating from the activist implications of his own ethical stance. The sociologist, he had said, should indeed be describing society as it is; ethical prescription was decidedly premature. Giddings' attack, and

71 H. H. Powers, "Terminology and the Sociological Conference," *AAAPSS*, 5 (March 1895): 705–17; Albion W. Small, "The Relation of Sociology to Economics," *PAEA*, 10 (March 1895): 106–7, and "Discussion," 110–11; Giddings, *Principles*, 12; Albion W. Small, "Review of Franklin H. Giddings, *The Principles of Sociology*," *AJS*, 2 (September 1896): 288–310, particularly 293–4, 297–300.
72 Franklin H. Giddings, "Sociology and Political Economy," *PAEA*, 3 (March 1888): 39; "Sociology in the Universities," *Popular Science Monthly*, 46 (March 1895): 698–9; Small to Ward, April 10, 1895, in Stern, "Letters of Small to Ward," 171–2.
73 Small, "Review of Giddings, *Principles*," 295.

political pressures closer to home, forced Small for a time to take a more radical position.

Edward A. Bemis was a Chicago economist and Ely disciple who had roused the ire of Harper, Laughlin, and local business interests. When Harper warned Bemis that he had jeopardized his position, Bemis complained to Small, who had all along befriended him. But according to Bemis, Small replied that

> I was injuring the department and the U'sity because of my participation in so many phases of public questions such as in the work of the Civic Federation. Said he 'Why you are more before the public than anyone here except President Harper.' ('more than even myself' was his remark to Sec'y Easley of the Civic Federation . . .) Prof. Small said . . . 'there is so much misapprehension of Sociology as a science of reform that although I hope to take up reform movements years hence, I am now going off in my lectures into transcendental philosophy so as to be as far as possible from these reform movements and thus establish the scientific character of my department.' Isn't that rich? With Prof. Small jealous and afraid of the trustees and of the flings of Laughlin, Harper is left free under the pressure of the trustees and moneyed men and of Laughlin to go back on all his pledges.

Harper did just that, and when Bemis went public and charged that he was being fired because of his political activities, Small denied the charge. When an open letter was sent to the *American Journal of Sociology* charging that the Bemis case made clear that no free investigation was possible at Rockefeller's university, Small countered angrily, denying that Bemis' case had anything to do with academic freedom and repeating his position that sociology simply did not know yet where the truth lay.[74]

But Small's conscience must have hurt. The "jealousy" Bemis sensed was token of Small's real desire to make good himself the ethical claim of sociology. In the next three issues of the *Journal*, Small dramatically changed his course. In "Private Business is a Public Trust" he delivered a blistering attack on the present system of property and inheritance. "The resources of the world are divided up among the members of the propertied caste, and the remainder of men depend upon the members of this caste for permission to get a share of nature by labor." Indeed Small did not leave much doubt about how close to home capitalist power had hit, for he noticed the plight of the doctor, minister, and teacher who, despite learning and skill had no legal claim if they were deprived of their charges or clients. He spoke for the "dissatisfied proletarian of all classes" against the denial of dignity, man-

74 Small to Ely, May 24, "Saturday Morn," June 15, and July 28, 1894; and Bemis to Ely, January 12, 1895, Ely Papers; Furner, *Advocacy and Objectivity*, 163–98; [Albion W. Small], "Free Investigation," *AJS*, 1 (September 1895): 210–14.

hood, and equality. The sociologist, he now asserted, must speak out for right principles in the hope that it will make change easier. "If, before pointing out possibilities of improvement, it were necessary to know the whole process by which the actual may be changed into the rational, hope would be forever dumb."[75]

Small followed up with a statement in favor of public control of corporations and municipal socialism along the lines set out by Henry Carter Adams, and then in "Scholarship and Social Agitation," took on Giddings. "The primary purpose of this paper is to challenge the claims of that type of scholarship which assumes superiority because it deals with facts." Such scholars have made science and evolution into gods, not seeing that evolution is still going on today. As to the problems of modern capitalism and ethics, "Scholars are shirkers unless they grapple with these problems. It is for this that society supports us."[76]

At the same moment, Small sent Lester Ward notes on his current work. He wanted to discover "more effective measures of social practice with distinct view to progress" by determining "the *attributes of progressive action* in general, so that we may oppose proposed actions if they betray nonprogressive characteristics." Did progressive action require structural change, or only "intensification of activity within structures already developed?" Was it necessary to change the fundamental character of the capitalist economy, monogamous family, and representative government, or could lesser reforms be successful?[77] Frightened by capitalist power and goaded by his own ignominious capitulation to it, Small briefly abandoned his flight into "transcendental philosophy," declared that the sociologist should play an active role in social change, and set about to determine whether structural change really was necessary for social progress to occur.

Exactly one year later, in March 1897, Small reversed himself again. "The shortest way to reach ability to solve social problems is not to try to solve them at all for a long time, but to learn how to state them." Small now agreed with "the men of scientific temper and the men of business methods ... that realistic study of social facts simply as facts, without any interposition of our opinions and feelings, is the only credible guarantee of the respectability of subsequent conclusions." The scholar must of course, as a citizen, act on imperfect evidence and take positions on such problems as the

75 Albion W. Small, "Private Business Is a Public Trust," *AJS*, 1 (November 1895): 281–2, 285, 289.
76 Albion W. Small, "The State and Semi-Public Corporations," *AJS*, 1 (January 1896): 398–410; idem, "Scholarship and Social Agitation," *AJS*, 1 (March 1896): 564, 569.
77 Notes enclosed in Small to Ward, March 10, 1896, in Stern, "Letters of Small to Ward," 327–30.

currency, taxation, and monopoly. But on the more fundamental issues, the "abiding relationships," he must hold off for more considered, scientific knowledge. Like Emerson, who had held back from abolitionism and then come to the cause later "with ten thousand disciples whom he had formed into large true men," the sociologist would someday return "not only to foresee but to foreordain" the future.[78]

What happened between March 1896 and March 1897 to so sharply reverse Small's stance? To some extent, what happened must have been his own attempt to reach definite conclusions on whether structural change was necessary. Given Small's underlying ambivalence, and the complexity of the problems which his synthetic vision disclosed to him, his reversal might well have been an admission of personal, and with it, sociological incapacity. But if political pressures pushed Small into his activist stance initially, one might expect that they played a part in his retreat. What happened in late 1896 was the election of McKinley, the defeat of Bryan, and with it, the sudden collapse of the widely feared radical threat.

To middle-class Americans, the election of 1896 presented the threat of democratic revolution. The accumulated passions of revolt and reaction flowed into the election, making it one of the most bitterly fought contests in the country's history. For economists and sociologists, it raised to fever pitch the question they had been asking for the past two decades, whether America was moving toward a socialistic future, and it posed the question in the realistic terms of electoral politics. As Columbia's Richmond Mayo-Smith wrote to Seligman in July,

> Politics is the absorbing topic here. We are going through the most extraordinary outbreak of anarchism and populism.... The silverites make such a clamor that it is impossible to say whether we are really on the verge of a social revolution. Is it the old devil of greenbackism or is it newer devils that have entered and taken possession? The great question is whether Silver has taken real hold on the farmers and laboring classes of the middle-central states. I doubt if we know until November.[79]

The shift of a critical percentage of northeastern workingmen to the Republican party and the defeat of Bryan answered that question. Industrialized labor, marginalized farmers, and a frightened middle class could not be brought together on a platform of producers' democracy. For the whole nineteenth-century tradition of radical reform, it was a final, deflationary

---

78 Albion W. Small, "The Sociologist's Point of View," *AJS*, 3 (September 1897): 152, 154–5.
79 Mayo-Smith to E. R. A. Seligman, July 21, 1896, Seligman Papers. On the importance of the 1896 election see Wiebe, *Search for Order*, 101–4.

blow. The broad native movement that had gathered around the ideal of a cooperative commonwealth rapidly dissipated after 1896.

Beyond the social-structural reasons for the decline of the native radical tradition, its rapid dissolution must have owed a great deal to the logic of American exceptionalism. Americans had believed since the beginning of their national existence that the actual course of American history was enacting the millennial ideal. Gilded Age radicals reactivated the transformative power of that ideal in the context of sweeping historical change, expecting the birth of a new world. When the election of 1896 finally made clear that transformation was not, in fact, impending, and when the potentiality for utopian change in American history grew more distant and uncertain, the temptation for Americans was to abandon their expectation of the Kingdom and hold fast to America.

Small left no record of his response to the election of 1896 and uncharacteristically published nothing between March of 1896 and 1897. But the election was widely perceived by the middle and upper classes as well as by the reformers themselves to be a decisive defeat for the native radical tradition. Small's writings in the deflationary years immediately after the election suggest a self-conscious acquiescence to "the men of scientific temper and the men of business methods" who urged "realistic study of social facts simply as facts." As a consequence, Small began to redefine the sociologist's "immanent ideal." He had always seen the ideal as inherent in history and, in the American tradition of commonsense realism, expected valid ideals to gain "general assent." Now he saw that the ideal must be based only on what the people actually want. "The power that estops or enforces all other social influence is the judgment that living men have accepted about what is desirable ... when action is necessary no other test of what is good for men is possible." Small's ultimate aim remained that sociological science be turned into action, but effective action now required acceding to what "living people think good for themselves."[80]

Discovery of the proper solution to social problems was the work of science, Small went on the next year, but for a discovery to be real, most men must agree to it. The labor problem could be solved by fair distribution, but what is fair distribution? Bellamy and the socialists – really only a small group of men – say that it requires equal pay for any hour's work; but most people do not agree with that. Therefore it is not a real discovery, and therefore it is "insane" for them to agitate on its behalf. "The obstinate fact is that nobody in the world is wise enough to convince a majority in any

80 Small and Vincent, *Introduction*, 267–8; Small, "The Sociologist's Point of View," 169–70.

nation today that he has a workable solution of the labor problem."[81] Though he continued to cling to his egalitarian and fraternal sympathies, he now saw no way to realize them except through people's "practical judgments of conduct," which "are the raw material of the only ethics that promises to gain general assent." The ethical task of sociology would henceforth be the combination into a synthetic whole of the partial values actually held by the different groups in society.[82] Small was probably aided in his move toward a naturalistic ethics by his colleague John Dewey, but his timing coincided with the collapse of radical transformation in 1896.[83]

For Ely too, the chastening experience of the nineties had marked a capitulation to "what is" and a recognition of the stubborn strength of historical reality. Ely originally preached that "society has some option, some choice, and a conscience to which an appeal can be made." By the turn of the century he admitted that there seemed to be "something inevitable in all these general tendencies. . . . When we have said all that we can about the power of the individual will, we still find that there are great social forces which compel us to act along certain lines." As the socialist millennium receded, the radical transformation of American history gave way to its actual historical course and Christian idealism gave way to scientific study of the historically given.[84]

It is therefore not surprising that Small coupled his retreat from ethical activism with the bravado claim that the sociologist would someday return "not only to foresee but to foreordain" the future. Small had from the start, in his category of dynamic sociology, embraced Ward's conception of sociology as an active agent in social direction and linked sociology's task to the achievement of a utopian social order. As the difficulties of that task became greater, Small's emotional and conceptual investment in it seemed to inflate. Small reenacted the strategy of Condorcet who, facing imprisonment by the French revolutionary government, added on to his account of

---

81 Albion W. Small, "Sanity in Social Agitation," *AJS*, 4 (November 1898): 338–42.
82 Albion W. Small, "The Significance of Sociology for Ethics," *Decennial Publications of the University of Chicago*, 1st ser., no. 4 (1903): 115. Drawing on Small's 1903 version of his theory, Dibble ignored the political context and suggested that except for some inconsistency here and there, this was Small's lifelong theory. Dibble, *Albion Small*, chap. 5.
83 In the year during which Small executed his retreat, he published an article in defense of the new pedagogy, "Some Demands of Sociology upon Pedagogy," *AJS*, 2 (May 1897): 839–51, that echoed John Dewey's reformist conception of education and his vocabulary. Small does not display Dewey's influence in his ethical theory, however, until the 1903 "Significance of Sociology for Ethics." On Dewey see below, Chapter 5.
84 Ely, *Socialism and Social Reform*, 176–7; idem, *Studies in the Evolution of Industrial Society* (New York: Macmillan, 1903), 97–8.

the progressive history of reason a utopian final stage of social scientific triumph.[85] With Small, the idea of the scientific control of history makes its appearance as a compensatory vision in a double sense. Forced to abandon the hope of immediate transformation, and no more able to accept historical uncertainty than Ward, he turned to science for assurance. In addition, scientific control promised future vindication for present failure. The present incapacity of the sociologist to exert even partial control would be compensated by the future ability of science to exert total control. The bravado of the chastened idealist joined the technological confidence of the positivist in laying the groundwork for American social scientists' vocational role.

By the end of the century, the leaders of the Gilded Age movement for a radical historical social science were in retreat. After his trial Ely never again assumed a major role in reform and his work grew increasingly conservative. Henry Carter Adams became chief statistician of the Interstate Commerce Commission, worked behind the scenes for expanded government regulatory power, and confined attenuated statements of his labor theory to his Michigan classes. Small went back to "transcendental philosophy," analyzing *the problem of thinking the whole human reality as a whole.*" When Harper complained about his meager enrollments, Small admitted "Quite likely I have dealt too exclusively with methodology, but I have a horror of letting men leave us under impressions which would permit them to pose, in the name of sociology, as extemporaneous readjusters of every unsatisfactory lot in life which demands reform." Let me know what you think of this policy, Small closed tartly. "I can easily give courses which would attract more students." Small remained an important figure in the profession, but the fortunes of historicism and of broadened social values in American social science would pass largely to other hands.[86]

## Conclusions

The gentry social scientists in the 1870s were the first generation to face the fact that industrialization was changing America, but they managed quickly to find unchanging historical and natural bases for the beneficent operation of natural law and republican institutions, and to affirm the continued power of those special conditions that in America defeated the destructive effects of time. In the 1880s and 1890s, the perception of industrial change could not

85 Keith Baker, *Condorcet* (Chicago: University of Chicago Press, 1975), 346–50, 370.
86 Ross, "Socialism and American Liberalism," 48, 52, 68–9, 76–8; Albion W. Small, "Methodology of the Social Problem," *AJS*, 4 (July–November 1898): 114, 392–4; Small to Harper, December 21, 1898, President's Papers.

be so easily contained. Young historical economists, spurred to radicalism by evangelical conscience, offered a new vision of America's millennial-republican destiny, one based on the historical transformation of American institutions into a cooperative commonwealth. Real historical change threatened to engulf even those who reacted conservatively to the radical threat, as Clark contemplated the destructive conflict between capital and labor and Giddings, the "broken and confused" lines of American social life. But the radicals were quickly stymied and the conservatives revived their faith in the ability of natural law and the exceptionalist heritage to put America once again on the road of unchanging progress. The actual course of American history remained normative, purged of its evangelical trans-formative power.

The ethical social scientists' bid for radical historical transformation was divided at the outset, bearing allegiance to individualistic as well as socialis-tic values, but that was true as well of the Fabian socialists who formed contemporaneously in England. American academic social scientists had also to contend with the power of respectable opinion, and behind it, the power of the capitalist class to enforce its will. That the Whiggish sons of ministe-rial families, in search of cultural power, should have succumbed to such pressures is hardly surprising. The constraints of American exceptionalism surely contributed to the outcome. The radicals carried the burden of urging qualitative change on people who were clinging to original perfection. Parading literally under the American flag in the campaign of 1896, con-servatives and moderates could speak not only for the eventual promise of capitalism, but for the continued promise of American institutions. The ethical social scientists themselves had grounded their ideal in the fulfillment of American history. For them as for their opponents, the ideal of a producers' democracy proved easier to abandon than the normative claim of exceptionalist history.

After 1896 class struggle was only temporarily in abeyance, and radical movements rose again to threaten mainstream political consensus. The dialectic of consensus and conflict continued. In academia, however, social-ism was forced to lead a more tenuous existence than in the society at large. It occasionally survived, most notably in the case of Thorstein Veblen, but for the most part, academic ties to capitalism and respectable opinion set the boundary of acceptable social science doctrine to the right of socialism. Though Sumner too was pressured, most of the coercion in the Gilded Age had been exerted against the left. So long as they wore a more smiling face than Sumner's, conservative social scientists could continue to put down roots. The inability of socialism to establish a respectable academic base deprived American social science of a continuing source of egalitarian values and historicist insight. The kind of social democracy that developed in England and the Continent within the domain of Fabian and revisionist socialism was in the United States largely forced into the domain of liberalism, where it was exposed to constant erosion.

Nonetheless, the Gilded Age conflict did lay the basis for a new liberalism and a new conservatism. The radical social scientists had by their sharp critique of American capitalism broken up the irenic harmonies of antebellum exceptionalism and exposed the inequality and conflict generated by industrial capitalism. Ironically, their insight probably made it easier to accept classical liberalism, with its recognition of conflicting interests and inevitable inequalities. New conservatives and new liberals both built upon the principles of classical liberalism. Clark and Giddings idealized the market society and argued that even within its rough lines, the harmonious vision of the American past could be recreated. New liberals would seek ways to moderate market inequalities and compensate for them, expanding liberal categories to embrace a social ethic. The antebellum exceptionalist ideal of wide distribution of property and power remained a powerful heritage, and social democrats would soon regroup on the left of the new liberal spectrum to try to realize democratic values within an industrial capitalist society. Moreover, historicism need not be entirely abandoned. The way was still open for liberal historicists to legitimate moderate change, contain the uncertainty of history within liberal bounds, and assure the promise of America's future through scientific control.

The Gilded Age conflict over socialism transformed the sociopolitical and historical bases of American exceptionalism and anticipated the terms within which the conflicts over its definition would be waged in the decades to come. It equally opened the social sciences to prolonged debate over the nature of their disciplines. Contemporaneously with their colleagues in Germany and Austria, American economists had opened a *Methodenstreit* which, less virulent, nonetheless persisted. Professional pressures allowed the economists to accept the legitimacy of both deductive and historical work, just as professional aspirations allowed the sociologists to continue searching for a productive focus amidst fundamental disagreement, but professionalism did not of itself command agreement. The problem of how to create a science of the sociohistorical world continued to generate conflicting answers.

# PART III

Progressive social science,
1896–1914

# 5

◁══════════════════════════════════════▷

# The liberal revision of American
# exceptionalism

During the Gilded Age, Americans faced for the first time the possibility of
historical change, and the chance that America might turn toward socialism
raised the issue of historical change in its most acute form. The major figures
of the Gilded Age who remained powerful into the Progressive Era – John
Bates Clark, E. R. A. Seligman, Albion Small, and Franklin Giddings – as
well as newer voices that emerged at the turn of the century – Irving Fisher,
Frank Fetter, Simon Patten, and Thorstein Veblen in economics; Edward A.
Ross and Charles Horton Cooley in sociology; John Dewey in philosophy –
were profoundly influenced by the Gilded Age crisis. Most of them struggled with socialism and tried now to escape its ideological polarization.
Revising the exceptionalist ideal, they reconstituted their disciplines on the
basis of liberal principles and liberal conceptions of history. The paradigms
they formulated – neoclassical economics, liberal economic interpretations
of history, a sociology and ideology of social control, and pragmatism – laid
the groundwork for twentieth-century social science. Thorstein Veblen was
the great exception to this liberal revisionism, for he retained his Gilded Age
socialism, and claimed for it the warrant not of ethics, but positivist science.
When we turn again to historico-politics, we will find that there too, a liberal
vision of American exceptionalism held sway among such new leaders as
Frank Goodnow, Woodrow Wilson, and Frederick Jackson Turner.

## The historical context of liberal exceptionalism

The industrial challenge and the "social question" it created remained the
salient historical context for American social science in the new century.
After the election of McKinley in 1896 and the end of depression in 1897, the
strains generated by industrialization appeared for a time to abate as the

economy entered a period of steadily rising prices and greater farm and business prosperity. Still, factory wages and middle-class salaries fell behind prices, and concentration of economic power in large corporations accelerated. In the merger movement of 1897–1902, entrepreneurs and finance capitalists engineered the consolidation of major producer and consumer industries into small numbers of giant firms that eschewed price competition for oligopoly. With their high fixed costs and complex coordination, large firms began to appreciate the value of a stable workforce, leading some to accept unionization. Most big businesses, however, like the smaller firms under severe competitive pressures, continued to both fight off unions and take minimal steps toward cementing their workers' allegiance to the firm, the beginnings of welfare capitalism.

After the collapse of the Knights of Labor, the American Federation of Labor (A.F.L.), a coalition largely of craft unions, emerged as the major arm of organized labor; yet in 1897, depleted by the depression, it included only 5 percent of the working class. Against the new industrial giants, the A.F.L. could make virtually no headway. Of native or older immigrant stock, they found themselves quickly swamped by new immigrants pouring in from southern and eastern Europe. The new immigrants and their children moved heavily into the industrial workforce and northern industrial cities. Still, the A.F.L. grew slowly during the Progressive Era and some more broadly based unions found immigrant support. Although the sense of impending labor victory that had accompanied the Knights was gone, the fear of class conflict continued. Capitalist intransigence bred violent confrontations and segments of the new workforce displayed fierce militance. The Industrial Workers of the World declared class war in the name of anarcho-syndicalism, and the new Socialist party of America, absorbing radical segments of the older native tradition, began to draw a wider constituency at the polls, winning almost a million votes for Eugene Debs in 1912. Hence, the socioeconomic problems of the Gilded Age – concentration of economic wealth and power, class conflict, and the threat of socialism – carried over into the new century.

What changed was the political context for dealing with them. Groups of reform-minded political independents began to force changes on the old party organizations, ushering in the Progressive period. The political reforms both weakened party structure and lowered popular suffrage, but they also gave new political force to the "public opinion" reflected in the popular media and to better-off businessmen, farmers, laborers, and reformers who were able to organize. This pluralistic politics, though weighted toward business interests, led to a series of legislative reforms, including the extension of economic regulation, modernization of the banking system, passage of the income tax, and the first hesitant steps to bring social welfare issues to the attention of the federal government. The social scientists themselves were among the organizing professional groups that composed the weighted-pluralist polity. Their growing university departments and the wide support for reform allowed numbers of them to become major figures in the Progressive movement, as experts for government and public-interest reform groups, as publicists and teachers, and notably in the case of Woodrow Wilson, as political participant.

The Progressive movement enlisted a wide segment of liberal support. On the right, even Clark and Giddings could embrace good government reforms and minimal programs of government regulation of monopolistic industry. Further to the left on the political spectrum, Progressives favored regulation of oligopolistic industries, antitrust enforcement, labor union organization, and social insurance. As the minimal Progressive program was enacted into law, the left Progressive program of more stringent corporate control and more ample support for labor and social welfare became more vocal. Advanced Progressives were strengthened by statistical reports documenting the severe inequality of wealth in America and the decline of real wages in manufacturing since 1900. As Progressive demands sharpened, however, moderate support fell away and conservatives mobilized to halt the movement. A series of violent labor confrontations between 1911 and 1913 and the substantial Socialist vote in 1912 further polarized popular opinion, as had happened in the mid-1880s and 1890s, bringing progressivism to its peak in 1914.[1]

Given the structure of social-economic change, the nature of Progressive reform, and the continued force of opposition to radicalism, the proscription of socialism remained as salient a task to social scientists in the Progressive period as it had been in the Gilded Age. For Clark, this purpose never wavered, from his first article in 1878 on "How to Deal with Communism" to his 1914 book, *Social Justice without Socialism*. For the new liberals, it was

---

1 This sketch of the Progressive period draws selectively on Robert Wiebe, *The Search for Order, 1877–1920* (New York: Hill & Wang, 1967); David Brody, *Steelworkers in America: The Nonunion Era* (New York: Russell and Russell, 1970 [1960]); James Weinstein, *The Corporate Ideal in the Liberal State, 1900–1918* (Boston: Beacon, 1968); Alfred Chandler, *The Visible Hand: The Managerial Revolution in American Business* (Cambridge, Mass.: Harvard University Press, 1977); Richard L. McCormick, *From Realignment to Reform* (Ithaca, N.Y.: Cornell University Press, 1981); Rhodri Jeffreys-Jones, "Violence in American History: Plug Uglies in the Progressive Era," *Perspectives in American History*, 8 (1974): 465–583. For contemporary discussion of inequality, see G. P. Watkins, "The Growth of Large Fortunes," *PAEA*, 3d ser., 8 (November 1907): 735–904; I. M. Rubinow, "The Recent Trend of Real Wages," *AER*, 4 (December 1914): 793–817; Frank H. Streightoff, "Review of Scott Nearing, *Financing the Wage-Earner's Family*," *AER*, 4 (June 1914): 438–41; Henry Pratt Fairchild, "The Standard of Living – Up or Down?" *AER*, 6 (March 1916): 9–25.

essential to draw the line between their own moderate proposals and the Socialist program. Jeremiah Jenks, who had been in the forefront of the call for corporate regulation, devoted his two presidential addresses to the AEA in 1906 and 1907 to setting the proper limits. In rousing support for reform, economists must not exaggerate the evils or minimize the benefits of capitalism, he warned. We must content ourselves with slow change rather than "some inclusive scheme of social reorganization." The American preference for "self-direction" had to be respected. Still, he closed bravely, when we advocate public regulation of business, "we ought not to be swayed at all by fear that we shall be called either socialists or scientific anarchists." The problem was compounded by the belief of some Progressives on the left that cumulative, liberal reform would create socialism.[2] The ideological limits of American exceptionalism continued to place social scientists on the defensive, even as they encouraged change. Liberal historians later came to see the reformers as progressives fighting a dualistic war against conservatives, but that political landscape required a considerable repression. They stood rather in the middle of a larger political spectrum and waged a two-front war.

Within the conflict of classes, the new liberals faced a widening array of social and cultural dissension during this period. The bonds of interest and function that created the Progressive Era's pluralist politics signified social fragmentation as well as organization. In beating back the efforts at democratic coalition, capitalist and political elites had exacerbated divisions. In the absence of stronger bonds of solidarity, each individual and group was left to save itself and to turn its frustrations and anxieties onto the competitor below. At the same time, the rise of evolutionary biology and racial anthropology added a level of legitimacy to racialist thinking. Racism took its most flagrant form in violence against African Americans and the passage of segregation and disfranchisement statutes throughout the South. In the North, the new immigration fueled a wave of nativism and racism.[3]

Francis A. Walker's reversal of a time-honored proof of American exceptionalism provides a neat index of these new fears. In his father's textbook and his own through 1884, statistics showing the higher birthrate of new

2 Kenneth McNaught, "American Progressives and the Great Society," *JAH*, 53 (December 1966): 504–20; Arthur Mann, "Socialism: Lost Cause in American History," *Criterion*, 19 (Autumn 1980): 11–16; Jeremiah W. Jenks, "The Modern Standard of Business Honor," *PAEA*, 3d ser., 8 (February 1907): 22; idem, "The Principles of Government Control of Business," *PAEA*, 3d ser., 9 (April 1908): 9, 20; John Martin, "An Attempt to Define Socialism," *Bulletin of the AEA*, 4th ser., 1 (April 1911): 347–54 and "Discussion," 355–67.
3 See John Higham, *Strangers in the Land* (New Brunswick, N.J.: Rutgers University Press, 1955); J. Morgan Kousser, *The Shaping of Southern Politics* (New Haven, Conn.: Yale University Press, 1974).

immigrant workers and decline in the birthrate of native American working-men appeared as proof of the improving effects of high wages in America and hence as an assurance that the Malthusian law would be evaded or counteracted. But in 1890 Walker saw in the new census figures – although they showed a similar configuration – a "monstrous" rise in the immigration of strange peoples and an even sharper drop in the native birthrate, prompting a fear of native decline and call for immigration restriction.[4]

In the Progressive Era, the traditional American fear of decay often centered on the new immigrants, presumably primitive and unassimilable. Although the confidence in America and cosmopolitan sympathies of some social scientists allowed them to face the new immigration with relative equanimity, others disdained the new immigrants, worried about "race suicide," and urged immigration restriction. Racial anxiety cut across the distinctions between positivists and historicists, left and right. Clark ignored racial issues, but his marginalist colleagues Irving Fisher and Frank Fetter, and his historicist opponents Simon Patten and John R. Commons, succumbed to them. Likewise, Albion Small stood above the fray, while his friend Edward A. Ross and his opponent Franklin Giddings were leaders of the racist charge.

The widening social discord was aggravated by the breakdown of Victorian gender roles. Women entered the workforce and the precincts of higher education in unprecedented numbers and mounted an increasingly aggressive campaign for suffrage. In the new factories and cities, traditional behavior patterns began to loosen and the divorce rate climbed. We have already noted that Albion Small declared the monogamous family contested ground. The sociologists were particularly sensitive to the ramifying social effects of industrialism, and Small tellingly described the resulting sense of value crisis. The problem, he said, was the breakdown of the older Protestant standard of values, the fragmentation of society into a multiplicity of ethnic groups and functional roles, each of which provided a different framework of values and viewpoints from which to understand the world. More than that, these conflicting values had polarized around a set of fundamental problems:

We are dealing in modern society with certain radical questions; e.g., Shall we aim for physical enjoyment, or for extinction of sensuous desire? Shall we posit an ideal of government or no government? Shall we plan for private property or communism,

---

4 Amasa Walker, *The Science of Wealth* (Boston: Little, Brown, 1866), 462–4; Francis A. Walker, *Political Economy* (New York: Holt, 1884), 282–3; idem, "Immigration and Degradation," in *Discussions in Economics and Statistics*, 2 vols., ed. Davis R. Dewey (New York: Augustus M. Kelley, 1971 [1899]), 2:424–5.

for monopoly or competition, for freedom of thought or for perpetual social chaperoning of mind and conscience? These are not questions of biology, or civics, or economics, or theology. They are not questions of ways and means. They are not problems of how to do things. They are questions of what is fit to do.[5]

The problem of values worked beneath the surface of Progressive optimism to deepen the sense of social dislocation.

As the national urban society brought the conflicting social and ethnic groups into contact, marks of individual and group status became more important and social tensions exacerbated. The era is filled with Veblen's "conspicuous consumption," with exclusive organizational and association-al patterns, and with conflicts between city, town, and rural district, as well as racial and ethnic hostilities.

Each class or section of the nation is becoming conscious of an opposition between its standards and the activities and tendencies of some less developed class. The South has its negro, the city has its slums, organized labor has its "scab" workman, and the temperance movement has its drunkard and saloon-keeper. The friends of American institutions fear the ignorant immigrant, and the workingman dislikes the Chinese. Every one is beginning to differentiate those with proper qualifications for citizenship from some class or classes which he wishes to restrain or to exclude from society.[6]

The observation is from Simon Patten in 1896 and betrayed – not quite as he intended – the divisive social tendencies of the time. Here was the destructive side of American pluralism that fueled the new liberal search for a social ethic.

By the turn of the century, social and industrial upheaval were producing a profound recognition of historical change. The new industrial nation that America had become was clearly visible and the rapidity of change was everywhere remarked. "One can hardly believe there has been a revolution in all history so rapid, so extensive, so complete," Dewey marveled in 1899. The sense of disjunction with the past was expressed on all levels of culture, and vividly in the public historical pageants that were mounted by Progressive reformers throughout the country. As David Glassberg has shown, "historical pageants imaginatively situated their audiences on the verge of a new era in which the customary relations between social classes, institutions, and interests would be transformed, while promising that the new society would be no more than the inevitable outgrowth of those of the past." Yet in spite of the effort to construct a reassuring vision of continuity, the pageants

5 Albion W. Small, "The Significance of Sociology for Ethics," *Decennial Publications of the University of Chicago*, lst ser., no. 4 (1903): 5–6, 23–4.
6 Simon N. Patten, "The Theory of Social Forces," *AAAPSS*, 7, Suppl. (January 1896): 143.

inadvertently disclosed how distant the past was becoming and how uncertain the future. Placing local American history within a symbolic framework chosen eclectically from classical, medieval, and modern history, from Europe and America, the reformers' artificial constructions betrayed their sense of disconnection from the past.[7]

Progressive social scientists found a more coherent way to understand and tame this new world, in liberal theories of history. Modernity was indeed different, but it was the outgrowth of progressive historical forces. America's ideal future could be attached to the great engines of modern progress: the capitalist market, social diversification, democracy, and scientific knowledge. Turning away from the original focus on advancing commercial and industrial corruption that threatened American perfection, they joined the general European movement toward modern development. In accepting the necessity and the promise of living in the new industrial world, social scientists expressed a new trust in the secular forces at work beneath the chaos of change and a new confidence in their ability to understand and shape the future. The decline of the Gilded Age sense of apocalyptic crisis and the Progressive confidence to address the problems of industrialization were bound up with this change in historical consciousness.

Many social scientists were aware of this shift, but no one addressed the new liberal historicism more directly and rejected the older exceptionalism more forcefully than E. R. A. Seligman, one of the architects of the new view. Speaking as president of the American Economic Association in 1902, he attacked

the opinion either explicitly or implicitly shared by many of our thoughtful fellow citizens that this country has in some way a distinctive mission to perform, and that we are marked off from the rest of the world by certain inherent principles, relative indeed, in the sense of being peculiar to America, but eternal and immutable in their relation to ourselves.

Well, said Seligman, "we have been largely living in a fool's paradise." There is nothing "inherent" in our democracy, Puritan character, or love of liberty. All these characteristics are dependent "on the shifting conditions of time and place." When economic conditions were ripe for slavery, as in the American South, our liberty-loving people embraced it: "What a ghastly mockery" of the "so-called Anglo-Saxon love of liberty." Indeed, the "boasted Anglo-Saxon individualism" was fast becoming socialism or close

---

7 John Dewey, *The School and Society* (1899), in *MW*, 1:6; David Glassberg, "History and the Public: Legacies of the Progressive Era," *JAH*, 73 (March 1987): 957–80; Timothy Dalton, "The Ever-Receding Past: Americans Review 'The Wonderful Century,'" Seminar paper, University of Virginia.

to it where conditions encouraged it, as in Australia and New Zealand. The historicity of the past, Seligman went on, cast the future into history. Many say that our future will be merely a new feudalism, or they point to Rome and say prosperity must be followed by decay and decline. But America should now be understood as a modern society and there were essential conditions which "differentiate modern industrial society from all its predecessors." More pointedly than anyone had before him, this Jewish-American cosmopolitan declared that "the American of the future will bear but little resemblance to the American of the past."[8]

Under the impact of liberal historicism, the idea of America itself changed in decisive ways. Liberal history located the American ideal more fully in the future than in the past and made achievement of the future into the distinctive American task. The American experience was no longer conceived as altogether exceptional, but was joined to the stream of Western liberal history. Given the long investment in the exceptionalist ideal, however, we will not be surprised to find that this effort to carry America into the mainstream of modern history was hardly complete or unequivocal. So long as the ideal of American perfection lived on, so long as Americans continued to fear the dangers of trusting that ideal to history, the logic of American exceptionalism remained relevant. Liberal history was itself premised on the recognition that most nations had failed to progress and had often tied liberal progress to natural law, and these characteristics of liberal discourse reinforced exceptionalist themes. Hence exceptionalism survived in the utopian ideal ambiguously both present and potential in American society. It survived in the willingness to place America at the forefront or the quintessential center of liberal change and to cast universal progress in specifically American shapes, so that America retained its exemplary or vanguard role in world history. It survived in the continuing need to deny the existence of class conflict. And it survived in the lingering fears of decline and the flight from history to nature, where science promised control.

Ironically, liberal historicism, designed to tame the uncertainty of history, deepened the gulf between the liberal future and the American past. Seligman soon recognized that the modern future had not fully arrived nor the exceptionalist past disappeared. America is "at once the youngest and the oldest of economic societies" he said in 1905. While still in many ways a frontier society, in industrial organization "America is leading the world and

---

8 E. R. A. Seligman, "Economics and Social Progress," *PAEA*, 3d ser., 4 (February 1903): 52–70, particularly 55–7, 59–60.

is showing other countries what stages they have still to traverse." This graft of "the modern industrial system" onto "persistent primitive stock" made the present "confusing."

> Because of this contest of the old with the new, we are in many respects still groping in the dark, dissatisfied in the more progressive communities with the survivals of old conditions, and trying to discern in the dim light of the future the final expression of the newer conditions which are soon to become universal.[9]

The uncertain valences of Seligman's language reveal the confusion, for in the older exceptionalist paradigm, the primitive and the agrarian stages were "new" and the advancing industrial stage, "old." Now, however, the primitive agrarian past became old and the industrial world, new. Americans were turning, to face forward into history rather than back toward nature.

Liberal historicism increasingly oriented them to the future and rendered their past obsolete. There was no more characteristic refrain of the Progressive Era than that economic changes had created a world unknown to the founders and that new industrial conditions required new practices. As Progressive reform advanced and then slowed, the desire to discard the outmoded American past for the liberal future was expressed with increasing urgency. That was the message of Herbert Croly's *The Promise of American Life:* If the American promise was to be fulfilled, American practice would have to change.

Croly's 1909 book, long considered the representative text of the Progressive movement, is also the representative text of the transformation of American exceptionalism. It was generated by the new historical consciousness and new exceptionalist task. Centered in a liberal understanding of modern history, it began to read all of American history in a liberal light. And it expressed its exceptionalist ideas in a modern language. For the social scientists we have thus far considered, the idea of American exceptionalism was rooted in a millennial and republican language that had remained vital in the education and public discussion of their youth and college years. During the Progressive period we begin to find younger social thinkers like Croly who seem to know that language but view it at some remove. The nationalist idea of America continued to animate them, but the older liberal-republican language that had provided the original context for that idea had begun to thin. Students in the new social science programs of the 1890s, they worked within the paradigms of their university professors and expressed their

---

9 E. R. A. Seligman, *Principles of Economics* (New York: Longmans Green, 1905), 108.

exceptionalist hopes or lingering fears of decline in one of the new languages of academic social science or a journalistic translation thereof.[10]

Croly began by defining the promise of America in terms that make clear that the national ideology of American exceptionalism was still very much alive. "The faith of Americans in their own country is religious," Croly began. "It pervades the air we breathe." It consists first of all, he said, in "a promise of comfort and prosperity for an ever increasing majority of good Americans"; then in liberty, "free political institutions," and finally, that these conditions would create "a worthier set of men." The experiment was of "more than national importance. The American system stands for the highest hope of an excellent worldly life that mankind has yet ventured." Croly emphasized that Americans had traditionally tied this universal ideal to the past. "Our national responsibility consists fundamentally in remaining true to traditional ways of behavior, standards, and ideals ... to continue resolutely and cheerfully along the appointed path." Americans believed that along that path "the familiar benefits will continue to accumulate automatically." They hold to an "optimistic fatalism."[11]

What is striking in Croly's book is the modern language in which the idea of America was expressed and its grounding in a liberal economic interpretation of history. Croly never thought to ask why Americans' civic faith was "religious" or why they constructed a "fatalistic" universal ideal tied to the past. For Croly, the promise of economic opportunity and prosperity was the foundation of the idea of America. Free political institutions "became in a sense the guarantee that prosperity would continue to be abundant and accessible." The central idea that economic ownership was the basis of both economic and political freedom was blurred, replaced by a generalized ideal of "comfort and prosperity." Croly seemed to be reading back to the

10 Paul Bourke suggests that Croly and his journalistic cohort developed "a new language for the expression of familiar propositions" in order to establish their new social role, that of "independent social criticism." Paul F. Bourke, "The Social Crisis and the End of American Innocence: 1907–1921," *Journal of American Studies*, 3 (1969): 57–73. Daniel Walker Howe has suggested that the decline of the traditional liberal-republican discourse was linked to the decline of classical education at the end of the nineteenth century – Latin being a major carrier of republican discourse. The collapse of moral philosophy in the colleges would have had correlative effects. Daniel Walker Howe, "Classical Education and Political Culture in Nineteenth Century America," *Intellectual History Group Newsletter*, no. 5 (Spring 1983): 9–14. John Patrick Diggins, *The Lost Soul of American Politics* (New York: Basic, 1984), chronicles the lingering death of republicanism in America from 1789 to World War I, a rather long demise. I believe that Diggins' insight into the pragmatic and Darwinian language of American social discourse during the Progressive Era, as well as his evidence of the persistence of old issues, can best be understood as consequences of the reformulation of the national ideology of American exceptionalism on a liberal basis.

11 Herbert Croly, *The Promise of American Life* (New York: Macmillan, 1909), chap. 1, particularly pp. 1, 10, 12, 13, 5, 17, 18.

beginning of American history the liberal economic conception of history that had emerged from the Gilded Age. "Specialized organization" was the central problem of the "current situation," but he skirted the issue of the overspecialized factory worker, and focused on the liberal problem of achieving cohesion among a society composed of special interests. Nationalism was a republican cure for this liberal malady, but speaking within a historical and linguistic context already separated from the liberal-republican discourse of the nineteenth century, he had begun to reconstruct American history in the liberal image.

Yet beneath this new, liberal substance, we can still sense the force of an older imagination. The idea of America remained the end toward which all Croly's history and politics moved. Nationalism remained the vital source of social solidarity for his liberal democracy, as it had always been for the earlier republic. And when at the end an apocalyptic note appeared, as Croly hoped for the appearance of some "democratic evangelist – some imitator of Jesus who will reveal to men the path whereby they may enter into spiritual possession of their individual and social achievements," we know that the millennial identification of the American Republic can continue to animate even the language of liberal individualism in the twentieth century.[12]

Progressive Era social scientists turned deliberately to the classical liberal tradition to revise their exceptionalist heritage. Classical economics and its marginalist revision provided a model of the capitalist market as a creation of freely acting individual wills. The ability to sell one's labor, not the ownership of productive resources, provided the basis of autonomy. Liberal theory cast political democracy as the work of sovereign individuals in voluntary association. The scientific enterprise was likewise premised on the rational capacity of individuals. Social scientists returned to these individualist foundations both to set the fundamental character of American society and to provide the basis for a socially harmonious order.

Some of the strategies that would be used to construct a new, socialized liberalism had already been broached by the turn of the century in Clark's modernized conception of the market as "invisible hand"; Henry Carter Adams' effort to enlarge the principle of personal responsibility to include workers' rights and the social actions of corporations; and Giddings' use of Adam Smith's concept of sympathy to create a socialized individual. We will see these and other similar strategies fully developed in the Progressive Era, along with the effort to make public authority more effective by rationalizing republican institutions of governance. In its historical form, liberal theory followed the lead of Herbert Spencer's evolution toward diversity, indi-

12 Ibid., 11, 126, 138–9, 453–4, and chap. 5.

viduality, and social harmony. The functional interdependence of the market and the increasing opportunities for social communication, exchange, and mobility were creating a modern society that supported both individual autonomy and the amelioration of conflict.

The liberal response to the crisis of American exceptionalism produced a wide spectrum of theory and belief. On the right, theorists argued that the capitalist market, with its competitive incentives, private goals, and unequal rewards, determined the character of individual autonomy and set the terms for social harmony. On the left, social democrats hoped that the liberal society and democratic polity would change the terms of competition, infuse private goals with public purposes, and redistribute income more equally, while still retaining the capitalist market under private ownership. Abandoning the political economy of the older exceptionalism, the social democrats retained its expansive ideal. "Self-possession" became a social product and sociality the test of individuality. It was precisely in the attempt to transform possessive individualism into social harmony that these theorists expressed their highest ideals, encountered their greatest difficulties, and opened themselves to ideological mystification. For left and right alike, the pressures of American exceptionalism repeatedly obscured the difficulties of transformation.

One support of the Progressive view of liberal history was the evolutionary anthropology that had reigned through the late nineteenth century. During this era we will see social scientists begin to exploit the resources of anthropology more deliberately to strengthen their theories of history as well as to develop a critical scientific method. Stretching the record of history back to its sources in nature, anthropology offered social scientists inclined to evolutionary theory what seemed to be a scientific grounding. Racial anthropology was taken up in support of biological theories of race. In other cases, what would soon be called "culture," the mores and folkways of different peoples, captured social scientific attention. Veblen, we shall see, was relatively unique among social scientists in adapting from anthropology not only its evolutionary theories, but also its stance of the alien observer.[13]

One new component of the liberal arsenal that will make its first appearance in Progressive social science is functional psychology. Psychology had played a central role in social science from its origins, when Hume urged a search for the universal constancies and variations of human nature and Mill reaffirmed that basis for the moral sciences. Historico-politics was thought to rest, at some distance, on the principles of human nature. Classical

13 On anthropology, see George W. Stocking, Jr., *Victorian Anthropology* (New York: Free Press, 1987) and *Race, Culture and Evolution* (New York: Free Press, 1968).

economics had been understood to build upon a selected set of psychological propensities and a major variant of marginalism claimed utilitarian psychology as its source. By the same token, historical and sociological critics of classical economics had turned to a wider range of psychological motives to reconstruct social science. When American psychologists in the 1890s began to develop a new functional psychology, therefore, the most alert social scientists began to explore its implications for their own traditions.

Functional psychology was developed in the work of William James and John Dewey, the seminal study of child development by James Mark Baldwin, and the studies of perception and attention emerging from the new psychological laboratories, but it owed its fundamental inspiration to Charles Darwin. Psychology had to be understood, according to the new functionalists, as a dimension of biological evolution. The mind was an organ of adaptation. This meant, first, that the mind was an active purposive agent in its transactions with the environment, and second, that the mind sought always to adjust to a changing social environment. From the first proposition psychologists and social scientists could construct an active individual, possessor of a unique will and capable of changing the surrounding environment to rational specifications. From the second proposition they could construct a socialized individual, habituated to the social environment and drawn toward the rational consensus adjustment enforced. Hence this model of self-acting components could approach either of the two poles of liberal and functionalist theory, by emphasizing the creative rationality of the actors or the rationality imposed by the environment, by pointing rational adjustment toward the ongoing parameters of the system or its changing character.[14]

Both poles were of use in the liberal theory of historical change in which functional psychology was often placed. As we have seen, the model of liberal progress offered by Smith and Spencer gave a key role to economic development and its increasing mastery over nature. The theory of progress developed in France made reason the dynamic power in history, and John Stuart Mill's essay *On Liberty* (1859) gave reason a social setting. Progress was generated by creative individuals who challenged the customary, conventional ideas that ruled the society around them. After Spencer, and

14 Edna Heidbreder, *Seven Psychologies* (Englewood Cliffs, N.J.: Prentice-Hall, 1961 [1933]); Robert J. Richards, *Darwin and the Emergence of Evolutionary Theories of Mind and Behavior* (Chicago: University of Chicago Press, 1987), chaps. 9, 10, and p. 6. The tendency of American social science to emphasize the social determinism in functional psychologies has been traced back to Talcott Parsons, but in fact began in the 1890s. See Dennis H. Wrong, "The Oversocialized Conception of Man in Modern Sociology," *ASR*, 26 (April 1961): 183–92.

particularly after Darwin, these classic models of liberal history were reshaped to Darwin's vision of evolution through adaptation and natural selection, a key text in the transformation being Walter Bagehot's *Physics and Politics* (1872).

The economic realm could easily be seen as the historical locus of natural selection. "The hist[orical] fact that Malthus suggested Darwin is significant," Dewey told his students. "Now biology transfers its ideas to economics."[15] In the hands of sociologists like Giddings, economics extended to society, so that the agent of selection became not only the economic struggle for existence but the social matrix of association and differentiation. At the same time, Mill's creative rationality was increasingly understood as Darwinian adaptation. Economic, social, and scientific invention became initiators of change and rational responses to a changing environment. Most Progressive social scientists, whether they emphasized selection or rational adjustment, found a progressive norm in historical evolution. Like Burke's prescriptive history, evolution was thought to carry forward those forms found useful or usefully adjusted in historical experience. At the same time, the changing historical environment put a premium on the creative rationality that produced readjustment. Historical evolution on the Darwinian model allowed for the normative course of American history and for liberal change.

For Progressive Era social scientists, as for their predecessors, the problem of historical change was bound up with the problem of intellectual authority. American social scientists had placed their faith in realism, science, and professionalism to provide authoritative knowledge of the modern world. If a sense of "disinheritance" had turned Gilded Age social scientists away from conventional knowledge to seek reality in the facts before them, realism became even more powerful as Progressive social scientists looked at the strange industrial world. The new concentrations of economic power, the teeming, polyglot cities, and the expansion of urban, state, and federal governance created new worlds that required detailed knowledge. The great preponderance of social scientists' publications during these years were empirical studies of the concrete operation of business, government, and social life.

Amid social fragmentation and disparate moral standards, science still appeared to promise agreement. The conception of scientific method that prevailed was best, and most influentially, articulated by Karl Pearson in his *Grammar of Science* (1892). At one level, Pearson's conception of science

---

15 "John Dewey, Political Philosophy Lectures, 1893," transcribed by Charles Horton Cooley, Charles Horton Cooley Papers, University of Michigan.

could be comfortably absorbed by American readers. He offered the assurance that social science could be every bit as "scientific" as natural science. "The field of science is unlimited ... every group of natural phenomena, every phase of social life, every stage of past or present development is material for science." This was true, he argued, because "The unity of all science consists alone in its method, not in its material."

The method Pearson offered was the reigning version of Baconian empiricism, presumably as exemplified in both Darwin and Newton. Science was a matter of collection and classification of facts, the formulation of laws by logical inference from those facts, and their critical scrutiny. "The smallest group of facts, if properly classified and logically dealt with, will form a stone which has its proper place in the great building of knowledge," he promised. Beyond this procedure, scientific method seemed to require only a resolute stance of objectivity. Science should banish all "metaphysics," all "personal feeling or class bias," all merely aesthetic goals. One of the defining characteristics of science and the measure of its usefulness was that it "leads us to classifications and systems independent of the individual thinker, to sequences and laws admitting of no play-room for individual fancy." The basic thrust of such a program was to encourage Progressive social scientists on the path they had started, and to strengthen their desire to prune "metaphysics" and bias from their formulations.[16]

The major Progressive thinkers continued to believe that human nature and historical evolution embodied norms that science would be able to reveal or construct. Some, like Albion Small, remained conscious of the ethical nature of that normative task and hence of the ethical role of the social scientist. Other Progressive social scientists, like Irving Fisher, believed they could speak prescriptively in the name of science, both in their theoretical and expert roles. Accepting the positivist caution against metaphysics and bias, they rejected not only an ethical social role but also an openly ethical interpretation of their subject. The norms they found in the market, social evolution, and history appeared to them to be the findings of science rather than ethics. One of the solvents of this view was the critical positivism Pearson advanced in his book, for the empirical positivist program was only part of what Pearson had to offer. Except for the philosopher Dewey, and Giddings, who was attracted to Pearson's statistical method, however, the first American social scientists to understand Pearson's more advanced ideas were those critics of progressivism we will meet in Part IV of this book. It will not be until the 1920s that critical positivism, disillusion

16 Karl Pearson, *The Grammar of Science* (London: Walter Scott, 1892), 15, 16, 39–41, ix, 9, 12.

with politics, and the anxieties of history will lead social scientists to try to divorce science from value altogether and to place the presumably neutral scientific expert at the disposal of other people's values.

Professionalism, like science, continued to promise Progressive social scientists intellectual and social authority, but again at a price. In part as a result of the concern for professional status, in part as a reflection of the prejudices that still dominated academia, those outside the respectable male white Protestant class were often denied access to professional careers. In terms of numbers, the chief casualty to professionalization were women. Between 1890 and 1900, the number of women taking graduate courses in all fields nearly doubled, to 30 percent, and a larger proportion than formerly were undoubtedly now enrolled in regular degree programs. Sociology matched the national average and most likely claimed a larger share of women than economics and political science. By and large these women graduates were steered to social work and reform activities or to the women's colleges, precincts the men were defining as outside the scientific and academic mainstream. There, despite pressure to adopt the trappings of science and professionalism, women social scientists sometimes managed to keep open the lines to social democratic activism and to explore heterodox ideas.[17]

In the national urban society that was forming around the turn of the century, the authority of professional social scientists stood more clearly than it had before on their function, their ability to purvey expert knowledge, rather than their ties to an authoritative class and culture. They had quickly put down roots in the expanding universities, established professional societies, and strengthened professional credentials, although public influence was slower in coming. As a class of intellectuals divorced from formal political power, they had to prove their usefulness. Still, by the turn of the century, conservative and liberal economists were starting to be called as experts to investigatory and regulatory commissions and America's entry onto the stage of international imperialism appeared to open a wide field to expert service. Progressive reform opened the gates further to social scientific expertise.

As academic professionals, Progressive social scientists spoke increasingly to each other in specialized journals and meetings, and as professional experts, they directed their advice increasingly to policy-makers and officials, rather than to the public at large. But it was not until the 1920s that

---

17 J. Graham Morgan, "Women in American Sociology in the 19th Century," *JHS*, 2 (Spring 1980): 7; Mary Jo Deegan, "Sociology at Wellesley College: 1900–1919," *JHS*, 5 (Spring 1983): 91–117; Ellen F. Fitzpatrick, *Endless Crusade: Women Social Scientists and Progressive Reform* (New York: Oxford University Press, 1990); and Chapter 4, n. 5, above.

professionalism dominated social science discourse. As in the Gilded Age, many social scientists continued to address respectable middle- and upper-class audiences in public journals, reform organizations, and educational convocations. The AEA no longer wanted to meet at Chautauqua, but some of its members continued to teach there. The social scientists' largest middle- and upper-class audience was their students, and it gave textbooks a large place in their scholarly production. Even as experts in reform organizations and before legislative and regulatory commissions, Progressive social scientists were less autonomous professionals, than one among many new middle-class participants in the political process. As a result, the moral and political implications of what they said remained extremely important to them, and their professional claim to objectivity continued to be vulnerable.[18]

The principal solution to the problem of objectivity remained in force: The academic disciplines narrowed the ideological spectrum permitted within their ranks. However, the Progressive center itself widened during the era, allowing a considerable range of ideologically freighted issues into the social scientific arena. The political scientists, with their more conservative sympathies, had the least difficulty with these issues, but even they, as progressivism advanced, occasionally erupted into conflict.

Professionalism itself provided a number of tactical defenses against ideological controversy. The simplest was retreat in the name of specialization or scientific standards. When a provocative paper at the AEA raised the possibility that liberal reforms were leading toward socialism, some commentators simply refused to address the issue on the grounds of "scientific modesty"; the economists themselves could neither reach nor enforce a definition of socialism, they said. Or when a controversial position was presented at meetings, the reformist position could be assigned to a popular reformer like Frederic C. Howe or Crystal Eastman, leaving the professionals free to point out the scientific difficulties in the way. The social scientists did, however, become increasingly accustomed to dealing with contested issues through the mechanism of balance. Albion Small made sure that whenever a left-liberal position appeared in his *American Journal of*

18 A. W. Coats, "The First Two Decades of the American Economic Association," *AER*, 50 (September 1960): 571–2; Mary Furner, *Advocacy and Objectivity* (Lexington: University Press of Kentucky, 1975), 265–72; Robert L. Church, "Economists as Experts: The Rise of an Academic Profession in the United States, 1870–1920," in *The University in Society*, vol. 2: *Europe, Scotland, and the United States from the 16th to the 20th Century*, ed. Lawrence Stone (Princeton, N.J.: Princeton University Press, 1974), 571–609. On the changing character of professions in this period, see Terence J. Johnson, *Professions and Power* (London: Macmillan, 1972); Magali Sarfatti Larson, *The Rise of Professionalism: A Social Analysis* (Berkeley: University of California Press, 1977), chaps. 1, 2.

*Sociology* it was soon followed by a conservative counter, and discussions at the professional meetings were often similarly structured. When a spokesman for the left or right could not be found in the profession, an outsider would be brought in. If biases could not be eliminated from a contested issue, they could at least be treated with impartiality. The professionals could claim that the issue, still laden with "opinion," had not yet achieved scientific formulation.[19]

They also put considerable trust in the immobilizing effects of scientific discourse. Albert Shaw may have been carried somewhat away when, speaking as president to the political scientists in 1906, he asserted that "Nobody cares any longer whether members of an association like this are classed as republicans or democrats ... socialists, or individualists; municipal traders, or anti-public-ownership men," but to some degree he was right about the workings of professionalization. We recognize, he went on, that scientific students have "a large common stock of sincerity and of intelligence, and a habit of mind which checks controversial attitudes and faddish enthusiasms."[20] Even where radical opinion survived, so long as activism was eschewed, it could occasionally be admitted within professional boundaries. When the conservative J. Laurence Laughlin sustained Veblen's appointment at Chicago or when Frank Taussig gave Veblen access to the pages of the *Quarterly Journal of Economics*, they were displaying not only a professional respect for intellectual standards but also a recognition that professional standards of intellectual discourse helped to contain the potentially explosive ideological impulse. Indeed we will see in Part IV that the economists paid for this strategy with two decades of controversy with Veblen's institutionalist disciples, but in the end, their confidence in professional containment was not misplaced.

The professionalization of American social science should be understood not only as an ally of science in the search for authority, but also as a product of the structure of American society. The extremely rapid growth and professionalization of the social sciences as academic disciplines in America clearly owes a great deal to America's expanding, decentralized university

19 Martin, "An Attempt to Define Socialism – Discussion," 355–6, 365; Frederick C. Howe, "The Case for Municipal Ownership," *PAEA*, 3d ser., 7 (February 1906): 113–32 and "Discussion," 133–59; Crystal Eastman, "The American Way of Distributing Industrial Accident Losses," *PAEA*, 3d ser., 10 (April 1909): 119–34 and "Discussion," 105–18, 135–57. See also the invitation to Lindley M. Keasbey to participate in the session on competition: "If a sober socialist can be found, let us invite him to share in the discussion." *PPASS*, 2 (1907): 33, and the exchange of letters between Frank Goodnow and Frank W. Taussig, June 3, 12, 13, 1905, and October 19, 1905, Frank J. Goodnow Papers, Johns Hopkins University.
20 Albert Shaw, "Presidential Address," *APSR*, 1 (February 1907): 185–6.

system and its capitalist and middle-class support. In England an aristocratic class resisted university innovation and expansion, and in France and Germany centralized state authority controlled growth and made appointments in new subjects adjunct to traditional fields. In contrast, American capitalists, modernizers, and politicians quickly recognized the economic and social benefits of modern knowledge and supported a rapid expansion of higher education. Between 1890 and 1940, the percentage of college-age students attending colleges or universities rose from 2 to 15 percent. The decentralized American colleges, competing for students and prestige, allowed the new disciplines to multiply quickly and establish their independence.[21]

It can be argued that this decentralized institutional structure was itself responsible for the scientistic orientation of American social science. In Europe, the social science disciplines were kept in close touch with philosophy and history through subordinate appointments and controlled examination systems. In American universities they were freed from traditional ties and able to drift toward the magnet of modern knowledge, natural science. But the decentralized university structure alone cannot account for this drift without taking into account the culture within which it existed. The social sciences in Europe were attracted to the better-developed disciplines not only by institutional ties but by intellectual force. In Germany and France philosophy and history had already broken from theology, established strong modern traditions of scholarship, and won national claims to cultural prestige. In England, the ideal of widely cultivated learning imbedded in aristocratic culture kept new subjects within the orbit of the traditional compartments of knowledge. In the United States, however, under the lingering influence of Protestant religiosity and exceptionalist historical consciousness, neither philosophy nor history had fully modernized in the nineteenth century and hence had developed neither the intellectual nor institutional power to attract their offspring.

Finally, we should note that professionalism and decentralized institutions produced increasing separatism in the social science disciplines, although diversity in substance and method continued within each of the disciplines and practitioners could still follow intellectual interests across disciplinary lines. Professionalism worked, however, upon traditions of inquiry that already had long and partially independent histories. It helped to draw those traditions apart, but along intellectual fault lines already present. The cultural context within which professionalization occurred will

21 Bernard Berelson, *Graduate Education in the United States* (New York: McGraw-Hill, 1960), chaps. 1, 2; Joseph Ben-David and Awraham Zloczower, "Universities and Academic Systems in Modern Societies," *European Journal of Sociology*, 3 (1962): 45–84.

be particularly important when we note, as we go on, some of the different patterns of development that occurred in the social sciences in the United States, England, France, and Germany.

## Dewey's pragmatism

John Dewey is in many ways the best exemplar of the development of Progressive Era social science. He surely demonstrates the still porous character of the social science disciplines in this period. A philosopher with some training in psychology, he taught and thought as many in this period did, across disciplinary lines. His interest in turning philosophy into a kind of social science as well as the far-ranging implications of his functional psychology, organic model of society, and pragmatist philosophy made his work influential on all the human sciences. Most important, Dewey's pragmatism, like the characteristic doctrines of Progressive social science, emerged directly from the Gilded Age crisis of American exceptionalism and revised the exceptionalist heritage to embody the new liberal and historicist awareness of change. Indeed, where Dewey parts company with most social scientists is precisely in the rapidity and the depth of his response to historicism. Dewey's influence appeared in the Progressive Era, but many social scientists were not prepared to appreciate his pragmatist solution or to fully embrace it. The distance that will remain between Dewey and the main body of American social science is a significant measure of how reluctant the social science disciplines were to come fully to grips with historicism. Yet Dewey himself is an exception who proves the rule, for his response to historicism remained in crucial ways linked to the exceptionalist heritage and the main line of social scientific advance.

Dewey was a liberal member of the ethically oriented generation of the 1880s, and like them, his mind was formed by the Gilded Age crisis in intellectual authority and politics. Raised to tender conscience by a pious mother, then drawn toward evolutionary science in graduate school, Dewey's moral earnestness grew as his faith in its traditional Christian support crumbled. His road from Christianity to naturalism was mediated by Hegelian idealism and Hegel also linked his philosophical and political concerns.[22] The economic and political conflicts of the Gilded Age were a

---

22 On Dewey's development, see Neil Coughlan, *Young John Dewey: An Essay in American Intellectual History* (Chicago: University of Chicago Press, 1975); Bruce Kuklick, *Churchmen and Philosophers: From Jonathan Edwards to John Dewey* (New Haven, Conn.: Yale University Press, 1985), pt. 3. George Dykhuizen, *The Life and Mind of John Dewey* (Carbondale: Southern Illinois University Press, 1973) is a reliable biography, which also provides entry into the voluminous literature on Dewey.

more important context for Dewey's pragmatism than most interpreters have recognized. He felt his "disinheritance," the strain between inherited dogmas and the world around him, as a profound separation of self and other, ideal and reality, which set him on a lifelong effort to abolish dualisms. His early essays show clearly that the threat to the American political tradition in the Gilded Age was one source of his unease and a principal dimension of his reconstructive efforts.

Sensing a "break between the beliefs of educated men, and the actual tendency of political organisms," Dewey entered the lists in the mid-1880s as a defender of democracy against its conservative critics. Bringing an Hegelian conception of history to the support of democracy, he argued that history was enacting the American millennial ideal. Democracy, he said, was "the one, the ultimate, ethical ideal of humanity." Progressively realized in history, it was at once potential in the present and the unrealized ideal toward which all history moved. Democracy "approaches most nearly the ideal of all social organization; that in which the individual and society are organic to each other." Such an organic society was not an authoritarian state nor a biological organism. The "type of an organism" was human society, because in it the parts are fully individualized, yet each voluntarily joins his will with the whole in cooperative, coordinated action. This is the theory "that every citizen is a sovereign, the American theory, a doctrine which in grandeur has but one equal in history, and that its fellow, namely, that every man is a priest of God." Indeed, going beyond the American Republic and the Protestant Reformation, Dewey located the ideal in Greek civic humanism.

> The Republic ... seizes upon the heart of the ethical problem, the relation of the individual to the universal, and states a solution.... Such a development of the individual that he shall be in harmony with all others in the state, that is, that he shall possess as his own the unified will of the community; that is the end both of politics and of ethics.... This is not loss of selfhood or personality, it is its realization. The individual is not sacrificed; he is brought to reality in the state.

If Dewey slid imperceptibly here from the Aristotelian and American Republic to the Platonic republic of "unified will," it is probably because behind this revival of civic humanism was the Kingdom of God. The idea of democracy, he closed fervently, is "a society in which the distinction between the spiritual and the secular has ceased, and as in Greek theory, as in the Christian theory of the Kingdom of God, the church and the state, the divine and the human organization of society are one."[23]

23 John Dewey, "The Ethics of Democracy" (1888), in *EW*, 1:227, 237–49.

As a young instructor at the University of Michigan, Dewey expanded his defense of democracy. The example of the striking worker soon became prominent in his ethical essays. "There is no need to beat about the bush in saying that democracy is not in reality what it is in name until it is industrial, as well as civil and political," he said. "A democracy of wealth is a necessity." During these same years he taught political science and welcomed "the growing emphasis upon ethics as a political science, and politics as an ethical science." If "personal insight and preference" are essential to moral conduct, then we must place "an equal emphasis upon securing such conditions of action as will bring personal insight and choice really and not simply nominally within the power of the individual."[24]

Dewey was encouraged by his colleague Henry Carter Adams, but more powerfully by two wandering reformers, Franklin and Corydon Ford, who settled in Ann Arbor between 1888 and 1892 and planned with him what they imagined to be a revolutionary newspaper, "Thought News." The Fords were dissatisfied journalists who believed that a newspaper that objectively disseminated social "facts" could hasten the movement of modern society toward organic interdependence and vaguely syndicalist organization. Dewey saw in this project a way to turn his democratic philosophy into practical action.[25]

Neil Coughlan has traced the breakthrough in Dewey's adoption of a pragmatic approach in philosophy to his 1891 philosophy syllabus, written during the "Thought News" period. In that syllabus Dewey claimed that philosophy is, like science, an inquiry into experience and he proposed to reconstruct philosophy along the lines indicated in experience.

In two directions, the whole is now more definitely realized than ever before.... On one hand, science has revealed to us, in outline, at least, the type action of the individual organism, the process involved in every complete act. On the other hand, as life has become freer, social action has revealed the principle involved in it. The action of the psycho-physical and of the political body, in other words, give us ... perception of the whole.[26]

Dewey is proposing here that experience be understood by an examination of action and that the most revealing models of action were the scientific model of the psycho-physical act of thinking and the organic sociohistorical model of progress. Dewey's dual focus, like the language he still used, owed

24 Ibid., 246; idem, "Moral Theory and Practice" (1891), *EW*, 3:105–9; idem, "Ethics and Politics" (1894), *EW*, 4:372–3. See also John Dewey, "Two Phases of Renan's Life" (1892), *EW*, 3:174–9.
25 Coughlan, *Young John Dewey*, chap. 6.
26 John Dewey, "Introduction to Philosophy: Syllabus of Course 5" (1892), *EW*, 3:212.

a great deal to Hegel. That there should be a "type action" revealed both in the individual psyche and in the movement of history is the vision of Hegel's phenomenology of mind and spirit. The movement of individual consciousness from ego to non-ego to constituted experience and the movement of reason in history from thesis to antithesis to synthesis followed an interactive, reciprocal, and dynamic pattern that knit together subjectivity and objectivity, individual and society, past and future. Dewey's pragmatic reason would follow the same paths and perform the same functions.[27]

Dewey reset this Hegelian philosophy in the evolutionary natural world disclosed by Darwin. The mind was an organ of adaptation, moved by interest and purpose, and aroused "only because of practical friction or strain somewhere." Thinking was "the critical point of progress in action, arising whenever old habits are in process of reconstruction, or of adaptation to new conditions." Drawing on James's pragmatic philosophy as well as his functional psychology, he proposed that truth was merely the solution that most fully resolved the friction or strain.

Nor was there a categorical difference between judgments of truth and value. All values were relative to changing experience. Moral action was simply the action that met most fully the needs of a concrete situation and most fully expressed the moral actor. The element of "oughtness" derived only from the demand for completeness: "the bad act is partial, the good organic." *All* the conditions, and the actor's *whole* self were involved, in a situation in which the individual was always growing, the self always realized in the larger organic community, and history always enlarging knowledge and social interaction. The only test of action, in ethics as in knowledge, was whether or not it worked. "We demand order in our experience. The only proof of its existence is in the results reached by making the demand. [The ethical command] is verified by being acted upon. The proof is experimental." Dewey placed the individual entirely in the ongoing flow of experience and denied the possibility of extracting from that flow any fixed standards except the process of action itself. Only if individuals were freed from all absolutes, he seemed to say, could they act responsibly in the uncertainty of history.[28]

Dewey himself could serenely inhabit that fluid world, however, only because he believed that discordant values were genuinely harmonized in each conscientious act and progressively in time, that the ongoing movement

27 Dewey's political and historical use of Hegel was influenced by the English philosopher T. H. Green. See John Dewey, "The Philosophy of Thomas Hill Green" (1889), *EW*, 3:14–35.
28 John Dewey, "Review of Lester Ward, *The Psychic Factors of Civilization*" (1894), *EW*, 4: 210; idem, "The Study of Ethics" (1894), *EW*, 4:234, 244–5; idem, "The Psychology of Effort" (1897), *EW*, 5:158–9, 162.

of society shaped individual and community, past and future, to harmonious form. Although he dropped the language of civic humanism, Christianity, and idealism, democracy remained the ideal toward which history moved. As James Kloppenberg has pointed out, it was the hidden teleology within the relativistic Deweyan philosophy that is prized by contemporary philosophers.[29] In Dewey's efforts to reconstitute his inherited ideals on a naturalistic and historicist basis, the millennial vision of American history was the bottom faith to which he clung.

In its specific political provenance, Dewey's pragmatism was a new liberal philosophy. Like the moderate Christian socialists of the Gilded Age, Dewey envisioned his ideal of democracy as a family community, in which individual initiatives and differences in status were harmonized by unity of purpose and interest. But he did not regard it as immediately impending. "Democracy is an ideal of the future, not a starting point," he said in 1888. "In this respect, society is still a sound aristocrat.... What is meant in detail by a democracy of wealth, we shall not know until it is more of a reality than it is now." His flirtation with Gilded Age radicalism was brief. When the announcement of the first issue of "Thought News" in 1892 brought ridicule from the Detroit newspapers, Dewey hastily abandoned the project. The Fords accused him of cowardice in the face of class opposition, but it seems likely that the man admired at Michigan for his fine "simplicity" of character had not fully appreciated what he was doing until opposition called it to his attention.[30]

During the next two years Dewey carefully located his theory at the mediating center between laissez-faire conservatism and socialist radicalism. With "Thought News" still in mind, he insisted that the true reformer must accept "the established facts of life" as well as change the forms of the past that its spirit might be preserved. "It is folly, it is worse than folly, it is mere individual conceit, for one to set out to reform the world, either at large or in detail, until he has learned what the existing world which he wishes to reform has for him to learn."[31] On the eve of leaving for the University of Chicago, Dewey, like Albion Small, came to a deeper appreciation of the "established facts of life," and along the same chastening path of normative American history. The radical Christian socialist George Herron did not realize, Dewey said, that "political, domestic and industrial institutions have become in fact an organized Kingdom of God on Earth, making for the

---

29 James T. Kloppenberg, *Uncertain Victory: Social Democracy and Progressivism in European and American Thought, 1870–1920* (New York: Oxford University Press, 1986), 43–4, 110–11, 131–2, 140.
30 Dewey, "Ethics of Democracy," 246; Coughlan, *Young John Dewey*, 88, 101–8.
31 John Dewey, "Reconstruction" (1894), *EW*, 4:103–4.

welfare of the individual and the unity of the whole." Progress was not automatic but was created by pragmatic intelligence. "Only action can reconcile the old, the general, and the permanent with the changing, the individual, and the new ... action as progress, as development, making over the wealth of the past into capital with which to do an enlarging and freer business."[32] The historical context to which pragmatic relativism binds itself is as open as the creative process of change and the hermeneutical construction of history. Dewey framed the relationship of pragmatism to history in liberal exceptionalist terms.[33]

During these same years, Dewey spelled out his commitment to the classical supports of liberal society. Science, democracy, and industrial capitalism were his motors of modern progress. Even before his conversion to Darwinian naturalism, Dewey had been an avid reader of the English liberal positivists in college. He believed that science was "a method of truth to which, so far as we can discover, no limits whatsoever can be put." Through democracy – the ideal "that every citizen is a sovereign" – the modern individual had become "a being who is self-possessed, an end in himself." Capitalism was the third liberal basis of modern society, for progress in industrial life could only be "effected through competition and struggle." Conflict could be directed "to reduce waste and secure its maximum advantage," he said, but it could not be eliminated. Dewey's psychological voluntarism, his Darwinian conception of thought as problem-solving activity stimulated by the "struggle for existence," was closely linked to his economic liberalism. He was willing to accept that capitalist competition necessarily involved "preferential advantage in the struggle for existence" and "preferential selection," because the range of struggle could be greatly lessened by "habits formed under the direction of intelligence."[34]

32  Ibid., 101; idem, "The Significance of the Problem of Knowledge" (1897), *EW*, 5:21.
33  Kloppenberg, *Uncertain Victory*, has drawn a compelling portrait of Dewey and his generation of social democrats in the United States and Europe which links their left-liberal politics to their philosophical critique of knowledge. I would emphasize that both their politics and epistemology developed together from the context of historical uncertainty and political conflict of the late nineteenth century. By classing together left-liberals like Dewey and revisionist socialists like Eduard Bernstein and the Webbs, Kloppenberg brings out their similarities, but not the national political context that circumscribed Dewey's politics and epistemology.
34  Dewey, "Reconstruction," 103, 99, 101; idem, "Review of Ward, *The Psychic Factors of Civilization*," 210, 212; Dykhuizen, *Life and Mind of John Dewey*, 11. Dewey spelled out his intention to both preserve and transcend capitalism and the liberal reformist, as opposed to socialist, implication of his theory, in "Evolution and Ethics" (1898), *EW*, 5:34–53. The competitive struggle for existence was not overthrown in society, but subjected to a larger social logic. This point was picked up in defense of competition and minimal reform by

Dewey's classical liberal roots were often obscured by his efforts to effect their organic transformation. He believed that industry, democracy, and science were together binding liberal society into closer harmony and began to work out how this harmony was achieved in his political science lectures at Michigan. Charles Horton Cooley's notes of those lectures provide a revealing record of how Dewey drew together the resources of individualist and organicist traditions in an effort to socialize liberalism. He formulated his views – as did virtually every social science college text of the period – in dialogue with socialism.

Dewey believed with Spencer that the foundation of society was the economic struggle for existence, that competition and the division of labor were organizing modern society on the principle of functional interdependence. Beyond Spencer, he projected from interdependence a social process of intelligence, education, and government action that mediated and completed social action. "The economic process ... constitutes the machinery by which on the whole the social organism is organized," Cooley recorded. "[The] intelligence function of Government, education, must be derivative finally, from the economic. Here again the fallacy of socialism, in opposing government and economic process."

Dewey's original contribution to this liberal program was his discussion of the "social sensorium," a mediating realm constructed by the conscious interaction of individuals and by language. Through this medium individual consciousness became social, for in it individuals were forced to define and accommodate their own actions to the actions of others. Social consciousness "is the recognition of individual activity so extended as to take into account claims made by the acts of others." A harmonious society could not be achieved, however, until individuals were fully socialized.

The falsity of anarchy is in not recognizing what a complex and continual interaction it requires to bring the individual to a consciousness of the whole and of his identity of interest with it.... This involves submission to social discipline, both reinforcing his activity and changing its direction. The truth of socialism is in recognizing the necessity of this social mediation. Its falsity in supposing that the aim of this social activity is to direct the individual; its true end being to put at the disposal of the individual facts to enable him to direct himself.

On one level, Dewey here is redefining individualism, arguing that individual self-realization and social progress lie only in the ongoing democratic experience through which individuals are forced to take account of other

Westal W. Willoughby, *Social Justice* (New York: Macmillan, 1900), 287–90. For another example of Dewey's careful centrism in these years, see "Academic Freedom" (1902), *MW*, 2:53–66.

persons' claims for respect. That is the open-ended Dewey. On another level, however, is the still Hegelian and exceptionalist Dewey, who conferred upon democratic experience the ability to turn individual self-interest into the interest of the social whole. "All opposition between the individual and the social side is apparent, historical, a phase of progress." The tendency toward the ideal became the real. Dewey was inspired by the American exceptionalist ideal to provide liberal individualism with a social ethic, but he was also led by it to transmute possessive individualism into organic social harmony by a kind of new liberal alchemy.[35]

The inclination in Dewey's work to identify pragmatic method, the American exceptionalist ideal, and the American liberal reality was given a notable formulation at the turn of the century by his collaborator and colleague, George Herbert Mead. Mead's pattern of development closely resembled that of Dewey's, save for the greater difficulty he had reaching a comfortable naturalism. Like Dewey, he still felt "the spirit of a minister" within him and wanted "to fight a valiant personal hand to hand fight with evil in the world." Reading *Looking Backward* and observing socialist practice in Europe, he came to see that the idea embodied in socialism – "the principle of corporate life" – marked the direction of future progress. When he arrived to teach at Michigan in 1891 he found Dewey in the midst of philosophical and political afflatus and was won over by Dewey's vision of pragmatic salvation.[36]

Mead's Christian social sympathies were like Dewey's attached to the liberal economy. As he wrote his father-in-law in 1892

The telegraph and land motive are the great spiritual agents of society because they bind man and man so close together that the interest of the individual must be more completely the interest of all day by day. And America in pushing this spiritualizing of nature is doing more than all in bringing the day when everyman will be my neighbor and all life shall be saturated with the divine life . . . when our functions and acts shall be not simply ours but the processes of the great body politic which is God as revealed in the universe.

Mead was writing the older man to present his work in its highest light, but the millennial language came easily to him. Both Mead and Dewey understood American history to be progressively realizing the millennial ideal already present in its liberal institutions.[37]

---

35 "John Dewey, Lectures," Cooley Papers. The MS is not paginated.
36 Coughlan, *Young John Dewey*, chaps. 7–9, is a fine account of Mead's development. The quotations are in Mead to Henry Castle, March 16, 1884, and October 21, 1890, George Herbert Mead Papers, The University of Chicago.
37 Mead to "Father Castle," June 18, 1892, Mead Papers.

At Chicago in 1899, writing in Small's *American Journal of Sociology*, Mead informed social scientists what social praxis was implied by Dewey's pragmatism. He began with the shrewd observation that socialism was the philosophy behind the reform measures of even the new "opportunists" who had succeeded to the utopian "programists." The opportunists believed "that it will be possible to effect by constructive legislation radical changes that will lead to greater social equality." But such expectations are false. Government had taken over some businesses like municipal utilities, but when it did so, "the government has become a business concern, which enters into the business world on a basis that is determined by the latter." Moreover, the functions of government "are merging with equal rapidity into the industrial world which it is supposed to control." The conclusion to be drawn from this miscalculation by socialistically inclined reformers, Mead said, was that

it is impossible to so forecast any future condition that depends upon the evolution of society as to be able to govern our conduct by such a forecast. It is always the unexpected that happens, for we have to recognize, not only the immediate change that is to take place, but also the reaction back upon this of the whole world within which the change takes place, and no human foresight is equal to this. In the social world we must recognize the working hypothesis as the form into which all theories must be cast as completely as in the natural sciences.

We have a method and a standard of application, Mead said, "that the hypothesis shall *work* in the complex of forces into which we introduce it ... not an ideal to work toward."

But how if we have no ideal to work toward, can we determine even the direction of our actions? Evolution required development, not mere perpetuation. Mead adopted Dewey's pragmatic method and shaded it to the existing world: "A conception of a different world comes to us always as the result of some specific problem which involves readjustment of the world as it is, not to meet a detailed ideal of a perfect universe ... and the test of the effort lies in the possibility of this readjustment fitting into the world as it is." Labor-union activity oriented toward higher wages and immediate conditions, rather than labor organizations designed to propagandize for socialism, Mead argued, met the standards of scientific reform.[38]

Mead's analysis holds an interesting inner contradiction. On the surface he is calling for social reform that is based on the recognition that change always escapes our imperfect ideal projections, producing unexpected novelties. But the content of his examples showed that America was not changing.

38 George H. Mead, "The Working Hypothesis in Social Reform," *AJS*, 5 (November 1899): 367–71.

Idealistic government reforms were being controlled by business considerations and absorbed into the structure of private capitalism. Only those labor activities were effective that fitted into "the world as it is." The liberal capitalist contours of the American world were in fact holding. Mead's text was that America lived in a historical world of ceaseless change and that pragmatism was the method of novelty. His subtext was that America would remain a liberal world nonetheless, and pragmatism serve as a method of accommodation to it. He gave the blessing of pragmatism to the 1890s proscription of socialism and return to the normative course of American history. Mead was not Dewey, of course, and Dewey was notoriously silent throughout his life in the face of widely varying readings of his work, but Mead's program is consonant with the political construction Dewey gave pragmatism in the Progressive Era, and which many of his followers have given it ever since.

# 6

◁ ══════════════════════════════ ▷

# Marginalism and historicism
# in economics


By the turn of the century, three different economic models emerged from the Gilded Age crisis of American exceptionalism and vied for support in the profession: marginalism, the liberal economic interpretation of history, and the socialist historico-evolutionary economics of Thorstein Veblen. Marginalism, as neoclassical economics, quickly established ascendancy. Veblen's theory was not considered a viable alternative by most of his economic contemporaries, exerting its greatest influence later, through the work of disciples. But the debate over historicism continued on a wide front.

## Marginalist ascendancy

The economists who moved economic discourse forward in the Progressive Era were in part the men, born in the 1850s and 1860s, who had already emerged in the Gilded Age as spokesmen in the debate.[1] John Bates Clark at Columbia University continued to work out the implications of marginalist

---

1 The only statistics I have found on the changing background of economists and other social scientists in this period are in the study of 171 leaders of the major disciplinary associations from 1865 to 1920 in Edward T. Silva and Sheila A. Slaughter, *Serving Power: The Making of the Academic Social Science Expert* (Westport, Conn.: Greenwood, 1984). Their figures suggest that the AEA leadership from 1904 to 1920 drew from slightly less elite and considerably less clerical background than the leadership from 1885 to 1903. However, because their sample is defined by officeholding in the AEA, it includes for the later period considerably more public figures who were specifically recruited for office to lend the AEA public legitimacy. Although 85 percent of the pre-1903 leaders were academic careerists, only 57 percent were in the 1904–20 period, the others being businessmen, lawyers, and journalists. Because the nonacademic types drawn in were less likely to be from clerical, old New England backgrounds, they may well have skewed Silva and Slaughter's findings. On AEA officeholders, see A. W. Coats, "The First Two Decades of the American Economic Association," *AER*, 50 (September 1960): 571–4.

theory. Both E. R. A. Seligman and Frank W. Taussig set out important paths in theory and practice by means of their positions at the major graduate departments of Columbia and Harvard, through their expertise in areas of public policy, and as the authors of popular textbooks. Simon Patten, chair of the Wharton School at the University of Pennsylvania, spoke in an idiosyncratic but revealing voice. Richard T. Ely, grown more conservative, remained a figure of significance largely through his revised 1893 economics text and a band of younger Wisconsin students and colleagues who carried on his reformist impulse. One of these was John R. Commons, heir to the evangelical-abolitionist tradition of Oberlin College, who studied with Ely at Johns Hopkins and joined him at Wisconsin in 1904.[2]

Other members of the Gilded Age cohort made their first professional appearance in the 1890s. Irving Fisher, the son of a Congregational clergyman of New England Puritan stock, was a student of William Graham Sumner at Yale and quickly emerged as an innovator in the marginalist school. Two other new spokesmen had gotten a late start on their productive careers in economics. Frank Fetter came to economics from business, took a degree at Halle, and after 1900 became a noted marginalist theorist. Veblen, after wandering in the wilderness for some years, began his academic career at the University of Chicago when it opened in 1892 and moved to Stanford and then the University of Missouri. Through his writings and his students, he defined an alternative economics and an alternative historical course for America.[3]

Between about 1890 and 1910 marginal economics became the dominant paradigm in American economics. The rapid victory of marginalism owed a great deal to its resonance with the historical and political aims of American economics. As a mathematical tool for calculating values, marginalism could be put to a variety of political uses, but marginalism had its origins and gained its force not simply as an analytical tool, but as a liberal world view. Still, marginalist theory had to achieve its victory in the face of considerable suspicion from those who wanted a greater degree of practical relevance than it seemed to offer and from those new liberal historicists who wanted

2 John R. Commons, *Myself* (New York: Macmillan, 1934); Lafayette G. Harter, Jr., *John R. Commons: His Assault on Laissez-faire* (Corvallis: Oregon State University Press, 1962).

3 Irving Norton Fisher, *My Father, Irving Fisher* (New York: Comet Press, 1956); Joseph Dorfman, *The Economic Mind in American Civilization*, 5 vols. (New York: Viking, 1946–59), 3:360–75; Jesse W. Markham, "Frank Albert Fetter," *DAB*, Suppl. 4, 267–8. Joseph Dorfman, *Thorstein Veblen and His America* (New York: Viking, 1934) is the best biographical study of Veblen and a mine of information on Veblen's generation. David Riesman, *Thorstein Veblen* (New York: Scribner, 1953) provides considerable insight into Veblen's complex personality.

economics to be sensitive to historical change and support new liberal reform. Marginalism also succeeded in America because it was able to both accommodate and co-opt the new liberal economists and to project its own style of realism.

One reason it was able to do so was because marginal economics presented itself to American economists after 1890 as a neoclassical paradigm, a perfection and completion of the classical model of political economy, rather than an abrogation of it. In large part, this neoclassical synthesis was the work of Alfred Marshall's *Principles of Economics* (1890), which showed how the economic transactions of the individual agent set equilibrium price in the short run and over the longer term. By analyzing the longer term, Marshall restored variations in supply as well as demand to market process, thereby linking marginalist analysis to the classical laws of supply and demand. Marshall also opened his analysis to some of the real conditions effecting supply and demand that critics of classical economics had identified. He recognized, for example, that the different bargaining strengths of partners in an exchange could affect the bargains struck on the way to equilibrium price, that laborers' greater need could place them at a starting and cumulative disadvantage in the labor market, and he suggested that under some circumstances the parties in an exchange could achieve maximum utility at other than equilibrium price. These discrepancies between real economic activities and the ideal tendencies of market law opened the way for marginalists to accept some kinds of liberal reform.[4]

Clark was a great admirer of Marshall's neoclassical synthesis and the evangelical idealism that suffused it. The gap between the real world of action and the ideal equilibrium toward which it moved allowed Clark, as well, to cast himself as a moderate Progressive. As against the more advanced Progressives, who denied that there was a meaningful distinction between monopoly and other corporations in which large size conferred a decisive market advantage, Clark considered real monopoly rare, the product of unusual circumstances or fraud. The great bulk of business consolidation was still under the control of competition, actual or potential. Hence neither ongoing regulation nor extensive trust-busting were necessary, but only the establishment of rules to prohibit unfair competitive practices. On labor, too, Clark took a right-Progressive stance. Labor like capital had to consolidate, but their tendency to strike and to push for gains beyond their fair market share made him distrust collective bargaining and urge a public

---

4 Alfred Marshall, *Principles of Economics* (London: Macmillan, 1890). The character of Marshall's neoclassical synthesis is particularly well drawn in A. K. Dasgupta, *Epochs of Economic Theory* (Oxford: Blackwell Publisher, 1985), chap. 7. See also Phyllis Deane, *The Evolution of Economic Ideas* (Cambridge University Press, 1978), 107, 111–13.

system of mandatory arbitration. Advanced Progressives were more inclined to worry about the weakness rather than the strength of labor and to urge legal action that would strengthen unions as well as government provision of social insurance. Nonetheless, the marginalist opening toward new liberal reform made it a viable contender in the Progressive Era.[5]

So too did its accommodation to realism. The abstract character of marginalist theory placed it at some disadvantage in the realist context. "The so-called theorist has a heavy and often undeserved load to bear," noted Seligman in 1902. "The term is redolent of condescension; it smacks of contempt." The marginal theorists responded by approving the search for facts, but emphasizing the higher importance of scientific law in understanding change. In 1904, referring to the rapid consolidation of industry, Clark admitted the need for empirical study to understand "the recent and startling movements in business life," but "if in the midst of the overturnings which result there can be detected the orderly working of economic law, nothing can be more important or practical than discovering it." Prediction required knowledge of both scientific law and the particular circumstances in which it operated, Fisher said. "Usually, however, failures in economic prediction are due to the lack of scientific rather than of historical knowledge." The road to reality, the marginalists claimed, was indeed through particulars, but more importantly through abstraction.[6] At the same time, Marshall's depiction of the businessman's calculation of market price on marginalist principles opened the way for another kind of realism. His analysis placed business deliberations and the businessman's language and expectations at the center of neoclassical economics. Quickly developing the links between marginalist theory and business behavior, marginalism soon offered its own kind of realism.

As in any paradigm shift, the older American economists moved more slowly toward marginalism than the younger. Among the economists who came of age in the 1880s, conservatives were more likely than new liberals to remain within the classical fold, for they were politically satisfied with the traditional paradigm. J. Laurence Laughlin and Arthur T. Hadley never felt the need of a new legitimation of capitalism and never liked the distance from practical affairs created by the more abstract language. In 1899 Hadley

5 John Bates Clark, "The Theory of Economic Progress," *PAEA: Economic Studies*, 1 (April 1896): 5–22.
6 E. R. A. Seligman, "Economics and Social Progress," *PAEA*, 3d ser., 4 (February 1903): 53; John Bates Clark, "Economic Theory in a New Character and Relation," in *Congress of Arts and Sciences, Universal Exposition, St. Louis, 1904*, ed. Howard J. Rogers, 8 vols. (Boston: Houghton Mifflin, 1906), 7:48–9; Irving Fisher, "Economics as a Science," *Science*, n.s. 24 (August 31, 1906): 260.

charged that this "metaphysical" theory "has been the most potent cause to weaken the influence of economists among statesmen and men of the world." Taussig, too, believed that "the subjective theory of value . . . is of less service for explaining the phenomena of the real world than is supposed by its votaries," but by 1911 he felt obliged to accept the new marginalist bottle, even while filling it with the old classical wine.[7]

Marginalism made most rapid headway among the economists who came of age in the 1890s and after. By 1894, Edward A. Ross saw the younger men moving in that direction and by 1900, Frank Fetter believed that marginalism had already won the allegiance of the younger generation and reoriented many older economists.[8] The favored explanation among historians of economics is that marginalism won out over classical economics because it was more "scientific," that is more analytically general, logically stricter, and further removed from philosophical and political assumptions. Still, since the 1850s, the marginalist concept was proposed by a variety of lone voices before it was "discovered" independently in the 1870s by Stanley Jevons in England, Carl Menger in Austria, and Léon Walras in France. Even then it was not until the 1880s and 1890s that it began to gain wide acceptance. Proponents of the scientific explanation point to professionalization as the operative context. According to George J. Stigler, the professionalizing economists, like the natural scientists before them, desired "a certain disengagement from the contemporary scene" and developed a taste for "non-vulgar instruments" that displayed rigor, elegance, and special technique.[9]

The professional-scientific explanation carries some degree of truth. As Edward A. Ross described his initial excitement about marginalist analysis in 1891, "I became very enthusiastic over the vista of mathematical economics opened up" and "could not tear myself away from the reductive charm of geometrical proof." He knew from his work with Ely that it was "reductive charm," but he was drawn to it nonetheless.[10] Still, Ross's momentary

---

7 Alfred Bornemann, *J. Laurence Laughlin* (Washington, D.C.: American Council on Public Affairs, 1940), 14, 89; Arthur T. Hadley, "The Relation between Economics and Politics," *PAEA: Economic Studies*, 4 (February 1899): 14–15; Frank W. Taussig, *Principles of Economics*, 2 vols. (New York: Macmillan, 1911), 1:viii, chap. 8; 2:112–23.

8 Frank A. Fetter, "The Next Decade of Economic Theory," *PAEA*, 3d ser., 2 (February 1901): 236–46 and "Discussion," 247–53.

9 "Papers on the Marginal Revolution in Economics," *History of Political Economy*, 4 (Fall 1972): Craufurd D. W. Goodwin, "Marginalism Moves to the New World," 551–70; George J. Stigler, "The Adoption of the Marginal Utility Theory," 577, 571–86. See also Joseph Schumpeter, *History of Economic Analysis* (Oxford University Press, 1954), 869–70.

10 E. A. Ross to Mrs. Beach, February 1, 1891, Edward A. Ross Papers, Wisconsin State Historical Society.

insight is significant. It was not everywhere that science and professionalism were measured by the rigor and elegant simplicity of natural science or by distance from historical particularity. Behind these judgments of science and professionalism lay the national cultural contexts that shaped them. In Germany and to a lesser extent in France, economists resisted marginalism well into the twentieth century, and it has never there shaped the discipline as fully as it has in England and America. To Gustav Schmoller, nourished on historicist cultural and professional traditions, Menger's atomistic marginalist approach seemed to violate the "indivisible totality" of the historical world.[11] Moreover, professionalization has as often embodied the aim of relevance to the contemporary scene as "a certain disengagement" from it. Neither professionalism nor science are univocal terms; rather they are shaped by cognitive, aesthetic, and value judgments imbedded in history.

Marginalism won its success in England and America not just because it embodied a sophisticated economic theory but because it met the standards of sophistication operative in those cultures. Marginalism can be understood as an extension of the process begun by Ricardo, of abstraction from and reification of the liberal capitalist world on the positivist model of science. It emerged as a reorientation of classical political economy and it proved most attractive to those professional cultures in which the classical economists' positivist scientific assumptions and liberal premises had the strongest professional and cultural support.

It also emerged at a time when the classical model of economics was under increasing political attack for its laissez-faire bias and failure to offer labor any hope outside the neo-Malthusian path of abstinence and moral improvement. This political dissatisfaction animated a great deal of dissent, from the historicist critique of economics in England and America in the 1870s and 1880s to the radical subversions of Ricardian theory by Karl Marx and Henry George. Clark recalled that it was the theory of Henry George that first put him on the path to marginalism, and we have seen how thoroughly his ideas were shaped by the political conflict. Frank Fetter too believed that "the political bearings of the value theory" was the major factor in its origins. Orthodox economics was in disarray and under "pressure of radical propaganda," he recalled. "Well I remember the confidence and gusto with which this demonstration of the truth of Marxism was still presented by socialist speakers in the nineties, as I listened to it from Berlin to San Francisco." The threat of radical theories founded on the labor theory of value had forced the founders of marginalism to revise the theory of value,

---

11 Karl Pribram, *A History of Economic Reasoning* (Baltimore: Johns Hopkins University Press, 1983), 219–24.

Fetter believed, and the continued threat had clearly drawn Fetter himself to the new ideas. As Mark Blaug has pointed out, the social and political relevance of marginalism was its great attraction.[12]

It was particularly relevant in the United States, where the crisis of American exceptionalism centered on the fate of labor in the new industrial world. Class conflict in America threatened both class interests and the national identity, and the Christian underpinnings of both national ideology and respectable culture required that there be a just solution. Professionalism in economics had emerged in that moral and political context, claiming the ability to solve the problem of class conflict and to modernize the exceptionalist heritage. Clark himself developed his utilitarian value theory in an effort to show the market as a beneficent social organism. After Haymarket he used the concept of marginal utility to remove the sting from the idea of surplus profit and started work on a full-scale theory of distribution, the core problem of the age. By 1894 the Columbia economist Richmond Mayo-Smith observed that "the whole world of economic theorists is groaning and travailing over a theory of distribution based on marginal utility. Economists are tumbling over each other in the race to be first in applying the doctrine of rent to the other shares in the distribution." Here was a perfect fit between scientific and ideological aim, and Clark soon took the honors.[13]

Many in Clark's audience responded accordingly, both within and outside the profession. As the historian Preserved Smith wrote him, ever since reading the *Distribution of Wealth* "your demonstration of the tendency of capital and labor to get just what the marginal unit of each earned ... has

12 John Bates Clark, *The Distribution of Wealth* (New York: Macmillan, 1899), viii; Frank A. Fetter, "Value and the Larger Economics," *JPE*, 31 (October 1923): 587–605, particularly 600–2. Mark Blaug, "Was There a Marginal Revolution?" in "Papers on the Marginal Revolution," 278–9. See also Ronald L. Meek, "Marginalism and Marxism," ibid., 502–3; and Dasgupta, *Epochs of Economic Theory*, chap. 6. Although emphasizing the historically and ideologically driven discontinuities between the marginalist and classical theories, Dasgupta recognizes that marginalist theory was still linked to classical economics by its social philosophy and was quickly incorporated into a neoclassical synthesis. John Maloney, *Marshall, Orthodoxy and the Professionalization of Economics* (Cambridge University Press, 1985) argues that in England the efforts of Alfred Marshall were central to the professionalization of economics around the marginalist paradigm. Maloney urges that the professional project and problems internal to the classical paradigm account for the rise and ascendency of marginalism and that political, ideological factors played a decidedly secondary role. However, he does not examine those factors nor their interaction with internal and professional considerations. His conclusion that the marginalist paradigm does have liberal ideological implications nonetheless, due to its philosophical and methodological premises, is left without historical basis. See particularly pp. 205–22.

13 Richmond Mayo-Smith, "Review of John R. Commons, *The Distribution of Wealth*," *PSQ*, 9 (September 1894): 570.

been a very living element in my intellectual life, and has kept me from being a thorough-going socialist, though my sympathies are with them on many points."[14] Marginalism supported the rejection of socialism and the egalitarian demand it had generated in Gilded Age America, arguing that capitalism produced maximum utility, allocational efficiency, and just distribution. It also offered Americans assurance that the new industrial world could still operate like the old, that competition could still control the massive industrial combinations coming into existence and the growing concentration of wealth. The deep reluctance to accept change in America made Clark's static model, with its traditional exceptionalist tones, compelling.

Clark's explicit ideological message is revealing of the sociopolitical roots of marginalism, but it is also, in part, misleading. Many of the marginalist economists who followed Clark were embarrassed by his overtly moral rhetoric. His tendency to read the laws of economics as normative natural law aroused criticism across the whole ideological spectrum, from Taussig to Veblen.[15] Particularly among the younger men who flocked to marginalism in the 1890s and after, marginalism must have been attractive because its higher level of abstraction seemed to escape the ideological contention of the Gilded Age and allow the legitimation of capitalism on the basis of science rather than moralism. The scientific-professional interpretation is correct in sensing that marginalism's success owed a great deal to its offer of "a certain disengagement" from contemporary politics. What should be emphasized, however, is that the kind of disengagement marginalism offered was politically relevant and ideologically committed.

Again Ross is informative. After his initial enthusiasm for the new academic toy, he rendered a more extended judgment in 1900, when he agreed with Fetter's marginalist forecast.

I believe we are on the eve of changes which will make economics a true science. The bane of economics in the past has been the persistence in it of physics. The distinction between service and good, or between land and capital, has been physical rather than economic. Professor Clark's great book is about the furthest removed from physics, and we all look upon it as a monumental contribution.... Another thing that has disturbed the development of our science has been the premature discussion of ethical questions ... I think that the ethical aspects of our economic system should come after a rational, cold-blooded explanation of what is.[16]

---

14 Preserved Smith to J. B. Clark, October 21, 1912, John Bates Clark Papers, Columbia University.
15 Frank W. Taussig, "Outlines of a Theory of Wages," *PAEA*, 3d ser., 11 (April 1910): 136–56 and "Discussion," 157–70; Thorstein Veblen, "The Limitations of Marginal Utility," *JPE*, 17 (November 1909): 620–36.
16 Edward A. Ross in Fetter, "The Next Decade of Economic Theory – Discussion," 252–3.

When Ross made this statement he had just been fired from Stanford University for making political statements offensive to the university's founder and was looking for a new job. Ross wanted to separate the "ethical" from "what is" in order to escape the ideological polarization that had divided the discipline and was still dogging his own career. Clark's obliteration of the "physical" distinction between goods and services, land and capital, could help to obliterate the moral and historical distinctions that generated ideological conflict. But Ross sought an escape from ideological conflict, not from ideology, for marginalism encoded the individualistic premises of classical liberalism. As we will shortly see, Ross himself was working his way back to those liberal premises and expanding them into a social framework for modern society. From that liberal perspective, marginalism could appear to be a "cold-blooded explanation of what is."

The leading marginalist thinkers who followed Clark also used the new science to legitimate liberal capitalism in America. Substantively, their research was directed not only at intellectual problems generated by a new paradigm of market function, but at solidifying the liberal capitalist bases of that paradigm in scientific law. Indeed Irving Fisher seems to have entirely by-passed the radical historicist mentality of the Gilded Age that had left its imprint on Clark; instead he carried the conservative positivist impulse of William Graham Sumner directly into marginalism.

By the time Fisher entered Yale College in the 1880s, his father's declining health had left the family impoverished. Like Sumner, he identified with the wealthy business class to which Yale gave him access and moved easily from religious belief to a secularized version of natural law. Socialists and labor leaders "must have their eyes opened to the great *laws* they are violating," he said, and he defended "Conservatism as Presented by the Comparative Study of Man." A major in mathematics, Fisher did graduate work under both Willard Gibbs and Sumner, and at Sumner's urging used his mathematical skills to explicate those laws. His doctoral dissertation, published in 1892, applied the mathematics of a mechanical equilibrium to the marginal theory of economic equilibrium. It was intended as a "systematic representation in terms of mechanical interaction of that beautiful and intricate equilibrium which manifests itself on the 'exchanges' of a great city but of which the causes and effects lie far outside." Grounded entirely in mathematics, Fisher's "beautiful" equilibrium ignored altogether the not-so-pretty history that had intruded itself even on Clark and Sumner.[17]

Fisher went on to spend a considerable portion of his time as an inventor,

17 I. N. Fisher, *My Father*, chaps. 1–3; Irving Fisher, "Mathematical Investigations in the Theory of Value and Price," *Transactions of the Connecticut Academy*, 9 (1892): 24.

businessman, and investor, and a major thrust of his theoretical effort was to show how marginalist theory was linked to the working categories of the modern businessman. He reconceptualized capital and income in accord with the accounting theory of double-entry bookkeeping, thereby supplying "a link long missing between the ideas and usages underlying practical business transactions and the theories of abstract economics." John R. Commons complained that Fisher had constructed a purely "business economics."[18]

Another path toward legitimation was taken by Frank Fetter, the leader of what became known briefly as the "American" or "psychological" school of marginalism. As Clark had originally seen, a principal advantage of grounding value theory in utility was to link the market choices of producers and consumers to people's wants. Fetter believed that the task of theory was to elaborate the psychological foundation of marginalism, and hence show how the market economy was at every level directed by people's desire to fulfill their needs. The marginalists' value theory was not just a theory of market price, but of "welfare." In his 1904 text he constructed the categories of the market economy from the wants of human nature, the feelings of desire and satisfaction that constituted and regulated those wants, and the processes of production, exchange, and consumption those feelings directed. Fetter came under increasing attack for his outmoded hedonistic psychology – indeed Fisher warned as early as 1892 against the effort to reduce economic utility to psychological categories – so that in his 1915 revision, he formally dropped the hedonistic premise: "the basis of value is conceived to be the simple act of choice and not a calculation of utility." But despite this redefinition he continued to consider feeling and gratification inherent in the act of choice and to link it to welfare. Even Fisher, in *Capital and Income*, borrowed Fetter's category of "psychic income" to show that after the physical accounts were balanced there was a "net income" of psychic gain that accrued from the economic process.[19]

Unlike Clark, however, these economists could no longer ground their work in natural law and justice, but tried to frame normative economic categories as scientific ones. Under the rubric of health or the general welfare, they claimed to judge by scientific rather than moral standards that the capitalist market was advantageous. Their textbooks were as clearly dialogues with socialism as anything written in the Gilded Age, but their

18 I. N. Fisher, *My Father*, chap. 10; Irving Fisher, *The Nature of Capital and Income* (New York: Macmillan, 1906), vii; John R. Commons, "Political Economy and Business Economics: Comments on Fisher's Capital and Income," *QJE*, 22 (November 1907): 120–5.
19 Frank A. Fetter, *The Principles of Economics* (New York: Century, 1904), pts. 1, 2; Fisher, "Mathematical Investigations," chap. 1; Fetter, *Principles of Economics* (1915), chap. 4; Fisher, *Capital and Income*, chap. 10.

tone was now one of balanced realism. Casting themselves not as defenders of the status quo, but as objective analysts of the strengths and imperfections of capitalism, they armed their readers against socialism and held open the door to some degree of liberal reform.

Fisher did not, as Commons feared, break all connection with the older political economy and its public values. "We must always distinguish between the ideal or *normal*, and the real or *average*," he said in 1907. The radical critiques of capitalism had forced many marginalists to confront the distinction between utility as what is desired and utility as "intrinsic worth." When Vilfredo Pareto formulated this distinction, Fisher recognized it as the ethical point of view of John Ruskin in another guise and approved it. But he appeared to think that the ethical judgment of "each actual case by our own ideal standard" was a judgment that economists could undertake on the basis of their scientific knowledge. Everyone's opinion of the ideal was not equal. "The world consists of two classes – the educated and the ignorant – and it is essential for progress that the former should be allowed to dominate the latter."[20]

Fisher was enabled to think of these judgments as scientific because he thought of the normal, the intrinsically desirable, as defining a state of "health." The metaphor of health and disease shaped all his discussion of normative economics. Fisher's early life was decimated by tuberculosis. Two of his siblings died in early childhood and his father finally died of the disease when Fisher was seventeen. In 1898, just after being appointed professor at Yale, he too came down with tuberculosis and left Yale for three years in the West to effect a cure. This last, close brush with death left him with "the urge of the preacher." On his return, he increasingly devoted his time to reform issues. The existence of current problems, he said, "suggest that something is wrong in the present economic order of society." There were "economic diseases," and with a knowledge of "the economic anatomy and physiology of society," it would be possible to treat those diseases.[21]

Fisher believed that he was rejecting natural law when he sided against Sumner and the old classical judgment that "the present state of society [is] a normal and desirable one because each man naturally 'seeks his own best interest'" and these interests "always thereby best serve society." The presumption of laissez-faire must be abandoned. Economic laws sometimes worked for social evil, and social and governmental action had to be mobilized against the evils. Unlike Clark, he talked about the detriments of

20  Irving Fisher, "Why Has the Doctrine of Laissez Faire Been Abandoned?" *Science*, n.s. 25 (January 4, 1907): 20.
21  I. N. Fisher, *My Father*, chaps. 1, 5, p. 214; Irving Fisher, *Introduction to Economic Science* (New York: Macmillan, 1910), 1.

economic inequality. Despite this rejection of laissez-faire, however, on the major economic issues of Progressive reform Fisher stood very close to Clark, for in the main, economic law worked to social advantage and government often did not. The government could regulate railroad rates, but he doubted the efficacy of the remedy. The governmental actions he approved were extensions of the police power over public health, safety, and welfare, such as child-labor regulation and conservation laws. In 1907, he felt America was already in danger of too much socialistic experimentation.[22]

Fisher's discrimination between health and disease in fact followed the old fault lines laid down by the natural laws of republican economics. His chief policy interest was in money. Besides writing an influential restatement of the quantity theory of money, he pushed for a "compensated dollar" to remedy fluctuations in monetary value, a scheme generally considered impracticable. All Fisher's reform interests – "the abolition of war, disease, degeneracy, and instability in money" – carried the same moral valence. Although he occasionally adopted the language of the liberal historicists, opting for "modern doctrines of governmental regulation and social control," what he was really concerned with was the social support of self-control, the web of personal and public morality that sustained the rationality of nature. Unhealthful and immoral living, prostitution, luxury, and "social racing," wasteful expenditure on armaments, unsound financial policies that allowed the value of money to fluctuate, uncontrolled immigration, and eugenically lax practices of reproduction were his chief evils, a list that fit easily with the evils proscribed by Amasa Walker's "right consumption." Fisher theoretically abandoned natural law and laissez-faire but he largely reconstituted the normative force and moral shape of traditional American economic doctrine.[23]

Fetter did not define a normative economics concerned with health, but he did, like Fisher, believe that the largest conclusions economists reached were objective judgments of public welfare. Carefully distinguishing between the value that accrued to individuals and the good of society, Fetter argued that the capitalist market had to be judged on the basis of "expediency," how well it contributed to the general social welfare. On the whole, he argued, it worked well according to that standard and on the whole, individuals gained

22 Fisher, *Introduction to Economic Science*, chap. 26; idem, "Why Has the Doctrine of Laissez Faire," 20–1.
23 I. N. Fisher, *My Father*, 222; Fisher, "Why Has the Doctrine of Laissez Faire," 18, 25; idem, *Introduction to Economic Science*, chaps. 25–6. Fisher popularized his moral prescriptions in a best-selling manual, *How to Live: Rules for Healthful Living Based on Modern Science* (New York: Funk & Wagnalls, 1915). During the teens and twenties he increasingly sank his energies and private fortune into his plan for monetary reform, a Life Extension Institute, and the pacifist crusade.

what their merits deserved. Only small and gradual changes in the system were justified. Fetter's chief reform interest, immigration restriction, echoed Fisher's. The recent decline in the real wages of labor, he said, proves that we have "passed the point of diminishing returns in the relation of our population to our resources." As in Sumner's man-land ratio, it was density of population that differentiated Europe from America, Canada, and Australia. Only by restricting immigration could we retain "that largeness of opportunity and of outlook which makes possible the traits most distinctive of American life."[24]

Besides offering a scientific defense of modern capitalism, the marginalists had also to offer Americans an assurance of continuity amidst the widening recognition of change. If they could show beneath the current "overturnings ... the orderly working of economic law," as Clark said, they had also to project on some level a vision of historical development that linked present and future. Clark himself addressed that need by outlining a dynamic economic theory to accompany his static one. In doing so, he showed how completely he had abandoned historicism. The dynamic factors in economics were the factors that "disturb the static equilibrium" and these were limited to the basic components of the static theory: population, capital, technology, organization of production, and consumer wants. Over time, Clark argued, these factors quantitatively grew and diversified, leading to increasing production. Hence the dynamic, like the static theory was "equally valid in all times and places," though society advanced under this economic regime from a primitive to civilized state. The more civilized the society, the more dynamic, and the closer it approached the static model. Thus America today "conforms more closely to a normal form than do the more conservative societies of Europe and far more closely than do the sluggish societies of Asia." Clark's theory of history was liberal exceptionalism, and his dynamic economics, a quantitative extrapolation of the few fixed categories of liberal economics.[25]

With his keen ear for cultural resonance, Clark also tried to assimilate the Progressives' "struggle for reforms" to his promise of continual economic progress. Although the laws of the market always put severe limits on how much human intervention Clark could accept, he admitted in 1914 that moderate liberal reform would always be possible and necessary. "The capacity for further improvement is the essential trait of the best condition now in sight. The reformer can point to his delectable mountains and trace

24 Fetter, *Principles of Economics*, 229–35, 365–6, 554; idem, "Population or Prosperity," *AER*, 3, Suppl. (March 1913): 9, 19.
25 John Bates Clark, *Essentials of Economic Theory* (New York: Macmillan, 1907), 197, 203–7, 555.

an unending route to and over them, as they rise range beyond range and lose themselves in the distance." A world perpetually improving was not a "progressive purgatory," he said, but a "progressive paradise."[26]

Irving Fisher ignored history altogether. Although Clark had been forced by his early beliefs to take the issue of historical change seriously, Fisher regarded it as a "mystery." As a minister's son who gave up the particulars of Christian faith for belief in God, and as a person repeatedly devastated by life's events, Fisher believed that the causes of things lay far above the human substance of history. Visiting his childhood home in 1903 after his recovery from tuberculosis, he made a revealing confession.

Of all the great mysteries the greatest to me is the mystery of history. Science explains the conditional, what would happen under different circumstances, but it does not explain the actual, what does and what did happen. When and how was the great machine we call the Universe set going and why was it prearranged in the particular way it was, so that out of it must have come all that did come out and will come out down to the minutest details.... Whatever its meaning, of one thing I am convinced: That it is for us to approve and not disapprove.... What we call mistakes are deviations from our provisional programs.... And so let be all the illness and disappointments with which my cup of Fate has been filled, and so let come what will come!

Fatalism has been available to individuals in Fisher's circumstances in many times and places, but it seems a particularly fitting outcome for someone educated as he was in an environment of secularizing Protestantism and conservative American exceptionalism.[27]

Moreover, Fisher entered a professional culture in which his desire to see through history to fixed law could gain considerable credence. As president of the economics section of the American Association for the Advancement of Science in 1906, he outlined a conception of economics very like the one Simon Newcomb and the classical traditionalists had put up against the historical economists in the 1880s. The aim of economics, he said, is like physics or any other natural science, to produce general laws. History was a classificatory enterprise that produced only rules or generalizations of fact.

---

26 John Bates Clark, *Social Justice without Socialism* (Boston: Houghton Mifflin, 1914), 14–15, 48–9.

27 I. N. Fisher, *My Father*, 83–6. Ironically, Fisher's fatalistic faith was inspired by the religion of healthy-mindedness in William James's *Varieties of Religious Experience* (1902). It is noteworthy that while John Bates Clark was in college, his father died of tuberculosis after a lingering illness, and his brother immediately after, in an accident. If Clark is to be believed that his underlying economic ideas took shape at that time, a period in which he was also contemplating entering divinity school, then the theistic underpinnings of Clark's and Fisher's views could have a similar personal source. *John Bates Clark: A Memorial* (privately printed, 1938), 6–8.

Real laws, empirically tested by the methods of Bacon, were "absolutely true to nature," even though conditional upon specified circumstances. Historical economists who complained that economic laws could not be universal because economic phenomena changed over time did not understand that all scientific laws were conditional upon specified circumstances. Ecnomists should simply apply themselves "to discover what conditions make the difference in the phenomena between modern and ancient or eastern and western civilizations."[28]

At bottom, of course, Fisher felt no need for history in economics because history was only an epiphenomenon of the "great machine we call the Universe," the "great machine" of the eighteenth century set on a progressive course by the divine hand. That he felt the need of a normative economics to distinguish ideal conditions from actual ones recalls the American jeremiad. The evils that threatened America were caused by moral declensions from the exceptionalist path, "deviations from our provisional programs."

Between the traditional determinism of Fisher and the dynamic exceptionalism of Clark, marginal theorists in America had ample grounds for ignoring history. If America was on a fixed course of liberal progress, and always had been, then marginalists could envision an ahistorical projection of present categories that required no attention to qualitative change. When confronted with a historicist critique in 1912, some younger marginalists simply retorted that of course they accepted the evolutionary point of view (Clark, after all, assumed an evolution from primitive to civilized society) or that of course the static model of economics would in time be supplemented by quantitative measures of dynamic factors.[29]

### Historical economics in alliance with marginalism

Clark's dynamic theory was not the only one available to marginalists. Seligman formulated an economic interpretation of history that became an important bridge between liberal historicists and marginalists. Seligman began his career in the Gilded Age sharing the historical economists' ethical idealism and political motive. As he wrote Henry Carter Adams in 1882, he

---

28 Fisher, "Economics as a Science," 258. Fisher claimed early to have learned from the discovery of non-Euclidian geometry that "The substratum of nature is for us always covered with the veil of thought" (I. N. Fisher, *My Father*, 38), but this view was compatible with a belief that scientific laws were "absolutely true to nature." See the discussion of Karl Pearson, below, Chapter 9.

29 See the replies of B. M. Anderson, Jr., and W. M. Adriance to Simon N. Patten in "Theories of Distribution – Round Table Discussion," *AER*, 3, Suppl. (March 1913): 90–4.

wanted economics to develop theories "in accord with the historical sequence and observed actuality of facts, and – much more important – to discuss the feasibility and means of many much needed reforms." He soon published studies of the Christian socialists and medieval guilds, and hoped that the principle of cooperation by which "every workman either was, or could in time become, his own master" might "one day revolutionize existing relations." In 1890 he still lamented that Americans did not sufficiently appreciate the importance of the labor problem. "When will people realize that free trade or protection is a matter of very small consequence compared with the momentous problems of the social question?"[30]

Seligman was also intent, however, that the economists stop short of socialism and that the principle of competition, softened by social action, remain at the core of the economy. When Henry Carter Adams published the reduced version of his theory of public regulation, he was full of praise: "It is the best proof of the fact that an abandonment of laissez-faire does not connote socialism or anything materially approaching socialism."[31] Seligman could not, however, have been satisfied with Adams' reasoning. The historicist strategy of Adolph Wagner and the German historical economists that Adams followed had been to subordinate economics to national history. For the Germans, this strategy opened up economic development to their statist national path. For Adams, American national history placed severe limits on social development. Seligman found a stronger support for social change in America when in 1893 he read Achille Loria's "remarkable" exposition of the theory "that the growth of law, politics and morals is based primarily on economic relations." Unlike the emphasis of the German historical school on particular national traditions, Loria showed that "Given like economic conditions, we must have similar legal systems."[32] Seligman

30 Seligman to Adams, November 30, 1882, Henry Carter Adams Papers; E. R. A. Seligman, in "A Symposium on Several Phases of the Labor Question," *Age of Steel*, 59 (January 2, 1886): 15–16; idem, "Owen and the Christian Socialists," *PSQ*, 1 (June 1886): 206–49; idem, "Two Chapters on the Medieval Guilds of England," *PAEA*, 2 (November 1887): 100–1; idem, "Review of *nouveau dictionnaire d'économie politique*," *PSQ*, 5 (June 1890): 336.
31 E. R. A. Seligman, "Review of H. C. Adams, *The Relation of the State to Industrial Action*," *PSQ*, 2 (June 1887): 353.
32 The influence of Loria on Seligman was less theoretical than substantive. He rejected out of hand, as did most economists (Edward A. Ross was an exception), Loria's theory that the development of capitalism was due to its suppression of free land. What he found "ingenious and interesting" was Loria's ability "to extend the [economic] explanation to so many well known social, legal and religious facts." E. R. A. Seligman, "Review of Achille Loria, *Les Bases economiques de la constitution sociale*," *PSQ*, 8 (December 1893): 751–3; idem, "Review of Achile Loria, *La Proprietà fondiaria a la questione sociale*," *PSQ*, 12 (September 1898): 531–2.

found a theory of history that would break the bonds of the American exceptionalist past.

Seligman also needed to secure the domain of historical economics against the attacks of Clark and Giddings. Though his was one of the strongest voices for compromise, he continued to spar with them, urging they recognize that economics was "an ethical and therefore an historical science, since ethical and social facts are the product of history."[33] Seligman found in the economic interpretation of history a way of legitimating historical economics. The significance of his thesis for economics, he said, was to reinforce "the one great acquisition of modern economics, which differentiates it *toto coelo* from that of earlier times," the recognition "that social institutions are products of evolution, and that they thus form historical and relative categories, instead of being absolute categories."[34]

Seligman drew his economic interpretation of history specifically from Marx's historical materialism but he turned it into a liberal view of history that justified both market capitalism and liberal change. Taking a lead from Engels' grounding of Marx in evolutionary theory, and from the Marxist revisionists, Seligman set history on a liberal Darwinian course. All of history to date has been subject to "the inexorable law of nature, with its struggle for existence through natural selection.... Individual competition, class competition and race competition are all referable to the niggardliness of nature, to the inequality of human gifts, to the difference in social opportunity." The system of private property and competitive capitalism had been civilization's way of gaining the benefits of that struggle. Although Seligman did not dwell on the subject, he made it clear that capitalist development necessarily involved class conflict and international contest.

As the motor of economic progress, however, capitalism was creating greater means and wider equality among the mass of people and between nations. On this economic and social basis, society could build ethical structures that would mitigate the struggle. Economic relations did not strictly determine politics and culture, but they did predominantly condition them and the modern economy of greater abundance and social consolidation would encourage collective ethical action. The reformer was a kind of "ethical teacher ... the scout and the vanguard of Society." But he had to

---

33 E. R. A. Seligman, "Review of *The Quarterly Journal of Economics*," *PSQ*, 1 (December 1886): 702–4; idem, "Review of Gustav Schmoller, *Zur Litteraturgeschichte der Staats- und Sozialwissenschaften*," *PSQ*, 4 (September 1889): 544; Franklin H. Giddings, "Review of Friedrich von Wieser, *Der Natürliche Werth*," *PSQ*, 4 (December 1889): 684; E. R. A. Seligman, "Review of Maurice Block, *Les Progrès de la science économique depuis Adam Smith*," *PSQ*, 5 (September 1890): 534–5.
34 E. R. A. Seligman, *The Economic Interpretation of History* (New York: Macmillan, 1902), 161.

move slowly, for "only if the conditions are ripe will the reform be effected."[35]

Seligman held out the hope that progress would someday abrogate scarcity and inequality and thereby end the domination of history by economic struggle.

When science shall have given us a complete mastery over means of production, when the growth of population shall be held in check by the purposive activity of the social group, when progress in the individual and the race shall be possible without any conflict except one for unselfish ends, and when the mass of the people shall live as do to-day its noblest members – then, indeed, the economic conditions will fall into the background and will be completely overshadowed by the other social factors of progress.[36]

Like Mill's stationary state, Seligman's vision of a harmonious social order at the end of liberal history was cast as the dominance of moral over economic motives. But Mill's future was a modest affair compared to Seligman's. The difference probably owed something to the larger hopes for abundance projected by late nineteenth-century industrial development. It also owed something to the millennial expectation even the skeptical Seligman could not deny himself and his audience. His utopia was placed safely in the distant future, yet not so far in the distance that its glow might not inspire and ennoble moderate reform efforts.

Seligman's economic interpretation of history provided an important model for historical economists who wanted to work within liberal exceptionalist boundaries. Equally important, it opened a well-traveled road along which historicists and marginalists could join together. Both liberal historicists and marginalists regarded the capitalist economy as the chief dynamic force of modern history. If the market was assumed to operate by marginalist law, then history could play an auxiliary role. The classical vision of basic market laws, whose operation was modified by the changing economic circumstances within which they acted, worked equally well for neoclassical economics. The beneficent tendency of the capitalist market put real restraint on the actions open to history, while the historical character of the market opened it to liberal reform.

Fetter's marginalist text, for example, defined "economic process" as an evolutionary process, to be understood through the economic interpretation of history. If value was created primarily by market factors, it also came under the "influence of lawmaking, of collective action, and of social institutions." The final arbiter of policy became "public opinion," itself

35 Ibid., 154–5, 131.
36 Ibid., 155–6.

shaped by changing economic conditions and ethical consciousness. Because the market worked very largely for public welfare, however, Fetter thought injustice the product of "survivals" or "historical accidents," which public opinion would remove.[37]

The liberal historicists who accepted marginalism gave more power to history than did the marginalists who proceeded from the other camp, and they used it more forcefully on the side of labor. The key difference was their concern for equality. Whereas those whose basic allegiance was to marginalism were likely to emphasize the link between poverty and moral failing, fear the weakening effects of social insurance on moral character, and the distorting economic effects of strong unions, those rooted in historicism emphasized the environmental determinants of poverty and the distributional benefits of social insurance and strong unions.[38] Equality required a stronger reliance on the norms generated by history than by the market.

That the new liberal historicists embraced marginalism has to be counted a major factor in the success it enjoyed in American economics. Through judicious combination of marginalist theory and liberal history, the historicists too were able to legitimate modern capitalism and reform it. In this context of accommodation, the ultimate viability of historicism depended on the ability of history to maintain a significant existence independent of the liberal market. To what extent could historicism modify or reshape the norms and methods of economic theory? To what extent could a consciousness of historical structure survive as a set of circumstances within which the market operated? How far could historicist assumptions escape the pervasive de-historicizing tendencies of marginalism and the American exceptionalist faith?

Seligman himself provides one kind of answer to these questions. As early as 1890, he conceded the contention of Giddings and Clark that there were "veritable economic laws, which are based on a broad foundation, and which are capable of lending themselves to the changing requirements of time, place, and condition." Not until 1901, however, after he had worked out his economic interpretation of history, did he begin writing as a marginalist. The aspect of marginalism he found most salient was Clark's "social" conception of marginal utility, with its benign ethical implications. By "social," Clark and Seligman meant that value was measured by ex-

---

37 Frank A. Fetter, "The Fundamental Conceptions and Methods of Economics," in *Congress of Arts and Sciences*, 7:18; idem, *Principles of Economics*, 249, 366, 555.
38 Compare Fetter, *Principles of Economics*, 248–53, 509–13, 554; and Fisher, *Introduction to Economic Science*, chaps. 25–6, with E. R. A. Seligman, *Principles of Economics* (New York: Longmans, Green, 1916), chaps. 37–8, and Richard T. Ely et al., *Outlines of Economics* (New York: Macmillan, 1916), chaps. 22–3.

change value, by the aggregative market judgment of value, rather than by personal utility to the individual. Seligman found confirmation in this aggregative function of the market for an organic conception of society. "The social theory of value carried out to its final conclusions would show us that only through society can the individual achieve his highest aspirations."[39]

In his popular textbook, published first in 1905, as well as in his more technical work, Seligman used "social utility" to fuse the operation of the market and liberal history. Ethical norms are social in origin, Seligman said, and therefore represent what is in the long-term interest of society. "Broadly speaking, and regarded from the point of view of society as a whole, what is economically advantageous must in the long run be right; and what is correct in ethics must in the end also be profitable to the business world."

Indeed, Seligman was not just "broadly speaking." The historical growth of private property as an institution reflected society's "dimly conscious" judgment that property redounds to "social welfare" or as he called it throughout, "social utility." Accepting Clark's sanguine judgment of business combination as a higher form of market competition rather than a limitation upon it, Seligman argued that "unless there are some real advantages in the combination it cannot endure; the mere fact of its continued and prosperous existence justifies its formation." Even in discussing taxation, when Seligman found the American practice of taxation of real property diverging from his theory that capacity to pay is the most equitable principle of taxation, he concluded that something must be wrong with his theory. Could we be drifting toward the unjust? No, he answered. "If this were true we might as well abandon the notion that at bottom there is an essential correlation between economic and moral law." In Seligman's normative synthesis, history controlled the market, but it was a history inextricable from the market itself.[40]

Seligman made room within historical determinism for human initiative. If the market was the chief determinant of ethical and political life, political and ethical action was still necessary to bring it to fruition. Government could enforce fair competition, unions could be strengthened to wring from employers the wage to which their market contribution entitled them, and although "America is manifestly not yet ripe," in time she would accept a broad system of social insurance and minimum-wage laws. Seligman placed

39 Seligman, "Review of Block, *Les Progrès de la science économique*," 535; idem, "Social Elements in the Theory of Value," *QJE*, 15 (May 1901): 347.
40 E. R. A. Seligman, *Principles of Economics* (1905), 34, 134, 341; idem, "Social Aspects of Economic Law," *PAEA*, 3d ser., 5 (1904): 62.

himself on the moving edge of historical progress. Whatever is was not right, but whatever is becoming was right. "It is always on the border line of the transition from the old social necessity to the new social convenience that the ethical reformer makes his influence felt," he noted. Philosophy as well as temperament placed Seligman at the strategic center of opinion among Progressive economists. According to Dorfman, he "moved just ahead of prevailing doctrines, along positions that accorded with those of the enlightened business community . . . his views were considered a good indicator of how far to go in making adjustments to the tides of public opinion."[41]

Allyn A. Young and Thomas S. Adams, the younger economists who revised Ely's textbook in 1908 and 1916, allowed liberal history a more independent existence than did Seligman. Marginalism was a smaller presence in the revised Ely text compared to its major explanatory role in Seligman's, and its near total dominance of Fetter's. The actual circumstances of economic transactions in contemporary America governed the discussions of processes and issues as fully or more fully than theoretical principle. This clear provision of factual information, a boon to teachers of elementary students and a warrant of realism, undoubtedly accounts for the popularity of the text. It was the single largest seller until World War II.

In its line of argument, the book laid out the principal tenets of marginalist doctrine, with strategic modifications from the side of history. The marginalist argument that "under free competition the pursuit of money profits leads to the best adaptation of productive efforts to the satisfaction of the wants of consumers" was accepted as a major argument for free enterprise as opposed to socialism. But it was immediately subjected to qualifications introduced by the actual inequality of income distribution, by entrepreneurial activity that ran "counter to the more permanent interests of society," and by the fact that the satisfaction of consumer wants must consider the quality as well as quantity of satisfaction, and hence ethical considerations. Ely's old historical law of the growing interdependence of society and hence the growing need for collective action – originally global and open-ended in its statement – became a circumscribed but still spirited dictum: "All indications point to a very considerable extension of organized social activity at precisely those points where the private pursuit of money profits has proven itself inadequate." There was no preestablished harmony between history, economy, and ethical judgment.[42] As befit an heir of Ely's radicalism, however, the message was not altogether clear. Unions should

---

41 Seligman, *Principles of Economics* (1905), 434; idem, *Economic Interpretation of History*, 131; Dorfman, *Economic Mind*, 4:267.
42 Ely et al., *Outlines of Economics* (1916), 538–40.

take increasing control of business in the interest of equality, but they must cooperate with the employer's drive for business success, for "in the long run, the institution that stands in the way of productive efficiency will perish."[43] Should the market, after all, rather than ethical ideals control historical action?

In its depiction of American history, the revised text still carried some of Ely's Gilded Age vision of loss of the past and sudden confrontation with "the evil possibilities of the new industrial system." But the reviewer in the *American Economic Review* was glad that the 1916 edition had gone a long way toward excising the "revolutionary" conception of economic change that had colored Ely's original – his sharp exposition of the change from artisanal to wage labor and from the old America to the new industrial age. Too much of Ely's old attitude still remained in the revised text to suit the reviewer, however. "It is not a revolutionary change in social relations, nor yet a revised standard of justice that causes changes," he scolded. "It is rather the sensible and necessary fitting of the legislation to vast changes in industrial and social organization."[44] The text, if not all its readers, salvaged a degree of historical transformation amidst the smooth workings of liberal evolution. For the moment, within some segment of the profession, historicism maintained a precarious, somewhat ambivalent, presence against the normative pull of marginal theory and liberal exceptionalism.

One final measure of the political and theoretical limitations of liberal historicism was the debate on the economists' role opened inadvertently by Arthur T. Hadley, the conservative Yale economist, in his presidential address to the American Economic Association in 1898. A follower of the older gentry path into economics, Hadley spoke from the standpoint of the natural aristocracy, urging the new generation to forsake their academic orientation and take on public roles. Earlier, under the threat of socialism, Hadley had tried to minimize the economist's public role, but now he could return to his native orientation. Moreover, he showed the shrewd insight of a modern conservative when he urged economists to concentrate their advice on the executive branch.[45]

In the discussion that followed, Seligman gave in effect the new liberal response, and historicism was the critical tool he used to undermine Hadley's updated conservatism. In a democratic society, the economists' primary function was to influence public opinion; the kind of experts Hadley had in mind flourished only in monarchical and aristocratic regimes.

---

43 Ibid., 468–9.
44 Charles Persons, "Review of Richard T. Ely, *Outlines of Economics*," *AER*, 7 (March 1917): 102.
45 Arthur T. Hadley, "The Relation between Economics and Politics," 7–28.

Moreover, the popularity of economic doctrine depended on the class interests it furthered and the actual distribution of class power. Classical English theory rose with the commercial-industrial classes it benefited, and gained wide popularity only so long as the great majority of working people believed they too benefited from it. Economic theory will again become popular when it "becomes broad enough to represent all interests, instead of the interests of only a single class." Seligman used his economic interpretation of history to characterize classical theory as the ideology of a dominant class and implied that current economists who held onto the theory were serving contemporary class interests. Yet he assumed that economists could now choose a theory that "represented all interests."[46]

John R. Commons called Seligman's bluff as well as Hadley's. Commons, who had already been let go twice from college positions because of his radical views, agreed with Seligman's class analysis of the old economic theory. "But a man cannot represent society as a whole. If he claims to do this, he really means that he wishes to have things as they are." There are always class interests involved in any economic position and the function of the economist was to show that "the standpoint of a class is the best standpoint."[47]

Commons' rejoinder roused a storm of debate and Hadley felt obliged to reply the following year. Economists could overcome "subjective" errors, or nearly so, Hadley said; they could come closer than any others to being the "champion of the permanent interests of the whole community."[48] Commons this time came prepared with a fully developed historical analysis. On the high road, he argued for a recognition of the partiality history imposed on every economist: "We should admit that we differ among ourselves, and that our fundamental differences coincide in general with class antagonisms in society. We are a part of the social situation. History alone will decide between us. Our present vision is limited. . . . Not the individual economist, but the *associated economists* represent the permanent interests of the nation as a whole." What this meant in practice, Commons said, is that economists can exert influence only in alliance with a class. If we had a government that represented real interests and classes, instead of localities, that struggle would be clear, and Taussig or Hadley might be elected to represent one set of interests and Ely another. As it is, the practical

46 "Discussion – The President's Address," *PAEA: Economic Studies*, 4 (April 1899): 108–11.
47 Ibid., 111–13.
48 Arthur T. Hadley, "Economic Theory and Political Morality," *PAEA*, 3d ser., 1 (February 1900): 45–61, particularly 49.

end to which Hadley's policy leads is for economists to become "court preacher to the political bosses and the irresponsible trustees."[49]

Seligman was taken aback. Commons' historical analysis, extrapolated from his own economic interpretation of history, and the naming of contemporary economists as representative of class interests pushed far beyond the point the new liberals wanted to go. All of them had found historicism a convenient tool for attacking the past and for proscribing socialism as utopian, but had not turned its critique upon themselves. Seligman tried again. True, class conflict was basic to history, but "democracy means ... that the interests of all are gradually being voiced in [a] higher union of common advance and social progress." The economist has to seek that union and try to represent "the common interest of society." Contrary to Hadley, the economist could not escape the subjectivity of his place in historical time. "But this equation is not so much the personal equation of any one particular class as the personal equation of the whole body of society as differing from that of other times and places."[50]

Seligman's historical vision makes sense only if we imagine the class-conflicted liberal society of the present to be already – at a deeper level of reality – the classless democracy it would someday become, only if we imagine the economist already able to place moral claims ahead of economic ones. He located the economist vanguard in the ideal democratic future that is always potential in the American present. Commons' willingness to place himself fully within history and to identify himself and the truth with a class position was unusual in the Progressive Era. The 1899 debate ended with Hadley expressing the consensus of the great majority of speakers, whether historicist, classicist, or neoclassicist in orientation, that the economist represented society as a whole.[51]

## Liberal historical variations

Not all American economists adopted marginalism, either in its pure form or in symbiotic relationship with a liberal economic interpretation of history. Simon Patten was one of the few leaders of the older generation who

49 "Discussion – The President's Address," 79–80, 73, 74. For examples of earlier, more cautious accusations of class bias in classical economics, see Francis A. Walker, "Recent Progress of Political Economy in the United States" (1888), in *Discussions in Economics and Statistics*, 2 vols., ed. Davis R. Dewey (New York: Augustus M. Kelley, 1971 [1899]), 1:321–9; Richard T. Ely, "Political Economy in America," *North American Review*, 144 (February 1887): 113–19.
50 "Discussion – The President's Address," 82–3.
51 Ibid., 87–8. One pro-Commons discussant is recorded on pp. 287–8.

continued throughout his life to seek a different way. Although accepting a utilitarian theory of value, he never regarded marginalism as more than a minor analytical technique. Instead, he tried to formulate a dynamic account of economic evolution using elements of classical and utilitarian theory and historical evolutionism. Idiosyncratic and convoluted as his formulations were, his work is highly revealing. As Clark recognized, Patten's vision echoed the "optimistic faith that is in all of us," though his keen mind and conflicted psyche led him to plumb the contradictions within the new liberal attempt to reconstitute American exceptionalism. The son of an ambitious Illinois farmer, raised both to Presbyterian righteousness and evangelical hope, to capitalist faith and democratic dissent, his struggles emerged from the central concerns of his generation.[52]

Indeed, Patten's work spans the whole course of crisis. His first treatise was intellectually contemporaneous with Francis A. Walker's reexamination of the fundamental principles of Ricardian economics so as to legitimate the old expansive version of American exceptionalism. Previous attempts to counter Ricardo had been unscientific, Patten began; he would attempt to do so on a scientific basis. Ricardo's theory of the diminishing returns on land was correctly based on certain physical facts, but it did not take into account important social facts that counteracted their effects; namely, the relative intelligence of the working class and the ratio of intelligent to ignorant workmen. Intelligent workmen not only increased the productivity of land directly in their work, but by their demand for a variety of products, stimulated maximum productivity, allowing the land to support an ever increasing population. This "natural" consumption of modest variety was contrasted with the debased consumption of the workmen willing to live on a meager diet of few items and with the ignorant consumption of the workmen striving after crude and expensively produced luxuries. Whether or not Patten had read Jevons at the time, his erection of the demand for certain kinds of pleasures into the driving force of the economy reflected the

---

52 Daniel M. Fox, *The Discovery of Abundance: Simon N. Patten and the Transformation of Social Theory* (Ithaca: Cornell University Press, 1967), is an insightful biographical and intellectual account. Unfortunately, it sows considerable confusion by declaring Patten the discoverer of "abundance." Fox reaches this conclusion by comparing him to the classical European economists and passing over the native discourse from which his work derives. Fox defines abundance as the end of scarcity, in turn defined as "the existence of mass poverty or the inability of a society to produce enough goods and services to guarantee everyone a standard of living which will support a healthy, productive life" (pp. 2–3). By that definition, American economists had denied scarcity and affirmed abundance in America since the early nineteenth century. Patten's concern, as his first book makes clear, was how to keep America on that exceptionalist course. That is why Patten's contemporaries did not seem to recognize his "discovery."

moral world of "right consumption" of American economists from Francis Wayland through Amasa and Francis Walker.[53]

Patten was driven to this analysis by the need to discover what had gone wrong with America. If Ricardo's law of diminishing returns held sway in the earliest stage of civilization, when small use was made of skill and capital, in the middling state of progress American exceptionalists had long inhabited, individual exertion produced an increasingly higher ratio of intelligent workmen, right consumption, and widely distributed benefits. How then explain "why there is at the present time such an unequal distribution of wealth, and why wages are low," why in short there is so much "social distress"? Patten's answer was that America was entering into that advanced stage of civilization England inhabited, which brought with it debased workmen, monopoly, and decline. Forces of retrogression were built into the forces of progress. "Every improvement which simplifies or lessens manual labor," Patten said, "increases the amount of the deficiencies which the laboring classes may possess without their being thereby overcome in the struggle for subsistence that the survival of the ignorant brings upon society." In as strict terms as it had for Sumner, capitalist progress depended on the survival of the intelligent and the elimination of the ignorant in the "struggle for subsistence." Yet unlike Sumner, Patten recognized that the social forces operating in the economy were open to human direction. The solutions Patten proposed in this first book belonged to the producer's liberal-republican logic: Ease the pressure of debt on workingmen, curtail speculation and excessive borrowing, encourage producers' cooperatives, and above all compensate for the specialized ignorance produced by the division of labor through education of all the faculties.[54]

As Patten came into contact with his German-educated cohort in the mid-1880s and joined the Wharton School at the University of Pennsylvania in 1889, he recast his theory on the basis of liberal historicism. The difficulties America faced were no longer, as in the republican historical imagination, the heralds of advanced decline, but rather the marks of a transitional period to a new and higher stage of civilization. The ignorant consumption habits that retarded progress now belonged to a primitive stage of civilization, to an economy of strong appetites disciplined by the pain of constant threat. As external threats receded and goods multiplied, however, people began to respond to pleasures rather than pains and to develop the

---

53 Simon N. Patten, *The Premises of Political Economy* (New York: Augustus M. Kelley, 1968 [1885]). Patten conceived the book between 1879 and 1882. Cf. Fox, *Discovery of Abundance*, 24–31.
54 Patten, *Premises of Political Economy*, 19, 14, 220, 216, 120, 222–44.

"weaker" appetites and more varied demands that fueled economic progress. Patten's originality lay in his recognition of the central roles consumption and consumer psychology would play in the new industrial economy.[55]

Still, the republican fear of decline lurked in the shadows of this liberal history. "Nation after nation has gone down" as they entered into a pleasure economy and without the old safeguards on character fell into vice and lethargy. Modern nations were in a long period of transition; although conditions had changed, the old habits and appetites persisted. Moreover, immigration brought in immense numbers of primitive peoples with primitive habits. Unwilling to accept the uncertainty of history, he declared that there must be a "normal" line of evolutionary progress leading to realization of the pleasure economy. Individuals might choose their own pleasures, "Yet their choices would of necessity conform to the conditions of social welfare or the race could not survive." Natural selection thus worked over time to perpetuate only those "social" motives which benefited the race. The pure pleasure economy that was developing would be a "social commonwealth."[56]

What became increasingly evident as Patten pushed further to the roots of his theory, was that despite his belief in their ultimate harmony, the law of natural selection of the capitalist economy was in conflict with the law of natural selection of the society that developed "social" motives. Capitalist competition created autonomous, intelligent workmen only when the dependent classes ended in "extermination," he said in 1889, although humanitarian feelings softened the process. In 1896 in his "Theory of the Social Forces" he emphasized on the one hand development of social bonds and higher democratic ideals that encouraged an inclusive sense of social responsibility. Yet at the same time he argued that only by creating invidious ties that excluded the ignorant could society move upward. Patten's observation quoted in Chapter 5 about the way in which groups in America were differentiating themselves from those below them, from the Negro, the "scab," and the immigrant, ended in approval. Although the lines "are not yet clearly or properly drawn, yet as now drawn they indicate the manner in which the growing civic instincts will act." Like Giddings, Patten believed

55 Simon N. Patten, "The Effect of the Consumption of Wealth on the Economic Welfare of Society," in *Science Economic Discussion*, Henry Carter Adams et al. (New York: Science, 1886), 123–35; Simon N. Patten, "The Theory of Social Forces," *AAAPSS*, 7, Suppl. (January 1896); Fox, *Discovery of Abundance*, chaps. 3–4. For a perceptive study of ideas about consumption, in the context of actual consumption patterns, see Daniel Horowitz, *The Morality of Spending: Attitudes toward the Consumer Society in America, 1875–1940* (Baltimore: Johns Hopkins University Press, 1985).
56 Patten, "Theory of Social Forces," 77, 84.

the United States was to move toward the inclusive bonds of the social commonwealth by selective and invidious competition.[57]

Unlike Giddings, Patten grew increasingly uncomfortable with this conflicted view. In 1899 he declared that "Progress is a higher law than equality, and a nation must choose it at any cost." The only sure way to progress was "eradication of the vicious and inefficient." In 1902 he was able to distinguish between those made poor by economic causes and those who failed to adjust; only the latter were true evolutionary losers requiring eugenic treatment. Although he concentrated his efforts on ameliorative rather than invidious reforms, he never abandoned the latter. It would be interesting to know whether the devoted army of social workers and reformers Patten trained at Pennsylvania shared or overlooked his ambivalence.[58] It is clear in our own day that his adherence to both invidious competition and inclusive democratic ideals was less a nineteenth-century hangover than a dogged recognition of the conflict embodied in the new liberal attempt to graft a social ethic onto competitive capitalism.

Patten was equally perceptive and equally unsuccessful in turning his vision of economic progress into a coherent theory of historical evolution. He was among the first to use the new functional psychology of William James and James Mark Baldwin to explain how "social forces" were formed. He showed how the "constructive activity of the mental mechanism" created ideals and "forms of thought" which then colored all perception, producing the "subjective" environment within which humanity lived. He set out to write a history of English thought, his own "economic interpretation of history," based on general biological, psychological, and social evolutionary principles he had deduced from theory. In the complex and changing conditions of history, these general laws could not be proved by inductive historical investigation, he admitted, only illustrated. The necessity of bridging general laws and historical particulars led him to rely heavily on the effect of climate on race psychology and of motor or sensory psychological orientation on different cultural epochs. The result was a more bizarre mixture than was usual, even for Patten.[59]

57 Simon N. Patten, *The Consumption of Wealth* (Philadelphia: T. and J. W. Johnson, 1889), 65; idem, "Theory of Social Forces," 133–43.
58 Simon N. Patten, *The Development of English Thought* (New York: Garland, 1974 [1899]), 302–3; Fox, *Discovery of Abundance*, 89, 93, 210–11n.; Steven A. Sass, *The Pragmatic Imagination: A History of the Wharton School, 1881–1981* (Philadelphia: University of Pennsylvania Press, 1982), 98–9, 102–9.
59 Patten, "Theory of Social Forces," 37, 54, 45, 70, 80–5, 126–33; Patten, *Development of English Thought*, v, vii. Patten distinguished between the general laws, which applied to the evolution of humanity on earth, and truly universal laws, which could only emerge from knowledge of other forms of life in the universe.

Although he tried again, Patten never succeeded in forging a viable historical competitor to marginalist economics. Nor was he alone in that failure. The widening appreciation of historical change had been proscribed or drawn off into liberal models of economics and history, where their historicist potential was contained or eroded. Yet historicism was still plainly available for use, and by economists less hopelessly conflicted than Patten. The problem was how to use it. Although some historical economists had believed that historical inquiry would generate economic laws comparable to those of classical theory, that expectation had largely disappeared by the turn of the century. Historical economics was widely criticized in America for having generated only formless empirical detail. The charge was not entirely true. Useful synthetic categories and models of historical anlysis had been generated by Gustav Schmoller's research, Sidney and Beatrice Webb's history of labor organization in England, the synthetic studies of Werner Sombart and J. A. Hobson, and by a host of socialist and semisocialist writers. Still, even sympathetic American economists had little sense of how to develop these methods and insights. Jacob H. Hollander, for example, who welcomed the Webbs' study of trade unionism in 1898 as a model for economics, could not form a coherent view of historical-empirical investigation, and his interest in the empirical grounding of economics soon drifted away from its origin in historicism and attached instead to the scientific demand for verified theory.[60]

Part of the difficulty faced by historical economists was the state of the historical discipline in America. Economists during this period often studied history as a minor field, and in graduate school chose empirical topics that encompassed some history. But this experience could not have given them much encouragement that they could reconstitute economics on a historical basis. As we shall see, the historians were busy providing the basic materials and detailed groundwork of historical study. Beyond this, decentralization and the structure of professional advancement imposed a pattern of disconnected monographic study on historians and economists alike. More basic was the empiricist epistemology and realist cultural impulse that steered historians toward factualism. Unable to recognize the conceptual nature of all knowledge and the heuristic value of theory in historical

60 Broadus Mitchell, "Jacob Harry Hollander," *DAB*, Suppl. 2, 310–12; J. H. Hollander, "A Study of Trade Unionism," *PSQ*, 13 (December 1898): 694–704; idem, "The Scope and Method of Political Economy," *Congress of Arts and Sciences*, 7: 64–5; idem, "The Present State of the Theory of Distribution," *PAEA*, 3d ser., 7 (February 1906): 40–3; idem, "Economic Theorizing and Scientific Progress, *AER*, 6, Suppl. (March 1916): 124–39 and "Tendencies in Economic Theory – Discussion," 162–9.

knowledge, they were ill-equipped to find in history the kind of analytical generalizations that could be useful to economics.

The response among historians to the various economic interpretations of history that arose at the turn of the century is revealing. Not only Karl Lamprecht's and Patten's idiosyncratic theories met with the historians' disapproval of single economic factors and economic determinism, but Seligman's did as well, even before he fused it with marginalist economics. Seligman had originally hoped that his theory would do "even more for history" than for economics, for he saw historians turning toward wider study of "social institutions." But even those sympathetic to the "new history" spoke out forcefully against his predetermined principles of classification and organization. Economic theory began to work its way into historical interpretation during the Progressive period only as it began to appeal to a younger cohort of more radical historians and proved itself in empirical investigation.[61]

To the extent that the historical economists absorbed the historicist vision and particularistic canon of the historians, they were drawn away from historical economics toward economic history, a field that narrowed after the turn of the century around the focus of business history. A number of talented historical economists who felt the bonds tighten slipped away. William J. Ashley, originally part of Oxford's historicist revolt, found himself at Harvard increasingly tied to detailed studies of medieval economic history. The real duty of detailed research, Ashley complained, as well as "indolence and scientific caution often combine to keep the professional historian within a somewhat narrow range of interests." Giving up the task himself for the chance of wider and more practical influence, he left Harvard for England to found a school of commerce. Edwin F. Gay, a learned historical economist trained by Schmoller, did the same thing at Harvard under Eliot's prompting, founding the Harvard Business School.[62]

Some historical economists who survived the Gilded Age, like John R.

61 Seligman, *Economic Interpretation of History*, 163–4; Edward P. Cheyney in "Discussion," to E. R. A. Seligman, "The Economic Interpretation of History," *PAEA*, 3d ser., 3 (February 1902): 393–7; C. W. Alvord, "Review of E. R. A. Seligman, *The Economic Interpretation of History*," *AHR*, 8 (April 1903): 517–19.
62 W. J. Ashley, "The Study of Economic History: After Seven Years" (1899), in *Surveys Historic and Economic* (London: Longmans Green, 1900), 29–30; Herbert Heaton, *A Scholar in Action, Edwin F. Gay* (Cambridge, Mass.: Harvard University Press, 1952). The creation of a branch of economic history separate from the kind of Progressive economic history developing within the historical profession is discussed by Steven A. Sass, "Entrepreneurial Historians and History: An Essay in Organized Intellect" (Ph.D. dissertation, Johns Hopkins University, 1977).

Commons, nonetheless continued the effort to reach synthetic conclusions. Commons was originally one of the evangelical band whose goal was "the Kingdom of God" on earth. Like others formed by the Gilded Age crisis, his chief concern was the inequality of the laboring class. Commons' distinctive viewpoint combined this stubborn recognition of inequality with traditional individualistic and exceptionalist premises. From the beginning he stressed that individuals were responsible for the use they made of their opportunities. Republican politics and the producers' economy, buttressed by free land, had once rewarded individual effort with economic independence and effective citizenship. By the 1890s politics had become corrupted and market gains monopolized by capitalists. America needed a massive effort of regeneration.[63]

At the turn of the century, Commons, like most of his generation, abandoned hope of impending transformation. Dismissed from academia, he began doing research for an independent business organization, the United States Industrial Commission, 1902–4, and the National Civic Federation, then in its new liberal phase of bringing together enlightened businessmen and conservative labor leaders. In that context he began to see that "There is no social movement of the past twenty years more quiet nor more potent than the organization of private interests." In the consolidated economy, lone individuals could no longer hope to exert their will, but joining together as a class and organized, they could protect their interests. Commons wanted to reorganize political representation around interest groups and to give the laboring class a fair place in the constitutional order. Joining the republican tradition's logic of balance to Clark's oceanic metaphor, he wanted to "get back to first principles."[64]

The great constitutional safeguards which we have asserted since the time of Magna Carta have been adopted in order to place a subordinate class on an equilibrium with a dominant class.... If this occurs, then no one class or part of a class will be big enough to swing all the voters. Like the waves on the ocean it may move up and down, but it comes back to the level of the massive bulk beneath.[65]

---

63 John R. Commons, *Social Reform and the Church* (New York: Thomas Y. Crowell, 1894), 4, 36–7, 92; Commons to Ely, January 30, 1894, Ely Papers; John R. Commons, *The Distribution of Wealth* (New York: Macmillan, 1893).

64 John R. Commons, "Representative Democracy" (1900), in *Representative Democracy* (New York: Bureau of Economic Research, 1900), 20, 23–4. On the balance of classes, see J. G. A. Pocock, *The Machiavellian Moment* (Princeton, N.J.: Princeton University Press, 1975), on James Harrington, 383–400.

65 John R. Commons, "Class Conflict: Is It Growing in America, and Is It Inevitable?" (1906), in *Labor and Administration* (New York: Macmillan, 1913), 82–4.

Classes had conflicting interests; politics and economics were arenas of class conflict; political power must be restructured to allow workers, through their unions, a fair fight. But classes were in the end aggregated interest groups and the struggle would go on within, and be kept in equilibrium by, the competitive market and the balanced republican Constitution.

At Wisconsin, funded by the Carnegie Institution's economic history project, Commons began work on a massive history of American labor which would support his political economy. He and his students opened the field of labor history to serious investigation, bringing to bear on it both the methods of historical scholarship and an analytic purpose informed by economic and political theory. The result was the creation of an exceptionalist interpretation of American labor. Commons' central argument was that American labor organization was unique, the product of competitive market conditions and America's unique historical circumstances. Contra Marx, Commons said, American workers organized before there were factories, to protect their economic position in the market. The stimulus was not capitalist exploitation but the extension of the market and the changed relations and "unfair" competition it introduced. European theorists had missed this central fact.

There are certain considerations in European history which have obliterated or confused the pure economic facts. Industrial evolution, considered as a mere economic process, had to work its way up through superimposed racial, military, tribal, feudal, ecclesiastical and guild regulations and restrictions.... It is this bald simplicity of American individualism, without much covering of races, armies, guilds or prelates, that permits us to trace out all of the economic structures in their evolution from infancy to manhood.

In short, the development of differing class interests and trade-union organization was a natural product of the competitive market, most natural in America, and hence could expect a distinctively American result.[66]

"As the outcome of history is known, its meaning is read," Commons said. The outcome toward which Commons' history moved was the American Federation of Labor, with its class consciousness limited to wage and job consciousness. What labor wanted was "wages, hours, and security, without financial responsibility, but with power enough to command respect." The history of American labor was a history of the increasing

66 John R. Commons et al., *History of Labour in the United States*, 4 vols. (New York: Macmillan, 1918–35); idem, "American Shoemakers, 1648–1895" (1909), in *Labor and Administration*, 259–61. See also idem, "European and American Unions" (1911), ibid., 149–57.

development of trade unions that reflected that philosophy. Humanitarianism, "intellectuals," had at times helped to improve the conditions of labor, but they had more often distracted labor from its true interests. The future of labor lay in collective bargaining and the judicial recognition of labor's gains. Making voluntary bargains was a historical, political activity; there was no predetermined harmony. But Commons trusted to that activity because it was a modern pluralist recreation of the liberal-republican's independent exertion of citizenship.[67] This was Commons' great problem with the flood of new immigrants. "Old-world traits incapacitate citizens for deliberative self-government," he believed, and without that, neither capitalist economy nor republican polity could work fairly.[68]

The exceptionalist theory of American labor Commons worked out during the Progressive Era quickly gained currency. Whatever broader influence its historical-analytic method could have had on economics was limited by the congruence Commons assumed between the natural market and history in America. Moreover, the increasing segregation of the study of labor, as of history, in subspecialties, neutralized its implications for economic theory. Commons meanwhile worked slowly toward a broader historical vision of economics that would capture his unique blend of radicalism and traditionalism.

As his example suggests, methodological invention was fueled by political will. It required a more critical perspective on modern capitalism and one's own national history, such as appeared in the theories of Hobson, Sombart, or Max Weber, to generate genuinely alternative views of capitalist development. Hence the most sustained challenge to the marginalists' dominance in America grew out of the socialist, evolutionary theory of Thorstein Veblen.

### Veblen's historico-evolutionism

Among the creative social scientists at the turn of the century, Veblen was the only true outsider, so much so that in his later years he identified with the alienated Jewish intellectuals of nineteenth-century Europe. The son of poor Norwegian peasants turned Minnesota farmers, Veblen felt painfully out of place in both his native and adopted worlds. He was also a profoundly passive-aggressive personality, turning in on his own impulses while turning

---

67 Commons, "Introduction," in *History of Labour*, 1:3–21, especially p. 9; idem, "The Opportunity of Management," in John R. Commons et al., *Industrial Government* (New York: Macmillan, 1921), 267–9; Jack Barbash, "John R. Commons and the Americanization of the Labor Problem," *Journal of Economic Issues*, 1 (September 1967): 161–7.

68 John R. Commons, "Review of Julius Drachsler, *Democracy and Assimilation*," *PSQ*, 37 (March 1922): 147; idem, *Races and Immigrants in America* (New York: Macmillan, 1907).

a brilliantly subversive intellect against the established orders of the world. Although most of the heirs of the Gilded Age left abandoned socialism for liberalism and tried to retain in some form its ethical stance, Veblen retained its socialism and disdained its ethicism. Despite his radical impulses, his personality so deflected them that he was partially insulated from attack. Though his ideas always made him suspect, he would be repeatedly fired less for radical views than for unconventional relations with women.[69]

After earning a doctorate in philosophy at Yale, Veblen was barred from a philosophical appointment by irreligion and spent seven desultory years back in the rural west. The agrarian radicalism of those years and Edward Bellamy's socialist writings, drawing on populist attitudes his family shared, sent Veblen to Cornell in 1891 to study economics. In that year, his first publication as an economist, "Some Neglected Points in the Theory of Socialism," was already a characteristic performance, both in its use of the Gilded Age left and its subversion of traditional forms.

Veblen's strategy was that of his first teacher at Carleton College, the young John Bates Clark, who had turned Herbert Spencer against himself. Beginning "in the spirit of a disciple," he ended showing the plausibility of the present industrial situation leading to the establishment of socialism in America. The form of social organization socialism seeks was not, as Spencer claimed, a reversion to a regime of status, but a system of "Constitutional government" already present in the political realm, "the boasted free institutions of the English-speaking people" which had become particularly in America, "democratic traditions and habits of mind." Three years later at the University of Chicago, he saw Coxey's army as an indication of the same direction of social evolution; the American constitutional system could turn into "the industrial republic of the socialists." His entry into the Gilded Age economic dialogue was at the now familiar point of connecting the evolution toward socialism to a democratic reading of American exceptionalism.[70]

The tone and substance of his argument was already distinctive, however. Rather than using the republican transformation as a device to soften the change, he exploited its irony. Nor was his vision the cooperative commonwealth of the ethical historical school. Socialism was to be created by the demand of the disaffected common people, and it meant unequivocally the nationalization of industry and its subordination to national democratic

---

69 Above, note 3, and Thorstein Veblen, "The Intellectual Pre-eminence of Jews in Modern Europe" (1919), in *Essays in Our Changing Order*, ed. Leon Ardzrooni (New York: Viking, 1934), 219–31.

70 Thorstein Veblen, "Some Neglected Points in the Theory of Socialism," *AAAPSS*, 2 (November 1891): 345–62, 359; idem, "The Army of the Commonweal," *JPE*, 2 (June 1894): 456–61, 458; Dorfman, *Thorstein Veblen*, 3–16.

government. With Ely clearly in mind, he noted caustically that those who took the socialist position primarily on ethical grounds, "the cis-atlantic line of the Socialists of the Chair, whose point of departure is the divine right of the state," were in fact moved by a paternalistic reactionary spirit, rather than a democratic one.[71]

Veblen's analysis of the new socialistic sentiments of the common people was the starting point of the striking line of argument he articulated at the end of the decade in *The Theory of the Leisure Class*. Socialism was founded at bottom in envy. Emulation was, after all, a universal trait of human nature: "It is a striving to be, and more immediately to be thought to be, better than one's neighbor." But what channeled that desire into material emulation was modern industrial society, by making wealth the common standard of success; making the means of acquisition and comfort easier; opening a wider field for emulation; and "widening the environment," so that one must adopt easily accessible signs of success. The "standard of living" in modern society is indefinitely expandable, and as each new generation is born into a society "already encrusted with this habit of mind" the effects will be cumulative. It was precisely this heightened emulation that produced the "feeling of injured justice" and "slighted manhood" and that generated socialism. In a socialist organization of society, emulation could turn to "perhaps nobler and socially more serviceable" activities. Socialism might even produce – though that surely was utopian – a feeling of the dignity of labor.[72]

In focusing on emulation, Veblen was, along with Simon Patten, one of the first American economists of his generation to sense the growing importance in modern capitalist society of consumption and its conventional character. For Patten and most of his colleagues, the focus on consumption led to an irenic view of how the spread of consumer goods would moderate class consciousness.[73] For Veblen, emulative consumption was more problematic. It generated the class conflict that might create socialism, yet it also generated what he was already portraying as a kind of false consciousness, an excessively stimulated materialistic emulation that socialism might replace with "perhaps nobler and more serviceable" aims. The problem of the existence of this false consciousness was one line of analysis carrying Veblen forward. Another was still a satiric aside in 1891, the dignity of labor, the central value in socialist philosophy, which was in need of theoretical legitimation.

71 Dorfman, *Thorstein Veblen*, 460.
72 Veblen, "Some Neglected Points in the Theory of Socialism," 345–62.
73 David B. Schulter, "Economics and the Sociology of Consumption: Simon Patten and Early Academic Sociology in America, 1894–1904," *JHS*, 2 (Fall–Winter 1979–80): 132–62.

Veblen recognized like Patten that he required a "theory of culture," and that also sent him to psychology. His thesis at Yale had been on Kant and he followed the path of neo-Kantian idealism to psychological naturalism, as Dewey had followed Hegelian idealism. Veblen appeared to equate Kant's regulative principle of the reflective judgment with the "guiding principle of inference" discussed by Charles Peirce, whom he heard at Johns Hopkins. "That which determines us, from given premises, to draw one inference rather than another," Peirce said, "is some habit of mind, whether it be constitutional or acquired." From his first analysis of material emulation and democratic constitutional preferences, Veblen saw "habits of mind" as products of historical experience.[74]

The context in which he developed his ideas over the next few years was his reading of socialist literature, particularly Marx and the Marxist revisionists. At Chicago he regularly taught a course in socialism and wrote all the book reviews on the subject for Laughlin's *Journal of Political Economy*. He soon recognized that Marx was the foremost theorist of socialism, identified Karl Kautsky's revisionism with the view he himself had taken of the "industrial republic," and praised Italian revisionists like Enrico Ferri and Antonio Labriola who were joining Marx to Darwin and evolutionary theory. By 1897 he was identifying these more modern and "sensible" Italian Marxists with the view that material conditions can affect institutions only by affecting "the individual's habitual view of things." Labriola's "materialistic conception" of history provided "a guiding principle (*Leitfaden*) in the study of social life and of social structure," he said. "Economic activities, and the habits bred by them, determine the activities and the habitual view of things in other directions than the economic one" by a process of "selective elimination." Veblen was the American Gramsci, drawn by the problem of false consciousness and training in idealist philosophy into a revision of Marx's theory of history.[75]

The other building blocks of Veblen's theory were functional psychology and racial anthropology. He found in the new psychology his fundamental norm of human nature. Man "is an agent seeking in every act the accom-

---

74 Thorstein Veblen, "Kant's Critique of Judgment" (1884), in *Essays in Our Changing Order*, 175–93; Stanley M. Daugert, *The Philosophy of Thorstein Veblen* (New York: Kings Crown Press, 1950), 16–23.

75 Thorstein Veblen, "Review of Thomas Kirkup, A History of Socialism," *JPE*, 1 (March 1893): 300–2; idem, "Review of Karl Kautsky, *Der Parlamentarismus, die Volksgesetzgebung und die Sozialdemokratie*," *JPE*, 2 (March 1894): 312–14; idem, "Review of Enrico Ferri, *Socialisme et science positive*," *JPE*, 5 (December 1896): 97–103; idem, "Review of Richard Calwer, *Einführung in den Sozialismus*," *JPE*, 5 (March 1897): 270–2; idem, "Review of Antonio Labriola, *Essais sur la conception materialiste de l'histoire*," *JPE*, 5 (June 1897): 390–1.

plishment of some concrete, objective impersonal end." The common view of the irksomeness of labor could only be a "conventional aversion," for no species could be instinctively averse "to whatever activity goes to sustain the life of the species." Veblen called this fundamental instinct toward "purposeful action" the "instinct of workmanship; negatively it expresses itself in a deprecation of waste." It is "this pervading norm of action" which "guides the life of men in all the use they make of material things," and therefore also it was the "guiding principle for any science that aims to be a theory of the economic life process." The propensity for "purposeful action" that created the active worker and his standard of human integrity also created, however, the conventional culture that molded his habits of thought. The way in which people come to see the world "depends upon the interest from which a discrimination of the facts is sought."[76] The tension between a natively creative and culturally determined human nature was at the center of his theory and the history it portrayed.

The racial theory that runs through Veblen's work is its least attractive aspect to current readers. Veblen accepted the theory of biological racial types that was used by some of his Darwinian-socialist sources and had begun to permeate American discussion of the Anglo-Saxon heritage and exceptionalist fate. This racial anthropology had important uses for Veblen, providing a stable biological basis for historical evolution and a link to American history. The "dolichocephalic blond" race was after all the creator and heir of "the boasted free institutions of the English-speaking people." The aggressiveness that created an obstreperous, freedom-loving character also made the capitalist elite that descended from this long-headed race the masters of chicanery, force, and fraud. Veblen's style was always to subvert, rather than discard, conventional wisdom. At the same time, he developed an interest in his own racial roots. He had a deep affection for Nordic myth, eventually publishing a translation of the Icelandic sagas. In the Progressive Era climate of racial prejudice, a defensive identification with race was not an uncommon response among the outcasts.[77]

Veblen brought these themes to fruition in 1899 in his evolutionary theory of the leisure class. The period of savagery, the earliest and longest period of time in which the human species had lived, was primarily a peaceful period, in which the interest of the group in survival took precedence over indi-

---

76 Thorstein Veblen, "The Instinct of Workmanship and the Irksomeness of Labor," *AJS*, 4 (September 1898): 187–90; idem, *Theory of the Leisure Class* (New York: Modern Library, 1934 [1899]), 9.

77 Veblen, *Theory of the Leisure Class*, 215. He quoted particularly from Georges Vacher de Lapouge, who had vaguely socialist leanings. See Linda L. Clark, *Social Darwinism in France* (University: University of Alabama Press, 1984).

vidual, self-interested motives. It was thus in that long, savage prehistory that the instinct of workmanship became through habit and natural selection the basic stratum of human nature. As the use of tools led to the creation of a surplus, predation became common and new standards of work and habits of thought emerged. The exploitive force of the hunters and warriors was admired, and the menial labor of gathering and agriculture was looked down upon. As wealth accumulated, a caste system developed along the lines first of sex and age – it was women and the young who were forced to menial labor – and then along lines of class. Under high barbarism or feudalism, the leisure class who owned the property and wealth displayed their power by developing to a high art their conspicuous disdain of work and usefulness.[78]

With the advent of the "quasi-peaceable" stage of industry Veblen brought home his shaft, for the successors to the feudal elite were the owners and managers of modern industry, whose concern with pecuniary gain led them to engage in and admire the same predatory behaviors as their ancestors, and adopt the same genteel standards of reputability. If in modern conditions they cared less for force, they rather excelled in fraud. If the development of modern industry had a new concern for productivity, so that all must make a show of work, "conspicuous consumption" replaced conspicuous leisure as the leading mark of reputability.

The working class in modern society was, like its servile predecessors, less touched by standards of pecuniary gain. Still, especially in industrial society, leisure-class standards of reputability filtered down through the social hierarchy adding a kind of false consciousness to the burden of exploitation the lower classes already bore. In one of his most chilling passages, Veblen argued

that the institution of a leisure class acts to make the lower classes conservative by withdrawing from them as much as it may of the means of sustenance, and so reducing their consumption, and consequently their available energy, to such a point as to make them incapable of the effort required for the learning and adoption of new habits of thought.

At the same time, "the imperative example set by the upper class in fixing the canons of reputability fosters the practice of conspicuous consumption." As an interpreter of American society, Veblen bore witness to Tocqueville's conjecture that an aristocracy might develop in the United States around the growing power of the capitalist class. In the class society America had become in the Gilded Age, democracy did not destroy classes, only widened the field of emulation, thereby strengthening upper-class hegemony.

78 Veblen, "The Instinct of Workmanship," 190–201, 197. Veblen covers the same ground in *Theory of the Leisure Class*, chaps. 1, 2.

But there was a contrary tendency at work. The machine process, with its relentless instrumental rationality, was coming to dominate modern culture. Industrialization was revitalizing the instinct of workmanship and was generating impersonal, matter-of-fact attitudes which undermined the older leisure-class habits of thought, particularly among the workers and lesser managers engaged in industrial employment. In the rise of science, the "new woman," and more functional aesthetic standards, as well as in working-class radicalism, Veblen could see the old leisure-class mentality crumbling. The game was close and he did not call it, but his evolutionary structure gave the future to the underlying industrial process, always the progressive force in history, and to the still fundamental productive instinct of human nature.[79]

Probably the most important economic idea in *The Theory of the Leisure Class* was the distinction between "industrial" and "pecuniary" functions. The legitimacy of productive labor and the illegitimacy of capital accumulation and profit-seeking runs through socialism, radical antebellum exceptionalism, and populism alike. Veblen transferred the distinction between honest labor and mere speculation, between the producers and the parasitic owners, middlemen, and money handlers to the whole course of capitalist development. In modern industry, he claimed, the split between the industrial function carried on by the workers and technicians and the pecuniary function of the owners and managers was becoming ever more salient. Veblen's distinction became the basis for an ongoing critique of American business institutions and of the acquisitive culture of American capitalist society.[80]

In 1904 Veblen developed that idea into a new theory of business enterprise. Drawing on historical categories of capitalist development worked out by Schmoller and Sombart, he analyzed what marginalism ignored: the shift after about 1870 in America from a market economy dominated by money exchange to one dominated by credit, and with it the increasing concentration of business control, particularly by the financiers, who purveyed credit. Veblen focused on the recurrent, increasingly virulent, cycles of prosperity and depression and his explanation rested on the sharpening divergence he saw between production and the business orientation of owners and managers. Using the report of the United States Industrial Commission to as good effect as Marx had used the English Blue Books, he

---

79 Veblen, *Theory of the Leisure Class*, chaps. 8–9, particularly pp. 196, 204; Alexis de Tocqueville, *Democracy in America* (New York: Vintage, 1954 [1835]), vol. 2, chap. 20.
80 Dorfman, *Thorstein Veblen*, 3–16; Thorstein Veblen, *The Theory of Business Enterprise* (New York: Scribner, 1904).

documented the exclusively pecuniary motives of the "captains of industry" as they created havoc in cutthroat competition, and as they bid up paper values beyond real values, generating cycles of boom and bust. He hardly had to recall to his readers the marginalists' bland account of prices seeking a normal equilibrium to create his ironic effect. The outcome of such a wasteful system, he predicted, was extinction, perhaps as Hobson warned, when "war and armaments and imperialist politics" sacrificed business profits "to the exigencies of the higher politics." The more likely outcome was socialism, for the machine process was reviving among workers the instinct of workmanship. The logical end of the "trade-union animus" – despite its many pecuniary "survivals" – was socialism.[81]

Veblen's theory, like the others we have been studying, was meant to shape the orientation of his discipline as well as the course of American history. The Darwinian Marxism of the Italians first prompted him to ask in 1896 why economics and sociology were not evolutionary sciences, and two years later he asked that question directly of his economic colleagues. Economics was not an evolutionary science, Veblen said, because classical economics was dominated by a very different approach, one which often drew on historical fact and causal explanation, but which pushed its analyses back to an essentially teleological explanation of economic processes in terms of "normality." Phenomena that worked along any other causal sequence were simply played off as "disturbing factors." Such an attitude of mind was essentially spiritual, derived from the older natural-law theories and hedonistic psychology, and beyond that, from an archaic, animistic habit of mind.

What economics should try to explain was a historical question: "the sequence of change in the methods of doing things, the methods of dealing with the material means of life." Because history was a cultural process, "an evolutionary economics must be the theory of a process of cultural growth as determined by the economic interest, a theory of a cumulative sequence of economic institutions stated in terms of the process itself." Here, presumably, was a call for a historicist mode of economic analysis.[82]

Yet Veblen quickly rejected the historical school of economics as a model. It had provided descriptive, narrative, and partially causal accounts of historical change, not a theory of historical change. The model he proposed was the evolutionary science used by biology, psychology, and anthropology, which provided "a genetic account of an unfolding process."[83] Veblen

---

81 Veblen, *Theory of Business Enterprise*, particularly chap. 7, pp. 328–55, 395.
82 Veblen, "Review of Ferri, *Socialisme et science positive*," 97–103; Thorstein Veblen, "Why Is Economics Not an Evolutionary Science?" *QJE*, 12 (July 1898): 384, 387–8, 390–1, 393.
83 Veblen, "Why Is Economics Not an Evolutionary Science?" 378, 388.

understood history as a single genetic process, a closed system, in which the primary variables were grounded in universal biological categories and their interaction traced over time. To treat history in this way is the method of evolutionary positivism. The "cumulative sequence of economic institutions" he traced often stood far distant from the historical evidence. Indeed, his view that cultural change operated by "selective elimination" allowed him to avoid close historical analysis. Still, Veblen had learned from Marx as well as Spencer and he had a sharp eye for cultural nuance and institutional change. When he focused on limited historical periods, as in his analysis of modern business enterprise, his wartime study of the institutional roots of German militarism, and his postwar book on absentee ownership, he produced work that was both historically grounded and widely significant.

The disjunction between his historicist and positivist premises came increasingly to trouble him. In the decade after *The Theory of Business Enterprise* he became aware that biology and psychology were destabilizing his categories of race and instinct and that historical change produced more complex and contradictory effects than he had accounted for. The result was a restatement of his theory in 1914 that tried to adjust for these complexities. Veblen admitted that there was no tendency in history for original human nature to work its way back to dominance, no period of history "more suitable to the untroubled functioning of these instincts than any phase that has gone before." Yet he was still able to trace the outline of the exceptionalist economic republic he had envisioned. He saw a connection "in point of time, place, and race, between the modern machine technology, the material sciences, religious skepticism, and that spirit of insubordination that makes the substance of what are called free or popular institutions." The architecture still stood, but it now stood on a historical conjuncture and it required wheels within wheels to make it go.[84]

Positivism informed not only Veblen's evolutionary model, but also his conception of science. For Veblen, science was the quintessential form of the impersonal, matter-of-fact attitude generated by industrial development. Like his closest friends on the Chicago faculty – the mechanistic biologist Jacques Loeb, the physicist A. A. Michelson, and William Caldwell in economics – he believed natural science, particularly psychology and anthropology, were leading the way for the social sciences. The blustering positivism of the anthropologist Georges Vacher de Lapouge was part of the

84 Thorstein Veblen, *The Instinct of Workmanship* (New York: Macmillan, 1914), 19, 201. See also Veblen, "Christian Morals and the Competitive System" (1910), in *Essays in Our Changing Order*, 200–18; idem, "The Mutation Theory and the Blond Race" (1913), and "The Blond Race and the Aryan Culture" (1913), in *The Place of Science in Modern Civilization and Other Essays* (New York: B. W. Huebsch, 1919), 457–96.

attraction of his racial theories to Veblen. "The social and political sciences must follow the drift, for they are already caught in it." If he carefully avoided predicting whether the industrial process would lead to socialism, he was willing to predict that it would lead to the triumph of modern science.[85]

After Veblen's positivist manifesto to the economists in 1898 he returned a few years later with a more modulated statement. The hard-boiled mechanist in Veblen never fully dominated the humanistic idealist. In "The Place of Science in Modern Civilization" in 1906 he tried to give science its due without allowing its positivist form to set all standards of life and mind. Echoing an idea of Walter Bagehot, he traced science to "idle curiosity," the playful mythmaking impulses which had their origin in savage life. In modern civilization, science came to see the world in the impersonal terms of cause and effect, but its idle and playful purpose remained, and modern humanistic scholarship remained a reservoir of this older and deeper human vision.

In tracing science back to "idle curiosity," rather than the instinct of workmanship, Veblen was perhaps sparing an already overdrawn source, but he seems also to be reacting against the linkage of pragmatism to the world as it is. He now went out of his way to divorce his own views and the functional psychology he had taken from the pragmatists, from their devotion to practical action and the conventional purposes that category contained. Science, he said, had nothing to do with the kind of practical conduct that was so much engaged in "personal advantage" or "expedient conduct." The science of idle curiosity "creates nothing but theories. It knows nothing of policy or utility, of better or worse.... This employment of scientific knowledge for useful ends is technology." Veblen wanted science to provide critical insight into the course of evolution, not become a tool to control it. Although in the end he could not keep fully to that proscription himself, it separated him sharply from his liberal colleagues' conception of their task.[86]

Where Veblen's positivism intersected that of his colleagues and in part reshaped it, was in his claim of objectivity. Veblen was disappointed that most reviewers read *The Theory of the Leisure Class* as a satire. He boasted to Ross that "several of the men in the natural sciences here speak of it as an example of true scientific method!" When his colleague John Cummings argued in a review that it was not objective science, but shot through with

85 Veblen, "Why is Economics Not an Evolutionary Science?" 373, 396; Dorfman, *Thorstein Veblen*, 93–4.
86 Walter Bagehot, *Physics and Politics* (New York: D. Appleton, 1873); Thorstein Veblen, "The Place of Science in Modern Civilization" (1906), in *What Veblen Taught*, ed. Wesley C. Mitchell (New York: Viking, 1936), 3–38, particularly 7–13, 21–6.

disguised moral judgment, Veblen defended the strategies he had used to achieve objectivity.[87]

To begin with, he eschewed overt moral judgment and prediction of the future. But as the conservative evolutionists had already shown, any account of the direction of evolution carried an implicit message. Moreover, he built his value system into original human nature through the instinct of workmanship and the category of waste, defined by whether the behavior or product "serves directly to enhance human life on the whole." When Cummings accused him of subjectivity in making those judgments, he replied that there was a considerable consensus on what constituted waste, which he was only echoing.

Some reason for this coincidence of views is to be found in a community of descent, traditions, and circumstances, past and present, among men living in any given community, and in a less degree among men in all communities. It is because men's notions of the generically human, of what is the legitimate end of life, does not differ incalculably from man to man that men are able to live in communities and to hold common interests.

The common sense of mankind of his old philosophy teacher at Yale, Noah Porter, resurfaced here and Veblen claimed that his linguistic strategy echoed common meanings. If terms like "conspicuous consumption" and "predatory" behavior carried moral connotations, they were only the moral attitudes which people themselves took "toward the institutional facts of which they speak."[88]

Veblen's final line of defense was to claim that the "trained scientist," in the interest of objectivity, could "view these categories of popular thought in a dispassionate light."[89] That he himself took that dispassionate attitude was proclaimed in the distance of his anthropological stance. Whether the young John Bates Clark first alerted him to the possibility, he saw that the anthropologist's viewpoint of the alien observer could be used to render the modern conventional world strange, opening that world to criticism at the same time that it claimed the objectivity of distance. Veblen projected scientific distance in his relentlessly impersonal rhetorical style. The formality of his language and his long, regular rhythms mimicked the "cumulative sequence of cause and effect" itself. Yet such formal, impersonal language also created the perfect deadpan persona for effective satire. Thus,

---

87 Veblen to E. A. Ross, December 7, 1899, Ross Papers; Thorstein Veblen, "Mr. Cummings's Strictures on *The Theory of the Leisure Class*" (1899), in *Essays in Our Changing Order*, 16–31.

88 Veblen, *Theory of the Leisure Class*, 99; idem, "Mr. Cummings's Strictures," 18–19, 30.

89 Veblen, "Mr. Cummings's Strictures," 30–1.

The leisure rendered by the wife … is, of course, not a simple manifestation of idleness or indolence. It almost invariably occurs disguised under some form of work or household duties or social amenities, which prove on analysis to serve little or no ulterior end beyond showing that she does not and need not occupy herself with anything that is gainful or that is of substantial use.[90]

Indeed, privately Veblen admitted that his purpose had in part been satirical. Even in his defense against Cummings, he could not resist calling his book at one point an "escapade." If confronted with this discrepancy, Veblen could have answered that scientific truth was always unconventional truth. To the conservative and professionally conscious, science and objectivity became identified with what was noncontroversial. Veblen took the subversive stance of the radical Enlightenment and the Marxist tradition, that science was inherently a tool of delegitimation, its truth always opposed to the conventional lies of the established powers. Because the rate of change of the various strata of economic and cultural institutions was always uneven, Veblen said, "Whatever is, is wrong." It was the task of an objective science to point that out.[91]

In Veblen's preference for the impersonal facts and tough-minded critique provided by natural science, we have one of the first instances of a hard-edged style of realism that would become very influential in twentieth-century social science. If "realism was the aesthetic of disinheritance" in the Gilded Age, by the early twentieth century the gap between inherited cultural traditions and current reality was much wider. Only a hard-boiled attitude could hope to dislodge the lagging conventional wisdom and grasp the reality of a world in which "Whatever is, is wrong." The old ideals could no longer be admitted to view as such, but had to be disguised. Veblen's cultural alienation allowed him to feel the distance and project the tough-minded realism that would soon engulf a generation.[92]

His work also provided the model for the institutional economists. He showed how economists could accept history and legitimate change, even radical change, while assuming a stance of scientific objectivity; how they could undermine convention, yet speak in the name of universal truth. If the

90  Veblen, *Theory of the Leisure Class*, 81–2.
91  Veblen, "Mr. Cummings's Strictures," 19; idem, *Theory of the Leisure Class*, 207. Ellsworth R. Fuhrman, *The Sociology of Knowledge in America, 1883–1915* (Charlottesville: University Press of Virginia, 1980), contrasts the dominant "social-technological" tradition in American social science with a "critical-emancipatory" Marxist tradition that assumes a stance of "critical unmasking."
92  A precursor in the style of tough-minded realism, though not satire, was Oliver Wendell Holmes, Jr. See Yosal Rogat, "The Judge as Spectator," *University of Chicago Law Review*, 31 (Winter 1964): 213–56, and Saul Touster, "In Search of Holmes from Within," *Vanderbilt Law Review*, 18 (1965): 437–72.

institutionalists eroded his historicist insight into structural change and turned his socialist evolution into a call for liberal social control, that was not what Veblen originally intended, though it was a result that positivism encouraged.

## Conclusions

Over the course of the Progressive period, most American economists adopted the marginalist neoclassical paradigm. As an intellectual construct it provided a simple, abstract logic for disparate economic phenomena and proved itself capable of wide elaboration. As an ideological construct, it provided a seemingly scientific defense of the liberal capitalist order coming into existence in America. As a historical construct, as a model of the economy which implicitly and explicitly projected itself through time, it envisioned a world of perpetual liberal change, of constant dynamic recreation of liberal order – in Clark's phrase, "a progressive paradise."

The liberal economists who had been attracted to historicism in the Gilded Age or who learned it at the turn of the century had seen in history a counterweight to the capitalist market, a realm of political, social, and ethical action that might modify and constrain capitalist development. Yet, by their underlying support of the market and their attraction to the fixed road to progress it marked out, the liberal historicists fell into an uneasy historical dualism. The liberal economy was the dynamic and controlling force in history; yet ethical-historical action was the ground and final arbiter of historical change. It is not surprising that Patten never managed to reconcile the conflicting demands of the market and of history, that Seligman fused them into a single normative process, or that liberal historicists who tried to maintain the adversarial independence of history often fell into market determinism. It had always been central to American exceptionalism, that nature and history were allied. Seligman was drawn to the same exceptionalist strategy as that of Sumner, even though the substance of his history was social democratic rather than libertarian. Ely projected a more vigorous history than Francis A. Walker, but they too conceived of history as limiting conditions upon fundamentally beneficent economic principle.

For radical historicists, capitalism remained central to history, but capitalism was changing into something different. On his own more rigorous terms, Veblen followed the route of the Gilded Age historical economists who turned the exceptionalist republic into the socialist utopia coming to be. If others soon responded to the receding utopian future by returning to the normative course of American history, Veblen retained hope, even while reluctantly giving it over to the uncertain dynamics of historical change.

Still, Veblen held onto his claim to science. Though he took evolutionary biology rather than physics as his model, he wanted economics to follow as fully in the footsteps of natural science as did his neoclassical opponents. Veblen's positivism, too, was an uneasy response to living in the dramatically changed history of industrial America.

The Gilded Age crisis in American exceptionalism spawned a variety of models for economic inquiry, but whether marginalist or historicist, liberal or radical, they all constructed theoretical support for what Croly now called "the American promise." Encouraged by industrial productivity, they could imagine the expansive exceptionalist ideal of American tradition realized in the approaching future. Clark, Seligman, Patten, and Veblen expressed, as Clark said, "the faith that is in all of us." But the different roads they took were no less sharply marked and defended because they shared a common destination. Marginalism occupied the professional mainstream, but it found thoroughgoing opposition in Veblen and a lively, if disparate, challenge among a variety of critics touched by historicism. The critics of marginalism remained scattered through the Progressive period. Institutionalism did not mark off something like a "school" in economics and mount a campaign until World War I. But American economists kept up the *Methodenstreit* begun in the 1880s. With the role of challenger reversed and with far less acrimony than the conflict in Germany and Austria, it became nonetheless a prominent feature of American economics.

The *Methodenstreit* characteristic of German and American economics was cut short in England. A group of historical economists and economic historians carried on the historico-ethical aims of Arnold Toynbee. But the stature of Alfred Marshall and the hierarchical character of English academic and cultural life made it possible for Marshall's neoclassical paradigm to absorb or entirely overshadow its competitors in English economics for two generations. In America a decentralized university system and cultural life allowed the proponents of historicism greater professional power and a wider audience.[93]

93 A. W. Coats, "The Culture and the Economists: Some Reflections on Anglo-American Differences," *History of Political Economy*, 12 (Winter 1980): 588–609, follows the exceptionalist practice of framing the difference between America and Europe as opposites, with the American model being one of liberal flux. Coats argues persuasively, however, that the professional structure in America was looser, open to competition between rival factions and communal pressures for political relevance. He may also be correct that academia in America recruited during this period from a wider variety of social backgrounds than in England. But Alon Kadish, *The Oxford Economists in the Late Nineteenth Century* (Oxford: Oxford University Press [Clarendon Press], 1982) shows that heterodox historical economists in England often came from lower-middle-class and upper-lower-class backgrounds; once recruited, their class and financial status hampered their advancement in the more hierarchical British society and culture. Kadish provides a suggestive study of the

There is, in addition, a deeper reason for this divergence. In both Germany and the United States, the late nineteenth-century traumas of state formation and rapid industrialization threatened to undermine the national identity. In America, the threat to exceptional historical identity made the issue of historical change central and galvanized a whole generation to meet its challenge. In contrast, the intellectual class in England, more secure in its national identity and having accommodated to industrialization over the course of a century, could more easily imagine modernity as a transformation within an ongoing stream of historical continuity and more easily stay within the boundaries of the neoclassical paradigm. Graham Wallas, who knew both countries well, believed that "in the space of one generation, a new environment had appeared, and the speed of the change forced it more strongly upon the American imagination than upon the Edwardian English mind." English economists at the turn of the century were concerned not with the birth of a new historical world but with the possibility that Britain, far advanced on the path of industrial development, was heading toward economic decline.[94] This greater sense of historical continuity in England showed itself, we will see, in a divergent pattern of development in all the social sciences. In the United States, as in Germany, disruptive historical change generated a disruptive intellectual response. The desire for a counterweight to marginal theory that would realistically register the changed industrial world bred a continuing historicist controversy in American economics.

failure of these English economists to effectively challenge Marshallian dominance. See also Alon Kadish, *Historians, Economists and Economic History* (London: Routledge, 1989). On Marshall's ability to withstand and disarm the diffuse historicist challenge, see Maloney, *Marshall, Orthodoxy and the Professionalization of Economics*, chap. 5.

94  Martin J. Wiener, *Between Two Worlds: The Political Thought of Graham Wallas* (Oxford: Oxford University Press [Clarendon Press], 1971), 168. For a revealing study of the narrow range of the late-nineteenth-century sense of historical discontinuity in England, see P. B. M. Blaas, *Continuity and Anachronism* (The Hague: Nijhoff, 1978). On British fears of economic and social decline from 1890 to World War I, see Mark Thomas, *The Edwardian Economy: Structure, Performance, and Policy, 1895–1914* (Oxford University Press, forthcoming), chap. 1. C. F. G. Masterman, *The Condition of England* (London: Methuen, 1909) was a popular expression of that view and, within that historical context, used the fall of the Roman Empire and the cycle of luxury and decay as his central figures.

# 7

◁=========================▷

# Toward a sociology of
# social control

In the summer of 1905 a sociological colleague of Lester Frank Ward's in
Washington, D.C., suggested that the sociologists form their own professional organization. Everyone agreed with Edward A. Ross that an American Sociological Society would help "to clarify our minds, acquaint us with
one another's opinions, and exalt the dignity of sociology in the public eye."
Deliberately adopting an ecumenical professional policy, the sociologists
eschewed any ideological or theoretical affiliation and opened membership
to social-work practitioners as well as academics, so long as they claimed a
"scientific" interest in sociology. Ward was named the first president and his
original rival, William Graham Sumner, the first vice-president and
president-elect. Both Franklin Giddings and Albion Small took active roles
in the proceedings. New converts to sociology, like Edward A. Ross and
Charles Horton Cooley, were also present. As we have seen happen in
economics, professional accommodation accompanied a substantive movement toward new liberal politics and the liberal exceptionalist vision of
American history.[1]

## Professional convergence

The polar positions Ward and Sumner, then Small and Giddings had staked
out in the Gilded Age shifted after the turn of the century to narrower
ground. After Small abandoned the possibility of socialist transformation, all
four envisioned the evolution of modern society, and America along with it,
in liberal terms. The question now became how far that evolution was open

---

1 "Organization of the American Sociological Society: Official Report," *AJS*, 11 (January
   1906): 555–69, particularly 556, 567; *PPASS*, 1 (1906).

to new liberal change. Was modern society on a fixed course, as Sumner had originally argued, determined by a natural process of selection linked to the market, and impervious to the intervention of reason, politics, and morality? Or could these fruits of human and historical action significantly shape the future, as Ward had countered? Under the influence of professional comity and of ideological convergence, the different answers to that question began to appear as differences in degree rather than in kind. "I think there is no longer cause to fear," a sociologist remarked at their first meeting in 1906, "that we may split up into warring sects like the theologians. Our sociological geniuses, though they seem to differ, are in reality only laying emphasis upon important phases of the whole subject."[2]

Giddings had originally stressed that the process of selection going on in society was a true form of natural selection, but he had always believed that "It is through the mediation of society that survival of the fit becomes the survival of the best." Consciousness of kind, operating through social values and institutions, carried on a process of social selection. Hence Giddings did not have to accept Herbert Spencer's mandatory prescription of laissez-faire. Social selection allowed conscious experimentation, and progress involved elimination of social extremes and the strengthening of consciousness of kind. During the Progressive period Giddings translated that mandate into moderate reforms that encouraged equal economic opportunity and social solidarity.[3]

Even William Graham Sumner receded somewhat from his evolutionary determinism in *Folkways: A Study of the Sociological Importance of Usages, Manners, Customs, Mores, and Morals.* Faced with his 1880s vision of American progress leading down a Ricardian path to republican decline, Sumner gave up the idea of progress and turned to the beginnings of human society, in anthropology. *Folkways* argued that evolution was governed by natural selection, that in human society selection was carried on by the

---

2 Frederick Morgan Davenport, in "How Should Sociology Be Taught as a College or University Subject? Discussion," *PPASS*, 1 (1906): 23. William F. Fine, *Progressive Evolutionism and American Sociology, 1890–1920* (Ann Arbor: UMI Research Press, 1979) is an insightful study of the evolutionary and reformist premises of Progressive Era sociology. Roscoe C. Hinkle, *Founding Theory of American Sociology, 1881–1915* (Boston: Routledge & Kegan Paul, 1980) places Progressive sociology within much the same boundaries but provides a formalistic analysis. Ellsworth R. Fuhrman, *The Sociology of Knowledge in America, 1883–1915* (Charlottesville: University Press of Virginia, 1980) is a careful study of the "social-technological" approach to sociological knowledge of the Progressive cohort.
3 Franklin H. Giddings, *The Theory of Socialization* (New York: Macmillan, 1897), 38–9; idem, *Inductive Sociology* (New York: Macmillan, 1901), 6; idem, "Sovereignty and Government," *PSQ*, 21 (March 1906): 1–27; Robert C. Bannister, *Sociology and Scientism: The American Quest for Objectivity, 1880–1940* (Chapel Hill: University of North Carolina Press, 1987), 79.

industrial process, by the struggle of classes, and by national warfare. "Might has made all the right which ever has existed or exists now." By implication, American history was part of an evolution that produced economic improvements but not moral progress.

Sumner interposed in this natural process the psychic constructions of folkways and mores, the latter more rational formulations of ethical standards. The general tone of *Folkways* was fatalistic, emphasizing the deterministic power of inherited folkways, but the mores were open to some degree of rational modification. These psychosocial formations were themselves created by evolution; they had "the character of a nature process," yet in a way that "defies our analysis," people who were determined by the mores could also act on them. "The statesman and social philosopher" could act *with* the mores, "sum up the forces which make them, and greatly help the result." Indeed, by the use of science, critical intelligence, and will, it might be possible to act *against* the mores, to construct a "science of society" that "could lead up to an art of societal administration which should be intelligent, effective, and scientific." History could no longer be trusted to produce progress; perhaps science could. Though only a momentary lull in an otherwise heavy sea of evolutionary determinism, this hint of scientific control brought even Sumner within the professional compromise.[4]

For his part, Small sought to present his own views as compatible with those of his conservative colleagues. At the first meeting of the American Sociological Society he suggested that all sociologists could now agree that the social evolutionary process differed, in degree or in kind, from the evolutionary process that produced the "flora and fauna." It was largely a difference of emphasis, he said, that led some sociologists to work on linking social phenomena to physical factors, while others like himself abstracted out the psychic factors in social evolution and concentrated their attention on them.[5] As had already occurred in economics, theoretical differences within the boundaries of liberalism could be transformed into a professional division of labor.

Although the elders showed little awareness as yet of its impact, younger sociologists recognized that the findings of August Weismann encouraged Small's compound view of evolution. Weismann's disproof of the inheritance of acquired characteristics led to a new awareness of the importance of social causation, and also to a new interest in eugenics, now the only way to exert social influence over biological heredity. As though to deny the

4 William Graham Sumner, *Folkways* (Boston: Ginn, 1906), 66, 117–18.
5 Albion W. Small, "Points of Agreement among Sociologists," *PPASS*, 1 (1906): 63–4.

consensus, a eugenicist arose to urge that sociologists should be doing the kind of research on race, gender, and reproduction pioneered by Francis Galton and Karl Pearson in England. Such unalloyed biologism was the exception, however. Most social theorists simply allowed a limited place for eugenics to deal with biological strains of unfitness, in Cooley's terms, "hereditary idiocy, or nervous instability tending toward vice and crime.... Only a shallow sort of mind will suppose there is any necessary conflict between biological and psychological sociology."[6]

Professional accommodation also involved adjustment between sociology and its social science neighbors, particularly economics. Small's sociology had been forged as a challenge to classical economics: sociology would bring the wider ethical interests of society to bear against economics; sociology was the synthetic social science to which economics was subsidiary. Even Giddings, who was an ally of neoclassical economics, implicitly challenged it by seeking in sociology a deeper legitimation of modern society and a more fundamental basis for social organization than economics provided. During the Progressive Era hostile comment continued sporadically across the new professional lines. Small kept up his barrage of synthetic claims against the narrower scope of economics. Other sociologists tried to phrase them more diplomatically. Ross, for example, asserted that sociology was the synthetic trunk of the social science tree, but like a banyon tree, the trunk was composed of stems that had independent roots.[7] For their part, economists continued to make known their disdain for sociological pretensions and doubts that it would succeed. Their opinions were not improved by the large student demand for sociology among those interested in social problems and social work. By 1909 one estimate showed sociology courses enrolling roughly 65 percent as many undergraduates as economics courses. At the University of Chicago, where there was a large graduate department in sociology, the combined enrollments almost equaled economics. Within the university, professionalization probably exacerbated rivalries.[8]

There was, however, little substantive interference from either side.

---

6 D. Collin Wells, "Social Darwinism," *PPASS*, 1 (1906): 117–30 and "Discussion," 131–8; Charles Horton Cooley, *Social Organization: A Study of the Larger Mind* (New York: Scribner, 1909), 296. See also William I. Thomas, "The Significance of the Orient for the Occident," *PPASS*, 2 (1907): 123.

7 Edward A. Ross, "Moot Points in Sociology, I. The Scope and Task of Sociology," *AJS*, 8 (May 1903): 770–3; reprinted in *Foundations of Sociology* (New York: Macmillan, 1905), chap. 1.

8 My figures are estimated from Luther Lee Bernard, "The Teaching of Sociology in the United States," *AJS*, 15 (September 1909): 188–9. See also Hamilton Cravens, *The Triumph of Evolution, American Scientists and the Heredity-Environment Controversy, 1900–1941* (Philadelphia: University of Pennsylvania Press, 1978), chap. 4.

Underneath the imperialist rhetoric, there was a de facto truce. With the marginalist neoclassical paradigm taking hold, and the historical impulse in economics largely tamed, sociology was not much of a threat to the economists. The only economist who found it important to substantively attack sociological theory was Simon Patten, who had rejected marginalism and was trying to construct his own sociology within economics. After the turn of the century, even he backed off.[9] The sociologists, as we will presently see, also refused to attack the economists on their own ground.

Within these new ideological and professional limits, sociologists struggled in the early twentieth century to achieve a disciplinary model they and their critical professional neighbors could approve. Their liberal conception of historical evolution united them around the capitalist market as a central progressive force, linked to social differentiation and republican government. Their sociological raison d'être required them to reject any deterministic economic interpretation of history, but the vague boundaries in new liberal theory between the market and society allowed considerable room for economic causation. Small found Seligman's premarginalist formulation so open to ethical action that "it would be extremely difficult to maintain dissent from his conclusion."[10] Sociologists nonetheless wanted to stress the broad social determinants of history which they were especially fitted to understand. This rooted self-conception may help explain their general disregard of Veblen's evolutionary theory as a model for their discipline. The socialist valence of Veblen's theory was probably reason enough. He was not a likely source for a discipline in search of academic respectability. But sociologists would also have been put off by his demonstration that the economic process, industrial and pecuniary, was the single determinant of modern consciousness, despite the promising leads that insight opened into American culture.

Barring economic determinism, the liberal exceptionalist parameters of the new profession left considerable room for controversy. As in economics, the methodological and political differences that had surfaced in the Gilded Age were reconstituted. Professionalism could not decide the weight or the bearings these divergent principles were to have. When a disciple of

9 Simon N. Patten, "The Failure of Biologic Sociology," *AAAPSS*, 4 (May 1894): 919–47; idem, "The Organic Concept of Society," *AAAPSS*, 5 (November 1894): 404–9; idem, "The Relation of Economics to Sociology," *AAAPSS*, 5 (January 1895): 577–83. For replies to Patten, see Franklin H. Giddings, "Utility, Economics, and Sociology," *AAAPSS*, 5 (November 1894): 398–404; idem, "Sociology and the Abstract Sciences: The Origin of the Social Feelings," *AAAPSS*, 5 (March 1895): 746–53; Albion W. Small, "The Organic Concept of Society," *AAAPSS*, 5 (March 1895): 740–6.
10 Albion W. Small, "Review of E. R. A. Seligman, *The Economic Interpretation of History*," *AJS*, 8 (November 1902): 417–18.

Giddings proudly surveyed the "synthetic tendency" in sociology in 1910, he had to simply list its components. "As no branch of the subject can rightfully claim precedence over another, the order of treatment can have no significance." For some years, generally at the instigation of Small, sociologists bombarded each other with survey questionnaires and roundtable meetings, hoping to elicit agreement on the nature of the field and how it should be taught, but to little avail.[11]

## Small's Chicago and Giddings' Columbia

Albion Small continued to mark out one major path toward a science of sociology. Although it never reached its destination, as always with Small, its failure is illuminating. Small was seeking a theory of the evolution of modern society that had the synthetic grasp and verisimilitude of history and yet, in the style of evolutionary positivism, built on "deeper" categories rooted in nature. Although he had abandoned the hope of imminent transformation, his ambivalence remained. He wanted both to reach and to transcend the class conflict that continued to cloud the American future. Small finally found a satisfying theory in Gustav Ratzenhofer's reflection on Austria's history of class and cultural conflict, mediated by an activist state. Ratzenhofer rooted history in the evolutionary struggle for existence and linked group conflict to the progressive differentiation of society. In modern society, as social groups entered into widening patterns of conflict, the "culture-state" and growing forces of socialization could produce greater equality and concord of interests. Ratzenhofer recognized the economic conflicts created by industrial capitalism, but subsumed them in a larger social process of mediation and diffused class conflict into a more particularistic struggle among economic, ethnic, and political groups.[12]

Adapting Ratzenhofer to American exceptionalism, Small redefined sociology as the study of the process of association in groups, a pluralistic process of conflict and accommodation that issued in wider harmony. Although he continued to berate the inequality and conflict of the present

11  Alvan A. Tenney, "Some Recent Advances in Sociology," *PSQ*, 25 (September 1910): 505; Frank L. Tolman, "The Study of Sociology in Institutions of Learning in the United States," *AJS*, 7 (May 1902): 797–838; 8 (July 1902): 85–121, (September 1902): 251–72, (January 1903): 531–58; Bernard, "The Teaching of Sociology in the United States," 164–213; F. Stuart Chapin, "Report on Questionnaire of Committee on Teaching," *PPASS*, 5 (1910): 114–25; "Report of the Committee of Ten," *PPASS*, 6 (1911): 40–59; "Round Table," *PPASS*, 7 (1912): 133–47.

12  Albion W. Small, *General Sociology* (Chicago: University of Chicago Press, 1905), pts. 4, 5; Don Martindale, *The Nature and Types of Sociological Theory* (Boston: Houghton Mifflin, 1960), chap. 8.

industrial order, he specifically rejected the inevitability of class conflict in America. Remembering his historicist beginnings, Small asserted that America is like every other country in that "Our future is still to be determined." But, he continued, radicalism was not warranted in America. "In spite of familiar Jeremiads to the contrary, with a small percentage of exception, there is opportunity for every man in America." There are evils, but they do not prove "structural defects in social order" and will not be solved by structural change. The real conflict in society, he concluded, was rather between intelligence and the status quo, between those willing to rethink and hence "socialize" social problems and those unwilling to change, a conflict which cut across economic classes and placed special importance on the intellectual function of his professional class.[13]

Small reoriented Ratzenhofer's sociology in still another way. By grounding social process in the evolutionary struggle for existence, Ratzenhofer provided a bridge between evolutionary positivism and history, but his theory ended in a thoroughgoing historical sociology. The conflicts in modern society were conflicts of "interests," understood as historically formed centers of power, including the state, the clergy, bureaucracies, extractive industry, wage labor, and so on. Small argued that these social interests issued from and were at bottom identical with the six basic "interests" in human nature: health, wealth, sociability, knowledge, beauty, and rightness. Retaining Ward's evolutionary psychological premises, he continued to believe that desires or wants were the true "social forces" and hence the proper basis for a scientific sociology. More importantly, they were the basis for his normative sociology. Interests were the units not only of social action but of social value, the ends enacted in the social process; the ends against which economics could be found wanting; the ends that sociologists must construct into a harmonious order. His desire for a philosophy of history led him away from the concrete groups struggling in history and back toward the normative categories of human nature.[14]

Small's political inhibitions led in the same direction. Ratzenhofer's theory directed the sociologist to empirical study of the conflicting interest groups in modern society. Small himself was, on his radical side, drawn in the same direction. He concluded his presentation of his new theory with the injunction that the "economic situation" was "the phase of society most requiring study."[15] But how, given his ambivalence, was he to come to grips with industrial capitalism, and how, given the problems of professional

---

13 Small, *General Sociology*, 375–9, 387–93.
14 Ibid., 249; chaps. 27, 31.
15 Ibid., 394.

specialization, was a sociologist to embark on the study of economic institutions? Small himself never tried. Nor, with one exception, did his students. The exception was a study of the Chicago publishing industry that was notably rich in its empirical detail and relatively insightful about the ways in which business considerations shaped publishing decisions. The author concluded that here the "aesthetic interest" depended upon the "business, or wealth-interest activities." Small's categories seemed to provide the author with his analytical thrust, yet in the end they became broad receptacles that blunted rather than sharpened analysis. The study suggests the weakness of Small's theory as a framework for sociological research. But it also confirms the concrete direction implicit in the theory, a direction taken by his most original follower, Arthur F. Bentley.[16]

The study is also interesting because it appears to be unique. As we shall see just below, Small's theory was no more clumsy to work with than Giddings', yet Giddings' students managed to apply it. Despite professional comity, sociologists could have found considerable unoccupied territory around the concrete processes of conflict and accommodation actually being generated by contemporary capitalism. Political inhibitions were surely as important. Chicago sociology under Small was noted in these years for its timidity, and it required a degree of political hardihood to give socio-historical specificity to even a liberal conflict theory of contemporary American society.[17]

The kind of concrete empirical work that flourished at the University of Chicago was the investigation of urban conditions, inspired by the charity and reform work of the city. Charles Henderson, Small's social-gospel colleague, was its chief source in the sociology department, and he was joined by philosophers George Herbert Mead and John Dewey, political scientists Ernst Freund and Charles Merriam, and others. The inspiration for their work came largely from Hull House and the urban charity movement. Hull House widened the sympathies of its academic visitors and the writings of Jane Addams, perhaps the most thoughtful of the Progressive social reformers, were regularly consulted by Cooley, Mead, and their colleagues. More specifically, *Hull House Maps and Papers* (1895) began the urban studies and use of maps for which Chicago sociology later became famous.[18]

16 Herbert E. Fleming, "The Literary Interests of Chicago, VI and VII," *AJS*, 12 (July 1906): 68–118.
17 Ross to Ward, September 16, 1905, in "The Ward-Ross Correspondence, 1904–1905," ed. Bernhard J. Stern, *ASR*, 13 (February 1948): 93.
18 The Hull House work was undoubtedly the source of suggestions for urban investigation in Albion W. Small and George E. Vincent, *An Introduction to the Study of Society* (New York: American Book Co., 1894), 165–6.

The Chicago School of Civics and Philanthropy, with funds for research from the Russell Sage Foundation, brought together Julia C. Lathrop of Hull House and two Chicago Ph.D.'s, Sophonisba Breckinridge and Edith Abbott, who taught part-time in the sociology department and directed extensive studies of living conditions among workers and immigrants. Although devoid of theory, premised on the belief that a recital of actual conditions would arouse the civic conscience and inform public action, the tradition of urban exploration and the research techniques these studies established led directly to the academic sociology of William I. Thomas, Robert Park, and Ernest W. Burgess.[19]

Small's Gilded Age rival, Franklin Giddings, was able to pass on his vision of sociology more directly to his students, although not unchanged. He stands as founder of what became "Columbia sociology" in a way that Small cannot stand for "Chicago sociology." Giddings' straightforward evolutionary positivism proved easier to transmit and transform in the American academic environment than Small's ambiguous and ambivalent historicism.[20]

Giddings came to a clearer conception of what he was trying to do at the end of the century, apparently as a result of reading Karl Pearson and one of the main influences upon Pearson, Ernst Mach. In the early 1890s Giddings was uncertain how sociology should combine induction and deduction on a field of study that was at once history and nature. In 1898 he cut through these dilemmas by asserting, following Pearson and Mach, that science was description. Theories, Mach said, were merely indirect descriptions, which allow us to grasp larger combinations of facts and lead back to the discovery of new facts. As science advances, the reach of theories is extended and interconnected. According to Pearson, society and history provided no barrier to the method of scientific description or to its absorption in the widening network of science.[21]

Defining science as description was a way to avoid the "metaphysical"

---

19 Steven J. Diner, *A City and Its Universities: Public Policy in Chicago, 1892–1919* (Chapel Hill: University of North Carolina Press, 1980). Mary Jo Deegan, *Jane Addams and the Men of the Chicago School, 1892–1918* (New Brunswick, N.J.: Transaction Books, 1988) is overly tendentious, but raises the interesting question of Jane Addams' relation to American sociology.

20 For my understanding of the Columbia school of sociology inaugurated by Giddings, I am much indebted to Bannister's excellent *Sociology and Scientism*, which restores a degree of balance to an internalist historiography of sociology hitherto largely in the hands of the Chicago school.

21 Franklin H. Giddings, "The Practical Value of Sociology," *AAAPSS*, 12 (July 1898): 3; Karl Pearson, *The Grammar of Science* (London: Walter Scott, 1892); Ernst Mach, "On the Economical Nature of Physical Inquiry," in *Popular Scientific Lectures* (Chicago: The Open Court, 1894), 186–213.

conception of innate force or cause in explanation. All science knew was the description of concomitant and co-varying facts. A pioneer in statistical method, Pearson emphasized that the reliability of such concomitance was always measured by degrees of probability. It was precisely its accuracy in determining concomitance and probability that made quantification so important to science and that suggested statistics as a central tool of social science. Sociology as a scientific description of society would be an empirical and statistical study of the variation and correlation of social facts. Pearson was also a pioneer in the mathematization of Darwin's theory of natural selection. By analyzing how individuals varied around a statistical norm, he hoped to prove Darwin true and to facilitate the eugenic control of reproduction. Giddings probably found Pearson's elitist social values, as well as his mathematical Darwinism, attractive. He adapted the method to his own sociological theory, hoping to find statistical evidence that racial and social characters showed increasing conformity to type, and hence that modern society was evolving in accord with his theory of social selection.[22]

On the basis of this understanding, Giddings quickly developed a concrete research program from his general theory. In *Inductive Sociology* (1901), he set out a research schedule for the study of contemporary communities that would presumably examine the workings of social evolution in modern society. He started even his freshman students on such research projects and his graduate students produced a series of urban and community studies in the first decade of the century. Giddings was looking for evidence of more cooperative standards of business behavior and more refined standards of social emulation. These were the processes that were to assimilate the mixed immigrant stock to Anglo-Saxon culture and moderate the class conflict introduced into America by industrial capitalism. James M. Williams' study of a northeastern town, for example, suggests that the effort to identify older and newer forms of social behavior and to look at the social effects of economic change opened up what could have been an interesting line of research. But Williams had to struggle with Giddings' elaborate categories of sociopsychological types, social activities, and forms of selection. Giddings' categories formed a fixed grid into which observation was pressed; they were more impediments than aids to analysis, and over time they disappeared from his students and his own work.[23]

What remained were the underlying evolutionary assumptions and quan-

22 Pearson, *Grammar of Science*, chap. 9; Franklin H. Giddings, "Review of Karl Pearson, *The Chances of Death and Other Studies in Evolution*," *PSQ*, 13 (March 1898): 156–61; Donald A. MacKenzie, *Statistics in Britain 1865–1930* (Edinburgh University Press, 1981), chap. 4.
23 Giddings, *Inductive Sociology*; James M. Williams, *An American Town* (New York: James Kempster Printing, 1906); Bannister, *Sociology and Scientism*, 80–1.

titative method. Although statistics in these early studies were largely descriptive, Giddings tried to use statistics analytically to advance his theory of the growing "consciousness of kind" in modern society. As early as 1897 he proposed a formula for measuring the "degree of sympathy" in American society through the degree of racial kinship, using census population figures. The four categories of resemblance, in order of increasing difference, were native born of native parentage, native born of foreign parentage, foreign born, and colored. In 1909 he proposed a more extensive "social marking system" to determine likenesses in religion, education, and conduct. Giddings' index numbers of social homogeneity remained exotic productions. But they were indicative of the deep fear among American sociologists of social fragmentation and of the growing impulse to quantify social experience. Giddings himself, increasingly pessimistic about the polyglot and permissive urban culture, suffered a nervous collapse in 1912. Amidst the uncertainties and stresses of this new historical world, numbers appeared to provide him a semblance of certainty and order.[24]

The sociological tradition that Giddings established at Columbia came to center on statistical method. The more fearful Giddings was of the American future, the more he propagandized for the scientific method of exact measurement. Columbia also provided greater opportunity for training in statistical methods than other sociological centers. Giddings and many of his students retained, however, as Small did, a historico-evolutionary conception of the subject matter of the discipline. Sociology, whether a philosophy of history or a positivist theory of evolution, concerned change over time and specifically the changes modern society was undergoing in America. Small partially turned that historico-evolutionary field into a recognizable historical world, but Giddings' methodology turned it into a homogenous field of statistically variable behavior. In one sense this was the familiar American ocean of atomistic individuals. In another, it was the last resort for someone who could no longer trust where America stood in time.

### The liberal exceptionalist sociologies of Ross and Cooley

While Giddings and Small were struggling along their historico-evolutionary paths, two newcomers to the discipline were refocusing these inherited traditions. Both Edward A. Ross and Charles Horton Cooley came to sociology from economics and both came to it to resolve the Gilded Age crisis of American exceptionalism. Their solutions drew sociology toward

---

24 Giddings, *Theory of Socialization*, appendix; idem, "The Social Marking System," *PPASS*, 4 (1909): 42–61; Bannister, *Sociology and Scientism*, 76–8, 81–2.

liberal premises and the study of sociopsychological processes. Ross took the first major step in this new direction with his idea of "social control." He defined the idea in a series of articles published in Small's *American Journal of Sociology* beginning in 1896, and then in a book by that name in 1901.[25] Social control was premised on the idea that there was a fundamental conflict between individual and social interests. In order to maintain itself, society had to modify individual feelings, ideas, and behavior to conform to the social interest. The formally and informally constituted processes through which this power was exercised – from law to social suggestion – Ross called social control. Ross remembered that he first thought of the idea in December 1894, and jotted down thirty-three ways in which society exercised social control. As he began to work out the idea, he believed he had made a "great new discovery in Sociology."[26]

The primary context for his discovery was the Gilded Age debate between capitalism and socialism, to which he was a party. Having won a Ph.D. degree in economics from Richard T. Ely at Johns Hopkins in one year, and started a close relationship with Lester Ward, Ross moved between economics and sociology, and between socialism and liberalism.[27] He identified himself with Ely's "new school" position: "abandonment of the faith in the identity of private and public interests; subordination of the individual point of view to the social point of view." He chided Ward for not appreciating the need for "sympathy to prevent the [socially] costly pursuit of individual gain.... I think we do not quite agree as to the importance of ethics to sociology."[28] He also quickly became interested in socialism. By December 1891, he was planning to write a book on modern European socialism, and was enlarging the socialistic principle in sociology. "Somebody ought to study and report upon the Socialism discoverable in history and in contem-

25 *AJS*, 1 (March 1896): 513–35, (May 1896): 753–70; 2 (July 1896): 96–107, (September 1896): 255–63, (November 1896): 433–45, (January 1897): 547–66, (May 1897): 823–38; 3 (July 1897): 64–78, (September 1897): 236–47, (November 1897): 328–39, (January 1898): 502–19, (March 1898): 649–61, (May 1898): 809–28; 5 (January 1900): 475–87, (March 1900): 604–16, "The Genesis of Ethical Elements" (May 1900): 761–77; 6 (July 1900): 29–41, (September 1900): 238–47, (November 1900): 381–95; Edward A. Ross, *Social Control* (New York: Macmillan, 1901).

26 Edward A. Ross, *Seventy Years of It: An Autobiography* (New York: D. Appleton, 1936), 56; Ross to Ward, September 16, 1895, in "The Ward-Ross Correspondence, 1891–1896," ed. Bernhard J. Stern, *ASR*, 3 (June 1938): 390.

27 The chief biographical sources for Ross are his autobiography, Ross and Stern, above, and Julius Weinberg, *Edward Alsworth Ross and the Sociology of Progressivism* (Madison: State Historical Society of Wisconsin, 1972).

28 Edward A. Ross, "The Unseen Foundations of Society," *PSQ*, 8 (December 1893): 722; Ross to Ward, February 22, 1892, in "Ward-Ross Correspondence, 1891–96," 368.

porary societies. I find lots of socialism and communism abroad everywhere. Family, Church, Free Schools, Science, etc." During his year at Cornell, however, in 1892–3, he experienced a breakdown, doctors said from overwork, and in cutting back, he abandoned the project. How much his decision was affected by the political danger of the subject is difficult to say. It is clear that the ethical Christian socialists led him to see social control as the process by which "an aggregate reacts on the aims of the individual, warping him out of his self-regarding course, and drawing his feet into the highway of common weal."[29]

Existentially, the conflict over socialism could have influenced Ross in another way. He was acutely aware of the social pressure being exerted on radical economists to modify their views, a phenomenon he would soon describe in his book as a rigid and unhealthy form of social control. He himself had played a close game, consenting to become secretary of the AEA after his mentor Ely was purged from the post in 1892 and at the same time declaring his sympathies for workers, radical farmers, and some form of currency inflation. He worried about academic freedom at each move up the academic ladder.[30] After Ely's trial in the summer of 1894, it would be surprising if unconsciously at least, Ross's sense of the pressure of society upon himself and his fellows did not inform his discovery of social control.

If it did, that was also because, far more than the evangelical social scientists, Ross's sympathy toward socialism and the supremacy of social values was balanced by sympathy for individuals in their contest with society. The text of Ross's book was a call for the social control of individual self-interest, but the sub-text was an uneasy fear that the individual would be ground down by social pressure. Orphaned at eight and raised by strangers on an Iowa farm, he was acutely conscious of his marginality and solaced himself with Carlyle's and Emerson's apotheosis of the creative individual and denunciations of social convention. Nor could he sustain the Christian idealism and millennial hope that allowed others to find a harmonious resolution of the conflict between individual and society. Reading Spencer sent Ross into a struggle between Christian belief and agnostic naturalism,

29 Ross to Ely, June 12, 1891; November 5, 1891; February 9, 1893, Richard T. Ely Papers; Ross to Ward, December 13, 1891, in "Ward-Ross Correspondence, 1891–96," 364; Edward A. Ross, "Social Control," *AJS*, 1:518.
30 Ross, *Social Control*, 398; idem, "The Standard of Deferred Payments," *AAAPSS*, 3 (November 1892): 293–305; idem, "The Unseen Foundations of Society," 722–32; Ross to Ward, March 27, 1892; August 31, 1892, in "Ward-Ross Correspondence, 1891–96," 371, 373; Ross to Mrs. Beach, May 14, 1892, Edward A. Ross Papers, Wisconsin State Historical Society.

which the latter won when he studied philosophy in Germany before arriving at Johns Hopkins.[31]

Ross's individualism was also strengthened by his study of marginalist economics at Hopkins. He was so taken with the subject that for a month or two, he did nothing but develop graphic models of economic problems using the declining curve of marginal utility. Although he was too much influenced by Ward to believe that economic competition was by itself an efficient process of natural selection, he was won over to marginal methods of analysis.[32]

Perhaps the most telling line of reasoning his marginalism opened up to him was an examination of the various standards of equity employed by proponents of socialism, an analysis he sent first to Ely in 1891. Using his graphs of marginal utility, he showed that no formal standard of equality could be just to individuals of dissimilar capacities. In his book version of *Social Control*, that insight stood at the center of his analysis of "the need for social control," and was applied not only to socialism but also to the capitalist system of private property. Competition inevitably rewarded some capacities over others which might equally well be considered meritorious. "Our institutions are not shaped by any one simple ethical principle that appeals to all men who are not bad ... they enclose hopeless contradictions. Neither the present inequality, nor yet the artificial, carefully protected equality of the communistic state, can enlist the fair-play sentiments of all." As a consequence, Ross said, some individuals would always be dissatisfied and social control would always be necessary.[33]

If we see Ross's development of the idea of social control in the ideologically charged context in which it occurred, we can see clearly what he did. Unlike the Christian socialists, Ross's moral sympathies were genuinely divided between individual assertion and social cooperation. He lacked the deep, religiously rooted desire for social equality that animated the evangelical social scientists like Ely and Small and that ultimately stymied their intellectual development in the American context. With a colder secular eye, and the sympathies of a liberal individualist, Ross turned their moral and political impasse into a sociological problem. He transcended the conflict between socialist and capitalist values by declaring it to be an objective

31 Edward A. Ross, "Turning Towards Nirvana," *Arena*, 4 (November 1891): 736–43; R. Jackson Wilson, *In Quest of Community: Social Philosophy in the United States, 1860–1920* (New York: Wiley, 1968), chap. 4. Wilson's perceptive account of Ross leaves out, however, Ross's work in economics and sociology from 1890 to 1896 and its influence on *Social Control*.

32 Ross to Mrs. Beach, February 1, 1891, Ross Papers; Ross, "The Standard of Deferred Payments," 293–305.

33 Ross to Ely, June 12, 1891, Ely Papers; Ross, *Social Control*, 54–5, 441.

feature of society itself, and thereby opened the process of socialization to intellectual analysis.[34]

To say that Ross surmounted the ideological polarization of the Gilded Age is not to say that he transcended ideology. The assumption that individuals are necessarily unequally rewarded, therefore inevitably dissatisfied and consequently in need of governance is the starting point of liberal theory. Claiming that his analysis ruled out the high degree of social morality necessary for socialism or assumed by anarchism, Ross's *Social Control* was an argument for a new liberalism.[35] It accepted as inevitable the inequality and conflict generated by capitalism, and sought to counter them with an enlarged vision of social control.

Social control was also a specific response to the Gilded Age crisis of American exceptionalism, as Ross's racial analysis revealed. Like Veblen, Ross transformed the Teutonic heritage into what appeared to be the more modern and scientific terms of biological racism. He had always taken the progressive vitality of the English race for granted and opposed unlimited immigration as a depressant to American labor. However, his original articles on social control, published between 1896 and 1898, contain few and relatively incidental references to race, as is also the case with his other writing and voluminous letters before 1898. If Ross noticed and feared the Mediterranean immigrants in America, it was his year in Paris in 1898–9 that introduced him to racial theory. As he wrote Ward, "The general result of my studies has been to convince me of the existence of moral varieties in the human species and to lead me to take as my problem the explanation of social order in the Aryan type of man particularly the Celto-German stock." In fact, examples of social control in non-Aryan cultures appear in the book. The Aryan context served chiefly to allow him to address directly the crisis of American exceptionalism.[36]

Ross stated at the opening of his book that his central concern was how the strong-willed "West-European breed" could be brought under social control. "The existence of order among men of this daring and disobedient breed challenges explanation. Especially is this true of the European man in

34 I am applying here a suggestion by David A. Hollinger, "The Defense of Democracy and Robert K. Merton's Formulation of the Scientific Ethos," *Knowledge and Society: Studies in the Sociology of Culture Past and Present*, 4 (1983): 1–15, that some social science theories can be understood as objectifications of conventional discourse.

35 Ross, "Social Control," *AJS*, 3:825–6.

36 Ross to Ward, December 12, 1898, in "The Ward-Ross Correspondence II, 1897–1901," ed. Bernhard J. Stern, *ASR*, 11 (October and December 1946): 593–605, 734–48, particularly 604–5. Ross cited the work of Georges Vacher de Lapouge, Guglielmo Ferrero and Edmond Demolins; see Linda L. Clark, *Social Darwinism in France* (University: University of Alabama Press, 1984).

America or Australia. The same selective migrations that made the Teuton more self-assertive than the docile Slav or the quiescent Hindoo, have made the American more strong-willed and unmanageable than even the West-European." As he refined his problem, the crisis of American exceptionalism came increasingly into view. He illustrated the need for social control by describing the original state of natural equality in the early mining camps of California.

> The equality that gives homesteaders or gold-diggers a few Arcadian days without bolt or bar, state or law, soon passes away.... Equality before the law, political equality, religious equality, – these may delay but they cannot stop the progress of economic differentiation.... Private property is, in fact, a great transforming force ... the thing that calls into being *rigid* structures.

We are at once in the Lockean and the American state of nature, witnessing the institution of government and the destruction of America's "Arcadian days" by industrial capitalism.

The danger was "a great inequality of opportunity." In America, "in the zone of new lands that belts Western civilization the doors of opportunity stand open ... The capable poor ... acquiesce in the *status quo*, because they hope to be possessors themselves someday." But in older societies, this source of social mobility tends to dry up: "The decline of public spirit, the decay of social solidarity, and the rise of the class as a moral authority are, as has often been remarked, the peculiar malady of an old society." The only escape was to become "once more dynamic." England had become the model, not the dystopia, of the American future. By expanding her markets and accelerating capitalist production, England had moderated class conflict, democratized, and preserved her traditional liberties. America too must "ease the upward pressure by founding colonies and by fostering industry and commerce."[37]

Although Ross still placed America at a familiar moment in time, facing the threat of liberal-republican decline, he also began to reformulate his fears in terms of a new sociological schema of historical transformation. Contemporaneously with the German sociologist Ferdinand Tönnies, Ross articulated a distinction between two kinds of social organization: the small community, what Tönnies called *Gemeinschaft*, with its face-to-face personal relations, and modern society or *Gesellschaft*, with its impersonal and rule-governed relations. In America as in Europe that analysis reflected the ambivalence social scientists felt toward the transformed urban world of industrial capitalism. The impersonal relations of modern society were

37 Ross, *Social Control*, 3, 53; 401–3.

precisely the voluntary, rational bonds that were the ideal of the diversified liberal society. But the small community, with its personal relations, provided an idealized locus for all the human values the new society threatened. Tönnies wholly regretted the passing of *Gemeinschaft* and even the liberals were ambivalent. Max Weber recognized in these impersonal, bureaucratic forms of social organization a new kind of tyranny, and Émile Durkheim saw that they created anomie as well as solidarity.[38]

Ross called the communal forms of social control "natural" and the societal ones "artificial," and the ambiguities he saw in that historical transformation echoed the traditional fears of American exceptionalism. The "artificial" controls were, by designation, fragile and they might not grow as rapidly as needed – very much the situation Patten feared in his transition to the pleasure economy. "The grand crash may yet come through the strife of classes, each unable to master the others by means of those influences that enable society to subdue the individual." To avoid the crash, modern society would have to develop more subtle and effective forms of control to deal with the "new, blind, economic forces we have not learned to regulate."

Then Ross's fear suddenly reversed to the other pole of the republican historical imagination. If strong controls were forthcoming, did we not then face the loss of energy and will? Without the "pitiless sifting" of the frontier, "will not a certain decay of character go on beneath our elaborate moral-educational regime – a decay which, in turn, may eventually revive in some form that ecclesiastical-governmental regime which we are supposed to have outgrown?" The sociological question posed at the outset of the book, how Aryan individualism could be controlled, turned at the end of the book into the traditional American question of how it could be preserved from decay. Ross's final hope rested with racial character, the innately "energetic, self-assertive, and individualistic" stock of the northern Aryans. Even under the social controls of modern society, he implied, they would not easily lose their *virtù*.[39]

Ross's idea of social control immediately assumed a vigorous and double life. In all the social science disciplines, it designated the new liberal reform program. Social control of individual self-interest meant public control of the private capitalist economy. The term had already been used in this sense by Henry Demarest Lloyd in 1884, in his sensational exposé of the "Lords

---

38 Harry Liebersohn, *Fate and Utopia in German Sociology, 1870–1923* (Cambridge, Mass.: MIT Press, 1988). See also M. J. Hawkins, "Traditionalism and Organicism in Durkheim's Early Writings, 1885–1893," *JHBS*, 16 (January 1980): 31–44.
39 Ross, *Social Control*, chap. 6, and pp. 432–8. In an earlier article, before going to Europe and before being fired at Stanford, Ross had written that the crash would be due to "mal-distribution of wealth." Idem, "Social Control," *AJS*, 3:815.

of Industry" who were fast destroying the free competition that had reigned in our "exceptional era in history." "Monopoly and anti-monopoly ... represent the two great tendencies of our time: monopoly, the tendency to combination; anti-monopoly, the demand for social control of it."[40] After Ross publicized it, the term was widely taken up by economists and political scientists to designate the new liberal economic task, and in time, it took on as wide a range of political and social purposes as the new liberalism itself. Adopted most enthusiastically by the most activist reformers, the language of "control," with and without the "social" prefix, became pervasive in American social science.

Ross's idea of social control had a more specific impact on sociology. Like Giddings' idea of consciousness of kind, which was first published the same year, 1896, social control began to focus sociologists on the distinctively social processes by which individuals were bound together in society. Like Ross himself, Progressive Era sociologists retained their central interest in the fate of modern society in time and the broad historico-evolutionary field on which that fate was enacted. But within that framework, they began to give special attention to the sociopsychological processes of social control. The terms "socialized" and "socialization," used in the broad sense Ross had identified, quickly appeared. Sociologists began to say that this social nexus between the individual and society – what they called variously "the social imperative," "social control," "the common mental life of the society" – was the key to sociology.[41] The later emphases in American sociology on social psychology, social interaction, and social disorganization all flowed from this original framework, in which sociology assumed the task of showing how the individual was drawn into the social order.

That task is, of course, a distinctly liberal one. Liberal theory required that sociologists start from an aggregate of atomistic individuals and construct society as a set of interactions or psychic influences between them. The problematic relation of the autonomous individual to such social bonds had been a central theme of liberalism since John Stuart Mill's classic essay *On Liberty*. Mill's is the first usage I have found of the term "social control" and it is used very much as Ross uses it, to designate the sociopsychological

---

40 Henry D. Lloyd, "Lords of Industry," *North American Review*, 138 (June 1884): 551–2.
41 John Dewey, "The Significance of the Problem of Knowledge" (1897), *EW*, 5:11; Daniel M. Fox, *The Discovery of Abundance: Simon N. Patten and the Transformation of Social Theory* (Ithaca, N.Y.: Cornell University Press, 1967), 77–8; Giddings, *Theory of Socialization*; Samuel Lindsay, "The Unit of Investigation or of Consideration in Sociology," *AAAPSS*, 12 (September 1898): 214–28; Albion W. Small, "A 'Unit' in Sociology," *AAAPSS*, 13 (March 1899): 81–5; Samuel Lindsay, "A 'Unit' of Sociology – a Reply to Professor Small," *AAAPSS*, 13 (March 1899): 86–9.

control that society exercises over individual conduct. The great difference is that Mill, while recognizing the necessity that society exercise such control, exerted his whole energy against it. The problem of modern liberal society, from his early nineteenth-century vantage point, was to keep social control to a minimum so that individuals may follow the line of their own self-development and so that society may progress. He wanted to extend the policy of laissez-faire from government to society.[42] Ross and his new liberal generation reversed the valences of traditional liberal theory. It was now social control that was sought, and individual autonomy a subsidiary theme. Indeed, under the multiplying lines of social control in modern society, the individual could no longer hope to wall off social influence. Ross was among those liberal social scientists who believed that autonomy could be preserved only by something impervious to this intrusive society: racial character, or later in the century, Freud's stubbornly egocentric biological drives.

The task of social control fixed new liberal norms in the analytical framework of American sociology. Abandoning the polarized ideological conflict of the Gilded Age, with its concern for the fundamental economic basis of society, sociologists turned toward examination of how the existing society – its economic institutions accepted as given – socialized its members. The action of the capitalist market, the loci of power in society, and structural changes over time tended to disappear from view in the search for harmonizing processes imbedded in society itself.[43]

These concrete historical configurations were in any case not clearly visible from the intermediate ground between exceptionalist history and positivist evolution the sociologists chose to occupy. Ross in some ways clung to history. Just as he had a stubborn sense of conflict between individual and society that social control never fully resolved, he had a keen sense for the concrete facts and conflicts of history. "I shall dispense as far as possible with both biologic and psychologic similes and concepts," he wrote

42 John Stuart Mill, *On Liberty* (1859), in *The Six Great Humanistic Essays of John Stuart Mill* (New York: Washington Square Press, 1963), chap. 3, particularly p. 181.

43 Geoffrey Hawthorn discusses the liberal character of American sociology in *Enlightenment and Despair: A History of Sociology* (Cambridge University Press, 1976), chap. 9, under the title, "History Ignored," but his treatment suffers from an extreme form of exceptionalism. American sociology is categorically different from European; it is not "intellectual" thought at all. "European social theory since the Enlightenment has in general been an attempt to secure a coherent liberalism on the ruins of a crumbling and decreasingly legitimate patriarchy. American social theory has been an attempt to secure a coherent liberalism on the basis of nothing at all" (p. 216). J. D. Y. Peel, *Herbert Spencer* (New York: Basic, 1971), 250, also assumes, though much less invidiously, that the relative absence of attention to social conflict and the dominance of liberalism in American sociology mirror a consensus in American society on liberal values.

Ward, "and call things directly by their ordinary names." Most of his text consisted of anthropological and historical discussion of specific instances of social control through law, education, religion, and custom. Yet these were just instances and except for the presumed ties between Western history, American history, and the evolution from *Gemeinschaft* to *Gesellschaft*, history was absent. Ross was aware of the absence.

> The sociologist who explains the growth and principal variations of the social equilibrating-apparatus, does not undertake to account for all the moral phenomena in history. Actual societies, and with them their systems of control, have been so shattered, mutilated, and deformed by war, famine, depopulation, immigration, race degeneration, and class conflict, that no laws can be framed for them that shall hold true of all cases and situations.

The sociologist, like the physiologist, he said, must confine himself to "states of health or of definite disease" in the "social equilibrating apparatus." He cannot account for such "catastrophes" as history regularly records. Ross too dissolved history into a natural process, one that skirted the troubling configurations of "actual societies" so as to find a harmonizing process at work within. His skeptical sense of conflict remained, but it had no theoretical anchor in the actual sources of conflict in modern society.[44]

The problem of binding liberal individuals into a harmonious society appeared to American sociologists to be preeminently a psychological one. With the structures of liberal society accepted as given, control lay in the realm of social consciousness, in education, and persuasion. The search for a liberal sociopsychological basis had sent Giddings at the outset back to Adam Smith's *The Theory of Moral Sentiments*. Smith's discussion of "sympathy" originated with David Hume, and its line of argument was developed by European theorists and critics of democratic society, in Gabriel Tarde's theory of "imitation" and Gustave Le Bon's theory of the crowd, and by the functional psychologists as "suggestion." Sympathy, imitation, and suggestion were mechanisms by which individuals shaped their conduct in accord with the desires and expectations of others. Ross drew on the idea of suggestion in *Social Control*. In modern society, the overt sanctions of punishment and reward would be less used, and suggestion, working through custom, opinion, and education, would be of increas-

---

44 Ross to Ward, March 11, 1896, and July 1, 1896, in "Ward-Ross Correspondence, 1891–96," 394, 397; Ross, "Social Control," *AJS*, 1:513–35; Ross to Ward, December 12, 1898, in "Ward-Ross Correspondence II," 604; Ross, *Social Control*, 409–10.

ing importance.[45] It is not surprising, therefore, that when Ross embarked on what he hoped would be a comprehensive theoretical work in sociology, he produced instead a pioneer text in social psychology.[46]

Ross's book translated the central problems of socialization and liberal social change to the plane of psychology. His models were Walter Bagehot and Gabriel Tarde. Bagehot had built on Henry Maine and Victorian anthropology to construct an explanation of how progressive societies broke "the cake of custom" through "discussion," the signature of both liberal progress and Anglo-American political institutions. Tarde formulated a view of liberal progress centered on the concept of imitation, the glue that bonded individuals into social likeness and that would increasingly dissolve modern conflicts into social agreement.[47] Drawing on his vocabulary of historical examples and his insight into the play of power, Ross showed how imitation worked in the phenomena of crowds and social convention, and across time, in the sway of custom. Then having created social minds, he set them in conflict and discussed the modes of conflict resolution. The key to both rationality in society and progress in history was discussion, the destroyer of custom, the seedbed of rational innovation, and the mechanism of peaceful accommodation.

Where Ross set his own stamp was in his refusal to accept the irenic view of Tarde that conflict could be fully resolved in social resemblance. He was too well convinced of the inevitability of conflicts of interest and too fearful for modern individuality and the "American Breed." Ross ended his social psychology in the same paradoxical position he had ended *Social Control*. The present was a time of "disequilibration," a time in which the pace of change was so great that the formation of a stable social consensus was impossible. Here was the cause of all our present difficulties. Yet here was the individual's saving grace. "A transition epoch is a halcyon time for individuality. For with the growth of the social mind in content it is a question what will be the fate of personal individuality."[48] After *Social*

45 Ross, *Social Control*, 25–6, 61, 71. Tarde linked imitation to Smith's sympathy in his *The Laws of Imitation*, trans. Elsie Clews Parsons (New York: Holt, 1903 [1895]), 79n. See also Robert A. Nye, *The Origins of Crowd Psychology: Gustave Le Bon and the Crisis of Mass Democracy in the Third Republic* (London: Sage, 1975), and Susanna Barrows, *Distorting Mirrors: Visions of the Crowd in Late Nineteenth Century France* (New Haven, Conn.: Yale University Press, 1981).
46 Ross to Ward, July 20, 1905, in "Ward-Ross Correspondence, 1904–1905," 92; Edward A. Ross, *Social Psychology* (New York: Macmillan, 1908).
47 Walter Bagehot, *Physics and Politics* (New York: D. Appleton, 1873); Tarde, *Laws of Imitation*.
48 Ross, *Foundations of Sociology*, 260–71; idem, *Social Psychology*, 363.

*Psychology* Ross postponed his big book. He began instead to visit the less developed countries and turn his travels into popular tracts. In part he was seduced by the notice his popular work on "race-suicide" had brought him. But his new venue also allowed him to thunder against "autocracy" and spy out the road toward progress without facing the downward turn he feared at the end.[49]

Cooley was more adept at erasing the conflict between his individualistic and organicist impulses, more sanguine about the course of liberal history, and more influential on the psychological course of American sociology.[50] Cooley's mind, like that of Ross, was formed by the Gilded Age labor conflict and the problem of socialism. As he approached graduate school in economics, he was convinced that "the unfavorable effect of industrial conditions upon the development of the individual is the most serious of present social questions.... What am I to do? I answer for myself, 'renounce all but a minimum of worldly goods and devote the rest of your energy to such reforms as you are fitted to further.'"[51] He soon admitted that in the comfortable home of his father, Thomas McIntyre Cooley, an eminent jurist, he would find renunciation impossible. Moreover, his temperamental calling was to intellectual rather than practical work. As he studied economics and read deeply in Romantic literature, his reformist leanings and humanistic interests led him toward sociology.[52]

The central issue facing sociology, he believed, had been defined by the conflict between capitalism and socialism, the problem of competition.

The classical school of English political economists ... held that it was the one universally benevolent process in the economic world. The socialists, on the other

---

49  Ross, *Seventy Years of It*, chaps. 12–17, particularly p. 161.
50  For biographical information on Cooley, see Edward C. Jandy, *Charles Horton Cooley: His Life and His Social Theory* (New York: Dryden Press, 1942); and two introductions by his nephew Robert Cooley Angell, in Charles H. Cooley, *Sociological Theory and Social Research* (New York: Holt, 1930), vii–xiii; and in Albert J. Reiss, Jr., ed., *Cooley and Sociological Analysis* (Ann Arbor: University of Michigan Press, 1968), 1–12. The chief source for all biographers is the "Journal" Cooley kept from adolescence throughout his adult life, now in the Charles Horton Cooley Papers, University of Michigan. Vernon K. Dibble, "The Young Charles Horton Cooley and His Father: A Sceptical Note about Psychobiographies," *JHS*, 4 (Spring 1982): 1–26, argued that the "Journal" alone, on which Jandy very largely relies, presents Cooley as more sickly, shy, neurotic, and ineffectual than he in fact was. Dibble's effort to eliminate any taint of depth psychology from Cooley's personality seems to me misguided, although he is correct that the "Journal" provides only partial insight. Indeed the "Journal" is a remarkable record of self-absorption upon which real life and its connections barely and belatedly intrude. Only Cooley's finished work, with its energetic display of a complex intelligence, can dispel the impression that is left by the rumination he clung to in his "Journal."
51  Charles H. Cooley, "Journal," vol. 6, May 9, 1890.
52  Ibid. May 28, 1890, June 2, 1890.

hand, maintain even more positively that it is a destructive and wasteful process, the bane of modern life.... The space between these two opinions is the battle ground of current social discussion. All other questions are subsidiary to it.[53]

When he entered this "battle ground," he already distrusted socialism and looked rather to "a betterment of social ideals" to bring about "something like equality." Raised on Emersonian individualism and his father's mugwump politics, and drawn to the fraternal and egalitarian ideals of the Christian socialist reformers, he set out to imbed the competitive individualism of the market in the higher organicism of society.[54]

The synthetic strategy he used was laid out by John Dewey's lectures at Michigan in 1893.[55] Cooley picked up on the core of economic individualism he found in Dewey and sharpened it with the influence of Franklin Giddings, who examined him on sociology at Michigan and encouraged his early work. Dewey had argued that competition governed the process of social differentiation and development. Cooley showed how it assigned each individual a place in the social system and drove the "sluggish multitude" and the elite engaged in higher forms of emulation to progress. Like Dewey, Cooley then argued that unity, association, and sympathy advanced with differentiation, individuation, and competition. The economic struggle was increasingly mediated by consciousness and competition could be elevated by public opinion and government action to higher and more ethical levels.[56]

Dewey pointed out that "the time-process is dependent on the space-

53 Charles Horton Cooley, "Competition and Organization," *Michigan Political Science Association*, 1 (December 1894): 33.

54 Cooley, "Journal," vol. 6, May 9, 1890. A revealing source for the values of Cooley's father is Henry Wade Rogers, "Biography of Thomas McIntyre Cooley," Thomas M. Cooley Papers, University of Michigan.

55 In his "Journal," vol. 11, June 28, 1897, Cooley set down the influences that had brought him to sociology. His greatest stimulus, he said, came from Macaulay, Emerson, and Dewey's psychology. In writing out his first lectures on sociology in 1894, he went on, he was chiefly influenced by Schäffle and "much influenced also by Dewey's lectures in Political Philosophy heard in the fall of '93." In an autobiographical statement written in 1928, Cooley gave a different impression. "John Dewey, whose lectures on political philosophy I attended in 1893–94, certainly left a lasting mark, but rather by his personality, I think, than by his lectures.... The chief thing I now recall from his lectures is a criticism of Spencer, in which Dewey maintained that society was an organism in a deeper sense than Spencer had perceived and that language was its 'sensorium.' I had already arrived at a somewhat similar view." Charles H. Cooley, "The Development of Sociology at Michigan," in *Sociological Theory and Social Research*, 6. In fact, virtually all the distinctive lines of analysis in Cooley's sociology were articulated first, albeit briefly, in Dewey's lectures, as recorded in Cooley's notes, "John Dewey, Political Philosophy Lectures, 1893," Cooley Papers.

56 Cooley, "John Dewey, Political Philosophy Lectures"; idem, "Personal Competition: Its Place in the Social Order and Effect upon Individuals; with Some Considerations on Success," *PAEA: Economic Studies*, 4 (April 1899); the "sluggish multitude" is on p. 156.

process.... No isolated society had ever been a progressive society." Both progress and sympathy would require increasing contact between communities, classes, and individuals. Cooley followed up with an intensive study of Albert Schäffle's elaborate analyses of the organic functions of society and wrote his doctoral dissertation on the theory of transportation, a study of economic place relations and of transportation as the basic communicative function of society.[57] As he moved fully into sociology, he turned his attention to the psychological forms of communication. History disclosed "rapid and accelerating social change," and behind that change was the multiplicity of accessible influences that created greater individuation, voluntary association, and sympathy. Primitive societies were like narrow strips of water, cut off from each other. "Modern society . . . is more like the uninterrupted ocean, upon which the waves of change meet with no obstacles except one another, and roll as high and as far as the propagating influence can carry them."[58]

During the 1890s the theoretical harmony Cooley was publishing in his studies of competition and communication was not matched by the private sentiments he expressed in his journal. There, the conflicting attractions of individualism and organicism still held sway. As social conflict peaked in 1896 he confided that "The universal antithesis between sympathy and inevitable competition is a tragic element in our society." Two years later as the country went to war in Cuba he rejoiced that America was still an aggressive Anglo-Saxon country and would not be eliminated by natural selection. The war "makes me proud of the race and the American stock." He saw in the "combative" faces of his students "the beneficent efficacy of a free and competitive social order." Cooley was soon ashamed of his "boyish excitement of war," but it was very much in character. He was confined by temperament to a largely cloistered and contemplative life and he longed in imagination for both the sympathetic common life of the organic society and the active self-assertion of competition.[59]

Cooley solved his theoretical problem by reconciling organicism and individualism on the level of psychology. The "selective principle" in evolution, he decided, was human nature and it was within human nature that the conflicting claims of individual and society could be reconciled.[60]

---

57 Cooley, "John Dewey, Political Philosophy Lectures"; idem, "The Theory of Transportation," *PAEA*, 9 (May 1894). On Schäffle, see Small, *General Sociology*.
58 Charles H. Cooley, "The Process of Social Change," *PSQ*, 12 (March 1897): 73, 79.
59 Cooley, "Journal," vol. 11, May 7, 1896; vol. 12, September 22, 1898; June 26, 1898; July 18, 1898; July 24, 1898.
60 Cooley, "Development of Sociology at Michigan," 5–6; idem, "Notes on Giddings' Outline," Cooley Papers; idem, "Process of Social Change," 81.

The achievement of a fully socialized liberal individual required a redefinition of the individual and the psychologizing of society. "If the person is
thought of primarily as a separate material form, inhabited by thoughts and
feelings conceived by analogy to be equally separate," Cooley said, "then
the only way of getting a society is by adding on a new principle of
socialism, social faculty, altruism, or the like." But society and individual are
not separable phenomena, merely different aspects of the same thing, and
that thing is mental. We know persons only as "imaginative ideas in the
mind." Indeed, we come to know ourselves as an individual only by a
process of mental intercourse with other persons. Our self-consciousness is
a process of communication through language and internalized in imagination; our identity is constructed from a "looking-glass self," a reflection of
how we imagine others see us. Society in turn "is a relation among personal
ideas ... they get together only as personal ideas in the mind."[61]

Having created an individual who is "all social ... all a part of the
common human life," Cooley could envision the progress of modern society
as a process of enlarging sympathy and justice. Hostility, emulation, and
rivalry could remain as impulses to self-assertion, but there was always a
common element that allowed for social communion. "If I come to imagine
a person suffering wrong ... he is my life, as really and immediately as
anything else." Hence "one who entertains the thought and feeling of others
can hardly refuse them justice; he has made them a part of himself. There is,
as we have seen, no first or second person about a sentiment; if it is alive in
the mind that is all there is to the matter." Virtue was nothing more than
"exerting the imagination." The liberal idea of sympathy, the organicist
insights of Dewey and the functional psychologists, the fluid and mentalistic
terms of William James's stream of consciousness, were all used by Cooley
to dissolve any fixed barrier between self and others. It was a fitting solution
for a man who lived largely in his own thoughts.[62]

Removing the psychological barriers to socialization was only half the
battle, however, as Cooley knew. The individual lived in a society shaped by
organization and history, and in extending his analysis from human nature
to social organization, he invented an intermediate formation. Human
nature was developed in each individual through experience in "primary
groups," specifically "the family, the play-group of children, and the
neighborhood or community group of elders." These were universal institutions and produced "what is universal in human nature and human ideals."
Here, intimate face-to-face association created "a certain fusion of indi-

61 Charles H. Cooley, *Human Nature and the Social Order* (New York: Scribner, 1902),
   89–90, 86, 152, 84.
62 Ibid., 12, 115, 366.

vidualities in a common whole." The unity of the primary group was "always a differentiated and usually a competitive unity, admitting of self-assertion and various appropriative passions," but "socialized by sympathy" and disciplined by "a common spirit." Here in short was the human nature for a new liberal society.[63]

Indeed Cooley was specific. The ideals generated in primary groups were those of loyalty, lawfulness, and freedom, including truth, service, kindness, democracy, and the ideals of the natural-rights philosophy: the right to personal freedom, to labor, to property, and to open competition. The most vital ideals of the present, democracy and Christianity, were based upon the ideals of primary groups, Cooley said. Democracy grew from the local community and "a right democracy is simply the application on a large scale of principles which are universally felt to be right as applied to a small group." Christianity too was based upon the family. To extend the ideals of the primary group to all society, to remake social organization on the new liberal pattern of human nature was "the great historical task of mankind."[64]

Cooley envisioned a source for liberal society that was virtually timeless. It was as enduring as primary groups themselves and "little affected by institutional changes." No matter what the conditions of society, the sociopsychological basis for liberal socialization was created anew with each generation. Cooley's was a romantic liberalism. He saw that the historical bifurcation Tönnies and Ross had made between communal and modern forms could be mitigated, that the communal form was imbedded in society itself in primary groups. From this perennial source, society would move forward to progress and backward to original innocence. "We are to become more as little children, more simple, frank and human." Indeed, at the present juncture, human nature "is apparently in a position to work itself out more adequately than at any time in the past." Formulating a concept that was already implicit in American sociology and would have a long future life, Cooley named the present a time of "disorganization," or disharmony between "human nature and its instruments." Such a state of affairs threatened the health even of the family and community, the basic primary groups in society, but it was transitional, created by rapid change. "The breaking up of traditions throws men back upon immediate human nature," loosing selfishness, sensuality, and skepticism. "But it also awakens the child in man and a childlike pliability to the better as well as the worse in natural impulse." Tendencies toward wider sympathy and higher organization were everywhere visible.[65]

63 Cooley, *Social Organization*, 23–4.
64 Ibid., 38–48, 51–3, 119, 200–5.
65 Ibid., 419, 113, 399, 318, 343, 347, 354–5.

It will come as no surprise that Cooley's romantic liberalism had the specific shape of American exceptionalism. In America, he believed, human nature has had "pretty much its own way." The American spirit is peculiarly "at one with the general spirit of human nature," and this he attributed to America's exceptional history. Cooley touched all the benchmarks of the exceptionalist literature: the example of Rome, the problem of founding a large and dynamic republic, the contrast of American individuality with French solidarity, the dialogue with Tocqueville. But the key link between human nature and America was almost too neat. The primary group ideals of mutual aid and democratic freedom had their historic origin in Teutonic village communities, the source of American institutions and racial inheritance; these ideals then developed further in frontier communities. "Our antecedents and training have been peculiarly fortunate." One result was that "on the whole, Americans may surely claim that there was never before a great nation in which the people felt so much like a family, had so kindly and cheerful a sense of a common life."[66] The primary group was Cooley's most influential idea, and Cooley himself was surprised at its influence because it was an afterthought. He wrote a complete draft of *Social Organization* without it, starting with his psychological theory of organic human nature and going directly to his liberal exceptionalist analysis of American society. Only afterward did he realize that there was a missing link in his argument.[67] The concept of the primary group was fashioned as the linchpin of the whole.

Cooley's exceptionalist reading of history placed America at the forefront of progress. America was born without the rich particularity of the European past. "When a populous society springs up rapidly from a few transplanted seeds, its structure, however vast, is necessarily somewhat simple and monotonous." In America the new industrial modernity "has had fuller sweep." America moreover is the first real democracy, a movement almost totally "different from anything in the past." America is "nearer, perhaps, to the spirit of the coming order." Cooley permitted himself some regret for the loss of the past.

That fine English sentiment that came down to us through the colonists more purely, perhaps, than to the English in the old country, is passing away – as a distinct current, that is – lost in a flood of cosmopolitan life. Before us, no doubt, is a larger humanity, but behind is a cherished spirit that can hardly live again; and, like the boy who leaves home, we must turn our thoughts from an irrevocable past and go hopefully on to we know not what.

66 Ibid., 168, 331, 114–16, 152–3, 160, 25, 51, 107, 144, 196.
67 Cooley, "Development of Sociology at Michigan," 12.

Standing on the verge of a new cosmopolitan history, Cooley could only hope that Jane Addams was correct that "the confused and deprived masses of our cities" would be "the initiators of new and higher ideals for our civilization." Torn from old traditions and mingled together promiscuously, "everything is cancelled but human nature, and they are thrown back upon that for a new start." One way or another, America retained the capacity of nature for new creation.[68]

Cooley was convinced that the United States would also retain the lineaments of democracy that were set out in her original institutions. The bulk of *Social Organization* was an examination of democracy and class in America. Using Tocqueville as his starting point, Cooley characterized these institutions by playing off American realities against Europe on the one hand and the democratic ideal on the other. As against the ideal, he found much wanting, but as against Europe, he slipped into the idealized vision of American exceptionalism. The American reality was at once ideal and less than ideal and the disparity drove him to nuanced exceptionalist analyses of political and social institutions.[69]

On the issue of class, for example, Cooley upheld Tocqueville's finding that there was no proletariat in America. Because classes in America were not hereditary, were "open," they meant only "specialization" within a common unity. Foreshadowing the analysis of American society by stratification, he urged that Americans commonly belonged to more than one class and could be graded along different scales of occupation, income, and culture. As a result, there would be no class war in America, only wholesome struggle. "In a society where groups interlace as much as they do with us a conflict of class interests is, in great degree, not a conflict of persons but rather one of ideas in a common social medium." Indeed, greater "specialization," class consciousness, and occupational tradition passed on through family descent were all to the good. In the "ascendency of a capitalist class" in America, he found both benefits and evils and in time, the evils would be subdued by democratic principles. Describing laborers as "handworkers," as he himself filled his spare time with handwork in carpentry, he viewed American society through the lens of his comfortable familial, professional, and small-town identity. After one visit to a settlement house, he saw that he ordinarily lived in "an upper-class atmosphere," but that bias was beyond remedy.[70]

68 Ibid., 166–7, 157, 169–70, 137.
69 Ibid., 279–80; pts. 3 and 6.
70 Ibid., 116–17, 248–9, 242, 180, 272, and chaps. 23–4.

Cooley was the Progressive Era complement of the Gilded Age William Graham Sumner; together they frame the liberal political spectrum that emerged from the crisis in American exceptionalism. Drawing round them traditional strands of republican political theory and exceptionalist history, Sumner spelled out the tenets of possessive individualism, as Cooley articulated the new liberal organicism. Cooley was as bold in revealing the sanguine premises of his organic creed as Sumner was in articulating the harsh bases of his competitive doctrine. Both drew immediate criticism from contemporaries for their extreme moods. Yet the analytical power and ideological resonance of both gave their work remarkable vitality through the twentieth century. Just as Sumner has remained a repository for libertarians in their battle against the new liberalism, Cooley's work has equally proven a resource for new liberal defenders of an idealized American democracy.[71]

## The meanings of social control

At the turn of the century the concept of social control framed the broad area of social psychology, social interaction, and social disorganization within which American sociology would begin to take shape. Social control as the sociologists defined it – society's sociopsychological control of individual conduct – meant something very different from what it has come to mean today. Recent historians and social scientists, using the work of Antonio Gramsci, have given the term a neo-Marxist signification; social control, in contemporary usage, means class domination, usually capitalist class domination through the medium of cultural hegemony.[72] To some degree, this neo-Marxist analysis can be applied to the sociologists' own use of the concept of social control. Social control inscribed and was intended to inscribe a normative vision of modern capitalist society at a time when that vision was seriously contested. As a result, liberal capitalist norms were fixed in the nature of sociality and glossed with the designation of science.

Ross himself defined social control as both social order in general and a particular kind of beneficent liberal order. Class control is not social control "in the true sense," he claimed. In a competitive society, in which those at

71 For an insightful account of Cooley's work and its later influence, written from within that tradition, see Marshall J. Cohen, *Charles Horton Cooley and the Social Self in American Thought* (New York: Garland, 1982).
72 T. J. Jackson Lears, "The Concept of Cultural Hegemony: Problems and Possibilities," *AHR*, 90 (June 1985): 567–93; Lois Banner, "Religious Benevolence as Social Control: A Critique of an Interpretation," *JAH*, 60 (June 1973): 23–41.

the bottom are the "weak and incompetent," no heavy system of class control will be necessary. Rather control "will show the sincerity, spontaneity, and elasticity that mark the control that is truly social." Here was an idealized version of competitive liberal society identified with, and legitimated by, the nature of society itself.[73]

Liberal social control was read into human nature, as well as society. The sharp edges of the conflict between individual and society often showed through Ross's analysis, but the idealist social scientists seemed to erase the conflict by locating the norm of social control in human nature itself. When George Herbert Mead declared that "man is essentially social," he also argued that "What society is struggling to accomplish is to bring this social side of our conduct out so that it may, in some conscious way, become the element of control." In this idealistic form, the control imposed on the individual by society was identified with the individual's own nature. Social control not only lost its coercive force, but was folded into the process of self-realization. In the concept of social control, the diverse sources and conflicting norms of social authority became blurred, obscuring just who was controlling whom.[74]

The tendency to obscure the issue of power was furthered by the sociologists' tendency to collapse political into social categories. John Dewey showed the way in his political science lectures of 1893. Rehearsing and discarding the traditional political theories of sovereignty, Dewey argued that sovereignty was merely an expression of the organic unity of society. The claim to rights and the exercise of authority rested wholly upon the organic interdependence of society. The reciprocal realization of individual and society was its final standard. The long accumulated discussion of the problems of political power dissolved in these organic metaphors. Dewey recognized that democracy required "Submission to social discipline"; that was the germ of truth in socialism. But in his sociopsychological language, submission became a problem not of political power but of "social mediation." Conceiving social control as a social process rather than an exercise of

73 Ross, *Social Control*, 376, 394.
74 George H. Mead, "Review of C. L. Morgan, *An Introduction to Comparative Psychology*," *Psychological Review*, 2 (July 1895): 401; George H. Mead, "Review of Gustave Le Bon, *The Psychology of Socialism*," *AJS*, 5 (November 1899): 406. Morris Janowitz, "Sociological Theory and Social Control," *AJS*, 81 (July 1975): 82–108; and *The Last Half-Century: Societal Change and Politics in America* (Chicago: University of Chicago Press, 1978), chap. 2, reviews one tradition of usage of the term among sociologists and attempts to revive it for current use. The analysis ignores and exemplifies, however, the fatal conceptual and ideological ambiguities imbedded in the term.

political will, the organic social scientists never applied to it the liberal-republican tradition of distrust of power.[75]

There is another reason for that oversight. When social scientists talked about society establishing social control over the individual and the economy, they were also talking about themselves. That is the final, and perhaps the most telling, signification of the concept of social control. When Ross picked up the term in 1894, it had just acquired another usage among sociologists. Small and his colleagues referred to "social control" as that "applied" portion of Ward's and Small's sociological program by which the new science was to use its knowledge to direct progressive reforms.[76] Ross telescoped the two concepts into a single term, implicitly identifying society's efforts to control its members with the sociologists' attempts to control society. By this identification, the social scientists, with their knowledge of the laws that controlled society, could speak for society; their means and purposes were but the socializing mechanisms and social purposes of society itself. By the same token, their efforts acquired the scope and power of society itself. The idea of social control that runs through so much of early twentieth-century social science generally carried that double meaning and double ideological freight.

A neo-Marxist analysis, therefore, does not capture the complexity of the idea of social control, unless Gramsci's concept of hegemony is defined broadly enough to allow for the relative autonomy of intellectuals and of culture.[77] For the class bias expressed in the concept of social control

---

75 Cooley, "John Dewey, Political Philosophy Lectures." Frank Tariello, *The Reconstruction of American Political Ideology, 1865–1917* (Charlottesville: University Press of Virginia, 1981), writing from a libertarian perspective, calls attention to this alarming consequence of the Progressives' emphasis on social control, but fails to place it in the wider contexts of their work.

76 Small and Vincent, *Introduction to the Study of Society*, 345; Bernard Moses, "The Nature of Sociology," *JPE*, 3 (December 1894): 27; George E. Vincent, "The Province of Sociology," *AJS*, 1 (January 1896): 487–8.

77 Lears, "The Concept of Cultural Hegemony," is an attempt to enlarge the concept in useful ways. See also Jerome Karabel, "Revolutionary Contradictions: Antonio Gramsci and the Problem of Intellectuals," *Politics and Society*, vol. 6, no. 2 (1976): 123–72, and on the relative autonomy of what Gramsci called "traditional" intellectuals, 147, 153–4. In using the concept of cultural hegemony, I assume that it has survived, in somewhat chastened form, in the debate in the *AHR* between Thomas Haskell, David Brion Davis, and John Ashworth. Haskell's claim that a rigorous standard of empirical proof must be applied at the level of individual motivation is reductionistic and would prevent the formulation of any analysis of the way interests and power relations shape historical choices. I would not, however, want to divorce hegemony completely from intentionality, as Lears's essay sometimes threatens to do. See vol. 90 (April 1985): 339–61 and (June 1985): 547–66; vol. 92 (October 1987): 797–878.

belonged less to the capitalists than to the academic social scientists, a class that was dependent upon the capitalists and whose interest in rationality often allied them with the capitalists, yet a class that retained some degree of autonomy. Like the gentry social scientists whose heirs they were, they took on the role of keepers of the American exceptionalist tradition and served as conscience as well as validator of the capitalist order. The idea of social control is a direct heir of the Whiggish belief in the subordination of individual rights to social and governmental definitions of the public good, a belief that permeated the Whiggish academic culture of American social science. Applied originally against the radical individualism of workers and farmers, it was in the Progressive Era extended to the acquisitive individualism of the capitalists. Social control was aimed at the classes above and below the professional social scientists. Moreover, social scientists were moved by the double goals of American exceptionalism; they sought both to protect the established course of American history and to draw it closer to its presumably inherent ideals.

That so many American social scientists adopted the language of social control owed a great deal to their uncertainty in history. From Henry Demarest Lloyd to Edward A. Ross, the crisis of American exceptionalism framed the call for social control. In American social science the term and the vocational role it embodied were promulgated by liberal social scientists who had opened up a limited sphere of history. Their recognition that America's future depended on creative historical action gave their new vocation its great importance and its great burden. We have already seen Lester Ward and Albion Small fill up that new space of historical uncertainty with the promise that social science would be able virtually to control the course of history, and the concept of social control neatly captured that aim.

In their way, the social scientists were only doing what prior generations of American intellectuals had done. As Sacvan Bercovitch has shown, clerical and republican elites have repeatedly faced crises in America's exceptionalist mission. Each time, they stilled their anxieties with a grandiose sense of calling and a breathtaking faith in their ability to yoke the power of Grace or Reason to America's historic purpose.[78] Unlike these previous generations, the social scientists had at hand neither Grace nor Reason to assure the course of history, only the positivist conception of science. Yet only the positivist conception of science now promised to escape the changing character of historical experience. Science alone prom-

---

78 Sacvan Bercovitch, *The Puritan Origins of the American Self* (New Haven, Conn.: Yale University Press, 1975), particularly 122–3, 132–6, 184–6; idem, *The American Jeremiad* (Madison: University of Wisconsin Press, 1978), 9, 24, 62–5, 86–92, 120, 135–6, 181, 190, 197.

ised to reach the nature that was beneath or within history and beyond its relativizing effect.

The positivist vision of science promised prediction and control, and prediction and control in turn gave a technocratic shape to their conception of their social role. By no means all American social scientists placed their faith in positivist social control. Charles Cooley, for example, remained to the end an outspoken critic of it, regarding social science as much akin to art as to science.[79] But a technocratic conception of social control did begin to take hold in the Progressive Era and we can see it in Ross's work.

Ross closed his discussion of social control with a revealing admission of the new sense of power he felt. He believed he had discovered the secret of how society controls its members and such knowledge in the wrong hands might subvert – just as in the right hands it might beneficently control – all social order.

The secret of order is, therefore, not to be bawled from every housetop.... The social investigator ... will venerate the moral system too much to uncover its nakedness. He will speak to men, not to youth. He will address himself to those who administer the moral capital of society; to teachers, clergymen, editors, lawmakers, and judges, who wield the instruments of control; to poets, artists, thinkers, and educators, who are the guides of the human caravan.

A rebel himself against the authority of priests and autocrats, Ross clearly sensed the radical potential of sociological knowledge. But there seems no doubt that he always identified with the political and cultural elite of "lawmakers" and "educators" that guarded the old republic. The new social scientists were to ally with the natural aristocracy, while subtly shifting its venue. In his book on social control, written for a popular audience, Ross described the social scientist in whose hands he placed the knowledge of control as a Nietzschean "Strong Man," who would choose to guard the "venerable corporation." Unlike the generalized and concentrated wisdom of the old elite, the social scientists' knowledge was a specialized and dangerous science to be given only in small doses to the people.

In his journal articles, he argued that the social scientist was justified in keeping this knowledge "half esoteric." "Surely the men of widest horizon and farthest vision who, making the joint welfare their own, wage perpetual war against predatory appetite, greedy ambition, unblushing impudence, and brutal injustice, may safely be intrusted with the secrets of control!" He urged the social scientists to press on with their studies. "The social system of control has been a dark jungle harboring warring bands of guerrillas; but

79 Charles H. Cooley, "The Roots of Social Knowledge," *AJS*, 32 (1926): 59–79.

when investigators with the scientific method have fully occupied this region the disorder and dacoity ought to cease." They will discover "some general principles" which will allow them to decide between the conflicting claims of the individual and society. "As soon as the conditions which reconcile order with progress are made clear to the leaders of opinion, the control of society over its members ought to become more conscious and effective than it now is, and the dismal see-sawing between change and reaction that has been the curse of this century ought to disappear."

In short, the purpose of social scientific knowledge was not to clarify and enlarge political judgments, but to decide them once and for all on authoritative scientific grounds. Once put into effect, their knowledge would straighten out the crooked path of history and place "scientific method" and reason in control. The social scientists could be trusted with such a science because as men who made "the joint welfare their own," they stood above the selfish interests of other groups in society.[80]

John Dewey was at the same moment a leading advocate of Ross's central premise, that the social sciences would produce the kind of positivist knowledge that could establish rational control over society and history. Dewey believed that philosophy must itself become a kind of social science, oriented toward social praxis. Its method henceforth must be the method of science and its field of interest chiefly "psychology and social ethics – including in the latter term all the related concrete social sciences, so far as they may give guidance to conduct." Keenly aware that the civic humanist ideal and the Kingdom of God must be realized in history, Dewey turned to science as the means to establish rational control of life.[81]

The methods of physical science have not yet been fully applied to life, Dewey said. When they are fully developed in psychology and "progressively applied to history and all the social sciences, we can anticipate no other outcome than increasing control in the ethical sphere – the nature and extent of which can be best judged by considering the revolution that has taken place in the control of physical nature through a knowledge of her order." Speaking as president to the American Psychological Association in 1899, Dewey argued that it was only the method of physical science, with its ability to "state things as interconnected parts of a mechanism," that could produce real knowledge of causes and permit control. Hugo Münsterberg, his predecessor in the chair, could criticize the application of scientific psychology to education, he said, only because the science is so little advanced. "If our teachers were trained as architects are trained; if our

80 Ross, "Social Control," *AJS*, 3:820–1; idem, *Social Control*, 441–2.
81 Dewey, "Significance of the Problem of Knowledge," 21–2.

schools were actually managed on a psychological basis as great factories are run on the basis of chemical and physical science . . . we should never dream of discussing this question." Here Dewey articulated even more vividly than the social scientists themselves a technocratic vision of their mission.[82]

Where Dewey differed from Ross and many social scientists was in his commitment to democratic process. Unlike Ross and Münsterberg, he believed that science should not remain the "half esoteric" preserve of the specialist elite, but could be translated for and reenacted at every level of society. He came to regard science as a refined form of the pragmatic intelligence, the model of "how we think." That is why teachers could be trained like architects in the science of their field, and why Dewey believed that science could inform and empower democratic process, rather than preempt it. Here, as in all things, Dewey's desire to erase divisions paid insufficient attention to real differences. The positivist conception of science, with its technical knowledge and manipulative approach to nature, is not easily reconciled with democracy, no more than are "great factories."[83]

If a technocratic conception of the social scientist's task is visible in Ross's and Dewey's concepts of social control, it is still a "soft" version of that role compared to what other social scientists would adopt, particularly after the outbreak of World War I. Ross's technocratic aim is barely sketched and linked to traditional moral purposes. He could still imagine himself leading the age-old caravan of humanity on its journey and succeeding to the guardianship of the republic. Some American social scientists even before the war, and many after it, would feel more deeply alienated from the past and driven to a more aggressive effort to control history through positivist science. Dewey's conception of social science and control ran a parallel course to theirs, but ultimately diverged from it.

## Conclusions

Like the Progressive economists, the Progressive sociologists forged new conceptions of their discipline from their experience of the Gilded Age crisis. Except for Sumner, who largely abandoned hope, the sociologists accepted the changed industrial world America had become and tried to relocate the exceptionalist ideal in the progressive stream of liberal history. Conflict they agreed was an inevitable feature of the development of modern society, but it was the conflict of economic, racial, and ethnic groups. At the St. Louis Congress in 1904, when Werner Sombart delivered a lecture on the

82 John Dewey, "Psychology and Social Practice" (1899), *MW*, 1:131–50, particularly 144, 149–50.
83 Ibid., 134–6.

"industrial proletariat" in modern society, it was translated for the American audience into "industrial group."[84] In America conflict was not and would not become class conflict in any meaningful sense. Indeed, the present state of social conflict marked a temporary transition between the old preindustrial society and the new industrial one. The direction of industrial society was toward liberal harmony: an increasingly peaceable, rational, and ethical adjustment of interests. That was the message alike of Small and Giddings, Ross and Cooley.

"Social control" meant that sociologists must use their new discipline to ease the historical transformation. The concept expressed their desire to explore the social and psychological means by which liberal society drew competitive individuals into the social order and by which America's time of troubles might be ended. Social control expressed as well their own professional ambitions, ambitions that already showed signs of moving in the direction of a technocratic science of prediction and control. The ideology of harmony often blinded them to the concrete historical reality and the difficulty of their task. In their desire for social unity, they often glossed over the divisions within capitalist society and human nature. Imagining themselves at the controls, they imagined a wholly beneficent exercise of social control.

Living in the new industrial world, American sociologists, like those in Europe, also began to reshape history into a succession of two ideal-typical stages, the community-centered traditional society and the modern, differentiated, industrial society. Sociologists in Europe constructed the same dichotomous view, which also thinned out the complex shapes of history and avoided actual historical analysis. In Europe, however, that modern sociological imagination overlay an already rich awareness of historical change.[85] In the United States it overlay a historical consciousness already thinned by attachment to exceptionalist metaphors. The two-stage model, with the present located at the point of transition, fit perfectly the historical sense of fundamental transformation that grew out of the Gilded Age crisis. The traditional fears of decline and the new sense of loss opened a search for ways to maintain traditional vitality in the threatening industrial world. Ross's resort to an "American Breed" echoed a parallel European resort to biological race. Cooley's primary group and wholly socialized, yet individualistic, human nature moderated the starker transformation portrayed

84  Werner Sombart, "The Industrial Group," in *Congress of Arts and Sciences: Universal Exposition, St. Louis. 1904*, ed. Howard J. Rogers, 8 vols. (Boston: Houghton Mifflin, 1906), 7:791–9.
85  Philip Abrams, "The Sense of the Past and the Origins of Sociology," *Past and Present*, no. 55 (May 1972): 18–32; Liebersohn, *Fate and Utopia*.

by continental theorists, a reflection of the romantic naturalism that in America lay ready to animate harmonial ideals.

American sociologists entered the Gilded Age with a more fragmented and less developed intellectual tradition than the economists, and they emerged from it with nothing like the paradigmatic clarity of neoclassical economics. Still, they established a firm foothold in academia and some clear directions for theory and research. As Philip Abrams pointed out, sociology never coalesced in England as a discipline until after World War II. If sociology answered a need for the legitimation of modern society, the relative continuity of English history dulled the need for ideological invention in sociology as in economics. Instead, government service and reform organizations offered careers to those interested in easing the way to social harmony, and drew off political concern into practical administration and reform, rather than social science. The need for theoretical legitimation flowed into the already well-developed channel of anthropology, which answered to England's imperial role.[86]

One might assume that just here was the difference between England and America. The presence of diverse races within the American heartland, rather than outside it, created a greater need in the United States for sociology. Yet the impetus to sociology came, as we have seen, before the impact of the new immigration made itself felt and was oriented first toward the social transformation of industrialization and the fate of the working class. American sociologists, more like the Durkheimians of the Third French Republic and the German sociologists around the Verein fur Sozialpolitik, were engaged in an effort to secure the national identity in the face of political and industrial transformation. The expanding and decentralized American university system offered an important base of support, one that both allowed and stimulated sociologists to forge a tenable intellectual field. Yet where the ideological will was present, as in France and Germany, academic sociology carved out a place even under less favorable institutional conditions.[87]

The combination of theoretical ambition and practical interest in social

---

86 Philip Abrams, *The Origins of British Sociology, 1834–1914* (Chicago: University of Chicago Press, 1968); J. W. Burrow, *Evolution and Society* (Cambridge University Press, 1966). Reba N. Soffer, *Ethics and Society in England: The Revolution in the Social Sciences 1870–1914* (Berkeley: University of California Press, 1978), argues that the social sciences in England underwent a revolution analogous to that in continental Europe, but inadvertently, I believe, supports the case for relative continuity in English social thought.

87 Anthony Oberschall, "The Institutionalization of American Sociology," in *The Establishment of Empirical Sociology*, ed. Anthony Oberschall (New York: Harper & Row, 1972); Terry N. Clark, *Prophets and Patrons: The French University and the Emergence of the Social Sciences* (Cambridge, Mass.: Harvard University Press, 1973).

betterment that was offered by American universities in the Progressive Era has been taken as the key to the particular combination of empirical research and theory that American sociology effected.[88] The combination required, however, the right blend of respectable ideology and scientific distance. Giddings' liberal evolutionary positivism was quickly able to make that operational leap. Small, with his political timidity and ambivalence, never managed it. With a new set of personnel, we will soon see Chicago sociology take up the slack.

88 Oberschall, "The Institutionalization of American Sociology."

# 8

◁==========================================▷

# From historico-politics to
# political science

I have paid little attention in the last several chapters to the students of
historico-politics. Economics and sociology enacted a two-stage drama of
challenge to the traditional disciplines established in the Gilded Age and
liberal revision of those traditions. The challenge raised the threat of
socialism and it was necessary first to understand that threat in order to
understand the new liberal versions of economics and sociology that formed
in its shadow. In historico-politics the two stages were combined in one. The
challenge to the gentry founders of historico-politics took shape more
slowly and from the beginning it projected a moderate liberal vision of
American exceptionalism.

## The liberal historicist challenge

As in economics and sociology, the younger generation in historico-politics
was born in the 1850s and 1860s, but their political orientation was more
conservative. Although disaffection in economics and sociology came from
egalitarian disillusionment with modern capitalism, in historico-politics it
came more largely from elitist disillusionment with democracy. From the
beginning, the younger generation sought a liberal historicist revision of
American exceptionalist principle, not a radical transformation.

The Gilded Age crisis, with its center in the social question, seems to have
steered young people who held more radical sentiments into economics and
sociology, where they could deal directly with the problems of industrialization, class conflict, and inequality. The younger generation in historico-
politics lacked the background in dissenting evangelical piety and social
millennialism so important to Richard T. Ely, Albion Small, and their
confederates. The fathers of Frank J. Goodnow, Henry Jones Ford,

257

Frederick Jackson Turner, J. Franklin Jameson, and James Harvey Robinson were active in business and politics, their orientation worldly and tolerant in religion. Herbert Levi Osgood was the only farmer's son in this cohort.[1]

In the few cases in which family religion was important, it led into moderate or conservative political channels. Woodrow Wilson was the son of a conservative southern Presbyterian minister who girded him to battle for personal righteousness rather than social perfectionism. Charles McLean Andrews was distant from his father, a roving preacher for an incipient fundamentalist sect with conservative political views, and he moved easily into liberal religion and moderate politics. Reared in an abolitionist Quaker family in Indiana and Iowa, Jesse Macy alone had the evangelical's sense of social mission, but its force was blunted. Encouraged by his father to read science and mathematics, he identified the candor and open-minded rationality he found in science with the peace-loving and truth-telling ideal of his Quaker community. Appalled by Civil War violence, he came to believe that scientific debate was "a method for dealing with all questions on which men differ in opinion," a method of communal discipline, which controlled conflict and banished "all liars, blunderers, and all who had a disposition to believe a false report ... from the charmed circle." Macy's Quaker pacifism channeled his concern for social righteousness into a consensual, scientific ideal, which moderated his social activism.[2]

In politics the new generation thus stood squarely within the Whig tradition of limited democracy that had dominated historico-politics from the early nineteenth century. Like the mugwump gentry, the strongest political impulse they displayed was the desire to salvage popular government from the corrupt party politics that dominated post-Civil War political experience. In the Gilded Age they showed only limited sympathy for the working class and no liking for socialism. Woodrow Wilson claimed in 1889

1 For biographical information, see Arthur W. Macmahon, "Frank Johnson Goodnow," *DAB*, Suppl. 2, 250–1; W. L. Whittlesey, "Henry Jones Ford," *DAB*, 3, 515–16; Ray Allen Billington, *Frederick Jackson Turner: Historian, Scholar, Teacher* (New York: Oxford University Press, 1973); Morey David Rothberg, "Servant to History: A Study of John Franklin Jameson, 1859–1937" (Ph.D. dissertation, Brown University, 1982); Harry Elmer Barnes, "James Harvey Robinson," in *American Masters of Social Science*, ed. Howard W. Odum (New York: Holt, 1927), 321–408; Dixon Ryan Fox, *Herbert Levi Osgood: An American Scholar* (New York: Columbia University Press, 1924).
2 Arthur S. Link, *Wilson, The Road to the White House* (Princeton, N.J.: Princeton University Press, 1947); Abraham S. Eisenstadt, *Charles McLean Andrews: A Study in American Historical Writing* (New York: Columbia University Press, 1956); Samuel J. Andrews, *William Watson Andrews: A Religious Biography* (New York: Putnam, 1900); Plato E. Shaw, *The Catholic Apostolic Church* (New York: King's Crown Press, 1946); Catharine Macy Noyes, ed., *Jesse Macy: An Autobiography* (Springfield, Ill.: Charles C. Thomas, 1933); Jesse Macy, "The Scientific Spirit in Politics," *APSR*, 11 (February 1917): 1–2.

that "ever since I have had independent judgments of my own, I have been a Federalist." J. Franklin Jameson while studying at Johns Hopkins confided to his diary that "every political meeting I have attended has had the same effect, to shatter my rising respect for the people, in their political capacity, and make me despise them." Whatever political attitudes they brought with them, the conservative milieu of the discipline encouraged moderation and enforced caution. Charles Kendall Adams wrote sympathetically to Ely in 1894 that for years "a large share of my intellectual efforts ... have been expended in efforts to guard against being misunderstood."[3]

The atmosphere was especially conservative at Columbia, under John W. Burgess. Daniel De Leon, a graduate student at Columbia in the mid-1880s, remembered his colleagues heaping contempt on a parade of victorious striking workers that passed beneath the university's windows. De Leon, indeed, is an exception to prove the rule of the conservative character of the historico-political vocation in the Gilded Age. A recent immigrant from South America of Jewish extraction, he stumbled into Columbia to study foreign relations. His brilliance was quickly rewarded with a prize lectureship in political science, but when his radical social sympathies emerged and drew him into public advocacy for Henry George and the Populists, his appointment was allowed to terminate, a conclusion by then satisfactory to De Leon, who never tired of taunting his former colleagues. In the 1890s, Burgess' juniors did not move far to the left. Herbert Levi Osgood, who developed an interest in socialism, struck the right note of considered but total rejection. Although Frank Goodnow would become a leading left Progressive by 1910, in the 1890s he gave little indication of popular sympathies. Originally a student of Burgess at Amherst and Columbia, he focused almost entirely on the reform of government institutions, not the purposes for which they might be reformed.[4]

At the University of Pennsylvania under Edmund J. James and Simon Patten and at Johns Hopkins, where Ely held forth under the more lenient Herbert Baxter Adams, the younger generation in historico-politics were exposed to the economic and social conflicts of the period. In addressing the

---

3 Wilson to A. B. Hart, June 3, 1889, quoted in Link, *Road to the White House*, 22; Rothberg, "Servant to History," 54; C. K. Adams to R. T. Ely, January 17, 1894, Ely Papers.
4 R. Gordon Hoxie et al., *A History of the Faculty of Political Science, Columbia University* (New York: Columbia University Press, 1955), 30–1, 71; L. Glen Seretan, *Daniel De Leon: The Odyssey of an American Marxist* (Cambridge, Mass.: Harvard University Press, 1979), 12–21; Fox, *Herbert Levi Osgood*, 31–5; Herbert L. Osgood, "Scientific Socialism: Rodbertus," *PSQ*, 1 (December 1886): 560–94. Frank J. Goodnow, *Comparative Administrative Law*, 2 vols. (New York: Putnam, 1893), Goodnow's first work on administration, spent four pages discussing such functions as public health and the collection of information under the heading, "The Socialistic Action of the Administration," 2:130–4.

issues of social justice and positive government, however, they carved out a centrist position. Wilson read Ely's *Labor Movement* and Clark's *Philosophy of Wealth* during the summer of 1887, when he did the basic work for his systematic treatise on *The State*. He came to recognize that socialism and democracy shared the same motive, "that every man shall have an equal chance with every other man." But he stopped short of the economists' advocacy of industrial cooperation and from the outset defined the democratic ideal in liberal terms, as an equal chance to compete.[5]

Only the towns and colleges of the Middle West seemed to encourage democratic enthusiasm among students of historico-politics, but even there mugwump distrust was not lacking. Frederick Jackson Turner's father was a rising Republican politician and businessman, sired in Jacksonian democracy. Young Turner expressed the approved sentiments in his high-school valedictory in Portage, Wisconsin, in 1878, during the first peak of the Gilded Age crisis, when he praised democracy and the people, but feared the rise of communism among the ignorant "masses."[6]

At Grinnell College in Iowa, Jesse Macy found himself in the middle, sympathizing with Granger attempts to regulate railroads, deploring greenback and silver monetary remedies, but resenting the excessive eastern condemnation of his neighbors. He retreated from publishing a critique of the American judiciary when the radical social gospeler in his department, George D. Herron, vigorously attacked the judiciary in the wake of the Supreme Court's decision against state railroad regulation. "For me to publish my article under such conditions would have been simply to add one more voice to what was looked upon as a wild-eyed fanatical attack upon a time-honored American institution." As Herron moved deeper into Christian socialism, Macy approved the interest in reform Herron stimulated, but disapproved his "emotional advocacy of impossible Utopias." Macy's consensual scientific ideal kept him to very general statements of a Progressive liberal position and within the orbit of "time-honored American institution[s]."[7]

Although the political attitudes of this younger generation were conservative or moderately liberal, not very different from the gentry founders of historico-politics, their political and disciplinary stance was nonetheless different enough to generate a challenge to their elders. This outcome was largely the result of their deeper commitment to historicism and realism. The

---

5 Arthur S. Link, ed., *The Papers of Woodrow Wilson* (Princeton, N.J.: Princeton University Press, 1966– ), 5:561–2; 6:303–9.
6 Billington, *Frederick Jackson Turner*, 11.
7 Noyes, *Jesse Macy*, 123–4, 131–2, 154–5.

gentry introduced these cultural elements into historico-politics, but their students more clearly understood the far-reaching implications they had for the traditional principles of American exceptionalism. Although they were likely to get their Ph.D. degrees in this country, sometimes with added study in Germany or France, the central historical tradition of their discipline, the deepening evolutionary enthusiasm of the culture at large, and the visible transformation of American society gave them a deeper sense of historical change than the gentry had. The chief import of their work was to show that American institutions were part of a changing history, not timeless exceptionalist principle.

The sharp recognition of change, the sense of inherited traditions no longer appropriate to a new reality, in turn gave new energy to the impulse toward realism. Wilson was the only advocate of a romantic epistemology that allied history and political science with literature. The recreation of life in language was a task of "insight and interpretation," he believed, requiring from the author a "personal equation." Wilson's colleagues were seeking to escape the "personal equation" and to find reality.[8]

The focus of realism on empirical facts may have been reinforced by the stricter scientific empiricism that emanated from such critical positivists as Karl Pearson, but the younger generation in historico-politics gained their sense of what science demanded more directly from the Rankean program for historical science, with its emphasis on the reconstruction of history from primary source materials, and from Darwin, who championed and presumably exemplified the empirical method. As heirs of the American tradition of commonsense realism, they easily concluded that induction from observed facts and skepticism regarding preformed generalizations was the highroad to historical science. Scientific method for this generation meant the abandonment of outworn ideals and the search for truth in the real facts of history.[9]

8 Woodrow Wilson, "Of the Study of Politics," *New Princeton Review*, 62 (March 1887): 188–99; Woodrow Wilson, "The Variety and Unity of History," in *Congress of Arts and Sciences, Universal Exposition, St. Louis, 1904*, ed. Howard J. Rogers, 8 vols. (Boston: Houghton Mifflin, 1906), 2:3–20. The speaker following Wilson at the St. Louis exposition opened with the observation that "It is assumed that the scientific study of history has entirely displaced history as literature." William M. Sloane, "The Science of History in the Nineteenth Century," in *International Congress*, 2:23. James Harvey Robinson concurred: "The Conception and Methods of History," in *International Congress*, 2:40.

9 The members of this generation, far more than the founders of historico-politics, deserve their designation as historical positivists. They believed in the ability of historical method, as a species of scientific method, to give them access to the real facts and, thereby, historical truth. I shall avoid the designation because of its easy confusion with the broader stream of positivism I have been discussing in this book. Historical positivism did not necessarily mean – and usually did not mean – a desire to follow the logical model of the natural sciences. On

Historicism itself could have called this faith into question, but its implications were not fully grasped. Recognizing that as history changed, each generation would have to rewrite history, the students of historico-politics conceived of the process as a progressive accumulation of truth, occasioned by changing circumstances but still part of a larger single truth. Like the historical economists, they failed to reach a reflexive historicism; in addition, no sharp political conflicts within their discipline forced the issue of historically rooted bias to their attention.[10]

The younger generation in historico-politics began around 1890 to articulate the new liberal historicist program for their discipline. Like their predecessors and contemporaries, they started from the crisis in American exceptionalism. Turner believed "we are approaching a pivotal point in our country's history." Macy anticipated E. R. A. Seligman in his fear that "for centuries we have been in a fool's paradise." He concluded that "to forestall in the new world the greater trials of the older communities" what was needed was "the new teaching of history."[11] The problem, they all agreed, was the old exceptionalist belief in America's perfect and unchanging institutions. The principles of the American polity had to be historicized, so they could be legitimated and preserved in the new world of historical change, and so they could submit to gradual liberal change.

In reviewing the work of the older school, Goodnow declared it a waste of time to trace Teutonic origins. Americans may have brought over English institutions but they soon reflected the "more primitive and democratic character of colonial society." Osgood followed suit. "It gratifies the pride of the masses to be told that the current dogmas about popular sovereignty are primordial truths," he declared. But that theory ignores "to a large extent the idea of historic perspective and development.... The democracy of a primitive, semi-nomadic people is quite a different thing from the democracy of the nineteenth century, and in the name of historical science it is time to protest against the confounding of the two."[12]

the founders, see above, Chapter 3 at n. 32. For a lucid discussion of the epistemology of American historians, see Ian Tyrrell, *The Absent Marx: Class Analysis and Liberal History in Twentieth-Century America* (Westport, Conn.: Greenwood, 1986), 8–9, 15–23, as well as Peter Novick, *That Noble Dream: The "Objectivity Question" and the American Historical Profession* (Cambridge University Press, 1988), pt. 1; John Higham, *History. Professional Scholarship in America* (New York: Harper & Row, 1973), pt. 2.

10 Novick, *That Noble Dream*.

11 Frederick J. Turner, "The Significance of History" (1891), in *The Early Writings of Frederick Jackson Turner* (Madison: University of Wisconsin Press, 1938), 61; Jesse Macy, "History from a Democratic Standpoint," *University Extension*, 3 (April 1894): 299.

12 Frank J. Goodnow, "Review of George E. Howard, *An Introduction to the Local Constitutional History of the United States*," *PSQ*, 4 (September 1889): 525; Herbert L. Osgood, "Review of James K. Hosmer, *A Short History of Anglo-Saxon Freedom*," *PSQ*, 6 (March 1891): 162, 164.

In 1892 Andrews published a study of the old English manor which made that point decisively for his generation, and placed it in the context of their disillusion with democratic politics and their new realism.

The liberal optimism of Europe, and, indeed, of America as well, before 1870, has taken on a more sombre hue since that time, and . . . the idealized primitive freeman has been gradually vanishing into the background. . . . As the world has learned that . . . the human nature of the individual and the combined action of the masses are pervaded with brute instincts and fallibility so it is willing to be told that primitive man, whether he were Saxon, Teuton or Aryan, was very much lower down in the scale of human development than the older view was willing to place him; that his freedom, of whatever nature it may have been, was still very different from that of the free citizen.

The growth of freedom had been slow, Andrews argued, and adjusted at each stage to the economic and social conditions of its existence.[13]

Andrews' purpose in historicizing the Teutonic chain was to show that while there was no "changeless code of morality," there was progress at work in the slow, organic movement of history. The study of history would enlighten the way. "It is fundamental to safe and conservative progress that our moral standard be a practical one; a standard always in advance of the fulfillment of its condition . . . [but not] too ideal." James Harvey Robinson, a young instructor at Pennsylvania, was more enthusiastic about reform, and on similar historicist premises. "The science of Politics has been at a practical standstill in this country for a hundred years," he complained. "The unreasoning and exaggerated faith in the perfection of existing institutions" had to give way "to an awakened interest and desire for advance." Though Robinson did not criticize the American Constitution, he had already in 1890 set the stage for change by breaking its connection with British models. The Constitution emerged rather from the founders' circumstances and the conditions of their time.[14]

Likewise Frank Goodnow, Burgess' prize student, pointed out that Burgess' own historical analysis of national sovereignty could be extended to all aspects of government and he proceeded to a liberal historicist analysis of American politics. Both preservationist and reformist in intent, Goodnow urged that his readers not decry all attempts at change "as indicative of our

13 Charles M. Andrews, *The Old English Manor, JHUSHPS*, extra vol. 12 (1892): 4.
14 Charles M. Andrews, "History as an Aid to Moral Culture." *National Education Association Journal of Proceedings and Addresses*, 33 (1894): 400–2; James H. Robinson, "The Original and Derived Features of the Constitution," *AAAPSS*, 1 (October 1890): 203–43; idem, "Review of Henry Sidgwick, *The Elements of Politics*," *AAAPSS*, 3 (September 1892): 212–13.

degeneration from the faith of our ancestors; but, frankly recognizing that new conditions need new measures, do what can be done."[15]

Macy joined the liberal historicist challenge only after an apprenticeship to traditional exceptionalism. When studying local governments in Iowa, he had made contact with Herbert Baxter Adams and been converted to the Teutonic germ theory. In an 1886 text he implied that self-governing villages were everywhere founded in America and that colonies were mere federations of them, as the national government was a federation of the colonies. After a year of study in England, however, he revised his text in 1890 to show that a variety of types of local institutions were brought over from England, that the colonies and the national government were original political entities of several kinds. Moreover, he added the discreet note that his book detailed the powers of the government in the past and present, but he could not predict from that what its powers might be in future. Macy's two texts graphically chart his change from Adams' exceptionalist conception of American history to liberal historicism, and its reformist consequences. Henceforth, his chief historical source was the work of the English historian S. R. Gardiner, which undermined in detail the English Whig myth of institutional continuity, yet supported a view of change in organic connection with the past. Macy found evidence in Gardiner that democracy is "in harmony with many fundamental beliefs and principles, which have their roots deep in the past, that are gaining control of the minds of men."[16]

Wilson, an avid reader of Edmund Burke, Walter Bagehot, and English history, came to Johns Hopkins with his liberal historicism in place. He was, like Burgess, a Unionist Southerner who was impressed by the growth of federal power; when he reviewed Burgess' book, he especially noticed the historicist premise of Burgess' nationalism and lamented that the historical analysis did not go deeper. Wilson understood that democracy was no absolute or God-given ideal, but a relative good. Still, it was produced by great, permanent causes in Western history and "still stands first" among the polities of the present and future. "I find myself exceedingly tolerant of all institutions, past and present," Wilson admitted, "by reason of a keen appreciation of their reason for being – *most* tolerant, so to say, of the institutions of my own day which seem to me, in an historical sense, intensely and essentially reasonable, though of course in no sense *final*." For those with a new sense of the shaping force of history and a deep complai-

15 Frank J. Goodnow, *Politics and Administration* (New York: Macmillan, 1900), 260–1.
16 Jesse Macy, *Our Government* (Boston: Ginn, 1886); revised ed., 1890, particularly p. 49; idem, "The Relation of History to Politics," *AHAAR* (1893): 185; idem, "Twentieth Century Democracy," *PSQ*, 13 (September 1898): 526. On Gardiner, see P. B. M. Blaas, *Continuity and Anachronism* (The Hague: Nijhoff, 1978), 40–3.

sance about the Teutonic institutions history had bequeathed to America, an eternal realm of truth was not necessary to guarantee America's political course. Wilson's Burkean historicism ratified gradual change, organically linked to the past.[17]

Perhaps the most notable statement of republican preservation through Burkean historicism was *The Rise and Growth of American Politics* in 1898, by Henry Jones Ford, a Buffalo newspaper editor. Ford's astute analyses so impressed the academic fraternity that they urged him to join their ranks, which he soon did, becoming a fellow at Johns Hopkins in 1906 and professor at Princeton in 1908. Ford's account of early American history is still capable of surprising historians, who can find in it conclusions only recently reached (again) by the profession; it seems to be the product of a traditional conservative understanding of the Constitution sharpened by a wide reading in the original sources. Ford showed that colonial American politics was an offshoot of aristocratic English society and American political ideas founded in Whig politics. The Constitution, he argued, embodied a conservative reaction of the gentry ruling class against the democratic and anarchic forces loosed by the Revolution and confederation. The party system was the work of this same class and was supported by popular "deference," but political contest soon led these gentry politicians to seek popular support and in the process, they democratized politics. The party system, he argued, performed the function of coordinating the different branches and levels of government the Constitution had separated. Under Walpole, the English party system too had been irresponsible and corrupt when it attempted to coordinate the legislative and executive branches, but the English had managed to alter their governing structures so as to make parties responsible. Such was the future task of American politics.[18]

One can see why the younger generation found Ford's analysis so attractive. While acknowledging the conservative basis of the Constitution, he showed how historical developments altered the political system as time went on, making it more democratic and opening the way to further development. At the same time, Ford managed to find grounds for hope that America's republican destiny would be fulfilled. By the Civil War, he concluded, "the ascendency of the race [was] reestablished." If our politics were corrupt, our immense industrial development implied that "resources of probity ... intelligence and skill ... heroic qualities which are the peculiar claim of militancy" were still present:

17 [Woodrow Wilson], "A System of Political Science and Constitutional Law," *Atlantic Monthly*, 67 (May 1891): 694–9; Link, *Papers of Woodrow Wilson*, 5:55, 61–2.
18 Henry Jones Ford, *The Rise and Growth of American Politics* (New York: Macmillan, 1898).

Such manifestations show that the sources of national greatness are uncorrupted, so that amid the baleful confusion of our politics patriotism may cherish the hope that a purified and ennobled republic will emerge —
'Product of deathly fire and turbulent chaos,
Forth from its spasms of fury and its poisons,
Issuing at last in perfect power and beauty.'

The people were still virtuous and the millennial republic could rise reborn from the current crisis.[19]

## Historicism and realism in history and politics

The liberal historicist attack on static exceptionalist principle occupied the entire younger generation in historico-politics, but their specific program soon divided in two. Although Albert Bushnell Hart at Harvard or William Dunning at Columbia divided their time and identities quite evenly between history and politics, most people in the field emphasized either the historical or political side of their joint task of finding in history viable principles for current political action.[20] The young political scientists and historians created from their shared premises different, though overlapping, agendas for the study of politics and for historical research.

The historians' program for historico-politics subordinated realism to historicism. To the historians, a real understanding of politics depended above all on a contextual understanding of the past. Over and over again in their studies, whatever the subject, the point on which their analyses hung was that the topic in question had to be understood not in terms of timeless principles or universal human nature, but in terms of the particular conditions of the time.[21] In embarking on their major studies of the history of colonial America as part of the British Empire, Andrews and Osgood were seeking to place it in the proper context of its time and place; to view it from the point of its origins in early modern British history rather than to read back into it the forms of modern American democracy. Turner had the same motive for his opposite strategy of abandoning the search for European

19 Ibid., 379–82.
20 Charles E. Merriam, "William Archibald Dunning," in Odum, *American Masters of Social Science*, 134; Robert L. Church, "The Development of the Social Sciences as Academic Disciplines at Harvard University, 1869–1900" (Ph.D. dissertation, Harvard University, 1965), vol. 1.
21 Robinson, "Original and Derived Features of the Constitution"; Edward P. Cheney, "The Recantations of the Early Lollards," *AHR*, 4 (April 1899): 423–38; Claude H. Van Tyne, "Sovereignty in the American Revolution: An Historical Study," *AHR*, 12 (April 1907): 529–45; Herbert L. Osgood, "The Political Ideas of the Puritans," *PSQ*, 6 (March 1891): 1–28.

origins and looking instead to the "American factors." Americans continually remade their heritage as they moved west across a continent of free land.
"The true point of view in the history of this nation is not the Atlantic coast,
it is the Great West."[22]

To reconstruct history in the context of the past required of the historians
a major commitment to discover the facts through research in primary
documents. Only if historians eschewed any narrow partisanship and built
their account from the sources themselves could they hope to determine, in
Ranke's phrase, "how things really happened." The premium on source
work turned a great deal of the energy of these historians into the discovery,
cataloging, printing, and examination of basic manuscript materials which
had hitherto been neglected. As chairman of the American Historical
Association's Historical Manuscript Commission, editor of the *American
Historical Review*, and for a time secretary of the Association, Jameson built
his career on implementing the Rankean methodological program. It was a
suitable vocation for someone so cautious that he hesitated to challenge the
germ theory in print, despite his disdain for it and for Herbert Baxter
Adams' scholarship.[23]

For a scholar determined to address a major topic and reach a synthetic
view, the demands of primary research could be overwhelming. Osgood
went through immense British and American archives for his history of
colonial America. The task took almost every waking moment of his life
after the mid-1890s, to the exclusion of virtually every other interest, and he
finished his last volume just before he died. His colleague E. R. A. Seligman
said "We all admired the way in which he resolutely refrained from all
extraneous tasks and potboiling in order to devote himself wholeheartedly
to his supreme object. We were proud of him." The ethic of research
scholarship was widely shared, but it could lead historians into "a service as
unrelenting as any monk."[24]

Although a realistic historicism sent the historians back to the sources, it
also led them to look beneath the surface of formal political institutions for
the fundamental social and economic forces in history. In the interdisciplinary environment of historico-politics, in which "the political sciences"
initially included economics and sociology, these young historians believed
that political principle must be grounded in the economic and social life of

---

22 Fox, *Herbert Levi Osgood*, 70–3; Charles M. Andrews, *The Colonial Period* (New York:
   Holt, 1912), v–vii; Frederick J. Turner, "The Significance of the Frontier in American
   History" (1893), in *Early Writings*, 187–8.
23 Rothberg, "Servant to History," chap. 2. The AHA *Annual Reports* attest to this concern,
   as do the publication records of Robinson, Hart, Andrews, and others.
24 Fox, *Herbert Levi Osgood*, 122, 143, 146, 112.

the people. Evolution, as well, pointed them to the long-term forces at work beneath the surface of history. As Morey Rothberg has discovered, the interest in developing social history affected even Jameson. His first ambition as a Johns Hopkins student, to write the history of the states of the union, was meant not only to exploit an unused body of documents, but to uncover the social basis of political history. In his 1891 lectures at Hopkins on Southern political history, his theme was the rise of democracy, a subject that led him to discuss the Enlightenment ideas of Jefferson, the egalitarian zeal unleashed by the Revolution, and the more democratic economic conditions of the old southwest. He followed up that insight in 1895 with lectures at Barnard on "The American Revolution as a Social Movement." Despite the desire of the Anglo-Saxon who made the Revolution not to "destroy or recast his social system," Jameson showed that the Revolution did recast land ownership, commerce, religion, and opinions of slavery.[25]

No one has known Jameson as an early social historian, however, because he did not publish these lectures. Finally, after thirty years, *The American Revolution as a Social Movement* appeared in print in 1925, to become Jameson's only major work of history. Rothberg concludes that it was as much political as intellectual caution that deterred him. With his conservative political beliefs, Jameson could not help but be troubled by the implications of his findings. That the American Revolution was a social revolution, not merely the limited affair of Whig principle the conservatives had valued, was a conclusion that carried disturbing political lessons in the crisis years of the 1890s. When at the end of his 1891 lectures he likened Jacksonian democracy to the current rise of populism, which "threatens to put the conduct of our public affairs in the hands of a vast horde of unintelligent farmers [and] demagogues," the remark was picked up by the Baltimore papers. Jameson's moral was impeccably conservative, but the Jacksonians, after all, had won. For a person of Jameson's politics and caution, social history was not safe.[26]

Andrews shared Jameson's ambition for social history and found an acceptable outlet for it in liberal historiography. Andrews argued at the AHA that courses in European history should extend right to the present and show "the changing conditions, political, social, and economic, under which we have entered upon the new era." The ultimate purpose of history, he maintained, as Andrew D. White had urged at their first meeting, was a "philosophical synthesis of history." History must be approached from the

25  Rothberg, "Servant to History," 64, 67–9, 123–6, 128–9. I am indebted to Rothberg's
     conversation and excellent thesis for highlighting this dimension of Jameson's work.
26  Ibid., 125–6, 129.

point of view of the past, extending generalizations forward, but its purpose was the understanding of "the present day."[27]

Andrews tried to carry out that prescription in a text on continental European history in the nineteenth century organized around "those movements that have made for progress." In the old republican account of European history, European failures were more instructive lessons to America than their successes. Andrews pointed out the excesses of revolution and the failure of utopian radicalism, but his account rested securely on the forward movement of history. He made his story the rise of liberalism in Europe, beginning with the French Revolution and ending with the still uncertain efforts at modernization of the central and Eastern European empires.[28] Robinson believed Andrews had succeeded, and enrolled him under the banner of a "new history," an "essentially modern and scientific conception of history."[29]

When Andrews turned to American colonial history, he felt the same need to introduce the underlying political, social, and economic factors which were working toward progress. Although his magnum opus was not published until 1934, his early thinking appeared in a brief text in 1912. Here his theme was, like Bancroft's, the democratic character of the American colonies and the emergence of American nationalism, but political experience, social attitudes, and economic conditions came into play, creating a more differentiated account of the colonial movement toward independence than appeared in the older histories. Though it focused on political institutions, Osgood's colonial history carried the same burden of tying American democracy and independence to differentiated historical conditions. Indeed, Osgood felt the need to justify his political approach. "The political and social sciences have now reached such development that it is impossible to present in a single view all known aspects of any period of history." So while

27 Charles M. Andrews, "Should Recent European History Have a Place in the College Curriculum?" *AHAAR* (1899), 1:547, 541–2.
28 Charles M. Andrews, *The Historical Development of Modern Europe from the Congress of Vienna to the Present Time*, 2 vols. (New York: Putnam, 1896–98), 1:iv, 25–8, 320, 447–8; 2:3–4, 278, 343–4, 349, 369. See also James T. Shotwell, "The Political Capacity of the French," *PSQ*, 24 (March 1909): 115–26.
29 James H. Robinson, "Review of Charles M. Andrews, *The Historical Development of Modern Europe*," *AAAPSS*, 9 (March 1897), 253–4. Robinson linked this "new history" to the work of Karl Lamprecht, who wanted to abandon the old history, which was "individualistic, descriptive, political" and given over to universal "ideas," and put in its place a history which was collective, evolutionary, social-cultural, and strictly empirical. Although Lamprecht's specific theory never carried conviction in America, his general orientation was similar to the younger historians who wanted to move toward social history. See Earle Wilbur Dow, "Features of the New History: Apropos of Lamprecht's 'Deutsche Geschichte,'" *AHR*, 3 (April 1898): 431–48.

he would focus on political institutions, he would include "material of a social or economic nature" that threw light on political growth.[30]

The truth is that Andrews did only marginally better than Osgood. While he organized his narrative around a synthetic view of colonial development rather than around the evolution of political forms, social and economic factors remained "background" to the mainstream of political development. Despite their broader aspirations, both Andrews and Osgood remained tied to the traditional political principles of their national ideology and disciplinary tradition. While joining American history to the stream of liberal historicism, they continued to tell the story of American exceptionalism. Not only did American colonial history remain an account of the rise of American liberty and nationality, but the contours of the Teutonic theory and its world-historical purpose also remained. When in 1895 Andrews reviewed the book of a French author that denied any special Anglo-Saxon link to liberty in England and America, he could not quite accept it. The author had not taken proper account of English political struggles, he said, nor explained "why the English nature responded so quickly to the democratic ideas." Osgood explicitly recognized an "analogy" between seventeenth-century America and the Saxon period in English history. Under the Saxons a foundation of English liberty had been laid "which was not lost during the entire subsequent course of English history," and, he added, American history. For many young historians, still attached to the traditional political historiography, the settlement of America remained "one scene in the development of English history, that longest, most continuous, and most momentous historical drama that the world has yet known."[31]

Turner was the first to base an account of American exceptionalism squarely on economic and social foundations. Alone among his historical cohort, he was willing to plant the exceptional American experience in the fast changing conditions of the American continent itself. His ability to make that leap owed something to his small town Midwest origins, where evidence of frontier life was still visible. His master's essay at Wisconsin, refurbished during his one year at Johns Hopkins for a doctoral degree, was on the Wisconsin fur trade. The frontier thesis also owed much to the

---

30 Andrews, *The Colonial Period*; Herbert L. Osgood, *The American Colonies in the Seventeenth Century*, 3 vols. (New York: Macmillan, 1904–7), 1:xxv.
31 Andrews, *The Colonial Period*, 66–7, 105; idem, "Review of Charles Borgeaud, *The Rise of Modern Democracy in Old and New England*," *AAAPSS*, 6 (September 1895): 306–8; Osgood, *American Colonies in the Seventeenth Century*, 2:440–2; Edward P. Cheney, "The England of Our Forefathers," *AHR*, 11 (July 1906): 778.

historicism he had learned at Wisconsin and Johns Hopkins, so that the germ theory never made much impression on him. He took several courses from Ely and caught the vision of the historical economists. In 1891 after his return to Wisconsin, he announced that "The age of machinery, of the factory system, is also the age of socialistic inquiry." Economic facts that affected "the great mass of the people" have often been "the secret of the nation's rise or fall, by the side of which much that has passed as history is the merest frippery." The economic experience of the people seemed from the vantage point of Wisconsin to be the settlement of free land.[32]

What made that insight salient was the sense he got at Hopkins that "we are approaching a pivotal point in our country's history." When the 1890 census reported the end of the frontier line they were confirming what the historical economists and just about every other social thinker had been saying since 1877, that the expansive stage of American history and its opportunity for widespread independence was coming to an end.[33] The rise of populism and the mounting crisis of the 1890s accentuated that crisis for Turner and his audience. Turner linked his theory to populism in his 1893 essay on "The Significance of the Frontier in American History" and when he restated it in 1896 for the AHA he emphasized the current political situation. It was during the 1896 hysteria over Bryan that his thesis first got public attention and picked up professional support.[34]

Turner's frontier thesis quite literally transcribed the crisis in national ideology into the objective terms of historiography. From the outset he wanted to account for "the peculiarity of American institutions" and "the distinguishing feature of American life." Picturing the frontier as the dynamic source of American *virtû*, he declared that "This perennial rebirth, this fluidity of American life, this expansion westward with its new opportunities, its continuous touch with the simplicity of primitive society, furnish the forces dominating American character." The most important effect of the frontier has been "the promotion of democracy here and in Europe."

32 Billington, *Frederick Jackson Turner*, 25–31, 60, 67; Wilbur R. Jacobs, ed., *The Historical World of Frederick Jackson Turner, with Selections from His Correspondence* (New Haven, Conn.: Yale University Press, 1968), 60; Turner, "The Significance of History," 51, 47, 48.
33 Turner, "The Significance of History," 61. Lee Benson, *Turner and Beard* (Glencoe, Ill.: Free Press, 1960) discovered the influence on Turner of the Italian economist Achille Loria, who also sparked the interest of E. R. A. Seligman in an economic interpretation of history. Loria's influence, like that of the 1890 census, probably brought to the front of Turner's consciousness a set of ideas already woven into the political culture and social science discussion of the Gilded Age.
34 Turner, "The Significance of the Frontier," 222; idem, "The West as a Field for Historical Study," *AHAAR* (1896), 1:282; Billington, *Frederick Jackson Turner*, 188–95.

Faithful to liberal-republican logic, he saw that "So long as free land exists, the opportunity for a competency exists, and economic power secures political power."[35]

An heir to mugwump anxiety as well, he saw some evil in frontier democracy: "strong in selfishness and individualism, intolerant of administrative experience and education, and pressing individual liberty beyond its proper bounds." The Populists were just the latest wave of "primitive" frontier radicals to appear in America, an analysis which promised that they too would be a passing phase. "They reflect the struggle of this society to adjust the old Western ideals, based upon American isolation, upon the nonexistence of classes, and upon freedom of opportunity, to the changed conditions of a settled nation competing with other settled nations and sharing their social tendencies." But Turner's analysis seemed to consign the frontier's exemplary virtues along with its recurrent vices to the past. "The frontier has gone, and with its going has closed the first period of American history."[36]

How could Turner, a man deeply committed to the exceptionalist ideal, link the American future to the past? Like his friend Wilson, he at first hoped that national character and imperialism would prolong "that dominant individualism."

> He would be a rash prophet who should assert that the expansive character of American life has now entirely ceased. Movement has been its dominant fact, and, unless this training has no effect upon a people, the American intellect will continually demand a wider field for its exercise.

He applauded American expansion into the Pacific and the opportunities afforded the expansive energies of the American character.[37]

Turner did not remain satisfied with a characterological and imperialistic basis for the American future, nor with the sketchy outline of the frontier thesis he presented in 1893. But he never managed to finish the magnum opus that would solidify his claims. He was drawn in part toward a positivist effort to read American history as exemplar of the universal process of social evolution. Achille Loria declared that "the land which has no history reveals luminously the course of universal history." Turner believed "He is right. The United States lies like a huge page in the history of society. Line by line

---

35 Turner, "The Significance of the Frontier," 186–7, 219, 221.
36 Ibid., 220–2, 228–9. The quotation beginning "They reflect the struggle" is from Turner, "The West as a Field for Historical Study," 1:282–3.
37 Turner, "The Significance of the Frontier," 228; Billington, *Frederick Jackson Turner*, 103, though Billington avoids this aspect of Turner's vision; Woodrow Wilson, "Democracy and Efficiency," *Atlantic Monthly*, 87 (March 1901): 289–99.

as we read from west to east we find the record of social evolution." Turning to just the right source. he began quoting Henry Adams to the effect that "North America was the most favorable field on the globe" on which to construct a universal science of history.[38]

Turner went principally to geography for his science. Recognizing that the moving frontier disclosed the existence of sections, he tried to transfer his thesis to the dynamic interplay of sectional forces. He wanted to draw from sectional analysis the main lines of American political history, the development of the democratic American character, and the assurance that in the continued diversity of sections and the continued democratic character of the west, the old American individualism would survive. His historicist impulse led him into the rich complexity of sectional experience, but his positivism kept him looking for a geographical determinism that would override demographic and cultural diversity and impose the mark of the American land indelibly upon its people. He was engaged in an exceptionalist effort to fuse nature and history, an effort easy to accomplish in rhetoric but beyond the powers of historicism.[39]

Turner's frontier thesis was the first visible fruit of the historians' efforts to construct a "new history," an effort both animated and stunted by the old history of American exceptionalism. It should also be seen as the first fruit among historians of the effort to reconceptualize the American past in wholly liberal terms. The frontier thesis defined the whole American experience before the Gilded Age by two terms, nature and individualism. What had made America was its repeated encounter with nature, not its political culture or economic institutions, not the ideas or social structures it brought from England and transformed in America. And from the start, nature had made America the home of liberal individualism. Traditional American historiography had always recognized individual liberty as a defining feature of the American experience. In Bancroft it was a central strand of American democracy, traced back to the Protestant Reformation.[40] But Turner made individualism the sole component of American character and political culture and stripped it of the ideas and institutions that

38 Turner, "Significance of the Frontier in American History," 198: idem, "The West as a Field for Historical Study," 284; idem, "Problems in American History," in *Congress of Arts and Sciences*, 2:185–6. Henry Adams' quotation is from the same section of his *History* in which he identified the American democratic "ocean." See above, Chapter 3.

39 Billington, *Frederick Jackson Turner*, chap. 9, pp. 351–2, 367, 372–4; Jacobs, *Historical World of F. J. Turner*, 57–8, 135; Frederick J. Turner, "Social Forces in American History," *AHR*, 16 (January 1911): 224–5.

40 George Bancroft, *A History of the United States from the Discovery of the American Continent to the Present Time*, 10 vols. (Boston: Charles Brown, 1834–74), vol. 1, chap. 10, vol. 2, chap. 18, 4:167–79, 8:474–5.

carried and modified it. Turner's romantic liberalism helped to efface, even as it transcribed, the old liberal-republican discourse. It opened the way to a liberal exceptionalist historiography that could celebrate the mindlessness of the American experience and its exclusive commitment to liberal individualism.[41]

Among the students of politics, the priorities in the program of realistic historicism were reversed. The new thrust of political science was historical realism. As Goodnow said, he wanted to show "particularly from a consideration of political conditions as they now exist in the United States, that the formal governmental system as set forth in the law is not always the same as the actual system." It was only through such recognition, he went on, that the actual system might be brought to conform more closely "to the political ideas upon which the formal system is based." History provided the key to this realistic analysis, as it set the terms of the problem, for it was historical change that transformed political institutions, turning old forms into useless shells and creating new functions that required new forms.[42]

Historical realism turned the young political scientists to study of political parties, administration, and city government, the black sheep of American politics. Their mugwump predecessors had been fully aware of the problems of political partisanship, municipal corruption, and inadequate administration, but they understood them as derogations from the norm, that did not in any way alter the fundamental principles on which republican government and political science rested. The younger generation recognized them as legitimate domains of political study, to be understood as functioning aspects of political life.

In one respect, however, they continued the critique of American politics begun by the mugwumps. The central difficulty they saw in American political institutions was the system of divided powers. Against that American problem, modern British government, with its concentration of political and administrative authority in Parliament, could serve as the model America should emulate, the governmental organization American institutions might be evolving toward. In his first exercise of historical realism, *Congressional Government* (1885), Wilson argued that the federal government was no longer one of balanced separate powers, but of congressional dominance. "The history of our Constitution is but another illustration of this universal principle of institutional change." Wilson approved the direction of change.

---

41 A leading example of the former is Daniel Boorstin, *The Genius of American Politics* (Chicago: University of Chicago Press, 1953); of the latter, Louis Hartz, *The Liberal Tradition in America* (New York: Harcourt Brace & World, 1955).

42 Goodnow, *Politics and Administration*, v, 2–3. See also L. S. Rowe, "The Problems of Political Science," *AAAPSS*, 10 (September 1897): 165–86.

He criticized the diffusion of party responsibility and weakening of debate in Congress in the hope that congressional government might evolve into a closer model of the parliamentary system.[43] The destructive effects of divided powers, with its corrective model of concentrated authority, was a central theme in the new political scientists' studies of administration, city government, and political parties.

Wilson issued the first call for the study of administration in 1887. Declaring that the era of constitution-making was closed "so far as the establishment of essential principles is concerned," he argued that future change would deal largely with administration. Although he defined that study to include what things "government can properly and successfully do" as well as how to do them efficiently, he spoke only generally about the inevitable expansion of government in complex modern conditions. Administration would be chiefly concerned with efficient execution. There were certain "stable principles" of administration – centralization of administrative authority and the grant of "large powers and unhampered discretion" – which produced both efficient action and clear-cut responsibility. He was echoing here what had become through the Napoleonic reforms and the influence of Jeremy Bentham, the accepted wisdom of administrative practice. Stressing that there was "but one rule of good administration for all governments," Wilson had to justify its centralized, hierarchical style to an American polity committed to popular sovereignty and divided powers. Taking the easy way out, he argued that administration was merely a field of "business," or "machinery." The methods of continental Europe could be borrowed freely without undermining American political institutions.[44]

The historical realist program for municipal reform was laid out in Goodnow's study of municipal problems. To discover "what the city really is," Goodnow argued, it was necessary "to treat the city rather as a part of the governmental system than as an isolated phenomenon." He concluded from a survey of European and American history that cities have always

---

43 Woodrow Wilson, *Congressional Government* (Boston: Houghton Mifflin, 1885), 5–7; Link, *Papers of Woodrow Wilson*, 4:6–13. A suggestive discussion of Wilson's political science is provided by Niels Aage Thorsen, *The Political Thought of Woodrow Wilson, 1875–1910* (Princeton, N.J.: Princeton University Press, 1988), a supplementary volume to *The Papers of Woodrow Wilson*, although Thorsen exaggerates the originality and significance of Wilson's work in political science.

44 Woodrow Wilson, "The Study of Administration," *PSQ*, 2 (July 1887): 197–222; A. Dunsire, *Administration: The Word and the Science* (New York: Wiley, 1973), 62–73. Dwight Waldo, *The Administrative State: A Study of the Political Theory of American Public Administration* (New York: The Ronald Press, 1948), sees public administration as an ideological vehicle for national American commitments to business, reform, and science, but does not quite see it as an ideological vehicle for the professional interests of political scientists and their Whiggish, antimajoritarian outlook.

been agents of state administration as well as centers of local needs. The call for complete home rule as well as the desire to remove the national parties entirely from municipal elections were therefore unrealistic. But local rule could be enhanced by applying the principles of administration, by drastically reducing the number of elected officials and centralizing responsibility in an elected city council and a strong mayor.[45]

On political parties, Ford's *Rise and Growth of American Politics* was the key document. Although the history of the English party system, the example of Walpole, and the emergence of the spoils system under Jackson had been staples in mugwump argument, parties had been treated simply as means of organizing opinion; their ideal function therefore was to represent elevated opinion, or principle. Against that ideal, the proliferation of party activity and corruption was understood as a more primitive historical impulse or as republican decay. Examining in historical detail the formation of parties in the new republic, Ford argued that the parties' rapid growth was due rather to the positive function it played in coordinating the peculiarly fragmented system of American government. Using history as a tool of analysis, he uncovered a central function of political parties that accounted for the persistence of political behavior the mugwumps could only deplore.[46]

Goodnow's *Politics and Administration* (1900) brought all these themes together in the most sophisticated form they were to achieve in the Progressive Era. There were, he said, two primary functions of government. They are the political, the expression of the people's will, and the administrative, the execution of that will. Administration was not merely a realm of business, he stressed, but a governmental function that had artfully to be coordinated with, as well as separated from, politics. Politics had to control administration to the extent of insuring its harmony with the people's will. But politics should not distort the administrative function; indeed centralized and hierarchical principles of administration would make the public will more effective and its leaders more accountable.

In sorting through his prescriptions for municipal reform, Goodnow also tried to keep the city's administrative and political tasks separate and integrated. Political parties had fattened on America's decentralized system of administration and the multiplication of elected officials, while the rigid constitutional structure of separated powers had prevented the parties from being brought under responsible control, as English parties had been. The

---

45 Frank J. Goodnow, *Municipal Problems* (New York: Macmillan, 1897), v, 22–32, 176–92, 195–9.
46 Cf. Dorman B. Eaton, *Civil Service in Great Britain* (New York: Harper, 1880), 116, 369, 382, and chaps. 1–2 passim.

sphere of democracy had to be cut back, and independent, centralized administration strengthened. Only when Americans adopt the principle of an independent administration, may the government "safely be intrusted with much work." But, going beyond Ford, he argued that parties also performed an essential political function in the selection of elected officials. That function must be made more responsible to the public through judicial control of party activity and such devices as legally protected primary elections.[47]

Twentieth-century political scientists have often berated their forbears for lack of realism without recognizing that realism is defined by historical context. They have also blamed that lack of realism on their forbears' attachment to historical method, without recognizing that historicism was the basis of their realism.[48] History provided the analytic wedge that separated eighteenth-century forms, nineteenth-century functions, and turn-of-the-century conditions. It supported Goodnow's insight into the multiplicity and integration of political functions. Although *Politics and Administration* served as the *locus classicus* for study of American politics, a good deal of its subtlety was lost as the discipline became more committed to scientific method. Wilson's separation of politics and administration was more often taken as the aim of political science than Goodnow's more subtle attempt at separation and integration. The underlying political function of expression of the people's will, which Goodnow kept in mind in municipal, party, and administrative reform, often faded from view as functional analysis was divorced from history and encased within natural-science models of the political system.[49]

Preoccupation with history and institutional restraints have together been blamed for the reluctance of early political scientists to engage in direct

---

47 Goodnow, *Politics and Administration*, chaps. 3–7 and p. 87.

48 Martin Landau, "The Myth of Hyperfactualism in the Study of American Politics," *PSQ*, 83 (September 1968): 378–99, rediscovers the realistic, functional analysis of Ford and his cohort, but fails to recognize the key role of historical and comparative analysis in that achievement.

49 Waldo, *The Administrative State*, 110–14 and chap. 8. Ford, for example, unlike Goodnow, believed that parties had one dominant function, that of administrative coordination. The conformance of government to public opinion was a subsidiary task and in any case, he believed, parties already performed it well enough. Henry Jones Ford, "Review of Frank Goodnow, *Politics and Administration*," *AAAPSS*, 16 (September 1900), 184–8. Landau, "The Myth of Hyperfactualism," appropriately found Ford's narrow functionalism more modern and scientific than Goodnow's. Compare also Austin Ranney, *The Doctrine of Responsible Party Government. Its Origin and Present State* (Urbana: University of Illinois Press, 1954), 107–10. Michael H. Frisch, "Urban Theorists, Urban Reform, and American Political Culture in the Progressive Period," *PSQ*, 97 (Summer 1982): 295–315, recovers some of the complexity of Goodnow's vision of urban reform.

investigation of contemporary politics.[50] There is some truth in that explanation. For his comparative study of modern Western political systems, *The State*, Wilson recognized that he needed at least three summers in Europe to study his subject "alive." When he could not finance that kind of research, he cribbed the accounts he needed from the latest German handbook. But for his earlier study of congressional government, he never went to nearby Washington to observe Congress in action.[51] The orientation toward history may have accustomed him to learning from books and periodicals, but the chief reason Wilson did not go to Washington was because he was convinced beforehand of the analysis he drew from Walter Bagehot and conventional mugwump wisdom. If realism required a perception of the inadequacy of inherited tradition, the realism of these students of politics was bound to be spotty, hampered by the political sentiments and exceptionalist principles they still shared with their mugwump and Whig forerunners. Tradition can blind the eye of the observer as well as the mind of the reader.

The program of historical realism set out by Goodnow and his colleagues was an extension of the traditional Whig program of historico-politics into a new age. American republican institutions were firmly imbedded in history; with moderate reform, a "purified and ennobled republic" might yet emerge. The old Whig prescription of organic governmental power, reduced democracy, and governance by the natural aristocracy still held good. In *The State* Wilson developed the old theme of "the absolute naturalness of government," its roots in kinship, and its legitimate moral aims, and this organic conception of government could be used against both striking industrial workers and lawless capitalists.[52] Although it was still a minor theme in their work, Wilson and his colleagues echoed the new liberal social scientists in their acceptance of capitalism and their willingness to extend the power of the state over it in limited ways.

The desire to contain democracy was a more powerful theme. Despite Goodnow's sensitivity to democratic concerns, he shared his tradition's fear that democracy "may be unsuited to anything short of the ideal conditions of human life." He believed that "The attainable in democratic government is not so much the deliberate choice of officers and the positive determination of policies by the people, as the power of veto and the power to change party leaders." This reduced vision of democracy, its sphere narrowed by

---

50 Albert Somit and Joseph Tanenhaus, *The Development of American Political Science: From Burgess to Behavioralism* (Boston: Allyn and Bacon, 1967), 69–76.
51 Woodrow Wilson to Herbert B. Adams, December 5, 1886, in Link, *Papers of Woodrow Wilson*, 5:416–17; ibid. 6:249–51; ibid. 4:12.
52 Ibid. 6:303.

administration and its authority limited to a kind of veto power, extended the deferential role mugwumps and Whigs had assigned to the people. Despite the demurrers of the more democratic political scientists, it provided an opening for capitalistic views of managed government according to business principles and for postwar theories of technocratic expert governance.[53]

The strongest theme in their work delivered governance not to capitalists but to themselves. If Goodnow's subtle relationships between politics and administration tended to disappear, it is also because his primary purpose, like that of his tradition, was to separate them, so that administration could be put into the hands of the "best men." In the new political science, the gentry program to train a class of educated leaders and expert civil servants came to center on the study of administration. Like "social control" for the sociologists and economists, administration for the political scientists focused both the reformist concern of their discipline and the vocational ambition of their profession, and carried with it that double ideological freight. The benign power of administration and the ability of administrators to act rationally in the public interest were no more questioned than were the similar benefits of social control. The social scientists' overestimation of their ability to control capitalism and socialize society was matched by the political scientists' overestimation of their ability to rationalize public decision-making and to separate politics and administration.[54]

One final measure of the power of the old Whig tradition over the new political scientists is the political theory they wrote in treatises and textbooks.[55] The substance of their theory remained the discussion of the state, its sovereignty and its enactment of limited government and civil liberty, in the Germanic and Whig terms first cast by Francis Lieber. Indeed,

---

53 Goodnow, *Politics and Administration*, 171, 248–9; Martin J. Schiesl, *The Politics of Efficiency: Municipal Administration and Reform in America, 1880–1920* (Berkeley: University of California Press, 1977). Cf. Henry Jones Ford, "Municipal Corruption," *PSQ*, 19 (December 1904): 680–1.

54 Raymond Seidelman with Edward J. Harpham, *Disenchanted Realists: Political Science and the American Crisis, 1884–1984* (Albany: State University of New York Press, 1985) captures this professional spirit of the new political science. Schiesl, *Politics of Efficiency*, provides an excellent account of how the institutional structures established by the administrative reformers became subservient to outside political interests and themselves centers of political interest.

55 The major treatise was Westal W. Willoughby, *An Examination of the Nature of the State* (New York: Macmillan, 1896). The four leading texts were James W. Garner, *Introduction to Political Science* (New York: American Book Co., 1910); Raymond G. Gettell, *Introduction to Political Science* (Boston: Ginn, 1910); James Q. Dealey, *The Development of the State* (New York: Silver, Burdett, 1909); Stephen B. Leacock, *Elements of Political Science* (Boston: Houghton Mifflin, 1906). See "Report of the Committee of Seven on Instruction in Colleges and Universities," *APSR*, 9 (May 1915): 368.

moved by Civil War nationalism and the desire to control industrial disorder, their writings emphasized the sovereignty of the state. The continued resilience of this tradition reflected its usefulness in the progressive effort to expand the functions of government yet limit them. Textbook writers began to pay less attention to the abstract discussion of sovereignty and more to the concrete functions of modern government. There was also a considerable range of new liberal views. Westal W. Willoughby, the most conservative, equated state and government and gave it absolute sovereignty. James Q. Dealey, the most democratic of the major writers, called the people subjects of the sovereign, "But they are not mere subjects; they are citizens also, for they have rights as well as obligations." Stephen Leacock, a Canadian, foresaw considerable expansion of state powers in the direction of social welfare; most were careful to permit only moderate extensions of government functions.[56]

The political usefulness of the old theory probably discouraged an effort to rethink its premises with the aid of liberal theory. Traditional Whig principles already provided a powerful government and a socialized individual. There seems no position more firmly and unanimously held by these writers than their opposition to "the obsolete individualism of the social contract theory."[57] To modernize individual rights, some theorists returned to the idealist liberal tradition Lieber and Bluntschli had used. Willoughby made use of T. H. Green's ethical conception of the state, although he coupled it incongruously to John Austin's conception of sovereignty. Walter Shepard based a theory of suffrage on Kant, urging that voting was an essential means to "the realization of the worth of human personality." For the most part, however, these writers struggled inconsistently to reconcile the moral claims of the individual with state authority.[58]

Within the framework of this conventional political theory the most basic disagreement was not over substance but over the epistemological status of theory. Here Willoughby, a student of Herbert Baxter Adams on whom

---

56 Dealey, *Development of the State*, 300; Leacock, *Elements of Political Science*, 386. Daniel Rodgers, *Contested Truths: Keywords in American Politics since Independence* (New York: Basic, 1987), chap. 5, presents an insightful, but too monolithic, account of Progressive Era political science as the apotheosis of the state. The theme of state sovereignty was treated with considerable modulation and was largely confined to theoretical texts, as against the wide interest of Progressive political scientists in political parties, municipal and state reform, administration, colonial governance, and legal interpretation.

57 James Q. Dealey, "Review of H. J. Ford, *The Natural History of the State*," *APSR*, 9 (November 1915): 798–9.

58 Thomas I. Cook and Arnaud B. Leavelle, "German Idealism and American Theories of the Democratic Community," *Journal of Politics*, 5 (August 1943): 227–8; Walter J. Shepard, "The Theory of the Nature of the Suffrage," *PAPSA*, 9 (1912): 106–36. See also Raymond G. Gettell, "Nature and Scope of Present Political Theory," *PAPSA*, 10 (1913): 56.

historicism seemed to have no effect, tried to establish a rationalist position. When he marked out the "essential nature" as opposed to the "mere appearance" of political institutions, he consigned "their actual operation in the arena of civic life" to the realm of appearance. Political philosophy was engaged in the "deduction of principles of universal applicability." The changing conditions of history did not produce "new truths (for that is impossible)" but rather disclosed errors and refinements that might be missed by "pure speculative thought." Unlike Henry Sidgwick in England, who attempted to justify his refurbished philosophical analysis of politics by declaring that historicism had sundered the understanding of past and present, Willoughby seemed untouched by historicism. His epistemology was the traditional one of the nineteenth-century American law he had studied before going to Johns Hopkins, with its belief that fixed rational principles lay beneath the changing forms of history, and that historical conditions merely disclosed them. Willoughby tried to defend his conception of theory "before the modern realistic world," but with little success. He and a number of other theorists drifted into the subfield of international law, particularly after World War I.[59]

As Willoughby drew Lieber's ideal-realism toward rationalism, most political theorists of the era drew it toward historicism. They argued that theory gave no access to a realm of absolute truth, nor was it mere abstract speculation. Theory was the product of history and changed with history. The principles of sovereignty and civil liberty they enunciated were the principles that animated modern Western nation states. In fact, their theories displayed only the loosest ties to history. Yet, in a discipline that honored the realistic study of political practice, the historical character of theory and its relevance to changing historical formations was the chief warrant of realism these theorists could give.[60] Still, as soon as their books were published, they were attacked by realistic colleagues for their "large amount of theorizing on a very narrow basis of information." Theory per se did not quite pass the test of realism.[61]

59 Willoughby, *Nature of the State*, viii, 4–5, 380–1; idem, "The Value of Political Philosophy," *PSQ*, 15 (March 1900): 76; William H. Hatcher, "Westal Woodbury Willoughby," *DAB*, Suppl. 3, 830–31; James W. Garner, "Westal Woodbury Willoughby: An Evaluation of his Contribution to Political Science," in *Essays in Political Science in Honor of Westal Woodbury Willoughby*, ed. John M. Mathews and James Hart (Baltimore: Johns Hopkins University Press, 1937), 3–32. On Sidgwick, see Stefan Collini, Donald Winch, and John Burrow, *That Noble Science of Politics* (Cambridge University Press, 1983), chap. 9.
60 Garner, *Introduction to Political Science*, 228–35; Gettell, "Nature and Scope," 50–2; Dealey, *Development of the State*, 210; Leacock, *Elements of Political Science*, 5–11.
61 Edgar Dawson, "Review of Raymond Gettell, *Introduction to Political Science*," *APSR*, 5 (May 1911): 311; William A. Schaper, "Review of James Garner, *Introduction to Political Science*," *APSR*, 5 (February 1911): 140–1.

## Professional division

Without the fuel of sharp political disagreement, these challenges to the gentry model of historico-politics did not arouse much acrimony. Herbert Baxter Adams did not approve of the "brutal" criticism practiced in German universities; he gave way silently to the chorus of opposition to his Teutonic germ theory, simply turning his energies to research in the history of American education. He did try to defend his conception of history as past politics. Politics should be understood in the inclusive Aristotelian sense, he said, and historico-politics could include any public aspect of civil society. Adams remained secretary of the AHA while the younger historians enacted their own program over his mild opposition. He had linked the Association to the federal government by having the Smithsonian publish (and occasionally censor) its *Annual Reports*, and by having the AHA meet each year in Washington. Taking matters into their own hands, the younger historians in 1895 established the *American Historical Review*, voted to hold meetings in other cities than the capital, and created a Historical Manuscripts Commission. They were giving institutional form to their Rankean methodological program and the pure historicism it required.[62]

The political scientists, too, moved cautiously, attacking Adams' germ theory more openly than Burgess' Hegelian principles. If Goodnow's *Politics and Administration* in 1900 was a declaration of independence, it was a muted one, and Burgess proved relatively tolerant of liberal positions that acknowledged the force of traditional American principle. The younger political scientists began to coalesce around their interest in administration and the opportunities it opened to act as experts on the problems of government. The Columbia political scientists had been particularly active in urban reform politics in the 1880s and 1890s, and the pace of expert activity for all the social scientists quickened around the turn of the century. In this context of practical administrative activity, the younger political scientists increasingly felt the need for more systematic collection and exchange of information on legislation at the municipal, state, national, and colonial levels. Spearheaded by Goodnow and Jeremiah W. Jenks, a Cornell economist, a committee was formed in 1902 to consider an association for this

---

62 Records of the Historical and Political Science Association and of the Seminary of History and Politics, Johns Hopkins University, p. 57; Herbert B. Adams, "Is History Past Politics?" *JHUSHPS*, ser. 13, nos. 3–4 (March–April 1895): 69–71; David D. Van Tassel, "From Learned Society to Professional Organization: The American Historical Association, 1884–1900," *AHR*, 89 (October 1984): 950–1.

purpose, which quickly turned into a move for a broader American Political Science Association (APSA).[63]

From its formation in 1903, when Goodnow was elected president, the APSA avoided conflict. Herbert Baxter Adams died prematurely in 1901; Burgess largely ignored the new association and fell back to his concern with Columbia, and Andrew Dickson White was given a ceremonial place on the Council. Goodnow's presidential address was careful to define political science in noncontroversial terms. He included concern for "what ought to be" as well as "what is," and legal institutions as well as "extra-legal" institutions. Neither science nor history were invoked as defining frameworks. The only category of political scientist he took the risk of offending was the "mere political philosopher" entirely given over to "philosophical speculation," for he knew no one present would admit to that offensive predilection. Debate over the public role of the social scientist, which had so occupied economists and sociologists, was strikingly absent. Advocacy was an issue in social science only when its controversial ideological bearings made it visible.[64]

With the formation of the APSA and the tendency of the younger generation in historico-politics to coalesce around either administration or the Rankean methodological program, we can no longer ignore the division of the joint discipline into political science and history. If politics, historicism, and realism united the younger generation in their attack on the gentry conception of fixed American principle, the different uses they made of these cultural elements were dividing them into historians and political scientists.

On one level, the split was simply a product of diverging interests, compounded by rising professionalism. Although political scientists were centrally concerned with contemporary politics, most historians, whether descended from the belles-lettristic tradition or simply engrossed in the demands of the Rankean reconstruction of the past, were not. In the rapidly enlarging and decentralized university system, specialization was relatively easy to effect and carried the status rewards of institutional and disciplinary independence. Historians, moreover, considerably outnumbered political scientists, adding to the tension on both sides.[65] Questions about the rel-

63 Hoxie, *History of the Faculty of Political Science*, 76–9, 102; Mary O. Furner, *Advocacy and Objectivity* (Lexington: University Press of Kentucky, 1975), 282–9.
64 "The Organization of the APSA," *PAPSA*, 1 (1904): 5–15; Westal W. Willoughby, "The APSA," *PSQ*, 19 (March 1904): 107–11; Frank J. Goodnow, "The Work of the APSA," *PAPSA*, 1 (1904): 42–3.
65 On the basis of rough estimates, I conclude that there were a third to a half as many doctorates awarded in political science as in history between 1882 and 1907, and that the

evance of political topics at AHA meetings or of the relative emphasis on historical or political training in the joint programs surfaced in the 1880s and broke into open conflict in 1895. The historians at Columbia, feeling slighted in Burgess' joint department of history and political science, requested a separate department, and Burgess obliged, dropping history from the title of his own chair. Adams' defense of his conception of history as past politics in 1895 was also a declaration that he would resist any separation at Johns Hopkins.[66]

It was probably the sting of this separation that prompted Burgess to make an unusual appearance at the AHA in 1896 and to lay down the gauntlet to historians. Although he stayed within his original conception of the joint field, he framed it around a provocative quotation from J. R. Seeley, the architect of historico-politics at the University of Cambridge, to the effect that history "is the name of a residuum which has been left when one group of facts after another has been taken possession of by some science." Political science would soon take possession of much that was still left, for it was political science that turned the facts of history into "the forms and conclusions of science."[67]

The historians could not very well accept such a formulation and both Andrews and H. Morse Stephens of Cornell University made extensive rebuttals to Burgess. The political scientists claimed too much for themselves, Stephens said. It was rather history, he implied, that occupied the imperial position. Although both sides made an effort to cool tempers, there were digs back and forth over the next years, and when the younger historians reviewed historical books by political scientists, they found them seriously wanting by the standards of historical scholarship.[68]

By the 1890s, however, there were deeper currents of opposition between

AHA was about twice as large as the APSA through the 1920s. Somit and Tanenhaus, *Development of American Political Science*, 55, 58, 91; John Higham, *History: Professional Scholarship in America* (New York: Harper & Row, 1973), 19, 27.

66 Charles K. Adams, "Recent Historical Work in the Colleges and Universities of Europe and America," *Papers of the AHA*, 4 (1889): 44–5; Anson B. Morse to Herbert B. Adams, March 29, 1893, Adams Papers; Hoxie, *History of the Faculty of Political Science*, 60–3; Herbert B. Adams, "Is History Past Politics?" 80.

67 John W. Burgess, "Political Science and History," *AHAAR* (1896), 1:207, 210.

68 H. Morse Stephens, ibid., 211–15; Charles M. Andrews, "The Teaching of History – Discussion," ibid., 256–7; "A Retrospect," *PSQ*, 10 (December 1895): 567; Albert B. Hart, "The Historical Opportunity in America," *AHR*, 4 (October 1898): 17; Frederick J. Turner, "Review of Harry Pratt Judson, *The Growth of the American Nation*," *AHR*, 1 (April 1896): 549–50; William Garrott Brown, "Review of Jesse Macy, *Political Parties in the United States, 1846–1861*," *AHR*, 6 (April 1901): 592–6; William Garrott Brown, "Review of John W. Burgess, *Reconstruction and the Constitution, 1866–1876*," *AHR*, 8 (October 1902): 150–2; William Garrott Brown, "Review of John W. Burgess, *The Civil War and the Constitution, 1859–1866*," *AHR*, 8 (January 1903): 368–70.

the historians and political scientists than were generated by specialization and professional ambition. The historians felt their effort to achieve historical truth threatened by the political scientists' search for political norms and involvement in contemporary politics. As Macy noted, historians "commonly assumed that politics is a perverter of history ... that in order to attain the true historical spirit the writer must be removed in time and space from the field of active politics."[69]

Although all historians wanted to avoid contemporary involvement in politics, they disagreed about what kind of history that entailed. Stephens spoke for a sharp break with political science. An Englishman who had moved to America just two years before, Stephens recounted for his audience the fight William Stubbs had made at Oxford against Seeley's subordination of history to political science. Stubbs taught us, he said, to study history "for its own sake." Looking for the truth in history was incompatible with looking for the political principles that occupied American historico-politics.

We should study history with the endeavor to find out the truth, not with the endeavor of understanding how free this or that or the other country is; not for the purpose of explaining how superior the government of our own country is to any other country, and still less for the purpose of justifying any particular theory of government.

The political scientists who engaged in that task wrote poor history. The solution was for political scientists to confine themselves to the study of existing political institutions, and to rely on historians for objective understanding of the past on which those institutions were based. Stephens was telling historians to abandon the joint task of historico-politics and to draw the line between an objective history and normative political science at the line between the present and the past.[70]

Andrews, speaking for those who were seeking a new history, tried to salvage the present for historians. History was more than a residuum, he said. It was really history that fulfilled Burgess' ultimate purpose of showing "the organic evolution of peoples." True, to achieve impartiality historians must begin by studying "that history which does not in any way concern us, either in our politics or religion." But the historian must end by showing the relevance of the past to the present and "the chief tendencies

69 Macy, "The Relation of History to Politics," 181.
70 H. Morse Stephens, "Political Science and History – Discussion," 213. For an excellent discussion of Stubbs's influence, see Doris S. Goldstein, "The Professionalization of History in Britain in the Late Nineteenth and Early Twentieth Centuries," *Storia della storiografia/ History of Historiography*, 3 (1983), 3–26.

of the present." In study of the last thirty years, he said, bias is not an insurmountable problem, so long as investigation is carried on by historians rather than by men of affairs. Indeed such study would moderate current partisanship and produce "fewer jingoes on one side and doctrinaires on the other." Andrews projected a program that retained the presentist focus and synthetic aim of historico-politics and hence offered the possibility of linking the new historicism to the diverging political and social sciences. But he, like Stephens, rejected the tutelage of political science, accepted the historicist program of Ranke, and sought to disconnect history from partisanship.[71]

The political scientists, no less than the historians, were becoming increasingly aware of the gap that was opening up between the historicist search for the past and the search for laws to direct political action. Jesse Macy, in his shrewd and naive way, was one of the first to demonstrate that historicism itself could erode the relevance of history to politics. When disabused of literal belief in Adams' germ theory, he was tempted to throw over the entire historical enterprise. Addressing the historical fraternity, he announced that if the Constitution or Magna Carta meant very different things in the past, then what was important about them was "what is believed and acted upon today." Macy also saw that history was in no way a privileged form of knowledge. It was often based upon biased reports and distorted in the writing by partisan passion. If history was past politics as Adams claimed, it had been perverted; the solution was to convert politics into a genuine science. Although Macy did not give up historical study of politics, he hoped that the consensual community of truth-seekers could turn it into science and thereby achieve the power of prediction and control. "History, as it becomes scientific, becomes more and more prophetic. Science reveals law, and a knowledge of law confers the power to forecast the future."[72] The impatience he felt with the complex differences and subjective screens of the past suggests the effect that the belated impact of historicism might have on minds long nourished on millennial republican history and commonsense realism. If historicism meant that the past could no longer be linked unequivocally to the present and future, it could no longer serve as the basis for action.

Indeed, Macy's more sophisticated colleagues also felt the need to leave the ground of history in search of political norms. Frank Goodnow opened his *Politics and Administration* with a universalistic analysis of his basic

71 Charles M. Andrews, "The Teaching of History – Discussion," 1:256–57; idem, "Should Recent European History Have a Place in the College Curriculum?" 547–8.
72 Macy, "The Relation of History to Politics," 184; idem, "Twentieth Century Democracy," 514.

categories. "The political life of man is largely conditioned by the fact of his humanity," he asserted. Although there are great historical differences, history appears to move in stages and political institutions will be similar at similar stages. Universal human nature, fixed on a universal course of change, is the ground of political life, and because of this ground, Goodnow continued, all theorists from Hobbes to his sociological colleague Giddings had been able to "conceive of the state as an abstraction," one which is like an organism, "endowed with life and capable of action." Because it is like an organism, it can be conceived as expressing its will and executing its will.[73]

With this proposition Goodnow came to the point of the argument, but he was not altogether satisfied. Whether the organic conception of the state is true or not, he continued, still "political functions group themselves naturally" under these two heads of the expression and execution of will; the division of labor and psychological efficiency seems to require it; the two functions and their organs can in fact be distinguished in all historical governments; and finally, quoting a French authority, "The mind can conceive of but two powers." The train of legitimating grounds merely accentuated Goodnow's uneasy need to find "in all governmental systems two primary or ultimate functions of government." And the purpose of so finding, of course, was to justify the separation of politics and administration, the foremost policy prescription of the political scientists.[74]

Goodnow was explicitly looking for a deeper justification than could be wrung from history. He had understood from his study of administration over the previous decade that Montesquieu's doctrine of the separation of powers was nowhere fully realized in history; that the three powers Montesquieu described and their governmental organs were never fully distinguished (the judicial power Goodnow divided between politics and administration). The doctrine could have effect as a theory of "what ought to be," he had concluded, but it must be applied according to the "history and political needs of the particular country."[75] Goodnow felt the need of a more absolute basis for "what ought to be" than history could provide.

Wilson, too, another predominantly historical thinker, resorted to univer-

---

73 Goodnow, *Politics and Administration*, 6–9. Goodnow introduced this section with an approving summary of Rudolf von Gneist's historicist argument that the formal constitutional principles and the underlying administrative processes of a people are linked, so that Germany, e.g., could not merely take over English constitutional forms at will. Goodnow drew the conclusion that "the political institutions of different peoples will show a much greater similarity than would be thought to exist were the consideration confined to the formal provisions of the constitutional law," and went on to posit a universal human nature at like stages of progress.
74 Ibid., 9–13, 22, 37–8.
75 Goodnow, *Comparative Administrative Law*, 1:23, 22.

sal claims when history could not secure his primary norm. Wilson believed that democracy was rooted in history but he learned from the historical economists that socialism was an authentic form of democracy. The historical process itself would determine the line between individualism and socialism in the future. But in the end Wilson was not satisfied to leave the decision to history or to historical analysis. Turning to anthropology and sociology, he argued that there had to be "natural limits to state action" in the nature of the individual, the family, and the state to rule out socialism.[76] In their implicit recognition that historicism could not provide them with fixed norms for political action and their resort to sociology and anthropology, Goodnow and Wilson were disclosing the attraction that science was beginning to have for American political science. The professional division between history and political science followed the faultline that was opening up between historicism and a search for political norms in the style of science.

### Scientific aspiration in political science

The scientific impulse in political science resulted in direct attempts to transform the study of politics into an independent science. It is noteworthy that these efforts came chiefly from two guardians of conservative exceptionalist principle. Like Clark and Giddings, they reformulated as scientific law the traditional basis of the American Republic in nature.

As the Progressive Era took shape, Henry Jones Ford became increasingly hostile to the current of reform. He disliked the devices of direct democracy, which tampered with the slow organic development of American republican institutions. He detested the Progressive Era changes in family and gender relations. His conservative responses were probably both cause and effect of his growing interest in Catholicism during these years and he ultimately converted. He also became a champion of a scientific political science that would provide "universal principles permanent in their applicability" instead of just "impressions received from 'accidents of development.'" The "type" of our republican institutions was gradually evolving in accord with evolutionary law. That evolution, he felt sure, contained "a principle of regeneration" strong enough to save America from the Roman fate. To find those laws political scientists must adopt the strategies and language of Darwinian evolutionary science.[77]

Ford issued a call in 1905 for a political science that could "supply general

---

76 Link, *Papers of Woodrow Wilson*, 6:303–9, 308.
77 Henry Jones Ford, "The Results of Reform," *AAAPSS*, 21 (March 1903): 224, 235, 237; "Necrology: Henry Jones Ford," *Catholic Historical Review*, n.s. 5 (October 1925): 450.

principles for the guidance of statecraft." Up until now American political science had focused exclusively on the Aryan-descended political forms of Europe and North America. "If we accept the national, popular state of Western civilization as the basis of political science what assurance is there of the possession of a true norm?" The modern Western state is hardly universal, and all political forms change. Political science "must take for its subject-matter the nature of public authority whatever forms it may assume.... It must detach its abstract terms from the historical accidents of their origin and provide itself with a systematic terminology." It must, in other words, take an "objective basis ... in orderly connection with natural history." Despite the difficulty of the endeavor, it must be attempted. "Success means attainment of the power to give rational determination to the destinies of nations."[78]

The difficulty of the task Ford had set himself and the character of the norm he sought became clear ten years later, when he attempted an evolutionary analysis of the state. He believed that Darwin himself had been unclear whether the basis of human evolution was the individual or the social group. Examining the latest evidence in biology, psychology, anthropology, and linguistics, he concluded that natural selection operated on traits useful to the survival of the social group, rather than the individual. It was possible therefore to define the state as an organism in the sense of a unit defined by the evolutionary process. The organismic nature of the state could in turn be used as a "determinant of the validity of social and political theories." The principal consequences of the social evolution of the state were:

The State is an organism.... The individual is a distinct entity in the unit life of the State. The Individual is not an original but is a derivative.... Government derives its authority from the State.... Rights are not innate but are derivative. They exist in the State but not apart from the State. Hence rights are correlated with duties. Liberty implies not absence of restraint but presence of order.... Individual life enlarges by participation in a larger life; ascends by incorporation in a higher life.

The most striking feature of these conclusions, coming on the heels of an extended examination of the latest scientific literature, is their familiarity. By 1915 they were the stock-in-trade of almost a hundred years of Whig political science, although they veered heavily to the conservative side of the tradition. Behind Ford's search for a science of politics was a traditional normative goal.[79]

78 Henry Jones Ford, "The Scope of Political Science," *PAPSA*, 2 (1905): 198–206.
79 Henry Jones Ford, *The Natural History of the State* (Princeton, N.J.: Princeton University Press, 1915), 170, 174–7.

American political scientists were more attracted by another positivist style. Abbott Lawrence Lowell, a Boston Brahmin thrice over, rejected the liberal historicist program for political science. He did not on the whole believe American institutions should change, and while an enemy of political corruption and advocate of expert administration, he had severe doubts about the ability of American democracy to sustain a professional civil service. Though he joined the new APSA, he took no part in its founding. Lowell's distinction in political science was in his restatement of a conservative version of American exceptionalism in the idiom of scientific natural law, bringing to it, as Giddings had to sociology, the use of statistical method.[80]

Lowell was an heir to Cambridge positivism. At Harvard he honored in mathematics and graduated from the Law School in 1880. He soon found the practice of law uninteresting – one of his law teachers thought he had "too mathematical a mind" – and he read after hours the English philosophical and legal positivists and their young American disciple, Oliver Wendell Holmes, Jr. He soon echoed Holmes's and Sir Frederick Pollock's distaste for German political science, with its conflation of law and morality. In general, he thought, political science needed more inductive studies; the German theories "which are so largely taught in our universities . . . seem to me of decidedly secondary importance," of relevance only to German institutions. Anglo-American institutions alone, we will see, fully reflected natural law.[81]

In the introduction to his first book of essays, Lowell temporarily abandoned the "scientific spirit" to state his political principles. In doing so, he made clear the political bearings of his dislike of ethical German theory and his desire for inductive methods. "The system of government which most promotes the moral and material welfare of the community," Lowell believed, was the American system of personal liberty and private rights. Only such a system encouraged and safeguarded "individual enterprise and exertion" and hence produced self-reliance and strong manhood. Like Sumner, Lowell centered American institutions on classic economic liberalism and its central premise of possessive individualism. Socialism was merely

---

80 The chief biographical source on Lowell is Henry Aaron Yeomans, *Abbott Lawrence Lowell, 1856–1943* (Cambridge, Mass.: Harvard University Press, 1948). One of many expressions of doubt regarding a civil service is in Lowell to Charles Homer Haskins, January 16, 1907, Lowell Papers, Harvard University.

81 Yeomans, *Lowell*, 42; A. Lawrence Lowell, *Essays on Government* (Boston: Houghton Mifflin, 1889), 172–3; Lowell to Albert Bushnell Hart, April 13, 1901, Lowell Papers. For a discussion of the positivist influence at Harvard Law School, see Mark De Wolfe Howe, *Justice Oliver Wendell Holmes*, 2 vols. (Cambridge, Mass.: Harvard University Press, 1957), 1: chap. 5; 2: chap. 5.

millennialism, he asserted, and the millennium would never come. Growth of "an inductive tone of mind" would erode such utopianism. In his subsequent studies, the reference to socialism fell away, but this inductive counsel continued to serve the same cautionary purpose.[82]

Lowell set out a remarkably candid analysis of American politics. He thought Wilson's *Congressional Government* was badly mistaken in its mugwump Anglophile wish that America move closer to British parliamentary government. The American adoption of parliamentary practices would either lead to nothing or would subvert the constitutional order, and that order reflected a sound intention. The aim was "to protect the individual, to prevent the majority from oppressing the minority," and only "within certain definite limits, to give effect to the wishes of the people." The aim of parliamentary government was quite different: to give direct voice to the majority of voters. Socialistic legislation was gaining ground in England precisely because parliamentary government could easily enact the will of the people. The American political system gave rise rather to "the demagogism of ambiguous phrases," which tried to unite all classes and bridge all issues in the interest of party spoils.

The result is, that party agitation in America does not in general involve any threat against the property or rights of private persons, and that those statutes which may be classed as socialistic rarely find a place in party programmes, and are not carried by party votes. This state of things is not an accident. It is the natural consequence of the political system of the United States.

Like Goodnow and Ford, Lowell was a realist, but his political intention was quite different; he showed that the "extra-legal institutions" of American party government were quite in accord with the antimajoritarian spirit of her legal ones and should remain that way.[83]

Lowell went on to develop the analytical possibilities of cross-cultural study. In 1896 he published a comparative analysis of the party systems of continental Europe, the first empirical study by an American of political parties as an integral part of the political system, and the following year became a lecturer and then professor in Harvard's department of history and politics. His most striking empirical study, one Goodnow called a "shining example" for political science, made extensive use of statistics to analyze party voting in America and England. Measuring party votes on legislation in the House of Commons, the United States Congress, and five state legislatures at intervals during the nineteenth century, Lowell showed that

---

82 Lowell, *Essays on Government*, 8–19; A. Lawrence Lowell, "The Influence of Party upon Legislation in England and America," *AHAAR* (1901): 1:350.
83 Lowell, *Essays on Government*, chap. 2 and pp. 22, 107–8.

after 1860 party voting was much stronger in England than in America. But if parties in America were in fact weak, according to the appropriate criterion of their control over legislation, why then were they so often decried as too powerful? The answer was that their very weakness, the absence in layered American government of any mechanism by which parties could enforce discipline, led them to turn to patronage as the means of survival.[84]

The realistic analytic wedge Lowell used was conspicuously that of comparative, rather than historical, context; he called himself a professor of "Existing Political Systems." He knew and incorporated into his analysis of American or English or French parties a great deal of history, but he analyzed them rather as single operational systems, playing off their differences across cultures rather than across time. His study of party voting in England and America, while noticing changes in English voting patterns through the nineteenth century, deliberately abandoned any historical attempt to understand the more shifting American figures, for they did not appear to follow closely any fixed law of evolution.[85]

Lowell thought of history as a repository of the relatively unchanging qualities of human nature. Cultures were fixed along certain tracks, and these tracks arranged along a single path of evolution, in a positivist version of American exceptionalism. To discover the "essential function in any democracy" of political parties, he said, one needed to examine the party systems in England and America, where "popular government has run a free course for the greatest length of time." The French multiparty system indicated partial evolution of popular government. The two-party system was "the normal condition of the party system ... among a people sufficiently free from prejudices to group themselves naturally." Here was American political principle as embodiment of natural law and the norm toward which historical progress moved. Later he used a mathematical model to illustrate the naturalness of the "mature" two-party system. Because political opinions were distributed along a bell-shaped curve, he said, the centrist tendencies of that system best represented opinion.[86]

As the Progressive Era dawned, Lowell recognized that American institutions must adjust to evolutionary change along the appointed path. Voluntary associations like political parties, corporations, and unions were becoming more important. Any solutions to current problems must accept "the

84 A. Lawrence Lowell, *Governments and Parties in Continental Europe*, 2 vols. (Boston: Houghton Mifflin, 1896); Lowell, "The Influence of Party upon Legislation."
85 Lowell, "The Influence of Party upon Legislation," 1:322.
86 Lowell, *Governments and Parties in Continental Europe*, 1:71, 84; A. Lawrence Lowell, *Public Opinion and Popular Government* (New York: Longmans Green, 1913), 65–6, 70.

natural tendencies of a progressive age instead of trying to run counter to them." The chief area in which American political institutions did not reflect the universal principles of historical evolution was in the lack of expert administration, a fault of American democracy that could no longer be tolerated in a complex modern state.[87]

Lowell thought of politics as an inexact, positive science rather than a historical one. Following the logic of John Stuart Mill, Lowell believed that political economy, by isolating a single motive, could achieve results "approximate enough to be of value." But in politics, two motives or institutions acting together could produce results quite different from what could be predicted from their action alone. "The only conclusion one can draw with certainty is that in a given environment a certain combination of causes produces the consequences that we observe." One mathematical problem in elliptic functions, he recalled, "has always clung in my mind, as an expression of the limits within which any principle is true." While Mill concluded that the contextual character of politics meant that it might never become a science, Lowell concluded merely that politics "must forever remain an inexact science."[88]

When Lowell formulated his program for political science, as president of the APSA in 1910, he therefore cast it as a program of scientific, rather than historical, realism. Political science must, like physiology, study the actual functions of political organs. Most of our books are on history, not on current function, he lamented. "The main laboratory for the actual working of political institutions is not a library, but the outside world of public life. It is there that the phenomena must be sought. It is there that they must be observed at first hand." Just as he expected to gain nothing from history, he declared abstract political thought barren as well. Progress would come from compiling, arranging, and classifying data, using statistics and the comparative analysis of existing conditions. Lowell severed the Progressives' program of historical realism, consigning history to the past and placing realism only in the present. He could follow that strategy because he trusted the natural course of historical evolution to sustain American exceptionalism.[89]

The tendency of American political scientists to seek universal principles that would provide norms for practice, and the attraction therefore of the model of natural science, was observed – and regretted – by no less an authority on America than James Bryce. An English proponent of the

---

87 A. Lawrence Lowell, "Social Regulation," in *Congress of Arts and Sciences*, 7:263–75.
88 A. Lawrence Lowell, *The Government of England*, 2 vols. (New York: Macmillan, 1908), 2:505–6; Lowell to Petrim Sorokin, January 14, 1933, Lowell Papers.
89 A. Lawrence Lowell, "The Physiology of Politics," *APSR*, 4 (February 1910): 1–15, particularly 7–8.

program of historical realism in political science, author of a distinguished study of American politics, and a great friend of Lowell and his American colleagues, Bryce was elected president of the APSA in 1909, while serving as British ambassador to the United States. He chose for his presidential address the subject of "The Relations of Political Science to History and Practice," and his message, though politely gloved, was clear: "I hope you will not think that I am 'giving away' your science if I say that it must not be expected to provide authoritative solutions for current problems and controversies."[90]

Bryce began by asking in what sense politics was a science and concluded that it was a historical science of the kind familiar to practitioners of historico-politics. Its fundamental laws were the laws of human nature, but the general and permanent tendencies of human nature were few and abstract. To understand their action at any time or place, they must be studied historically. "Every political organism, every political force, must be studied in and cannot be understood apart from the environment out of which it has grown and in which it plays. Not all the facts of that environment are relevant, but till you have examined them, you cannot pronounce any irrelevant." The result is that the kind of knowledge political science will produce can do only what historical knowledge has always done. It can "create in the class which leads a nation the proper temper and attitude towards the questions which from time to time arise in politics." It can broaden their views, enlarge their sympathies, and moderate their narrower passions, as well as provide a knowledge of facts and general principles. More than that, Bryce warned, it cannot do. In the "interpretation of historical facts and their application to a concrete controversy," there was no way to escape the subjectivity of personal or party bias. "Cherish no vain hopes of introducing the certitude or the authority of science into politics."[91]

There is a note in Bryce's warning that deserves particular attention. He sensed among American political scientists a desire to wield "the certitude or the authority of science" in the concrete controversies of contemporary politics. It is not just the norms of American politics made insecure by historical change that were involved, but the contested norms of practical politics. Although historico-politics was a more conservative disciplinary environment than economics or sociology and avoided a socialist challenge within its ranks, it lived in a public world in which the threat of socialism remained real, so that Wilson had to call upon nature to combat it. Political

90 *APSR*, 3 (February 1909): 1–19, particularly 16.
91 Ibid., 8, 16–18.

scientists were desirous of making their ideas felt in the practical world of American politics, traditionally hostile to the advice of intellectuals and outsiders. Among themselves no prescription could have been less controversial than the separation of politics and administration, but in the political world at large, it needed all the help it could get, as Goodnow must have sensed when he tried to ground it, in every possible way, in the nature of things.

Political scientists were also being drawn increasingly into reform activity and the orbit of the activist social sciences, while Progressive sentiment itself was advancing in controversial and polarized directions. The two political scientists who were most aggressive in their call for a science of politics were conservatives who felt beleaguered by the increasingly liberal tenor of Progressive society and politics, and hence felt the strongest need for the authority of science. Both Lowell and Ford pictured a scientific study of politics as one that abandoned the current hasty search for improvements and turned instead to an objective "search for truth."

Bryce's warning went unheeded, but the language of science was still a long way from capturing the discipline. Administration, with its roots in a tradition of educated prudence, of management rather than control, would seem an unlikely field for the development of positivist science, as unlikely as the value-laden field of politics itself. The prescriptive role chosen by political scientists and the absolutist demands of American exceptionalism were nonetheless leading them in that direction.

The most likely alliance for political science as it pulled away from history toward science was sociology. Sociologists too were engaged in a search for normative laws and many of them, like Small, had stressed the historical side of that historico-evolutionary enterprise. Progressive sociologists showed no hesitation in claiming political science as a dependent realm within synthetic sociology. Just as Dewey had quickly seen the possibility of collapsing political theory into a theory of society, sociologists declared sovereignty merely one form of social control or social cohesion.[92] For their part, the political scientists seemed inclined toward the sociologists. The four major texts of the Progressive period all agreed that political science was a part of the larger sociological science of society.[93]

The overlapping subject most thoroughly exploited was public opinion. Edward A. Ross discussed it initially as a modern tool of social control, and

92 Edward A. Ross, "Moot Points in Sociology, I: The Scope and Task of Sociology," *AJS*, 8 (May 1903): 774–5; Franklin H. Giddings, in "The Study and Teaching of Sociology," *AAAPSS*, 12 (July 1898): 7.
93 Dealey, *Development of the State*, 53; Leacock, *Elements of Political Science*, 11; Garner, *Introduction to Political Science*, 31; Gettell, *Introduction to Political Science*, 4.

his analysis of Walter Bagehot's "discussion" linked public opinion to both social action and political institutions. The tenor of Progressive discussion was optimistic, taking account of the irrational features of popular mentality, but recognizing that abstract rationality was not necessarily the appropriate standard for political choice. Charles H. Cooley, for example, argued that popular sentiment, common sense, and good judgment of personality were sufficient to arm ordinary people for their task of setting basic moral directions and choosing leaders.

Lowell, in probably the first book on public opinion by a political scientist, acknowledged that political opinions, like most opinions, were not formed by independent rational reflection, but were rather – and quite appropriately – adopted because they were "in accord with a code of beliefs already in the mind." They fit into the person's "conception of the universal fitness of things" as handed down to them in their milieu. Although Walter Shepard enthusiastically foresaw "government by public opinion without the interposition of representative bodies other than very extended electorates," Lowell showed how public opinion was effectively contained within its proper limits by legislatures, parties, and experts. But the tone of the Progressive analysis, by sociologists and political scientists alike, differed markedly from the condemnation of popular irrationality that emerged with World War I.[94]

Despite common interests, the ties between political science and sociology were still tentative and superficial. Sociology was itself too divided and unsure to provide a model for scientific study of politics. A decade after he had looked to Giddings' organic conception of society, Goodnow doubted sociology could help him understand municipal government. It was impossible to frame a model of city government for "most cities," he said; the model must be adapted to the particular conditions of each city. Moreover, there was no general agreement on how social conditions affect government. Social psychology was not very advanced and had to be used with great care. Nor could there ever be laboratories for experimental social psychology. "The only way, therefore, in which the inductive method may be used is to study the past. Through such a study we may be able to formulate certain general principles, which may, prima facie, have much to commend them." Goodnow expressed the considerable skepticism about sociology and the considerable attachment to historical method that still existed in political science.[95]

94 Charles H. Cooley, *Social Organization* (New York: Scribner, 1909), pts. 3, 6; Lowell, *Public Opinion*, 18–22; Walter J. Shepard, "Public Opinion," *AJS*, 15 (July 1909): 60.
95 Goodnow, *Municipal Government* (1909), 41–4.

The sharpest antagonism to sociology was voiced by Ford. He blamed the rise of sociology for the explosion of popular rights and licentiousness in the Progressive Era and published a scathing attack on "The Pretensions of Sociology" in the *Nation* in 1909. The disintegrative doctrine of natural rights was built into sociology from the start by the fundamental individualism of Ward and Spencer, he argued. The only way to avoid such consequences was through his own reading of Darwin, Aristotle, and political science; namely, that the state, not society, was the basic social unit and that the individual was the creation of the state and its institutions.[96] Ford's extreme animus was idiosyncratic. His theory of the priority of the state to society seems to have been unique to him, so that like Patten in economics, he was forced to contest the sociological field. But his conservatism and his desire to protect the political turf from sociological imperialism were undoubtedly more widely shared in the profession and set limits on the attraction of sociology.

## Conclusions

In historico-politics, as in economics and sociology, a younger generation of scholars challenged the gentry conception of fixed American principle and revised American exceptionalism. But without the threat of a socialist challenge, neither the revolt nor the transformation were as marked as in economics and sociology. The students of historico-politics had as their subject matter the sacred republican government. They did not have to face so directly the new industrial machine and urban polyglot society. Moreover, as Ian Tyrrell has pointed out, the historicist program of the nineteenth century emphasized the uniqueness of national historical traditions. Among "historical individuals," the state was preeminent, so that the incursion of historicism in the 1890s need not have turned historians' attention away from the unique story of the American Republic, only change the basis of exceptionalism to the ongoing forces and changing conditions of history. The American identity became more fragile and uncertain, but history could still be searched for assurances that it would survive.[97]

Adopting a program of historical realism, political scientists tried to get beneath the traditional structure of constitutional principle and examine

96 Henry Jones Ford, "The Pretensions of Sociology," *AJS*, 15 (July 1909): 96–104. The controversy broadened: Charles A. Ellwood, "The Science of Sociology: A Reply," ibid., 105–10; Henry Jones Ford, "The Claims of Sociology Examined," ibid. (September 1909): 244–59; Charles A. Ellwood, "The Origin of Society," ibid. (November 1909): 394–404.
97 Ian Tyrrell, "American Exceptionalism in an Age of International History," paper delivered at the Organization of American Historians, April 1989.

how party politics, city government, and administration actually functioned in American political life. They began to bring to bear on these subjects Western historical experience with administrative structures, urban powers, and party conflict. But their categories of analysis and prescriptions, like the topics themselves, followed their inherited tradition, with its antimajoritarian conception of liberty, its desire to expand elite governance, and its focus on institutional analysis. A political science constructed on the self-interested motives of liberal, interest-group politics still lay in the future.

Historians too did not quite transfer their allegiance from the exceptional conditions of the American past to the new forces of liberal modernity. They were moving in that direction, seeking an economic and social basis for American politics, but they held to the antebellum vision, most often linking America's unique principles to their English heritage. Turner's frontier thesis was a transcription of the exceptionalist faith in the continent of virgin land. When Turner presented his sectional interpretation of American history to the American Sociological Society and forecast that sectionalism would remain a major, democratizing force that perpetuated the American character, he got no support from the sociologists. They, like the economists, had come to believe that the democratic ideal would be brought to fruition by nationalization and industrial capitalism.[98]

Yet Turner's frontier thesis fit perfectly into the liberal vision the Progressive economists and sociologists were constructing. Their allegiance to the industrial future made them look upon America's agrarian past as a fast-vanishing world. Ely, Seligman, and many others quickly adopted Turner's frontier thesis, characterizing the American past as a realm of simple agrarian nature, wholly individualistic in character, outmoded by the new industrial world and its need for social control.[99] Turner's receding agrarian past made it easier for the economists and sociologists to thin out American history into a variant of *Gemeinschaft* or to reconstitute the historical American past as nature, where it could serve as romantic liberal ideal.

Although historians and political scientists ratified the gulf between past and future that historicism had opened, there were still many historicist political scientists and presentist historians who shared a contextual understanding of the past and a desire to put history to analytical and synthetic uses. Professional division did not require that political scientists abandon a historical understanding of their political task. The novelty of the real

98 Billington, *Frederick Jackson Turner*, 229–30; Frederick J. Turner, "Is Sectionalism in America Dying Away?" *AJS*, 13 (March 1908): 661–75 and "Discussion," ibid. (May 1908): 811–19.
99 E. R. A. Seligman, *Principles of Economics* (New York: Longmans Green, 1905), chap. 7; Richard T. Ely et al., *Outlines of Economics* (New York: Macmillan, 1916), chaps. 5–6.

political world emerging in the Progressive Era did not have to be divorced from the past. But the desire to still the relative and conflicting voices of history with the authority of science led the political scientists to reexamine their affiliations. They began to see themselves as part of a sociological, rather than historical, synthesis and seek ways to make their work scientific.

The historians, for their part, became increasingly aware of the distance between themselves and what had become the social sciences, properly so called. In 1903, still smarting from the departure of the political scientists, they were attacked by the sociologists for resisting the evolutionary methods of biological science. Giddings' brief account of his own evolutionary theory of history based on consciousness of kind left them aghast at his method of "universal generalization." Instead they argued, with one reference to Dilthey and Rickert, that history required an individualizing method.[100]

George Burton Adams summed up the sense of many historians that they were the object of "an attack . . . systematic and concerted, and from various points at once." This "hostile movement" included political science, geography, the economic interpretation of history, sociology, and social psychology. Far from being scientific in the sense of using the careful methods of science to determine facts, it was a speculative movement that sought to construct a science of history on the model of Comte or Buckle, or a philosophy of history that revealed the destiny of the race. As against this speculative tendency, Adams stressed the historian's commitment to the "discovery and recording of what actually happened." Holder of a degree in divinity as well as history, and historian of those Anglo-Saxon political institutions that were to be the "permanent" and "final free institutions of the world," Adams retained, however, the larger synthetic aims of historico-politics. Recalling Andrew White's opening address to the AHA in 1884, he believed a philosophy of history should live on as a "source of inspiration and of courage," though separable from scientific work. The historian was now laying foundations and furnishing materials for a later scientific synthesis.[101]

Adams was not entirely negative, however. Historians should not ignore the social scientific movement, he said. "The new interpretation of history brings us too much that is convincing, despite all the mere speculation that goes with it; its contribution to a better understanding of our problems is already too valuable; we are ourselves too clearly conscious in these later

100 Franklin H. Giddings, "A Theory of Social Causation and Discussion," *PAEA*, 3d ser., 5 (May 1904): 139–99, particularly 192–3. See also "The Meeting of the American Historical Association at New Orleans," *AHR*, 9 (April 1904): 9–22.
101 George Burton Adams, "History and the Philosophy of History," *AHR*, 14 (January 1909): 224, 236, 234–5; idem, *European History* (New York: Macmillan, 1899), 511.

days of the tangled network of influences we are striving to unravel." The historian should rather use the new work with "discrimination." It was the older men in the profession, he said, already set in their ways who could take comfort in the value of their limited search for facts. It was for the younger men rather "to meet the leaders of the new movement ... with their own weapons, and to turn some of their positions into a part of our own line of defense ... to find a common standing-ground for all workers at what are really common tasks."[102] Adams in fact laid out the road the new historians would take over the next decades, a road divided from the social sciences in its adherence to historicist assumptions and the Rankean methodological program, yet keeping a somewhat parallel course to the social sciences, by means of its synthetic hopes and continued development of the new history.

If the historians, unlike the social scientists, were able to historicize the American Republic, that was to some degree a product of their training and their exemption from current practice. They could find in history a useable past and leave the difficulties of its uses to others. If they trusted history, it was a history made over by the canons of American exceptionalism, a history that still linked American experience to age-old Anglo-Saxon principle and to the unique American land. They trusted history to keep America the same even amidst its changes. But change was encroaching on social consciousness at an ever more rapid rate, and among some social scientists its effects were already becoming more dramatic.

102 G. B. Adams, "History and the Philosophy of History," 230, 235.

# PART IV

◁══════════════════════════════════════▷

## American social science as the study of natural process, 1908–1929

# 9

# New models of American
# liberal change

During the second decade of the new century, as progressivism advanced and collapsed into worldwide conflagration, a number of social scientists responded more profoundly than their contemporaries to the currents set in motion by the crisis of American exceptionalism. Imagining themselves in a wholly new world, they looked for the utopian shape of modernity within the process of liberal change itself. The concepts and paradigms they developed are still among the most fundamental and characteristic of twentieth-century American social science, among them Robert F. Hoxie's and Wesley Clair Mitchell's institutional economics, William I. Thomas' and Robert Park's urban social research, and Arthur F. Bentley and Charles Beard's group politics. Beginning with Bentley's *The Process of Government* in 1908, these new programs were intended to grasp the character of liberal historical change. Yet framed as sciences of natural process, they often abandoned historical context, structure, and time. In this chapter we will examine this innovative cohort and the bearings of their new work; in Chapter 10 we will take a broader look at how the balance shifted toward scientism in the social disciplines.

## The historical context of natural process

This late Progressive cohort was not entirely defined by age. Although many were younger, born in the 1870s and a few fast-starters in the 1880s, others were no younger than the more conventional Progressives. Thomas and Park, like Edward A. Ross and Charles H. Cooley, were born in the mid-1860s.[1] So too, this cohort had its social roots largely in the native Protestant middle-class – business, clerical, occasionally rural – that had produced earlier generations of social scientists. Similarly, the reformist social conscience of the Progressives, with their concern for the industrial transformation of labor and the unequal distribution of wealth, was clearly visible among these new recruits. Bentley, the son of a small-town Nebraska banker who was mindful of the credit squeeze on his farmer customers, grew up with Populist sympathies. Beard, scion of a well-to-do Indiana family of Quaker, abolitionist heritage, went off to graduate study at Oxford and immediately found his way to Toynbee Hall, the movement for workers' education, and Fabian politics.[2]

For many in this cohort, including the social democrats, the ongoing social question was joined to the social and cultural issues that had emerged in the Progressive Era. In the liberal exceptionalist context, in which classes were understood as groups, it was easy for many social scientists to subsume the older exceptionalist problem of equality under the liberal problem of pluralist order. Both Thomas and Park considered the problems of industrial labor and class conflict less central than the problems of race, ethnicity, and deviance. Thomas stood close to the Progressive center in his views on labor and the reform of capitalism, Park to the right of center. Thomas always included the labor problem and capitalism in his description of the crisis of

1 The chief biographical sources on Thomas are Fred J. Baker, "The Life Histories of W. I. Thomas and Robert E. Park," *AJS*, 79 (September 1973): 243–60, and Morris Janowitz, "Introduction," *On Social Organization and Social Personality*, by William I. Thomas (Chicago: University of Chicago Press, 1966), vii–lviii. Additional primary source material is available in Herbert Blumer, *An Appraisal of Thomas and Znaniecki's "The Polish Peasant in Europe and America"* (New York: Social Science Research Council, 1939), 103–6, and Winifred Raushenbush, *Robert E. Park: Biography of a Sociologist* (Durham, N.C.: Duke University Press, 1979), chap. 8. There is suggestive material about Thomas' early milieu in *The Holston Methodist*, a newspaper co-edited by his father, the Reverend Thaddeus Peter Thomas, from roughly 1872–5; and in Lucile Deaderick, ed., *Heart of the Valley: A History of Knoxville, Tennessee* (Knoxville: East Tennessee Historical Society, 1976). Park is well served by an insightful biography, Fred H. Matthews, *Quest for an American Sociology: Robert E. Park and the Chicago School* (Montreal: McGill-Queen's University Press, 1977). See also Baker, "Life Histories"; Robert E. Park, "An Autobiographical Note," in *Race and Culture*, ed. Everett C. Hughes et al. (Glencoe, Ill.: Free Press, 1950), v–ix; and Raushenbush, *Robert E. Park*.

2 The only published biographical source on Bentley is Sidney Ratner, "A. F. Bentley's Inquiries into the Behavioral Sciences and the Theory of Scientific Inquiry," *British Journal of Sociology*, 8 (March 1957): 40–58. Ratner can be supplemented by Bentley's brief "Epilogue" to *Life, Language, Law: Essays in Honor of Arthur F. Bentley*, ed. Richard W. Taylor (Yellow Springs, Ohio: Antioch Press, 1957), 210–13. On Bentley's father see the Charles F. Bentley Papers, Lilly Library, Indiana University. On Beard there is an informative biography, Ellen Nore, *Charles A. Beard: An Intellectual Biography* (Carbondale: Southern Illinois University Press, 1983), and, among several accounts of those who knew him, Mary R. Beard, *The Making of Charles A. Beard* (New York: Exposition Press, 1955).

modern American society; Park always tried to justify the capitalist order. But both subordinated issues of equality to those of pluralism.

The experiences the late Progressive social scientists shared with their predecessors were filtered through a new historical mesh, woven of professionalism, urbanization, and political crisis, and created a new temper, more skeptical, impatient, and iconoclastic. To begin with the professional context, the late Progressives were products of the new graduate programs of the 1890s and early twentieth century, programs that enforced a specialized focus, scientific aim, and academic orientation. Once the academic career was established, it began to attract and reward people whose deepest allegiance was not to social justice, like the preachers manqué of the Gilded Age, nor to power among men of affairs, like the more worldly Whiggish class, but to intellectual work. Mitchell was in many ways characteristic. The son of a respectable middle-class family constantly battling precarious finances, he early turned to books and the hope of a professional career. At the University of Chicago he became a star student and upon graduation "knew definitely that I had found my work in research."

Mitchell's attraction to the scientific ideal was the deepest intellectual current of his life. Raised in a tolerant Protestant household, he liked best to puncture traditional religious belief. Veblen's iconoclasm was immediately attractive to him at Chicago, and Jacques Loeb, the eloquent champion of a positivist, technological conception of science, became a lifelong idol. But there is no evidence of any political concern in his family or youth, and at Chicago, through the bitter years of economic depression and labor conflict, he was wholly taken up with his studies. He confessed that for him, "To do work well is to practice virtue." Mitchell nonetheless was strongly idealistic and gradually, after the turn of the century, his idealism took on some of the sharper contours of Veblen's socialistic vision, but these social goals were sublimated in his scientific ideal. "It is not lack of will that impedes progress, but lack of knowledge. We putter with philanthropy and coquette with reform.... What we need as a guide for all this expenditure of energy is sure knowledge of the causal interconnections between social phenomena." Science, not Progressive reform, was the need of the hour.[3]

The scientific aspiration of these professional programs now regularly attracted young people whose studies had been in science and engineering, a desirable career option for middle-class young men in the new industrial world. Economics had throughout the nineteenth century attracted trained

---

3 The chief biographical source on Mitchell is Lucy Sprague Mitchell, *Two Lives. The Story of Wesley Clair Mitchell and Myself* (New York: Simon & Schuster, 1953), chaps. 1–2, 5; pp. 183, 167, 187.

mathematicians, but reformed universities increased the pool and gave them increased access to economic careers. Irving Fisher's move from mathematics to economics at Yale in 1890 was a noteworthy beginning. By 1920, economists were remarking that more students were entering the field from a background in the exact sciences, and that they were inclined to display impatience with the lack of certainty and exactness in their new field.[4] The gap between rhetorical aspiration and reality was far greater in sociology. Cooley and Park had started college on the popular engineering track, and realized their talents lay in other directions. But F. Stuart Chapin, who graduated from Columbia College in science and engineering in 1909, had strong mathematical skills and, under the prompting of Franklin Giddings, quickly discovered their usefulness in sociology.[5]

Chapin reflects as well a certain narrowing effect of the new specialized training. Two years after graduation he had a Ph.D. degree in sociology, by which time he was already publishing manifestos on education, evolution, and the preeminence of statistical method. Chapin was quick and motivated, and he took graduate courses from James Harvey Robinson in the new history and Franz Boas in anthropology, as well as from Giddings. The more extended and roundabout training of the earlier generations in America and Germany, with its path through history and philosophy, was not necessarily more thorough. But the professional apparatus seemed to lend an inflated authority to increasingly specialized and sometimes shallow learning.

Like professionalism, the social experience of the urbanizing middle class profoundly shaped the late Progressive cohort. The move from small town or farm to city had been a staple of nineteenth-century experience, and given the prominence of Columbia University, Johns Hopkins, and the University of Chicago in the new social science disciplines, a staple of social scientists' experience as well since the Gilded Age. What was new for this cohort was the experience of the Progressive Era city, with its polyglot population and loosening social standards, and even more striking, their attraction to it. Many of them came from backgrounds that prepared them in some way for a cosmopolitan urban experience.

Born in the Mississippi River town of Red Wing, Minnesota, Robert Park early befriended Scandinavian immigrants and became a skeptic in religion. At the University of Michigan he studied philology and literature, taking as his highest goal, after Goethe's Faust, the knowledge of life in all its diverse

---

4 "The Teaching of Elementary Economics: Round Table Conference," *AER*, 11, Suppl. (March 1921): 175.
5 On Chapin see Robert C. Bannister, *Sociology and Scientism: The American Quest for Objectivity, 1880–1940* (Chapel Hill: University of North Carolina Press, 1987), chap. 10.

vitality. After graduation he satisfied that desire as a newspaperman covering the city beat in Detroit, Chicago, and New York. He also thought of going into "the think business like Emerson and Carlyle" and in 1892, visiting Dewey in Ann Arbor, he stumbled into the midst of the "Thought News" project, which he enthusiastically joined. It was the appetite kindled in that project, to study "the philosophical aspects of the effects of the printed facts on the public" that sent him finally in 1898 to Harvard to study philosophy with William James. After earning a doctorate in Germany and returning to Harvard, however, James concluded that Park did not think well enough to become a philosopher.[6] Despairing of an academic appointment, he became publicity agent to the Congo Reform Association and then to Booker T. Washington at Tuskegee. For seven years Park lived mostly at Tuskegee, and "became, for all intents and purposes, for the time, a Negro, myself."[7] Living among America's lowly, yet engaged in a great social task, the ambiguous and romantic situation seemed to suit Park perfectly.

William I. Thomas met Park in 1912 at a conference on the Negro at Tuskegee and they became instant friends. "My Dear Brother in Christ," Thomas greeted him, capturing perfectly the facetious, worldly tone and sublimated idealism they shared.[8] The following year he brought Park to the University of Chicago. Thomas too had spent his childhood in the woods, but in southwestern Virginia. His first interest, he remembered, was "rifle shooting, which was the sport of the mountain people." During adolescence and college he lived in Knoxville, Tennessee, a fast-growing industrial town of the New South, where his father was a businessman and preacher in the Methodist Episcopal Church South, and where he witnessed the intense racial conflicts of the Gilded Age. Studying philology and literature at the University of Tennessee, he now took to the woods to collect Chaucerian and Shakespearean words "surviving in the speech of the mountaineers."[9] Through graduate study in Germany and his own reading he moved toward *Volkpsychologie* and anthropology, interests that ultimately led him to a degree and faculty position in sociology at Chicago. Over the years he had also traveled from religious belief to worldly skepticism.

Thomas in addition had an interest in the loosening social relations the city displayed. His work in sociology was on gender differences and sexual behavior, as well as race and ethnicity. Becoming something of a debonair, with an interest in urban lowlife, he was also a consultant to the city's vice

6 Matthews, *Quest*, 57.
7 Baker, "Life Histories," 258.
8 William I. Thomas to R. E. Park, April 23, 1912, Robert Ezra Park Papers, University of Chicago.
9 Baker, "Life Histories," 246–7.

commission and an advocate of liberalized sexual relations. Educated early in the ambiguities of America's racial and ethnic diversity, and in romantic and cosmopolitan sympathies, both Thomas and Park took to Chicago, and brought its diversity and urban character fully into social science.

The pursuit that most captured the urban spirit of these social scientists was journalism. Itself one of the new professions of the college-educated middle class, it offered a sanctioned path into the exciting and dangerous urban world.[10] Park was not alone in his attraction to journalism. After spending one year as an instructor in sociology at the University of Chicago and failing to get reappointed, Bentley spent the next thirteen years of his life as a reporter and editor in Chicago. Even Mitchell, after successfully covering a United States Steel strike for the Chicago *Tribune*, thought briefly of a journalistic career. None of this cohort were muckrakers, but muckraking shaded into urban realism, a style that explored the seamy side of life, valued "objective" facts, and affected a knowing cynicism. The uselessness of moralistic Progressive reform, the stupidity of do-gooders, and the superior realism of their corrupt enemies were daily discoveries of these men, as they were for Lincoln Steffens. Bentley's *Process of Government* in 1908 is heaped with the fruits of urban realism. If a man steps in and saves a boy from a bully we praise him for his kind heart, Bentley complained. But the same man tolerates child labor and the abuse and starvation of workers all around him.

I see the bitter draught come from the honey hive, and the sweet savors come from rancid life.... I have my doubts about the net growth of human kindness. I want to know why the mixed mass of loves and hates and wants which, we say, make up man have taken this new form of action.

The extension of this temper into academia fell harshly upon the Progressive elders of the social science disciplines, and encouraged the desire for a clean scientific sweep among some of the young professionals.[11]

Despite this resonance, the urban temper of this cohort did not fit easily into the professional academic world. At the most basic level, the conventional gentry culture of the academic professions discouraged the kind of direct contacts and sympathetic associations that were demanded by urban realism. A remarkable group of women, determined to escape conventional

---

10 See Michael Schudson, *Discovering the News: A Social History of American Newspapers* (New York: Basic, 1978), chap. 2.
11 Arthur F. Bentley, *The Process of Government*, ed. Peter Odegard (Cambridge, Mass.: Harvard University Press, 1967 [1908]), 8–9. Daniel T. Rodgers, *Contested Truths. Keywords in American Politics since Independence* (New York: Basic, 1987), chap. 6, describes the change in temper in political science marked by Bentley's book.

constraints, had entered the city, but male academics followed more slowly. In the conservative and genteel culture of political science, in particular, the oft-repeated desire for realistic study of politics was inhibited by the vulgarity and illegitimacy of American, and particularly, urban political practice. When A. Lawrence Lowell urged his colleagues to study contemporary politics firsthand, he noted pointedly that it would involve sympathy for all the actors, for all kinds of men and their activities. It is noteworthy, however, that the advice came from the assuredly Brahmin Lowell, whose own contacts were with European rather than American politicians.[12] The worldly temper of this cohort, in the persons of Bentley and Beard, for the first time made interest-group politics the center of political science.

Sociology had greater tolerance for urban exploration, but not for the kind initiated by Thomas. He admitted that his pursuit of knowledge involved "association with prostitutes, thieves and bums. It involves the possibility of being seen in places and with persons in which and with whom you are not supposed to belong ... I have met many women in many places which would be called compromising."[13] When realistic study produced some degree of advocacy, academic constraints were compounded. "I feel that my associates picture me as afflicted with periodic brain-storms – a sort of *folie circulaire*," Thomas confessed, "and are wondering how long I will remain quiescent and when I will break out again." A major outbreak occurred in the summer of 1915, when he addressed the Women's Equal Suffrage Association in Chicago and spoke in favor of enlarging access to birth control, removal of the legal status of "illegitimate birth," and the right of unmarried women to bear children. Thomas said his audience included "some of the most serious persons in Chicago" who approved his speech, but others were shocked and complained to the university.[14]

The ordeal Thomas was put through stood as warning to less hardy souls. Albion Small tried to defend him to President Henry Pratt Judson, a more narrow-minded ruler than William Rainey Harper, and Thomas tried to defend his work, but in the end, he had to back down. "I showed poor judgment in addressing this audience in this way," he wrote Small. They did not belong to the "'universe of discourse' of the more advanced public" and the university. Indeed Thomas had to remember that the university had been "particularly generous" in releasing his time for research. When he did his next book, which would likely be on prostitution, "it will be on the basis of an endowment, and I will not undertake it as a member of the University

---

12  A. Lawrence Lowell, "The Physiology of Politics," *APSR*, 4 (February 1910): 9.
13  "Thomas Tells His Own Story," *Chicago Herald*, April 22, 1918, pp. 1, 4.
14  William I. Thomas to Albion Small, June 17, 1915, President's Papers, University of Chicago.

without a detailed exposition of the plan and the cordial approval of the University."[15] When contact and advocacy turned to personal behavior, the university finally repudiated such cosmopolitan values. Park was a man of conservative personal and family morals. Thomas was not. In April 1918, he was arrested in a downtown hotel with a young married woman, charged with disorderly conduct, and pilloried in the press.[16] Before the charges were dismissed, the university fired him and the Chicago University Press ceased publication of his classic study, *The Polish Peasant in Europe and America*, with just two of its five volumes in print.

Thomas' case is the most dramatic instance of the conflict between the advanced temper of this new cohort and academic constraints. Beard, as we shall see, left Columbia and a regular academic position in protest at wartime political repression. Bentley turned to journalism only after failing to secure reappointment at Chicago, a failure his friend attributed to Chicago's political and intellectual timidity.[17] If Bentley, Beard, and Thomas suffered truncated academic careers, Park left voluntarily. The University of Chicago was a twenty-year interlude for Park and he returned in 1933 to the environs of Tuskegee, where he spent his last active years.

The constraints of academia, however, were not unique. Journalism allowed wide contact with the city, but capitalist owners and a mass readership imposed heavy restraints as well. Journalism was an attraction and for some a haven, but not a free one. Bentley felt increasingly frustrated by his editorial writing and as soon as he came into an inheritance, he became a gentleman Indiana farmer and independent scholar. The truth is, this cohort, among the most creative in the annals of American social science, found itself ill at ease or unwanted in academia, yet not altogether happy or secure outside it. Mitchell was a thoroughly academic man, but most of them could have answered to Small's astute remark about Bentley, that he was "at home" neither among scholars nor on the street. "He rather cultivates the attitude of an amused analyzer of the whole process, while he is gravely discharging his vocational function within the process."[18]

The ambivalent role academic professionalism played in the life of this cohort echoed the more profound ambivalence of the city itself. Their temperament was not entirely formed by attraction to the city. Most of these

15 William I. Thomas to Albion Small, June 23, 1915, President's Papers. See also Henry Pratt Judson to Albion Small, June 19, 1915; William I. Thomas to Albion Small, July 5, 1915, President's Papers.
16 "Thomas Tells His Own Story."
17 Sidney Sherwood to A. F. Bentley, August 3, 1896, Arthur F. Bentley Papers, Indiana University.
18 Albion Small, "Review of Arthur F. Bentley, *The Process of Government*," *AJS*, 13 (March 1908): 698.

social scientists came to it as adults, from small towns and farms, and from homes of Anglo-Saxon respectability and sometimes religious conservatism. As we shall see in their theoretical work, their fascination with the city and its diversity was fueled by repulsion as well as attraction. Their sympathies were often limited by respectable norms and the fears they generated. Each of them struggled personally with contradictory impulses. Thomas found peasant cultures interesting but he found the Poles in America "very repulsive."[19] Park lamented the disorder of the city even as he praised it. When released from academia, he and Beard followed Bentley into the countryside.

The stress of conflicting sexual standards caused special havoc in this cohort. One of Bentley's earliest concerns was the problem of social control of individual sexual impulses.[20] The subject was most central, perhaps, to Luther Lee Bernard, Chicago's match for Chapin in the category of scientific *Wunderkind*. As Robert Bannister has shown, Bernard was in his private life an obsessive sexual athlete, while in his public pronouncements, a critic of the feminist liberation and sexual license of modern society. Raised on orthodox fundamentalist Christianity in a small West Texas town and conflict-ridden home, it is no wonder that he felt in Chicago a desperate need for control.[21] Thomas endlessly sounded the same theme. Sexuality answered a legitimate need for excitement and vitality, he said, but his aim was to bring the subject, like all else in modern life, under "rational control." In the defense he wrote of his conduct in 1918, the term "efficiency" continually recurred.[22]

Control was the central theme of the science-oriented social sciences that appeared in the late Progressive period and bloomed during the 1920s. In the hands of this cohort the idea of social control took on greater insistence and harder contours, stressing objective, quantitative methods and behaviorist psychology.[23] The principal inventor of American behaviorism, John B. Watson, was a member of this cohort in psychology and his background perfectly epitomized theirs. Watson grew up in rural South Carolina under the influence of fundamentalist Christianity, and attended a Baptist college in a nearby New South mill town. The ambitious son of a broken home, he

---

19 William I. Thomas to Dorothy Swaine Thomas, "How the Polish Peasant Came About," January 1935, Archival Biographical File, University of Chicago.
20 Arthur F. Bentley, "On the Social Discredit of the Sexual," and "On Social Discredit of the Sexual (Second Attempt)" [1894], Bentley Papers.
21 Bannister, *Sociology and Scientism*, chaps. 8, 9.
22 Thomas to Small, July 5, 1915; "Thomas Tells His Own Story."
23 Bannister, *Sociology and Scientism*, has insightfully explored the themes of urbanization, sexual conflict, and control for the objectivist sociologists.

carried his demons with him to the Chicago metropolis, where he entered graduate school and suffered a nervous breakdown before finishing. Working with animals was the only activity in which he was ever really comfortable, whether in the laboratory or on the farm to which he later retreated. Behaviorism represented his revolt against orthodox religion and his unconscious reproduction of its norms; his effort to gain rigid control over the strange outer world he encountered and his own conflict-ridden inner world.[24]

Watson articulated an extreme behaviorism that denied any recognizance to consciousness in scientific psychology and taught that all mental action could be ultimately explained as reflex responses to the environment. But his more general premises were widely influential; namely, that mental life was significantly displayed in behavior and had to be measured in behavioral terms; that behavior was chiefly guided not by rational thought but by biological impulses combined with conditioning. Behaviorism promised the scientific control of life to a generation who felt their lives increasingly out of control.[25]

### Modernist historical consciousness

The urbanizing experience of the early twentieth century accentuated the late Progressives' sense of historical dislocation. The disorder of the city was a dimension of the disorder of history, and the desire for control a measure of disorientation in the changing liberal world. Thomas opened the *Polish Peasant* in 1918 with what was by then a truism of American social science: "This demand for rational control results from the increasing rapidity of social evolution."[26] With this cohort, the historical consciousness that had been forming in the Progressive Era entered a new phase. When asked to write an autobiographical statement in 1928, Thomas gave vivid witness to the distance history had opened between past and present.

24 Kerry W. Buckley, *Mechanical Man: John Broadus Watson and the Beginnings of Behaviorism* (New York: Guilford Press, 1989); Paul G. Creelan, "Watsonian Behaviorism and the Calvinist Conscience," *JHBS*, 10 (January 1974): 95–118; David Bakan, "Behaviorism and American Urbanization," *JHBS*, 2 (January 1966): 5–25.
25 Franz Samelson, "Struggle for Scientific Authority: The Reception of Watson's Behaviorism, 1913–1920," *JHBS*, 17 (July 1981): 399–425; Lucille T. Birnbaum, "John Broadus Watson and American Social Thought, 1913–1933" (Ph.D. dissertation, University of California, Berkeley, 1965).
26 William I. Thomas and Florian Znaniecki, *The Polish Peasant in Europe and America*, 2 vols. (New York: Alfred Knopf, 1927 [1918]), 1:1. This reprint is the edition most widely accessible and cited; it was printed from the original plates, although the autobiography has been moved from the middle to the end of the book.

When it is suggested to me that I review my past for sociological purposes this past seems very remote to me. The changes in ways of life have recently been so great as to separate all of us from our early years profoundly, and in my case this separation seems to be the more profound because I was born in an isolated region of old Virginia, 20 miles from the railroad, in a social environment resembling that of the 18th century, and I consequently feel that I have lived in three centuries, migrating gradually toward the higher cultural areas.

Starting from his youth "in the woods," Thomas went on, he ultimately "reached civilization."[27] In a few decades he had traversed three centuries and the whole history of America from nature to civilization. Bernard and Watson, whose origins were also rural and orthodox, could feel that the railroad to the city traversed three centuries. With the exception of Chapin, the others in this cohort from less isolated towns and more moderate Christian homes, could well feel they had traveled two. By the second decade of the century, the sense of rapid historical change and distance from the past were pervasive. In the world of this cohort, and increasingly during the 1920s, the past seems so far gone that it can be discounted altogether, and change so pervasive that it can itself become the norm. "The one thing that 'all history' really teaches," said Mitchell, "is that social conditions and social organizations are subject to a ceaseless process of change."[28]

Under the strain of this intense awareness of change, historicism itself began to decompose. One of the most striking evidences came from James Harvey Robinson in 1908 as he launched a renewed campaign for a "New History."

Let us suppose that there has been something worth saying about the deeds and progress of mankind during the past three hundred thousand years at least; let us suppose that ... a single page were devoted to each thousand years. Of the three hundred pages of our little manual the closing six or seven only would be allotted to the whole period for which records, in the ordinary sense of the word, exist, even in the scantiest and most fragmentary form.

By 1912 Robinson had found another figure to express the shortness of historical time even more vividly.

Let us imagine the whole history of mankind crowded into twelve hours, and that we are living at noon of the long human day.... For over eleven and a half hours, nothing was recorded.... At one minute before twelve Lord Bacon wrote his

---

27 Baker, "Life Histories," 246.
28 Wesley Clair Mitchell, "Social Problems and the Social Sciences," January 27, 1920, Wesley Clair Mitchell Papers, Columbia University, p. 4.

*Advancement of Learning* ... and not half a minute has elapsed since man first began to make the steam engine do his work for him.[29]

The figure was constructed on the acceleration of historical change. Progress, said Robinson, "tends to increase in rapidity with an ever accelerating tempo." He was struck by the novelty of the present. We were just at the beginning of progress, and that made us contemporaries of the ancients.

From this point of view, the historian's gaze, instead of sweeping back into remote ages when the earth was young, seems to be confined to his own epoch; Rameses II, Tiglath-Pileser, and Solomon appear practically coeval with Caesar, Constantine, Charlemagne, St. Louis, Charles V, and Victoria; [moreover] Bacon, Newton, and Darwin are but the younger contemporaries of Thales, Plato, and Aristotle. Let those pause who attempt to determine, the laws of human progress or decay. It is like trying to determine, by observing the conduct of a man of forty for a week, whether he be developing or not.

History had passed by so quickly that it was not much help in getting one's bearings. To gain perspective, one had to look not at the compressed foreground, but at the long background of humanity's prehistory in nature and forward to the prospect of future change. The new message from history, he said, is that "it was only at about one minute to twelve *that [man] came to wish to progress, and still more recently that he came to see that he can voluntarily progress, and that he has progressed.*" The historian's task lay in recounting recent progress and encouraging reform. Either way, whether the vision of rapid change led back toward nature or forward to the future, the historical past itself faded in significance.[30]

In this cohort we thus begin to see the effects of a new, modernist, historical consciousness. Modernist historical consciousness was the product of historicism itself, with its concept of history as the continual creation of

29 James H. Robinson, *History* (New York: Columbia University Press, 1908), 22; idem, *The New History: Essays Illustrating the Modern Historical Outlook* (New York: Macmillan, 1912), 239–40. Robinson picked up the figure of the clock from Lester Frank Ward, *Pure Sociology: A Treatise on the Origin and Spontaneous Development of Society*, 2d ed. (New York: Macmillan, 1907), 38–40, who in turn adapted it from Ernst Haeckel. Ward, like Haeckel, was still largely rooted in the evolutionary historicism of the nineteenth century and interpreted it to show that history was a process of slow accumulation: "the sociologist may forget the paltry littleness of each increment to civilization ... and study the monument that the race has thus created." Ward also saw, however, that in relation to geologic time, "the sociologist deals with a fresh young world. He can see it grow, and he has a perfect right not only to speculate as to the future of society but also to try to accelerate its growth."

30 Robinson, *New History*, 240, 57–8, 251. Robinson's sense of historical continuity led him to stress the gradual, cumulative character of change, but as part of the idea of continuous change, not as Ward's increments to the "monument" of "civilization." See pages 16 and 256 in *New History*, and the discussion of "process" below.

novelty. After 1870 historicism in Europe entered a period of crisis brought on by the relativistic implications of historicism, ambivalence over the character of modern society, and the accelerating tempo of historical change. While professional historians found ways to ward off the crisis and maintain allegiance to historicism, the historical consciousness of leading cultural sectors in Western Europe turned toward modernism. The past began to seem an outmoded burden and the present a moment of perpetual transition to an unknown future. Value could not be sought in the past; it had to be created at each moment of the present, at each moment of the future. According to Renato Poggioli, modernist historical consciousness rested on a sense "of belonging to an intermediate stage, to a present already distinct from the past and to a future in potentiality which will be valid only when the future is actuality." In the words of Carl Gustav Jung, "Today is a process of transition which separates itself from yesterday in order to go toward tomorrow. He who understands it, in this way, has the right to consider himself a modern." Out of this new perception of historical time, came a range of historical attitudes we have come to associate with modernist culture: rejection of the past, affirmation of the future, the dissolution of history itself into a timeless existence, whether as primitive nature, abstract, spatial forms, perpetual transition, or perpetual self-creation.[31]

By the late Progressive period, expressions of this new sense of historical time appeared in the United States. One of the most apt came from a young institutional economist, Walton H. Hamilton, in 1916. In America, he said, "Change was everywhere," in society, economy, population, and culture. "The onward tide of the highly dynamic forces ... were drawing industrial society into an unknown future.... The mark of reality seemed much more legible in tendency than in existing fact. The less important 'being' was swallowed up in the more important 'becoming.'" Contemporary America, he concluded, was in "perpetual transition."[32]

Perhaps the most influential expression of modernist historical consciousness came from John Dewey. Although Dewey's social psychology and pragmatist philosophy had begun to affect a few social scientists earlier, it is during the second decade of the century that his ideas were widely cited and

---

31 Renato Poggioli, *The Theory of the Avant-Garde* (Cambridge, Mass.: Harvard University Press, 1968), especially pp. 66–7, 72–4, and chap. 10; Joseph Frank, "Spatial Form in Modern Literature," in *Criticism*, 2d ed., ed. Mark Schorer (New York: Harcourt Brace, 1958): 379–92; Gerald Graff, "Literary Modernism: The Ambiguous Legacy of Progress," *Social Research*, 41 (Spring 1974): 104–35.

32 Walton H. Hamilton, "The Development of Hoxie's Economics," *JPE*, 24 (November 1916): 860. Hamilton believed that this sense of historical change was responsible for Hoxie's historical vision of economics, but we will see below that Hoxie was eventually led toward a more modernist vision of "perpetual transition."

his stance often taken as examplary for American social science. Pragmatism had originally been cast as a means to knit together past and future. Now it was a tool for discarding the past and entering upon a perpetually changing future. "The influence of Darwin upon philosophy resides in his having conquered the phenomena of life for the principle of transition." He effected a "transfer of interest from the permanent to the changing." What this meant for philosophy, Dewey said, was the need to discard the whole past two thousand years of philosophical discourse, with its search for a permanent and unchanging reality. Instead philosophy must turn to the contemporary changing world and become "a method of moral and political diagnosis and prognosis."[33]

In *Creative Intelligence* (1917) he was most eloquent about his modernist reorientation to the future. "Since we live forward ... what should experience be but a future implicated in a present!" Dewey exclaimed.

To catch mind in its connexion with the entrance of the novel into the course of the world is to be on the road to see that intelligence is itself the most promising of all novelties, the revelation of the meaning of that transformation of past into future which is the reality of every present.

If Dewey now seemed willing to discard the normative force of past history, he retained its normative force as the present that was becoming the future. "The secret of success – that is, of the greatest attainable success – is for the organic response to cast in its lot with present auspicious changes to strengthen them." When Dewey's wartime exuberance passed, this note of following the lead of the present remained. *Reconstruction in Philosophy* was a more sober statement of the thesis he had set out over the previous decade. He urged "faith in the active tendencies of the day" and "the courage of intelligence to follow whither social and scientific changes direct us."[34]

Dewey's desire to tie the future to the course of present history maintained the connection of pragmatism to new liberal politics and to the normative course of American history. He called pragmatic intelligence "America's ... own implicit principle of successful action" and the means to "our salvation."[35] From the point of view of the long history we have been studying, what is most striking about the modernist sense of time is its

---

33 John Dewey, "The Influence of Darwin on Philosophy" (1910), *MW*, 4:7, 13.
34 John Dewey, "The Need for a Recovery of Philosophy" (1917), *MW*, 10:9, 47, 16; idem, *Reconstruction in Philosophy* (1920), *MW*, 12:201.
35 Dewey, "The Need for a Recovery of Philosophy," 47–8. It is noteworthy that the young socialists who, inspired by Dewey, rejected historical laws in the name of a creative future, ended by capitulating to the American present. See Mark Pittenger, "Science, Culture and the New Socialist Intellectuals before World War I," *American Studies*, 28 (Spring 1987): 73–91.

resonance with America's exceptionalist historical consciousness. If historicism ran against the grain of the nationalist ideology for most of the nineteenth century, modernism was in many ways attuned to the revised liberal exceptionalism of the twentieth century. Indeed modernism cut short the brief historicist interlude in America, quickly drawing social thinkers toward a vision of American history, past and future, as perpetual liberal change. In the idiom of modernism, qualitative historical change could disappear and exceptionalist strategies of nature continue in force.

Both the modernist experience of history as perpetual transition and the American vision of that history as perpetual liberal change were reflected in the rising saliency of the concept of process. The term has already appeared in progressive sociology, in marginal economics, and in Mitchell's "ceaseless *process* of change." According to Hannah Arendt, the idea of process emerged within historicism from the increasing recognition of history as continuity, as a series not of discrete events but of means-ends relationships, each segment of history producing the next by an orderly series of changes. As historical process, history embodied more deeply the continuity, the movement, the forces within it. Ultimately, Arendt believed, the pursuit of the deeper continuities of history resulted in events losing their meaningfulness in themselves to the process of history.[36]

Process, moreover, is the "common denominator" between nature and history, allowing both to be understood as series of ordered changes working toward some result. Hence the idea of process marked a point of convergence between the historicist effort to understand the continuous changes of history and the social scientific effort to understand history as natural evolution. The earliest American social scientists to talk about process in sociology and economics were trying to grasp an exceptionalist experience they understood as both historical and natural. The full effects of that convergence appeared when the flow of history accelerated and its parameters became uncertain. Modernist history lost its distinctiveness to the ceaseless process of change and history blended into nature. Robinson's vision of the continuity of history and prehistory, taking the process of historical change back toward the process of nature and forward to continual progress, enacted one kind of displacement of history into nature. Social scientists came to understand American history as a self-renewing natural process inhering in the character of liberal society.[37]

36 Hannah Arendt, *Between Past and Future* (New York: Viking, 1954), 61–2.
37 Ibid.; and the insightful discussion of this concept in Paul Kress, *Social Science and the Idea of Process: The Ambiguous Legacy of Arthur F. Bentley* (Urbana: University of Illinois Press, 1970). See also Max Lerner, "Social Process," in *Encyclopaedia of the Social Sciences* 1930 ed., 14:148–51; C. Wright Mills, "The Professional Ideology of Social Pathologists,"

As the name itself indicates, modernism referred to a critical stage in the evolution of modernity and to a problem in historical time. In common usage, the term has come to designate only the aesthetic response to that problem. Cultural modernists were determined to find through artistic creation and self-creation a realm of value that, lying within the transitory world, nonetheless evaded the relativity and impermanence of history. As David Hollinger has shown, the role of aesthetic "artificer" was in essential ways different from that of the scientific "knower" whose history we have been tracing. Both scientism and aestheticism, however, were responding to the crisis in historical consciousness that emerged in Western culture around the turn of the twentieth century. In the American social science traditions, where the problem of historical change was of central concern, the modernist acceleration of historical time heightened traditional anxieties and intensified the desire for control. Social scientists sought permanence and value by reconstructing transitory historical experience into natural process and by exerting rational control.[38]

If process meant a loss of significance for events in themselves, as Arendt indicated, it necessarily began to alter the realism that had reigned in American social science since the Gilded Age. The realistic search for concrete experience continued as a new reality continually presented itself for observation. In the context of building academic and scientific professions, moreover, empirical research was a likely warrant of true scientific work. Among this late Progressive cohort, anxious to dismantle the moralistic generalizations and speculative theories of their elders, empirical research into the changing facts of contemporary society was a hallmark of their new programs. Theory remained suspect. Bernard, whose talents lay in that direction and never managed a respectable piece of empirical research, felt constantly on the defensive.[39] Yet even realism began to change under the impact of modernism. As the social scientists began to see facts as process, the concrete reality they sought to grasp receded into flux. In a striking reversal of the gender conventions of realism, for example, the economist Albert B. Wolfe criticized Edward A. Ross's latest book for being "inductive and superficial," rather than searching for "deeper psychological causation." Ross, he said, "is quick as a woman in catching concrete details." A science of natural process tended to drive beneath the level of concrete facts

*AJS*, 49 (September 1943): 165–80; William F. Fine, *Progressive Evolutionism and American Sociology, 1890–1920* (Ann Arbor, Mich.: UMI Research Press, 1979), chap. 2.

38  David Hollinger, "The Knower and the Artificer," *American Quarterly*, 39 (Spring 1987): 37–55.

39  Bannister, *Sociology and Scientism*, 137.

to causal process, and render problematic what was surface or substance, concrete or abstract, male or female.[40]

The modernist conception of historical time was also influenced by new developments in anthropological theory. Historicism had been intertwined with evolutionism during the nineteenth century; now the work of Franz Boas and others challenged the fixed, unilinear model of evolutionary development. Aided as well by the disproof of the inheritance of acquired characteristics, one of the supports of the older theory, the fixed structure of evolution was dismantled. Attention turned to the particular interacting factors that produced human variety and progress, increasingly to the study of culture. The evolutionary depiction of long-term change over time began to be replaced by short-term study of the process of change. At the same time, the critical use of anthropological method begun by Veblen was developed in new ways by sociologists seeking access to urban realities.[41]

### Political crisis, 1912–1920

The gathering effects of social and economic change on historical consciousness were compounded during these years by the mounting effects of political crisis. The first American generation to find themselves in a world that was certain only of ceaseless change, they were also the first to ride that change on the troubled current of twentieth-century history. The years from about 1912 to 1920 put American social scientists on a roller-coaster of expanding idealism and bitter frustration. The combination of progressivism and war worked in a number of ways to distance Americans from their past and to strengthen the call for sciences of social control.

The first cycle of thwarted hope was precipitated by the climax and decline of Progressive reform. Between 1912 and 1914, while support for an advanced reform agenda grew stronger, conservative opposition limited legislative action, the Supreme Court abrogated Progressive legislation, and capitalist power was mobilized to repress labor, control the press, and bring pressure on the academic left. The social scientists were often part of the leftward movement and felt the sting of reaction. In 1914 AEA President John H. Gray of Minnesota, in a tone of angry frustration, issued a ringing call for social control. Sociologists like Cooley, who had denied the exist-

---

40 A. B. Wolfe, "Review of E. A. Ross, *The Outlines of Sociology*," *APSR*, 18 (August 1924): 639–40.

41 On the transformation of evolutionary theory in anthropology, see George W. Stocking, Jr., *Race, Culture and Evolution* (New York: Free Press, 1968), and *Victorian Anthropology* (New York: Free Press, 1987).

ence of true classes in America, now asserted that the American capitalist class "dominates the weaker classes in much the same way as stronger classes have always done."[42] Perhaps the surest sign of heightened ideological warfare was a return by Albion Small to his semisocialist mode. In his presidential address of 1912 Small once again accused his colleagues of failing to come to grips with capitalism and in 1913 published his most radical political statement. Written in the form of a novel, its ironic and fragmented authorial voice is a testament to Small's frustrated radical conviction, tortured ambivalence, and self-reproach.[43] The political scientists for their part gathered around the problem of judicial review: Beard's *An Economic Interpretation of the Constitution* (1913) was only part of a wider professional protest.[44] The failure of Progressive action to keep pace with economic and social change accentuated the desire to throw over the useless past and establish social control.

The outbreak of war in Europe in 1914 turned American attention away from domestic reform and sealed the fate of progressivism. Yet most social scientists did not abandon their domestic idealism but invested it in the war. Whether like John Dewey, they felt the need to "connect conscience" with the forces that were moving America into war, or whether caught up in the Allied cause and crusade to make the world safe for democracy, social scientists hoped that the nationalist sentiment, expansion of government powers, and manifest disorder of the Western world would lead to a fundamental "reconstruction" of American as well as European society after the war. Irving Fisher's address to the economists in 1919 was a good measure of the radicalizing effect of the war on social-scientific reform sentiment. A marginalist who had been right of center, he now anticipated "the impending world-reconstruction," urged heavy inheritance taxes, mixed public-private control of large corporations, and extensive social insurance programs.[45] But the end of the war produced no surge of domestic

---

42 John H. Gray, "Economics and the Law," *AER*, 5, Suppl. (March 1915): 3–23; Charles H. Cooley, "The Institutional Character of Pecuniary Valuation," *AJS*, 18 (January 1913): 554–5.

43 Albion Small, "The Present Outlook of Social Science," *PPASS*, 7 (1912): 34–7; idem, *Between Eras: From Capitalism to Democracy* (Chicago: Victor W. Bruder, 1913).

44 Frank J. Goodnow, *Social Reform and the Constitution* (New York: Macmillan, 1911); Roscoe Pound, "Courts and Legislation," *APSR*, 7 (August 1913): 361–83; Horace A. Davis, "Annulment of Legislation by the Supreme Court," *APSR*, 7 (November 1913): 541–87; Charles A. Beard, *The Supreme Court and the Constitution* (New York: Macmillan, 1912).

45 John Dewey, "Conscience and Compulsion" (1917), *MW*, 10:264; Irving Fisher, "Economics in Public Service," *AER*, 9, Suppl. (March 1919): 5–21. For a representative sample of the "reconstruction" literature, see Frederick A. Cleveland and Joseph Schafer, eds., *Democracy in Reconstruction* (Boston: Houghton Mifflin, 1919).

reform; instead it loosed reactionary movements against labor, internationalism, and expanded national power. The social scientists could only wonder at how little they understood the turnings of history and how little they mattered in them. In 1920 some economists asked themselves "why the teaching of economics has had so little influence upon public life."[46]

Not only the failure of domestic reform, but the growing ideological polarization profoundly disturbed these social scientists. Amid repeated evidence that social opinion, inside academia as without, was governed by ideology rather than science, they began to talk of the need for a harder science, a science of facts and numbers that could moderate or dispel the pervasive irrational conflicts of political life. Mitchell, for example, early recognized the moral animus driving the work of his teacher, J. Laurence Laughlin, and soon discovered that Veblen's work too was widely dismissed as biased speculation. The only answer, Mitchell concluded, was quantitative facts.

I want to *prove* things as nearly as may be and proof means usually an appeal to the facts – facts recorded in the best cases in statistical form. To write books of assertion or shrewd observation, won't convince people who have been in the habit of asserting other things or seeing things in a different perspective.... This feeling has been growing upon me as I have realized how slight an impression Veblen's work has made upon other economists. To me he seems straight and clear; but when others contest his conclusions I often find that the only real answer lies in doing a lot of work with statistics.

When the United States Commission on Industrial Relations issued separate and opposed reports from its expert labor, business, and public members, Mitchell was led to a deeper recognition of the intractability of social conflict. There was no way to resolve "the class war" on the basis of science, but conflicting assertions could be reduced in some degree to questions of fact that science could resolve.[47]

So too the awful violence of the war, its glaring denial of modern progress, exposed the inadequacy of social science. "It would perhaps be an exaggeration to say that the European war ... has rendered every text in social science thus far published out of date," an economist declared, "but it would not be a very great exaggeration." For the first time social scientists recognized that the advance of the natural sciences was not an unmitigated

---

46 "The Teaching of Elementary Economics," 171. John A. Thompson, *Reformers and War: American Progressive Publicists and the First World War* (Cambridge University Press, 1987), provides a close analysis of the disillusionment provoked by the end of progressivism and the course of the war.
47 L. S. Mitchell, *Two Lives*, 186, 176; Wesley Clair Mitchell, "Social Progress and Social Science," September 6, 1915, Mitchell Papers.

good. In the form of technology, it had "enormously complicated the industrial and political problem," Dewey said in 1917, and created devastating weapons of destruction. "We apparently do not control them; they control us and wreak their vengeance upon us." Still, Dewey concluded, "The recourse of a courageous humanity is to press forward ... until we have a control of human nature comparable to our control of physical nature." The possibility that such control could produce equally devastating results did not reach the surface of Dewey's text. What did appear, and was echoed by many of his readers, was his assertion that there was no such thing as assured progress, progress in the "wholesale" form of evolutionary law or improving human nature. There was only the possibility of "retail" progress, to be bought in small quantities by individual human effort.[48]

One reflection of the shock of wartime violence and the doubts it threw upon historical progress was the increasing currency of irrationalist psychologies. The disclosure of brute human nature in the midst of twentieth-century progress probably accounts for the rush of so many social scientists to behaviorism and Freudian psychology. Despite the different conceptions of rationality and conscious experience these two psychologies formulated, they were quickly coupled by their emphasis on biological, subrational factors in human behavior. Indeed the war revived interest in eugenics, for much the same reasons: A biological disease required a biological cure. In the period of rising Progressive reform, Chapin looked to education to reform "the lagging mores," even though that would take a very long time. In 1915, however, the European war led him to doubt the sufficiency of education. "Moral conduct is often but a thin veneer which covers up unsuspected depths of primitive brutishness and crude impulse." Only natural selection could permanently improve the moral quality of the racial stock, and that meant eugenics. By 1919 things were no better, indeed class conflict had sent America into a state of "social confusion, self-deceit, hypocrisy and pessimism" almost as severe as that in Germany, and Chapin now reformulated his worries in the language of Freudian psychology.[49]

48 A. B. Wolfe, "Review of W. H. Hamilton, *Current Economic Problems*," *AER*, 7 (March 1917): 106; John Dewey, "The Need for Social Psychology" (1917), *MW*, 10:62–3; idem, "Progress" (1916), ibid., 234–43.

49 F. Stuart Chapin, "Education and the Mores," in *Studies in History, Economics and Public Law, Columbia University*, 43 (1911): 103; idem, "Moral Progress," *Popular Science*, 86 (May 1915): 467; idem, "Democracy and Class Relations," *PPASS*, 14 (1919): 100–10. The wartime resurgence and convergence of psychoanalysis, behaviorism, and eugenics around the power of biology is by-passed by the principal secondary works: Birnbaum, "Behaviorism"; Nathan G. Hale, Jr., *Freud and the Americans. The Beginnings of Psychoanalysis in the United States, 1876–1917* (New York: Oxford University Press, 1971); Mark H. Haller, *Eugenics: Hereditarian Attitudes in American Thought* (New Brunswick, N.J.: Rutgers University Press, 1963).

Minus the turn to psychoanalysis, Mitchell followed a similar path. As he wrote his English friend Graham Wallas in 1915, he was shocked how the war had diverted interest from constructive problems "and thrown us back into a muddle of feeling strongly about issues which we have not the capacity to think out clearly." His instinctive response to this resurgence of irrationality was to reach for more powerful tools of social control. Although Wallas worried that the war would bring encouragement to the eugenicists, Mitchell countered that he hoped the war would break down "the old taboos.... I should hail it as a fine result if England suddenly made up her mind to replenish her wasted population from the best breeding stock that she has left."[50]

The negative effects of Progressive failure and war, their accentuation of anxiety and irrationality, and their exposure of the inadequacy of social science are most strikingly exemplified by W. I. Thomas. Thomas had early adopted a scientific idiom, hoping to find in anthropology "the laws of social physics," and at Chicago he worked extensively with Jacques Loeb. As someone who prided himself on lack of interest in philosophy, however, Thomas barely mentioned his scientific premises in his work. Moreover, he was at first confident of American progress. In 1907 he addressed the growing labor, ethnic, and racial problems in America, made worldwide by colonialism and the rise of Japan – "The oriental world is large enough to overwhelm us and smite us with a sword which we have put into his hands." But Thomas was sure that America was safe from the kind of decline that had afflicted the Roman Empire. "We are safe because we have the habit of seeking change." His confidence remained intact until his ordeal at Chicago in 1915 and World War I.[51]

An altogether new note appeared in Thomas' work in 1917. Smarting from the public clamor that had greeted his views on sexuality, he sarcastically dismissed the primitive moralism of Christianity, Progressive reform, and patriotism. "Society is in a hypnoidal state with lucid intervals." For the first time he articulated the self-conscious scientism that would appear the following year in the long and influential methodological introduction to the *Polish Peasant*. In the face of so much obscurantism, he was no longer confident that America would change. Change came from the individual, but society repressed the individual. Change came from the "creative man" who, adapting to change, created "norms of a superior social value." Change in

50 Graham Wallas to W. C. Mitchell, January 4, 1915, and W. C. Mitchell to Graham Wallas, February 3, 1915, Mitchell Papers.
51 Baker, "Life Histories," 248; William I. Thomas, "The Scope and Method of Folk-Psychology," *AJS*, 1 (January 1896): 434, 440–1; idem, "The Significance of the Orient for the Occident," *PPASS*, 2 (1907): 119, 122.

the modern world came above all from science, a science which would disturb all norms and eventually establish "the most general and universal norms, namely scientific laws." Behind Thomas' personal sense of urgency was the present world crisis, and the feeling that historical change had erased the signposts of the past. "We live in an entirely new world, unique, without parallel in history." The only thing that can help us, he said, is a science of social control. "Then we can establish any attitudes and values whatever." Thomas emerged from the war sounding like a technocratic utopian.[52]

Anxiety and disillusion formed only one path to sciences of control and only one side of the political experience of these years. The other side, often alternating and coexisting in the same people, was a positive faith in social science and in American nationalism. Most social scientists were quickly caught up in wartime patriotism. Deploring the nationalist bias of German academics and the emotional excess of the American masses, they all the while displayed both themselves. The heightened wartime patriotism was soon augmented by the powerful world position America assumed at war's end. Even when it took the form of calls for greater internationalism and critiques of the "return to normalcy," a resurgent American nationalism raised social scientists' expectations and gave them confidence in their world-historical task.

They also had some reason during these years to feel confidence in their scientific abilities. Social scientists had increasingly participated as experts in the Progressive movement and their scientific expertise was given a considerable boost by the war. Economists moved into the new statistical agencies that coordinated the war effort; political scientists followed up on the prewar beachhead they had established in Washington as experts in budgeting and administration, or worked on propaganda and international organization. Historians were called in particularly to the propaganda effort and planning for peace negotiations. Sociologists, when not attached to these enterprises, could, like Chapin, put their local knowledge to use in community organization.[53]

Mitchell is the best example of the confident turn to science. By January 1920, he was still keenly aware of the problems America faced, but the note of impatience was gone. What inspired him was in part the patriotic

52 William I. Thomas, "The Persistence of Primary-group Norms in Present-day Society and Their Influence in Our Educational System," in *Suggestions of Modern Science Concerning Education*, by Herbert S. Jennings et al. (New York: Macmillan, 1917), 191–2, 179–80, 185, 188–9, 196, 107.

53 Carol Gruber, *Mars and Minerva: World War I and the Uses of the Higher Learning in America* (Baton Rouge: Louisiana State University Press, 1975); Paul B. Cook, *Academicians in Government from Roosevelt to Roosevelt* (New York: Garland, 1982), 80–92, 172–5.

nationalism of America's successful war effort. "The spirit of our forefathers has not been lost and we shall recover from our recent fit of hysteria and presently begin work in earnest." He was impressed with the strengths of American industry: "Our own country is in a more favorable position than any other great power in the world."

Even more, Mitchell was hopeful that his ambitions for science could be fulfilled. As he knew from personal experience, "The war gave a powerful impetus to statistical work in Washington." Moreover, he had personal experience of increasing private opportunities for statistical work. Mitchell, along with Edwin F. Gay, dean of the Harvard Business School and director of the wartime statistical service, was about to launch the National Bureau of Economic Research, funded by the Russell Sage Foundation. "It begins to look indeed, as if economic research might soon come to rival medical research as a fashionable beneficiary of philanthropy." Mitchell put on the bureau's board of directors representatives from business, labor, and academia, from the Socialist League for Industrial Democracy to the American Bankers Association, in the hope of making "exact and impartial investigations." He emerged from the war with a deeper awareness of the difficulties involved, but nonetheless convinced that statistics provided a royal road to economic science and social control.[54]

The final dimension of the political experience of these years that shaped the transformation of American social science was the suppression of dissent. The wartime reaction removed from academia a number of adventurous individual voices, like that of Charles Beard. Beard resigned from Columbia, he recalled bitterly, after "a very humiliating inquisition" from the board of trustees, "in the presence of three or four of my colleagues ... who seemed to think the process quite right and normal." Three years later he had to resign as director of the New York Bureau of Municipal Research when the Carnegie Foundation informed the bureau's trustees that no money would be forthcoming as long as he remained. "So I retired to agriculture in Connecticut." Beard's remained a formidable voice, but his fate stigmatized even his mild radicalism and his influence within the academy was curtailed.[55]

Radical women who had established footholds in the women's colleges

---

54 Wesley Clair Mitchell, "Social Problems and the Social Sciences," January 27, 1920, Mitchell Papers, pp. 3, 7, 11, 14, 16; Herbert Heaton, *A Scholar in Action, Edwin F. Gay* (Cambridge, Mass.: Harvard University Press, 1952); David M. Grossman, "American Foundations and the Support of Economic Research, 1913–29," *Minerva*, 20 (Spring–Summer 1982): 59–82.

55 Social Science Research Council, Hanover Conference, 1926, transcript, p. 499, Charles E. Merriam Papers, University of Chicago.

were also among the casualties. At Wellesley, Katherine Coman and Emily Balch had created a respected social science program with strong reformist leanings before the war. Always under careful watch for her political views, Balch was forced out of Wellesley when she became a pacifist during the war, and the social science program was virtually closed down for a decade. The Wharton School at the University of Pennsylvania suffered a similar fate. During the Progressive period Patten had continued his uneven support of the social welfare agenda and brought a number of activists to his faculty. The economist Scott Nearing, with his aggressive support of child-labor legislation and increasingly pointed attacks on the city's inequality of wealth roused the opposition of business interests, particularly those with financial ties to the university. In 1915, aided by the distraction of ethnic and religious hostilities and fundamentalist revivalism, the trustees fired Nearing and then pressured Patten and his young Turks into retirement or departure. When the war was over, Wharton was free to turn its attention wholly to "business science."[56]

Within this pruned academic field, the heterodox political impulses that survived were channeled into the new disciplinary programs. The late Progressive cohort had themselves been moved by heterodox political as well as intellectual impulses. In economics the new institutionalists were self-consciously left of the neoclassical mainstream. So too the pioneer analysts of group politics stood on the left of traditional political science. In sociology, Small and Giddings spanned the Progressive mainstream of the profession, so the new movements came from a number of points on the political spectrum, including the cultural radicalism and political quietism of Park and Thomas.

### New concepts of science

In addition to history and politics, these social scientists were influenced by new theories of science. Committed at the outset to developing social sciences, and by 1920 urgently determined to create real sciences, they paid greater attention to the philosophers and scientists who were revising positivism. Karl Pearson's *Grammar of Science*, reissued in 1911, was one exemplary text in the reconstruction of positivism. Although his work supported the traditional Baconian emphasis on empirical method, Pearson reexamined the implications of the positivist determination to derive knowl-

56 Mary Jo Deegan, "Sociology at Wellesley College: 1900–1919," *JHS*, 5 (Spring 1983): 91–117; Steven A. Sass, *The Pragmatic Imagination: A History of the Wharton School, 1881–1981* (Philadelphia: University of Pennsylvania Press, 1982), chap. 4.

edge only from phenomenal experience. Auguste Comte, Herbert Spencer, and their disciples had believed it possible to extrapolate synthetic systems of knowledge from science. They had often assumed that the lawlike regularities they found existed in nature and operated by natural necessity. As against this "systematic" positivism, Pearson, following in part the lead of Ernst Mach, outlined a "critical" positivism that more rigorously dispelled metaphysics.[57]

The truths of science were not mirror representations of reality, Pearson said, but conceptions and propositions formed from sense-experience. Their truth was a product of their universality, and that in turn a product of the universality of normal human sense organs and the logical mental process. Hence science consisted only in its method of tested observation and logic. Its characteristic products were laws of cause and effect, but such laws were only statements of phenomenal sequence and their recurrence a matter only of probability. Moreover, science produced laws for pragmatic reasons. Science was "an economy of thought" to expedite activity, a brief "formula" that aided "forethought." Still, despite this philosophical pruning, science remained for Pearson the only avenue to "genuine knowledge" of the universe. Constructed of bits of truly observed and logically arranged phenomenal experience, it had the only guarantee there was of truth. Besides reaffirming the privileged position of science, Pearson's work also reinforced the behavioristic tendency of the new social sciences. Pearson assumed that social science would consist of statistical description of the measurable characteristics of aggregates of individuals. As we have seen, Giddings quickly picked up on that assumption and by 1920 he had renamed his sociology "pluralistic behaviorism."[58]

The other influence we find at work on the understanding of science was pragmatism, particularly the work of Dewey. Pragmatism is today understood to deny that there is any privileged form of knowledge. Knowledge is socially constructed and its validity determined by its usefulness to human purposes, purposes that are plural and changing. If science is defined by its method, it is not because that method provides special access to phenomenal experience, but because that method leads to practical knowing in the world and is sustained by a socially organized world of experience. As Stephen Toulmin has suggested, the logical outcome of Dewey's radical rejection of fixed truths was to turn the philosopher toward exploration of "the rational

---

57 Maurice H. Mandelbaum, *History, Man, and Reason: A Study in Nineteenth Century Thought* (Baltimore: Johns Hopkins University Press, 1971), 10–20.
58 Karl Pearson, *The Grammar of Science*, 3d ed. (London: Adam and Charles Black, 1911), 77–8, 110; Franklin H. Giddings, "Further Inquiries of Sociology," *PPASS*, 15 (1920): 60–7.

functions, methods of argument and criteria of judgment relevant to practical argumentation" in the various fields of human knowledge. But Dewey never fully entered upon that field. In most of his work, the method of natural science appears explicitly or implicitly as the model for all kinds of knowing. If natural science was not a privileged form of knowledge, it "set a standard for knowing."[59]

It was often unclear in Dewey's work whether he was urging all fields of knowledge to adopt the abstracting, generalizing, quantitative method of natural science, or so reducing the method of natural science to generic inquiry that all the distinctive approaches to knowledge could be included within its terms. He was, for example, intrigued by Veblen's model of evolutionary analysis, and in 1902 outlined a conception of knowledge that would encompass both natural scientific and historical method. Although historical method sought the causes of unique rather than general events, he said, it provided causal insight into the genesis of events similar to that of natural science, by isolating a single common factor at the origins of a historical phenomenon, and using the complicating processes of history as an analogue to controlled experiment. Dewey himself used genetic analysis as a critical tool to expose the irrelevance of past ideas to present needs. His account of the origins of philosophy, he admitted in *Reconstruction*, "has been given with malice prepense. It seems to me that this genetic method of approach is a more effective way of undermining this type of philosophic theorizing than any attempt at logical refutation could be." Genetic analysis appeared to be a propaedeutic to scientific work rather than scientific method itself.[60]

Dewey continued to urge the model of natural science. "Only when nature is regarded as mechanical [can it be] subdued to human purpose." Only "when qualities were subordinated to quantitative and mathematical relationships" did they become manageable. Although he criticized the extreme behaviorism that insisted on translating mental into physical terms, he endorsed the broader "behavioristic movement" in social psychology, for as Condorcet understood, "social phenomena are of a kind which demand statistical mathematics."[61] As the humanities and positivistic sciences pulled

59 Stephen Toulmin, "Introduction," to *The Quest for Certainty* (1929), by John Dewey, *LW*, 4:xxi; John Dewey, *LW*, 4:172. See also Richard Rorty, "Dewey's Metaphysics," in *Consequences of Pragmatism: Essays, 1972–1980* (Minneapolis: University of Minnesota Press, 1982), 72–89.
60 John Dewey, "The Evolutionary Method as Applied to Morality" (1902), *MW*, 2:3–38, particularly 7–11; idem, *Reconstruction in Philosophy*, 93.
61 Dewey, *Reconstruction in Philosophy*, 120; idem, "The Need for Social Psychology," 57.

apart, Dewey became more aware of the sharp difference between the abstracting, generalizing method of natural science and the sympathetic observation of concrete particulars required in the moral and practical use of knowledge. But he continued to rely on the concrete social problem to which inquiry is addressed and the social purpose for which it is addressed to draw together these two kinds of knowledge.[62]

The advancing authority of science, with its model of generalized, abstract knowledge, had left historical knowledge without a firm legitimation. The historicist crisis generated efforts to explain the character of historical knowledge, particularly among historians and philosophers in the German-speaking world. Friedrich Dilthey developed hermeneutic theory and the concept of *Verstehen* as a distinctive mode of historical understanding. Wilhelm Windelband and Heinrich Rickert characterized history by its individualizing logic, and Max Weber, following their lead, showed how to construct a historical social science. Faced by the growing distance between present and past that historicism had opened up, these theorists offered means of understanding the past and permitting the twentieth century to reorient itself in historical time. Dewey's pragmatic premises could lead to Dilthey's hermeneutic conclusions, as James Kloppenberg has shown, but Dewey himself did not follow them out in that historicist direction. Intent upon unities, wedded to the promise of control offered most forcefully by the positivist model of natural science, and firm in his belief that American society contained the seed of a democratic future, Dewey largely avoided the problem of how the historical world, as a specifically *historical* world, could be understood.[63]

Dewey thus left social scientists on an indeterminate pragmatic ground, on which they could move in a variety of directions. Robert F. Hoxie, while working under the influence of Veblen, used Dewey's legitimation of genetic analysis to develop a historical method. Mitchell, Bentley, and Park used pragmatism to develop heterodox but still positivist conceptions of social science. For most social scientists of this period, pragmatism appears as a more superficial influence, reinforcing the relativistic lessons of the eco-

---

62 Dewey, *Reconstruction in Philosophy*, 179.
63 James T. Kloppenberg, *Uncertain Victory: Social Democracy and Progressivism in European and American Thought, 1870–1920* (New York: Oxford University Press, 1986), 101, emphasizes the "muted harmonies" between Dewey and Wilhelm Dilthey. Kloppenberg argues that they shared a radical theory of knowledge, a theory that "entailed" historicism and "logically culminates in a hermeneutics." However, Dewey's mechanistic conception of science as control was at odds with the hermeneutical sensibility and turned much of his influence in a different direction. See David Hollinger, "The Problem of Pragmatism in American History," *JAH*, 67 (June 1980): 88–107.

nomic interpretation of history and the call for a "policy of opportunism" in social reform.[64] The upshot of the new theories of science, pragmatist and positivist, was to encourage the effort to turn the social sciences into genuine sciences of social control, while leading the more thoughtful social scientists to examine how natural scientific methods could be applied to the historical field of social experience.

### Bentley and Beard's political science

In political science the most innovative members of the late Progressive cohort were Arthur Bentley and Charles Beard, but in comparison to their counterparts in economics and sociology, they held relatively marginal places in their discipline. Bentley was already an academic outcast when his book was published, and his ideas made their way tangentially and slowly into political science. Beard, though an important figure in the discipline, produced his most original and important work in historiography and increasingly influenced historians rather than political scientists. In the more conservative ranks of political science, the iconoclastic temper of this cohort had less appeal. Yet Bentley's *The Process of Government* (1908) was not only the first major work in the new style, but the work with the widest range of influence.

### *Bentley's interest-group politics*

Bentley himself came at politics sideways, with no academic background in political science. He was trained first as an economist and developed many of his ideas while teaching sociology under Albion Small. The most immediately striking feature of his book was its attack on just about everyone. The political science tradition was pronounced "dead," and hardly rated a serious critique. But nearly every major figure in sociology sustained a blow. There was "the utter uselessness" of Small's theory for anything "except verbiage"; Giddings' consciousness of kind appeared as a "bare tautology"; Pearson's school of biological sociology had no warrant for assuming that "lumps of mental or moral qualities can be compared as individual possessions, and can be inherited as such." Nor could Giddings or any of the theorists of social progress justify their belief that ideas or ideals or self-consciousness were more powerful in the modern than in the ancient world. The elaborate schemes of social evolutionary categories they had constructed to sustain that progressive conclusion had to fall along with it.[65]

---

64 For example, Goodnow, *Social Reform and the Constitution*, 3–4.
65 Bentley, *The Process of Government*, 162, 35–7, 100n., 106, 128–36.

Already spurned by academia, Bentley burned his bridges. He had managed to get his book published by the University of Chicago Press without Small reading the manuscript, although unlike his colleagues, Small responded to the intellectual challenge seriously, if feebly.[66] The subterranean impact of Bentley's critique and his positive ideas, however, were soon apparent.

Bentley's own starting point was economics. "My interest in politics is not primary," he said, "but derived from my interest in the economic life."[67] The key to that economic interest, and to Bentley's mind, is its simultaneous drive toward the concrete and the abstract, the realism of fact and process. Bentley started out in historical economics, as a student of Richard T. Ely at Johns Hopkins, and he had the historical economist's interest in capturing the concrete particulars of economic experience. His first work set out to understand the Populists' complaints by closely examining the history of a Nebraska township. "Where the figures are on a very large scale, all sense of the actual economic life of the individual is lost." He discovered that only the original settlers who purchased land at cheap prices could make an adequate profit. The rising price of land was not a measure of its profitability, but of the demand for land, and that in turn was fed by traditional ideas, not economic reality. Bentley learned the generic lesson of historical economics: One needed to study the whole historical field to understand human actions, even in the market. The theorist Bentley most admired in *Process* was Rudolf von Jhering, the scholar of historical jurisprudence. "The real question – the question we must face," he said, "is why the living, acting men and women change their forms of action, cease to do now what they did formerly, use their 'qualities' in some places and not in others, in short live the particular social lives they do live." It was that historical sense of changing, "particular social lives" that made Bentley so critical of the theorists who explained social activities by universal characteristics of human nature.[68]

Bentley also took from historical economics its political problem. An interest in economic inequality originally led him to study with Ely and fueled his desire to "solve the puzzle of human society." His friend Hutchins Hapgood, who studied with him in Germany, described him as "an unhappy restless soul, bitterly critical of himself for his inability to reach the heights." Hapgood recalled that

66 I draw this conclusion from evidence in K. Miller to A. F. Bentley, October 12, November 1, November 4, and December 2, 1907, Bentley Papers. Small's review of the book is in *AJS*, 13 (March 1908): 698–706.

67 Bentley, *Process of Government*, 210.

68 Arthur F. Bentley, "The Condition of the Western Farmer as Illustrated by the Economic History of a Nebraska Township," *JHUSHPS*, 11th ser., no. 7–8 (1893): 9–10; idem, *Process of Government*, 56–91, 18.

Sometime later, when he was in London, I got an eloquent letter from him about his passionate disappointment in not being able to solve the mystery of sociology. He had been wandering through the slums of London, and had seen such a mass of suffering human beings, he said, so unhappy that they didn't know they were unhappy; an objective impersonal misery that put him into a state almost of insanity.

Bentley's unhappiness with society extended across a wide sphere, as his early essay on "The Social Discredit of the Sexual" suggests. The "puzzle of human society" that he had to solve was "the opposition between the individual and society." Given to him in political and personal experience, that opposition had to be resolved in theory if a science of society were to become possible.[69]

The other side of Bentley's economic interest led to abstraction. He was attracted not only to historical economics' search for the concrete but also to Carl Menger's abstract marginalist theory. He wanted to develop a theory that would apply to social as well as to economic behavior, and he took his cue from Menger's method. "I have endeavored," Menger said, "to reduce the complex phenomena of human economic activity to the simplest elements that can still be subjected to accurate observation." Bentley apparently took the same lesson from Pearson. He set out to find the basic "units of investigation" in social science, and then *the* unit, that would be not simply the most useful in method but the simplest ontological unit of social reality. He was seeking a "phenomenal monism" that would for scientific purposes resolve social phenomena into like social units and at the same time resolve his existential opposition between individual and society.[70]

Bentley was always sure that the elemental unit was not organic society as a whole, but at first he thought it was its opposite, the ideas of individuals. Sometime after he left the university and went into newspaper work in Chicago, he reacted sharply against his former individualism and idealism. He attended Dewey's lectures while teaching and later assigned the change "to a literal-minded taking of Dewey's lecture assertions about individual-person."[71] Still Dewey seemed to take effect only later, when Bentley was rethinking his scientific problem during off hours and "all the politics of the

69 Hutchins Hapgood, *A Victorian in the Modern World* (New York: Harcourt Brace, 1939), 84, 99, 112; Arthur F. Bentley, "The Units of Investigation in the Social Sciences," *AAAPSS*, 5 (June 18, 1895): 915.
70 Carl Menger, *Principles of Economics* (New York: New York University Press, 1981 [1871]), 46–7; Bentley, "Units of Investigation"; idem, "Phenomenal Monism as the Basis for the Study of Society" [1895], Bentley Papers; Arthur F. Bentley to Albion Small, November 26, 1910, Bentley Papers.
71 Arthur F. Bentley, "Memorandum," February 8, 1941, attached to "On the Relation of the Individual to Society in the Social Sciences," November 1894, Bentley Papers.

country, so to speak, was drifting across my desk."[72] The ideas of individuals now seemed like so much self-interested "talk." The basic unit of social investigation he announced in 1908 was the activity of groups.

Drawing on the pragmatism of James and Dewey and the social psychology of Baldwin and Dewey, he defined all social phenomena as activities, and all activity as social, purposive, and situational. Activity could thus resolve all the factors that entered into social situations, including "the troublesome human soul states," into a single kind. It could also be read externally through the observational methods of science. Using a tactic Watson would adopt for conscious states, Bentley included in his framework not only "external" activities, but "potential" activities and "tendencies of activity" for those not manifest. In social life, activity was always the activity of groups, manifest and potential. The nation was composed of "groups of men, each group cutting across many others, each individual man a component part of very many groups." The ideas of individuals were pale and faulty reflections of the groups, "indeed the only reality of the ideas is their reflection of the groups." The groups were not fixed; they were composed not of individuals but of activities. All science required measurement, and groups could be measured by their numbers, intensity, and technique, and their causal relations with other groups could be traced. "When the groups are adequately stated, everything is stated," and echoing Pearson, "The complete description will mean the complete science."[73]

Bentley's group activities were the product of both abstract discussion of the nature of social reality and concrete observation of Progressive politics. For five years or so, he wrote Small, "I didn't read anything but newspapers ... I simply soaked Chicago." His subject matter was political life. "Dewey has unified experience in analyzing individual conduct, starting with it as he finds it day by day in himself and his associates. I have, or claim to have, done, or at least begun, the same thing starting with what happened politically in the United States, 1900–1908, Roosevelt being the symbol thereof." What happened politically in the United States, 1900–8, Bentley concluded, was interest-group politics. The purposive activities that formed groups were interests, he said, following the lead of Small and Ratzenhofer. The term group and the term interest were synonymous. Politics was a study of group "pressures," and in an appendix, he showed how concrete studies could be carried out. Using votes in a city referendum, the city council, and the state legislature, and matching votes to urban maps, he analyzed the group pressures at work on the issue of municipal socialism. Except for

72 Bentley, "Epilogue," 211.
73 Bentley, *Process of Government*, 191, 184–6, 204, 206, 208–9.

dealing with votes rather than land prices, and seeking the weight of various group interests instead of the weight of various factors shaping economic choice, his method was the same one he had used in his first historical study of a Nebraska township.[74]

To his readers in political science, Bentley's vision of interest-group politics was the most recognizable feature of his book, for in many respects he presented an entirely novel vision. It was, as its title declared, a vision of government as process, a term Menger too had used. There was a "limitless criss-cross of the groups" and a limitless field on which to chart them. "There are no political phenomena except group phenomena" and group phenomena were processes. Politics as process dissolved most of the familiar features of the political science tradition. In process terms, the difference between organization and function was simply a difference between longer and shorter lines of activity. History constituted one among many "lines of activity," and not the most essential. The political world, as in a modern painting, was inscribed on a flat surface.

The normative dimension of politics disappeared as well. "The society itself is nothing other than the complex of the groups that compose it." There was no such thing as the interest of society as a whole and no such thing as "the public good." All the fine rhetoric of politics were rationalizations of group interest and tools in the war of interests. There was no more telling feature of the book than the minimal attention given to administration. Administrators were part of the political process, like everyone else. They represented certain interests over against others. "There is no such thing as a totality group in government." Bentley destroyed at one stroke the traditional principles and professional goal of political science. The selfish interests, the corrupt bargains, the ceaseless play of pressure was all there was left.[75]

Yet that was not quite all there was. The process of government was a liberal process. His vision of "groups of men, each group cutting across many others, each individual man a component part of very many groups," came from the German sociologist, Georg Simmel, with whom he had briefly studied. Simmel refined the liberal view of modernity as a period of both increasing individuation and interconnection. In modern urban life, Simmel showed, individuals joined in innumerable associations and voluntary groupings, what he called "social spheres," so that each individual participated in cross-cutting affiliations. Modern individuality was born at the intersection of spheres, where individuals experienced a new kind of

74 Bentley to Small, November 26, 1910, Bentley Papers; Bentley, *Process of Government*, chap. 7 and appendix.
75 Bentley, *Process of Government*, 206, 220, 243, 219–20, 222, 354.

freedom. Class was one " social sphere" among others, one which could but did not necessarily fix or preempt participation in other spheres, although Simmel himself believed that class conflict was becoming more pronounced in modern industrial societies.[76]

Bentley used Simmel to argue that "class" was not a viable category of scientific analysis. "It would only be in a rigorous caste organization of society ... that the groups would so consolidate in separate masses of men that a classification ... would serve for all the leading purposes of investigation." Indeed, despite what the socialists say, there are no real classes "in great modern nations." No one has ever proved "that this hard grouping exists," he insisted. "The socialism that extends itself to large portions of the population is, wherever we know it, a socialism that ends in political compromises. And compromise – not in the merely logical sense, but in practical life – is the very process itself of the criss-cross groups in action." What was true of modern society generally was especially true of America. In the United States, where group process was well-developed, "groups are freely combining, dissolving, and recombining in accordance with their interest lines."[77]

For Bentley, modern society, and quintessentially modern American society, was classless, and the analysis was quickly picked up by American social scientists. Charles Horton Cooley's discussion the following year of American "open classes" and the contrasting principles of caste and class already took its cue from Bentley and Simmel, and we will see Park and Hoxie follow suit. Although Bentley never paid any special attention to the South, Cooley and Park did. It may be that the new caste system of the segregated South was the unspoken standard against which class appeared to be fluid. If so, they were repeating the Civil War experience in which capitalist labor was named "free" as against the labor of slaves.[78]

76 Progressive sociologists learned this view of modern society from Georg Simmel, *Über sociale Differenzierung* (Leipzig: Verlag von Duncker & Humblot, 1890), as well as Albion Small's partial translation, "Superiority and Subordination as Subject-Matter of Sociology," *AJS*, 2 (September 1896): 167–89, (November 1896): 392–415. Nicholas J. Spykman, *The Social Theory of Georg Simmel* (Chicago: University of Chicago Press, 1925), is a good introduction in English to the work of Simmel that interested American sociologists; for Simmel's views on class, see pp. 118–19. Simmel's term for social spheres is *Kreise*, literally "circles," but I follow P. A. Lawrence in thinking "spheres" the better rendering of his meaning: *Georg Simmel: Sociologist and European* (Sunbury-on-Thames: Thomas Nelson, 1976), 95ff.

77 Bentley, *Process of Government*, 206–8, 358–9.

78 Charles H. Cooley, *Social Organization* (New York: Scribner, 1909), pt. 4, especially pp. 248–9. Cooley's reference to "circles" is one direct mark of Simmel's influence. Bentley circulated his copy of Simmel to Giddings and Clark, at least, when he returned from Germany and probably introduced Small to his work. Franklin H. Giddings to Arthur F. Bentley, April 23, [1895], Bentley Papers.

Bentley's analysis also set out the model for American pluralist politics, along with the classlessness of American society, the mainstay of liberal exceptionalist ideology in the twentieth century. Progressive politics was a particularly good example. "Instead of conditions corresponding to class domination, we have ... the breaking down of set classes, and a technique which helps to keep free the avenues of group approach." Bentley constructed an idealized vision of American pluralism:

> In governments like that of the United States we see these manifold interests gaining representation through many thousands of officials in varying degrees of success, beating some officials down ... subsiding now and again over great areas ... rising in other spots to dominate.... Withal, it is a process which must surprise one more for the trifling proportion of physical violence involved considering the ardent nature of the struggles.

Here was, in substance if not in form, the American ocean, the freely moving atoms of American liberal society now recast as the freely acting interest groups of the American polity.[79]

What held this motion in place was "system." Bentley spent a good part of the book arguing that "the activities are all knit together in a system." All activity, he said, "is systematized. Even the simplest motion with which the physicist deals is part of a system of motion. When the geometrician gives position to a point, he admits system. In living beings there is no function that is not systematized." Process belonged to system, and "government is the process of the adjustment of a set of interest groups in a particular distinguishable group or system." Although he denied that the system had any "self-realizing capacity," he recognized that it did have a capacity to produce "the adjustment or balance of interests." In the style of marginal economic theory he described the pressures as working themselves through "to a conclusion or balance," though it was an abstract balance, never complete or final, always readjusting through "the equilibration of interests, the balancing of groups."

What resulted was order. "Order is bound to result, because order is now and order has been, where order is needed, though all the prophets be confounded." On the one hand, order was whatever resulted from group conflict. All pressures counted in the governmental balance, even if silent. "No slaves, not the worst abused of all, but help to form the government." Yet on the other hand the resulting order was the nonviolent compromising

---

79 Bentley, *Process of Government*, 358, 453. For a critique of pluralist theory, see William E. Connolly, ed., *The Bias of Pluralism* (New York: Atherton, 1969).

"equilibration of interests" of liberal society. The interests were "harmonizing themselves." We are in the familiar exceptionalist world of mirrors, in which the generic and the American, the ideal and the real, come together.[80]

Bentley's imposition of system on his analysis of process reflected not only his liberal political intentions but his desire to find permanence amid change. System is process rendered static. The seeming "turmoil" was "organized." Within the ebb and flow, the liberal contours of American society remained. Bentley's desire for permanent structure appeared strikingly in his conclusion, when he suddenly changed his metaphor from the flat surface of process to the three-dimensional world of history. What he had been doing, he said, was "formulating the backbone of history."

> We often hear it said that history must be rewritten with each generation [but that] is not true. There have been forming underneath the various dressings of history a substantial backbone and skeleton of accepted relations.... We can easily conceive of a solid structure of group relationships as they have developed in historic times becoming known to us, which must inevitably define the fundamental shapes which the history-writing that varies with the generations must take, if it is to have meaning and value at all beyond the meaning and value of the most narrowly partisan outcry.

Historicism had originally led Bentley to seek an explanation for changing, "particular social lives." Now, through a science of flux, he hoped to escape the relativity of history. The flux after all "easily" disclosed "a substantial backbone and skeleton of accepted relations," clearly the structure of liberal society that formed his categories. On the surface his vision of American politics was shockingly novel, particularly in a discipline still largely devoted to historical realism, but beneath the surface it carried a familiar message.[81]

Bentley's double vision also suffered from the instability of fact and process. His theoretical concerns led him to stress the continuous, processual nature of group activity, in which there were no discrete individuals, ideas, or groups of people apart from the process of activity itself. But his concrete understanding of economic life and American politics led him to locate social reality in palpable interest groups. His theory was intended to clear the way for an empirical science of the activities of such groups. As Kress has pointed out, by reducing groups to activity and activity to "homogeneous, continuous action," Bentley really had no basis for reintroducing discreteness or for determining "units of investigation." At least into

---

80 Bentley, *Process of Government*, 218, 285, 260–3, 287, 264–7, 271–2, 274, 301–5.
81 Kress, *Social Science and the Idea of Process*, chap. 5; Bentley, *Process of Government*, 481–2.

the 1920s, Bentley himself did not seem to recognize this problem. He maintained both his theoretical and his concrete purposes and he continued to think the former would facilitate the latter.[82]

After *The Process of Government* was published he was not satisfied that he had fully carried out his theoretical intention. He wrote Small in 1910 that "I have been busying myself exclusively of late with the problem of knowledge. Also that the possibilities of a restatement of the Dewey type of pragmatism in social terms are attractive to me." In continuing to use the term social, he feared he had not fully extirpated the widely accepted opposition between individual and society. "I must have a term which will permit social and individual to exist within it as phases, or differences of emphasis." Although he claimed to have abandoned his ontological search for a methodological one, he was still being driven by the desire to unify experience and harmonize the individual and society in a monistic theory.[83]

Within a few years, Bentley left Chicago for a rural existence in Indiana, but his experience as a small farmer and the war soon reactivated his concrete purposes as well. He became head of the Indiana Red Cross and when the fighting was over he became an active supporter of the Nonpartisan League that was forming in the north central states. In 1908, filled with the rising optimism of the Progressive movement, he had been sanguine about the success of American liberal politics, but by 1920, with Progressive reform and postwar reconstruction stymied, he moved into radical politics and a harsher vision of American society.

Bentley wrote a long analysis of the political crisis in 1920 that puts in sharp relief the concrete facts he tried to unite with his abstract theory. He intended it as a study in group process. "Its main reliance is upon facts that can be quantitatively stated.... So far as it is possible, they will be stated objectively ... in terms of groups, of their interests as related to one another." Based on a statistical analysis of the distribution of wealth, the book documented the profiteering and waste of the corporate class and urged the middle class, acting on their interest in opportunity and efficiency, to curtail their power.

It is equally striking that Bentley framed his group analysis with a historical one. The extreme concentration of wealth and power in a class of

---

82 Kress, *Social Science and the Idea of Process*, 71. Kress implies that Bentley's fundamental position was the abstract, processual one, and that his concrete proposals for group interest study were meant only as imperfect examples. Norman Jacobson, "Causality and Time in Political Process: A Speculation," *APSR*, 58 (March 1964): 15–22, discounts the concrete in Bentley's work altogether.

83 Bentley to Small, November 26, 1910, Bentley Papers; Bentley to Richard P. Baker, October 3, [1910], Bentley Papers.

large capitalists evolved only after the Civil War; it constituted a revolution in the power structure of American society and government. The middle class had to mount a "counter-revolution" to restore constitutional government. "Is it American human nature to submit? Americans will not submit." Bentley might well say that in writing as a member of the middle class for a middle-class audience, as he admitted doing, he was resorting to political "talk," using historical narrative and historical principle in its proper role of political persuasion. But he also claimed a scientific purpose. The manuscript suggests the poverty of a science of groups without an interpretive historical structure to give it meaning, a poverty Bentley implicitly recognized when he placed it within history. The history he chose, of course, was exceptionalist. He saved the liberal model of America as a land of equal opportunity by making capitalist power a temporary aberration that could be erased, a revolution against the grain of American history. His sharper view of class structure in the United States, as for Cooley, did not alter the main lines of his theory.[84]

Bentley's manuscript was turned down by every publisher to whom he submitted it. It was too radical and too long. The more sanguine liberal analysis of *The Process of Government* lived on, anticipating by a decade the behavioristic social science of Thomas, Park, and Watson; by two decades the study of contemporary interest-group politics among political scientists; and by four decades the systems analysis of pluralist politics that claimed its paternity. Bentley could see the implications of modernist liberal exceptionalism at its inception and, without any ties to historico-politics, erase the older tradition at a stroke.

### Beard's historical science of interest-group conflict

Charles Beard tried rather to modernize the inherited tradition. In 1901, while studying for a degree in history at Oxford University and mounting a project in worker education, he wrote a short history of the industrial revolution, which in many ways set the course and the problems he would encounter during his whole career. Beard placed the West within the wide stream of liberal history. That stream was in major part economic, quickened in the last one hundred and fifty years by the discoveries and inventions that fueled the industrial revolution. It was a development, however, that had concentrated the means of production in the hands of a small class of

---

84 Arthur F. Bentley, *Makers, Users, and Masters*, ed. and "Introduction" by Sidney Ratner (Syracuse, N.Y.: Syracuse University Press, 1969), chaps. 19–24, and pp. 2–3, 282. Charles H. Cooley, *Social Process* (New York: Scribner, 1918), chap. 8, again conceded that classes in America were not completely open, but the trend was toward increasing openness.

capitalists. Liberal progress also meant the advance of democracy, the movement from primitive tyranny to modern liberty in religion and politics and ultimately to collective control of the "material environment." The outcome would be "the reorganisation of industrial society upon a democratic basis."

Just what that meant, Beard did not say. Standing on what was still the open ground between radical liberalism and Fabian socialism, he quoted Ruskin, urged that economics was an ethical science, and struck a decidedly utopian note of the end of conflict in a future of economic unity and organization. Quite appropriately, the young Wesley Mitchell, in the style of Veblen, put the book down as a product of the benighted ethical school of historical economics. Beard thus enters our scene at the tail end of the Gilded Age hope for social transformation. When he moved to Columbia University to finish his graduate work in political science he learned to cast his work in the objective style of what is, rather than the prophetic prediction of the future. But the future of industrial society and its potential for democratic transformation remained his central problem.[85]

Beard also enters our scene at the tail end of historico-politics. Trained in the Rankean methodological program, he presented to John W. Burgess a thesis on the evolution of the office of justice of the peace in medieval England, part of "that long process by which all men and all institutions were brought under the direct and supreme authority of the state."[86] As history and political science diverged, Beard remained one of the few and certainly the most important scholar to bridge the two disciplines. He worked both on the historicist reconstruction of the past and the practical reform of contemporary politics and saw no conflict between the two. Indeed it is impossible to understand his work or his place within the diverging disciplines, without recognizing that Beard retained the compound purpose of historico-politics. His history always served a practical political aim and his political science was conducted through historical analysis.

Beard's originality came from the intersection of his liberal conception of modern history, his disciplinary purposes, and his special hopes for America. Although the connection was only implicit in 1901, Beard included America in the category of industrial society. It was already common among

85 Charles A. Beard, *The Industrial Revolution* (London: George Allen & Unwin, 1901), Introduction, 86; Wesley Clair Mitchell, "Review of Charles Beard, *The Industrial Revolution*," *JPE*, 9 (June 1901): 459–60.
86 Charles A. Beard, "The Office of Justice of the Peace in England in Its Origin and Development," *Studies in History, Economics and Public Law, Columbia University*, 20 (1904): 11.

historical economists and sociologists to place American history within the evolution of industrial society, but it was a novelty in the more conservative realms of history and political science. Indeed, no historian had yet framed an account of American democracy as a product of that economic development, for Turner had continued to attribute democracy to the unique economic basis in free land. At Columbia Beard came under the influence of Seligman's *Economic Interpretation of History*, which had already specifically linked American history to that larger dynamic course.[87] Seligman too viewed political democracy and ethical action as a concomitant of economic progress, and believed liberal capitalism would in the end transform itself into a more harmonious and cooperative society. Beard's greatest originality would be in working out for the first time an economic interpretation of American history that grounded democracy in the development of industrial capitalism.

Within political science, Beard played a similar mediating role. Standing within the Progressive tradition of historical realism, he incorporated into it Bentley's emphasis on politics as the conflict of group interests. Giving *The Process of Government* a rare positive review, he assimilated its message to the realist impulse of his discipline and his own economic interpretation of history. Bentley "has made effective use of the idea of 'group interests,' as distinguished from class interests in the Marxian sense," Beard said. His argument was not original, but it was salutary. It would "help to put politics on a basis of realism, where it belongs." In his 1908 lecture on political science, he used the group theory to construct a more realistic vision of politics, translating sovereignty into the dominance of an economic group or class. His 1910 text on American government, which quickly dominated the field, incorporated interest-group analysis into a traditional compendium on the organization and functions of federal, state, and local government.[88]

Beard's interest-group analysis deepened the program of historical realism, but it created tensions within that tradition that Beard never fully faced. To begin with, Beard combined his new social democracy with the traditional Whiggish politics of his profession and his father, a "rock-ribbed Federalist-Whig-Republican." Beard's first priority for political practice was large use of the national government to control corporate capitalism. For that, he turned like his colleagues to centralized political power. Like Goodnow, he advocated the use of administrative experts, the centralization

87 Nore, *Charles A. Beard*, 30–2.
88 Charles A. Beard, "Review of Arthur F. Bentley, *The Process of Government*," *PSQ*, 23 (December 1908): 739–41; idem, *Politics* (New York: Columbia University Press, 1908); idem, *American Government and Politics* (New York: Macmillan, 1910), particularly 35–58, 100, 118–19, 134–45, 250, 721.

of administrative authority, and the reduction of electoral and party control, so that officials would be responsible to the democratic electorate. In accordance with the Whig tradition, Beard distrusted direct majoritarian democracy and the mere rule of numbers at the ballot box. The Progressive movement for the initiative, referendum, and recall made matters worse, increasing the number of electoral issues and dispersing popular attention. The corrupt parties meanwhile distorted the expression of real interests. At one point he urged, like Commons, that representation be based on economic interests rather than on territory, through proportional representation or some other device. When the Supreme Court was under attack, Beard defended the power of judicial review as imbedded in original intent. What was needed was a strong national government, capable of overriding both localism and temporary majorities. It was not the power that was at fault, but its current usage. Within the context of Progressive politics, Beard's program held together and amplified the democratic purpose already marked out by Goodnow. But his social democratic aspirations sat oddly with his antimajoritarian skepticism.[89]

The tension between Beard's socioeconomic analysis and his politics went deeper. Beard wanted to develop a science of causation based on the underlying conflicts of interest groups. That goal led, as it led Bentley, to a theory of politics as social process, and Beard applauded the tendency to treat politics as a branch of sociology. But at the same time he opposed the "dissolution of the subject into history, economics and sociology" and retained a normative conception of politics. The state was "the highest form of human association yet devised." Political science should not only strengthen causal analysis, but also generate ideals, wisdom, statesmanship, and popular virtue.

These conflicting purposes reappeared at the level of causation. The liberal economic interpretation of history, as we have already seen, left the relation between economics and politics ambiguous and the autonomous power of political action uncertain. Beard believed that politics as well as economics was part of the underlying process of historical evolution. "Every citizen is a part of the social organism," he said, "capable, according to his knowledge

---

89 Nore, *Charles A. Beard*, 3. The most insightful account of the logic of Beard's politics is Pope McCorkle, "The Historian as Intellectual: Charles Beard and the Constitution Reconsidered," *American Journal of Legal History*, 28 (October 1984): 314–63. For Beard's position on the democratic side of progressive political science, see Jane S. Dahlberg, *The New York Bureau of Municipal Research* (New York: New York University Press, 1966), and Charles A. Beard, "Reconstructing State Government," *New Republic*, 4 (August 21, 1915): 1–16. For more examples of Beard's ambivalence regarding majoritarian democracy, see Charles A. Beard, *The Economic Basis of Politics* (New York: Knopf, 1922), 79–80, 84, 86–7.

and effort, of modifying its structure and changing its varied functions." But economics and politics together made "that great and indivisible natural process which draws down granite hills and upbuilds great nations." How, in this "indivisible natural process," could politics control economics? If citizens' knowledge and effort only reflected their economic interests, in what sense was politics normative? How would economic interest turn into political wisdom, the interest of the parts into that of the whole? The main thrust of his work was always to reduce politics to economics, but he could never be easy or unambivalent about doing so.[90]

On one level, Beard's message was positive. American politics was the product of group conflicts and should be, for real democracy was the fruit of conflicts between interest groups, working through the state apparatus. Beard's central work, *An Economic Interpretation of the Constitution* (1913), made that point in the most striking way possible. The Constitution was pushed through and ratified by groups having strong economic interests in a national government, groups whose wealth lay in credit in the national debt and public lands. It was opposed by groups whose wealth lay in land and whose politics was therefore localistic. The broad principle of strong national government the founders established was sound, and all the sounder because it rested on their real interests. From the outset the Constitution provided a national mechanism for the control of a national economy.[91]

If economic interests provided the national Constitution a measure of historical legitimation, however, they also delegitimized it. Beard's vivid demonstration of the historical basis of the American Republic was meant to desacralize it. Like Seligman, Beard constantly hammered away at "the familiar notion that we are living under a peculiar dispensation in the matter of political institutions."[92] American institutions, like all others, were formed in the clash of economic interest. The Constitution was originally formed to control, not empower, democracy. In the current impasse over

90 Beard, *Politics*, 6, 15, 33–5, 10. The quotation "Every citizen is a part . . ." is from Beard, *Industrial Revolution*, 99. Many of Beard's interpreters have seen economic determinism as the demon with which Beard struggled, usually placing the conflict on the level of historical causation, between economic interests and ideas. The sources of the discussion are William Appleman Williams, "Charles Austin Beard: The Intellectual as Tory-Radical," in *American Radicals: Some Problems and Personalities*, ed. Harvey Goldberg (New York: Monthly Review Press, 1952), 295–308, and Lee Benson, *Turner and Beard: American Historical Writing Reconsidered* (Glencoe, Ill.: Free Press, 1960). I am suggesting that in the broader field of history and political science that Beard inhabited, the conflict ran at every level through economics and politics, nature and history.
91 Charles A. Beard's *An Economic Interpretation of the Constitution* (New York: Macmillan, 1913) needs to be read in conjunction with his *The Supreme Court and the Constitution*. See also Beard, *American Government*, 46, and McCorkle, "The Historian as Intellectual."
92 Beard, *Politics*, 21.

Progressive legislation, that historicist message had a particularly important political bearing: The eighteenth century was not the twentieth and its principles were not sacrosanct.

Beard's effort to desacralize the Constitution required, moreover, that economic interest be based in personal financial interest. As we have seen, the antimajoritarian character of the Constitution was a fixture of Whiggish political science, if not of popular political rhetoric, and would hardly have shocked his colleagues. The personal self-interest of the founders was essential if Beard was to break through the mythology he saw encrusting contemporary politics. Yet Beard specifically exempted Hamilton and Madison, his nationalist heroes, from personal interest, in favor of a larger political view.[93] On close reading, Beard is trying simultaneously to embrace and escape economic interest.

Beard followed *An Economic Interpretation of the Constitution* with a historical survey of *Contemporary American Politics* in 1914, which did for the present very much what he had done for the founding period. Lest any myths survive, the Gilded Age development of industrial capitalism was described in terms that deliberately punctured the traditional view of American exceptionalism. What industrialization meant was "the transformation of vast masses of the people into a proletariat, with all the term implies." Corruption and special privilege existed on a massive scale and "the 'natural aristocracy' became the agents of capitalism." Yet Beard left no doubt that industrial development was inevitable and brought immense benefits. Indeed its consolidation was inevitable, and attempts to restore competition were reactionary. What was necessary was the activation of political democracy. But at this point Beard could only trace the action of limited class programs. There was first of all, the Progressive movement launched by Theodore Roosevelt.

Just as the Protestant Revolt during the sixteenth century was followed by a counter-reformation in the Catholic Church which swept away many abuses, while retaining and fortifying the essential principles of the faith, so the widespread and radical discontent of the working classes with the capitalist system hitherto obtaining produced a counter-reformation on the part of those who wish to preserve its essentials while curtailing some of its excesses.

Elsewhere Beard identified this "counter-reformation" as the Bismarckian strain of progressivism. The other strains of the Progressive movement were equally grounded in partial economic interests and partial political visions. Beard did not predict the future, but neither could he clarify how the

93 McCorkle, "The Historian as Intellectual," 335.

melange of class and interest groups could inaugurate the humane political democracy he sought.[94]

The mature style of Beard's work was set by this problem. Beard was the master and victim of realism. Beard the iconoclast stated in his most provocative language those objective facts that confounded the popular dogmas of his audience. The Founding Fathers were lining their own pockets. American workers have become a "proletariat." Progressivism, said this Indiana Quaker, is like the Catholic Counter-Reformation. And this is good his objective language said, this is the way history is, this is the realistic force of economic interests. Yet the irony is that Beard was violating his own as well as his audience's beliefs. He no more than they could accept in America the sufficiency of economic self-interest, the degradation of workers to the status of a proletariat, or the triumph of counter-reformation. Holding tightly to the hope of liberal capitalist progress, Beard stretched the language of realism to cover his conflicting values. The style gave him his historiographical force, but it masked rather than resolved his intellectual and normative conflicts.

Beard's Progressive historiography brought to fruition the New History proclaimed by James Harvey Robinson. The effort to turn American historiography toward the social and economic forces of modernity and to make it relevant to present politics had been going on since the 1890s. Beard and Robinson announced its arrival and their work set the agenda for American historiography into the 1960s. Progressive politics galvanized the new movement, but the underlying energies reflected the desire to relocate contemporary history, with its shattered traditional bearings, in the underlying process of history, whether as Beard's "indivisible natural process which draws down granite hills and upbuilds great nations," or as Robinson's continuity of history and nature, or as Turner's more traditional moving frontier as a process of perennial rebirth. The New Historians addressed the past from the present, aware that in the rapid stream of change there was nowhere else to stand. This recognition was an important advance in historical thinking and it is not surprising that Beard later became one of the few historians or political scientists to seriously question those disciplines' claims to objectivity.

The New Historians spoke the language of the late Progressive cohort and exploited the connections between history and the social sciences. The social scientists in turn commented very favorably upon the movement. "Like the changing Chinese," Small said in 1912, the historians were finally moving,

94 Charles A. Beard, *Contemporary American History, 1877–1913* (New York: Macmillan, 1914), 33–5, 303.

and might even someday catch up.[95] But the New History remained firmly anchored in Rankean methodology and historicist reconstruction. The social scientists, adding behaviorist sciences of natural process to the already naturalized process of marginalist economics, were moving away at an even faster clip. Unlike the situation in France, where history was in a sufficiently powerful intellectual and professional position to co-opt the sociologists' scientific impulses, the American disciplines diverged.[96]

The comparative framework offers us a final perspective on the consequences of American exceptionalism. As Ian Tyrrell has so well shown, the American New History stood in many ways at a point midway between the historiographies of England and France. While English historians remained engaged in the particularistic reconstruction of their political tradition, the New Historians, like the French *Annalistes*, whose origins date from the same period, entered upon a more venturesome effort of social realism. But the new French historiography, far more than the American, embraced the analytic aim of the social sciences and grappled with the challenge posed by Marx. The result was a historiography more theoretical, more structural, and more wide-ranging in its cultural curiosity. The New Historical exploration of social reality was confined to the workings of liberal process and the story of American democracy.[97]

History, like economics and sociology, was shaped by the crisis of American exceptionalism, a crisis that pushed American gentry intellectuals and their professional successors into a more intense awareness of national change than existed in England, and therefore, a more strenuous effort to come to grips with social reality, whether as institutional economics, or sociology, or the New History. But the desire to retain America's exceptional place in history steered American thinkers away from the Continent's more structural and historicist traditions and toward the apotheosis of liberal process. It was a movement akin to European modernism, but one that used modernist flux to reestablish national permanence.

### Chicago and Columbia sociologies: Thomas, Park, and Chapin

While Beard was beginning to incorporate the idea of liberal process into the traditional frameworks of historiography and political science, similar

95 Albion Small to Edward A. Ross, October 15, 1912, Albion W. Small Papers, University of Chicago.
96 William R. Keylor, *Academy and Community: The Foundation of the French Historical Profession* (Cambridge, Mass.: Harvard University Press, 1975).
97 Ian Tyrrell, *The Absent Marx, Class Analysis and Liberal History in Twentieth Century America* (Westport, Conn.: Greenwood, 1986), 23–8, 47–50, 62–3.

efforts were underway in sociology. Bentley's systems' analysis of group process was still too novel a vision for sociology as it was for political science, but sociologists found considerable resonance in Bentley's behavioristic approach and his idealized conception of fluid groups and a classless American society. At Chicago, where we begin, the new iconoclastic temper appeared first in a series of attacks on Small's conception of sociology. Bentley's critique in *The Process of Government* was part of a wider scientific revolt against a synthetic, normative sociology grounded in universal categories of human nature.

Robert F. Hoxie, trying to carve out his own social field within economics, opened the debate in 1906. Hoxie argued that each social science dealt with "human experience as a whole," but from the point of view of a particular problem or interest. Science was "explanation, interpretation" and "a thing cannot be explained in terms of itself." In seeking a synthetic explanation of society as a whole, Small had to be thinking of some "extra-experiential end or ideal of life." When Small did not understand the criticism, Hoxie told him that their disagreement stemmed from Small's ignorance of pragmatism. Pressed further, Small sent off a questionnaire, starting with "Do you believe that reality is fixed in its ultimate nature and constitution?" He got very few, and very different, replies, but he concluded that most social scientists no longer believed as he did in "an underlying moral economy in the affairs of men."[98]

That same year Small also began to hear about his "social forces error." Edward C. Hayes, a Chicago graduate with a ministerial background who had been reading Pearson, wanted sociology to adopt "strictly scientific methods" and study observable behavior rather than mental states. To refer to motives as " social forces" was to resort to a metaphysical explanation, much like resort to "vital force" in biology. By 1910, when he issued a full-blown attack at the sociological meetings against the "social forces error," one commentator thought he was kicking a dead horse, although Small and Edward A. Ross still rose to defend the older view.[99]

### Thomas' social psychology

The Chicago sociologist who did the most to create a new model for sociology did not bother to attack Small but simply went his own way.

98  Robert F. Hoxie, "Sociology and the Other Social Sciences: A Rejoinder," *AJS*, 12 (May 1907): 739–55; Albion Small, "Are the Social Sciences Answerable to Common Principles of Method?" *AJS*, 13 (July 1907): 1–19, and (September 1907): 200–23, particularly 219; "The Relations of the Social Sciences. A Symposium," *AJS* (November 1907): 392–401.
99  E. C. Hayes, in "Discussion," *PPASS*, 1 (1906): 74–7; idem, "The 'Social Forces' Error," *PPASS*, 5 (1910): 77–89 and "Discussion," 90–100.

William I. Thomas extended the psychologically oriented sociology of liberal change that had begun to form in the Progressive Era under Ross and Cooley, and turned it into a research paradigm. Like Cooley, Thomas was a Romantic, in his childhood love of the woods and in the kinship he felt for the mountaineers, folk peoples, and savages he liked to study. One of the attractions of *Volkpsychologie* was its emphasis on "the identity of human spirit in all zones." From the beginning he relished the iconoclastic power of that message and pricked civilized man for "the conceit that he had nothing in common" with the lower orders of nature. Thomas' course of study had taken him progressively back toward nature, toward biology and anthropology, "because the beginning of the whole process is most significant. [We] are there nearer to the source and secret of life itself." His first major work was a sociological study of savage society, *Source Book of Social Origins* (1909).[100]

Thomas' romanticism, however, was that of a modern liberal. Whether from his New South Methodist background or his reading in Spencer, he early accepted the liberal view that modern history was driven forward by the economic struggle for existence, capitalist accumulation, and the division of labor. Like his new liberal colleagues, he believed America was poised at a critical moment of "divided consciousness." Rapid change had broken up old habits without yet creating new ideals. His solution was to break down barriers of communication, of class consciousness, sexism, "race prejudice and tribal arrogance" toward a world of harmonious, pluralistic liberal exchange. The key to America's future was progressive change. Indeed, the "secret of life" that "the nature-peoples" would disclose was the secret of their failure to progress. "In the very fact that they have not become like us we may hope to find the laws of social physics which raised us above them."[101]

The laws Thomas found were refinements of the liberal theory imbedded in Henry Maine, Walter Bagehot, and in functional psychology. Change supervened upon habit and crisis, in savage society as in our own. The only real difference between modern Western societies and others was that science, democracy, and industrialization had made change itself into a habit. Thomas found in original nature not a principle of permanence or

100 Thomas, "Scope and Method of Folk-Psychology," 440, 434; idem, *Source Book for Social Origins: Ethnological Materials, Psychological Standpoint, Classified and Annotated Bibliographies for the Interpretation of Savage Society* (Chicago: University of Chicago Press, 1909), 4.
101 Thomas, "Significance of the Orient," 117–18; idem, "Scope and Method of Folk-Psychology," 441.

a perennial reservoir of unchanging ideals, but a principle of perpetual change.[102]

Thomas deliberately sought that principle in nature rather than in history, arguing that mankind's long savage development was far more fundamental to the understanding of society than was the study of mankind "in historical time." For support he quoted seven pages from Robinson's "brilliant" 1908 essay, the section in which Robinson, using the figure of the book, had foreshortened history against the background of nature. Prehistory as nature also offered the basis for science. Anthropological evidence drawn from myths was a more reliable indicator of "social consciousness" and "certain general principles of change," than was the indirect evidence of happenings provided by the imperfect historical record. Although Cooley's liberal romanticism seems to have been a response to the lengthening distance between the American past and present, a way to reinstate the past within the present, Thomas, in response to the more extreme acceleration of time, substituted the assured and ordered change of nature, the process of change, for the uncertain and unfathomable changes of history.[103]

If from the beginning change was Thomas' problem, psychology was his mode of solution. Thomas worked out his basic psychological approach under the tutelage of Jacques Loeb, champion of a mechanistic conception of biological response. Influenced by Mach's engineering model of science, and fighting what he thought was the *Naturphilosophie* still inhabiting evolutionary theory, Loeb sought the secrets of evolution in the interaction between environmental agents and a life substance characterized chiefly by irritability. "Given the property of irritability," Thomas said, "which from being purely mechanical becomes more and more purposive, we have a starting point for the interpretation of the psychical energies of man." Once language is invented, the individual is influenced by social rather than natural forces: "words, ideas and sentiments are substituted for light, gravity and acid," and intelligence is able to mediate reaction into new action. It was precisely this mechanical process of stimulus and response that gave Loeb his hope of experimental control and Thomas the hope of social control.[104]

Thomas at first assumed that biological endowment set the direction of response. His doctoral dissertation was a study of the metabolic difference between the sexes – males predominantly katabolic, females, anabolic – and

---

102 Thomas, "Significance of the Orient," 122.
103 Thomas, *Source Book*, Introductory.
104 Thomas, "Scope and Method of Folk-Psychology," 442–3; Philip J. Pauly, *Controlling Life: Jacques Loeb and the Engineering Ideal in Biology* (New York: Oxford University Press, 1987), 49–51, 75–86.

traced the origin of both social feeling in the race and the division of labor between the sexes to this basic physiological difference. Very soon, however, he began to place more weight on the character of environmental experience than original biological inclination. As Rosalind Rosenberg has shown, Thomas' experience with university women at Chicago and the studies of Helen Thompson on sex differences in intelligence had a major impact on his thinking. Thomas began to argue that conventional gender roles and racial prejudices were the products of cultural habits formed in earlier stages of evolution, and now outmoded. Supported by functional psychology and the findings of Franz Boas in anthropology that primitive peoples had the same mental capacity as civilized ones, he concluded that "Differences in intellectual expression are mainly social rather than biological."[105]

When Thomas turned to functional psychology, he found a number of basic concepts ready at hand: "attention, interest, stimulation, imitation." He soon developed another, which became central to his own work and to American social psychology, the concept of attitude. It made its first appearance in 1907 in his study of the psychology of sex, where it specified the relationship between the individual and the environment: a "mental attitude" was formed when "an associational and sympathetic relation is set up between the individual and certain parts of the outside world to the exclusion of others." Like the functional psychologists who were breaking down fixed categories of mental faculty, Thomas recognized that this response to the environment mobilized both mental associations and feelings. But the importance of the term attitude as he came to use it over the next decade was its ability to represent the relation of mind to a changing environment. Control of change is the object of all purposive activity, Thomas said in *Source Book*, and attention is the means of establishing control. "Attention is the mental attitude which takes note of the outside world and manipulates it; it is the organ of accommodation." Through attention, as "mental attitude," Thomas soon poured all those "attitudes" which responded to sociocultural change.[106]

105 William I. Thomas, "On a Difference in the Metabolism of the Sexes," *AJS*, 3 (July 1897): 31–63; Rosalind Rosenberg, *Beyond Separate Spheres: The Intellectual Roots of Modern Feminism* (New Haven, Conn.: Yale University Press, 1982), 120–31; William I. Thomas, "The Mind of Woman and the Lower Races," *AJS*, 12 (January 1907): 435–69.
106 William I. Thomas, "Race Psychology: Standpoint and Questionnaire, with Particular Reference to the Immigrant and the Negro," *AJS*, 17 (May 1912): 726; idem, *Sex and Society: Studies in the Social Psychology of Sex* (Chicago: University of Chicago Press, 1907), 105–6; idem, *Source Book*, 17. In "Attitude: The History of a Concept," *Perspectives in American History*, 1 (1967): 287–365, Donald Fleming pointed out the pioneer role played by Thomas in forging the concept of attitude and argued that the concept marked a characteristic line of development in twentieth-century American social science, namely,

At this point, Thomas' interests took a fateful turn. From his first studies in Europe, he had thought of examining European peasant peoples comparatively in their homeland and in America. In 1908, Helen Culver, a Chicago philanthropist, gave him $50,000, a then unheard of sum for social science research, to study the problem of the new immigration. Thomas decided after a wide survey to study the Poles, largely because the nationalist movement in Poland had developed considerable documentation of the peasantry. We have already seen that he was pursuing an interest in American blacks as a peasant people when he went to Tuskegee and met Park in 1912. That year he published the founding document of Chicago sociology, a research protocol entitled "Race Psychology: Standpoint and Questionnaire, with Particular Reference to the Immigrant and the Negro." It addressed the central issue that would occupy the ethnic and urban sociology of Thomas and Park, "the backwardness and forwardness of different social groups." The theoretical standpoint Thomas had constructed was crucial to the enterprise, for it placed his subjects in the midst of a changing liberal society and assumed racial equality.[107]

Thomas' research protocol was designed to send students out into the city to talk with their subjects and to track down all sorts of evidence, from histories to the kind of "undesigned" sources familiar to historians, "letters, diaries, newspapers, court, church, and club records, sermons, addresses, school curricula, and even handbills and almanacs." In developing this research stance, Thomas had taken a great deal from anthropology, not only from Boas' theory of the biological equality of races, but also from the combination of distance and sympathy the strangely human materials of anthropology provided him. When Park tried late in life to explain how Thomas had founded Chicago sociology, he traced his influence to his popular anthropological course on social origins. It gave students "a point of view from which society, with its codes, conventions, and social programs, was regarded as a natural phenomenon." It emancipated students from "traditional and practical interests." Park's language of "natural phenomenon" was his own rather than Thomas', as we shall see, but what Park sensed was anthropology's ability to simultaneously make the strange

the modernist movement away from rationalism and toward psychological depth analysis. It is important to note, however, that Thomas and American social scientists generally were ambivalent about depth analysis. The chief context in which Thomas worked was Darwinian and directed at the naturalization of human function and the problem of progressive change. See Janowitz, "Introduction," xxii, and David Shakow and David Rapaport, "The Influence of Freud on American Psychology," *Psychological Issues*, 4, no. 13 (1964).

107 W. I. Thomas to D. S. Thomas, "How the Polish Peasant Came About"; Thomas, "Race Psychology," 725.

familiar and the familiar strange. Veblen had already exploited half of that dialectical possibility, and Thomas had in him a streak of Veblen's radical conception of science. Thomas also was involved with Hull House, where sympathetic contact with the city's peoples and respect for immigrant cultures was a way of life. If Thomas' own attitude toward the Poles was compounded of attraction and repulsion, that did not prevent him from assuming a degree of sympathy as well as distance and sending his students into the city as anthropological explorers.[108]

In his research protocol, Thomas warned students about patronizing assumptions and the strangeness of the material. Differences had to be understood as the product of attitudes, not dismissed as biological inheritance. One revealing touch was his discussion of "Family, Community and Gang." Although he quoted Cooley's definition of the primary group, he gave as example a Russian peasant family under matriarchal rule, where the mother had her son beaten to death for violation of community-sanctioned family norms. Without directly saying so, he had neatly disposed of Cooley's idealized, Americanized human nature. The knowledge of most use to sociology, Thomas was saying, was the knowledge of contextually based attitudes.[109]

When *The Polish Peasant in Europe and America* appeared in 1918, it quickly became a paradigmatic work for the new empirical social science this cohort was creating. It was known for the power of its analysis, far superior to anything that had previously appeared in its discipline, but also for the ambiguity of its intention and reception. On one level the direction of the book was clear, visible in its form. A massive work of over 2,200 pages, it testified to the importance of detailed empirical knowledge of the people sociologists studied. Like Thomas' *Source Book*, his *Polish Peasant* was a compendium of brief theoretical statements followed by illustrative documents, including long series of family letters between Poland and America, and a three-hundred-page autobiography composed on command by a Polish-American immigrant. That form allowed the reader to hear just the language and see just the context to which the theoretical point referred. Given the still fluid character of sociology, it performed the task of standardizing basic observational data and conceptual references. But on a

108 Thomas, "Race Psychology," 770–2; "Robert E. Park's 'Notes on the Origins of the Society for Social Research' [1939]," introd. Lester R. Kurtz, *JHBS*, 18 (October 1982): 336–7; Rivka Shpak Lissak, *Pluralism and Progressives, Hull House and the New Immigrants* (Chicago: University of Chicago Press, 1989), chap. 2.
109 Ibid., 726, 730–1, 753–5.

deeper level, the form disclosed Thomas' principal task. He was engaged in the interpretation of texts.

Thomas clearly announced his work as a study in social psychology, in turn defined as the study of attitudes, as distinct from sociology proper, which studied social rules. His subject was broadly the problem of social change, but particularly the response of a peasant people to what, in effect, he described as modernization, both in Poland and America. As modernization occurred, Polish peasant communities and the individuals within them underwent a process of readjustment that could be charted on a cycle of organization-disorganization-reorganization, with disorganization defined as decreased influence of social rules on individual behavior. Thomas showed that Polish immigrants did not come to America with a blank slate that could then be imperiously "Americanized." They came with habits and attitudes formed in Poland and they reconstituted their community in America. "The striking phenomenon, the central object of our investigation," Thomas said, was *the formation of a new Polish-American society* out of those fragments separated from Polish society and embedded in American society. This Polish-American society as a whole is, indeed, slowly evolving from Polonism to Americanism. . . . But this 'assimilation' is not an individual but a group phenomenon." By locating Polish peasants in a stream of social change in Europe as well as America, and in a legitimate ethnic as well as American society, Thomas enormously enriched the popular and scholarly discourse on immigration and assimilation. Fittingly, he urged that there was no one ideal organization of culture in the world. "Every nation should simply try to bring its own system to the greatest possible perfection" and through mutual learning, develop tolerance of historical differences. His own social science should be a contribution to that end.[110]

Both in method and message, however, there were important ways in which Thomas undercut his enlightened cosmopolitan liberalism and his sensitivity to the contextuality of social experience. The *Polish Peasant* conveyed the self-conscious scientism that he had adopted between 1912 and 1918 in the face of public and university censorship, wartime hysteria, and historical anxiety. "We must have an empirical and exact social science ready for eventual application," he announced in the book, "and such a science can be constituted only if we treat it as an end in itself." Or again, "there is not a single phenomenon within the whole sphere of human life that conscious control cannot reach sooner or later." The effort to construct a science of

110 Thomas and Znaniecki, *Polish Peasant*, 1:31–5, 85–6; 2:1469.

control now led Thomas to repudiate even his past use of anthropology. Ethnology was no more reliable than history as a source of social knowledge. We use our knowledge of the present to understand the past, rather than vice versa. The only object of scientific study was the present, "the actual civilized society."[111]

Beyond the political and historical crisis that intervened in the years before 1918 to reshape Thomas' views toward scientism, there was also Florian Znaniecki, a young Polish philosopher Thomas had met in Poland, who turned up on his doorstep in Chicago at the outbreak of World War I. Thomas put him to work on the Chicago Polish community and he drafted, for Thomas' revision, a good deal of the final book. In the course of this effort, Thomas made him a full collaborator and Znaniecki turned himself into a sociologist. Although it is impossible to be certain just what he contributed, it does seem clear that Znaniecki's philosophical training and concerns gave him far less sense of the concrete than Thomas had, and that he came to the study with ideas about the Polish peasantry already well-formed from his experience in the aristocratically based Polish nationalist movement. Znaniecki appears to have strengthened Thomas' interest in sociological laws and he may have confirmed his distaste for the Polish peasants in America.[112]

Thomas' positivistic scientific aim worked at cross-purposes to his interpretive task. The aim of social psychology, as of all social science, he announced at the outset, was to become a "nomothetic science ... to interpret as many facts as possible by as few laws as possible." The problem of social science was precisely to predict behavior in changing situations, and to do this, social laws had to take attitudes into account. The failure of Progressive reform had shown him that changing material conditions was not enough, for how conditions were used depended upon the attitudes of the people who used them. Thus a new attitude was always the product of two factors, a change in social elements and "the pre-existing attitude upon which it has acted." General laws of behavior formulated in the study of one culture would in future be amended and supplemented by studies in other cultures, yielding ultimately, universal laws. Thomas collected a rich array of concrete attitudes only to extract from them the universal process of organization and disorganization. That abstracting scientific purpose largely accounts for the oft-noted "underanalysis" of the documents. His dense collection of sources yielded more than American sociologists had ever

111  Ibid. 1:15, 66, 17–18.
112  W. I. Thomas to D. S. Thomas, "How the Polish Peasant Came About"; Florian Znaniecki, "William I. Thomas as a Collaborator," *Sociology and Social Research*, 32 (March–April 1948): 766.

before seen, but it was still a thin harvest compared to what could have been gleaned.[113]

When Thomas analyzed the autobiographical document he printed and tried to deal adequately with the complexity of a single life, his interpretive sense came visibly into conflict with his positivist aims. Attitudes, he said, could not be taken from isolated instances, but needed to be interpreted in the context of a whole life. Thus the life record or case study was "the *perfect* type of sociological material," far more so than statistics, which were, "taken in themselves ... nothing but symptoms of unknown causal processes." Reformulating his conception of law, he now expected it to combine the greatest possible generality with "the greatest possible concreteness.... to use as few general laws as possible for the explanation of as much concrete social life as possible." Thomas later regretted the heavy-handed discussion of "laws" in the methodological introduction and attributed it to Znaniecki, but the *Polish Peasant* was thoroughly imbued with, and divided by, the positivist intentions that Thomas had announced before and continued to articulate after the book was published.[114]

Thomas' natural science model also thinned out his historical context, although a great deal of the concrete richness of the analysis came from its de facto use of history. He located his attitudes theoretically in shifting "situations" rather than in historically specified contexts; whatever social structure we see is created by attitudes, not attitudes by structure. But the Polish context he constructed was rooted in historical formations.[115] Poland was rendered with far greater historical specificity than America – indeed Poland took up two-thirds of the book – no doubt because Thomas took the American historical world for granted. The only specific character given to American society was the generic liberal modernity being created by capitalism.

When Thomas turned to Polish America, there was again underanalysis. He described briefly the secular nationalist organizations and the church-oriented organizations that vied for leadership of the community, but gave little insight into some of their most striking features or into the attitudes of their Polish-American followers. The chief point at which he provided access to attitudes was in the discussion of disorganization, the lapse of individuals into vice, crime, unemployment, dependency, and violence.

113 Thomas and Znaniecki, *Polish Peasant*, 1:62, 13, 42–5; Norbert Wiley, "Early American Sociology and *The Polish Peasant*," *Sociological Theory*, 4 (Spring 1986): 35; Blumer, *An Appraisal*, 38–9.
114 Thomas and Znaniecki, *Polish Peasant*, 2:1832–4; W. I. Thomas to D. S. Thomas, "How the Polish Peasant Came About."
115 Thomas and Znaniecki, *Polish Peasant*, 1:68–9.

Whereas later historians have emphasized the relative stability of the Polish-American community, Thomas pictured a high degree of demoralization.[116]

Part of the problem was Thomas' own attitude toward his material. "It is rather strange," Thomas noted later, "that while I collected all the materials in Poland, Znaniecki collected all those relating to the Poles in America . . . And he wrote that volume, with my revisions." Thomas, of course, had wandered informally through Chicago slums for some years, and he oversaw Znaniecki's research. But it is indeed curious that the father of hands-on Chicago sociology, who now spoke Polish himself, kept his distance from Polish-Americans. There is surely an echo here of Woodrow Wilson not going to Washington to observe Congress. Thomas recalled no substantive disagreement with Znaniecki on Polish America, although in Poland, Thomas had quickly seen through the nationalist propaganda he was being given, as a result of which, "I distrusted the Poles and they distrusted me." In Chicago both authors appear to have looked on the peasants as objects rather than agents, and this attitude governs their analysis of Polish America.[117]

Whereas in Poland Thomas saw disorganization and reorganization, in America Thomas and Znaniecki saw only disorganization. Indeed, "The natural tendencies of an individual, unless controlled and organized by social education," inevitably led to "abnormal" behavior. Even for the average immigrant in America, there was "a certain lowering of his moral level." In the second generation that situation could only worsen, and Thomas noted the high crime rate in second generation children. There would never be adequate reorganization unless the second generation was "brought into direct and continuous contact with better aspects of American life."

In a 1921 book on assimilation that he drafted, Thomas made clear that assimilation, not pluralism, was his goal. The immigrants' "attitudes and values, their ideas on the conduct of life" must be "brought into harmony with our own." America already had considerable "undeveloped" cultural material in the Negroes, Indians, Southern mountaineers, and other groups. "There is a limit . . . to the amount of material of this kind that a country can

---

116 Note the failure to take historical-cultural attitudes into account regarding the lack of charitable institutions, the public character of the organizations, and their growing membership despite their seeming loss of function. Ibid., 2:1534, 1538–44, 1622–3. A sociological explanation of some of these features is provided by Helen Znaniecki Lopata, *Polish Americans: Status Competition in an Ethnic Community* (Englewood-Cliffs, N.J.: Prentice-Hall, 1976), particularly p. 54. On disorganization, see Thomas and Znaniecki, *Polish Peasant*, 2:1476 and Wiley, "Early American Sociology and *The Polish Peasant*," 35–6.

117 W. I. Thomas to D. S. Thomas, "How the Polish Peasant Came About"; Thomas and Znaniecki, *Polish Peasant*, 2:1526–1623.

incorporate without losing the character of its culture." Americanizers should use the immigrants' attitudes, memories, and organizations, rather than destroy them, but in the end, immigrants would have to lose their separate identities and the immigrant communities would have to disappear. Thomas could envision a pluralistic world but not a pluralistic American nation.[118]

By the time the *Polish Peasant* was fully published, Thomas had fled to New York City, where he entered upon a career of freelance social science research. His 1921 manuscript on assimilation had to be published under Park's name. During the coming decade, the *Polish Peasant* exercised its influence on its own, urging a science that was both interpretive and nomothetic, cosmopolitan and parochial. Through the work of Robert Park, that divided method and message gained wider currency, for Park was a man of even sharper divisions. He felt as deeply a humanistic and romantic interest in particular experience, and transmuted it even more decisively into objectivist science.

## Park's sociological naturalism

When asked to discuss a paradigmatic theorist for contemporary sociology, Park chose two, Thomas and William Graham Sumner. Thomas provided a paradigm for research into changing attitudes; Sumner echoed Park's fatalistic sense of the power of social process. The liberal economic spine of historical evolution was more important for Park than for Thomas. In his personal attitudes toward success, his early admiration for the German army, and his later sociology, the competitive struggle for existence, waged through the market and social conflict, remained at the center of his thinking. He was also more protective of the exceptionalist status of America, and held out less hope for reform, for he believed that liberal evolution worked with the slow necessity of nature, a lesson surely reinforced at Tuskegee. Sumner's tragic fatalism was as close to Park's sensibility as Thomas' romantic curiosity.[119]

Park's first venture into sociology, his doctoral dissertation of 1904,

---

118 Thomas and Znaniecki, *Polish Peasant*, vol. 2, pt. 3, particularly pp. 1649–51; Herbert A. Miller and Robert E. Park, *Old World Traits Transplanted* (New York: Harper, 1921), 262–5. The book was drafted by Thomas.
119 Robert E. Park, "The Sociological Methods of William Graham Sumner, and of William I. Thomas and Florian Znaniecki," in *Methods in Social Science: A Case Book*, ed. Stewart A. Rice (Chicago: University of Chicago Press, 1931), 154–75; idem, "The German Army: The Most Perfect Military Organization in the World," *Munsey's Magazine*, 24 (December 1900): 376–95.

*Massen und Publicum, The Crowd and the Public*, was nonetheless a move in the direction of Thomas. A survey of the new field of sociology, informed by lectures from Simmel, Park discerned even before Thomas the outlines of a sociology of liberal change. It was technically a thesis in philosophy and it conflated philosophical distinctions, undoubtedly to William James's dismay, but it captured brilliantly the implications of the liberal sociology taking shape in America. Because sociology studied social relationships among individuals, Park began, the explanation of those relationships had to be sought in the psychology of interacting individuals. Because neither the individual nor the social group were fixed entities, but were constantly changing, neither could serve as the ultimate unit of social psychology. Nor could institutions, themselves composed of shifting individuals and purposes. The basic unit of social psychology therefore had to be *Willenshaltungen*, "volitional attitudes," a term which could also encompass the ideas and desires that earlier theorists had treated as the basic units of their subject. At one stroke, Park had discerned that a sociology of a fluid liberal world was a study of attitudes.[120]

With similar discernment, he argued that the process by which attitudes were communicated and social groups formed was the process of "sympathy," stated first by David Hume and Adam Smith, and elaborated in such later concepts as Tarde's imitation and Giddings' consciousness of kind. This was a formal concept, Park stressed; it joined all human sentiments and attitudes, not those that were specifically social or altruistic. It included the suggestion that linked the crowd and the partly more rational processes that linked the public. Finally, Park set off the crowd and the public, as fluid and transitional social groupings formed by sympathy, from more fixed institutions like the state and the church, which generated authoritative norms. It was precisely the plasticity of these fluid social formations that allowed for social change. The crowd activity of the French Revolution and the public opinion of modern society could revise norms and their institutional forms. For Park, too, the mechanisms of social psychology were enlarged into a theory of liberal social change.[121]

---

120 Robert E. Park, *The Crowd and the Public, and Other Essays*, ed. Henry Elsner, Jr. (Chicago: University of Chicago Press, 1972), 24–31.

121 Ibid., 31–6, 43–81. Leon Bramson, *The Political Context of Sociology* (Princeton, N.J.: Princeton University Press, 1961), particularly pp. 49–50, 62, 70–2, 90, discusses the liberal usage Park and other American sociologists made of the more conservative European crowd theories. Following Louis Hartz, Bramson attributes the difference in sociologies to the exceptionalist American reality. America had no "social problem," i.e., the problem of relations among social classes, only "social problems." Americans being liberals, Bramson attributes the conservative elements present in Park and his colleagues, such as emphasis on "group cohesion, status, and consensus," to the inherent conservative

When he arrived at Chicago in 1913, after his years at Tuskegee, Park was prepared for Thomas' social psychology of attitudes and disorganization and quickly adopted it, but he also felt the need of a more fundamental "theoretical scheme."[122] This he set out in *Introduction to the Science of Sociology* (1921) with his colleague Ernest W. Burgess. Constructed like Thomas' *Source Book* and *Polish Peasant*, the Park and Burgess text performed their standardizing functions. As the dominant text in the field for the next twenty years, it also widely disseminated Park's conception of sociology.

The heart of the text was a group of chapters on competition, conflict, accommodation, and assimilation. Park and Burgess presented competition as the most basic form of "interaction" at work in society. Competition "invariably tends to create an impersonal social order" in which each individual, pursuing his own profit, contributes "to the common welfare." Pointing to the ecological theory he would prominently develop over the next decade, he used the plant community as his model of "competitive co-operation," declaring that "The economic organization of society, so far as it is an effect of free competition, is an ecological organization." There were, however, common interests of the community that could not be enacted in the market, and that called for a political level of organization. Both the competitive and political struggle created conflicts, and the social order was constructed of "accommodations" to competition and conflict. "The rights of property, vested interests of every sort, the family organization, slavery, caste and class, the whole social organization, in fact, represent accommodations." Accommodation was "associated with the social order that is fixed and established in custom and the mores." Assimilation, in turn, involved a "more thoroughgoing transformation of the personality" which derived from intimate contact.

One result of Park and Burgess' model of society was to turn social structure into social process. Indeed structure hardly appeared directly in the book, and class, not at all. The structure implied in the process, however, was the capitalist structure of liberal society. Economic competition was identified as a natural process leading to a natural order of competitive cooperation. The social processes of accommodation themselves took on the necessity of a natural process. It is at this social level, Park said, "rather than in the formal procedures of governments, that we must look for the

bias of sociology's founding concepts, inherited unwittingly from nineteenth-century Europe. I have argued that America did indeed have a "social problem" and that the American political tradition contained its own organicist resources and conservative inclinations for dealing with it.

122 Baker, "Life Histories," 259.

fundamental mechanism of social control." "Nature" designated for Park that realm of economic and social experience that lay beneath the level of conscious political choice and that carried with it the necessity of natural law. But Park was often unsure of the boundaries of nature in society, and unsure of what nature portended for America.[123]

The first issue Park addressed when he arrived at Chicago in 1913 was racial and ethnic assimilation. He began with his model of liberal society, in which alien people assimilated as individuals. Adopting the superficial manners and customs of the society, the alien individual could enter into the competitive processes of the market and voluntary associations of the society and find individuality. Park was keenly aware, however, that the superficial mark of skin color had prevented American Negroes from taking that individualistic route. Moreover, particularly in the South, Negroes were a subject people. Since formal emancipation, "Common interests have drawn the blacks together, and caste sentiment has kept the black and white apart." Therefore, "under . . . conditions of individual liberty and individual competition, characteristic of modern civilization, depressed racial groups tend to assume the form of nationalities." Their road to assimilation, like the subjugated Slavic peoples of eastern Europe, would have to be through the development of cultural nationalism. The segregated condition of the American South was in fact encouraging the development of racial pride and ambition. But separatism would also perpetuate differences. Just as the nationalities of Austria-Hungary were seeking federation, in the South "the races seem to be tending in the direction of a bi-racial organization of society. . . . What the ultimate outcome of this movement may be it is not safe to predict."[124]

Park's racial analysis of 1913 carried all the ambiguities of Booker T. Washington's, with its overt message of accommodation to segregation and its undercurrent of corporate militance. But it carried in addition a real uncertainty about the outcome. By 1921, when he revised and published Thomas' study of assimilation under his own name, he accepted Thomas' conclusion that the peasant peoples of Europe would in the course of several generations abandon their separate cultural identities and assimilate into American society. Park's chief concern was the racial groups, African Americans and later Orientals, for whom visible racial marks blocked the

123 Robert E. Park and Ernest W. Burgess, *Introduction to the Science of Sociology* (Chicago: University of Chicago Press, 1921), chaps. 8–11, particularly pp. 509–11, 668. One source for Park's view of sociology as a study of social process, and for the centrality of the competitive economic process, was probably Cooley's *Social Process*.
124 Robert E. Park, "Racial Assimilation in Secondary Groups, with Particular Reference to the Negro," *PPASS*, 8 (1913): 70–1, 77, 82, 83.

natural processes of liberal society, and on this subject Park began, and in the end remained, uncertain.[125]

Park's racial analysis gave him another problem. Could there be assimilation in a modern society composed of "widely different mental capacities"? Assimilation had most often been taken to mean likemindedness, which required a rough equality, "a standard grade of intelligence." He urged instead that assimilation did not require likeness, but only loyalty – the habits and sentiments formed from "the mutual interdependence of parts." After all, "there is no greater loyalty than that which binds the dog to his master," Park said.

A dog without a master is a dangerous animal, but the dog that has been domesticated is a member of society. He is not, of course, a citizen, although he is not entirely without rights. But he has got into some sort of practical working relations with the group to which he belongs. . . . It is this practical working arrangement, into which individuals with widely different mental capacities enter as co-ordinate parts, that gives the corporate character to social groups and insures their solidarity.[126]

Whatever this egregious metaphor reveals about Park's unconscious racial attitudes, it clearly reveals the political implications of his Spencerian social theory of functional interdependence. Assimilation did not imply a single body politic among equal citizens, but minimal social cohesion among generically different kinds of people. Park's old teacher Josiah Royce, whose concept of loyalty he revised, would have been appalled. On one level, Park resolved this difficulty in his text by distinguishing accommodation, the social organization that results from competition, and assimilation, a process more akin to acculturation. Assimilation did not require likeness, but it did require participation in a "common life," both political and social. Still, Park never explored how a functionally integrated society of unequals was to engage in a truly democratic "common life."[127]

Park's most distinctive contribution to Chicago sociology was his focus on the city. In a research protocol published in 1915, he declared that the city was the characteristic feature of modern society and the appropriate locus for sociological investigation. The city was an institution, he declared, and institutions were "a product of the artless processes of nature and growth." Fundamentally, the natural process at work was the market. "The city, particularly the modern American city" was created by "the inevitable

125 For an insightful discussion of Park's wavering on this subject, see Stow Persons, *Ethnic Studies at Chicago, 1905–45* (Urbana: University of Illinois Press, 1987), chaps. 4–5.
126 Park, "Racial Assimilation," 69–70.
127 Park and Burgess, *Introduction*, 739–40, 763–8. See also Miller and Park, *Old World Traits*, 260–2.

processes of human nature," by which Clark meant the economic and social choices of competing individuals:

Under our system of individual ownership, for instance ... we leave to private enterprise, for the most part, the task of determining the city's limits and the location of its residential and industrial districts. Personal tastes and convenience, vocational and economic interests, infallibly tend to segregate and thus to classify the populations of great cities. In this way the city acquires an organization which is neither designed nor controlled.

The city was the product of the growth of capitalism, and for Park capitalism was a natural process, rooted in "the inevitable processes of human nature." The "American city" and "our system of individual ownership" were archetypal, the generic modern city and the generic economic process.[128]

Nonetheless, this natural economic process occurred in a thick social medium that amplified conflict and put the American fate somewhat in doubt. Park's liberal vision was always clouded by lingering republican fears. Because the market distributed preferences, it collected racial and class feelings into neighborhoods that could become segregated and isolate its inhabitants from competition. Indeed, "In the older cities of Europe, where the processes of segregation have gone farther, neighborhood distinctions are likely to be more marked than they are in America."

Park lessened the threat that America would follow suit by adopting Bentley's strategy. He dismissed class as a viable category of analysis "in the modern democratic state." Liberal society did tend to organize increasingly around "vocational interests" and artisans (note the archaic term), businessmen, and professionals did tend to group themselves in "classes." But, he asked rhetorically, "Do social classes tend to assume the character of cultural groups? That is to say, do the classes tend to acquire the exclusiveness and independence of a caste or nationality; or is each class always dependent upon the existence of a corresponding class?" So long as class was not caste, Park echoed Bentley, class was not an operative category of analysis. Even "socialism [had] never succeeded in creating more than a political party." Sociologists therefore should investigate "vocational types."

Among the types which it would be interesting to study are: the shopgirl, the policeman, the peddler, the cabman, the night watchman, the clairvoyant, the vaudeville performer, the quack doctor, the bartender, the ward boss, the strikebreaker, the labor agitator, the school teacher, the reporter, the stockbroker, the pawnbroker; all of these are characteristic products of the conditions of city life;

---

128 Robert E. Park, "The City: Suggestions for the Investigation of Human Behavior in the City Environment," *AJS*, 20 (March 1915): 577–9.

each, with its special experience, insight, and point of view, determines for each vocational group and for the city as a whole its individuality.

It is hard to imagine a better way to dissolve the bonds of class than this particularistic and promiscuous array. Park's interest in urban variety was real, but it here served a distinctly liberal exceptionalist function.[129]

Finally, Park exempted America from European forms of social control. Liberal society had to develop secondary forms of social control to substitute for the decaying controls of primary groups. In the city that meant increasing use of positive law, administration, and new mores among segregated urban groups. But, he warned, "it is important to know whether the motives which are at present multiplying the positive restrictions on the individual will necessarily go as far in this country as they have already done in Germany. Will they eventually bring about a condition approaching socialism?" The answer Park expected was clear.[130]

Park modeled his study of the city on an essay by his German teacher, Simmel, "The Metropolis and Mental Life," but it diverged from it in striking ways. The costs of modern progress that Simmel counted were those of the upper-class metropolitan, who sensed the inner reserve individuals had to develop to survive the overwhelming stimulation of the city. Against this indifference, against the objective weight of modern culture, the individual had to summon "the utmost in uniqueness and particularization, in order to preserve his most personal core." The evils Park noticed were those of the middle-class American reformer, the "disintegrating" influence of the city on church, school, and family, the rise of crime and vice, the transformation of the neighborhood into a segregated, isolated area by means of racial antagonisms and class interests. Simmel's ultimate concern was to protect the autonomy of the individual in modern liberal society; Park's program was oriented toward "social control," in his case, the social control of nature.[131]

In Simmel's essay, therefore, the autonomy of subjective experience was the focus of analysis. In Park's it was the objective and deterministic process. Individuals did not act against the forces of the city and create their own individuality; rather the city created "individual types." At his most individualistic moment, Park pictured the individual attracted to the city by "a sort of tropism," and finding "the moral climate in which his peculiar nature obtains the stimulations that bring his innate qualities to full and free

129 Ibid., 583, 586–7.
130 Ibid., 600.
131 Ibid., 593–4; Georg Simmel, "The Metropolis and Mental Life," in *The Sociology of Georg Simmel*, ed. Kurt H. Wolff (Glencoe, Ill.: Free Press, 1950), 422–4.

expression." In short, Simmel's work was a study of "mental life," and Park's a study of "human behavior in the city environment." Drawing on Jacques Loeb, the behaviorists, and Sigmund Freud, Park made a point of emphasizing the importance of subconscious processes, "instinctive, senso-motor, or ideo-motor." He did not deny the existence of consciousness but he was determined to transform it into a natural object.[132]

Simmel's analysis was linked to history and Park's, to nature. "The metropolis reveals itself as one of those great historical formations," Simmel concluded. Not only was the money economy itself the creation of history, but the individualism of the metropolis was formed by the cultural forces of eighteenth-century Enlightenment and nineteenth-century liberalism and Romanticism. The twentieth-century metropolis thus presented "peculiar conditions" that "gain a unique place, pregnant with inestimable meanings for the development of psychic existence."[133] For Park, the city was the product of a natural process working itself out most fully on American soil, and pregnant with meanings for a behavioral science of society.

In making his commitment to nature, in defining an "institution" as a work of "nature," Park was not being naive. The problematic relationship between nature and history was, in fact, one of his central and lifelong concerns. Because of his graduate training in philosophy, he was more interested in the theoretical issues involved in constructing a science of society than most of his colleagues. While studying philosophy at Harvard, he recalled, he had been "impressed by Münsterberg's discussions of the distinctions between history and natural science." In Germany, he had decided to take his degree from Wilhelm Windelband when he discovered that the Heidelberg philosopher was engaged in "an attack upon the methodological problem that I had come to regard as fundamental."[134]

Windelband was working out a logical basis for the empirical sciences based on the formal character of their cognitive goals. Sciences were distinguished not by the nature of their subject matter, but by the logical stance taken toward their subject. Sociology could be a natural science as well as physics. What characterized a natural or nomothetic science was its

132 Park, "The City," 608, 598, 610–11. See also Robert E. Park, *The Principles of Human Behavior* (Chicago: Zalaz Corp., 1915).

133 Simmel, "The Metropolis," 423. Simmel formulated both a "general" and a "special" sociology, the former conceived as a method of social analysis applicable to all of historical life, the latter as a study of the abstract "forms" of social life. In both cases, however, he remained aware that his analyses were abstracted from history and pointed out the relationship between sociological and historical categories. See Georg Simmel, "The Social and the Individual Level: An Example of General Sociology," and Kurt Wolff, "Introduction," in *Sociology of Georg Simmel*, xvii–xlii, 26–39.

134 Baker, "Life Histories," 256.

search for the general in the form of laws of nature. The historical, or ideographic, sciences, in contrast, sought the particular in the form of what is historically determined. Park opened his doctoral dissertation in 1904 with Windelband's distinction and he quoted it at length in his 1921 text. He read it as an enabling charter for sociological science. Sociologists studied the same subject matter as historians, but took events "out of their historical setting ... out of their time and space relations ... to emphasize the typical and representative." Any subject that could state facts in that way, and verify them, was "so far as method is concerned, a natural science."[135]

The problem for Park was the cost Windelband extracted. Science achieved its laws, and the practical power they conferred, by creating a world of abstract concepts, "despoiled of all their earthly sensuous qualities." In contrast, history portrayed life with its "characteristic vivacity," and the uniqueness of events was the source of all the interests and values of life.[136] Park was attracted to both and declared both had equal value, but he misconstrued this distinction in an important way. Windelband had left his conception of historical knowledge somewhat undeveloped, but his student Heinrich Rickert, whom Park also read, made clear that historical knowledge like scientific knowledge was conceptual knowledge; the distinction was in how historians located and developed their concepts. Rejecting Dilthey's view that historical knowledge was based on a different kind of knowledge, Rickert and Windelband denied that history employed a special kind of intuitive insight or sympathy with human motives.[137]

Park, however, always understood Windelband and Rickert in the light of his original mentor at Harvard, Hugo Münsterberg, who, more like Dilthey, emphasized the intuitive, experiential character of historical knowledge. Thus history and geography, as concrete sciences, "enlarge our experience of life ... arouse new interests and create new sympathies ... call out ... instincts and capacities." The abstract sciences, however, are "tools for converting experience into knowledge and applying the knowledge so gained to practical uses." Like Münsterberg, he placed a high rhetorical value on history. History interprets, he said, and "it is upon the interpretation of the facts of experience that we formulate our creeds and found our faiths." But "natural science explains" and it was on the basis of such explanation that we learned to control "nature and human nature." For all his concessions to the interpretive or experiential task of history, he cast

135 Park and Burgess, *Introduction*, 8–12.
136 Ibid.
137 Herbert Schnädelbach, *Philosophy in Germany, 1831–1933* (Cambridge University Press, 1984), 57, and Heinrich Rickert, *The Limits of Concept Formation in Natural Science*, ed. and Introduction by Guy Oakes (Cambridge University Press, 1986).

sociology as a positivist, nomothetic science and gave it alone the status of explanatory knowledge.[138]

One result of Park's formulation was to make interpretation a problematical pursuit in sociology. He tended to describe history and interpretation as propaedeutic to sociology, providing only the "experience," which it converted into "knowledge." Another result was to obscure and conflate the distinction between historical and universal generalization. Sociology appears, Park said

as soon as the historian turns from the study of 'periods' to the study of institutions. The history of institutions ... leads inevitably to comparison, classification, the formation of class names or concepts, and eventually to the formulation of law. In the process, history becomes natural history, and natural history passes over into natural science. In short, history becomes sociology.

Park's example here was Westermarck on marriage, who derived universal types of marriage from "the responses of a few fundamental human instincts to a variety of social situations." In this formulation, historical institutions and historical generalization lost their historical character unremarked and slid over into universal laws and types. "By nature," Park said, "we mean just that aspect and character of things in regard to which it is possible to make general statements and formulate laws." Sociology was supposed to study natural and not historical types, though Park often seemed not to recognize the difference. And "by nature," as we have already seen, Park meant a good deal more than a logical category.[139]

Park's 1921 text with Burgess was in some ways the high point of his positivism. In 1913 he had ventured that the case study provided the kind of insight into the "inner life" that history yielded, and that the case study was useful to practical sociologists in showing how to apply sociological science in specific circumstances, but none of this appeared in the text.[140] As the scientistic movement gained power in the 1920s, he tried to find a more secure place within sociology and within his dualistic scheme of knowledge for interpretive knowledge, though he always retained his positivist aims as well. It is tempting to concur at this point with James's judgment of Park as a philosopher. It is more instructive, however, to compare his positivist reading of Windelband and Rickert, by way of Münsterberg, to the way Max

138 Max Weber, *Roscher and Knies: The Logical Problems of Historical Economics* (New York: Free Press, 1975), 129–52; Hugo Münsterberg, "The Position of Psychology in the System of Knowledge," *Psychological Monographs*, 4 (1903): 641–54; Park and Burgess, *Introduction*, 15–16, 23–4.
139 Park and Burgess, *Introduction*, 11, 16.
140 Robert E. Park in "Informal Conference: Is It Possible for American Sociologists to Agree upon a Constructive Program?" *PPASS*, 8 (1913): 167–8.

Weber, at the same moment, was using these sources to develop a historical conception of sociology.

Weber argued that a natural science of society was logically possible, but pointless. "The real question is *whether* the generally valid laws which may eventually be discovered make any contribution to the *understanding* of those aspects of cultural reality which we regard as *worth knowing.*" What we want to do in the sociocultural sciences, as in history, is to understand concrete reality, the *"meaningful* and essential aspects of concrete patterns" and their "concrete causes and effects." The logical ideal of natural science, however, "would be a system of *formulae* of absolutely general validity. This system would constitute an abstract representation of the features common to all historical events. It is obvious that historical reality, including those 'world-historical' events and cultural phenomena which we find so significant, could never be deduced from these formulae." Following the lead of Rickert, he argued that historical knowledge was just as conceptual and explanatory as the knowledge of natural science. It sought, however, concepts that captured the individual character of cultural phenomena, and it offered a kind of intelligibility, through knowledge of motives, unavailable in the natural sciences. Working within the concrete configurations of history, sociology had ample room to study general (not universal) processes and historical (not natural) types.[141]

Weber no less than Park sought a way to develop sociology as a science and to balance the claims of explanation and of sympathetic understanding. But Weber was raised in a culture in which for over a century the unique configurations of his national history had been set off against the recurring laws of nature. What he saw as significant in the sociocultural world were the concrete events of history and their unique patterns of causes. Raised in a culture in which for over a century the unique configurations of his national history had been identified with the recurring laws of nature, Park valued the individual particularities of history, but subordinated them to and conflated them with the regularities of nature.

### Objectivism in sociology

By 1921, when his text was published, Park was assuming the leadership of the sociology department at Chicago. Both he and Thomas had set out the

---

141 Weber, *Roscher and Knies*, 217n., 64–5. On Weber see Thomas Burger, *Max Weber's Theory of Concept Formation*, exp. ed. (Durham, N.C.: Duke University Press, 1987), and Lelan McLemore, "Max Weber's Defense of Historical Inquiry," *History and Theory*, 23, no. 3 (1984): 277–95.

main lines of the sociological work they and many students would pursue. Outspoken advocates of a behavioristic sociological science that could assert social control, they were at the same time aware of the complexities of transforming historical and mental life into objects of science and of translating scientific findings into programs of reform. There were a number of younger people in the profession, however, who seemed far less aware of the complexities and far more certain of a direct and simple path to science, and who were close at their heels. Robert Bannister has called them the objectivist wing of American sociology. In background and temperament and in the objective programs they developed, they carried the impulses and characteristics that were widely present among their cohort to more extreme conclusions.[142]

Luther Lee Bernard arrived at Chicago in 1907 from West Texas, Pierce Baptist College in St. Louis, and a master's degree program at the University of Missouri. Objectivism emerged full-grown in his doctoral dissertation of 1911, *The Transition to an Objective Standard of Social Control*. Bernard argued that Small, and indeed all previous theorists, had extracted that standard from utilitarian psychology. Society was understood as interaction among individuals; individuals were assumed to act on the wholesome promptings of pleasure or pain; and the social good was compounded from individual judgments of happiness. Bernard denied this chain of reasoning at every point. Society was an organism; feeling was a totally unreliable guide for individual activity; and individual feelings – whimsical, subjectivistic, hedonistic – were inadequate measures of the social good. Individual feelings could not set the standard "in a world where training must modify instinct, where the cultural and artificial rather than the habitual and 'natural' set the standard, in a social and moral world in the best sense."

The true social standard according to Bernard, lay in the fullest development of the organic society, and only science could discover and enforce its conditions. "Where a social fact is established it should become as obligatory as the laws of astronomy or physics." This would involve some coercion, though no more than the coercion of scientific experts in a democracy, as Lester Ward had imagined. And it would allow individual liberty. True freedom could not be created by "subjective or personal initiative, but only where all the conditions of activity are uniform and thoroughly controlled,

---

142 Bannister's *Sociology and Scientism* is an excellent account, which errs only in identifying scientism and its historical context with the more extreme behaviorists and quantifiers, whereas their historical experience and desire for sciences of control were widely shared by their cohort.

where the individual is not subjected constantly to unexpected stimuli and impulsions which he cannot guard against."[143]

Bernard's total distrust of untutored human nature, his belief in the absolute transcendance of society, his desire for complete control of way-ward human experience, and his straightforward equation of scientific laws and moral norms, all bespeak the sudden transformation of Christian orthodoxy into scientism and a conflict-ridden experience of the modern liberal world. They also bespeak the wider desire among social scientists less severely afflicted for a science of social control. When Edward C. Hayes reviewed Bernard's thesis he did not deny the possibility of an objective standard of social control, only that Bernard had found it. Bernard was undemocratic. Social aims had to be composed of individual values, Hayes said. Bernard's later efforts to defend his position suggest that he met with considerable doubts, but he seems also to have had support.[144]

The main thrust of the new program, however, was less the moral objectivism of Chicago, than the methodological objectivism that Giddings had been nurturing at Columbia. Giddings' emphasis on statistics had developed from his interest in biological evolution. Like Karl Pearson he believed historical evolution was governed by a selective process, natural and social, that could be measured in the statistical distribution of population characteristics. Giddings' students, and to some extent Giddings himself, were by this time losing faith in the elaborate map he had drawn of this process for modern society, but they continued to believe that evolutionary selection was going on and that sociologists studied it. Given its problemat-ical modern outcome, however, statistical study of society became even more important, for it was only through objective, quantitative measures that a true map could eventually be drawn.

Stuart Chapin accepted Giddings' viewpoint, but his 1913 text on social evolution stopped short of modern society, where Giddings' theory was problematical, and cast doubt on the racial theory that was so important to his teacher. He presented side by side Giddings' and Boas' theories of the origins and character of racial differences, and came down gently on the side of Boas. The evidence favored equal mental capacity and equal capacity for progress. If the combination of natural, social, and sexual selection had not

---

143 L. L. Bernard, *The Transition to an Objective Standard of Social Control* (Chicago: University of Chicago Press, 1911), 27, 82, 92.
144 Edward C. Hayes, "Review of Luther L. Bernard, *The Transition to an Objective Standard of Social Control*," *AJS*, 17 (May 1912): 852–3; L. L. Bernard, "The Objective Viewpoint in Sociology," *AJS*, 25 (November 1919): 298–325; L. L. Bernard, "The Function of Generalization," *Monist*, 30 (July 1920): 623–31.

worked, as Giddings imagined, to create innate differences between the progressive and nonprogressive peoples, how important were these racial differences in modern society?[145]

The only answer to this and other questions in sociology would have to come through statistics. In 1912 Chapin presented a statistical study to his colleagues as a model for future work. Using election statistics, he measured variability of the popular vote in presidential elections since 1856. He discovered a substantial increase in variability in 1876 and 1896, produced by both an increase in the percentage of people voting and in shifts in party voting. Assuming that increased variability in voting marked increased "intelligent voting," he claimed to substantiate, *pace* Bentley, one of the great desiderata of evolutionary social science – the growing rationality of public opinion and its "flexibility in adjustment."[146]

Two years later he issued a programmatic call for the use of statistics in sociology. "There has been too much deductive philosophic generalization and far too little inductive verification," Chapin charged. Statistics offer the best means to amass large numbers of observations and also to reduce bias and individual error. In the statistical "average," moreover, sociology had available an objective standard. Generalizations that emerge from such study, he claimed, "will be fairly comparable as regards validity and accuracy with the generalizations of applied science." The resolutely objective style of Chapin's language barely masked the utopian enthusiasm he felt for this royal road to a science of sociology. It is fitting that an expert statistician felt it necessary to tell the sociologists in reply that statistics were useful but not a panacea. By using voting data, Chapin had avoided one of the chief difficulties for sociology – how to quantify human phenomena. The seeming exactness and certainty of number, its very nakedness of qualitative distinction, promised to "do away with all the uncertainties or doubts that beset the path of social science."[147]

In 1917 Chapin issued a methodological statement that made clear the outcome of this method for history. He began with the central feature of successful natural science, experiment. "The fundamental rule of the experimental method is to vary only one condition at a time and to maintain all other conditions rigidly constant." Sociologists in the past have had to rely

145  F. Stuart Chapin, *An Introduction to the Study of Social Evolution: The Prehistoric Period* (New York: Century, 1913), chap. 7. In the "Preface," Chapin justified his prehistoric time period by quoting Thomas and Robinson on time.
146  F. Stuart Chapin, "The Variability of the Popular Vote at Presidential Elections," *AJS*, 18 (September 1912): 222–40.
147  F. Stuart Chapin, "The Elements of Scientific Method in Sociology," *AJS*, 20 (November 1914): 371, 391; F. A. Dewey, "An Application of Statistical Method," *AJS*, 21 (November 1915): 334–8.

on "natural experiments," like the relative isolation of Appalachian peoples; on social experiments, like the nineteenth-century utopian communities; and on the social experimentation carried on through enactment of social legislation. But in all these cases, the results are "indefinite and inconclusive." The problem is that "social units are complex as compared with the relatively simple units of other sciences." Sociological units are not homogenous; they are unique. "Welfare experiments ... though successful in Germany and England, prove nothing final and conclusive for Americans." There is always more than one varying condition in the situation, and conditions are always changing. The answer was use of the statistical method, which could discover the separate effects of different factors and overcome the heterogeneity of aggregates by means of correlation and sampling techniques.[148]

Since Comte sociologists had spoken of history as the sociologist's substitute for and repository of experiments, but in Chapin's hands, history began to turn into a box from which pieces could be picked out for examination, their character and context defined entirely by statistical correlation. In the same way, mentality would be absorbed by measurable behavior. In reading Thomas' methodological prescriptions the following year in the *Polish Peasant*, one can hear a dialogue going on with Chapin. Social facts are not more complex than natural ones, Thomas replied. However, in social phenomena, the variable is never just one factor, but two, the attitude of the subject as well as the changing condition. The life history is the method of choice for sociology, not statistical method. For all their shared allegiance to scientism, Thomas and Park were trying to develop a science of human experience.

### From Veblen to institutional economics: Hoxie and Mitchell

After the decline of the Gilded Age movement of historical economics, realism had remained a powerful force in economics both within and outside the neoclassical mainstream. The new realists of iconoclastic temper were inevitably drawn to the influence of Veblen. Besides Mitchell, we will look at Robert F. Hoxie, Veblen's successor at Chicago in 1906, and Herbert Davenport, a somewhat older and idiosyncratic recruit to economics from business. Together they drew Veblen's historico-evolutionism toward the naturalistic models of liberal process that were forming in sociology and political science.

---

148 F. Stuart Chapin, "The Experimental Method and Sociology," *Scientific Monthly*, 4 (February 1917): 133–44, (March 1917): 238–47, particularly 133, 135, 240, 244.

Veblen offered a positivist, as well as radical, model of historical economics. From the start, he had pronounced the historical school a failure and proposed instead a "theory" of history modeled on evolutionary biology and grounded in anthropology. On one level, Veblen's conception of theory, informed by his early studies of Kant and Peirce, put him and his heirs ahead of most historians in their willingness to bring synthetic and analytic constructs to history. On another level, however, his positivism led him toward a closed model of human experience, in which history was generated by fixed categories of instinct and race. Mitchell was stimulated by Veblen to study ethnology, not history, and sent off on a long detour through instinct psychology. When they attempted to dig deeper into the historical basis of Veblenian theory, Mitchell and Hoxie both found themselves unprepared and had to develop new methodological strategies on their own. As the catalyst for an alternative historical economics, Veblen's evolutionary economics was not altogether promising.

## Hoxie's changing theory of labor economics

Veblen's work nonetheless opened up several lines of inquiry that were promptly taken up by younger economists. The first was the study of labor and the "trade-union animus" he identified as the means toward socialism. During the peripatetic early years of his teaching career, Robert F. Hoxie moved into position to address that issue. A disciple first of Laughlin's classical economics, then of Fetter's marginalism, Hoxie also accepted Veblen's argument that economics needed a historical dynamic theory. After 1906, settling down at the University of Chicago, he concentrated on studies of the American labor movement in the light of Veblen's hypothesis.[149]

Faced with a historical task, Hoxie had to deal first with the difficulties historical method presented to economists. It had degenerated, he claimed, into "a mere heaping up of facts in the hope that principles would somehow spontaneously arise out of them." There was some truth in the historian's contention that we do not yet know enough, but that need not stop us from reasoning upon what we did know. More importantly, because of the difference of the past, what the historian told us about past causes could not automatically be applied to present problems. Still, only history could distinguish continuity and change. By 1906 Hoxie was ready to define the "historical method," as opposed to mere "historical narrative," as an

---

149 Hamilton, "Development of Hoxie's Economics," 862–71; Robert F. Hoxie, "The Demand and Supply Concepts: An Introduction to the Study of Market Price," *JPE*, 14 (June 1906): 337–61, (July 1906): 401–26.

analytical tool linking the present and the past. Apparently informed by Dewey's conception of genetic analysis, he argued that the "historical method of science" was a species of purposive scientific investigation.

> Is it not true that in reality all scientific investigation is undertaken in furtherance of some definite, vital, human interest? We wish to control the forces at hand so as to better realize some human purpose, therefore we seek to comprehend the existing situation from the standpoint of the purpose or interest in question.... It follows that all scientific investigation is bound to be highly selective.

Hoxie was not saying that the interpretation of the problem necessarily shaped "the facts," it only selected them. Still, the "historical method of science" was selective in a double sense, for it required independent observation of the present problem that was the focus of inquiry and then a pointed investigation of the past to determine just why the present situation had come to be what it is. The recognition that one had to approach history with a well-formulated question, that historical method was an analytical tool yielding explanation was a decided advance over his colleagues' conceptions.[150]

Hoxie proceeded according to this method to study labor history and also to investigate union activities and labor's response to scientific management, as a participant observer and through innovative interview and questionnaire techniques. He created a model for Chicago sociologists as well as institutional economists. Using Veblen's distinction between industrial and business employments, he found in the American Federation of Labor a strong "pecuniary" spirit, defined as concern for immediate economic gains and particularistic interests that linked the worker to his employer and craft rather than to other workers. Hoxie was uncertain, however, what conclusions to draw from his findings. They could mean that "in this country real class consciousness and class conflict are absent," or they could rather point to faulty leadership of the labor movement and to the severe economic necessity that made workers the slave of the "need for immediate results" and forced them to forgo their class-conscious feelings. "If so it emphasizes most the tremendous counter force set up by the very economic conditions that breed classes and class conflict."[151] By 1916, after further contemporary

---

150  Robert F. Hoxie, "On the Empirical Method of Economic Instruction," *JPE*, 9 (September 1901): 481–526, particularly 500; idem, "Historical Method vs. Historical Narrative," *JPE*, 14 (November 1906): 569–70.
151  Hamilton, "Development of Hoxie's Economics," 873–5; John P. Frey, "Robert F. Hoxie: Investigator and Interpreter," *JPE*, 24 (November 1916): 884–93; Robert F. Hoxie, "The Convention of the Socialist Party," *JPE*, 16 (July 1908): 442–50; idem, "President Gompers and the Labor Vote," *JPE*, 16 (December 1908): 693–700, particularly 700.

and historical studies, he rejected this dialectical view of history and instead opted for the American exceptionalist explanation.

Hoxie's historical analysis of American labor organization was in some ways astute. He found several types of unionism that had appeared at various stages of economic development. The craft or "business" union, pecuniary in spirit, he found at the start of labor organization in the 1820s and still dominant in the A.F.L. The utopian, social-uplift union had appeared almost at once in the 1830s and persisted in the Knights of Labor, with its attempt to include in its ranks the whole "people." But the Knights was utopian in a second sense, not only behind but ahead of its time, for it also tried to weld craft workers into a sense of working-class solidarity. The most developed form of union organization, the industrial union, both built and reflected that kind of class consciousness, but it was a minor element in America then and for the discernible future. American workers lacked class consciousness.[152]

The reason, Hoxie argued, was because there were no classes in America.

Whatever operates to make individuals like-minded tends to draw them together into a group. . . . Whatever emphasizes or creates difference of character, belief or interest tends to repel individuals and to force them into diverse and opposing groups. These groups, therefore, are the outcome of the attractive and repellent interaction of all the characteristics of individuals, relatively permanent and relatively temporary and shifting, in all the infinity of their specific manifestations and combinations.

Amid this atomistic ceaseless movement, the economic interest was prominent in the formation of groups, but not predominant, at least in America.

In a society like our own, democratically organized, characterized therefore by much and varied contact between the individuals of the different mechanical groups, exposed by intercourse to the ideas and ideals of every nation, changing in its composition by the influx of every race and order of men . . . enlarging and shifting its wants, constantly developing new social problems and new social issues, there is little opportunity for the development of caste or class.

Here was the idealized image of America as classless democracy that Bentley and Park had developed. Constant motion was erasing all structural difference. What had happened to the economic constraint that made workers the slave of the "need for immediate results"? Hoxie did not investigate how much class mobility there was in America, nor raise the possibility that classes could persist, even if some individuals moved in and out of them. That American workers had political and ethnic identifications that could work at

---

152  Robert F. Hoxie, *Trade Unionism in the United States* (New York: D. Appleton, 1917), chap. 4, especially p. 95.

cross-purposes to their sense of class solidarity might mean that they had a different kind of class consciousness, rather than none at all. Hoxie rightly argued that Veblen had placed "too much stress upon the economic environment as a formative force . . . there are no such rigid economic environments and disciplines. There is much more social interaction than is supposed." But did economic determinism have to be transformed into social motion so random and atomistic? Was the only alternative to "European" class consciousness an idealized image of American democracy? And was this always true in America? In 1830 or 1880 as in 1917?[153]

Hoxie's scientific presentism and concern with typology also worked against a historicist differentiation of the past. It is easy, though not necessary, when doing history backward from present conditions, to read the present into the past. Hoxie made the business union the earliest and most persistent American type and to do so, he split off from it the utopian, uplift features current historians recognize as integral to it through the 1870s, a reflection of an earlier and different form of class consciousness than Hoxie was looking for. Thus Hoxie's vision of ceaseless change had the same covert message that George Herbert Mead's had in 1899. As his editor noticed, Hoxie had found "relatively stable union types." The ceaseless change of American experience kept reproducing the same pluralistic individualism.[154]

In fact, Hoxie did not give up his hope for ultimate change. When he could no longer accept Veblen's theory, he came to accept a more hard-headed version of what he acutely identified as the Progressive uplift theory of organicist social control. Society was moving toward greater social interaction and hence greater democracy. If we forgo the hope of complete consensus, Hoxie urged, we can expect increasing social agreement on the "rules of the game" that govern group conflicts and hence the moderation and elevation of those conflicts. Given American conditions, wageworkers would only be able to organize effectively and achieve "constitutional government in industry" under the auspices of a larger social control. Employers' groups were themselves softening and beginning to think about the welfare of their workers. Presumably public opinion and legislation could establish "maxima" and "minima" in labor-employer conflicts, on the

153 Ibid., 355–8, 367. For a careful study of Hoxie's abandonment of Veblen that does not take exceptionalism into account, see Paul J. McNulty, "Hoxie's Economics in Retrospect: The Making and Unmaking of a Veblenian," *History of Political Economy*, 5 (Fall 1973): 449–84.
154 Hoxie, *Trade Unionism*, "Introduction," by E. H. Downey, xxiv. On current labor historiography, see David Montgomery, *Beyond Equality: Labor and the Radical Republicans, 1862–1872* (New York: Knopf, 1967), chaps. 4–6.

principle of the minimum wage. When in his last study he saw the new methods of scientific management deskilling and atomizing workers so that labor organization was becoming even more difficult, he countered with a plan of public vocational education that would somehow restore the moral and intellectual stamina the workers were losing and allow them to organize.

This was, unfortunately, Hoxie's last word. After a lifetime of recurring depression, he committed suicide in 1916 at the age of forty-eight; his last book was a posthumous collection. John R. Commons believed that his suicide was a reaction to the loss of sponsorship for his study of scientific management. The economist Alvin Johnson, who deeply distrusted Veblen, reported seeing Hoxie shortly before his death, depressed over the fact that Veblen's theory had misdirected his work on labor. But from Hoxie's written work it would seem that before his death he had worked out an alternative theory. Perhaps he did not quite believe that liberal individualism and social control would work either.[155]

### The irregular Veblenian paths of Davenport and Mitchell

At the same time that Veblen's labor theory was taking this exceptionalist turn, so too was his theory of business enterprise. Herbert Davenport began to study economics in his thirties, after he lost his fortune in South Dakota in 1893. From the beginning Davenport was interested in working within the new marginalist theory and figuring out the flaw in socialism. By 1896 he had produced perhaps the first marginalist college text in America, and in 1898 earned a doctorate at Chicago. There also he became a student and friend of Veblen. Davenport was impressed by Veblen's criticism of the hedonistic psychology in neoclassical economics and of the value-laden apologetics still visible in the old-style classical economics.[156] As a personal victim of financial crisis, he agreed with Veblen's indictment of the credit system and its financial manipulations. But Veblen's insistence on the dominance of money values in the capitalist economy had an ironic outcome. It reinforced Davenport's belief that marginalism, as an analysis of value based wholly on market price, provided an objective account of the capitalist economy.

Davenport constructed a unique blend of Veblenian and marginalist eco-

155 Hoxie, *Trade Unionism*, chaps. 8, 10, 12, 14, especially pp. 367–72; John R. Commons, *Myself* (New York: Macmillan, 1934), 177–81; Alvin S. Johnson, *Pioneer's Progress* (New York: Viking, 1952), 204–7.

156 M. Slade Kendrick, "Herbert Joseph Davenport," *DAB*, Suppl. 1, 224; Joseph Dorfman, *The Economic Mind in American Civilization*, 5 vols. (New York: Viking, 1946–59), 3:375–90.

nomics. He began with Veblen's historicist premise that the market was a historical creation, constantly changing. From that he drew an ahistorical conclusion: The task of the economist was to pay as little attention as possible to past and future and to study "the situation as it actually is." What existed was a money economy. Davenport cleared that field of the historical, institutional changes that were central to Veblen's analysis of business enterprise. "Combination and monopoly may be regarded as merely secondary aspects of competition and of individual initiative." To say that the economy was now becoming a credit economy said "merely that in new and marvelous ways money is taking on a still greater emphasis." Economic science could become simply the study of the money economy as expressed in price. In his appreciation of the complex interrelation of market calculations he won Irving Fisher's admiration, but in explicating market process from the point of view of the entrepreneur and his search for gain, he also drew on Veblenian iconoclasm. One of his most influential ideas was the importance of the "loan fund." Capital, he stressed, came from banks, not from abstinence.[157]

Davenport returned to Veblen when he allowed himself a few remarks on the "art" of economics rather than its "science." Here one could take account of the "social significance" of the money economy and here Veblen's attack on the money handlers and acquistive rich meshed perfectly – given its own populist sources – with Davenport's liberal antimonopoly sentiments. At least two-thirds of total American wealth, Davenport estimated, was "made up of one form or another of . . . capitalized predation," most often in the form of corporate stock manipulation. Through "serious inheritance taxes" and controls on corporate management the competitive field could be cleared of illegitimate advantage. "The pressing problem is to establish equality of opportunity – the elimination of handicaps." It is not surprising to find beneath Davenport's judgments a traditional American exceptionalist view of history. Out of the long history of the world, mired in poverty, he began,

there has finally emerged the modern civilization. . . . The Anglo-Saxon is now exploiting the almost inexhaustible wealth of the richest continent in the world. . . . No new continent is left to be opened. . . . But both the science and the opportunity are still with us . . . yet there is dire poverty for hordes of hard-working men. For this . . . there is only one possible line of explanation, the prodigal incomes of the rich.

---

157 Herbert J. Davenport, *The Economics of Enterprise* (New York: Macmillan, 1913), 26, 21–2; Dorfman, *Economic Mind*, 3:386–7.

American history, like the money economy, stood suspended in time, at the apex of world history, but under threat of corruption.[158]

Most of Davenport's readers were confused, as well they might be, by his mixture of Veblen and marginalism, historicism and ahistoricism. But in one respect he had hit on a line of analysis the young institutionalists would attempt to develop in a more historicist direction. According to Wesley Mitchell, the business point of view adopted by marginalists like Davenport, Fisher, and to some degree Frank Fetter, confirmed Veblen's analysis that business values dominated the money economy. What was needed was an effort to work out the implications of that insight in historico-evolutionary rather than marginalist terms, and that task Mitchell undertook.[159]

As an undergraduate and graduate student at Chicago, Mitchell worked chiefly under the conservative Laughlin, whose continued devotion to empirical, historical study as an adjunct of classical theory reflected unchanged the mentality of Charles Dunbar and the economic traditionalists of the 1870s. In the 1890s, when the currency issue came to a head, Laughlin emerged as a public spokesman against monetary inflation and a professional critic of the quantity theory of money that was used to defend it. He set Mitchell to work on an empirical study of the economic effects of the issuance of greenbacks during the Civil War, which he hoped would confirm the ill effects of paper money and disprove the quantity theory. Mitchell's study came to both those conclusions, but his research also became the unlikely vehicle of professional success, for it demonstrated his superb talents as an empirical analyst.[160]

What turned Mitchell decisively toward Veblen was his idea of the divergence between pecuniary and industrial employments, set out in a 1900 article and *The Theory of Business Enterprise* in 1904, the year Mitchell went to the University of California at Berkeley. That book, he believed, disproved the popular view that Veblen's work was "based on sheer imagination rather than upon observation and reason." In 1906 Veblen moved to Stanford and began to see Mitchell often and the following year Mitchell

158 Davenport, *Economics of Enterprise*, 519, 525–8.

159 Wesley Clair Mitchell, "The Role of Money in Economic Theory" (1916), in *The Backward Art of Spending Money, and Other Essays* (New York: McGraw Hill, 1937), 156–60.

160 Alfred J. Bornemann, *J. Laurence Laughlin* (Washington, D.C.: American Council on Public Affairs, 1940); Wesley Clair Mitchell, "A History of the Greenbacks, with Special Reference to the Economic Consequences of Their Issue: 1862–65," *Decennial Publications of the University of Chicago*, 2d ser., no. 9 (1903); idem, "Gold, Prices, and Wages under the Greenback Standard," *University of California Publications in Economics*, 1 (1908).

began work on a manuscript on the evolution of the money economy, "the highly organized group of pecuniary institutions" that had come to dominate modern society and culture. Mitchell was going to bring his formidable empirical talents to a demonstration and development of the theory Veblen had set out in broad strokes. In December 1908, when he attended for the first time the annual meeting of the American Economic Association, he found reformers and marginal theorists, but no one who wanted to follow through on Veblen's historico-evolutionary theory as he did.[161]

To do the subject properly, he plunged into early modern European history – "I am brutally ignorant of economic history" – which he found tedious and fascinating by turns. At the same time he had been working up statistical material on how the price system operated. In March 1909, he decided to postpone the larger manuscript and the historico-evolutionary analysis it demanded and publish as a separate work the statistical analysis of contemporary business cycles. He also issued a call for a new historico-evolutionary economic theory of the kind he was having difficulty writing. The leading problem of that new economics was "to account for the actual human types which are found in every nation, by tracing the processes by which habits and institutions have grown out of instincts, and by examining the fashion in which the new acquisitions and the old traits combine in controlling economic conduct." Working on Veblen's evolutionary model, with its instinct psychology, he concluded that economists needed more psychological training. Most likely, this stumbling block encouraged him to drop the larger project and turn his attention to the modern business process.[162]

Published in 1913, *Business Cycles* was Mitchell's masterwork, a rallying point for all advocates of empirical research in economics, as Thomas' *Polish Peasant* would be a few years later in sociology. That same year he was appointed at Columbia as the successor to John Bates Clark. To his new colleagues he seemed a man "equipped to attack theoretical problems in a truly scientific spirit." Just what Mitchell accomplished in *Business Cycles*, however, was a source of considerable confusion, and still is. Upon the quality and suggestiveness of his analysis there has been no disagreement. As his appreciative student, Arthur Burns, pointed out, what Mitchell brought to economic analysis was the power of a good historian, the ability to move back and forth between generalizations and particulars, estimate evidence,

161 Wesley Clair Mitchell, "Review of W. J. Ghent, *Mass and Class: A Study of Social Divisions*," *JPE*, 13 (March 1905): 283; L. S. Mitchell, *Two Lives*, 167–71.
162 L. S. Mitchell, *Two Lives*, 171–3, 175–7; Wesley Clair Mitchell, "The Rationality of Economic Activity," *JPE*, 18 (February 1910): 97–113, (March 1910): 197–216, particularly 216.

and construct and manipulate data imaginatively to test hypotheses regarding what, in detail, is happening. Where readers, and he himself, were confused was over the larger bearings of his work.[163]

Mitchell's own intention has to be understood within the Veblenian framework in which the project originated. The analysis he made of business cycles was distinctly Veblenian. Basing his examination on data from 1890 to 1911, from England, France, Germany, and the United States, he focused on the period of developed finance capitalism Veblen had identified. He began the book with a description of the contemporary economy, in which capitalism was defined as a historical form whose central feature was making money rather than making goods. Hence the industrial functions of the economy were controlled by the price system and the search for profit. Like Veblen, Mitchell described the operation of the price system from the standpoint of its unquiet experience rather than any inner law, tracing how disturbances moved through the economy's interlocking business institutions. He concluded that Veblen's theory of business cycles was generally sound, though it could be modified and augmented in various ways.

> The theory propounded is fairly close to Veblen's on the most important point – a decline in prospective net earnings leads to a shrinkage of business credit and thus brings on a liquidation of outstanding accounts. But my statistical apparatus affords a more cogent demonstration of the whole process – tho of course a tamer one.

Tamer and despite the Veblenian framework, different.[164]

Veblen was clear that he was presenting a historico-evolutionary "theory," a closed model of history that specified the causal factors moving history forward. Mitchell sometimes conceived of his work as an account of the business cycle, at other times as an account of the forward movement of the whole historical economic process. At times he called his work a "theory" of business cycles, at other times, a "descriptive analysis," a wider, essentially historical analysis that used theories heuristically to enrich and focus inquiry rather than to pre-define it; hence an account that might provide evidence for some theories over others, but not itself a "theory." He therefore was unsure of the extent to which he had provided, or ever could provide, a "causal" theory of the business cycle. He described his method

---

163 Henry R. Seager to E. R. A. Seligman, May 14, 1913, quoted in Joseph Dorfman, "A Professional Sketch," in *Wesley Clair Mitchell: The Economic Scientist*, ed. Arthur F. Burns (New York: National Bureau of Economic Research, 1952), 133; Arthur F. Burns, "Introductory Sketch," ibid., 11–15. Compare opinions on the bearings of Mitchell's methodology given by John Maurice Clark, Milton Friedman, Alvin Hansen, and Joseph Schumpeter in ibid., 193–206, 245, 306–7, 329–35.

164 Wesley Clair Mitchell, *Business Cycles, Memoirs of the University of California*, 3 (1913), especially chap. 2 and pp. 579–81; L. S. Mitchell, *Two Lives*, 178.

as putting "speculations ... to the pragmatic test," but Dewey's blanket formula could not have helped him disentangle scientific and historical method.[165]

Mitchell's uncertainty regarding method was related to a fundamental ambiguity in the substance of his analysis. His Veblenian analysis of the money economy, with a slight shift in angle, a Gestalt-switch in perception, turned into a neoclassical view of the price system. He analyzed the search for profit in the money economy as a phenomenon of business calculation in an implicitly neoclassical market. Mitchell's businessmen did not deal in real utilities, but they calculated profit margins just as neoclassical businessmen did. The money economy he described responded to competition actual and potential, and took into account the substitutability of goods.[166] Marginalist theorists could, and did, read Mitchell's analyses with perfect comprehension and agreement, something they could not do with Veblen's account of profit seeking as predation.

Mitchell also praised the price system for its flexibility and stimulus to individual efficiency and cooperation. It was "unquestionably the best system of directing economic activity which men have yet practiced." Still, like the new liberals, he saw that it had "serious limitations." He defined two kinds of deficiencies in the money economy. The first criticism was common to all the new liberal economists: The general welfare was not the same as individual welfare, measured by profit. But the chief cause of "recurrent disorders" was imperfect planning. Here, in the concept of planning, Mitchell was enlarging the new liberal regulatory impulse under the influence of his own commitment to scientific control. Planning was efficient within the individual firm but not between firms. Ruling out state socialism, he suggested that the government collect and publish more, and more accurate, barometers of economic activity so that individual firms could plan better and also resist the powerful financiers, who were tempted to manipulate the market for their own benefit. Mitchell envisioned a market economy in which individual actors would calculate profits more rationally by avoiding the ignorance and irrational expectations that aggravated the

---

165 W. C. Mitchell, *Business Cycles*, 19–20, 449–50. Abraham Hirsch draws a sharp contrast between Laughlin's empirical, and Dewey's more hypothetical, style of investigation as models for Mitchell, but I do not think this difference gets to the heart of Mitchell's difficulties. See Abraham Hirsch, "The American Setting and Wesley Clair Mitchell's View of Traditional Economics," *Journal of Economic Issues*, 1 (June 1967): 74–85; idem, "Mitchell's Work on Civil War Inflation in His Development as an Economist," *History of Political Economy*, 2 (Spring 1970): 118–32; idem, "The *A Posteriori* Method and the Creation of New Theory: W. C. Mitchell as a Case Study," ibid. 8 (Summer 1976): 195–206.

166 W. C. Mitchell, *Business Cycles*, 27–9, 31.

sharp swings of the business cycle. Planning produced a more perfectly functioning liberal market.[167]

Finally, Mitchell inscribed the neoclassical market in his analysis by defining the business cycle as a self-righting mechanism, a cycle that always moved from depression into a new swing toward prosperity. Veblen had proposed that since the start of the credit economy, business cycles had grown more severe and downward stresses in the economy accumulated. The economy might be headed toward a chronic state of depression. But by definition Mitchell ruled out Veblen's open-ended view.

Prices, then, form a system – a highly complex system of many parts connected with each other in diverse ways, a system infinitely flexible in detail yet stable in the essential balance of its interrelations, a system like a living organism in its ability to recover from the serious disorder into which it periodically falls.

The business cycle emerged within an "organism" or self-regulating system. "Instead of becoming chronic, [business cycles] lead after a time to the return of prosperity." Mitchell clearly did not understand the implications of that view. Like Veblen, he chided his colleagues that in the real world there was no such thing as a "static" or "normal" state, a balance toward which prices converged. "Affairs are always undergoing a cumulative change, always passing through some phase of a business cycle into some other phase." He did not see that the "cumulative change" he had described was not really cumulative, but was self-enclosed. "I shall never forget his speechless surprise," Joseph Schumpeter recalled, "when I tried to show him that his great book of 1913, so far as the bare bones of its argument are concerned, was an exercise in the dynamic theory of equilibrium."[168]

Mitchell certainly did not think that was what he had done. He repeatedly described the change within each cycle as a historical process, and noted also the change between cycles. No business cycle is ever quite like any other. Business history repeats itself, but with a difference. "That is precisely what is implied by saying that the process of economic activity within which business cycles occur is a process of *cumulative* change." Moreover, at the end of the book he suggested that the chief causes of variation in business cycles lay outside the business system, in war, peace, tariffs, and changes in economic organization. "Being cumulative, their dominating influence upon

167 Ibid., 31–40, 585–96. On planning, see Ellis Hawley, *The Great War and the Search for a Modern Order* (New York: St. Martin's Press, 1979), 120–3, and Guy Alchon, *The Invisible Hand of Planning: Capitalism, Social Science, and the State in the 1920's* (Princeton, N.J.: Princeton University Press, 1985).
168 W. C. Mitchell, *Business Cycles*, 31, 39–40, 86; Joseph Schumpeter, "The General Economist," in *Wesley Clair Mitchell*, 329.

the phenomena of business cycles stands out clearly in the lapse of years. Hence it is probable that the economists of each generation will see reason to recast the theory of business cycles which they learned in their youth." Yet in his analysis Mitchell dismissed the variation between the cycles he studied, finding certain essential features at work in all of them. Nor did he analyze changes over time. Indeed the reader would have to assume that after "the lapse of years," if business cycles remained, they would remain by definition, self-righting mechanisms.[169]

That Mitchell depicted the economic process of modern history as an ever recurrent cycle is surely of interest. The language of American exceptionalism does not appear in his work, but the assumption of a happy outcome is deeply imbedded in his thinking. While he was working up his analysis, he was planning to present it to his class the following year. "What do you think of the plan?" he asked his future wife.

Will it be impossible to thrill a class of 150 freshmen with the delicate harmonies of the system of prices? Will they fail to grasp the aesthetic perfection of hair-poised adjustments between the raging forces which push wages up and down? Will they miss that sense of impending doom hanging over the fair fabric when the stresses begin inexorably to accumulate within the system? Will the panic have no terrors for their frivolous minds, and the long-drawn liquidation – will it be a matter to sleep through? And when the wholesome readjustments have been worked out will they miss the joy of a happy ending and a fresh beginning?[170]

Mitchell's tone was facetious, but the emotions expressed were not altogether feigned. He believed that the "disorders" of the money economy always produced "a happy ending and a fresh beginning." The liberal economy was to Mitchell, as it had traditionally been to American economists, a source of endless vitality. It is thus not surprising that, as Alvin H. Hansen remembered, "the term 'business cycle' became a popular and agreeable concept. Businessmen found it no reproach to describe the system of free enterprise as moving in continuing and self-generating cycles. Rather, they regarded these oscillations as the 'heart throb' of a lively, dynamic system."[171] In his own way, Mitchell effected as peculiar a blend as Davenport. Business cycles existed in history, but history was confined to the neoclassical market and endlessly renewed itself in recurrent cycles. The liberal image of the market and the American vision of perennial vitality were hard to expunge, even for the disciples of Veblen.

After *Business Cycles* was published and he had succeeded Clark at

169 W. C. Mitchell, *Business Cycles*, 449, 582–3.
170 L. S. Mitchell, *Two Lives*, 175–6.
171 Alvin H. Hansen, "Social Scientist and Social Counselor," in *Wesley Clair Mitchell*, 302.

Columbia, Mitchell found himself in an important professional position, soon to be augmented by his leadership of the National Bureau of Economic Research. He set about to clarify his premises, starting first with the old problem Veblen had bequeathed him, psychology. From Edward L. Thorndike he concluded that Veblen's instinct of workmanship could not be a single heritable trait, but at most a stable disposition shaped and passed on by cultural experience. Mitchell soon found, moreover, that psychology did not give unequivocal aid. Watson had a different view of instinct from Thorndike. What did seem to emerge from the psychologists was rather the emphasis on studying behavior.[172]

Mitchell also was probably influenced by Dewey to move in this direction. At Chicago Dewey had reinforced the respect for the concrete activities of people, as opposed to rationalistic theories about them, which he was simultaneously learning from Laughlin and Veblen. On arriving in New York, he reestablished ties with Dewey and read all his work as it appeared. A series of Mitchell's notes, probably from 1914, suggest that a review of Dewey's social psychology reinforced his sense that economic science ought to be about the real activities of people and the whole range of activities in which they engage. Mitchell would also have known of Dewey's support of a behavioral point of view in psychology. He was soon urging that behaviorist psychology offered a new psychological foundation for economics.[173]

Mitchell included under the category of "behavior" a number of very different things. To study economic behavior meant to study all behavior involved in the economic process, not simply profit taking. One could study, as he did in a noted essay, the consumption choices of housewives. Under this broad psychological rubric Mitchell also meant to include the study of economic welfare, labor relations, and the kind of long-term institutional changes studied by Veblen, the Webbs, and Sombart.[174]

If behavior meant study of all economic activities, it also meant study of the outwardly visible actions of people. Economists could abandon esoteric searches into both instinct psychology and "that dark subjective realm" of

---

172 Wesley Clair Mitchell, "Human Behavior and Economics: A Survey of Recent Literature," *QJE*, 29 (November 1914): 10, 16, 22–3; idem, "Prospects of Ecics," Notes, March 24, 1920, p. 6, Mitchell Papers.
173 Lucy Sprague Mitchell, "Personal Sketch," in *Wesley Clair Mitchell*, 92; [Wesley Clair Mitchell], Notes, [1914]: "Use of Dewey's scl psy in Ecic Th," "Problems of Ecic Th," "Ecic Method," "Charac of Ecic laws," "Two types of explan in Ecics," Mitchell Papers.
174 Wesley Clair Mitchell, "The Backward Art of Spending Money" (1912), in *Backward Art*, 3–19; idem, "Prospects of Ecics," Mitchell Papers. Mitchell was also influenced by Charles H. Cooley, "Institutional Character of Pecuniary Valuation"; idem, "The Sphere of Pecuniary Valuation," *AJS*, 19 (September 1913): 188–203; idem, "The Progress of Pecuniary Valuation," *QJE*, 30 (November 1913): 1–21.

hedonistic satisfactions. One could now study economic behavior "in the light of common day." Economists were not dependent upon psychologists, but partners. They could use psychological findings when applicable, but could contribute their own analysis.[175]

Finally, behavior, unlike motive, could be studied by objective methods. Indeed the most important method for the study of economic behavior was statistics. By the end of World War I, statistics took at least equal place with behavior in Mitchell's view of his discipline. Declaring the social sciences to be still "immature," perhaps "more like metaphysics than like mechanics," he urged that quantitative analysis offered the social sciences their best hope of becoming like the natural sciences.

Social statistics ... has many of the progressive features of the physical sciences. It shows forthright progress in knowledge of fact, in technique of analysis, and in refinement of results. It is amenable to mathematical formulation. It is capable of forecasting group phenomena. It is objective.... [It contributes to] the task of developing a method by which we may make cumulative progress in social organization.

Mitchell's praise of statistical science fittingly ends with a shift in the context of his favorite word from the "cumulative change" of history to the "cumulative progress" of scientific rationality.[176]

Mitchell's growing emphasis on behavior and statistics thus extended the ambiguities he had displayed in his study of business cycles. Behavior and statistics were to be the watchwords of a new kind of economics, the kind his younger colleagues were already starting to call "institutionalism." Economics ought to be, Mitchell was saying, an empirical study of economic behavior, as his own study of business cycles had been. Statistics was a tool for studying the ongoing historical process, a way of studying not what according to rationalistic theories people should do, but what in fact and unforeseen, they did do. But if historical behavior was understood as market behavior in the money economy, then statistics measured the activities of market aggregates, not historical actors.

Even within the framework of the market, Mitchell expected empirical study of actual economic processes to yield new generalizations, a new framework of theory that would remain close to the facts. Economic theory would become "consciously an analytic account of economic behavior" so that the "viewpoint will be the same in a book on the theory of value and theory of rate making." On the other hand he saw that neoclassical

175 W. C. Mitchell, "The Role of Money in Economic Theory," 175.
176 Wesley Clair Mitchell, "Statistics and Government" (1919), in *Backward Art*, 51–53.

economics roughly "worked" because it mirrored the calculating rational behavior instilled by the market. Precisely because money rationalized economic behavior, "the use of money lays the foundation for a rational theory of that life."[177] How different then would his empirical theory be? Why would it not yield, as *Business Cycles* had yielded, an account of market behavior consonant with qualified neoclassical premises? Was he developing tools for charting the historical processes that were changing the neo-classical market or tools for the general analysis of that paradigmatic market?

In his first major programmatic speech to the AEA, in 1916, Mitchell took an inclusive line, leaving room for marginalist economists to study the rational logic of business and for historical economists to study institutional change. The institutional character of the market allowed economic theory and economic history to work on "a common plane," he believed.[178] He did not see that the common plane would have to be set up either inside or outside the market paradigm, and would mean in each case something different.

What is perhaps most striking in this story of Veblen's first disciples is their departure from his theory. Davenport, coming to Veblen with an older exceptionalist view intact, simply clung to it. Hoxie and Mitchell, when they came face to face with the ambiguous historical conditions Veblen's own categories had allowed them to identify, reached for the liberal exceptionalist vision of the perpetually changing, self-renewing market society. When they could not find the American utopia in Veblen's socialist scheme, they rejected his analysis wholesale and turned to a vision that could preserve their exceptionalist ideal. That vision made some sense of their observations and data, but not the only sense that could have been made of them. Indeed, to reach that view, they had to contradict facts they had previously seen or logic they continued to hold. Diluted as the liberal "promise of America" had become, it retained the power to draw American social thinkers into exceptionalist paths.

## Conclusions

The cohort of creative social scientists who appeared in the late Progressive period remade the contours of American social science. Though extending the direction of work already begun, they created powerful new models of social science that have shaped their disciplines ever since. Hoxie, Mitchell,

---

177 W. C. Mitchell, "Prospects of Ecics," pp. 6–7, Mitchell Papers; idem, "The Role of Money in Economic Theory," 170–71.
178 W. C. Mitchell, "The Role of Money in Economic Theory," 175–6.

Thomas, Park, Chapin, Bentley, and Beard originated concepts and methods fitted to the liberal understanding of modern American society. Their inventions were responses to the historical change going on around them: to the polyglot, urban, secular world that was engulfing them, the concatenating political crises of the decade, and the acute sense of change itself, amplified at every turn. But it is the argument of this chapter, as of this book, that their new concepts and methods shaped that historical change as deeply as they reflected it. This cohort worked in a society in which the structural power of capitalism was heavily felt and visibly present, in which the reinforcement of ethnicity and class was as palpable as its divergence, in which the rapidity of historical change opened up a space for dialogue with the past, not just abandonment of it. Their choices were the choices of liberal American exceptionalists, drawn toward the inclination of their national, disciplinary, and professional discourses.

The emphasis on fluid process in their work constituted perhaps its chief novelty, whether as the movement of Mitchell's cumulative business cycle spreading through the money economy; Thomas' social psychology of attitudes and sociology of disorganization; Park's sociology of urban competition, conflict, accommodation, and assimilation; Bentley's equilibrating interest-group pressures; or Beard's historical rendering of the struggle of economic interests. Process placed them at the intersection of history and nature, seeking to capture both the concrete particularities of experience and universal natural forms, both the changing shapes of modern society and an unchanging dynamic at its core. A great deal of the creative richness of their work, as well as the contradictions they never resolved, grew out of these divergent impulses locked together in the metaphor of process.

In the idiom of American exceptionalism, America too stands at the intersection of history and nature. Part of the attraction of process was its ability to project an idealized liberal vision of modern American society. Society was the product of interacting individuals, forming and re-forming in groups – perhaps not quite freely forming, but forming under fluid rather than fixed constraints. Class disappeared in that solvent; race alone threatened to withstand it. For such a society, the statistical study of aggregates and the external observation of behavior seemed peculiarly appropriate. So too did the two figures of liberal exceptionalist process that have recurred in this text. One figure was that of cyclical change, as in Mitchell's business cycle and Thomas' cycle of social organization-disorganization-reorganization. We will soon see Park as well develop cyclical theories of assimilation and ecological growth, and Chapin, of historical change. The second figure was that of Henry Adams' and John Bates Clark's democratic and liberal ocean, the image of perpetual atomistic motion held in equilibrium. The society of mobile, criss-crossing individuals of Bentley, Park, and Hoxie looked very much like that ocean of jostling atoms. Indeed Irving Fisher's eighteenth-century mechanism, which had by-passed history altogether, could produce a similar image of perpetual self-adjusting motion. In America, where history and nature converged, social scientists could go through historicism or around it to reach a simulacrum of the modernist dissolution of history.

Fluidity, then, marked only one aspect of their work, for process produced stasis. Flux was contained by the liberal shape of American society, by economic, social, or political systems that rendered conflict harmonious, business downturns temporary, and progress likely. Yet even within the lineaments of liberal democracy and American nationalism, the ceaseless process of historical change required control and many of these social scientists resorted to more rigorous sciences of social control. The young cohort that had appeared on the cutting edge of historical change in the 1880s to challenge disciplinary traditions had united under the banner of historicism. These later challengers, even when urging an analogous move toward the realistic understanding of change, united largely under the banner of positivist science. History was no longer the solution; it was the problem. Only a hard, technological science seemed capable of controlling so fast-moving a society or so slow-moving and retrograde a public consciousness as existed in America. The gap between the present and past was also a gap between themselves and the lagging body of public policy and public understanding, and increasingly they looked to science to close the distance.

The innovative work of this cohort marked a major shift in outlook that would become increasingly visible in the 1920s. The interaction of the major historical changes we have been charting – the movement toward modernist historical consciousness, the growing power of professional specialization, and the sharpening conception of scientific method – produced a slow paradigm shift in the social sciences.[179] The result was a broad move away from historico-evolutionary models of social science to specialized sciences focused on short-term processes rather than long-term change over time.

179 The case for this paradigmatic shift has been made most persuasively in anthropology by George W. Stocking, Jr., *Race, Culture, and Evolution* (New York: Free Press, 1968). Hamilton Cravens, *The Triumph of Evolution. American Scientists and the Heredity-Environment Controversy, 1900–1941* (Philadelphia: University of Pennsylvania Press, 1978), argues for the central importance of professionalization in promoting the shift in anthropology and sociology. The fact that economics can be included in this broad transformation, however, confirms that an underlying change in historical consciousness, rather than evolutionary theory *per se*, is most fundamentally at work. Professionalization also needs to be placed in the larger context of intellectual transformation. For a thoughtful discussion of this paradigmatic shift and its causes, see Fine, *Progressive Evolutionism*, 190–207.

These several factors interacted differently in each social science discipline. The marginal economists were the first to fully disengage from historicism. Indeed, classical economists had begun that disengagement early in the nineteenth century. By the 1890s, historicism was tied to political radicalism and the uncertainties of historical contingency, and the marginalist economists, well advanced in specialization, rejected it. Sociologists, political scientists, and the institutional economists who had resisted marginalism reacted a decade or two later. Coming from traditions that had absorbed some degree of historicism, they often followed the insight of historicism itself into the fluidity and relativity of modern experience. In economics, where he faced the static, neoclassical paradigm, Mitchell sometimes spoke in the name of historicism. In sociology, where he faced a long tradition of historico-evolutionary speculation, Thomas turned against history altogether. Sociologists were influenced as well by the critique of evolutionary determinism that dismantled genetic evolutionary paradigms in anthropology. In all the social science fields, historicism was turning toward modernism and the historical perspectives that remained were giving way to natural process and sciences of social control.

# 10

◁═════════════════════════════════════════════▷

# Scientism

The sciences of liberal change that were forged during the second decade of this century captured substantial support in the social science disciplines. Inherently unstable, designed to grasp the reality of historical change by reaching to a natural process within history, they did not survive intact. The self-conscious search for scientific method, which they had themselves inaugurated, quickly gained ascendancy and transformed them, as it transformed the larger disciplinary traditions.

## The advent of scientism

Like aestheticism, scientism was a response to the modernist historical crisis, an effort to make the achievement of science an end in itself and thereby to find order amid historical flux. It was also the result of a long-standing commitment perennially deferred, an effort to make good on the positivist claim that only natural science provided certain knowledge and conferred the power of prediction and control. With science now defined by its method, scientism demanded that the requirements of natural scientific method dominate the practice of social science. In examining the postwar context in which scientism arose in the United States, we will look first at the increasing strength of professionalism; then at the historical anxieties and disillusion with politics that professionalism channeled into science; and finally, at a range of institutional and conceptual supports for scientism in the 1920s.

### The professional context of scientism

The leaders of debate in the 1920s included the innovators of the late Progressive period, others born in the 1870s, and a still younger group born in the 1880s and trained in American graduate schools during the Progressive Era. In population, the academic social scientists of the 1920s were somewhat more diverse than those of the Progressive period, opening out from the core of New England respectability to a somewhat broader range of the middle class, to women, and to different ethnic backgrounds. Members of the American Sociological Society during the 1920s were very much like a sample of all college professors in that period in tracing their origin more heavily to the Middle West and the South than the earlier generation, and including a slightly higher proportion of people born outside the United States. It seems likely as well that the 1920s sociologists were like all college professors in drawing from a wider range of ethnic backgrounds, more women, and fewer clerical families, as well as being less religious and less heavily Republican in political affiliation than the previous generation.[1]

The 1920s sociologists do show interesting differences from the sample of all college professors, however, and anecdotal evidence would suggest noticeable differences between the social sciences as well. As against the academic profession in general, sociologists still drew more heavily from clerical families and twice as frequently from academic families, while their fathers were significantly less frequently businessmen, farmers, or workers. Sociologists also recruited significantly more women. With its traditional concern for social problems and its accrediting function for social work and reform organizations, sociology had its center of gravity in the sons and daughters of a professional class that carried on the public ethic of the older Protestant gentry.

My impression is that economics was much less open to women, more attractive to the sons of businessmen, but also more open to the aspiring sons of new immigrant families. The number of young economists from new immigrant families who were already visible in the profession during and after the war was striking: Alvin Johnson, son of a Danish immigrant farmer; Jacob Viner, Isador Lubin, and Selig Perlman, among others, from Jewish immigrant background. Fifteen percent of sociology students at the University of Chicago in the 1920s were also from new immigrant backgrounds, but this was higher than the average in sociology. Columbia under the racist Giddings would have discouraged such students. Political science seemed to follow the "worldly" profile of economics in drawing more heavily from business and legal families than from clerical and academic ones and in being inhospitable to women, but it was also far less open

---

1 James T. Carey, *Sociology and Public Affairs: The Chicago School* (Beverly Hills: Sage Publications, 1975), chap. 2. Carey's figures on sociology are the only reliable comparative figures I have been able to find.

to ethnic diversity than either economics or sociology. Like history, political science maintained a heavily Anglo-Saxon gentility. Johnson tells that when he arrived at Columbia University and told John W. Burgess of his interest in political science and economics, Burgess sent him automatically to economics. Opportunity even in economics, however, was a matter of degree, for racism, sexism, and anti-Semitism still pervaded all the academic professions.[2]

The demographic diversity that entered the social sciences was countered by the growing strength of the professional structure of the disciplines and their consequent power to socialize recruits into professional norms. In part the power of professionalism may have been a matter of size. Although full figures are not available, the membership of the professional associations may be taken as a guide. Beginning in the Gilded Age with between one and two hundred members each, they numbered by 1920 between 1,000 members in sociology, 1,300 in political science, and 2,300 in economics. Despite the continued membership in these associations of interested nonprofessionals, the numbers of teaching and practicing social scientists must have been considerably larger. The disciplines were able to take on some of the character of subcultures.[3]

The professional structure also changed. When the young evangelical economists arrived in the 1880s, they encountered political barriers and established intellectual traditions, but informal and malleable professional organization. By 1910, students found a professional structure in which norms of behavior, patterns of preferment, and hierarchically ordered career tracks were already in place. Outlets for activist and reform interests now existed in the form of expert roles within liberal pluralist boundaries. John Maurice Clark, the institutionalist son of John Bates Clark, drew a striking portrait of the proliferation and containment of activist roles in the economics "Guild" in the 1920s.

A Doctor of Philosophy from one great university may, on behalf of the Federal Trade Commission, match his wits and his grasp of facts and principles against a Doctor of Philosophy from another great university, employed by a large corporation.... A railroad's accounts, kept on a system installed by a professor from the

---

2 I rely here on impressions gathered from many sources, including Anthony Oberschall, "The Institutionalization of American Sociology," in *The Establishment of Empirical Sociology*, ed. A. Oberschall (New York: Harper & Row, 1972), 187–251; Joseph Dorfman, *The Economic Mind in American Civilization*, 5 vols. (New York: Viking, 1946–59), vols. 4, 5; and the sources listed above, Chapter 6, n. 1. On history, see Peter Novick, *That Noble Dream: The "Objectivity Question" and the American Historical Profession* (Cambridge University Press, 1988).

3 The membership of the associations was published in their annual reports.

University of Michigan, or its statistics, supervised by a graduate of the University of Wisconsin, may in the natural course of events be used against the road by a former professor turned valuation expert, or by an economist in the employ of the railroad brotherhoods.

Having learned to confine political dissent within exceptionalist bounds, to distinguish scientific technique from political ends, and to define impartiality as pluralism, the guild provided considerable scope for activism at the same time that it standardized that activism through university education and career networks.[4]

There remained nonetheless considerable tension between activism and professionalism, particularly if activism had a radical political tinge. Economics, too, provided more acceptable outlets for expertise than sociology and political science, in which labor among the poor and in politics was not as highly regarded. When William Fielding Ogburn got his Ph.D. degree in sociology from Columbia in 1911 and went out to teach at Reed College and the University of Washington, he was drawn toward civic and labor activities, contacts with the International Workers of the World, and an interest in socialism. Even though the Reed College president encouraged his public advertisement of the college, Ogburn worried that his activism prevented his doing scientific work and threatened his professional advancement. He also worried that his activities, being controversial, were "likely to get the university in disfavor" and thus were not "fair to my employer." Moreover, he had his own professional standards. "Why give up my training for something I had no training in?" When he went to Washington during the war to do cost-of-living studies, he suddenly had the time and institutional support to turn out seventeen articles. An appointment at Columbia in 1919, at the apex of the professional hierarchy, sealed his decision. He was "resolved to give up social action and dedicate myself to science."[5]

### Historical and political anxieties

The stronger professional structure of the social sciences served not only to contain diversity and activism, but also to help steer the anxieties generated by history and politics into science. The personal experience of historical

4 J. M. Clark, "Recent Developments in Economics," in *Recent Developments in the Social Sciences*, ed. Charles A. Ellwood et al. (Philadelphia: Lippincott, 1927), 218. See also Wesley Clair Mitchell, "Economic Research as a Career," March 30, 1922, Wesley Clair Mitchell Papers, Columbia University.
5 "A Few Words by Professor Ogburn," June 9, 1951, Banquet in Honor of Ernest W. Burgess and William F. Ogburn, William F. Ogburn Collection, University of Wyoming. A copy of this talk was kindly given me by Barbara Laslett.

displacement, like the national one, continued into the 1920s. The social distance traveled b ʳ the younger social scientists who came from the South or the smaller towns of the Midwest often spanned the industrial transformation of American society. Ogburn, reared in small Georgia towns, had one year in Savannah and a summer in Paris before reaching New York City in 1908. He had, moreover, been fatherless since the age of four and was raised in social and familial circumstances that invited dependency. At Columbia he at once idolized Giddings, "a marvellously persuasive preacher for science," and when Ogburn came to Columbia he took on the same role.[6] "My worship of statistics has a somewhat religious nature," he said. "If I wanted to worship, to be loyal, to be devoted, then statistics was the answer for me, my God." As an authority principle, it provided a desperately needed means of control. Like Thomas, Bernard, and Watson, Ogburn reported troubling sexual conflicts, as well as wildly erratic work habits. Against emotions he could not quite understand or regulate, he began a "long fight for reality." He found distance and control in a structure of professional authority and scientific objectivity.[7] The children of immigrants who moved into the social science disciplines may also have found the universalism, impersonality, and discipline of science attractive, for it could erase invidious ethnic differences as well as structure their experience of rapid social change.

The historical transformations of the Progressive Era and war years also broke down traditional gender roles and unleashed fears of feminization. The masculine identity Ogburn shored up with scientism and the aggressively masculine language he and so many of his colleagues used to describe science and its purpose of control, suggest that gender fears were among the anxieties loosed by historical change that scientism could allay. This seems particularly the case in sociology, which attracted so many women students and so many men of unusual cultural sensitivity, and where professional status was especially insecure. Scientism helped to set the masculine boundaries of sociology against the feminine precincts of social work and reform and against the expressive values of the new urban culture. Stuart Chapin,

---

6 Ibid.
7 My understanding of Ogburn comes from the insightful study by Barbara Laslett, "Unfeeling Knowledge: Emotion and Objectivity in the Rhetoric of Sociology," unpublished paper furnished by the author; and Robert C. Bannister, *Sociology and Scientism: The American Quest for Objectivity, 1880–1940* (Chapel Hill: University of North Carolina Press, 1987), chaps. 11–12. The quotations on statistics are from Ogburn's journals in the University of Chicago Library, quoted in Laslett, 35–6; "the long fight ..." is from the same source, quoted in Bannister, 166.

who took academic positions linked to training female social workers, was determined to scientize social work practice, as well.[8]

For the postwar turn from politics to scientism, the most revealing evidence came from the political scientist Charles E. Merriam. Unlike the late Progressive cohort who early experienced and responded to the sense of accelerating change, Merriam was a thorough Progressive. Born in 1874, he made his way from Iowa to Columbia and from Presbyterian orthodoxy to skepticism without suffering a severe break with the past. Merriam grew up steeped in his father's Republican politics and political ambitions, and at Columbia, following the lead of Frank Goodnow and William Dunning in political theory, he made the conventional critique of socialism and moved quickly into new liberal historicism.[9]

Merriam had little analytical depth, but he had a shrewd sense of the lay of the land. With the help of Dunning's notes he wrote his first and best book in 1903, a short history of American political theory that fully caught the new perspective. He showed that political ideas in America were rooted in a changing history, from their original Puritan roots, to the English liberal individualism of the Revolution, Jefferson, and Jackson, and finally to "a new theory of republican institutions, fundamentally different," the theory of Lieber and the Civil War nationalists who abandoned the idea of the social contract and based the state on the organic, evolutionary character of the nation. "There is little in either the industrial or the colonial situation to indicate a departure from the line of democratic progress," he concluded. To this sanguine historical reading Merriam appended the new political science as a development and heir of the nationalist democratic tradition, thus enclosing it within progressive history. He sustained this vision throughout the Progressive period.[10]

By then, Merriam was devoting his energies to Progressive politics. Now at the University of Chicago, he was elected in 1909 to the city council and became a leader of municipal reform and a potential mayoral candidate in

8 There is suggestive material bearing on this view in Laslett, "Unfeeling Knowledge," Bannister, *Sociology and Scientism*, and Donald C. Althouse, *The Intellectual Career of F. Stuart Chapin* (Ann Arbor, Mich.: University Microfilms, 1964). For a similar example of the role of scientism in supporting masculinity, see Dorothy Ross, *G. Stanley Hall: The Psychologist as Prophet* (Chicago: University of Chicago Press, 1972), chap. 5.

9 Barry D. Karl, *Charles E. Merriam and the Study of Politics* (Chicago: University of Chicago Press, 1974), is an insightful biography of Merriam, though it does not pay close attention to Merriam's scientism.

10 Charles E. Merriam, *A History of American Political Theories* (New York: Macmillan, 1903), 201, 343; idem, "Outlook for Social Politics in the United States," *PPASS*, 7 (1912): 113–25.

1915. But his hopes were cut short by the rise of a new demagogic boss, and in 1919 Merriam sustained a final, decisive defeat at his hands. As Barry Karl has shown, this was the turning point in Merriam's life, the source of a new level of disillusionment with politics and a decision to turn his ambition fully into professional channels. Like John Adams, whose faith in the people fell with his own electoral fortunes, Merriam for the first time questioned the ability of liberal history and liberal historicism to guarantee American democracy. If political doctrines were determined by history, the "by-products of environment," then what truth could they have? "Systems may justify themselves as sounding boards of their time, but what becomes of the validity of the underlying principles?" Moreover, profound ideological conflict still afflicted politics and political science. If even professional students of politics could not discuss fundamentals without violent disagreement, "might it not suggest remodelling and reorganization of their methods?"

With his shrewd sense of the conventional trend, Merriam turned to science. He was particularly sensitive to the professional implications of this choice. If political science ignored the fatal infirmity of historicism, it would lose "the *locus standi* of a science." The great problem with ideological conflict was that it prevented political science from speaking "with some authority." The problem to which Merriam most often recurred was his sense that political science was falling behind the latest advances in natural and social science. Merriam's older brother was the biologist John C. Merriam, named in 1918 to head the National Research Council, a clearinghouse for the natural sciences inaugurated by World War I. Merriam's contacts with his brother and a circle of colleagues gave him his new vision of the power of natural science and the possibilities of professional organization. Whereas in the progressive mode he had offered a science that was part of history and encouraged reform by informing the people about the interdependence of society, he now proposed a science defined by "method," oriented to "control," and sustained by organized professional structures to promote research.[11]

Although Merriam's recognition of the uncertainty of history was belated and his appropriation of professional scientism sudden, his disillusioned transfer of allegiance from politics to science reflected a widespread shift in viewpoint. Part of the shift was due to the effects of the war itself, which called into question the idea of historical progress. In the United States, as in Europe, the war destroyed the idea of what John Dewey called "wholesale"

---

11 Charles E. Merriam, "The Present State of the Study of Politics," *APSR*, 15 (May 1921): 174, 177, 176.

progress, but the shock of the war and fear for the future did not cut as deep in the United States. Most Americans' experience of the war, like that of Merriam, had spared them its full horror. Moreover, America emerged from the war with a degree of economic and international power that made its own future, in comparison to that of Europe, look promising. And in comparison to Asia, the liberal vision of progress looked even better. The number of American social scientists who visited China and Japan during the years before and after the war is striking, and the effect seems to have been, as it was for Edward A. Ross earlier, to solidify their belief in the progressive character of modernity.[12]

That said, however, the war precipitated a distinct change in the idea of progress, one of degree if not of kind. Even before the war American social scientists had come to reject historical determinism and had cast historical progress as the outcome of favorable historical tendencies and voluntary human effort. After the war the balance of forces between historical tendencies and voluntary action shifted, so that what once seemed to come at "wholesale," now seemed available only at "retail." History counted for less and human reason counted for more. The greater uncertainty of progress brought on by the war strengthened the modernist rejection of history. It also made the achievement of scientific control seem all the more important. Yet, under the increasingly rigorous scientific canon, the existence of progress could not be proved; indeed, it seemed to be one of those sentimental ideas that had blinded earlier social scientists and prevented the construction of a true science. Hence in the 1920s social scientists, like Ogburn, most often spoke of social "change" rather than social "progress." It was necessary to examine the implicit meanings of their work and its hidden norms to discover the still strong American belief in the possibility and likelihood of progress.

Professionalism helped to channel the political anxieties of the postwar world into scientific aspiration. In the first years after the war the mood was still charged with hopes of reconstruction and dire fears. Strengthened by wartime organization, labor fought bitterly to retain its wartime gains against capitalist counterattack and postwar economic depression. One of the first acts of Wesley Clair Mitchell's National Bureau of Economic Research (NBER) was to publish an authoritative study of the distribution of income in the United States, a study that shocked many social scientists by the meagerness of the standard of living provided to the overwhelming

---

12 The list of Far Eastern visitors includes Henry Carter Adams, Charles A. Beard, John Q. Dealey, John Dewey, Frank J. Goodnow, and Robert E. Park. On Dewey's "wholesale" and "retail" progress, see above, Chapter 9 at n. 48.

majority of people and by its extremely unequal distribution. Allyn A. Young, perhaps the most respected neoclassical economist of the period, conceded "the injustice of existing conditions.... Has much of our talk about democracy, equality of opportunity ... been idle? Is it for nothing that men from the old countries have built up a new civilization here?" However, in the next few years the economy recovered, the labor offensive was broken, and evidence appeared that the prewar decline in real manufacturing wages had been reversed. When Young republished his article in a 1927 collection, he omitted his indictment of capitalism.[13]

The economic recovery only compounded the widespread disillusion with politics. In the midst of "normalcy," with union membership declining, uneven but visible prosperity, and experiments proceeding in welfare capitalism and voluntary business planning, some social scientists could hope that capitalism would, after all, come through for them, without strong state action. For others, however, the Treaty of Versailles, the rejection by the Senate of American membership in the League of Nations, the election of a reactionary administration in 1920, and the defeat of organized labor extended rather the sense, apparent even before the war, that politics was inadequate to its current tasks. The young political scientist Harold F. Gosnell noted in 1924 the widespread pessimism among social scientists on the left about achieving social democracy. Walton Hamilton, a leading young institutional economist, felt that "the poor as well as the rich have shrunk from the immediate penalty" of trying to change capitalist institutions. That meant that the experts would have to do it, and they could only do it by means of a science of control such as they had not had before.[14]

The turn away from politics did not come easily, however, and it left its mark on both politics and social science. There is a revealing autobiographical analysis of this rejection and sublimation by Stuart A. Rice, one of the leaders in the movement for objective scientific methods in social science. Rice attended the University of Washington until 1915 and during the war years was active in welfare administration and radical politics in the northwest. After both seemed to fail and after taking his doctorate under Franklin Giddings at Columbia, he had nothing but contempt for his former self.

13 Wesley Clair Mitchell et al., *Income in the United States: Its Amount and Distribution, 1909–1919*, vol. 1, *Summary* (New York: Harcourt Brace, 1921); Allyn A. Young, "Do the Statistics of the Concentration of Wealth in the United States Mean What They Are Commonly Assumed to Mean?" *AER*, 7, Suppl. (March 1917): 144–6, 155–6; A. A. Young, "The Concentration of Wealth and Its Meaning," in *Economic Problems New and Old* (Boston: Houghton Mifflin, 1927), 95–107.
14 Harold F. Gosnell, "Review of Fred Haynes, *Social Politics in the United States*," *APSR*, 18 (August 1924): 627; Walton H. Hamilton, "The Price System and Social Policy," *JPE*, 26 (January 1918): 65.

Middle-class and upper-class radicals, he said, were people who had failed to attain emotional satisfaction within their own class. They unconsciously sought in radicalism release from thwarted emotions and satisfaction of their own "egoistic impulses." Rice had learned something of psychoanalysis and it had extended his reaction against politics into his own political motives. But behind this psychological sensitivity were the effects of class, the nonexistent class in American society, that so separated a middle-class youth from his working-class constituents that he could not with a whole heart identify his motives with theirs and recoiled at the insincerity of his position.[15]

The psychological distrust of radicalism and politics was objectified as science in what seems to have been the first quantitative study of political attitudes in the United States. Floyd H. Allport, a Harvard-trained social psychologist, studied the political opinions of his college students and concluded that there were greater similarities than differences between the "atypical" opinions, the radicalism and conservatism on the left and right. The results were due to psychological similarities in the style of conflict resolution, and might suggest similar psychological conflicts underneath. Allport's psychological distrust of ideological politics of the left and right brought a new scientific tool to an old exceptionalist theme of centrism and opened what would become a rich vein of social-scientific defense of centrist politics, employed variously against radicalism, ideology, and totalitarianism.[16]

The depth of the reaction from politics to science placed added emotional freight on science. Rice believed that "civilization no longer has time to wait for undirected trial-and-error progress." Nor was "cold rationality" sufficient. The solution was to make science itself *the object of emotional attachment.* Science was a field for unflinching heroism and devotion. "There can be no worthier 'cause' of social reform." Allport, one of the leading proselytizers for behavioral science in sociology and political science, brought the religious intensity of his upbringing to his scientific mission. Rexford Guy Tugwell, an idealistic disciple of Simon Patten, declared that the institutional economists, like everyone else, had rejected the possibility of panaceas and turned their backs on utopia, yet he claimed that in the construction of a new economic science "lies the possibility of a

---

15 Stuart A. Rice, "Motives in Radicalism and Social Reform," *AJS*, 28 (March 1923): 577–85. See also Harold F. Gosnell, "Stuart Rice," in *International Encyclopedia of the Social Sciences*, 1968 ed., 13:512–13.
16 Floyd H. Allport and D. A. Hartman, "The Measurement and Motivation of Atypical Opinion in a Certain Group," *APSR*, 19 (November 1925): 735–60.

remade world – no less." Lester Ward and Albion Small had accurately foreshadowed the compensatory uses of scientism.[17]

Sinclair Lewis' *Arrowsmith*, perhaps the classic American text of scientific hero worship, attests to the wide moral authority of science in the 1920s. To an intellectual class that watched their native religion turn to fundamentalism, patriotism to chauvinism, and politics to reaction, science appeared to be the one pure and sustaining discipline in the modern world.[18] In the social sciences, the reaction against involvement with politics and reform also sharpened the distinction between pure and applied science, but it drew the line in a distinctive way. Social science was to be an autonomous body of knowledge, pursued in a way to develop its scientific character, yet it was to be directed at and constituted in accordance with the technological capacity for control. Application in politics was to be left to others, or to that other "expert" self of the social scientist who provided advice to government or business, but the capacity for application, for control, remained the hallmark of the pure science they wanted to create.

## Scientism gains support

The professional base of scientism was strengthened during the 1920s by the investment of large sums of money in social science by capitalist-funded charitable foundations. The movement for a more scientific social science was already under way before the big money hit. But until the war the major foundation in the field, Russell Sage, had funded social welfare-oriented studies rather than social science per se. The Carnegie Foundation had begun to fund major projects in economics, including a multivolume economic history of the United States and then Mitchell's National Bureau of Economic Research. The Rockefeller Foundation massively entered the scene in the early 1920s. The Rockefellers wanted to combat the opprobrium to which the Rockefeller fortune was subjected. They wanted to help solve social problems in a way that would spare the family name controversy and spare the country more radical changes. For all their purposes, the emerging scientific idiom of social science was attractive, promising both distance from political controversy and knowledge that would allow the real control of social change.

17 Rice, "Motives in Radicalism," 585; Floyd H. Allport, "The Religion of a Scientist," *Harper's Magazine*, 160 (February 1930): 365–6; Rexford G. Tugwell, "Introduction" to *The Trend of Economics*, ed. Rexford G. Tugwell (New York: Knopf, 1924), ix–x. On Tugwell, see Michael V. Namorato, *Rexford G. Tugwell* (New York: Praeger, 1988).
18 Charles Rosenberg, "Martin Arrowsmith: The Scientist as Hero," in *No Other Gods: On Science and American Social Thought* (Baltimore: Johns Hopkins University Press, 1976), 123–31.

The person who guided the Rockefellers to the social scientists was Beardsley Ruml, twenty-six years old and a Chicago Ph.D. in psychology, who shared much of the social scientists' vision. From their side the key figure was Charles Merriam. A "virtuoso of nonspectacular promotion," Merriam had the political skills and contacts as well as his new-found interest in science. He was in a position to sense and act upon the keen feelings of inferiority that afflicted political scientists and sociologists in the presence of more scientific sister disciplines. Ruml's own interest in promoting interdisciplinary work and the National Research Council suggested the model. In 1923 the Social Science Research Council (SSRC) was founded, funded by Rockefeller money, launching inquiries into social science methods, organizing summer conferences and advisory councils for problem areas, and dispensing individual fellowship money.[19]

The SSRC institutionalized a pattern of independent cooperation among the social science disciplines. The ability to join together was itself a sign of confidence on the part of each social science discipline in its own distinctiveness. The research projects funded and devised by the SSRC were not generally interdisciplinary in conceptualization. What brought disciplines together was their joint concern to promote their own fields. Membership in a professional society denoted a deeper identification, and the great majority of social scientists belonged only to a single one by 1929. About 7 percent of the sociologists and political scientists were also members of the American Economic Association and the economists – 17 percent of them – affiliated with the American Statistical Association.[20] Although the SSRC did not break down this hardening of disciplinary focus, it did serve as a medium for the exchange of ideas across borders, substituting for the movement of personnel that had occurred when the disciplines were more porous.

SSRC funds and exchange were a major catalyst for the focus of social science on scientific method. Perhaps the most characteristic product of the decade was the volume the SSRC sponsored, *Methods in Social Science*, organized and edited by Stuart Rice. Rice worked over the whole decade to commission critiques of the methodology of key works, classic and contemporary, in all the fields included within the Council. Although there was no

19  David Grossman, "Philanthropy and Social Science Research: The Rockefeller Foundation and Economics, 1913–1929," *Minerva*, 20 (Summer 1982): 59–82; Karl, *Merriam*, chap. 7; Barry D. Karl and Stanley N. Katz, "The American Private Philanthropic Foundation and the Public Sphere, 1890–1930," *Minerva*, 19 (Summer 1981): 251–7. The description of Merriam is by Harold Lasswell, *"The Cross-Disciplinary Manifold: The Chicago Prototype,"* in *The Search for World Order*, ed. Albert Lepawsky et al. (East Norwalk, Conn.: Appleton-Century-Crofts, 1971), 419, 426.
20  Stuart A. Rice and Morris Green, "Interlocking Memberships of Social Science Societies," *AJS*, 35 (November 1929): 439–44.

single point of view among the contributors, there was a single message; namely, that methods to date had been insufficiently scientific, even the methods of the most determinedly objective. Here and there fileopietism triumphed. By and large the historians let each other off easy, too anxious to claim improved scientific standards for history, but the rule was politely to point out severe shortcomings. Rice saw to it that even the quantifiers were judged by more knowledgeable statistical experts, who could call their claims into question. The SSRC made it plain that devotion to scientific method would be a high calling.[21]

Between 1922 and 1929, the Laura Spellman Rockefeller Memorial that Ruml headed and the SSRC dispensed about forty-one million dollars to American social science, social work, and their institutions. By organizing its own separate social science departments into a joint research committee and stepping up the Chicago-based projects already under way, the University of Chicago got in on the ground floor, though of course it had in addition the persons of Merriam and Park. Chicago received by far the largest institutional grants, almost three and a half million dollars, including direct staff support. Chicago also received a lion's share of the fellowship money and a new social sciences building. By the time the building was dedicated in 1929, however, the Memorial was beginning to cut back its support for Chicago, the SSRC, and their style of social science. For the amount of money expended the results in the actual solution of social problems seemed thin. New voices steered the Rockefeller money toward medical research, public health, and child development, areas equally noncontroversial and more directly and visibly beneficial.[22]

The effect of this sudden incursion of funds was felt in many directions. The rapid development and influence of "Chicago" sociology and political science in the 1920s clearly owed a good deal to these resources. The foundation support that went to Mitchell's NBER contributed substantially to establishing statistical economic research at a time when the federal government was dismantling its wartime statistical units.[23] The foundation money could not create something that lacked support within the disciplines, but it could greatly strengthen some things rather than others.

21 Stuart A. Rice, ed., *Methods in Social Science: A Case Book* (Chicago: University of Chicago Press, 1931).

22 Raymond B. Fosdick, *The Story of the Rockefeller Foundation* (New York: Harper, 1952). Martin Bulmer, *The Chicago School of Sociology: Institutionalization, Diversity, and the Rise of Sociological Research* (Chicago: University of Chicago Press, 1984) is useful, but underestimates the effects of funding.

23 On the NBER see Arthur F. Burns, "Introductory Sketch," in *Wesley Clair Mitchell: The Economic Scientist*, ed. Arthur F. Burns (New York: National Bureau of Economic Research, 1952), 3–54; and Grossman, "Philanthropy and Social Science Research."

That is particularly true of the scientific direction of American social science. The centrality of scientific method was established by the social scientists themselves, mediated largely through Ruml, and not altogether congenial to the Rockefellers. Merriam, for example, tried repeatedly to sell them the idea of a separate institute of politics, but his confidence that the work could be suitably scientific was not shared by his benefactors.[24] The withdrawal of funds at the end of the decade bespeaks the foundation's inability fully to share or shape the social scientists' goal. On the other hand, there was substantial agreement on the scientific direction – it served the basic purposes of all concerned – and the unprecedented financial support to the chief advocates of science added enormously to their legitimacy and power.[25]

Moreover, the social scientists' interest in science was itself designed to escape the proscriptions of, and to exert political authority in, the centrist political world of American capitalist society. When Harold Lasswell, a brilliant young disciple of Merriam, visited England in 1923 he was dismayed to find Graham Wallas, a friend of American social science, scornful of the Americans' large scientific dreams, all the while trimming their practical proposals. "To Graham Wallas the growth of the private foundations for scientific research offers a lucrative milch cow with a sedate temper when nothing pink or red is in the same pasture."

Lasswell had to agree that the contrast was striking between the "extreme opinionation" of the English scholars and the "diffident" Americans, with their "nice little verbal packages" of "social process." In some cases, he thought, the worshipers of science were indeed motivated by "prudence." But, he went on, there was a deeper reason. "Here in England these academicians have a sense of power. They actually feel that they have a hand on the wheel of state. . . . In politics they find the boys they knew at Oxford or at the Settlement." They could influence them "at dinner parties, club lounges, week-ends." By contrast, look at the United States. "Scattered over three thousand miles . . . Lacking traditions of the Lord and Professor . . . relatively impotent, and driven to vagaries in consequence." Lasswell's sociological explanation is shrewd, and we have noted before the effects of a cohesive class-based British culture with access to power as against the decentralized American academics with only tangential access to power. But Lasswell's analysis takes as given the Americans' desire for power, and his

24 Charles E. Merriam to F. Stuart Chapin, July 9, 1923; Charles E. Merriam to Charles A. Beard, October 23, 1924; Charles E. Merriam to Robert S. Lynd, April 18, 1929, Charles E. Merriam Papers, University of Chicago.
25 Franz Samelson, "Organizing for the Kingdom of Behavior: Academic Battles and Organizational Policies in the Twenties," *JHBS*, 21 (January 1985): 33–47.

own and his colleagues' pursuit of that aim through science. In the American context, social science required the imprint of "objective" science to build an institutional power base in capitalist society.[26]

The importance of such financial support can be easily seen in comparison to the fate of the New School for Social Research. The New School was founded in 1918 by and largely for left Progressive social scientists who were chafing at restraints on academic freedom: Charles Beard, just dismissed from Columbia University, his sympathetic colleagues James Harvey Robinson, Wesley Mitchell, and John Dewey; and Thorstein Veblen, again without an academic home. They were all committed to the scientific development of the social sciences and except for Robinson, whose primary concern was adult education, they all wanted the school, as its name declared, to promote social scientific research by its faculty and students. Unlike the mainstream social scientists, however, they overtly linked their science to a social democratic philosophy. Hence they could not expect support from the large conservative foundations, but had to live in "chronic indebtedness," dependent upon the gifts of the maverick progressive children, chiefly daughters, of the lesser rich. Such gifts were never large enough to support the research institute they had hoped to found and Dewey and Mitchell soon returned full-time to Columbia. The New School, under Alvin Johnson, turned largely to adult education and increasingly to culture rather than the social sciences. Hence foundation money gave to research conducted under the apolitical veneer of science a distinct advantage in the 1920s and solidified its institutional bases of support for the future.[27]

During the 1920s the cultural authority and social power of scientism pushed the center of gravity in the social science professions toward a harder and more technocratic conception of social science. One witness at an SSRC conference in 1925 reported the great emphasis being placed on "behavior." It was "a rather striking and genuine intellectual revolution," an "important shift in scientific interest and emphasis, a shift from understanding to control."[28] The late Progressive innovators who had developed institutional economics, social interactionism, and group-interest analysis had themselves begun that movement for sciences of behavior and control. After the war a younger generation carried the program to greater extremes, to a behavioral psychology based on a reflex model of mind; to the primacy of objective methods and statistical technique; and to the belief that science was value-

---

26 Harold D. Lasswell to Charles E. Merriam, October 8, 1923, Merriam Papers.
27 Peter M. Rutkoff and William B. Scott, *New School: A History of the New School for Social Research* (New York: Free Press, 1986), chaps. 1–2.
28 Frederick J. Woodbridge, quoted in Franz Samelson, "Organizing for the Kingdom of Behavior," 42.

free, divorced by its method from human bias and practical purpose, and hence useable by experts for all purposes.

Although they probably did not command the majority in numbers, the aggressive proponents of scientism commanded the moral authority of purists, those who could claim to carry out most fully the common creed. Their harder line put not only the upholders of disciplinary traditions, but the initiators of scientism, on the defensive. The situation was different in economics, where traditional neoclassicism could also claim the scientific high ground, but in sociology and political science, while Bentley moved with the behaviorist tide, Thomas, Park, and Beard had to struggle with its implications, and Beard ultimately turned back.

The range of sophistication about scientific method varied greatly across all camps. Ogburn's call for the accumulation of facts appeared to reflect a naive empiricism which was widespread among social scientists. Mitchell's initial faith in the ability of statistics to "prove" things with certainty, like Chapin's and Ogburn's continuing faith that statistics would reveal the natural laws at work within society and history, seemed hardly to have advanced beyond the faith of the early nineteenth-century champions of statistical science. There were also, however, knowledgeable efforts to ground social scientific practice, such as the attempt of Stuart Rice to revise Karl Pearson's critical positivism. Rice and others used the new concepts of physical science that emerged in the 1920s to both inform and free the social sciences, on the assumption that the uncertainties of observing the social world were after all not so different from those faced by the physical sciences. Philosophical agnosticism could also free the social sciences to pursue their scientific aims, a note struck by Rice and the young political scientist, Harold Lasswell. Philosophy had always – mistakenly – told science what it could or could not do, Lasswell said. No one could tell what social science could do until it was tried. Past failure was only a sign of past incapacity. This was a new world.[29]

Dewey's pragmatism served a variety of uses. Rice drew on it to develop the idea of "scientific fictions" in his revised positivism. Dewey was more frequently called to the support of the softer behaviorists, the historical and relativist side of Veblen and Mitchell rather than to Mitchell's quantitative, behaviorist message. Dewey himself spoke out against the hard-line behaviorists who tried to reduce mental to physical categories, but on the issues of quantification, the behaviorist ambition of control, and the level of

29 Stuart A. Rice, *Quantitative Methods in Politics* (New York: Knopf, 1928), 3–47; Harold Lasswell, "The Comparative Method of James Bryce," in *Methods in Social Science*, 478–9. On the early enthusiasm for statistics, see Theodore M. Porter, *The Rise of Statistical Thinking, 1820–1900* (Princeton, N.J.: Princeton University Press, 1986).

abstraction appropriate for the social sciences, he did not throw his weight to one side or the other.[30] From the right, we will see, Dewey's pragmatism was blamed for the whole movement toward science. Indeed, the range of views with which pragmatism was identified mirrored the broad range of scientism in the decade.

The advent of scientism – and "advent" properly conveys the momentous meanings science was meant to carry – was the social-scientific conclusion to the crisis of American exceptionalism begun in the Gilded Age. There are of course longer lines to be drawn. The problems of liberal exceptionalism were worked out into the 1950s, are still being worked out, but they were worked out in an industrial world no longer defined by the trauma of the break with the American past. A central statement of this conclusion came from Dewey, whose pragmatism had emerged from the Gilded Age crisis in the 1890s and deepened as that crisis ran its course. Dewey's 1929 *The Quest for Certainty* was the classic statement of his own pragmatism, a philosophic version of the social scientists' credo of the 1920s, and a powerful reformulation of the American determination to combat the uncertainties of historical time.

The world of perpetual change that Dewey had announced in 1910 and 1920 was still the basis of his thinking. But what now impressed Dewey even more than change was the failure of Americans to accept it, their continued resort to the ancient strategy of seeking an eternal, universal, and perfect truth within or beyond the changing natural world. The peril of living in the uncertainty of time was, he argued, the central problem of the human condition, the problem which had driven all of Western thought into a quest for certainty. He proposed a "Copernican revolution which looks to security amid change instead of to certainty in attachment to the fixed." For Dewey "security amid change" came only from the exercise of pragmatic intelligence, that is to say inquiry, hence scientific method, hence "the supremacy of method." The power of method was in turn the power of action. "Action is the means by which a problematic situation is resolved. Such is the net outcome of the method of science." Dewey stood in the historical world in a familiar American position. Though he sought security rather than certainty, he was reasserting the power of action – Dare I say *virtù*? – against the uncertainties of historical time. For Dewey always imagined intelligence as action in history, an intervention in the ceaseless flow of time that both loosed and mastered innovation. Like the *virtù* of the

---

30 Horace M. Kallen, "Political Science as Psychology," *APSR*, 17 (May 1923): 181–203; George H. Sabine, "The Pragmatic Approach to Politics," *APSR*, 24 (November 1930): 865–85; John Dewey, "Philosophy," in *Research in the Social Sciences: Its Fundamental Methods and Objectives*, ed. Wilson Gee (New York: Macmillan, 1929), particularly pp. 254, 256, 262–5.

republican tradition, scientific method, as pragmatic action, was Dewey's great antagonist to the disorder of history.[31]

Dewey retained the national basis of security. The problem of the present hour was "the confusion of tongues, beliefs and purposes that characterizes present life." What Dewey hoped most from scientific method was consensus about the bases of value judgments. "Attainment of this consensus would mean that modern life had reached maturity in discovering the meaning of its own intellectual movement." The American future was now modernity and modernity would find its realization in the harmony of an organic liberal society. Dewey's politics moved left slowly with the social democratic tide, and in the 1930s he enlarged his categories to embrace democratic socialism, but he continued to speak within the discourse of American exceptionalism. More deeply influenced by historicism than most, he sensed and solved the problem that discourse posed at its deepest levels. Other social scientists could follow their historical anxieties, the logic imbedded in their disciplinary discourses, and the pressures of their professional lives to a shallower but similar end.[32]

### Institutionalism versus neoclassicism in economics

The institutional economics inaugurated by Robert F. Hoxie and Wesley Clair Mitchell became a distinctive feature of American economics during the 1920s and early 1930s. Institutionalism entered a discipline in which the neoclassical paradigm had already achieved predominance, however, and neoclassicism again withstood the challenge. By the end of the 1920s, the institutionalist assault was already losing force, undermined by its own commitment to the market and to positivist science. Moreover, the neoclassical paradigm had become entrenched in the professional structure. While offering Americans an escape from history and the market's guarantee of liberal society, it also made room for some degree of realism and liberal change. So long as they stayed within the liberal and new liberal purview of American exceptionalism, critical impulses could be absorbed into neoclassicism, in much the same way that the historicist revolt had been earlier.

---

31 John Dewey, *The Quest for Certainty* (1929), *LW*, 4:245, 195. For an early example, see Dewey, "Moral Theory and Practice" (1891), *EW*, 3:109. Cf. Rexford G. Tugwell, "Experimental Economics," in *The Trend of Economics*, 421: "Our civilization ... may slip and regress, falling into the mad desuetude of ruin that overtook Assyria and Egypt, Greece and Rome ... fall from the tree of time and rot like a withered leaf in the mold of common earth. There is that chance. But alternatively we may think of ourselves in different metaphor, not as a leaf on the tree of time but as an historical force, with power over time, over space, over mankind itself. We may master our fate."

32 Dewey, *Quest for Certainty*, 248–50.

## The neoclassical orbit

We can look briefly at three economists who were born like Mitchell in the mid-1870s and who shared many of the concerns of his cohort, yet who chose a neoclassical rather than institutionalist allegiance. When Alvin Johnson arrived at Columbia, he found John Bates Clark utterly opposed to the racial attitudes of John W. Burgess and Franklin Giddings, and he was drawn to Clark's ethical, universalist vision of capitalist progress. Precisely by its subjection of human life to economic calculation, Johnson said, capitalism rode over "national, racial and religious prejudices" and created "toleration, liberty and fraternity." Capitalism may now be "material, gross, ugly," but it was still in an early stage. It had just begun its "liberation of human nature." The liberal dynamic was toward "greater variety and wealth of beauty," personal liberty and toleration, and universality. Like Clark, he admitted that "of the revolutionary trinity only equality remains beyond the visible horizon," but even that was possible in the future.[33]

In 1909 Johnson wrote a marginalist text that, according to Joseph Dorfman, "presented the reigning orthodoxy so well that teachers complained that it left nothing for them to discuss." But at the same time, Johnson did not forget his populist sympathies. He became an ardent Roosevelt Progressive and an ardent antisocialist. He found in the historical interconnection of the legal and economic systems and in the imperfect functioning of the market ample grounds for proposing government regulation and some welfare provision without vitiating the basic mechanisms of competition or the basic structure of inequality that undergirded the market system. The market's distribution of income embodied a "tendency toward fairness" and its imperfections were correctable.

As Johnson's experience suggests, the neoclassical paradigm made a widening allowance for Progressive reform and had its own universalist appeal to upwardly mobile ethnic Americans. Like others in his cohort, however, Johnson wanted to influence the popular mind, and he found a market for his ideas in the cosmopolitan intellectual community in New York City. His paean to capitalism in 1914 brought him to the attention of Herbert Croly at the *New Republic* and began a shift from economics to journalism and the New School.[34]

---

33 Alvin S. Johnson, *Pioneer's Progress* (New York: Viking, 1952), 41, 48, 122–3, 225, 232; idem, "The Soul of Capitalism," *The Unpopular Review*, 1 (April–June 1914): 233, 240, 242–3. On the pluralistic cosmopolitan ideal espoused by Johnson, see David A. Hollinger, "Ethnic Diversity, Cosmopolitanism and the Emergence of the American Liberal Intelligentsia," *American Quarterly*, 27 (May 1975): 133–51.
34 Dorfman, *Economic Mind*, 3:421; Alvin S. Johnson, *Introduction to Economics* (Boston: D. C. Heath, 1909), 9–10, 378–80; Johnson, *Pioneer's Progress*, 147, 218, 232.

Allyn A. Young was, in contrast to Johnson, a more typical professional economist. Born of old New England stock, he made a distinguished academic career that took him to Harvard University and briefly, the London School of Economics in the 1920s. Young took his doctoral degree with Richard T. Ely and was the principal reviser of Ely's text, the leading college textbook in economics through World War II. Like many in his generation, he wanted economics to develop in a realistic direction. In his first major articles he declared that economics had enough of general equilibrium theory, and should turn rather to study of "the price-making process." The systematic formulations of Frank Fetter and Irving Fisher were too abstract and unreal. Theory should not "attempt to formulate concepts so general and abstract that the whole economic process may be viewed as a relatively simple mechanical system."[35]

Young understood realism as an adjunct of neoclassical theory, however, not an alternative, and he was anxious to dissociate himself from the general critique of abstract theory mounted by Veblen and Mitchell. As he wrote Mitchell in 1911, the Ely text already had an established place, so he wanted to "improve it in as many ways as possible," but it was not the kind of book he himself would write "if I were doing all the work." A master of statistical method, Young believed that statistical study of "the price-making process" had to be carried on in conjunction with neoclassical theory, and would refine and extend theory, rather than replace it. "The purpose is ... that the fabric of theory shall be a yielding garment, fitting the varied and complex reality of economic life as closely as is demanded by the criterion that the conclusions to which theory leads shall be both useful and general." In politics as in method Young took a centrist position. He mounted an influential critique of A. C. Pigou's retreat from competition, arguing that the link in traditional theory between competition and maximum product held good, yet he was open to the Progressive range of regulatory reforms.[36]

Thomas S. Adams, the second reviser of Ely's text, took still a third path into mainstream economics. Adams began working as an economic expert, at the U.S. Census Bureau and in Puerto Rico, even before getting his Ph.D. from Johns Hopkins University. After going to the University of Wisconsin, he investigated labor problems and increasingly, problems of taxation.

35 Frank W. Taussig, "Allyn Abbott Young," *DAB*, 10, 619–20; Joseph A. Schumpeter, "Allyn Abbott Young," *Encyclopaedia of the Social Sciences*, 1930 ed., 5:514–15; Allyn A. Young, "Some Limitations of the Value Concept," *QJE*, 25 (May 1911): 418–19, 424; idem, "Pigou's *Wealth and Welfare*," *QJE*, 27 (August 1913): 686.

36 Young, "Some Limitations," 411; Allyn A. Young to Wesley Clair Mitchell, December 8, 1911, Mitchell Papers; Young, "Pigou's *Wealth and Welfare*," 683, 686.

Appointed at Yale in 1916, Adams became the chief tax advisor to the U.S. Treasury Department during and after the war, and was the architect of the federal income tax, "a fit successor to David A. Wells." Adams took the impulse toward realism and reform into the practical development of special areas of policy expertise, areas that maintained tangential links to neoclassical theory while at the same time developing specialized and relatively autonomous bodies of knowledge and principle. In this world of expertise, success depended on practical skill in negotiating the political world and sensitivity to the complexity of affairs rather than to mastery of theory. Yet the common training in neoclassical theory, already part of professional certification and socialization, provided a common language and style of thinking that could keep these practical specialists broadly within the neoclassical fold. So too, the liberal and new liberal political spectrum it covered opened a wide variety of expert positions. Large numbers of practical economists followed centrifugal tendencies toward specialization, but were not necessarily carried out of the orbit of the neoclassical paradigm.[37]

### Institutionalist challenge and decline

A considerable number of economists, however, threatened to leave the neoclassical orbit. Although Mitchell had tried in 1916 to describe work on different aspects of the money economy as cooperative endeavors, by the end of the war younger dissidents were announcing an "institutional" economics that would construct a new theoretical basis for economics. The attack was sounded first by Walton H. Hamilton, who named as his precursors Henry Carter Adams, Charles H. Cooley, Veblen, and Mitchell. A colleague for a few years of Hoxie at Chicago, where he came to admire Hoxie's "genetic method," Hamilton claimed that the genetic study of economic institutions "is" economic theory, and that in perhaps a decade or so of work, the new theory would emerge. Tugwell, an even greater enthusiast, also called for a new experimental, inductive, historical science.[38]

The most noteworthy of the younger group was much more circumspect. John Maurice Clark had been nurtured and taught by his distinguished

---

37 On Adams see "Special Resolutions," *AER*, 24, Suppl. (March 1934): 213–14; "Tommy Adams," *Saturday Evening Post*, June 3, 1933, p. 20; and W. Elliot Brownlee, "Economists and the Formation of the Modern Tax System in the United States: The World War I Crisis," in *The State and Economic Knowledge, The American and British Experience*, ed. Mary O. Furner and Barry E. Supple (Cambridge University Press, 1990). The quotation is from "Tommy Adams."

38 Walton H. Hamilton, "The Institutional Approach to Economic Theory," *AER*, 9, Suppl. (March 1919): 318, 309; Tugwell, "Experimental Economics."

father. When he entered the profession he joined the rising call for "facts" and dynamic theory, but he never wanted to attack the core marginal theory his father had done so much to construct. When Hamilton issued his institutionalist challenge in 1919, and critics objected to his seeming willingness to abandon marginalist analysis, John Maurice Clark denied that the institutionalists intended to drop the static doctrines. He himself was only revising their premises to allow their enlargement, in accord with his father's *Philosophy of Wealth* of 1885. Clark always harked back for inspiration to that ethical and historicist moment in his father's career.[39] But even he got caught up in the revolutionary rhetoric of the movement, suggesting paradigmatic differences and claiming in his major institutionalist effort, the study of overhead costs in 1923, that he was laying one stone of a new foundation for economics.[40]

By this time, Mitchell was speaking to informal groups in the same way, and when he gave his presidential address to the AEA in 1924, he made clear that he expected the behavioral point of view and statistical and institutional study to create a new science of economics. As president of the American Statistical Association, he was even more explicit, putting his faith primarily in statistical method.[41]

What fueled the institutionalist ambition was an overflow of realism and new liberal idealism that could not be contained by neoclassical practice. Impatient with the incapacity of economic theory to lead the way to real social democracy, the institutionalists gathered up the hopes and discontents of the war years into a call for a new kind of economic science. The war and its aftermath only heightened the problem of historical change that had emerged before the war. Hamilton, like Hoxie, believed a society in "perpetual transition" needed a historical approach to economics. Tugwell cast his whole analysis in the historical terms he had learned from Patten, except that the accelerating force of industrialism had already created a new world. World War I, said Mitchell, had brought home the problem of historical change. "Even in days of reaction, we cannot regain implicit faith in the

---

39 J. M. Clark, "Review of A. C. Pigou, *Wealth and Welfare*," *AER*, 3 (September 1913): 623–5; idem, "Davenport's Economics," *PSQ*, 29 (June 1914): 322; J. M. Clark in "Discussion" of Hamilton, "The Institutional Approach," 323. On J. M. Clark see Joseph Dorfman, *Economic Mind*, 5:438–63.

40 J. M. Clark, "Soundings in Non-Euclidian Economics," *AER*, 11, Suppl. (March 1921): 132–43; idem, *Studies in the Economics of Overhead Costs* (Chicago: University of Chicago Press, 1923), ix–x.

41 Wesley Clair Mitchell, "Prospects of Ecics," Notes, March 24, 1920, Mitchell Papers; idem, "The Prospects of Economics" (1924), in *The Backward Art of Spending Money, and Other Essays* (New York: McGraw Hill, 1937), 342–85; idem, "Quantitative Analysis in Economic Theory" (1925), in *Backward Art*, 20–37.

stability of our prewar institutions.... Living amidst such uncertainties, we cannot be content with an economic theory of the 'static state.'"

The uncertainties of history in turn demanded social control. Hamilton turned to institutions, he said, because he wanted "an economics relevant to the problem of control." Institutions, Mitchell repeated, were the "changeable element in control over behavior." And control in turn meant science. "The whole modern movement may be interpreted as a demand for procedure which appears more adequately scientific," J. M. Clark said. Using pragmatism loosely to argue for a more catholic conception of science than neoclassicism recognized, Clark argued that the economy, unlike the materials of natural science, changed over time, hence uniformity and exactness were impossible. "In such a situation the pragmatic philosophy is a natural ally of the harrassed economist." There was no reason to exclude evidence that was relevant just because it could not be treated with accuracy. The proper standard of science was comprehensiveness.[42]

If the ceaseless change of history required a new science, so too did social democracy. On the left of new liberal politics, the institutionalists' lineage tended to be dissenting Protestantism, either through parentage or academic mentors, or new-immigrant ethnicity. They looked toward more inventive and thoroughgoing ways to reorganize the market in the interest of general social welfare. The neoclassicists were too fundamentally satisfied with the workings of the market and its long-term ameliorative trend, too protective of its workings, to assert the claim of history, ethics, and democracy to control the market in the public interest. Hence the need of a real theory of sociohistorical economics to provide a counterweight to market theory.

To that end, the institutionalists restated the logic of social control.[43] That logic had been repeated now for two decades and the neoclassicists believed that they had accepted it. But they had accepted it as a qualification of neoclassical theory, as secondary considerations to the needs of the market itself. Even when the institutionalists urged at some points the removal of monopolistic barriers to competition, they sensed that without a historical theory to ground their prescriptions and relativize the demands of the market, they would never be able to counter the authority of the neoclassical model and its legitimation of existing capitalist practice.

The attempt to achieve social democracy through construction of a new economic science produced a curious mixture of rhetorical radicalism and

---

42 Mitchell, "The Prospects of Economics," 373–5; Hamilton, "Institutional Approach to Economics," 313; Mitchell, "Prospects of Ecics," 6; J. M. Clark, "Recent Developments in Economics," 221–2, 235.
43 For example, Rexford G. Tugwell, "The Economic Basis for Business Regulation," *AER*, 11 (December 1921): 643–58.

political caution. Tugwell said the institutionalists could remake the world, if only change was "slow enough." The institutionalists made a high art of the new liberal determination to work out from the world as it is. Pragmatic experimentalists, they distrusted the tendentious character of socialist and Veblenian theory, as well as neoclassical theory. A great part of their making haste slowly was their own commitment to the market. The long-term rise in living standards created by industrialism, the relative prosperity of the twenties, and the beginnings of reform had its effect on them as well as their neoclassical opponents.[44]

The institutionalists were not agreed on how to proceed; they were not yet in possession of the paradigm they wanted to construct. The two principal models of institutionalist practice in the 1920s came from Mitchell and J. M. Clark, and they were different. Mitchell, as we have seen, believed that the wide study of economic behavior would produce a new empirical and dynamic theory. In practice, he continued his statistical description of economic processes in the money economy, chiefly the business cycle, along the same lines he had set out in 1913. As director of the National Bureau of Economic Research, and the President's Commission on Economic Trends, he organized an extensive program of statistical study. Mitchell's *Business Cycles* was greatly expanded in revision but never completed. As he refined his techniques of statistical economic analysis, he became increasingly impressed by the complexities of the problem, the inadequacies of the data, and the need for more extensive research.[45]

On the other hand, J. M. Clark was interested more in qualitative analysis than quantitative research. As he wrote Mitchell, "I'm not so thoroughly inductive as you are, and I'm ... not a behaviorist at all." The main thrust of his work was to use the resources of neoclassical theory itself to determine the "discrepancies between market value and a more comprehensive view of social values," an effort already begun by J. A. Hobson and A. C. Pigou. His most extensive contribution to that effort was focused on "inappropriables," or externalities, those "costs and services that are not fully compensated because our legal system does not or cannot surround them with the rights and protection that go with full private property."

Clark developed one way to get at them through expansion of the concept of overhead costs. Overhead costs were the costs of unused capacity, the product of big business's high fixed capital investment and the unpredictably fluctuating market. The reapportionment of overhead costs could ease the

---

44 Tugwell, "Experimental Economics," 391; Wesley Clair Mitchell, "Is Capitalism Decaying?" *New York Evening Post*, April 7, 1923, sec. 3, pp. 577–8.
45 On Mitchell's career in the 1920s and 1930s, see Burns, "Introductory Sketch," and Dorfman, *Economic Mind*, 4:360–77.

pressures toward cut-throat competition and thereby flatten the business cycle and curtail unfair competitive practices. His most far-reaching proposal – greeted by an "ovation" at the AEA, when he made it in 1920 – was to include labor as an overhead cost, for "the laborer's health and working capacity ... must be borne by someone, whether the laborer works or not." Under the wage contract, laborers now bore that overhead cost, but it was far more "scientific" for employers to bear it, as by a yearly salary, for employers then would have an incentive to maintain steady employment, just as now, through payment of workmen's compensation, they had an incentive to reduce accidents. Clark's effort here, and always, was to redefine social values as market values so that they could be brought into the neoclassical scheme.[46]

The flurry of institutionalist activity in the mid-1920s stirred up a counterattack from mainstream economists. AEA meetings featured institutionalist papers countered by neoclassical discussants and vice versa, as in the Gilded Age during the historical economists' challenge. Tugwell brought out a volume of institutionalist essays in 1924 and included in it a searching critique of institutionalism from Frank Knight, to whom we will shortly turn. Allyn Young, in reviewing the Tugwell volume, brought his formidable powers of discrimination to bear on every author, Knight included, but the thrust of his attack was to dismiss everything that could not be appropriated for neoclassicism. Referring slightingly to Veblen, he attacked Mitchell for his claim to be doing something different from neoclassical economics. Mitchell's substantive work "fits into and amplifies the general structure of economic knowledge that has been built up ... The assumptions, the modes of thought, are such as are familiar to economists." He had been confused by Veblen into thinking that he was doing something else.[47]

The turning point came in 1927. At a roundtable at the AEA eight eminent economists and statisticians, including Mitchell, debated the role of statistics in economics and all seven of Mitchell's colleagues attacked his position, arguing that statistics offered a useful empirical and analytical tool but could not remake theory. Jacob Viner accused him of reopening the devastating quarrel over historical economics that had begun sixty years earlier in Germany. Mitchell's reply has been taken as a recantation, but it recants only his

46 J. M. Clark to Wesley Clair Mitchell, April 21, 1927, Mitchell Papers; J. M. Clark, "Economic Theory in an Era of Social Readjustment," *AER*, 9, Suppl. (March 1919): 286–90; idem, *Overhead Costs*, 15–16; Dorfman, *Economic Mind*, 5:453. See A. C. Pigou, *Wealth and Welfare* (London: Macmillan, 1912); J. A. Hobson, *Work and Wealth: A Human Valuation* (New York: Macmillan, 1914).
47 Allyn A. Young, "The Trend of Economics, as Seen by Some American Economists" (1925), in *Economic Problems*, 232–60, particularly 250–1, 259–60.

inclination to fight. As he claimed afterward, he had said nothing different from what he had been saying during the past three years. He had said, if only briefly, that quantitative and qualitative work were interrelated and that qualitative work would continue. If we remember that Mitchell regarded the generalizations of neoclassical economics as approximations that worked fairly well because the money economy encouraged rational profit-seeking behavior, then we can see how he might think that neoclassical generalizations could be used in research, yet in time be superseded by more exact empirical generalizations. Still, he returned to a conciliatory tack, regretting the conflict over methods and saying "we have tasks of many sorts to perform." Mitchell continued to do what he had always done, and in the same vocabulary. But he did largely withdraw from polemics and he never again cast his own program in so ambitious a light as he had done in the mid-1920s. Henceforth he would rely on the long-term strategy to which his method bound him in any case; namely, boring from within.[48]

That same year J. M. Clark backed away from whatever heterodox implications his work contained. He had always defended the viability of marginal theory and he now emphasized his adherence to the consensus that maintained it at the core of economic theory. Neoclassical theory was necessary to reveal when government was "violating economic law." The whole Veblenian emphasis on the contradiction between profit and service was encouraging class conflict and hence becoming counterproductive.

One thing can confidently be predicted: the 'older economics' will not vanish utterly. That is assured by its pedagogical compactness, its logical coherence and availability, and its large measure of pragmatic truth. It can be presented within the limits of an academic unit of instruction, as dynamic or social economics cannot. It is available to the logical intellect without the need of mastering wide areas of facts. And its analysis of the elements of cooperative efficiency in an individualistic system will remain usefully relevant so long as that system works at all, and so long as 'red' radicalism on the one hand or modern mercantilism on the other, threaten us with something worse.

Clark was making clear that henceforth his institutionalism would proceed in a way that did not challenge the political, professional, and intellectual consensus of mainstream, neoclassical economics.[49]

The public assurances of Mitchell and J. M. Clark removed the two most eminent and established economists from the leading edge of institutionalist

48 Wesley Clair Mitchell, "Present Status and Future Prospects of Quantitative Economics," *AER*, 18, Suppl. (March 1928): 28–45; idem, "Remarks from the floor," December 27, 1927, Mitchell Papers.
49 J. M. Clark, "Recent Developments in Economics," 232, 270–1, 305–6.

debate, but it did not stop the younger economists from continuing to speak out, and criticism of the movement continued. Young issued a "protest against the fruitless quarrels of the methodological sects, against their intolerance, and against their pretensions to exclusive possession of the only right points of view and the only effective methods of research." He wanted tolerance, though tolerance on classical terms. "Mathematical physics has not abdicated to descriptive genetics its place as the perfect type of science, and in a manner the ultimate type." At the 1932 meeting of the AEA, institutionalism was debated again, but by then there was an even greater note of impatience in their critics. Paul Homan, who had been critical of the institutionalists in 1928 but not wholly unsympathetic, by 1932 had had enough. They had, to be sure, stimulated useful revision of systematic theory, but their work was indistinguishable from the rest of the economists. The school turned out to be "an intellectual fiction," motivated chiefly by the left political interest in planning. We will not follow the quarrel further, nor is it necessary to do so, for the outcome was by this time settled.[50]

As the debate already indicates, the institutionalists felt considerable professional pressure to back down. The open conflict disturbed not only Young and Homan, but J. M. Clark as well, who in his 1927 defense of orthodox theory regretted that "a veritable clamor of voices has arisen," each voice offering a different program. Clark, of course, also had strong personal reasons for his guild feelings. As he wrote to Mitchell in 1926, "I remember what you said about my father's attitude: that whatever I might do, he would construe it in terms of his system. I hope nothing I do will ever break through that attitude of his: and so long as my work is constructive, I'm sure nothing ever will."[51]

If not as powerful as paternity, professional friendship too could encourage moderation. Mitchell and Young worked at their differences. Young was on Mitchell's NBER board and they exchanged work in manuscript. At Mitchell's suggestion Young toned down his criticism of Veblen. And Young kept up a critique of Mitchell's distinctive vocabulary:

What I didn't like in your recent Natl. Bureau of Econ. Research chapter was the miscegenation of a philosophy of history, of a type which I don't like and which I *think* wrong (but which I can't prove to be wrong – no one can) with what seems to me to be strictly scientific analysis of a high order. I don't like your eugenics, and I

50 Allyn A. Young, "Economics," in *Research in the Social Sciences*, 63, 60; Paul T. Homan, *Contemporary Economic Thought* (New York: Harper, 1928); Paul T. Homan, "An Appraisal of Institutional Economics," *AER*, 22 (March 1932): 10–17; "Round Table Conferences: Institutional Economics," ibid., Suppl. 105–16.
51 J. M. Clark, "Recent Developments in Economics," 220, 258; J. M. Clark to Wesley Clair Mitchell, April 8, 1926, Mitchell Papers.

don't like your "Industrial Revolution," and I don't like your "cumulative change," but I like your figures!

Mitchell persisted but he had now to be very conscious of how far to press his claims.[52]

Political pressures were also at work on the institutionalists. Hamilton was named director in 1924 of the new Brookings Graduate School, formed in tandem with the Institute for Government Research (IGR) in Washington. For three years he made the school a center of interdisciplinary education informed by the institutionalist vision. He also prepared a research report on the bituminous coal industry that recommended virtual nationalization of the industry. Pressures from the coal companies and the conservative political scientists of the IGR combined to bring Hamilton down and to eliminate the graduate school altogether. The new Brookings Institution was put in the hands of a moderately conservative neoclassical economist and Hamilton joined the faculty of Yale Law School.[53]

In some cases, political pressures on institutionalism were so thoroughly interwoven with professional ones that it is difficult to disentangle their influence, as J. M. Clark's defense of orthodox theory made clear. It is noteworthy, however, that his and Mitchell's tactical retreat occurred in 1927, the year that marked, for many intellectuals, the return of political radicalism and political conflict.[54] The specter of "'red' radicalism" that disturbed Clark was undoubtedly raised by the Sacco and Vanzetti agitation and "modern mercantilism" could well have been the McNary-Haugan agricultural tariff, forced through by farmers who did not share the prosperity of the 1920s. These domestic events threatened the intrusion into America of the radicalism and economic nationalism starkly visible in Europe. Politics, of course, helped to fuel the institutionalist impulse, but it exerted an even stronger force in favor of established institutions.

The decline of institutionalism was the product of internal weakness as well as external opposition. The most striking feature of American institutionalism was that, for the most part, it did not study institutions. Mitchell, J. M. Clark, and others generally listed the work of Marx, Sombart, Veblen,

---

52 Allyn A. Young to Wesley Clair Mitchell, June 22, 1927, February 27, 1929, Mitchell Papers. Young appears to be referring to a draft of Mitchell's summary chapter in *Recent Economic Changes*, 2 vols. (New York: McGraw Hill for the NBER, 1929), in which Mitchell's eugenics is his conclusion that the rise in living standards over the decade had been the result of families having fewer children, so that reproduction was traded for consumption.
53 Donald T. Critchlow, *The Brookings Institution, 1916–1952* (DeKalb: Northern Illinois University Press, 1985), 63, 75–81.
54 Malcolm Cowley, *Exile's Return* (New York: Viking, 1951), 218–21.

and the Webbs as one type of study included under the institutionalist umbrella, but they themselves did not engage in it. Suspicious of historical method as unscientific and wedded to the single institution of the money economy, they lacked the political will and the intellectual desire to enter fully onto a relativizing historical ground. Mitchell, as we have seen, was increasingly drawn to statistical study of aggregate behavior in the money economy in the name of science. His work was appropriated by neoclassical economics, where it provided realistic analysis of market functioning that could amend, extend, and render practical the abstract generalizations of theory.

The institutionalism of J. M. Clark directly offered neoclassicism extension and amendment, but his extensions of neoclassical logic had the potential to undermine major features of established capitalist practice, as in his argument that labor be treated as an overhead cost. The younger economists who were pressing the radical claims of institutionalism heralded his work as a "genuine logical revolt." As one of them regretfully noted, however, "the issues between his position and direct-cost economics are now implied, now barely sketched." Hence it was understandable that an orthodox reviewer "read the book with perfect equanimity" and concluded that it succeeded only in "correcting certain minor inaccuracies of doctrine." Clark did not in fact press the radical implications of his work. Increasingly suspicious of labor, he became increasingly protective of market prerogatives.[55] Mitchell and J. M. Clark could not subvert the market paradigm from within because the market and its values had already subverted their own discourse.

Institutionalism did nonetheless leave a legacy of work outside the neoclassical mainstream that retained some capacity for challenging orthodox theory and method. J. M. Clark's effort to bring externalities into market analysis has taken on new life in the current era of environmentalism. The tradition of descriptive statistical research Mitchell established at the NBER has continued a vigorous existence and pressed the claim of empiricism against deductive theory. In the 1920s and 1930s John R. Commons developed a voluntaristic species of institutionalism, organized around the political and economic "bargain," that has attracted intermittent interest, although it found little resonance among the social democrats of the era. More importantly, Veblen's writings, with their analysis of absentee ownership and division between making money and making goods, remained a

---

55 Morris A. Copeland, "Review of J. M. Clark, *Studies in the Economics of Overhead Costs*," *PSQ*, 40 (June 1925): 299; C. Addison Hickman, *J. M. Clark* (New York: Columbia University Press, 1975).

source of insight for the analysis of business institutions and a stimulus for social democratic impulses in economics.[56]

Institutionalism as a movement, however, fell victim to the Great Depression and its Keynesian remedy. For self-proclaimed experts in historical change, their inability to come to any better understanding of the Depression than their neoclassical colleagues was a considerable deficit. Mitchell in particular, who predicted like everyone else that the downturn would right itself within a year or two, was driven deeper into his program of empirical research by this proof of ignorance.[57] Whether a more powerful and genuinely historical institutional economics would have done better is impossible to say. Like the left-liberal economists generally, the institutionalists were drawn into the Keynesian revision of neoclassicism.

Analyzing aggregate categories of income and expenditure for the economy as a whole, and using marginalist analytic techniques, Keynes showed that the economy could stabilize at levels below full employment. To function at full employment the market needed the intervention of government to regulate and supply investment. Keynesian economics was thus a proof – by the extension of neoclassical technique itself – of the institutionalists' claim that the market was not an optimum self-equilibrating process and that the intervention of government was necessary to achieve democratic social goals. The Keynesian analysis of aggregate income and expenditure also reconstituted neoclassicism into macroeconomic analysis of the national economy as a whole and marginalist microeconomics. Institutionalism had helped to prepare the way for Keynes's governmentalist solution and to provide the statistical information on which macroeconomics was built. Keynesian macroeconomics in turn built onto the neoclassical paradigm those new liberal public goals that had been shown to be compatible with and necessary for optimal market function, such as governmental rules for fair competition, a welfare safety net, and fiscal stimulation of the market.[58]

As one economist ruefully explained, Keynes "promises something that

56 Simon Kuznets, joining European traditions of historicism to Mitchell's program, is perhaps the best example of the empirical and historical capacities of the NBER tradition. See Kuznets, *Economic Development, the Family, and Income Distribution: Selected Essays* (Cambridge University Press, 1989), particularly the "Foreword" by Richard Easterlin and the "Afterword" by Robert W. Fogel. The best study of Commons' institutionalism is Neil W. Chamberlain, "The Institutional Economics of John R. Commons," in Joseph Dorfman et al., *Institutional Economics: Veblen, Commons, and Mitchell Reconsidered* (Berkeley: University of California Press, 1963), 68–91. An excellent source for all the major institutionalists is David Seckler, *Thorstein Veblen and the Institutionalists: A Study in the Social Philosophy of Economics* (Boulder: Colorado Associated University Press, 1975).
57 Dorfman, *Economic Mind*, 5:266–9.
58 On the Keynesian revision of neoclassicism, see Phyllis Deane, *The Evolution of Economic Ideas* (Cambridge University Press, 1978), chap. 12.

cannot be resisted: full employment and high levels of consumption without serious dislocation of our institutions." He was rueful because the claims of democracy remained subordinate to market requirements, logic, and premises.[59] Moreover, Keynesian neoclassicists in America, unlike the Marxist-influenced Keynesians in England, inserted the concept of equilibrium into macroeconomics, removing it still further from the exigencies of history. Over time, the core microeconomic theory has become progressively more massive and more mathematical, and its ahistorical conceptual world increasingly dominates macroeconomics. In that disciplinary context, the presence of history remains adventitious. As the institutionalists originally recognized, without the countervailing power of a historically grounded theory, the historical and institutional dimensions of economic life and the values they embody become vulnerable and unreal.[60]

### Frank Knight and the final turn against history

The denouement of this story of the weakening of historical consciousness within economics requires that we return to the 1920s. Frank Knight was one of the most powerful theorists among the neoclassical economists of that decade. The product of a rural, religious Illinois family and uneven formal education, Knight's journey from the nineteenth century was more like Simon Patten's than that of his own cohort of adopted urbanites. Like Patten, Knight drew traditional orthodox materials in new directions and ruthlessly exposed unwelcome contradictions, so that he was somewhat at odds with all economic camps.[61] But Knight pushed his logic to conclusion in a way that Patten never managed to do, and became a founder of the libertarian Chicago school of economics. His work extends well beyond the 1920s and cannot be given here the rounded treatment it deserves. But we can see from his early work how he brought to heterodox fruition some of the principal strands of the exceptionalist tradition of economics we have

59 John S. Gambs, *Beyond Supply and Demand: A Reappraisal of Institutional Economics* (New York: Columbia University Press, 1946), 3.
60 Deane, *Evolution of Economic Ideas*, chaps. 13, 14; R. A. Gordon, "Institutional Elements in Contemporary Economics," in *Institutional Economics*, 123–47; Peter Temin, "The Impact of the Depression on Economic Thought," in *Economics in the Long View*, vol. 1, ed. Charles P. Kindleberger and Guido di Tella (London: Macmillan, 1982). One measure of the decline both of history and macroeconomics vis-à-vis microeconomics and mathematics is the evolution of Paul Samuelson, *Economics* (New York: McGraw Hill) from the first edition in 1948 to the editions of the 1970s and 1980s.
61 For biographical information on Knight, see Richard S. Howey, "Frank Hyneman Knight and the History of Economic Thought," *Research in the History of Economic Thought and Methodology*, 1 (1983): 163–86, and Donald Dewey, "Frank Knight before Cornell: Some Light on the Dark Years," ibid., forthcoming, a copy kindly given me by the author.

been studying and opened a path that leads toward complete elimination of the historicist countercurrent in American economics.

The first expression of Knight's mind to survive, his junior-class oration at Milligan College, Tennessee, in 1910, starts with the premise from which all his thinking flowed: "The life of man ... consists of a series of choices, the intelligent ordering of which is his part and function, the essence of his nature as an intellectual and moral being."[62] This focus on the free and rational act of choice as the essential feature of humanity was the chief moral lesson of his religious training. His family and the small, struggling colleges he attended were adherents of the Disciples of Christ, a denomination that eschewed elaborate theologies for the reasonableness of Biblical Christianity and the centrality of its original message to come to Christ. While at Milligan, Knight praised one of the leading Disciples ministers, Peter Ainslie, and his book, *God and Me*, a primer for the aspiring Christian. Its message was, amidst all the distractions and temptations of the world, to choose God, "for by God's grace I possess the strength for freedom and I will again claim friendship with God." Temptation was the "furnace-house" in which "God proves character," and life was above all an arena of moral choice: "The daily round in my life is *my workshop*, where God and I are making my character." Ainslie and the Disciples tradition stressed not only the freedom to choose but the rational ability to choose. The Disciples emerged from an early nineteenth-century combination of restorationist evangelism and Enlightenment rationality and emphasized the individual's ability to reason and the commonsense rationality of the community.[63]

In his junior-class oration, Knight was already using economistic language, and the following year he studied economics from Charles J. Bullock's marginalist text. Bullock began with consumption as wants that impel men to economic activity and as choices individuals make, choices involving intelligent ordering and moral considerations. Bullock's treatment of consumption combined marginalist insights with the older American moral tradition in which "right consumption" formed the apex of the system, for he emphasized the development of higher wants, the ill effects of "injurious consumption" such as luxury, and the importance of saving.[64] The moral emphasis on choice Knight found in this American tradition of economics

---

62 Frank H. Knight, "Culture and the Classics" (1910), p. 4, Frank H. Knight Papers, University of Chicago.

63 Dewey, "Frank Knight before Cornell," 35–6; Peter Ainslie, *God and Me* (New York: Revell, 1908), 22–3, 30; Samuel C. Pearson, "Faith and Reason in Disciples Theology," in *Classic Themes of Disciples Theology*, ed. Kenneth Lawrence (Fort Worth: Texas Christian University Press, 1986), 101–29.

64 Charles Jesse Bullock, *Introduction to the Study of Economics*, 3d ed. (New York: Silver, Burdett, 1908), chap. 4.

undoubtedly made a deep impression because it confirmed the chief lesson of his religious training. The moral and the economic message became one for Knight: Autonomous choice was the highest characteristic of human nature and the generic characteristic of the market.

The Christian foundation of Knight's libertarian vision can be missed because of his aggressive religious skepticism. He apparently doubted the literal Christian story early in life, and when he made his way to Cornell to study philosophy the Christian idealists who ruled the department could not face his corrosive skepticism and refused to teach him. When he then turned to economics, his teacher Alvin Johnson recognized, no doubt from his own rural background, the temperament of the self-taught intellectual who battled his way out of a backwater milieu: "I knew your type," Johnson remembered, "You came out of a malodorous environment where every man with a mind doubts everything. You doubted every statement I made."[65] But as Donald Dewey has shown, that skepticism never freed Knight from his attachment to religion. He maintained a formal Christian affiliation and a deep religious preoccupation throughout his life. Doubting the letter, he absorbed the spirit; he very much admired Edward Scribner Ames, a Disciples minister and University of Chicago philosopher who liberalized Disciples' Christianity, emphasizing the moral message of Christ's life and Christian faith.[66]

Knight's major and still classic theoretical work, *Risk, Uncertainty and Profit*, was his doctoral dissertation of 1916, revised and published in 1921. It described the market in moral, libertarian terms: "The very essence of free enterprise is the concentration of responsibility in its two aspects of making decisions and taking the consequences of decisions when put into effect." His originality was in his analysis of making decisions. He was surprised to discover how little had been written about the process of making "ordinary practical decisions," and got his chief help from the discussion of probability in Pearson's *Grammar of Science*. "The fundamental fact underlying probability reasoning is generally assumed to be our ignorance." Knight concluded that "The actual procedure of making decisions in practical life is a rather inscrutable or 'intuitive' formation of 'estimates,' subject to a wide margin of error or uncertainty." Estimates of probability that were measurable constituted "risk"; the remainder was true "uncertainty."[67]

65 Alvin S. Johnson to Frank H. Knight, December 6, 1967, Knight Papers.
66 Dewey, "Frank Knight before Cornell." On Ames see William R. Barr, "Christology in Disciples Tradition: An Assessment and a Proposal," in *Classic Themes of Disciples Theology*, 18–19.
67 Frank H. Knight, *Risk, Uncertainty and Profit* (Boston: Houghton Mifflin, 1921), 349, 211, 212n., 218, 314.

Working within the paramaters of John Bates Clark's marginalist analysis, Knight could see that perfect competition, the condition of ideal equilibrium, implied perfect knowledge, and the absence of uncertainty. "The 'tendency' toward perfect competition is at once explained, since men are creatures endowed with the capacity to learn, and tend to find out the results of their acts, while the cause of the failure ever to reach the goal is equally evident so long as omniscience remains unattainable." The world of striving occurred in the interval, in the world of risk and uncertainty. "It is a world of change in which we live.... We live only by knowing *something* about the future; while the problems of ... conduct ... arise from the fact that we know so little."[68] Knight's specific topic had been to explore the concept of profit as Clark had left it, and he could conclude that profit was the product of uncertainty, the fruit of superior intuitive judgment or luck.

Knight's stance in economics developed within the contemporary Progressive context of the dialogue with socialism and the emerging conflict between neoclassicism and institutionalism. Bullock's was a typical Progressive text in its effort to address the strengths and weaknesses of both capitalism and socialism, and Knight's teachers at Cornell, Johnson and Young, extended that tendency further, staying within the confines of neoclassicism but trying to meet its critics and enlarge its reformist and realist resources. Knight wrote in that context, as his reference to "a world of change" suggests. He prefaced his book with a defense of "pure theory" as against "the pragmatic, philistine tendencies of the present age," but his aim was "to isolate and define the essential characteristics of free enterprise as a system" so as to determine "where if at all it is at fault." It was the weight of Christian moralism on him that made him aware of "fault" and sympathetic to the criticism of capitalism from the left, so that he distinguished between the proximate morality of market choices and the higher morality of the choice of ends, and judged the market by the standards of that higher morality.[69]

Knight concluded that there were substantial "inherent defects" in the system. But at the same time he was impressed by "the fatuousness of over-sanguine expectations from mere changes in social machinery." The force with which Knight expressed that double message – drawing out the moral weaknesses of capitalism and at the same time condemning any political solutions as productive of even greater harm – became his personal, disconcerting signature. A contrarian truth-teller by temperament, determined to carry through the logic of his premises, he ended time and again

---

68 Ibid., 20–1, 199.
69 Bullock, *Introduction*, chap. 17; Knight, *Risk, Uncertainty and Profit*, vii–viii.

in paradox. In commenting on J. M. Clark's idea of overhead costs, for example, Knight praised him for identifying "an inherent and far-reaching weakness in the competitive system" and then concluded that "any provisions which promise to deal adequately with this disharmony and to iron out the disastrous fluctuations of industry must carry us no inconsiderable way in the direction of socialism."[70]

The furthest point Knight reached in this style was his essay, "The Ethics of Competition" in 1923, in which he deliberately set out the "fundamental weaknesses of competition from the standpoint of purely ideal standards, and so to establish bases for comparison with any other possible system." There was first of all the many ways in which the ideal of perfect competition and its undoubted values were not realized in practice. In addition competition was a game, one that rewarded and created behavior that could not be considered worthy by accepted ethical standards. Knight was torn by "the contrast between the enticing plausibility of the case for the 'obvious and simple system of natural liberty,' and the notoriously disappointing character of the results which it has tended to bring about in practice." But the meager results did not tarnish the ideal, for "many of the evils and causes of trouble are inherent in all large-scale organization as such" and alternatives were likely to be "vastly worse."[71]

Knight's doubt of Scripture had forced him to examine "the kind of folks people are" and "the kind of world it is."[72] It was a world in which the free-enterprise system provided whatever possibility there was for "living intelligently," both by maximizing "the intelligent use of means" and maximizing the "economic provision" prerequisite to the intelligent choice of ends. Yet that possibility was never wholly realized in this world. "I am not surprised at the extent of sin in the world," Peter Ainslie had said, "neither will I be discouraged if there is more, for the capacity for man to sin is tremendous." Evil was ingrained in the world and the attempt to eliminate it was futile.[73]

Through the 1920s Knight fought to protect free enterprise against the new liberals in his profession. The principle of social control meant political control by democracy or majority rule, and he equated social organization

70 Knight, *Risk, Uncertainty and Profit*, viii; idem, in "Economic Theory and Practice – Discussion," *AER*, 13, Suppl. (March 1923): 105–7.
71 Frank H. Knight, "The Ethics of Competition" (1923), in *The Ethics of Competition and Other Essays* (New York: Harper, 1935), 74, 47, 58.
72 From a letter to his wife, quoted in Donald Dewey, "The Uncertain Place of Frank Knight in Chicago Economics" (December 1987), p. 9, unpublished paper, a copy kindly provided by the author.
73 Frank H. Knight, *The Economic Organization* (New York: Augustus M. Kelley, 1951 [1933]), 4–5; Ainslie, *God and Me*, 23.

by this principle with socialism. The crash of 1929 and the New Deal destroyed his hope and by 1934 he drew a bleak picture. Free enterprise now seemed a brief utopian moment in modern history, confined to the late eighteenth and early nineteenth century. Since then, greed and power had eroded the rules of the game and the measure of equality needed to play it fairly. Even then, the crash was not indicative of a fatal flaw in the system, only the result of monetary mismanagement.[74]

The greater problem was the encroachment of politics. Laissez-faire democracy had originally supported the free market, but politics, like the market, was a game, one played for power. Discussion was the form of free, rational exchange in the political arena and rational consensus its ideal outcome. Without the limitations of material reality that enforced rationality in the market, however, it was far more easily corrupted. Persuasion, as a form of coercion, had debased rational discussion and given rise to demagogues like Franklin D. Roosevelt. American democracy was moving toward fascism. In this tale of decline, the old lines of American exceptionalism reappeared. The temporary efflorescence of liberal enterprise had been due to "the open frontier." But the history of economic individualism and political laissez-faire "almost from the start was a race between growth and decline." Political corruption was, as Plato and Aristotle saw, "a cyclical oscillation, from freedom to autocracy." After the Second World War Knight's gloom lifted, though unlike many of his libertarian followers, he continued to believe that not only politics, but the market itself carried seeds of the imperfect world within it.[75]

Knight's treatment of politics requires further notice, but we first must go back to the early 1920s and look at his methodological writing, which occupied a great deal of his attention. Knight was a major opponent not only of new liberal social control but of its most vocal support in the profession, institutionalist economics. What is often spoken of as his antiscientism should be clearly circumscribed, for his methodological views were formed in opposition to the scientism of the institutionalists, not against the positivist, classical conception of economic science propounded by Mill. Indeed, Knight's views on method can be regarded as an attempt to solidify Mill's separation of the science and art of economics, thereby denying to the institutionalists the possibility of a genuine science of social control.[76]

---

74 Knight, *The Economic Organization*, 23–30; idem, "Economic Theory and Nationalism" (1934), in *Ethics of Competition*, 277–359.

75 Knight, "Economic Theory and Nationalism," 289, 299.

76 Cf. Allyn A. Young to Frank H. Knight, March 11, 1927, Knight Papers: "I am more and more impressed with the fundamental soundness of the position which we both take, namely that the social sciences must be art as well as science, and rather more so."

Knight called neoclassical economics "a science of economics, a true, and even exact, science, which reaches laws as universal as those of mathematics and mechanics." Through a high degree of abstraction, economic science reached the form of all rational activity and of all "social relations arising through the organization of rational activity." Such rational laws could not predict the "*content* of economic behavior," they could not tell what goods an individual would prefer, but they could predict that "within limits he will prefer more of any good or less." This separation of the formal rationality enacted in the market, based on the matching of means to ends, and the substantive rationality of the choice of ends, marked off the proximate morality of the market from the higher morality of life. Nonetheless, the laws of market rationality were based on intuitively known, axiomatic characteristics of the world and they allowed the economist to project the necessary conditions of a free enterprise system and sharply circumscribe the sphere of political intervention.[77]

The kind of science the institutionalists wanted, an empirical science of actual economic behavior, a science not of formal economic rationality but of substantive choices, was impossible. Knight drew on his analysis of "ordinary practical decisions" to declare that empirical judgments of human behavior had to be essentially intuitive, artful refinements of common sense and hence "categorically different" from the kind of exact judgments that could be made about the rational component of economic behavior. Such intuitive judgments could be educated by history; they could be improved by statistics; William I. Thomas' caution that attitudes had always to be taken into account was clearly more correct than the behaviorists' attempt to ignore consciousness, but in no case could they be transformed into science. They were rather part of the art of applying the abstract laws of economic science to particular contexts. As a result of his engagement with the institutionalists, Knight added a third division of economics, "the philosophy of history" or "the cumulative changes of institutions." This was a field exclusively for "informed judgment. . . . The movements of history are to be 'sensed' rather than plotted and projected into the future." But even trained judgment did not go very far and was more likely to be wrong than right. Such a history Knight in fact gave us in 1934.[78]

Knight presented himself as an antipositivist, declaring always that ethics described a higher realm of existence than economics and that economic science could describe only a restricted sphere of life. He repeatedly attacked

77 Frank H. Knight, "The Limitations of Scientific Method in Economics," in *The Trend of Economics*, 256–60.
78 Ibid., 267, 250, 264–6.

John Dewey's scientism and its brief for social control.[79] But in fact the picture of "intuitive" judgment Knight drew was of an inferior form of knowledge, categorically fenced off from scientific rationality. Applied economics could be somewhat useful. Historical economics was a fascinating exercise in guesswork. But only the exact science of economics could reach the inherent nature of rational organization and lay down the rules by which society should be organized.[80]

It is not surprising, therefore, that when he saw those rules broken and turned his attention to the invading realm of politics, he tried to understand what happened by transforming politics into another kind of market, a market formed by autonomous rational agents exchanging words rather than goods, a game of power rather than wealth, and inferior in its ability to maximize rational choice. The metaphorical use of economistic language to describe the social and political world had been present among American social scientists for some time, but except for the idea of a social equilibrium, it was casual and occasional. Knight's effort to reduce politics to the dimensions of the market was more sustained, and opened up, notably through his students James M. Buchanan and Gary Becker, the now substantial effort to understand social and political behavior on the model of economic behavior and hence to expand economic theory to cover the social and political world. Knight thus stands at a fundamental turning point in political economy. He first expressed the position taken by Mill and developed in America from the time of Francis A. Walker onward, that consigned all the wider human purposes, and the changing social and institutional world in which they acted, to a vaguely delineated realm of history, exterior to the realm of market rationality. Under the pressure of profound disillusionment with that historical world, however, Knight turned and began to colonize it for market analysis. In the work of his students, history as anything other than the utility-maximizing behavior of individuals has disappeared.[81]

---

79 Knight summed up his critique in "Pragmatism and Social Action" (1936), in *Freedom and Reform* (New York: Harper, 1947), 35–44.

80 Knight retained an interest in history and translated Max Weber's *General Economic History* in 1927. He proposed, contra Weber, that the essential spirit in modern capitalism was the spirit of progress and improvement: "The real revolution separating and differentiating modern (especially American) economic life from all that has gone before is this spirit of 'bigger and better,' the constructive transformation of the world and of individual life through knowledge, technique, and organization." Knight in "Round Table on Economic History," *AER*, 19, Suppl. (March 1929): 158.

81 On Knight as libertarian, see John McKinney, "Frank H. Knight and Chicago Libertarianism," in *The Chicago School of Political Economy*, ed. Warren J. Samuels (University Park, Penn.: Association for Evolutionary Economics, 1976), 191–213. On Buchanan, see Dennis C. Mueller, "Mueller on Buchanan," in *Contemporary Economists in Perspective*, ed. Henry

## The influence of instrumental positivism in sociology

In sociology, with no established paradigm to bar the way, the new empirical science models of liberal change took immediate institutional root. But the absence of a dominating paradigm also gave free reign to scientism and made the focus on method far more central than in economics. Against the behaviorist and statistical current created by scientism, the humanistic and contextual elements in Chicago sociology were put on the defensive, where they fell prey to the sociologists' own divided purposes. Their visions of liberal history, subordinated to method and systematically distanced from the movements of concrete history, fell into confused or simplistic exceptionalist shapes.

### The expanding influence of sociological scientism

The movement toward scientism hit the sociologists about the same time as the economists. In 1918 Lucille Eaves, director of research at the Woman's Educational and Industrial Union, proposed the appointment of a committee on the standardization of research, reflecting the growing body of social research by public and philanthropic organizations and the growing scientific orientation of such work created by university education. John L. Gillin, a Giddings student who became a rural sociologist at Wisconsin, was named chair of the committee and turned it to the task of promoting scientific research in academic sociology, hopefully with financial support from "rich men" and foundations.

Gillin's own understanding of science was meager and naive, but he expressed the sources of scientism that had long been at work in the field and upon which the new scientism could draw. Sociology must be "relieved of the charge that it is a pseudo-science"; science offered "the Promised Land of wholesome social life"; and "rigidly scientific methods" would free sociology of its association with socialism.[82] That same year the sociologists

W. Spiegel and Warren J. Samuels (Greenwich, Conn.: JAI Press, 1984), pt. B, 557–69. Buchanan's appropriation of the name "neo-institutionalism" forms an ironic coda to the story of American institutionalism, for his work is not only hostile to new liberal social control and aggressively antiempirical, but it destroys the fundamental purpose of institutionalism and of the historicism on which it distantly rested, namely to relativize and constrain the atomistic individualism of market analysis. See also Gary Becker, *The Economic Approach to Human Behavior* (Chicago: University of Chicago Press, 1976).

82 John L. Gillin, "Report of the Committee on the Standardization of Research of the American Sociological Society," *PPASS*, 14 (1919): 252–9; John L. Gillin, ibid. 15 (1920): 231–41. Quotations are on p. 241 and in John L. Gillin, "The Development of Sociology in the United States," ibid. 21 (1926): 24–5.

began to meet in subject- and method-centered roundtables that would allow the focused discussion of ongoing research, and Small began to warn of the new "cant" about research and methods. By 1923 the formation of the Social Science Research Council and the Rockefeller largesse had stilled most qualms and plunged the profession wholesale into empirical research, from which they hoped a basic science of social control would emerge.[83]

The sociologists were still left the question, however, of what constituted science. The hallmark of science was now its method. The underlying desire for control oriented method toward behavioristic premises and replicable, exact measurements. Statistics became the visible mark of science. Christopher G. A. Bryant has aptly termed this American sociology "instrumental positivism." The presumed rigors of natural-science methodology became the primary goal of social-scientific practice, dictating what was to be studied as well as how. Instrumentalism meant a preoccupation with statistical technique, an individualistic conception of society, inductive-research strategy, the belief that science was value-free, and eventually the growth of team research.[84]

In truth, the individualism, empiricism, and search for objectivity that accompanied this methodological preoccupation were as much its cause as effect, the liberal and exceptionalist ground on which social scientists, increasingly pressed by the uncertainties and disappointments of history, sought a science of control. As Bryant makes clear, the key to instrumental positivism was not the use of statistics, per se. Statistics had been a method of historical as well as positivist science, where it was subordinated to a historical conceptual framework. Instrumental positivism decreed that the statistical study of aggregate behavior would itself define the field of social inquiry. When Mitchell, for example, declared the statistical study of market behavior to be the preferred method of institutionalism, he was following the lead of this new sociological canon, and in practice, if not intent, reducing the historical-institutional field to the terms of measurable market aggregates.

In 1926 the sociologists' committee on research remarked on "how objective the work of the members of this Society is today." Of the reported research projects, "31 per cent either explicitly (or implicitly, in the opinion of the chairman of this committee) involve the use of statistics." Quantita-

83 Albion Small, "The Future of Sociology," *PPASS*, 15 (1920): 181–2; "The Work of the American Sociological Society – A Symposium," ibid. 16 (1921): 257–63. As Ogburn noted, the devotion to a single topic at previous meetings had meant invitations to write on assigned topics, rather than discussion of research.
84 Christopher G. A. Bryant, *Positivism in Social Theory and Research* (New York: St. Martin's Press, 1985), chap. 5.

tive method was for some time "implicit," for it required a degree of specialized expertise that took time to develop in the profession. And as its practitioners soon realized, the complexity of applying statistical techniques to social phenomena required ever-increasing sophistication. Chapin was occupied during the 1920s trying to develop objective measures of social status, dependency, and social change. By 1929 he recognized that "measurement, far from being that step in scientific study that lies close to the solution of the problem, is itself a problem because of the confusion of meaning and looseness of usage." Like Mitchell, Chapin was discovering that statistical technique could absorb his best efforts. So despite the difficulty of the task, and because of it, statistical method became increasingly the desideratum. Chapin wanted it "emphatically stated" that measurement still had "undoubted advantages as a form of scientific description."[85]

The statistical orientation also had a strong institutional source. According to Robert Bannister, Columbia was turning out almost twice as many Ph.D.'s as Chicago and placing them more effectively to multiply Giddings' influence and propagate the statistical message. Two of Bernard's and Chapin's students, Read Bain and George Lundberg, quickly became aggressive spokesmen for hard-line objectivism in sociology.[86]

The preeminent case of Columbia's expanding reach was the appointment of Ogburn at Chicago in 1927, where he became a major advocate of instrumental positivism. There was already at Chicago considerable interest in statistics through Merriam. Park himself, and his chief collaborator in directing Chicago research, Ernest W. Burgess, routinely used elementary statistics to measure such things as the growth of immigrant newspapers or the patterns of land use in the city. Park was also interested in the possibility of quantifying attitudes. But Ogburn's arrival at Chicago sharpened the issue and forced Park into efforts to contain statistical method. Ogburn in turn grew increasingly wedded to it. Professional rivalry and personal dislike seem to have hardened both their positions, but the logic of scientism itself forced them apart as it increasingly threw into doubt all qualitative techniques of analysis.[87]

Ogburn himself struggled with scientism. He was fascinated by psychoanalysis and entered into analysis with Trigant Burrow during the war. At first psychoanalysis strengthened Ogburn's attraction to radical politics. The economic interpretation of history from Marx to Beard, with its exposure of

85 C. E. Gehlke, "Report of the Committee on Social Research of the American Sociological Society," *PPASS*, 21 (1926): 279; F. Stuart Chapin, "The Meaning of Measurement in Sociology," ibid. 24 (1930): 83, 94.
86 Bannister, *Sociology and Scientism*, 56, 78, 152–4, 204–5.
87 Ibid., 174–5.

repressed economic motives, was a proof of psychoanalysis and "a good working instrument" for social science. But he quickly became aware that his own attraction to that economic theory might have psychological roots.[88] When he turned from politics to science at Columbia, he turned ever more deeply against wishful thinking. John Dewey, he said, gave "a totally inadequate idea of the great part emotion and desire play in thinking." Ogburn was now ready to label all social philosophies the product of childhood "complexes," and to banish theory from social science. "We understand by a theory 'hypotheses unsupported by facts,' otherwise we would call it a law." The only way to achieve science, therefore, was to abjure theory for facts and to develop a rigorous, quantitative scientific method. Yet even to write about psychoanalysis forced him to go back on himself. On this subject "I shall not be limited by rigid scientific tests of proof, for if I did there would be little to talk about in either social psychology or psychiatry (or, indeed, in much of social science)."[89]

The extreme objectivism of Ogburn's presidential address to the sociologists in 1929 was thus a defensive maneuver. The solution he advocated, and tried in his own life, was to separate social science from life and to bifurcate the social scientist into two rigidly separated compartments. As a scientist,

it will be necessary to crush out emotion and to discipline the mind so strongly that the fanciful pleasures of intellectuality will have to be eschewed in the verification process; it will be desirable to taboo our ethics and values (except in choosing problems); and it will be inevitable that we shall have to spend most of our time doing hard, dull, tedious, and routine tasks.

But then the scientist could "temporarily shut the door to his laboratory and open for a while his door to the beauty of the stars, to the romance of life, to the service of his fellow-men." Only that rigid separation would control bias and, under the exigencies of control, "the result will be pure gold," a science that "grows by accretion, by the accumulation of little bits and pieces of new knowledge." Ogburn admitted that he struggled his whole professional life to maintain that separation, with only mixed success, yet he never abandoned the ideal or retracted the obsessive vision of social science as an accretion of empirical, numerical facts devoid of color, emotion, theory, or

88 Laslett, "Unfeeling Knowledge," 39; William F. Ogburn, "The Psychological Basis for the Economic Interpretation of History," *AER*, 9, Suppl. (March 1919): 305; idem, "Capital and Labor," in *Democracy in Reconstruction*, ed. Frederick A. Cleveland and Joseph Schafer (Boston: Houghton Mifflin, 1919), 326.
89 William F. Ogburn, "Bias, Psychoanalysis, and the Subjective in Relation to the Social Sciences" (1922), in *On Culture and Social Change*, ed. Otis D. Duncan (Chicago: University of Chicago Press, 1964): 294–7, 299–300; idem, "The Contributions of Psychiatry to Social Psychology," *PPASS*, 21 (1926): 83.

value. As a statement of aspiration, it is a remarkable testament to the desperation and futility of scientism.[90]

The ideal nonetheless grew through the 1920s, and perhaps the most important measure of its power was the fate of Chicago sociology.[91] Thomas' work immediately felt the impact of the new methodological imperatives. Thomas understood attitudes as cognitive, as well as affective, dispositions that always shaped the individual's response to the environment. Attitudes defined the situation to which individuals responded and actions could only be understood in the context of such definitions. In 1928 Read Bain argued that attitude research, and specifically Thomas' use of it in the *Polish Peasant*, was inconsistent, incoherent, and untrustworthy. Personal testimony of "hypothetical subjective states" told little about how a person will act under given circumstances. Attitudes ought to be defined as and measured by overt behavior.[92]

At the same time, there were efforts on several fronts to develop techniques for the measurement of attitudes. Park initially led the effort. In his 1921 text he developed the idea, apparently from Simmel, of "social distance." Attitudes, as tendencies to act, could be understood as "contrasting tendencies to approach an object or to withdraw from it," and given his spatial imagination, he graphed the concept along two dimensions. Park encouraged his student Emory Bogardus to develop survey techniques for ethnic and racial attitudes that would measure the social distance between groups in America. When Park heard reports of the political science meeting at which Allport told about his study of political opinions, and the scaling technique he had developed for measuring opinions, he urged Bogardus on. "If we can develop methods of measuring the social attitudes, which determine the status of the different immigrant groups, on racial minorities in our population, we will have done something that the psychologists have not yet succeeded in doing." Bogardus worked out a method of measurement over the next few years, but he became skeptical of his subjects'

90 William F. Ogburn, "The Folkways of a Scientific Sociology," *PPASS*, 24 (1930): 10–11, 5; idem, "A Few Words by Professor Ogburn." Bannister, *Sociology and Scientism*, points out the bifurcation between public science and private feelings that developed among many of the objectivists.

91 Bulmer, *The Chicago School of Sociology*, is an informative account of Chicago sociology in the twenties that stresses its diversity. The most revealing source on the political context of Chicago sociology is Carey, *Sociology and Public Affairs*. Dennis Smith, *The Chicago School: A Liberal Critique of Capitalism* (New York: St. Martin's Press, 1988) takes a fresh look at the Chicago tradition from a comparative, European perspective. Robert E. L. Faris, *Chicago Sociology, 1920–1932* (Chicago: University of Chicago Press, 1970 [1967]), is a useful, but uncritical, survey.

92 Read Bain, "An Attitude on Attitude Research," *AJS*, 33 (May 1928): 949.

self-knowledge and hence the adequacy of their direct reports of attitudes. Interviews and life histories provided deeper material for analysis.[93]

Park too seems to have dropped the idea. He could not understand Bogardus' statistics, and the growing influence of instrumental positivism put the subject in a new light. A major factor would also have been Floyd Allport's decree in 1927 that "the methodology of natural science" required that sociology drop the concepts of "group" and "institution" altogether and study merely the measurable, aggregate behavior of individuals. Bogardus replied for the social interactionists, that the individual was no more a fixed unit than the group and that intersocial stimulation and social relationships affected social behavior.[94]

Nonetheless the kind of research Allport proposed, which in fact viewed social behavior as merely aggregated individual behaviors, quickly developed, though more at the hands of social psychologists trained in psychology than by sociologists. The most important figure was L. L. Thurstone, a psychologist brought to Chicago by Merriam, who was inspired by Allport to develop a more sophisticated technique for measuring opinions. Using a large number of judges, Thurstone scaled opinions on a continuum from those most strongly in favor to those most strongly against an issue, marked off by "equal-appearing-intervals." Thurstone was aware that opinions thus measured were not the only indicator of attitude – actions might provide other and different indicators – but he and those who followed did see themselves as providing one objective technique for the measurement of attitudes.[95]

From the point of view of Thomas' initial formulation, opinions thus measured were not attitudes. Attitudes were formed in the individual in the course of a series of specific situations, in the context of a whole life, and they were expressed in complex and specific social situations. The opinion survey or questionnaire assumed a reified, unitary, and simple construct that could be abstracted out of context. Thus Thomas advocated the use of the case-study method, the detailed life history of the kind he had used in the

---

93 Robert E. Park and Ernest W. Burgess, *Introduction to the Science of Society* (Chicago: University of Chicago Press, 1921), 286, 440–1; Robert E. Park to Emory S. Bogardus, August 2, 1924, February 4, 1925, Robert E. Park Papers, University of Chicago; Jean M. Converse, *Survey Research in the United States. Roots and Emergence, 1890–1960* (Berkeley: University of California Press, 1987), 56–67.

94 Floyd H. Allport, "The Group Fallacy and Social Science," *AJS*, 29 (May 1924): 688–703; and Emory S. Bogardus in "Discussion," 703–4. See also Floyd H. Allport, "'Group' and 'Institution' as Concepts in a Natural Science of Social Phenomena," *PPASS*, 22 (1927): 83–99.

95 L. L. Thurstone, "Attitudes Can Be Measured," *AJS*, 33 (January 1928): 529–54; Converse, *Survey Research in the United States*, 68–75.

*Polish Peasant.* As against opinion surveys, the case study could tell you what attitudes were, and hence what overt behavior might be expected from them. As against statistics of overt behavior, the life history could tell you what behavior meant, what attitudes and purposes it expressed. As the sociologists increasingly focused on method, the life history became the center of controversy, for its open-ended, free-ranging character made it difficult to reduce to standardized, measurable units and hence to submit to objective verification.[96]

Thomas never abandoned the case study, but he gave it a diminishing role in relation to statistics. Thomas' personal situation in the 1920s left him extremely sensitive to the opinion of his colleagues, which is to say, subject to the behavioristic drift of the profession. More important, the one secure tie he made in that decade was to Dorothy Swaine, an Ogburn student who became his wife. Committed to statistical method and rigorous behavioristic premises, she and Thomas worked jointly in the 1920s. Thomas and Thomas took a position of moderate behaviorism in 1928. Declaring themselves in pursuit of a science of prediction and control, they used a probabilistic model of science that could have been adapted from Pearson. The changing and complex character of human beings would prevent the formulation of the kind of causal laws and complete description that natural science achieved. But a science of behavior would be able to make inferences, "to determine that in certain situations certain reactions will usually follow," and thus provide "not a *complete* but an *adequate* causal explanation of behavior."

Because the aim of scientific research was to make inferences and predictions, statistical study was crucial, but the Thomases were equally aware of the immense complexity and interrelations of the factors involved. Statistics had thus far measured only a few of the many factors and often made "premature" predictions. The solution was to include

case-histories and life-histories ... along with the available statistical studies, to be used as a basis for the inferences drawn. And these inferences in turn must be continually subjected to further statistical analysis as it becomes possible to transmute more factors into quantitative form.... But the statistical results must always be interpreted in the configuration of the as-yet unmeasured factors and the

---

96 A doctoral dissertation by an Ogburn student helped to make the behaviorists' case by concluding that the two methods produced similar results: Samuel A. Stouffer, *An Experimental Comparison of Statistical and Case History Methods of Attitude Research* (New York: Arno, 1980 [1930]), but Stouffer discounted or failed to take account of the many ways his study prestructured the results. On the "behavioralization" of Thomas' concept of attitude, see Norbert Wiley, "Early American Sociology and *The Polish Peasant*," *Sociological Theory*, 4 (Spring 1986): 20–40.

hypotheses emerging from the study of cases must, whenever possible, be verified statistically.

In this formulation the life history and the mental life it records must be taken into account, but they are the subject matter and the raw material of behavioral science, to be progressively transformed into statistically measured attitudes and actions. The kind of studies the Thomases recommended in the 1920s were more sophisticated statistical studies of behavioral, social, and cultural variables using control groups.[97]

In 1938 the *Polish Peasant* was voted by social scientists the most influential work written since the war, and the SSRC convened a conference to reappraise it. The conference, however, spent its time criticizing, rather than celebrating, the book. Thomas and supporters of the life-history method could not effectively contend against the more rigorous behavioristic tide, and Thomas' own sympathy for statistical method left his allegiance unclear. Both Thomas and Park's paternity have been claimed by the one cohesive school to emerge from Chicago sociology, the symbolic interactionists. Disciples primarily of George Herbert Mead, they formed in the 1930s in opposition to the behaviorists, arguing that all social interaction involved an irreducible level of symbolic meaning. Thomas would probably have agreed with that general proposition, but he did not believe that the symbolic character of social interaction determined the logic appropriate to its understanding. Nor could he ever leave his base in individual psychology, so as to ground attitudes in the holistic conception of culture anthropology made available. In method as in liberal philosophy, Thomas' subjects acted like atomistic individuals collecting into aggregates in response to shifting situations.[98]

Park turned away from the statistical study of attitudes, only to develop his own positivistic study of ecological process. In 1925 he and a student

---

97 William I. Thomas and Dorothy Swaine Thomas, *The Child in America* (New York: Knopf, 1928), chap. 13, particularly pp. 553–4, 571; William I. Thomas, "The Behavior Pattern and the Situation," *PPASS*, 22 (1927): 1–13.

98 Herbert Blumer, *An Appraisal of Thomas and Znaniecki's "The Polish Peasant in Europe and America"* (New York: SSRC, 1939), particularly pp. 83, 86–7, 166–74; Evan A. Thomas, "Herbert Blumer's Critique of 'The Polish Peasant': A Post Mortem on the Life History Approach in Sociology," *JHBS*, 14 (April 1978): 124–31. On Thomas' move toward behaviorism see Stephen O. Murray, "W. I. Thomas, Behaviorist Ethnologist," *JHBS*, 24 (October 1988): 381–91, and compare the symbolic interactionism of Herbert Blumer, "Social Psychology," in *Man and Society: A Substantive Introduction to the Social Sciences*, ed. Emerson P. Schmidt (Englewood Cliffs, N.J.: Prentice-Hall, 1937), 144–98. A useful but highly selective account of the Thomas–Park tradition, from a post-1960s vantage point, is Berenice M. Fisher and Anselm L. Strauss, "Interactionism," in *A History of Sociological Analysis*, ed. Tom Bottomore and Robert Nisbet (New York: Basic, 1978), 457–98.

whom he had steered into ecology introduced the subject to the sociologists. "We are almost the founders of a new science, McKenzie and myself," he wrote his wife. "Everyone . . . is now talking about the 'ecological aspect' of everything." Park claimed that the city, "as a product of natural forces," was an ecological unit, and the pattern of settlement in the city, moving out in concentric circles, mapped an ecological process. But if ecological process was determinative, if it governed the social processes of organization and disorganization, then why study attitudes?[99]

As the hard-line behaviorists rose to prominence, Park tried to defend his dual allegiance. "It is not impossible," Park began, "that all we ordinarily conceive as social may eventually be construed and described in terms of space and the changes of position of the individuals within the limits of a natural area; that is to say, within the limits of an area of competitive co-operation." In effect, sociology would become, "what some persons have sought to make it, a branch of statistics." Having gone so far, Park then shifted gears. The problem was that individuals were not constant and homogenous units. Society was formed by communication and individuals changed in the process of communication, accumulating memories and habits. "Not individuals, but attitudes, interact to maintain social organizations and to produce social changes." Calling up Simmel's concept of individuality, Park now emphasized that unique life experiences created in every person a reserve of privacy, which that person strove to protect. For that reason "social distances cannot always be adequately measured in purely physical terms."

Park unannounced now shifted gears again. This social world had its own social and moral order and he described it by a metaphor of liberal (and ecological) competition: "The conception which each of us has of himself is limited by the conception which every other individual, in the same limited world of communication, has of himself, and of every other individual." Hence the individual's position in society and self-conception – "the core of his personality" – were socially determined. "A person is simply an individual who has . . . social status; but status turns out finally to be a matter of distance – social distance." And finally, social distance is "so frequently and so inevitably correlated with spatial relations" that statistics have significance for sociology. Park had gone up the hill and back down. Individual subjectivity and social attitudes were specified as the significant area of sociology only to be declared in the end to mirror and largely depend upon

99 Robert E. Park to Clara Park, January 2, 1926, Park Papers. See R. D. McKenzie, "The Scope of Human Ecology," *PPASS*, 20 (1925): 141–54.

the competitive ecological process.[100] As the decade proceeded and the controversy over method escalated, Park repeatedly tried to defend subjective experience, and every time he slipped into determinism, subordinating subjective to social process, and social to the natural ecological process of economic competition. Park was prevented by his own positivism from adequately defending or enlarging the role of interpretive and historical method in sociology.[101]

### History as nature

If historical method did not fare well in sociology, neither did the understanding of history. The Thomases reiterated in 1928 that "the past contains no models on which we may build in the present."[102] Moreover, the 1920s disillusionment with national politics turned a great deal of sociological attention away from the larger movements of history and toward the community, rural or urban, where society might be rebuilt from the bottom, or from the primary group. For most sociologists, however, history did not disappear, even within the more limited local focus. The liberal exceptionalist hope, the new fragility of progress, and the centrality of the evolutionary sociological tradition all combined to keep the historical fate of modern society at the center of sociological attention.

Park's view of history, like his method, was held hostage to his view of natural process. Sociology turned history into "natural history," which was the history of types or species. The importance of dealing with "temporal relations," he wrote R. D. McKenzie, was that "we believe we can ultimately reduce them to types and measure the factors that speed up or slow down the process of culmination of a type." The message Park always drew from this vision, however, was to let nature take its course. In his "natural history" of the immigrant press in America, for example, he argued that immigrant newspapers were themselves evolving, censorship and all, toward the commercial, mass circulation American type as the result of an economic struggle for existence. Under the influence of ecology, Park extended the cyclic character of ecological change. Within the parameters of type, he said, social change was always scientifically described as a cycle. When his stu-

---

100 Robert E. Park, "The Concept of Position in Sociology," *PPASS*, 20 (1925): 13–14.
101 Robert E. Park, "Magic, Mentality and City Life," *PPASS*, 18 (1923): 109; idem, "Culture and Culture Trends," *PPASS*, 19 (1924): 30, 35; idem, "Human Nature and Collective Behavior," *AJS*, 32 (March 1927): 734, 739–41; idem, "Sociology," in *Research in the Social Sciences*, 3–49. For an astute comment on the last, see Herbert Blumer, "Review of William Gee, ed. *Research in the Social Sciences*," *AJS*, 35 (May 1930): 1107–9.
102 W. I. Thomas and D. S. Thomas, *The Child in America*, 575.

dents studied revolutions or strikes they found a cyclical pattern that ended in the dissipation of conflict and adjustment to a changing environment.[103]

The one area of social life Park had not been able to subdue to his vision of liberal history was race relations. Ecology had its most profound effect on Park's attitude toward race, though it operated in tandem with a transforming personal experience of race relations on the West Coast and in Hawaii. Until the mid-1920s Park remained uncertain about racial assimilation. His books on immigrant assimilation and the immigrant press indicated that the new ethnic immigrants would assimilate to American society. The liberal-ecological process would, in its own good time, wear away their group identities, particularly as immigration from Europe halted. But Negro-white race relations could be different, and after the Chicago race riot of 1919, he sensed a growing "class consciousness" and "race consciousness" in the cities.[104]

What apparently changed his mind was his study of Japanese-American relations, in which he encountered "the younger generation of Orientals." Listening to a young Japanese-American woman, he felt that he was listening to "an American woman in a Japanese disguise." Park went on to a conference in Hawaii, where he was astonished at the mixing of races and described his meetings with the Japanese delegation as "an adventure in friendship." Park's encounter led him for the first time to declare unequivocally the triumph of ecological determinism. "The forces which have brought about the existing interpenetration of peoples are so vast and irresistible that the resulting changes assume the character of a cosmic process.... The race relations cycle ... of contacts, competition, accommodation and eventual assimilation, is apparently progressive and irreversible."[105]

For Park, it was always the determinism of natural process that was liberating. In that cosmic vision, he was able to let go his exceptionalist fears of decline and his exceptionalist attachment to the Caucasian visage of the American type. "Races and cultures die – it has always been so – but civilization lives on." He was also able for the first time to declare his faith

103 Robert E. Park to R. D. McKenzie, June 14, 1924, Park Papers; Robert E. Park, *The Immigrant Press and Its Control* (New York: Harper, 1922), 354–6, 467; idem, "Introduction," to *The Natural History of Revolution*, by Lyford P. Edwards (Chicago: University of Chicago Press, 1927), xiii; Ernest T. Hiller, *The Strike* (Chicago: University of Chicago Press, 1928).

104 Robert E. Park, "The Concept of Social Distance" (1924), in *The Collected Papers of Robert Ezra Park*, ed. Everett C. Hughes (Glencoe, Ill.: Free Press, 1950), vol. 1: *Race and Culture*, 259.

105 Robert E. Park, "Behind Our Masks" (1926), ibid., 244–6, 254–5; idem, "Our Racial Frontier" (1926), ibid., 149–50; idem, "Human Migration and the Marginal Man," *AJS*, 33 (May 1928): 881–93.

that African Americans would be included. "In America ... humanly speaking, there are no class distinctions." From Lindbergh to Al Smith, "the spectacle of American life is amazing and inspiring." Democratic personal relations would lead to personal acquaintance and render invisible even "the racial mark."[106]

Park's inevitable "race relations cycle" was immediately taken up in the sociological literature and assumed an important place in the ambiguous history of race relations in America. It fueled the optimism toward integration that, growing in the more egalitarian politics of the 1930s and 1940s, helped to open American society to the new immigrants and end racial segregation in the South. Park also contributed to the field of African-American sociology and its tie to racial reform. A native tradition of inquiry into their community developed early among African Americans and W. E. B. DuBois' *The Philadelphia Negro* (1899) was among the first academic examples of an urban social survey. Allied to communal and Progressive reform, programs in sociology developed at black colleges in the South, under DuBois at Atlanta, Booker T. Washington at Tuskegee, and a Giddings disciple at Hampton Institute. Under Park, Chicago became a center for training black sociologists, including Charles S. Johnson and E. Franklin Frazier, and a source of the movement for African-American improvement embodied in the National Urban League, a northern successor to the Booker T. Washington tradition of self-help.[107]

Park's cosmopolitan vision was not a true pluralism, however, but a species of liberal exceptionalism, and extracted for assimilation the price of cultural homogeneity. From African Americans it extracted the even higher price of continued segregation. Park's conservative reliance on natural process required that the intermediate stage of conflict and caste accommodation be allowed to proceed. Segregation was a form of "etiquette" that seemed "essential to social organization and effective collective action" in the midst of rapid social-industrial change. Under segregation, he said, Negroes already had begun to develop a business and professional class, so that stratification was parallel in both communities and ties were forming across racial lines. Segregation was now vertical rather than horizontal. As

---

106 Park, "Our Racial Frontier," 151; idem, "The Bases of Race Prejudice" (1928), in *Race and Culture*, 233, 238.

107 Stow Persons, *Ethnic Studies in Chicago, 1905–1945* (Urbana: University of Illinois Press, 1987); Paul Jefferson, "The Antebellum Origins of Afro-American Sociology: Research, Rhetoric and Reform, 1787–1865"; "Sociology, Race and the New Liberalism: 'Doing Good after a Plan' at Hampton Institute, 1893–1917"; "Inventing Afro-American Studies: Charles S. Johnson and the Social Construction of a Sociology of Race Relations, 1922–1930," unpublished papers; Nancy J. Weiss, *The National Urban League, 1910–1940* (New York: Oxford University Press, 1974).

John Kneebone has shown, Park's overly sanguine account of vertical segregation, with its postponement of basic change, was important to the white southern liberals who between the wars urged improvement in race relations but proscribed political action. The final ambiguity in the tale is that Park himself could not sustain the optimism that had forged his cyclical theory, but returned in the 1930s to the possibility of permanent racial solutions short of assimilation.[108]

The divergent implications of Park's naturalism also appeared in the urban sociology produced at Chicago during the 1920s, although ambiguity emerged from many sources. With its crime syndicates and slums, Chicago attracted students both for its social needs and its local color. The young sociologists became adept at taking visitors on "slumming visits."[109] Park's naturalism allowed Louis Wirth, one of the new ethnic recruits to sociology, to present the Jewish ghetto and its characteristic "types" sympathetically, as the product of social isolation rather than race. For many others, the anxiety over social disorganization led to one-sided views of social pathology.[110]

Harvey Zorbaugh's *The Gold Coast and the Slum*, an instant best-seller in Chicago, suggests as well as any single work the strengths and weaknesses of Chicago urban sociology. Zorbaugh studied Chicago's near north side, which included a welter of disconnected districts – the "gold coast"; an old section of houses turned into furnished rooms for the young, single, and poor; a patch of bohemia; and an ethnic slum. He laid down an ecological underpinning in mapped patterns of population density and land values. He did extensive interviewing and collected written reports and life histories, many of which were reprinted in the book and which provided genuine insight into disparate urban lives. But his insight was limited by the pathologist's viewpoint and he spent a good deal of the book showing and lamenting that this urban region was not a genuine "community." The *Gemeinschaft* of the old New England town was recalled to judge the disorganization of modern urban *Gesellschaft*.

108 Park, "The Bases of Race Prejudice," 241–3; John T. Kneebone, *Southern Liberal Journalists and the Issue of Race, 1920–1944* (Chapel Hill: University of North Carolina Press, 1985), 10–13, 84–92, 199–200; Persons, *Ethnic Studies at Chicago*, 72–3, 86–8; Robert E. Park, "The Race Relations Cycle in Hawaii" (1937), in *Race and Culture*, 189–95. Persons' excellent study emphasizes the ambiguities in Park's thinking about race. For a different view, see R. Fred Wacker, *Ethnicity, Pluralism, and Race: Race Relations Theory in America before Myrdal* (Westport, Conn.: Greenwood, 1983).
109 Faris, *Chicago Sociology*, 65, 72, 83.
110 Louis Wirth, *The Ghetto* (Chicago: University of Chicago Press, 1928); C. Wright Mills, "The Professional Ideology of Social Pathologists," *AJS*, 49 (September 1943): 169–70, 180.

Rehearsing Park's account of modernization as individuation, Zorbaugh saw only the disappearance of a "common body of experience and tradition, no unanimity of interest, sentiment, and attitude which can serve as a basis of collective action." For collective action Zorbaugh was forced to look at politics and, in a telling instance of the apolitical stance of Chicago sociology and its ignorance of the American political tradition, he resorted to Webster's dictionary for a definition of parliamentary government and praised the purity of earlier American politics. In the end, his solution was to activate the civic consciousness of the gold-coast elite, the only people in the city who could see the city as a whole. Park himself would not have written that book. In the introduction he subtly dissociated himself from the communitarian nostalgia and the solution of elite activism. But then his conservative naturalism did not provide much guidance to the activist students who flocked to sociology. The book is fairly a product of the contrary tendencies Chicago sociology propagated rather than resolved.[111]

Perhaps the last word on the subject is that the best book in the field to be written in the 1920s – Robert and Helen Lynd's *Middletown* (1929) – did not come from the Chicago tradition. It seemed to one reviewer to be a masterpiece that emerged full-blown from nowhere. In fact, the Lynds had been educated in the activist tradition of social research and egalitarian experience that had emerged from the settlement houses and the ministry, and in academia had been shunted into social work and divinity schools. Their description of the "pecuniary" culture and class-segregated experience that dominated American lives was informed by Veblen and achieved a verisimilitude that still resonates in modern America. Their chief debt to academic social science was to anthropology; they subtitled the book *A Study in Contemporary American Culture*. Robert Lynd shrewdly recognized that he could use the new concept of culture to legitimate his critical, holistic analysis, against the doubts of the sociological positivists.

It is true, of course, that the Lynds deliberately chose a small city, with a population untainted by ethnic admixture, so as to capture the pure effect of industrial change on America. The Chicago sociologists at least struggled with the cosmopolitan complexity of modern America and their ambivalence toward it. The Lynds also, like the Chicago sociologists, imagined a transition from *Gemeinschaft*, although they located that community in the Middletown of the 1890s rather than in colonial New England, a striking token of the new, modernist, historical consciousness emerging in the 1920s. To the Lynds, born in the 1890s, the Gilded Age upheaval was no longer

---

111 Harvey W. Zorbaugh, *The Gold Coast and the Slum* (Chicago: University of Chicago Press, 1929), 227, 250–1, 253; and Robert E. Park, "Introduction," ibid., vii–viii, x.

visible. In a world of perpetual transition, the real past quickly disappeared to be replaced by the typological shift from community to society, a shift that could be located virtually anywhere in time.[112]

The sociologists who continued in the 1920s to cultivate the larger evolutionary field of Western history were often Giddings' students, but they brought to it an ahistorical method. Ogburn's major work was his 1922 book, *Social Change*, an attempt to reformulate the problem of evolutionary progress Giddings' sociology had left him. An important influence on his redefinition of evolutionary sociology was Boasian cultural anthropology. Boas, like Ogburn, was at Columbia and young anthropologists influenced by Boas – Robert Lowie and Alexander Goldenweiser – had begun to publish in the *American Journal of Sociology* as early as 1912, spreading the word not only of Boas' argument for biological racial equality but also of his historical conception of culture.[113]

Ogburn found particularly compelling a study by Alfred Kroeber on "The Superorganic," Herbert Spencer's term for the realm of culture. If progress were divided into its biological and cultural components, Kroeber said, the biological component had enlarged very little if at all since prehistory. But the realm of culture had expanded enormously. Nor could the expansion of culture be explained by individual psychological characteristics, for the variation of human capacities in any culture must have always been roughly the same. What explained culture was a cumulative tradition and "great currents of history," visible in the pattern of inventions that not only grew cumulatively greater through time but frequently disclosed multiple, simultaneous discoveries. "The presence of a majestic order pervading civilization will be irresistibly evident."[114]

Ogburn used Kroeber's analysis to free evolution from Giddings' biological and racial heritage. In 1921 he declared himself an advocate of "the

112 Robert S. Lynd and Helen M. Lynd, *Middletown: A Study in Contemporary American Culture* (New York: Harcourt Brace, 1929); Norman J. Ware, "Review of Robert Lynd and Helen Lynd, *Middletown*," *AER*, 19 (June 1929): 328–9. Note also Ware's doubt whether 1890 was "as simple as it looks from here." Yet because "change is everywhere," he thought the idea of "cultural lag" appropriate. For an excellent analysis of the Lynds' book, as well as for their use of culture, see Richard Wightman Fox, "Epitaph for Middletown: Robert S. Lynd and the Analysis of Consumer Culture," in *The Culture of Consumption: Critical Essays in American History, 1880–1980*, ed. R. W. Fox and T. J. Jackson Lears (New York: Pantheon, 1983), 143–73.
113 Robert H. Lowie, "Review of Franz Boas, *The Mind of Primitive Man*," *AJS*, 17 (May 1912): 829–35; idem, "Social Organization," ibid. 20 (July 1914): 68–97; idem, "Psychology and Anthropology," ibid. 21 (September 1915): 217–29; A. A. Goldenweiser, "Culture and Environment," ibid. 21 (March 1916): 628–33.
114 A. L. Kroeber, "The Superorganic," *American Anthropologist*, n.s. 19 (April–June 1917): 198, 201.

historical method in the analysis of social phenomena," and defined historical sociology as "the history of society, the development of culture, and the evolution of social institutions." Bypassing the question of epistemology altogether, Ogburn focused on freeing the realm of culture from racial and biological interpretations. In method, however, Ogburn stuck with Giddings. In the sociological study of evolution and social problems, he said, historical method was an increasingly statistical, analytical method. Here Ogburn's model was institutional economics. He had pored over Mitchell's book, with its cyclical economic trend line, and now at Columbia he undoubtedly heard Mitchell's defense of a historical economics that used statistical method. As in the study of business cycles, Ogburn said, "the problem is not so much to determine ... what the psychological or the cultural factor is; but the problem is to find which of several possible cultural factors are effective and the degrees of their effectiveness," and this was a problem for statistical analysis.[115]

The problem of "what the psychological or the cultural factor is," was precisely the problem of Boasian anthropology and of history. Ogburn used anthropology's concept of culture to delimit the cultural field, but he never recognized the holistic character it bestowed upon that field or the difficulties it raised for statistical method. He continued to look at history to find statistical evidence of the laws at work beneath it. The central problem of sociology was to uncover the secret of the growth of civilization. "Can the nature of its growth and change be described in a few simple processes?" Not yet, he admitted, but "eventually the processes, causes, and laws will become clearer."[116]

Ogburn's contribution to that problem was the theory of cultural lag, which he developed from Kroeber's analysis and statistics of inventions. Pronouncing inventions to be the cause of social change and their measure,

115 William F. Ogburn, "The Historical Method in the Analysis of Social Phenomena," *PPASS*, 16 (1921): 71, 82; idem, "A Few Words by Professor Ogburn," 4.
116 William F. Ogburn, *Social Change, with Respect to Culture and Original Nature* (New York: B. W. Huebsch, 1922), 55, 58. On the historian's interest in "what" rather than "why," see Allan Megill, "Recounting the Past: 'Description,' Explanation, and Narrative in Historiography," *AHR*, 94 (June 1989): 627–53. Another variation on the use of culture in sociology is Dorothy P. Gary, "The Developing Study of Culture," in *Trends in American Sociology*, ed. George Lundberg et al. (New York: Harper, 1929). A historical materialist, Gary believed culture offered a way to study institutions, classes, and structures, the patterned and constraining social medium in which individuals lived. Lundberg, a hard-line instrumental positivist with a leftist inclination to social control, must have found Gary's politics, if not her method, congenial. On the changing use of the culture concept see John S. Gilkeson, "The Domestication of 'Culture' in Interwar America, 1919–1941," in *The Estate of Social Knowledge*, ed. JoAnne Brown and David van Keuren (Baltimore: Johns Hopkins University Press, 1990).

he reflected that "in modern times they have been occurring faster and faster until to-day mankind is almost bewildered in his effort to keep adjusted to these ever-increasing social changes."[117] The problem was not merely the speed of change, but its uneven speed. Drawing on the anthropological distinction between material and nonmaterial culture, he located inventions and rapid change primarily in the sphere of material culture. Because nonmaterial culture was correlated with material culture, but changed much more slowly, there were constant lags. Ogburn's theory was a refinement of the most pervasive historical idea of his era; namely, that American society was lagging in its response to increasingly rapid economic change.

The problem with his theory, as he sensed, was how to gauge the correlation of material and nonmaterial culture, and what would count as an "adjustment." Ogburn gave as a detailed analysis of cultural lag the change in industrial machinery and work conditions that led at the turn of the century to so many workers' injuries and deaths. The adjustment was workmen's compensation laws. "People can live, society can exist, under very varied combinations of different parts of culture," he admitted. "Thus there are possible many different degrees of adjustment. But varied conditions under which people live furnish evidence as to what are the most harmonious combinations." What counted as adjustments were described by such terms as harmonious, better, scientific, and just. To the end of his life Ogburn argued that there were objective standards by which adjustment could be measured and that adjustment was necessarily improvement.[118]

The wide and immediate currency of Ogburn's theory of "cultural lag" hardly reflected its analytical power. It gave a name and shape to the widespread sense of historical malaise and it expressed in seemingly scientific form the new liberal hope for progress by incremental change. Denying the ability to chart the overall course of evolutionary progress, Ogburn could still document by statistics of invention a rising trend line of social change. Given the chastened postwar view, he recognized the futility of the idea of social control. "It appears like a grandiose dream to think of controlling according to the will of man the course of social evolution." But social control as adjustment would itself constitute "social progress" and forestall revolution. Park was quick to pit his conservative naturalism against the new liberal theory of cultural lag. The kind of changes Ogburn called adjustments were not "the result of design, or consciously intended by the persons who brought them about.... Nothing inspiring or uplifting seems to follow

117 Ogburn, *Social Change*, 199–200.
118 Ibid., 267, 214, 268; idem, "Cultural Lag as Theory" (1957), in *On Culture and Social Change*, 86–95.

from the cleavage [between material and nonmaterial culture] . . . there is no immediate practical significance."[119]

Ogburn continued to believe, however, that a statistical sociological science had profound practical uses. He began to put out a yearly statistical survey of social trends in the hope of providing greater "security" in "the uncertain time of change. The best prediction in social changes is usually that based on a projection of past trends." His scientific and practical aims came together in his directorship of the massive report prepared for President Herbert Hoover on *Recent Social Trends*. Commissioned in 1929 before the crash and published as Hoover was leaving office, the report turned out to be a monument to the distances between political and scientific purpose and to the hazards of predicting social change "on a projection of past trends." The report was nonetheless, and remains, a rich compendium of useful information on early twentieth-century America, useful for history and social analysis alike. It is information that also points up the dependence of statistics on the categories in which they are collected and the questions they are designed to answer, on having a good sense of "what the psychological or the cultural factor is," which is to say on historical interpretation, social theory, and contextual understanding. Ogburn, still the heir of Giddings, had too much the sense that quantitative facts would speak for themselves, disclosing simple processes directing the course of evolutionary progress.[120]

The same can be said of another Giddings student, F. Stuart Chapin, but Chapin disclosed even more graphically the difficulty of submitting historical evolution to quantitative method. Chapin's 1928 *Cultural Change* followed Ogburn's lead in delimiting the historical field of sociology, but he took the history more seriously than Ogburn did. Chapin examined, briefly but with an effort at specificity, the historical stages of Western civilization from Greece and Rome to medieval Europe, the industrial revolution – the most sudden and transforming change in material culture in history – and the modern reaction to industrialization. His point was that although each stage of civilization had followed a cyclical pattern of rise and decline, history did not exactly repeat itself. Solutions had been found to the problems of decay in the past and the modern industrial period was essentially different from earlier stages. Given the accelerating rate of change there were now maladjustments, but social institutions were not fixed and

---

119 Ogburn, *Social Change*, 346, 280; Park, "Culture and Culture Trends," 34–5. For a more extended discussion of Ogburn's theory of social change see Dorothy Ross, "American Social Science and the Idea of Progress," in *The Authority of Experts*, ed. Thomas H. Haskell (Bloomington: Indiana University Press, 1984), 157–75.

120 "Recent Social Changes," *AJS*, 34 (July 1928): 2. On *Recent Social Trends* see Karl, *Merriam*, 210–25; and Bannister, *Sociology and Scientism*, 181–7.

could be changed. In short, the history Chapin discovered was the new liberal historicism of about 1900.

True to that genre, Chapin's liberal history was progressive. Adapting Ogburn's theory of invention, he stressed "how culture elaborates, accumulates, piles up, at what appears to be an ever-accelerating rate." For Ogburn this cumulation remained abstract, charted on a trend line. For Chapin it was a substantive vision of liberal historical progress that would incorporate the old America into the new and surmount the threat of cyclical decline through material and social invention. The frontispiece of his book was a striking picture of the Chicago Tribune Tower, thrusting into the sky. "This Beautiful Structure," read the caption, "Representing a Modern Skyscraper Made of Reinforced Steel Construction; with the Gothic Motif Superimposed, Epitomizes and Summarizes the Chief Theory of This Book – That Cultural Change is Primarily Accumulative." Chapin may have called his subject "change" but it was really progress, progress that would harmoniously blend the best of the past and present into a powerful modern future.[121]

The largest part of Chapin's book was not history, however, but attempts to find quantitative measures of cultural change. Everywhere he turned, to the business cycle, dependence on charity, patents, the growth of state government in Minnesota, the spread of the city commission form of government, he found the same cyclical curve, representing early rapid growth, leveling off, and then decline. Aware of the difficulty of combining together for statistical analysis units that were not homogeneous or uniform, he relied on a recent model of biological organic growth that showed the same curve. The curves were the product of social learning, he thought, and he developed on their basis "working hypotheses" for further statistical verification, hypotheses that displayed the same degree of superficial generality as his cycles. Finally, he turned to Chicago social psychology and redefined its operative concepts in the hard behavioristic language of "speech reactions" and "muscular behavior patterns."[122] Chapin hoped for a Tribune Tower, but with his mixture of tongues, he had created a tower of Babel, a symbol of the disjunction between his liberal historicist aspiration and his chosen path of instrumental positivism.

One final example of the effort to transform sociology's traditional problem of historical evolution into science was Frederick J. Teggart, an exception who proves the rule. Teggart – and after him, his students Kenneth Bock and Robert Nisbet – developed a tradition of criticism of

121 F. Stuart Chapin, *Cultural Change* (New York: Century, 1928), 56–8, 275, 51.
122 Ibid., 380–1, 427–36.

sociological scientism. A scholar of intellectual history, among many other things, Teggart traced back to Aristotle's conception of organic growth the aspiration of sociology to seek beneath the concrete particularity of history for the essential "nature" of things and for natural, regulative laws of development. Teggart's criticism of sociology's scientific path did not have much impact on the profession during his lifetime. Ensconced at Berkeley in his own department of Social Institutions, he made no effort to reach the sociologists and zealously kept them out of his department. But Teggart was equally disliked by the historians, with whom he taught until they expelled him in 1916, for he was equally critical of history. Using the historians' own words, he showed how deeply culture and subjectivity colored their work. But that was as it should be, he said, for history as it was traditionally practiced was a form of literature that recalled the past to each age anew, a depiction of events that recreated experience, not a generalizing science. Robert Park appropriately found sustenance in Teggart's separation of science and history.[123]

The trick was that Teggart believed history – concrete, particular history – should be made the subject of a science. A scientific historian had first to abandon Western ethnocentricity and the dream of progress and to recognize that history, like the sociologist's "society," was not a single unit, but a plural concatenation of histories. Then by close comparative study, generalizations could be built up about the process of historical development that held true for all times and places, for beneath diverse histories there was "the fundamental homogeneity of history." Teggart worked out the theory that political organizations and civilizations emerged from contact, pressure, conflict, or war, processes that tended to occur at certain kinds of geographical crossroads and that liberated individual initiative. Arnold Toynbee later claimed inspiration from Teggart.[124]

The animating passion behind this theory was far less idiosyncratic than the method. "The cardinal point is that the conflict, in breaking up the older organization, liberated the individual man, if but for a moment, from the dominance of the group, its observances, its formulae, and its ideas.... The individual became, in some measure, a law unto himself. This, at bottom, is the fact upon which all history turns." It meant the release of initiative, the

---

123 On Teggart, see Robert Nisbet, "Teggart of Berkeley," *American Scholar*, 48 (Winter 1978/79): 71–80; Stephen Murray, "Resistance to Sociology at Berkeley," *JHS*, 2 (Spring 1980): 61–84; and Margaret T. Hodgen, "Frederick J. Teggart," *International Encyclopedia of the Social Sciences*, 1968 ed., 15:598–9. For his critique of history, see Frederick J. Teggart, *Prolegomena to History: The Relation of History to Literature, Philosophy, and Science* (Berkeley: University of California Press, 1916).
124 Frederick J. Teggart, *The Processes of History* (New Haven, Conn.: Yale University Press, 1918); the quotation is on p. 80.

development of personal responsibility, and the fundamental right of disposing of one's own property without interference. Here was the familiar liberal idea of social change as individual initiative, freed from the "cake of custom." With his usual historical acuity, Teggart traced it to John Stuart Mill's *On Liberty* and Walter Bagehot. Teggart had been born in Belfast and took from his favorite literature of the Scottish Enlightenment and English liberalism his theory, values, and aspiration to turn history into a science. It is only fitting that in 1932 he launched into a critique of the Veblenian tradition of "social control of economic activity" and deplored the abrogation of the "American," the "naturalistic theory" that "progress pertains to the lives of individuals." Teggart's was a road not taken by American sociology, but it wound through the same territory.[125]

As we leave it in 1930, that territory was both divided and fragmented. Chicago sociology left a bifurcated tradition, attached to naturalistic assumptions of ecological process and natural types on the one hand and to a social psychology of symbolic interaction on the other. The large-scale historical focus of Giddings' tradition broke up into disjointed studies of empirical trends. The one steady development in both traditions was instrumental positivism, decreeing a narrowed focus, naturalistic premises, and the primacy of quantitative methods. It has remained, through the rise and decline of structural-functionalism, the defining feature of mainstream American sociology.[126]

## Conversion and resistance in political science

Political science, like sociology, lacked a dominant paradigm, but it had a dominant tradition in historical realism. The discipline entered the 1920s with its conservative traditionalism still visible. As late as 1924 Harry A. Garfield marveled at "the contrast between conditions in the late eighties and the present time," but assured his colleagues that "we need not modify any fundamental principle." The minimal reforms he suggested "will make

125 Ibid., 86–90; idem, *Theory of History* (New Haven, Conn.: Yale University Press, 1925), 190; idem, "Thorstein Veblen. A Chapter in American Economic Thought," *University of California Publications in Economics*, 11 (1932): vii, 2–3.
126 On the thirties and the rise of Parsons, see Henrika Kuklick, "A 'Scientific Revolution': Sociological Theory in the United States, 1930–1945," *Sociological Inquiry*, 43, no. 1 (1973): 3–22. Both Kuklick, p. 16, and Bannister, *Sociology and Scientism*, chap. 15, argue that the hard scientific program triumphed in only a narrow segment of the profession. My interpretation follows the broader definition of instrumental positivism and the conclusion of Bryant, *Positivism in Social Theory and Research*, chap. 5, as well as Patricia Wilner, "The Main Drift of Sociology between 1936 and 1982," *History of Sociology*, 5 (Spring 1985): 1–20.

for progress almost without change. We have been heading toward that goal from the beginning."[127] But Garfield seems to be the last representative of the older American exceptionalism to preside at the American Political Science Association.

### Merriam's scientific program

Merriam's call in 1921 for a new science of politics found an instant response. His student Arnold Bennett Hall at the University of Wisconsin took the lead in organizing annual summer conferences on the science of politics, beginning in 1923. The conferences were organized as roundtable meetings focused on how to bring scientific method to bear on specific problems and the following year the same format took over the APSA annual meetings. The summer conferences came to an end in 1928, but by then they had done their work of reorienting the discipline.[128]

Merriam's scientific program included an important qualification. He recognized the traditional basis of his discipline in "political prudence," by which he meant "the conclusions of experience and reflection regarding the problems of the state." Though not "demonstrably and technically exact," this body of knowledge was still "a precious asset of the race." Read carefully, Merriam's call was not to abandon this heritage, but to supplement and refine it by the use of scientific method, "the practice of measurement, comparison, standardization of material." Yet the thrust of his message was not preservation or enlargement, but change, and Hall conveyed the scientistic spirit with which his students took up the call. It is the business of political science, Hall told his colleagues, "so to extend and perfect its technique and increase its activities, that more and more of the field now

127 Harry A. Garfield, "Recent Political Developments: Progress or Change?" *APSR*, 18 (February 1924): 1, 16–17.
128 An excellent account of Merriam and the "regenerated science" of the 1920s, which stresses the continued normative commitment to democracy and reform, is Raymond Seidelman with Edward J. Harpham, *Disenchanted Realists: Political Science and the American Crisis, 1884–1984* (Albany: State University of New York Press, 1985), chap. 4. The still classic account of the scientism of American political science is Bernard Crick, *The American Science of Politics* (Berkeley: University of California Press, 1959), although see Chapter 3, note 73. Dwight Waldo, "Political Science: Tradition, Discipline, Profession, Science, Enterprise," in *The Handbook of Political Science*, ed. Fred Greenstein and Nelson Polsby (Reading, Mass.: Addison-Wesley, 1975), 1–130, is useful, as is – particularly for professional development – Albert Somit and Joseph Tanenhaus, *The Development of American Political Science: From Burgess to Behavioralism* (Boston: Allyn & Bacon, 1967). David Ricci, *The Tragedy of Political Science: Politics, Scholarship, and Democracy* (New Haven, Conn.: Yale University Press, 1984), is a critique of scientism in American political science, although the author appears to retain a positivist conception of science.

preempted by political prudence will be occupied by a science of politics."
Along with technique came a sometimes utopian language of "social control
... by which the true course of social progress may be more prophetically
discerned."[129]

The political scientists' early discussions suggest they were largely un-
familiar with the demands of science. One scholar expected that new studies
of voting would soon permit "final judgment on such expedients as compul-
sory voting with all the assurance of a chemist proving the quality of a new
paint-remover or a biologist testing a germicide." Others began to struggle
with the complexity of measuring political phenomena and evaluating
political solutions. Even more than in sociology, statistical technique had to
be supplied from the outside.[130]

The most sophisticated research plan of the first conference was presented
by the constitutional scholar Edward S. Corwin. Corwin's presence was
evidence of the potentiality for systematic research within the historical and
normative tradition of political science. Taking as his problem the effects of
the Supreme Court practice of judicial review, he discussed the need to
specify criteria in the light of value judgments about political outcomes and
outlined a sophisticated series of questions, taking into account differences
in historical period, field of constitutional law, interplay of state and federal
courts, and changes over time in canons of interpretation. The study may
have seemed as daunting to Corwin as to his audience. Not altogether
welcome among the aspirants to behavioral science, he did not participate in
the conferences again.[131]

The roundtable on law was taken over by Hall, who endorsed simple
attempts to find a basis for "prophesying judicial action." Although he
cautioned that quantitative measures could not be taken alone, he approved a
study of a single court over the next ten years that focused on things that
were measurable – length of opinion, number of precedents cited, length
of briefs submitted, and so on – because they might, when measured and
cross-tabulated, prove important. The move from Corwin to Hall provides a
revealing example of the consequences of instrumental positivism: focus on a
short span of the present rather than change over time, and ten years spent

129  Merriam, "Present State of the Study of Politics," 176, 179–80; "Reports of the Second
    National Conference on the Science of Politics," *APSR*, 19 (February 1925): 105; "Reports
    of the National Conference on the Science of Politics," ibid. 18 (February 1924): 121.
130  A. N. Holcombe, "Review of C. E. Merriam and H. F. Gosnell, *Non-Voting*," *APSR*, 19
    (February 1925): 202–3; "Report of the Third National Conference on the Science of
    Politics," ibid. 20 (February 1926): 139–43; "Reports of the Second National Confer-
    ence," 108.
131  "Reports of the National Conference," 148–54; Robert T. Crane to Charles E. Merriam,
    [July 3, 1923], Merriam Papers.

collecting measurable data on the chance they might measure something, as against ten years beginning on complex questions known to be significant.[132]

One traditional area of political science that proved particularly interested in technique was administration. Carrying the issue of budget reform from localities and states to the federal government, the IGR was established in Washington in 1916 to try to develop an executive budget. The director, W. F. Willoughby, brother of the theorist, reflected both the conservative and scientific temper of administrative experts of the postwar period. Progressive budget reform had been part of the popular movement for good government and had often worked to broaden public services as well as to make them more efficient. "The work of administration," Willoughby now assured his colleagues, "is, if not a science, a subject to the study of which the scientific method should be rigidly applied." Repudiating the political techniques of progressivism, he would work by cooperation with national officials, not by "public indictment of present conditions and the conduct of a public propaganda." Expert elite governance was the center of his vision, in substance as well as technique. "The government best administered is best." Willoughby was relatively successful in urging federal budgetary reforms and he played a key role in killing the Brookings Graduate School under Walton Hamilton. But his desire to avoid policy issues increasingly narrowed the scope of his work and influence. Economists, with their more confident expertise, pushed the older accountants and political scientists out of the budget arena. When the IGR was folded into the Brookings Institution in 1927 it took decidedly second place to economic research.[133]

Political scientists were also handicapped in the area of civil-service reform. The development of mental tests during the war was quickly taken up by civil-service experts, who wanted tests for personnel selection and techniques for measuring personnel efficiency, but here the psychologists had most of the relevant expertise. L. L. Thurstone was working on a test for the selection of policemen when Merriam found him and brought him to Chicago. Not until the idea of "scientific management" moved from blue-collar to white-collar work did the field of administration get its own body of presumably scientific principles. Scientism meanwhile simply strengthened the separation of administration from politics that had been all along part of the effort to legitimate the principle of elite governance in the democratic polity. The consistently Whiggish class basis of political

---

132 "Report of the Third National Conference," 128, 132–4.
133 Critchlow, *Brookings Institution*, 32–40, 63–6; W. F. Willoughby, "The Institute for Government Research," *APSR*, 12 (February 1918): 49, 60–1, 62. Henry Jones Ford very much approved the more conservative tack, in "Review of W. F. Willoughby, *The Problem of a National Budget*," *APSR*, 13 (August 1919): 505–6.

science is nowhere more evident than in the persistently sanguine view of administration as the desideratum of American politics. Max Weber's pessimistic vision of bureaucracy had no impact on American students of administration until the 1950s.[134]

At the same time that Merriam's scientific program began to transform the traditional concerns of political science, it also opened a new field to scientific investigation. Psychology was Merriam's chief interest and his scientific Trojan horse. He brought Thurstone and other psychologists into the political science conferences and meetings. Floyd Allport and Stuart Rice presented their work to them, as they had to the sociologists. But Merriam's interest in psychology, like that occasionally expressed by other Progressive political scientists, had roots within his own discipline.

The effort to revise the tradition of political "prudence" in the light of the new psychology had been initiated by the Englishman Graham Wallas in *Human Nature in Politics* (1908). Using James's functional psychology, Wallas hoped to substitute for the old discredited intellectualist psychology, a view of the nonrational bases of thought that was serviceable for democratic mass politics. He also emphasized nurture rather than nature, in support of his new liberal/Fabian politics, and called for an increase in quantitative thinking about politics. Thinking in terms of numbers, estimates, and averages would dispel the absolutes of rational and conventional political traditions. Wallas' book was widely heralded in America, more so than in Britain, and as he developed his ideas in two later books, he picked up some of the American language of control as the aim of politics – "the control of national cooperation" for example.[135]

Merriam and his colleagues credited Wallas with opening the field, but they felt that he had not himself entered. Indeed, the differences between Wallas' work and Merriam's movement were as striking as the similarities. What turned Merriam to psychology, as to science, was his sudden disillusionment with American politics. With the decline of progressivism and the hysteria of the war years, even traditional Progressives like Merriam came to believe that democratic voters and leaders operated on a psychology of irrationalism. Walter Lippmann, an iconoclastic young journalist who before the war used Wallas to urge the constructive and liberating use of impulse in politics, after the war turned sharply against the rational capacity

134 "Reports of the National Conference," 125–33; A. Dunsire, *Administration* (New York: Wiley, 1973), 92–4, 80; Dwight Waldo, *The Administrative State. A Study of the Political Theory of American Public Administration* (New York: Ronald, 1948), 92, 163, 41n.
135 Graham Wallas, *Human Nature in Politics* (London: Constable, 1908); idem, *The Great Society: A Psychological Analysis* (New York: Macmillan, 1914); idem, *Our Social Heritage* (New Haven, Conn.: Yale University Press, 1921), 102–3.

of the people. In *Public Opinion* (1922) and *The Phantom Public* (1925), with wide approval among the social scientists, he offered an acid analysis of popular inattention, irrationality, and manipulability.[136] Merriam never adopted Lippmann's harsh language or abandoned democracy. But the old Progressive faith in the educability of the people turned into the need for scientific techniques by which leaders could lead and the public could be trained into accepting the correct path. Science became increasingly a substitute for political prudence.

Wallas, in contrast, made no distinction between professional and public thinking about politics; his new psychology and quantitative thinking were meant for professional political scientists, statesmen, and ordinary voters alike. He never lost his central focus on political reasoning and "discussion," so that realistic, quantitative thinking was meant to raise the rational level of discussion rather than displace it. He wanted to understand psychology in order to educate citizens in it, so that they could resist manipulation. Not surprisingly, Wallas expressed chagrin at the excessively scientistic direction taken by American political science in the 1920s, particularly with the way in which its deterministic and behavioristic assumptions denied to individual citizens free will and initiative.[137]

Merriam's scientized politics grew out of his new sense of the insecurity of history and politics: "Society is dissolving every moment, and the question is, How shall the reconstruction of authority in the minds and lives of men be made?" His answer was the Progressive answer – more effective political leadership and civic education – but he now looked to scientific psychology for understanding and control. Merriam pressed his brother and the psychologist Robert M. Yerkes for a psychological test of "leadership."[138] Meanwhile, he embarked on a study of American political leaders, although the resulting book revealed how little able he was to follow the scientific path he pressed on others. Merriam presented "only a sketch, not a complete scientific analysis," of the careers of Lincoln, Roosevelt, Wilson, and Bryan.

136 A. N. Holcombe, "Review of Walter Lippmann, *Public Opinion*," *APSR*, 16 (August 1922): 500–1; Arnold B. Hall, "Review of Walter Lippmann, *The Phantom Public*," *APSR*, 20 (February 1926): 199–201; Robert E. Park, "Review of Walter Lippmann, *Public Opinion*," *AJS*, 28 (September 1922): 232–4. Lippmann's earlier work was *A Preface to Politics* (New York: M. Kennerly, 1913).

137 Wallas, *Human Nature*, 155–6, 188–90; idem, *Great Society*, 244–5, 281–6; idem, *Social Heritage*, chap. 11, particularly pp. 255–7. On Wallas, see Martin J. Wiener, *Between Two Worlds: The Political Thought of Graham Wallas* (Oxford: Oxford University Press [Clarendon Press], 1971), particularly 170–1, 205–6, 208–10.

138 Charles E. Merriam, "Review of Zachariah Chafee, *Freedom of Speech*," *AJS*, 27 (July 1921): 98; Charles E. Merriam to Robert M. Yerkes, October 14, 1921; January 23, 1923; Yerkes to Merriam, January 23, 1923, Merriam Papers.

As sketches they show something of the idealism and catholic sympathies that made Merriam a good Progressive politician, but the extent of his "science" was a list of six "attributes" of the political leader which began with sensitiveness to social and industrial tendencies and ended with courage. A reviewer in the American Political Science Review, either hoping to make his name or lacking all political sense for his own career, easily made mincemeat of the book.[139]

Merriam's complementary interest in civic education came in part from his participation in the wartime propaganda effort. He had been in charge of American "publicity" in Italy, where his task was to articulate America's altruistic war aims and disseminate "facts" about American preparedness and determination to fight. Returning home in 1919 with a clear conscience, he announced that "Our information did not consist of lies, misstatements, half truths, or exaggerations." He returned also with a clear sense that such techniques might be extremely effective if applied to civic education.[140]

The most important aspect of Merriam's discussion of civic education during the 1920s was the conceptual framework in which he began to put it. By the end of the Progressive period, Hoxie, Commons, Dewey, and others had begun to talk about the possibility that consensus in America rested not on a consensus of specific values, but rather on the processes of adjusting conflicting values, on the rules of the game, or on a common framework of knowledge or attitudes that lay beneath conflict. Faced with persistent labor violence and class and ethnic conflict, they were determined to develop and legitimate the ability of culture to defuse it. Merriam understood this move and recognized the importance of what came to be called political culture. "The character of the party system is dependent upon the political *mores* of the community, upon the standards, the appreciations, the values, found in the mass of the political people.... Class and group conflicts are inevitable, in the struggle for economic and political power, but what is the common standard in the war?" It was education to this "larger group loyalty and allegiance," the fundamental mores of American politics, that Merriam hoped for.[141]

The problem was that as Merriam repeated and refined the Progressive understanding of politics, he was also encouraging the development of a very different political language. As he bombarded his colleagues with pro-

139 Charles E. Merriam, *Four American Party Leaders* (New York: Macmillan, 1926), xiv, xi–xii; Ralph S. Boots, "Review of Charles Merriam, *Four American Party Leaders*," *APSR*, 21 (May 1927): 450–2.
140 Charles E. Merriam, "American Publicity in Italy," *APSR*, 13 (November 1919): 541–55, particularly 554.
141 Charles E. Merriam, *The American Party System* (New York: Macmillan, 1922), 429, 431.

grammatic surveys of scientific – particularly psychological – methods, he conveyed an increasingly technological and utopian vision of a science of politics. Quickly impressed with the achievements and hopes of the new animal psychologists, testers, behaviorists, and psychoanalysts, he believed they were "on the verge of definite measurement of elusive elements in human nature hitherto evading understanding and control by scientific methods." Although always including qualifications, he began to discuss politics in terms of eugenics, "tropisms," mental measurement, and large-scale statistical studies.

The high point of utopian scientism for Merriam was his *New Aspects of Politics* in 1925. He believed himself to be in "a new world, with new social conditions and with new modes of thought and inquiry." While "the race is rushing forward with incredible speed," it was not prepared to deal with the pace of change. The solution Merriam offered was education and eugenics.

We are very rapidly approaching a time when it may be necessary and possible to decide not merely what types of law we wish to enact, but what types of person we wish to develop, either by the process of education or of eugenics ... to determine what sorts of creature are to be born, within important limits at least.

Merriam's forecast of a "new world made over by modern science," a bit closer and a great deal more frightening today, is a good measure of the unwarranted innocence that created the scientism of the 1920s.[142]

The heir of Merriam's technological imagination was Harold D. Lasswell. The son of a Presbyterian minister as passionately devoted to politics as religion, young Lasswell transferred his own faith to science without incident. He arrived at Chicago in 1918, a precocious and fluent young man, having already read Freud and prepared to absorb everything. He became Merriam's graduate student just as the SSRC was getting under way and was quickly favored with fellowships that took him to Europe and to study psychology at Harvard. After writing a thesis on propaganda, he joined the Chicago faculty in 1927, one of the group of young men open to innovation whom Merriam brought to Chicago in the 1920s.[143]

Lasswell had the new generation's capacity to dismiss out of hand the idealism and constraints of the older political tradition. In Rice's compendium on method, he dissected the inadequacies of James Bryce, discounting Bryce's claim that politics could not be a natural science because its

142 Merriam, "Present State of the Study of Politics," 181; idem, *New Aspects of Politics* (Chicago: University of Chicago Press, 1925), 19, 125, 2, 155, 21–2.
143 On Lasswell, see Dwaine Marvick, "Introduction: Context, Problems, and Methods," in *Harold D. Lasswell on Political Sociology*, ed. Dwaine Marvick (Chicago: University of Chicago Press, 1977), 1–72.

phenomena did not behave the same under different circumstances of time and place. That was only because we are still dealing with gross phenomena, Lasswell countered. We will make progress when phenomena are "resolved into relatively permanent components." A science of politics will examine the "elementary situation in which 'unrest' or 'dissent' arises, and a loosely knit pattern of social action commonly named 'democracy' or 'oligarchy' may turn out to play a very subsidiary role in the matter."[144]

Lasswell also had the capacity to absorb and develop the psychological concepts that Merriam could only imagine. "Propaganda," he informed the political scientists, "is the management of collective attitudes by the manipulation of significant symbols." It was the inevitable accompaniment of the argument and persuasion that existed in democracy.[145] Hence any ethical system adequate to democracy must approve propaganda. Indeed propaganda was not only necessary, but salutary. It would puncture "eulogistic democracy" and promote the "engineering frame of mind."

The political implication of this cultural iconoclasm lay not simply in its Menckenesque desire to debunk "the will of the people," but more deeply in its aim to substitute technocratic social control for political conflict. The political philosophy of conflict, of "nation versus nation, class versus class, leader versus leader, party versus party," is out of date, he said. The propagandist understands that society is rather "a process of defining and affirming meaning," that by use of cultural symbols, the situation can be redefined, so that what occurs is neither a victory nor defeat for conflicting parties but rather a new "integration." Lasswell was using here the influential work on social interaction of Mary Follett that obliterated the distinction between elite direction and democratic initiative. This was, in effect, how democratic society always works, Lasswell said, and how propagandists consciously work. The problem, then, for "the few who would rule the many under democratic conditions" was not to resolve or compromise economic, social, and political conflicts, but to redefine them through cultural symbols that rendered them harmless.[146]

Lasswell's interest in psychoanalysis deepened his iconoclastic realism. Merriam kept abreast of the latest work in psychiatry and early admired the social psychological work of Elton Mayo and R. D. Henderson at Harvard. After failing to get them to Chicago, he started sending his students to them. When he sent off Lasswell in 1925 he told Mayo that Lasswell should "learn the language of psychopathology" so that he could make "useful combina-

144 Lasswell, "The Comparative Method of James Bryce," 478–9.
145 Harold D. Lasswell, "The Theory of Political Propaganda," *APSR*, 21 (August 1927): 627.
146 Harold D. Lasswell, "The Function of the Propagandist," *International Journal of Ethics*, 38 (April 1928): 258–68.

tions" of psychopathology and politics. Lasswell obliged, producing in 1930 *Psychopathology and Politics*, a pioneer effort to develop systematically the reductive insight of his cohort into politics. Public ideals were displaced private motives, requiring therapy to deflate, he believed, rather than discussion to adjudicate. In Lasswell, Merriam found the psychological and scientific capacity he himself lacked and perhaps also found a voice for the disappointment in politics he could not quite express.[147]

It was after all the tone more than the substance that changed in the transfer, a difference of degree rather than kind. The moderate Progressives' belief in the power of education and culture to dispel economic conflict, as well as in the need for elite leadership and social control, was taken literally by a generation in a seemingly new world, a world in which idealism had conspicuously failed and science alone promised control. The liberal hopes of American social science, always on the defensive, turned from "soft" to "hard." Merriam was occasionally aware of the "Machiavellian" possibilities of this science of politics, but it did not temper his program. As he wrote Mayo, "There is no way of inventing a new tool that the burglar cannot use."[148] Lasswell became the father of the 1950s behavioral movement in political science, an extension and elevation of scientism in the profession, and by that lineage Merriam was rightly the grandfather.

One other line of research should also be taken into account in Merriam's scientism. One of his major projects, supported by Chicago's Local Community Research Committee and Rockefeller, was a study with his student Harold F. Gosnell of nonvoting in Chicago. If Lasswell picked up on the hard side of Merriam's Progressive message, Gosnell developed the soft side. He tried to discover "the attitude of the non-voter" in hope of widening intelligent political participation. Upon finding that the half of the electorate that failed to vote were often ignorant of how or when to vote, and that the largest single group was newly enfranchised women, he urged that voting be made more convenient and the full electorate directly informed. In the interest of this democratic message Gosnell employed a new armory of scientific tools: attitude surveys by interview and questionnaire, collections of demographic data for his sample of 6,000 voters, and the statistical tabulation and analysis of results. It is striking, however, that Merriam and Gosnell avoided differentiating the nonvoters. They deliberately matched their sample to proportions in the public at large, except for the category of women, so that they began and ended with the innocuous premise that "the

147 Charles E. Merriam to Elton Mayo, March 21, 1925, October 22, 1926, Merriam Papers; Harold D. Lasswell, *Psychopathology and Politics* (Chicago: University of Chicago Press, 1930).
148 Charles E. Merriam to Elton Mayo, March 11, 1925.

traits of the non-voter are often only the slight enlargement of the traits of the voter."[149]

Despite their shared premise that the body politic could be mapped by categories of aggregates, Merriam's work had a very different focus from the political science of interest groups that had been proposed by Arthur F. Bentley and Charles Beard. The analysis of interest-group politics was not high on Merriam's scientific agenda, for it was linked through Beard to the outmoded historical method and through both of them, to left-liberal politics. Merriam was associated in the 1920s not with Bentley's Non-Partisan League or Beard's *New Republic* crowd of advanced Progressives, but with the National Civic Federation, now a conservative organization that had abandoned its earlier attempt to meet labor halfway. The Federation was conducting a campaign to encourage citizen participation in politics and did not hide its desire to staunch "the tendency of American voters to stray out of the regular party folds into the limbo of 'third parties.'" Although Merriam had mild misgivings, he joined the effort, for "we are moving in the same direction, i.e. of more effective political interest." He could not, however, go along with Beard and the Commission on the Social Studies when they urged an education designed to resist received pieties and encourage political change. Merriam wanted to make the liberal civic culture more effective, not reduce it to the play of interests or change it.[150]

### For and against scientism

The work of Bentley and Beard had considerable influence in the 1920s and the study of interest-group politics began to attract some younger political scientists.[151] But the influence the two men were able to exert was limited

149 Charles E. Merriam and Harold F. Gosnell, *Non-Voting, Causes and Methods of Control* (Chicago: University of Chicago Press, 1924), particularly chaps. 1, 4, and pp. 1, 15, 48–50.

150 Charles E. Merriam, "Progress in Political Research," *APSR*, 20 (February 1926): 1–3; idem, "Recent Developments in Political Science," in *Recent Developments in the Social Sciences*, 320–5; Ralph M. Easley to Charles E. Merriam, March 30, 1925, and Merriam to Easley, February 12, 1925, Merriam Papers; Karl, *Merriam*, chap. 10. Note also Charles E. Merriam to Harry Elmer Barnes, October 13, 1922, Merriam Papers: "If you examine Small's 'General Sociology' and also Ratzenhofer it seems to me you will find nearly all of Bentley. Dr. Small did not have a very high regard for Bentley's ability or originality. I went over his work at the time I wrote my 'History of American Political Ideas' but did not find very much that is significant."

151 One source of influence came through the radical professor of political science at the University of Washington, J. Allen Smith. During the war years Rice, Ogburn, and a young institutional economist, Carleton Parker, all had contact with the University of Washington. During the 1920s Smith trained Peter Odegard, who did one of the first interest-group studies. See the Introduction by Odegard to *The Process of Government*, by Arthur F. Bentley (Cambridge, Mass.: Harvard University Press, 1967 [1908]).

and went in different directions. Bentley had virtually no contact with the academy. Einstein's theory of relativity inspired Bentley to again seek a public voice, though he had to pay himself for the publication of *Relativity in Man and Society* (1926). Although the same program of group analysis was visible in the text, it was now joined to a discussion of the principle of relativity in physics and to a new vocabulary: the "man-society" field, "cross-sectional activity," "dominance: clots: survivals." Perhaps spurred by his failure to get his concrete and radical attack on industrial capitalism published, Bentley seemed more than ever driven to grasp the concrete world of human interests by means of a generalizing and atomizing abstraction that destroyed all particularity. "Why use a term like clot instead of talking directly of a type of business organization, a form of government . . . a great religious system? Just in order to get away from any pretense to uniqueness in any one of these structures or systems. Just to get down to what is common to them." Although social science had still a long way to go, he believed the new emphasis on function, process, and behavior was moving in the right direction.[152]

The book led to a brief flurry of interest. He was asked to contribute an article on method to the *American Journal of Sociology*, and replied with a delphic series of epigrammatic statements. Thereafter his submissions were uniformly refused by American journals; only an occasional European journal published him. Returning to his epistemological studies, his holistic vision finally gave way and he worked with John Dewey on a transactional analysis that tried to identify the basic units of communication in a conversational situation between two persons. Bentley was rediscovered and honored during the 1950s as another progenitor of the new scientism, but his work and his influence had suffered from the absence of students and an audience.[153]

Charles Beard was also handicapped in his ability to direct the course of political science in the 1920s. Living on a Connecticut farm and with no academic connection, Beard at first avoided professional contacts and nursed his "psychic injuries." Merriam tried politely to draw him into association affairs and the scientific movement, but he replied stiffly that "Having no academic means of support," he had to give his time to "personal economic

---

152 Arthur F. Bentley, *Relativity in Man and Society* (New York: Putnam, 1926), 90, 91, 179, 182; Arthur F. Bentley to S. A. Sanders, November 16, 1925, Arthur F. Bentley Papers, Indiana University.

153 Arthur F. Bentley, "Remarks on Method in the Study of Society," *AJS*, 32 (November 1926): 456–60. On Bentley's late work on transactional theory, see Paul Kress, *Social Science and the Idea of Process: The Ambiguous Legacy of Arthur F. Bentley* (Urbana: University of Illinois Press, 1970), chap. 4.

considerations." When he was asked in September 1926 to talk to the comfortable men of the SSRC about his own research and what obstacles hindered it, he discussed the importance of studying economic interests and by way of obstacles, retold the story of how his own courage, capitalist pressures, and the silence of his colleagues had driven him into exile. If I read rightly between the lines, his audience was stunned.[154]

Beard's ability to direct the study of interest-group politics was in any case hampered by his own ambivalence. He hoped politics would reform capitalism, but he had reduced politics to economics, and he did not wholly trust either. Lippmann had caught a large piece of the problem when in 1922 he said that he could not discover in Beard's work "a clear conception of how he thinks economics determines politics." Beard could only give the anguished reply that he had no intention of going into the "metaphysics" of the subject.[155]

That same year Beard published an essay he had been working on since 1916. He argued so vociferously that no utopian consummation of history was possible, that he revealed how important that ideal had been to him over the years. He had envisaged something like E. R. A. Seligman's utopian transformation, in which moral ends would finally supersede economic ones. Now he was dissuaded by the war and by his observation of the Russian Revolution, where even under the utopian inspiration of communism, classes had reemerged. Returning to the American heritage of realistic politics from Aristotle, to Machiavelli, Harrington, Locke, and the founders, he declared that there was nothing else in politics but the play of interests. "There is no rest for mankind, no final solution of eternal contradictions. Such is the design of the universe."[156]

Beard nonetheless could not quite give up hope of the subordination of economic interests to normative politics. He confessed to his colleagues at the SSRC that he was "baffled about the implications of the economic process itself." He felt economic development to be part of "this enormous thermodynamic process that seems to constitute the substance of the universe." He was not sure whether "all of our talking and running up and down and politics" could affect it at all. Yet economic analysis, he hoped,

154 Charles E. Merriam to Charles A. Beard, March 6, 1924, and Beard to Merriam, March 10, [1924], Merriam Papers; Social Science Research Council, Hanover Conference, 1926, transcript, pp. 504, 498–501, Merriam Papers.
155 Walter Lippmann, "Mr. Beard on Property and Politics," *New Republic*, 31 (August 2, 1922): 282–3; C. A. Beard, "The Economic Basis of Politics," ibid. 32 (September 27, 1922): 128–9.
156 Charles A. Beard, *The Economic Basis of Politics* (New York: Knopf, 1922), 44–5, 95–9. Cf. Charles A. Beard, *Politics* (New York: Columbia University Press, 1908), 9–10.

would "get a more realistic view of politics, emancipate ourselves from a lot of the most primitive emotions that arise from our economic interest, clarify our minds, and prepare the way for that day which the idealists have always hoped for, when the dreams of men will control their economic operations. The idea is fascinating." Beard now had to work through these problems in popular writing and in history books that would sell. *The Rise of American Civilization* (1927) by Charles and Mary Beard was in the latter category and gave Beard his chief influence in history rather than political science. Determinedly optimistic, Beard and his wife constructed a modernization theory in which democratic politics was loosely linked to economic progress through such mechanisms as popular education. The ambivalences that still plagued him were encoded in a provocative language of realism and covered over with rhetorical flourish.[157]

There would increasingly be a third obstacle to Beard's influence. Beard had been a staunch wartime patriot, very much in favor of American entry into World War I. After the war, as he learned of the imperialist betrayal of democratic hopes and marveled at America's new position as the leading economic and political power in the world, he began to think that America was leading, indeed through fortunate circumstances had always led, the industrial-democratic evolution. America should play a continental, not an international politics, carry forward the development of liberal democracy, and the world would follow in her wake.[158] In 1901 Beard had pictured the United States riding in the wake of European social transformation. Now, though the economic process remained universal, it was recast in the image of American liberalism and America took the lead.

The exceptionalist stance that emerged from the war was a permanent turning point for Beard and the basis of his later historiography and politics. If his "confessions" to the SSRC in 1926 can be believed, he was also influenced by his postwar trip to China and Japan, where he became "convinced – not for publication – that the whole of the Orient is not worth the bones of an American doughboy." He expressed "great admiration for the Japanese and Chinese" but he shuddered at the thought of "three hundred and forty-two people to the square mile." Beard's resort to the

157 SSRC, Hanover Conference, 500–1, 510, Merriam Papers; Charles A. and Mary Beard, *The Rise of American Civilization*, 2 vols. (New York: Macmillan, 1927).
158 Beard, *Economic Basis of Politics*, 29, 32; Ellen Nore, *Charles A. Beard: An Intellectual Biography* (Carbondale: Southern Illinois University Press, 1983), chaps. 6–7; David W. Noble, *The End of American History: Democracy, Capitalism, and the Metaphor of Two Worlds in Anglo-American Historical Writing, 1880–1980* (Minneapolis: University of Minnesota Press, 1985), chap. 3.

man-land ratio was appropriate, for he was returning to the historical vision of traditional American exceptionalism. He feared that agriculture was falling too far behind industry, destroying that "balanced system of national economy" that would maintain America's "economic independence" and free her from the entanglements of economic imperialism. "If this keeps up for another hundred years at the present rate, we shall pass the point now reached by England.... The cultivation of the soil will pass mainly into the hands of colored races and white tenants." If from no other source, the documents of the early Republic in which Beard was steeped gave him a language with which to express his nationalist anxieties, and at a time when he felt himself personally victimized and isolated.[159]

During the 1930s Beard became increasingly hostile to American international commitments and aggressively opposed entry into World War II, so that he was in the end cut off from the historians as well as the political scientists. I do not, however, want to make Beard too much the victim, for the SSRC meeting marked for a time his return to professional affairs. He regained some of his confidence when he became president of the APSA in 1926 and when *The Rise of American Civilization* was published in 1927, and he soon became a vocal critic of scientism.

For a good part of the 1920s, scientism, and Merriam's version of scientism, seemed to carry all before it. Older theorists like Westel W. Willoughby and Raymond Gettell, could not mount an effective reply. A Progressive stalwart like John A. Fairlie simply avoided the issue, declaring the new scientism continuous with the science of politics begun by Aristotle. Still, there was considerable resistance to the imperialism of psychology. Merriam took care at the APSA to try to head off opposition, laughing at his own "obsession" under the figure of the rape of political science by the "penetralia of biological and psychical nature."[160]

Others soon spoke out. William Bennett Munro, Canadian-born, with a Harvard doctorate and professorship, stood squarely in the old tradition of historico-politics and conservative Whiggish values. In his presidential address to the APSA in 1928 he urged political scientists to divorce themselves not only from philosophy and law, but also from psychology and sociology. We are sometimes told to wait on social psychology, he observed. "If so, it will be a long wait." He ridiculed the technical jargon of Lasswell's

159 SSRC, Hanover Conference, 514; Charles A. Beard, "Agriculture in the Nation's Economy," *Nation*, 125 (August 17, 1927): 150–1.
160 Raymond G. Gettell, "The Nature of Political Thought," *APSR*, 17 (May 1923): 204–15; John A. Fairlie, "Politics and Science," *Scientific Monthly*, 18 (January 1924): 18–37; Charles E. Merriam, "Progress in Political Research," 13.

definition of propaganda, and on another occasion dismissed out of hand Allport's declaration of psychological hegemony.[161]

Munro nonetheless thought political scientists should imitate the objective attitude and procedures of the natural scientists. There was a universal human nature and there were laws of politics. "Obviously it is racial determinism that explains, in large measure, the higher and more stable plane upon which the political system of the northern continent has moved." His own contribution to science was the "law of the pendulum," the cyclical tendency of political attitudes to run to extremes and thereby generate their opposites. Thus the cycle from drift to action to normalcy in the decade 1910 to 1920. If Munro's address was "universally acclaimed" by the political scientists, it was undoubtedly a reflection of dislike for the newfangled psychological language that Merriam was imposing upon them, and belief that with a little metaphorical dressing the traditional Teutonist historico-politics could become a science on its own terms.[162]

The more serious attacks on Merriam's program were aimed at scientism and came from those most deeply oriented to philosophy and history. One critique of positivism named pragmatism the enemy. Opening what would be an extended defense from the right of "coherent logic and normative values," William Yandell Elliott identified pragmatism as the source of positivism in political science. Positivism led to the empiricism of "facts" in method and to the fascistic states of Mussolini's Europe, in practice. Although Elliott mentioned objectivist method, his attack was largely against the European pluralist and syndicalist political theorists who fragmented national authority and denied a normative public good, giving over national order to mere force. There was some interest in America in the pluralist theory of sovereignty, particularly in the work of Harold Laski, whose pluralism was inspired by guild socialism and the desire to legitimate the diverse organs of popular will. Most American theorists, however, even when sympathetic to pluralist values, refused to abolish an overriding central

161 William Bennett Munro, "Physics and Politics – An Old Analogy Revised," *APSR*, 22 (February 1928): 8–10. On Munro, see Harvey Eagleson, *William Bennett Munro, 1875–1957* (privately printed, 1959).
162 William Bennett Munro, *The Invisible Government* (New York: Macmillan, 1928), 42, 33–7; William Y. Elliott, "The Possibility of a Science of Politics: With Special Attention to Methods Suggested by William B. Munro and George E. G. Catlin," in *Methods in Social Science*, 74. Catlin's attempt to formulate a science of politics is worth exhuming, for it marks a path from the classic theory of possessive individualism to the new behavioral, statistical science. Besides Elliott and the commentary by Catlin that followed, see Catlin's *The Science and Method of Politics* (New York: Knopf, 1927) and *A Study of the Principles of Politics* (London: Allen & Unwin, 1930).

sovereignty. The political theorists were not, in any case, Elliott's enemy, but the more numerous and powerful advocates of scientism, whom he linked broadly to Dewey. Most political scientists had to be provided with an explanation of what pragmatism was before they could begin to disentangle the debate.[163]

A more effective defense of the political scientists' ethical role came from Edward Corwin. What are the implications for democracy if we accept this vision of natural science, he asked, especially in alliance with "behaviorism, which repudiates ... the most fundamental assumption of the democratic dogma, the assumption that man is primarily a rational creature?" The behavioristic attack on popular rationality, he pointed out, extended a long-standing critique and laid down an impossible intellectualist standard of rationality. In fact, the half of the American electorate that did not vote in the 1920s did so for good reasons. Their indifference arose from "the average American's sense of well-being and his consequent confidence in his governors, from the general homogeneousness of political sentiment as to fundamentals," as well as from the recent fact that "politics has largely lost its capacity to entertain and amuse." Even if the half that did vote was as manipulable as the behaviorists claimed, that was all the more reason for political scientists to continue their traditional task of public education. If human nature is a "white wall ... is there any reason why effrontery and self-interest alone should wield the pencil?" Corwin's exceptionalist defense of American democracy had the cynical conservative flavor of A. Lawrence Lowell's realism. But the temper of the times, if equally cynical, was not happy with American democracy or patient enough to accept the political scientists' traditional role of an educative elite.[164]

A third line of criticism came from Charles Beard. When he turned to an exceptionalist view of liberal history after the war, Beard had to place his faith in the special conditions of history that gave the United States its leading position in the world. The Beards' *Rise of American Civilization* attributed American democracy to such historical accidents as colonial origins in England, the first modern, bourgeois culture, and the virgin land of the Mississippi Valley. For all his determined optimism, however, Beard

163 William Y. Elliott, *The Pragmatic Revolt in Politics: Syndicalism, Fascism, and the Constitutional State* (New York: Macmillan, 1928), 53; Sabine, "The Pragmatic Approach to Politics." For representative responses to pluralist philosophies see Walter J. Shepard, "Review of Harold J. Laski, *Authority in the Modern State*," *APSR*, 13 (August 1919): 491–4; Ellen Deborah Ellis, "The Pluralistic State," *APSR*, 14 (August 1920): 393–407; Francis W. Coker, "The Technique of the Pluralistic State," *APSR*, 15 (May 1921): 186–213.
164 Edward S. Corwin, "The Democratic Dogma and the Future of Political Science," *APSR*, 23 (August 1929): 569–92, particularly 570, 577, 592.

could not trust the uncontrollable course of history. His presidential address to the political scientists in 1926 was, like Dewey's *Quest for Certainty*, a remarkable restatement of the anxiety of living in historical time that the republican imagination had bequeathed to modern American liberals.

Under the title "Time, Technology and the Creative Spirit in Political Science," Beard urged that contemporary political science train its students for an unknown future. "Time and technology ever stream forward." Our job was to connect "political science with the flowing stream of time and technology." Here was the liberal historical consciousness, "the consciousness of an irresistible flow of seconds, hours, days, years, and centuries – to which is now coupled that fruitful eighteenth-century concept, the idea of indefinite progress – the continuous conquest of material environment by applied science." To bring political science into this "world stream," Beard recommended not "research under scientific formulas in things mathematically measureable or logically describable," but rather greater exercise of "the deductive and imaginative process." Given the stream of change, "constructive imagination [was] necessary for any harmonious adjustment of humanity to its destiny," as well as critical, Socratic questioning of accepted political wisdom.

What makes Beard's talk so interesting is that the liberal forward flow of time was heavily laden with republican foreboding. He opened his talk with an imaginary lecture by an eighteenth-century professor on the future, thus anchoring historical consciousness in the founding of the Republic. Though he spoke of progress, it was "the pitiless reality of the time-sense," he described. Technology moves with "terrifying rapidity," it goes "pouring" through time with "convulsive pressures." And time itself is "unsparing," an "onrushing stream of years that devours us all," an infinity of "doomful possibilities." Beard urged his colleagues to constructive imagination, to make "the effort to meet destiny with triumph," but he seemed to be whistling in the wind. Indeed, while calling for a critique of the present and imagination of the future, he kept hoping for "immortal" work, for a permanent body of principles, for a "Jovian role of interpreter and director" that would escape the bounds of time. A science of what is and what is becoming was adequate for Beard when history was progressing toward a harmonious consummation, but now Beard feared that the "great hydraulic system" of economic progress was in fact heading for a crash.[165]

It is Beard's anomaly that while in substance he mounted a traditional exceptionalist effort to stay the hand of time on the American continent, in

165 Charles A. Beard, "Time, Technology, and the Creative Spirit in Political Science," *APSR*, 21 (February 1927): 1–11.

method he entered on a novel path. Reading advanced philosophies of science and history, he concluded that students of history and politics could not know, in any objective scientific sense, the past or future. His skepticism, in fact, despite its unsettling implications, may have been a form of defense, a distancing, from the "doomful possibilities" of history. In 1929 he told his colleagues unequivocally that "No science of politics is possible; or if possible, desireable." Political science had held three visions of such a science. Ranke's ideal of describing history as it really happened was, he now saw, impossible. Quoting Benedetto Croce, he concluded that "reality cannot be described without philosophic implications." As to Henry Adams' idea of a science of history that might grasp "known tendencies projected in time," that, even if we had it, would be undesirable. "We should imprison ourselves in an iron web of our own making." Finally there was the new "engineering" model of political science, the desire to determine "exact facts," and their "proportional weight," and to determine public policy by them. Here Beard showed, from "facts" to "policy," the impossibility of objective determination. But Beard's move toward relativism, identified as he was with the outmoded historical method, made more impact on the historians than the political scientists.[166]

It seems doubtful that Beard, Corwin, and Elliott had much effect on the opposition. Munro, at the traditional center of the discipline, would have been alienated by Beard's relativism and left-liberal politics; he might have found Corwin and Elliott's traditional premises and conservative values more congenial, but their sophisticated historicism and philosophy would have gone over his head. The most able theorists of scientism like Stuart Rice and Harold Lasswell had constructed an impregnable wall of positivist faith and philosophic agnosticism. Merriam stood somewhere between Munro and Lasswell. It was only after his public pronouncement for science that – stimulated by criticisms of his loose statement – he began to read in the philosophy of science. He shrewdly decided that he would henceforth not attempt to explicate scientific method.[167] Merriam simply ignored the contradiction between positivist inquiry and normative principle, which the critics had exposed, and continued to couple objective science with a Progressive defense of American democracy.

The new scientism and the deeply rooted traditionalism of political sci-

166 Charles A. Beard, "Political Science," in *Research in the Social Sciences*, 269–91; Nore, *Charles A. Beard*, chap. 12; Ian Tyrrell, *The Absent Marx: Class Analysis and Liberal History in Twentieth Century America* (Westport, Conn.: Greenwood, 1986), 36–9; Novick, *That Noble Dream*, chap. 9.
167 Lawrence K. Frank to Charles E. Merriam, February 5, 1926, and Merriam to Frank, February 10, 1926, Merriam Papers.

ence reached a stalemate, each blocked and infiltrated by the other. As the decade ended and Rockefeller funds declined, Beard and Merriam joined forces to mount a research effort based in the APSA that was acceptable to both. They could not, however, get it funded. The Depression crisis and the New Deal drew Merriam, as they had Ogburn, away from science and into government consulting. The heightened political concern brought money to the APSA for work on civic education, rather than scientific research. And the political crisis allowed the reassertion of the strong normative tie of political science to American political institutions, a tie expressed from right to left and not much loosened by scientism.[168] The scientific impulses launched by Bentley and Merriam survived, however, and in the political climate of World War II and its aftermath, emerged as the liberal scientism of behavioral science, systems analysis, and public management.

## Conclusions

The advent of scientism in the 1920s marked in many ways the resolution of the Gilded Age crisis in American exceptionalism. From the early decades of the nineteenth century, when Daniel Raymond, Francis Wayland, Francis Lieber, George Fitzhugh, and Henry Carey had revised European models of social science to address the fate of the American Republic, American history had been given special access to nature and special exemption from the corrosive effects of time. The Gilded Age crisis shattered that millennial world and forced social scientists into the industrial mainstream of Western history. But the continued force of the national ideology, its sustaining institutions and its ahistorical cultural traditions led American social scientists to contain the possibility of radical change and to find a source of permanent sustenance within or outside the novelty of history.

Neoclassical economists first found a paradigm, modeled on physical science and presumably rooted in the necessities of nature and human nature, that exempted American experience from history, at least any history other than the track of perpetual liberal progress that could be extrapolated from the paradigm itself. Institutional economists, most sociologists, and some political scientists, more deeply strained by the rapidity of change and

---

168 Somit and Tanenhaus, *The Development of American Political Science*, 88, 134–40, pictures Thomas H. Reed, chairman of the Committee on Policy at the end of the decade, as carrying off a kind of coup for civic education as against Merriam's scientism. The shift seems rather a result of the changing political context. Once the Rockefellers pulled back, Reed, Merriam, and the committee tried to get a more scientifically oriented agenda funded, but could not. See Thomas H. Reed to Charles E. Merriam, December 18, 1928; Merriam to Reed, July 18, 1929; and Reed to Merriam, May 14, 1930, Merriam Papers.

the insecurity of American ideals, sought a different kind of science, an empirical science of the changing liberal world that would allow them technological control. The anxiety to control the careening new world on the one hand, and the narrowed focus and comfortable opportunities of professionalism on the other, turned that scientific impulse toward scientism. Social scientists began to construct a naturalistic social science as an end in itself, and under the influence of instrumental positivism, erected positivistic scientific method into the chief standard of inquiry. The new scientific outlook, technical language, and political counsel the social scientists offered often seemed hopelessly distant from both popular perceptions and the American past, making the new world seem even newer. Only the disciplinary tradition of historico-politics and political science had nurtured sufficient respect for and knowledge of history and philosophy to generate a considerable resistance, and there the resistance was vitiated by traditionalist complacencies and fears.

By the 1920s the relationship between the national ideology of American exceptionalism and the discourse of the social sciences had itself been transformed. Until well into the Gilded Age crisis, exceptionalist language explicitly shaped the social science disciplines; national ideals and social-scientific traditions shared a common liberal-republican language and with it, a common set of problems and strategies. By the turn of the century, as Americans abandoned faith in widespread ownership of productive resources and the possibility of escaping modernity, both the national discourse and the specialized social sciences forming in the universities began to lose that original language. Professionalization and scientism distanced social science discourse from national ideals. The new, liberal language of social science joined America to the modern liberal world. But that language continued nonetheless to express a revised version of American exceptionalism, and the national myth, still powerful in the culture at large, continued to cross professional boundaries. The linkage between American exceptionalism and social science discourse was looser and more diffuse, yet still capable of shaping the problems and solutions social scientists addressed.

Living in what seemed to be "perpetual transition," the language and strategies of American exceptionalism continued to be useful. The work of Dewey and Beard, who grew up on the crisis and relearned in maturity its classic sources, remained centered on the fate of the American Republic in time. The American promise animated all Park's and Merriam's work, and the traditional fears that promise carried became explicit when they discussed such problems as class. Occasionally a younger person, like Tugwell, would reincarnate the older republican language of a mentor, or like Knight, link an older tradition to modern theory.

Perhaps those most wedded to the language of American exceptionalism and its traditional purpose of nationalist defense were the political scientists, those directly assigned the task of caring for American republican institutions. These schooled historicists could not encode their vision in the language of natural law and natural progress and therefore clung all the more tenaciously to traditional principles and exceptionalist soil. For most social scientists, however, exceptionalism exerted its influence by way of political ideals and unexamined nationalist mythology, such as Ogburn tried so resolutely to separate from his professional work. Or it worked within the new disciplinary language, which unbeknownst to its users, recast the staples of exceptionalist discourse in scientific terms: the fluid statics of "process," Thomas' jeremiad of social disorganization, Ogburn's lag between technological and cultural change. The end product of the crisis of American exceptionalism was the disciplinary traditions themselves, which by their individualistic or pluralist premises and their fixed liberal boundaries of social process and historical change, steered practitioners toward the normative understanding of American history.

Yet the 1920s, like every decade before and since, was full of conflict. Much of the conflict between disciplines had been halted or muted by professional accommodation, but conflict continued within disciplines, and internal conflict in some ways carried on older cross-disciplinary disagreements. The institutionalists were successors to the sociologists' original war on classical economics, and Beard carried on the historians' attack on the scientism of political science. The chief source of conflict was the ideal of scientism itself. In economics, the outline of that conflict was blurred, because both neoclassicists and institutionalists claimed authentic, but different, kinds of scientific credentials. Well-entrenched in a disciplinary paradigm and professional institutions, the neoclassicists dismissed the institutionalist revolt as mere leftist politics rather than science, ignoring the liberal exceptionalist politics built into their own paradigm and institutions. But the scientism of the institutionalists, as well as their attachment to the neoclassical vision of liberal progress, made them vulnerable to a Keynesian compromise and they abandoned construction of a historical theory that would relativize neoclassical values.

In sociology a hard-edged behaviorism and uncompromising instrumental positivism set the terms for debate. Since the decline of Small's influence, there was no historical school left in sociology to mount a counterattack that was untainted by evolutionary positivism. Interestingly, it was the heirs of Giddings' evolutionism like Ogburn and Chapin, the most aggressive spokesmen for instrumental positivism, who directly addressed historical change over time and identified their statistical method with both science and history. For Chicago sociologists, liberal evolutionism remained implicit, but they focused on shorter term processes. What they retained of history was the contextual "situation" and sensitivity to the symbolic meanings through which individuals perceived and transformed their situations. The characteristic premises of historicism were divided between the two schools, and in both cases, subordinated to the demands of scientism.

In political science the influence of scientism was slowed by the historical realism and normative commitment of historico-politics. The traditional descriptive empiricism allowed study of the pluralist processes of American politics, but the psychological theories of Merriam and Lasswell and the more radical implications of the work of Bentley and Beard, both political and methodological, did not make much headway. Nor did the overtly historical and normative models of political science put forward by spokesmen for public law and political theory. Although they commanded a great deal of philosophical, and in Corwin's case historical, sophistication, they came from fields increasingly marginalized by the mainstream science of politics. More importantly, their defense of public values and historical experience, conservative in professional as well as political terms, did not speak to the impatient demand for a new world of control to match the new world of change.

# Epilogue

To trace the "origins" of American social science to 1929 is in some ways an arbitrary exercise, for its history is a continuing development before and after that date. But 1929 takes us far enough into that history to recognize both the continuing characteristics of American social science and its distinctive twentieth-century features.

My intention has been to historicize American social science, to show that its effort to naturalize the historical world is itself a historical project. To say this is to deny its positivist self-description as objective science. Like John Dewey, I use this historical strategy with "malice prepense," but I am aware that positivists are well armed to slough it off. In science, they say, there is no connection between the context of discovery and the context of verification. Even if that were true, and I do not believe it is, it assumes for the social sciences precisely what is in question; namely, the likeness of its practice to the natural sciences.[1]

What my history shows is that American social science has consistently constructed models of the world that embody the values and follow the logic of the national ideology of American exceptionalism. The exceptionalist vision has continually responded to the changes of history itself, and it has been open to a considerable variety of disciplinary interests, political pur-

---

1 On positivist disbelief in the significance of origins for science, see Milton Friedman, "The Methodology of Positive Economics," in *The Philosophy of Economics*, ed. Daniel M. Hausman (Cambridge University Press, 1984), 210–14; and Don Martindale, *The Nature and Types of Sociological Theory* (Boston: Houghton Mifflin, 1960), 128. For contrary views, see Warren J. Samuels, "Ideology in Economics," in *Modern Economic Thought*, ed. Sidney Weintraub (Philadelphia: University of Pennsylvania Press, 1977), 467–84; and Anthony Giddens, "Positivism and Its Critics," in *A History of Sociological Analysis*, ed. Tom Bottomore and Robert Nisbet (New York: Basic, 1978), 270–83.

poses, and personal experiences. But the exceptionalist stance has withal produced remarkable continuities within and across these disciplines. Both the differences and similarities, it seems to me, confirm the historical character of the social science enterprise and the power of the exceptionalist vision to shape history to its purposes.

The most striking outcome of exceptionalist history has been scientism itself. The aim of scientism has been to establish prediction and control of the historical world and perhaps its most conspicuous accomplishment has been a set of quantitative techniques for information gathering and analysis that are used to manipulate such things as the money supply, consumer choices, votes, and remedial social therapies. As substantial as these uses are in complex societies, there has been loud and consistent criticism of their use. What concerns most critics is the relative ineffectiveness of these techniques, because of their determined reliance on quantitative measurement and abstract bodies of theory far removed from the institutional and cultural contexts in which they must work. Blind to what cannot be measured, they are often blind to the human and social consequences of their use. The manipulators of social scientific technique, intent on instrumental rationality, cannot notice the qualitative human world their techniques are constructing and destroying.[2]

Although less conspicuous than the technical function of positivist social science, its more powerful function has been to influence values and shape the language within which people understand the sociohistorical world. However much the social sciences deny the normative character of their presumably scientific theories, such theories necessarily construct worldviews, and most often they are propagated as worldviews. For most of this century social scientists have been engaged in uncovering the impersonal webs of influence that shape urban industrial society in America. Analyzing the social determinants of race, poverty, and political activity, and the economic conditions and limitations of government regulation, they were active participants in the new liberalism that led up to and beyond the New Deal, as well as conservative defenders of the slow course of nature that worked in American history.

More recently, under the impact of scientism, the two most influential

---

2 Good examples are Charles E. Lindblom and David K. Cohen, *Useable Knowledge: Social Science and Social Problem Solving* (New Haven, Conn.: Yale University Press, 1979); Robert A. Scott and Arnold R. Shore, *Why Sociology Does Not Apply: A Study of the Use of Sociology in Public Policy* (New York: Elsevier, 1979); Robert H. Nelson, "The Economics Profession and the Making of Public Policy," *Journal of Economic Literature*, 25 (March 1987): 44–91; Peter B. Natchez, *Images of Voting/Visions of Democracy* (New York: Basic, 1985).

paradigms in American social science have become instrumental positivism and neoclassical economics, with its offshoot of social and public choice theory, the paradigms that most clearly embody the individualistic and ahistorical premises of liberal exceptionalism.[3] These paradigms project an idealized view of self-propelling individuals and interest groups, imbedded in nature, dynamically recreating on American soil a progressive liberal society. Systematically excluding attention to the historical structures of the modern world and the power relations that sustain them, these paradigms provide only such critical purchase on the future as the established structures allow. Its prophecies are self-fulfilling. Its norms now play an active role in the turn back from the new liberalism, shearing away the precarious graft of a social ethic on the liberal stem.

The desire to achieve universalistic abstraction and quantitative methods turned American social scientists away from interpretive models available in history and cultural anthropology, and from the generalizing and interpretive model offered by Max Weber. Had American social scientists followed such models, they need not have abandoned a generalizing aim or the appropriate use of statistical methods of analysis. Systematic study of the oligopolistic market of finance capitalism or of representative democracy in a mass-communications society could be imbedded as ideal-typical analysis in a Weberian social science, where they would keep their relation to changing historical formations and keep open the possibility of other kinds of analysis.[4] Conscious of the interpretive character of their knowledge, social scientists would not deliberately forget their own history, but develop the capacity of that history to generate critical self-awareness and conceptual sophistication.

There have, of course, been strong historical countercurrents in American social science, but they have always functioned at disadvantage to the

---

3 A revealing view of recent American social science and the universe it constructs is given by a National Academy of Science study, Dean R. Gerstein et al., eds., *The Behavioral and Social Sciences: Achievements and Opportunities* (Washington, D.C.: National Academy Press, 1988).

4 Max Weber, *Roscher and Knies: The Logical Problems of Historical Economics* (New York: Free Press, 1975) and idem, *The Methodology of the Social Sciences*, ed. Edward A. Shils and Henry A. Finch (New York: Free Press, 1949). See Thomas Burger, *Max Weber's Theory of Concept Formation*, expanded ed. (Durham, N.C.: Duke University Press, 1987) for a rather skeptical view of the possibilities of Weberian social science, and for a friendlier view, Guenther Roth and Wolfgang Schluchter, *Max Weber's Vision of History: Ethics and Methods* (Berkeley: University of California Press, 1979). Given the undeveloped state of historical social science, the tensions between the interpretive and generalizing aims of Weberian social science have not been much explored. See also *Interpretive Social Science, A Reader*, ed. Paul Rabinow and William M. Sullivan (Berkeley: University of California Press, 1979); and idem, *Interpretive Social Science. A Second Look* (Berkeley: University of California Press, 1987).

scientific claims of positivism. The ability of scientism to repeatedly command the mainstream of American social science nonetheless owed a great deal to the complicity of heterodox social scientists and their failure to develop a fully historicist understanding of their task. There are again today vigorous dissenting groups, oriented in various ways to Marxism, historicism, phenomenology, or hermeneutic theory, but they again face a daunting scientism.[5] If the social sciences are to develop a more genuine diversity than scientism has hitherto allowed, they will need a critical understanding of their own history.

The historical profession, I must admit, has not been much help. Since the early twentieth century, when it separated from the social sciences, it has been relatively insular. In recent years that tendency has changed somewhat. The newer history that has emerged from the New History has wonderfully expanded the range of historical understanding, sometimes adapting the quantitative techniques and systematic models of social science to historical use. Such joint efforts as the Social Science History Association, however, have focused almost exclusively on exchanging methods and have not adequately addressed the positivist stance that so often accompanies the methods. Most important, historians for a long time nourished their own dreams of objectivity, in the interest of which they largely confined their view to the past and abjured theoretical discussion. Like the social sciences, academic history has not accepted a fully historicized view of itself and hence not fully recognized its dialogic relation to the past. That relation must include the re-creation of the contextual experience of the past, indeterminate as that experience ultimately is – otherwise historians would be carrying on a dialogue only with themselves – but historians also carry that re-created past into present discourse and they could do so in a more widely informed and self-conscious way.[6]

The problems of both social scientists and historians suggest that they look once again at the modernist historical crisis at the turn of the twentieth century. Historicism did indeed bequeath us an ineradicable difference

---

5  It is worth noting that an earlier study by the National Academy of Sciences, *Behavioral and Social Science Research: A National Resource*, Part I, ed. Robert McC. Adams et al. (Washington, D.C.: National Academy Press, 1982), paid attention to both a "dominant" and an "alternative" historical vision of the social sciences (p. 27). The current study, *The Behavioral and Social Sciences*, pays attention to only the dominant vision.

6  The possibilities of contextualism and dialogue are currently being explored by historians. Variations range from the work of J. G. A. Pocock, cited in the Introduction, to Dominick LaCapra, *Rethinking Intellectual History: Texts, Contexts, Language* (Ithaca, N.Y.: Cornell University Press, 1983), and in another direction, the few contributors oriented to historicism in *Vision and Method in Historical Sociology*, ed. Theda Skocpol (Cambridge University Press, 1984).

between past and future, the need to act for the future without the assurance of the past. But not all the modernist solutions to that problem have worn well over the course of the twentieth century. We can only pretend to stand free of history in the self-created space of imagination, or in a mechanical realm of nature, or in a self-contained past. It is not just that history is there to wreak its vengeance nonetheless. In a real sense it is not there unless we continually re-create it. The modernist turn against the past made a virtue of necessity, but in the increasing disorientation of the modern world, it has become a vice. I take to heart Hannah Arendt's warning against the tendency of modern man, as she calls us, to rebel "against human existence as it has been given, a free gift from nowhere (secularly speaking), which he wishes to exchange, as it were, for something he has made himself."[7] We do not make the world, we find it and remake it. In the presentist confusion of twentieth-century American culture that distinction is particularly important. To systematically train our most serious students of the modern world in the metaphors of nature, seems to me to invite both inhumanity and disorientation.

A return to history will do us little good, however, if it is a return only to the ideological national history. My effort to historicize American social science is part of a gathering effort to historicize the idea of American exceptionalism itself. On a simple generic level, the idea of American uniqueness is probably inexpungible. All countries nourish a nationalist sense of "specialness" and as a historical fact, all countries are to some degree unique. But American exceptionalism goes well beyond those simple parameters. It originated in and has been kept alive by the peculiar characteristics of our nationalism. American nationality formed in order to separate the United States from Europe and has been fueled by the tendency to view America and Europe as polar opposites. Europeans themselves began that polar vision long before we were a nation, projecting onto America, the New World, their utopian – and dystopian – fantasies, and they have often continued to encourage it for their own reasons. Hegel excluded America from "world history," because history was about the past and "America . . . is the country of the future . . . the land of desire for all those who are weary of the historical arsenal of old Europe."[8] Beyond such lyric dreams, there has also been the fixed trajectory of historical development and rigid vision of class structure developed by Marxists. Such views have led to exaggeration of the divergence of American from European history and the fluidity

7 Hannah Arendt, *The Human Condition* (Chicago: University of Chicago Press, 1958), 2–3.
8 G. W. F. Hegel, *Lectures on the Philosophy of World History, Introduction: Reason in History*, trans. H. B. Nisbet from the Hoffmeister ed. (Cambridge University Press, 1975), 170–1.

of American society, and American celebrants have been quick to concur.

A second characteristic support of the discourse of American exceptionalism might be called the metaphysics of idealism, the tendency to conflate the ideal and the real. From the beginning, American nationalists attached to their history the values of individual liberty, political equality, social harmony, and to some variable degree, social equality as well. The millennial underpinnings of American exceptionalism made it possible to see those values as both present and potential, both the reality of American society and the ideal toward which reality moved. We have in the course of this book often seen a hegemonic impulse at work in such conflation. But we have also seen exceptionalism generate expansive visions of economic and political democracy, and at moments reach beyond liberal harmony to solidarity. Abandoning exceptionalist history has often seemed tantamount to abandoning these worthy ideals and the hope that American society was moving closer to their realization.

It is not accidental that the hold of American exceptionalism on the national imagination has weakened just as the historical ascendancy of the United States has come under challenge. Living as we now do in a world of many histories and many modernities, many democracies and many nationalisms; standing among the world's multiracial societies, as well as alongside Europe, we are obliged to reexamine our similarities and differences from others. Nor can we claim any longer to be unaware of the moral ambiguities of our own history, and of the heavy exceptionalist overlay that encrusts our characteristic languages of liberalism, history, and social science. A more differentiated understanding of our national history will give us a better chance to discern what liberty, equality, and solidarity in the world could mean.

# Bibliographical note

## Manuscript sources

The following is a list of the manuscript collections I consulted:

Herbert Baxter Adams Papers, Special Collections, Johns Hopkins University.

Henry Carter Adams Papers, Michigan Historical Collections, University of Michigan.

Arthur F. Bentley Mss., Lilly Library, Indiana University.

John Bates Clark Papers, Rare Book and Manuscript Library, Columbia University.

John R. Commons Papers, State Historical Society of Wisconsin.

Charles Horton Cooley Papers, Michigan Historical Collections, University of Michigan.

Charles William Eliot Papers, Harvard University Archives, Pusey Library.

Richard T. Ely Papers, State Historical Society of Wisconsin.

Daniel Coit Gilman Papers, Special Collections, Johns Hopkins University.

Frank J. Goodnow Papers, Special Collections, Johns Hopkins University.

William Rainey Harper Papers, University of Chicago Special Collections.

Albert Bushnell Hart Papers, Harvard University Archives, Pusey Library.

Philip M. Hauser Papers, University of Chicago Special Collections.

Frank H. Knight Papers, University of Chicago Special Collections.

A. Lawrence Lowell Papers, Harvard University Archives, Pusey Library.

George Herbert Mead Papers, University of Chicago Special Collections.

Charles E. Merriam Papers, University of Chicago Special Collections.

Wesley Clair Mitchell Papers, Rare Book and Manuscript Library, Columbia University.

William F. Ogburn Papers, University of Chicago Special Collections.

Robert E. Park Papers, University of Chicago Special Collections.

Presidents' Papers, 1889–1925, University of Chicago Special Collections.

Records of the Historical and Political Science Association and of the Seminary of History and Politics, Special Collections, Johns Hopkins University.

Edward A. Ross Papers, State Historical Society of Wisconsin.

Albion W. Small Papers, University of Chicago Special Collections.

Edwin R. A. Seligman Papers, Rare Book and Manuscript Library, Columbia University.

William I. Thomas Archival Biographical File, University of Chicago Special Collections.

Graham Wallas Papers, British Library of Political and Economic Science, London School of Economics and Political Science.

Many of these collections afford access to a wider range of information than the life and work of their subject. For American social science in the Gilded Age, the Herbert Baxter Adams Papers, together with the Gilman Papers and the "Record" of the Hopkins seminar, provide an excellent account of the first major social science center in the country. The comparable source for the University of Chicago in the 1890s is the Albion Small Papers, the personal papers of William Rainey Harper, and the Harper materials in the Chicago Presidents' Papers. Small, in addition, was in touch with Ely and others on the ethical, historical wing of Gilded Age social science. The combination of Lowell's personal papers and the Hart and Eliot Papers need to be supplemented with Robert L. Church's dissertation to give as complete a picture of early developments at Harvard. The most revealing record of the anguished journey from cooperative socialism to liberalism is the Henry Carter Adams Papers. The Ely Papers are useful on that subject, but they consist largely of incoming mail and hence are a better source for the range of social gospel reform in and out of the social science disciplines.

For Progressive Era social science and on into the 1920s, the Small Papers and Presidents' Papers at Chicago and the Lowell Papers at Harvard continue to be useful for their individual subjects, their respective disciplines, and the political pressures on social science. The Commons Papers provide some insight into the breadth of social science activity at the University of Wisconsin. As records of individual intellectual development, both the Ross and Cooley collections are exceptionally valuable. In addition, the Cooley Papers contain notes of John Dewey's political philosophy lectures in 1893, an important document of Dewey's relationship to social science.

The manuscript collections available for the period 1910–29 contain considerable material still to be exploited by historians. Given the dearth of published work on Bentley, his papers are an indispensable source. The same is true of Knight, although the collection is a difficult one to use. Knight's notes of Alvin Johnson's lectures and Allyn Young's comments on Knight's thesis also cast a wider net. Despite the considerable number of Mitchell letters already published, the Mitchell Papers contain notes and manuscripts useful for tracing his intellectual development and correspondence that is important for understanding the network of relations within economics. Unfortunately for the history of sociology, there are only a few Thomas letters at Chicago in his file and in the Small, Park, and Presidents' Papers, although they are important documents.

There are rich sources for the social sciences in the 1920s at Chicago. The Park Papers are useful chiefly for Park's own work and the Chicago sociology of race relations and ecology, although they provide considerable insight as well into the changing interpretation of Chicago sociology after 1930. The Merriam Papers have the widest reach because of Merriam's many contacts in political science and government affairs and his central role in the SSRC. The collection contains verbatim transcripts of SSRC conferences in the 1920s that are wonderfully revealing. Ogburn's papers are useful for his career and his sociology; on the *Recent Social Trends* project, his papers contain an indispensable document, verbatim transcripts of the project committee meetings. Finally, the Wallas Papers include some interesting correspondence with American social scientists.

The reader should be warned that the list of manuscript collections I consulted is not a complete guide to those available on the subject of American social science to 1929. In a number of cases there are strong secondary works based on manuscript sources that can provide considerable access to the mansucripts, for example, Donald Bellomy's detailed dissertation, based on the voluminous William Graham Sumner Papers at Yale, and Robert Bannister's *Sociology and Scientism*, based in part on the extensive papers of Luther Lee Bernard at Chicago and Pennsylvania State University. For some of the early figures in this book, such as Francis Lieber and John W. Burgess, manuscript collections are available but there is also much useful published primary and secondary work.

## Published primary and secondary sources

The published primary sources on which this book is based include published letters, articles, and books by the social scientists themselves, and the major social science journals. This last is an especially useful source, not only for articles, but equally for book reviews, which often reveal opinions and divisions of opinion more freely than formal writings. The list of footnote abbreviations can also serve as a list of the major social science journals I consulted. Access to the principal primary sources for each of the social scientists and specific topics I deal with can best be gotten through the footnotes accompanying the relevant text.

The same holds true for the secondary sources I have used. The Index, I hope, is sufficiently detailed to lead the reader to the place in the text where specific persons, subjects, and periods are discussed. Where there are secondary sources that are commented upon in the footnotes and cover more than the period or subject dealt with in one chapter, the Index will indicate where the relevant citations are to be found. For example, under the heading "Political Science" there will be a subheading for "general sources" that will locate the primary references to general histories of American political science.

# Index of names

Subheadings are indiated by a dash.

481

# Index of subjects

Subheadings are indicated by a dash.

497

# Ideas in Context

Titles in series

Richard Rorty, J. B. Schneewind, and Quentin Skinner (eds.), *Philosophy of History*

J. G. A. Pocock, *Virtue, Commerce and History: Essays on Political Thought and History**

M. M. Goldsmith, *Private Vices, Public Benefits*

Anthony Pagden (ed.), *The Languages of Political Theory in Early Modern Europe**

David Summers, *The Judgment of Sense: Renaissance Nationalism and the Rise of Aesthetics**

Laurence Dickey, *Hegel: Religion, Economics and the Politics of Spirit, 1770–1807**

Margo Todd, *Christian Humanism and the Puritan Social Order*

Lynn Sumida Joy, *Gassendi the Atomist: Advocate of History in an Age of Science*

Edmund Leites (ed.), *Conscience and Casuistry in Early Modern Europe*

Wolf Lepenies, *Between Literature and Science: The Rise of Sociology**

Terence Ball, James Farr, and Russell L. Hanson (eds.), *Political Innovation and Conceptual Change**

Gerd Gigerenzer et al., *The Empire of Chance: How Probability Changed Science and Everyday Life*

Peter Novick, *That Noble Dream: The "Objectivity Question" and the American Historical Profession**

David Lieberman, *The Province of Legislation Determined: Legal Theory in Eighteenth-Century Britain*

Daniel Pick, *Faces of Degeneration: A European Disorder, c.1848–c.1918*

Keith Baker, *Approaching the French Revolution: Essays on French Political Culture in the Eighteenth Century**

Ian Hacking, *The Taming of Chance**

Gisela Bok, Quentin Skinner, and Maurizio Viroli (eds.), *Machiavelli and Republicanism*

Forthcoming titles include works by Martin Dzelzainis, Mark Goldie, Noel Malcolm, Roger Mason, James Moore, Nicolai Rubenstein, Quentin Skinner, Martin Warnke, and Robert Wokler.

This series is published with the support of the Exxon Education Foundation.

Titles marked with an asterisk are also available in paperback.